MULTIMEDIA BASICS

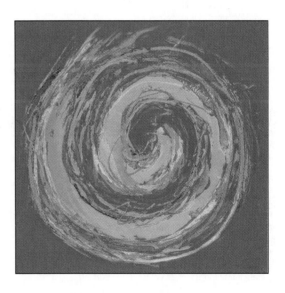

Suzanne Weixel

THOMSON

COURSE TECHNOLOGY

Australia • Canada • Mexico • Singapore • Spain • United Kingdom • United States

Multimedia BASICS, Second Edition

by Suzanne Weixel

Executive Director, Learning Solutions
Nicole Jones Pinard

Senior Acquisitions Editor
Jane Mazares

Product Manager
Jodi Anderson

Marketing Coordinator
Julie Schuster

Editorial Assistant
Jon Farnham

Development Editor
Rose Marie Kuebbing
Custom Editorial
Productions, Inc.

Production Editor
GEX Publishing Services

Compositor
GEX Publishing Services

How to Use This Book

What makes a good computer instructional text? Sound pedagogy and the most current, complete materials. Not only will you find an inviting layout, but also many features to enhance learning.

Objectives— Objectives are listed at the beginning of each lesson, along with a suggested time for completion of the lesson. This allows you to look ahead to what you will be learning and to pace your work.

Step-by-Step Exercises—Preceded by a short topic discussion, these exercises are the "hands-on practice" part of the lesson. Simply follow the steps, either using a data file or creating a file from scratch. Each lesson is a series of these step-by-step exercises.

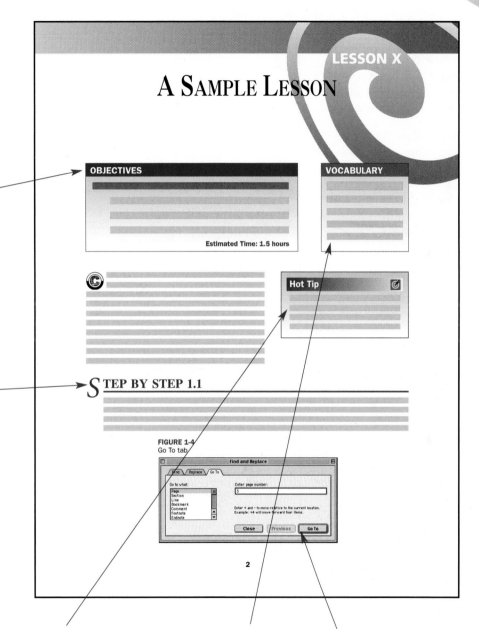

A SAMPLE LESSON

LESSON X

OBJECTIVES

Estimated Time: 1.5 hours

VOCABULARY

Hot Tip

STEP BY STEP 1.1

FIGURE 1-4
Go To tab

Find and Replace

Go to what:
Page
Section
Line
Bookmark
Comment
Footnote
Endnote

Enter page number:

Enter + and – to move relative to the current location.
Example: +4 will move forward four items.

Close   Previous   Go To

2

Marginal Boxes— These boxes provide additional information, such as Notes, Hot Tips, fun facts (Did You Know?), advanced concepts (Extra for Experts), and warnings (Important).

Vocabulary—Terms identified in bold-face/italic throughout the lesson and summarized at the end.

Enhanced Screen Shots—Screen shots now come to life on each page with color and depth.

How to Use This Book

Summary—At the end of each lesson, you will find a summary to prepare you to complete the end-of-lesson activities.

Vocabulary/Review Questions—Review material at the end of each lesson and each unit enables you to prepare for assessment of the content presented.

Lesson Projects—End-of-lesson hands-on application of what has been learned in the lesson allows you to actually apply the techniques covered.

Critical Thinking Activities—Each lesson gives you an opportunity to apply creative analysis and use various resources to solve problems.

End-of-Unit Projects—End-of-unit hands-on application of concepts learned in the unit provides opportunity for a comprehensive review.

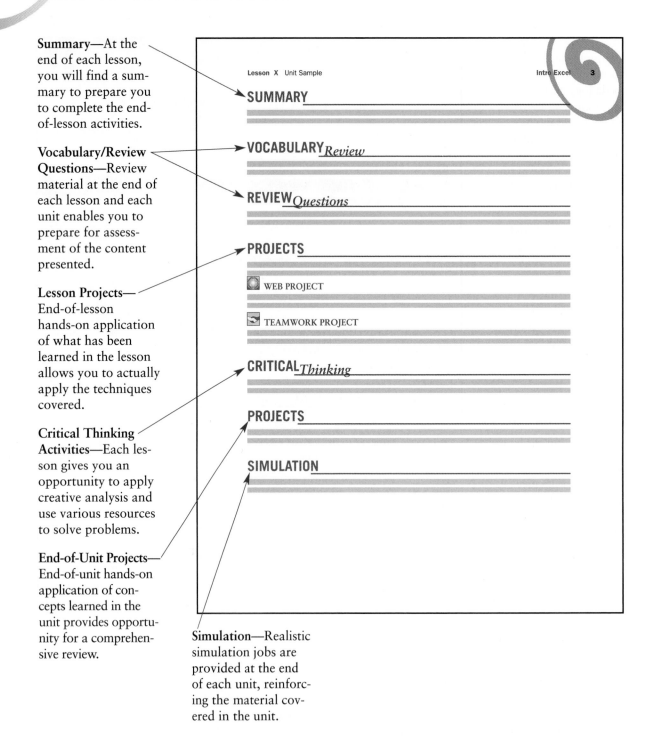

Lesson X Unit Sample

Intro Excel **3**

SUMMARY

VOCABULARY*Review*

REVIEW*Questions*

PROJECTS

WEB PROJECT

TEAMWORK PROJECT

CRITICAL*Thinking*

PROJECTS

SIMULATION

Simulation—Realistic simulation jobs are provided at the end of each unit, reinforcing the material covered in the unit.

PREFACE

In today's fast-paced, media-driven business environment, it is essential to understand how to take a multimedia approach to capture an audience and deliver a message. Whether it involves presenting a slide show to a prospective client or developing a Web page for a non-profit organization, success depends on being able to create a product that effectively incorporates graphics, animation, video, text, and sound.

Multimedia BASICS takes a generic, non-software-specific approach to learning the most popular multimedia tools. This text covers the following applications: Macromedia Fireworks 8, Adobe PhotoShop CS2, Macromedia Flash 8, Adobe Premiere Pro 2.0, Adobe Premiere Elements 2.0, Microsoft PowerPoint 2003, Microsoft Publisher 2003, Adobe InDesign CS2, Macromedia Dreamweaver 8, and Microsoft FrontPage 2003. You may also find it helpful with other programs.

By completing the lessons and activities in this book, you will learn to use multimedia in a variety of applications. Topics include individual and integrated coverage of graphics, animation, video, presentation systems, desktop publishing, and Web page development. Multimedia BASICS is divided into units and lessons. You will learn a concept and then apply it through hands-on step-by-step activities. The book will take you through each step in a logical, easy-to-follow manner.

In the Graphics unit, we will introduce you to the fundamentals of creating and editing graphics images. You will learn to work with both bitmap and vector graphics to develop eye-catching pictures that can be used in print, on the Web, in animations and video, and in presentations. Lessons incorporate the basic principles of design and color while covering techniques that even artistically challenged learners can use to create exciting and informative computer graphics. Concepts in this unit are illustrated using screen captures from Macromedia Fireworks 8.

In the Animation and Video unit, graphics and video clips come to life on your computer screen. You will learn the basics of generating frame-by-frame, motion, and path animations as well as how to create, import, and edit video files. In addition, you will explore the fundamentals of sound and find out how to optimize files for different uses. Lessons cover the basics of both computer animation and video, as well as how to incorporate the files in presentations and Web pages. Concepts in this unit are illustrated using screen captures from Macromedia Flash 8 and Adobe Premiere Pro 2.0.

In the Presentation Systems unit, you will learn how to design and create slide shows and computer-generated presentations. Lessons cover all aspects of presentation development, including planning, topic management, and the generation of support materials, as well as the technical details of creating, organizing, and formatting content. You learn how graphics and animation, special effects, and color affect the quality and impact of a presentation. Finally, you learn different methods for displaying a presentation, including presentation conferences, slide shows, and Web site access. Concepts in this unit are illustrated using screen captures from Microsoft PowerPoint 2003.

In the Desktop Publishing unit, printed materials take center stage. Before you even start using a software program, you will learn the importance of identifying an audience and selecting the right materials. You will find out how to plan and schedule a publication from start to finish, including how to select a publication type and printing method, and even how to stay within a budget. Lessons cover such topics as creating a publication from scratch, using a design template, working with type, selecting and applying colors and special effects, and incorporating graphics. You will also learn how to use the principles of design to organize content on a page so that it is both appealing to look at and easy to read. Concepts in this unit are illustrated using screen captures from Microsoft Publisher 2003.

In the Web Site Development unit, you will learn how to design and create Web pages and link them into a Web site. Lessons cover the importance of page layout and design in capturing a visitor's attention and delivering a message, as well as how to use color, text, graphics, and animations to enhance a page. You will learn how to key HTML code in a text editor to create a Web page as well as how to use a Web site development program. Other topics include how to incorporate navigation tools, when and how to make use of sound, and methods for previewing and testing a page prior to publication. Concepts in this unit are illustrated using screen captures from the Notepad text editor and Macromedia Dreamweaver 8.

The book culminates with the Integrated Simulation which includes exercises and activities that combine aspects from all five units to challenge the learner and reinforce the covered skills. For example, you will have the opportunity to practice developing graphics for print and then using them in a publication, or importing a graphic image into an animation, then using the animation in a presentation.

For those who need a refresher on Windows, Appendix A covers Windows basics such as working with folders, launching a program, and installing hardware and software. Appendix B identifies the many projects in the book that can be used in cross-curriculum activities.

Acknowledgments

I would like to thank the many people who helped me with this book by providing technology or talent, including Becca Baur for her camcorder, Nathaniel Weixel for his voice and pictures, and Evan Weixel for his music. In addition, I could not have completed this project without the help of everyone at Course Technology, Custom Editorial Productions, Inc., and GEX Publishing Services. Putting this book together has been a delightful and fun experience due largely to the good work of the people whose names appear here.

- Jodi Anderson, Product Manager, Course Technology

- Rose Marie Kuebbing, Developmental Editor, Custom Editorial Productions, Inc.

- Sarah McKay and Marisa Taylor, Project Managers, GEX Publishing Services

About the Author

Suzanne Weixel is a self-employed writer and editor specializing in the technology industry. Her experience with computers began in 1974 when she learned to play football on the Dartmouth Time-Sharing terminal her brother installed in a spare bedroom. She graduated from Dartmouth College in 1981 with a degree in art history and currently lives in Marlborough, MA, with her family. Suzanne has written or contributed to numerous books including, but not limited to, *Multimedia Basics,* published by Course Technology, *Learning Microsoft Office XP, Learning Microsoft Word 2003, Learning Flash 8, Learning Microsoft Office 2003 Advanced Skills: An Integrated Approach,* and *Personal Computing Essentials,* published by Pearson Education.

GUIDE FOR USING THIS BOOK

Please read this Guide before starting work. The time you spend now will save you much more time later and will make your learning faster, easier, and more pleasant.

Conventions

The different type styles used in this book have special meanings. They will save you time because you will soon automatically recognize from the type style the nature of the text you are reading and what you will do.

ITEM	TYPE STYLE	EXAMPLE
Text you will key	**BOLD**	Key **Don't litter** rapidly.
Individual keys you will press	**BOLD**	Press **Enter** to insert a blank line.
Web addresses that you might visit	*Italic*	More information about this book is available at *www.course.com*.
Web addresses that you should key	**BOLD**	Start your browser and go to **www.course.com**.
Glossary terms in book	***Bold and Italic***	The ***menu bar*** contains menu titles.
Words on screen	*Italic*	Click before the word *pencil*.
Menus and commands	**Bold**	Choose **Open** from the **File** menu.
Options/features with long names	*Italic*	Select **Normal** from the *Style for following paragraph* text box.

Review Pack and Instructor Resources CD-ROMs

The *Review Pack* CD-ROM contains all the data files needed to complete the exercises in the text. Data files for the Graphics unit are in Macromedia Fireworks 8 or Adobe Photoshop CS2 format, or formats supported by one of those programs. Data files for the Animation and Video unit are in Macromedia Flash 8 (animation), Adobe Premiere Pro 2.0, and Adobe Premiere Elements 2.0 (video) formats, or formats supported by those programs. Data files for the Presentation Systems unit are in PowerPoint 2003 format. For the Desktop Publishing unit, data files in Microsoft Publisher 2003 and Adobe InDesign CS2 formats are provided. And for the Web Site Development unit, data files are all in formats compatible with Macromedia Dreamweaver 8 and Microsoft FrontPage 2003.

The *Instructor Resources* CD-ROM contains a wealth of instructional material you can use to prepare for teaching this course. The CD-ROM stores the following information:

- Data and solution files. Data and solution files for the Graphics unit are in Macromedia Fireworks 8 format, Adobe Photoshop CS2 format or formats supported by one of these programs. Data and solution files for the Animation and Video unit are in Macromedia Flash 8 (animation), Adobe Premiere Pro 2.0, and Adobe Premiere Elements 2.0 (video) formats, or formats supported by those programs. Data and solution files for the Presentation Systems unit are in PowerPoint 2003 format. For the Desktop Publishing unit, data and solution files in Microsoft Publisher 2003 and Adobe InDesign CS2 formats are provided. And for the Web Site Development unit, data files are all in formats compatible with Macromedia Dreamweaver 8 and Microsoft FrontPage 2003.

- ExamView® tests for each lesson. ExamView is a powerful testing software package that allows instructors to create and administer printed, computer (LAN-based), and Internet exams. ExamView includes hundreds of questions that correspond to the topics covered in this text, enabling learners to generate detailed study guides that include page references for further review. The computer-based and Internet testing components allow learners to take exams at their computers. They also save the instructor time by grading each exam automatically.

- Electronic Instructor Manual that includes lecture notes for each lesson, lesson plans, Quick Quizzes, and troubleshooting tips.

- Answers to the lesson and unit review questions, and suggested/sample solutions for Step-by-Step exercises, end-of-lesson activities, and Unit Review projects.

- Copies of the figures that appear in the text, which can be used to prepare transparencies.

- Suggested schedules for teaching the lessons in this course.

- Additional instructional information about individual learning strategies, portfolios, career planning, and a sample Internet contract.

- PowerPoint presentations that illustrate objectives for each lesson in the text.

System Requirements

The concepts and exercises in this book are designed to be compatible with many different software programs, including, but not limited to, the following:

- Graphics unit: Macromedia Fireworks 8, Adobe Photoshop CS2

- Animation and Video unit: Macromedia Flash 8, Adobe Premiere Pro 2.0, Adobe Premiere Elements 2.0

- Presentation Systems unit: Microsoft PowerPoint 2003

- Desktop Publishing unit: Microsoft Publisher 2003, Adobe InDesign CS2

- Web Site Development unit: Macromedia Dreamweaver 8, Microsoft FrontPage 2003

Computer systems that support these programs include PCs running Microsoft Windows. (Adobe Premiere Pro 2.0 and Adobe Premiere Elements 2.0 require Windows XP or later.) In order to complete some of the Step-by-Step activities and projects in this book, you should have access to the Internet via a modem or a direct connection.

TABLE OF CONTENTS

UNIT 1 GRAPHICS

UNIT 2   ANIMATION AND VIDEO

UNIT 3   PRESENTATION SYSTEMS

UNIT 4   DESKTOP PUBLISHING

UNIT 5 WEB SITE DEVELOPMENT

GRAPHICS

Unit 1

Estimated Time for Unit: 10.5 hours

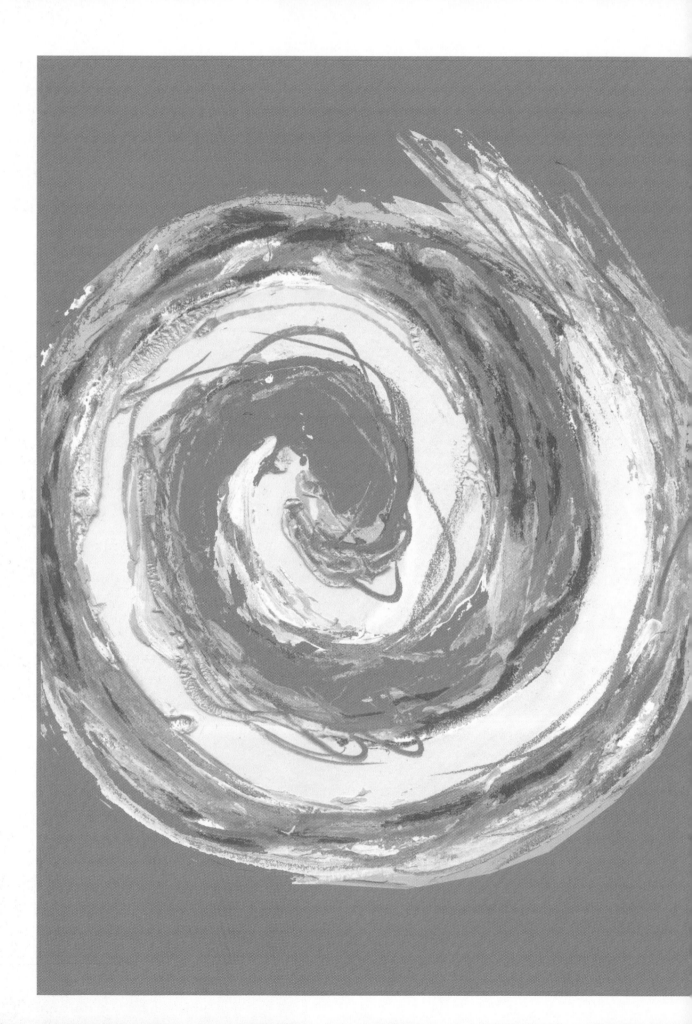

CREATING GRAPHICS

VOCABULARY

Active

Bitmap

Default

Drawing area

Fill

Graphics

Hexadecimal code

Layer

Objects

Pan

Panels

Pixels

Points

Resolution

Selection handles

Stroke

Toggle

Vector

View

Zoom

Graphics are building blocks for developing exciting and informative multimedia documents, presentations, and publications. They are the images you use to enhance the work you do on your computer, and include drawings, photographs, cartoons, charts, and maps. For example, a newsletter that includes pictures is more inviting to a reader. Inserting a chart into a slide show makes the content easier for viewers to understand. And a Web page that includes an animated drawing is more likely to hold a visitor's attention.

Graphics programs provide the tools you need to create, edit, and manipulate images on your computer. There are many different types of graphics programs available. Some programs, such as Adobe Illustrator and Macromedia Freehand, are designed specifically for creating graphics that can be printed, while other programs, such as Adobe Photoshop and Macromedia Fireworks, are designed for creating graphics that can be printed or displayed electronically in a file or on a Web page. There are programs intended for home use and programs designed for professionals. Some graphics programs are available only as part of other programs such as the drawing and picture editing tools that come with Microsoft Office. These usually do not have as many features as the stand-alone programs. In this book, you will learn how to use a full-featured graphics program to create and modify original artwork as well as to work with existing images of all different types.

The first step in mastering the use of graphics is to learn how to create drawings. In this lesson, you will learn how to use a graphics program to draw basic shapes, to save the drawings in a graphics file, and to print a graphics file.

Understand Vector and Bitmap Graphics

Y̲ou will find that there are two basic types of graphics used in computer applications: *bitmap* and *vector*. Vector graphics consist of lines and curves—called vector paths—that are defined by mathematical objects called vectors. Shapes you draw using computer programs are vector graphics. Vectors use geometric characteristics such as size, position, and shape, as well as color, to describe graphics. To edit a vector image, you change the individual vectors. For example, you change the diameter of a circle, or the position of a curve. Bitmaps, which are sometimes called raster images, use colored dots—called *pixels*—arranged in a grid to define an image. Each pixel has a specific location and color that, when combined with the other pixels, create the image. To edit a bitmap, you have to edit the color and/or position of the individual dots.

Vector files are usually smaller than bitmap files because they consist of a series of mathematical formulas rather than many pixels, so they are easier to store and incorporate in other applications. The images also retain their original definition and perspective when resized, so they can be displayed at different resolutions without losing quality. This is useful if you need to show the same image on different monitors, such as when different users access the same Web page. Bitmaps tend to lose definition as they are resized, because the individual dots become visible. Usually, photographs and clip art graphics are bitmaps. Figure 1-1 shows the difference between a vector circle (on the left) and a bitmap circle (on the right) that have been magnified. The edges of the bitmap are rough because you can see the individual pixels at this magnification.

FIGURE 1-1
Vector graphics retain their quality when enlarged, whereas bitmaps do not

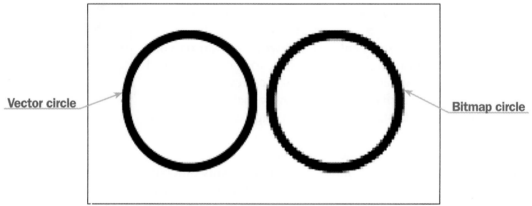

Vector circle
Bitmap circle

Full-featured graphics programs such as Adobe Photoshop and Macromedia Fireworks can be used to create and edit both vector drawings and bitmaps for use on Web pages and in presentations as well as in printed documents. Programs such as Adobe Illustrator and Macromedia Freehand are designed specifically for drawing and editing vector images. Vector graphics programs do not have tools for editing bitmap images; and programs designed for working with bitmaps have few tools for working with vectors. If you are using a vector graphics-only program, or a bitmap graphics-only program, you may find, as you work through the lessons in this book, that some of the features are not available in your program.

Create, Save, and Close a Graphics File

Before you can begin working with graphics, you must learn how to create and save a graphics file. Some graphics programs start with a new blank file already open. In that case, you can simply begin using the available tools to create a picture. Some graphics programs start without a file open so you can open an existing file or create a new one. In any case, you can create a new file without closing and restarting the graphics program. Once you create the file, you must save it so you have it available for use in the future.

Create a Graphics File

To create a new graphics file, use the New command on the File menu or click the New button on the Main or Standard toolbar. Some programs automatically create the file using the *default* size, color, and *resolution* settings for the *drawing area*, whereas other programs display a dialog box where you can select the settings you want to use. Default settings are the standard options already selected in the program. Resolution is the quality or sharpness of an image, usually measured in pixels per inch or per centimeter. Pixels—short for *picture elements*—are dots used to define some images on a computer screen. The drawing area is the area within the document window where you draw and edit the image. Some programs call this area the *canvas* or the *stage*. You may change the settings when you first create the file or at any time in the future.

When you select the New command, the program creates a new blank file similar to Figure 1-2. In addition to the standard screen elements such as a document window, menu bar, toolbars, and scroll bars, most graphics programs include a drawing area, a collection of drawing tools, and panels or palettes where you can select options. The appearance of the screen depends on the program you are using as well as the default options set for your computer, so don't worry if your screen doesn't look exactly the same as the one in the illustration.

FIGURE 1-2
Typical graphics program window

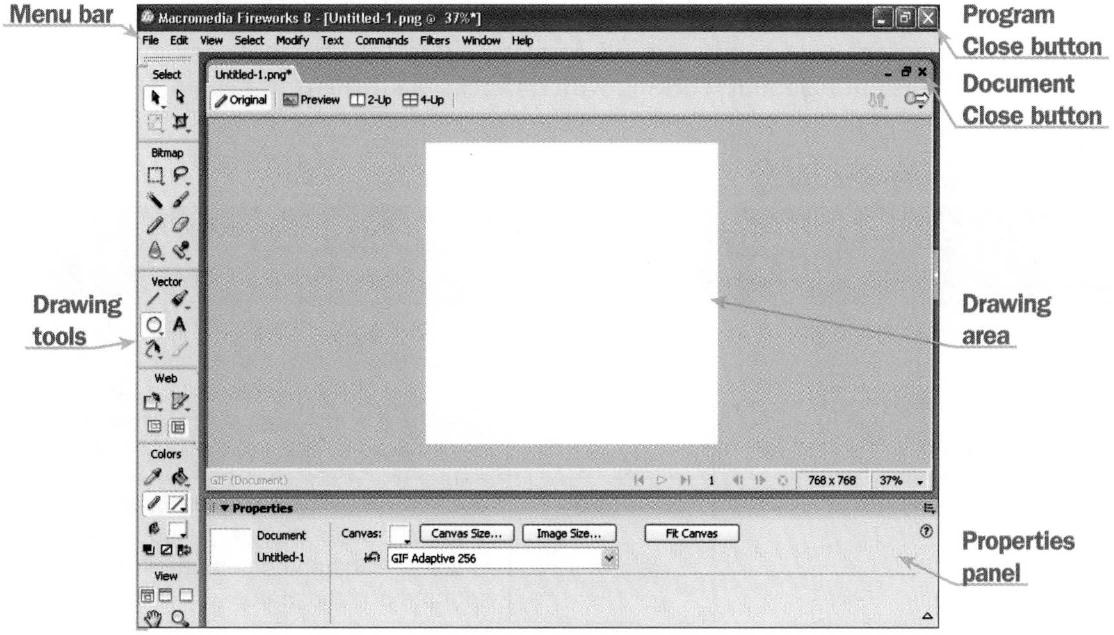

New files usually have a generic name such as Untitled or New File, and are numbered consecutively. So, the first file you create is Untitled-1, the second is Untitled-2, and so on. You customize the name of the file when you save it. Most graphics programs let you have more than one file open at a time, although only one can be *active*. The active file is the one in which you are currently working.

S TEP-BY-STEP 1.1

1. Launch your graphics program.

2. Click **File** on the Menu bar, and then click **New**. This command may open a new file or a New Document dialog box.

3. Click the **OK** button in the dialog box to create a file with the default drawing area settings. Leave the new file open to use in the next exercise.

> **Note**
>
> Don't worry if there is no New Document dialog box, or if the dialog box has a different name. You may be using a graphics program different from the one used to illustrate this book. Your program version or operating system may also affect the contents of the dialog box.

Save a Graphics File

You can use the Save As command on the File menu to save a graphics file for the first time. When you save a file for the first time, you give it a name and select a storage location. You should use filenames that help identify the file contents, and, of course, you must follow standard filename rules. That means you cannot use the following characters in the filename: /, \, >, <, *, ?, ", !, :, ;.

By default, most programs will save a new graphics file in the My Pictures folder on your local hard disk, or in the same folder where you most recently saved a file. However, you can select a different location. You can save a file on a local hard disk, on a network drive, or on removable media, such as a floppy disk, a flash drive, a DVD, or a CD.

Different programs save in different file formats. Table 1-1 lists some common graphics file formats. You'll learn more about working with different file formats in Lesson 2.

TABLE 1-1
Common graphics file formats

GRAPHICS FILE FORMAT	FILE EXTENSION	DESCRIPTION
Portable Network Graphic	.png	This format is often used for graphics on the World Wide Web. It can support up to 32-bit color as well as effects such as transparency. It is the native file format for Macromedia's Fireworks graphics program.
Joint Photographic Experts Group	.jpg or .jpeg	This format is used for photographs and other high-color images. It supports millions of colors and can be compressed. It does not support transparency.

TABLE 1-1 Continued
Common graphics file formats

GRAPHICS FILE FORMAT	FILE EXTENSION	DESCRIPTION
Graphics Interchange Format	.gif	GIF files are popular for use on the World Wide Web. They can contain up to 256 colors. They are used for cartoons, logos, graphics with transparent areas, and animations.
Bitmap	.bmp	BMP is the Microsoft graphics file format and is used frequently for bitmap images.
Wireless Bitmap	.wbmp	The Wireless Bitmap format is used for displayed images on Wireless Application Protocol (WAP) pages on mobile devices such as personal digital assistants (PDAs). It uses a 1-bit format, so it can display only two colors—black and white.
Tagged Image File Format	.tif or .tiff	TIFF files are used for storing bitmap images. This format is commonly used in desktop publishing and other multimedia applications.
PICT	.pict	PICT is the file format used by programs that run on Apple Macintosh computers.
Photoshop	.psd	PSD is the native file format used by the Adobe Photoshop graphics program. Most other graphics programs can open .psd files, as well.

STEP-BY-STEP 1.2

1. Click **File** on the Menu bar, and then click **Save As**. The Save As dialog box opens, as shown in Figure 1-3.

FIGURE 1-3
Save As dialog box

2. In the File name box, with the default name already selected, key **Drawing**. This will be the name of the new file.

3. From the Save in list, select the location where you want to store the file.

4. Click the **Save** button in the dialog box. The file is saved with the new name in the selected storage location. Leave **Drawing** open to use in the next exercise.

Save Changes to a Graphics File

Once you have saved a file for the first time, you can quickly save changes by clicking the Save button on the Main or Standard toolbar, or by using the Save command on the File menu. Saving changes ensures that you don't lose your work if there's a problem with your computer or the software. Whenever you choose to save, the existing file will be overwritten with the current file. To keep the original file unchanged, you can use the Save As command to save the file with a new name or in a new location.

Close a Graphics File

When you have finished using a graphics file, you should close it. You can close a file by using the Close command on the File menu, or by clicking the Document Close button on the document's title bar. After you close a file, the graphics program remains open so that you can continue using it.

If you have not saved the file before issuing a close command, the program displays a dialog box asking if you want to save. Click the Yes button to save the changes and close the file. Click the No button to close the file without saving the changes. Click the Cancel button to close the dialog box and continue working in the file. If you close the file without saving, all changes that you made since the last time you saved the file will be lost.

S TEP-BY-STEP 1.3

1. Click **File** on the Menu bar.

2. Click **Close**. The Drawing file closes. Leave your graphics program open to use in the next exercise.

> **Note** ☑
>
> You can close the program and all open files at the same time if you are finished using the program. Use the **Exit** command on the **File** menu or click the **Program Close** button. If you have not saved an open file, the program prompts you to save before closing.

Open an Existing Graphics File

To work again with a file you have closed, You must open it in your graphics program. You can use the Open button on the Main or Standard toolbar or the Open command from the File menu to display the Open dialog box. By default, the Open dialog box displays the files in the My Pictures folder. Or the dialog box may display the location from which you last opened a file. You can use the Open dialog box to locate and select the file you want to open.

> **Did You Know?** 💡
>
> Some programs also have a command for opening recently used files. In some cases, the most recently used files are listed at the bottom of the File menu, so you can just click the File menu and then click the name of the file you want to open. In other programs, the recently used files are listed on a submenu. If that is the case, you must open the File menu, click the Open Recent command to display the submenu, and then click the name of the file you want to open.

S TEP-BY-STEP 1.4

1. Click **File** on the Menu bar, and then click **Open**. The Open dialog box displays the list of files in the folder, as shown in Figure 1-4. (Don't worry if your Open dialog box does not look exactly the same as the one in the figure. Your program may be set to display the filenames differently.)

FIGURE 1-4
Open dialog box

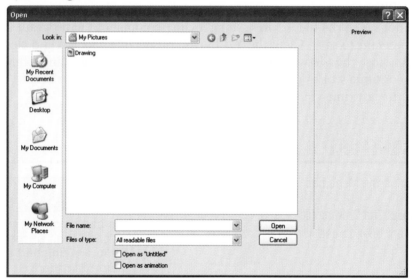

2. If the Drawing file is not listed in the dialog box, click the **Look in** list drop-down arrow and then select the location where the file is stored.

3. In the list of files, click **Drawing**.

4. Click the **Open** button in the dialog box. The file opens in the program window. Leave **Drawing** open to use in the next exercise.

Use Drawing Tools

To create a vector drawing in a graphics program, you use drawing tools to insert *objects* in the document window. In general, an object is any element, such as a shape or a line. The drawing tools are a collection of buttons from which you select the specific type and style of object you want to create. Although some tools vary from program to program, most programs offer a set of tools for drawing basic shapes such as rectangles, ovals, and lines; for drawing freehand objects; and for creating different polygons. Some programs also have options for modifying the way a tool works, such as adding rounded corners to a rectangle, and for changing or reshaping an object that has already been drawn.

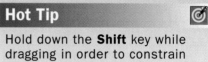

Tools are usually available on a toolbar, in a toolbox, or in a tools panel along the edge of the program window, and are often grouped according to function. For example, one group may be for drawing basic shapes, another may be for modifying existing shapes, and another may be for selecting existing shapes.

To use a drawing tool, click on it to select it. The mouse pointer changes to a crosshair. Hold down the mouse button and drag in the document window to create the shape. The shape is inserted in the drawing using the current *stroke* and *fill* settings. The stroke is the line used to draw a shape, and the fill is the area inside a shape. You will learn about changing the stroke and fill settings later in this lesson. In addition, small rectangles called *selection handles* are displayed around the shape. These handles indicate that the shape is selected, and you can drag one to resize the shape.

In many programs, some tools in the toolbox display a small triangle or drop-down arrow. This means that the tool that is currently displayed is only one of a set of related tools. For example, if the Rectangle tool has the drop-down arrow, it probably hides a set of basic shapes, such as the Ellipse tool, the Rounded Rectangle tool, and the Polygon tool. To see the entire set, position the mouse pointer on the tool, then press and hold the mouse button to open the hidden toolbar (you can release the button once the toolbar is displayed). Click a tool to select it, or press Esc to close the toolbar. Figure 1-5 shows the Basic Shapes toolbar from Macromedia Fireworks 8.

> **Hot Tip** ◎
>
> Hold down the **Shift** key while dragging in order to constrain the shape. For example, use it with the Ellipse or Oval tool to draw a perfect circle. Use it with the Rectangle tool to draw a perfect square. Use it with the Line tool to draw straight lines along any of the 45-degree angles.

FIGURE 1-5
Basic Shapes toolbar in Macromedia Fireworks 8

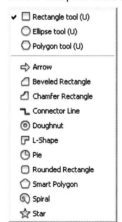

Table 1-2 illustrates and describes some of the common graphics drawing tools. (The icons shown are from Macromedia Fireworks 8 tools panel.) Keep in mind, however, that not all programs have the same tools, or use the same names for tools. You may have to experiment or consult your program's Help information to find the specific purpose of each tool.

TABLE 1-2
Common drawing tools

ICON	TOOL NAME	DESCRIPTION
◢	Line tool	Use to draw straight lines
◯	Ellipse or Oval tool	Use to draw ovals and circles
▢	Rectangle tool	Use to draw rectangles and squares
▢	Rounded Rectangle tool	Use to draw rectangles and squares with rounded corners
⬡	Polygon tool	Use to draw multisided shapes such as stars or octagons
✎	Pencil tool	Use to draw freehand as if using a pencil
✒	Pen tool	Use to draw precise vector lines and curves by plotting and connecting points
🖌	Brush tool	Use to draw as if using a paintbrush
▱	Eraser tool	Use to remove objects or parts of objects from a drawing
A	Text tool	Use to insert text in a drawing
✐	Vector Path tool	Use to draw freeform vector lines and curves
▲	Pointer, or Selection, tool	Use to select objects in a drawing

STEP-BY-STEP 1.5

1. Click the **Ellipse tool**. (You may need to use the hidden toolbars to locate the Ellipse tool.) If you are using Adobe Photoshop you may use Shape layers for this exercise.

2. Position the mouse pointer in the upper-middle part of the drawing area. Don't worry about placing the pointer in a precise spot. Just estimate the correct location.

Note

In Adobe Photoshop you can draw in either Shape layers mode or in Paths mode. In Shape layers mode, objects are filled with the foreground color, but you may not be able to apply strokes. In paths mode you must select the path in the Paths palette and then apply fills and strokes. To select a mode, click the appropriate button on the Options menu.

Did You Know?

You can identify tools using ScreenTips. Rest your mouse pointer on a tool button to display the tool's name.

STEP-BY-STEP 1.5 Continued

3. Hold down the mouse button and drag down and to the right to draw the shape, as shown in Figure 1-6. Release the mouse button when you are finished.

FIGURE 1-6
Draw an oval

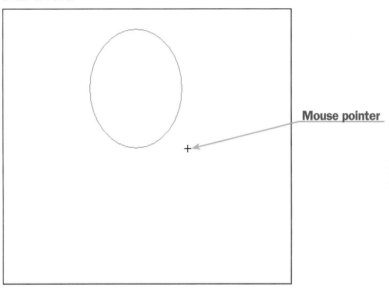

Mouse pointer

4. Click the **Line tool**. Some programs have different types of lines, such as curves and freeforms. Select the tool for drawing straight lines.

5. Move the mouse pointer to the left edge of the drawing area, below the ellipse.

Did You Know?

You can draw outside the boundaries of the drawing area. Objects drawn outside the drawing area are saved with the file but do not print. Use this "scratch area" to practice techniques or store objects for future use. Objects drawn in the scratch area can be dragged onto the drawing area at any point in time.

STEP-BY-STEP 1.5 Continued

6. Click and drag to the right across the drawing area to create a horizontal line, as shown in Figure 1-7. (Press and hold **Shift** while you drag to create a perfectly horizontal line.) Release the mouse button when you are finished. Don't worry if the color or stroke of the shapes in your drawing are different from those in the figure.

FIGURE 1-7
Add a line shape to the drawing

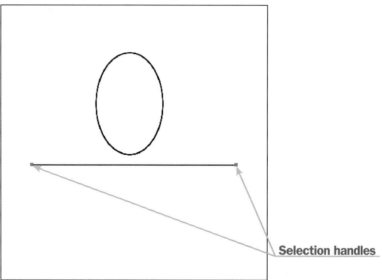

Selection handles

7. Click **File** on the Menu bar and then click **Save**. The changes are saved. Leave **Drawing** open to use in the next exercise.

Select Vector Objects in a Drawing

To make changes to a vector object, you must first select the object. The easiest way to select an object is to use a selection tool. The tool usually looks like a black pointing arrow, and has a name such as Pointer, Path Selection, or Selection. To select the object, click the selection tool and then click the object. (If the object is on a different layer, click once to select the layer, then again to select the object.)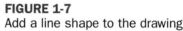

By default in most programs, shapes are placed on the same *layer* in the image. A layer is a transparent plane used to separate objects in a file. In some programs, such as Adobe Photoshop, new shapes are placed on separate shape layers. To select an object, you must first select its layer in the Layers palette.

When an object is selected, selection handles are displayed around its edges. To select more than one object at a time, select the first object, press and hold Shift, and select another object. Or, just drag the selection pointer around all the objects you want to select. (Usually, you cannot select multiple objects on different layers.) To cancel a selection, click a blank area of the drawing or in the scratch area.

Graphics programs usually have other selection tools designed for specific purposes, such as the Marquee tool, which is used for selecting bitmaps; the Subselection or Direct Selection tool, which is used for selecting a single object that is part of a group; and the Select Behind tool, which is used to select an object that has another object overlapping it. Some programs have a Select menu that lists commands specific to selecting and deselecting objects.

S TEP-BY-STEP 1.6

1. Click the selection/pointer tool. This makes the tool active so you can use it to select objects.

2. Click the ellipse shape in the drawing. The ellipse is selected, as indicated by the selection handles displayed around its edges.

3. Click the horizontal line. Now the line is selected, and the ellipse is not.

4. Press and hold **Shift** and then click the ellipse. Both objects are selected.

5. Click a blank part of the drawing area or in the scratch area. The objects are deselected. Leave **Drawing** open to use in the next exercise.

> **Hot Tip**
>
> To delete an object from a drawing, click it to select it, and then press Delete.

Use Undo and Redo

If you are unhappy with the results of your drawing efforts, most graphics programs have commands you can use to reverse — or undo — your most recent action, or, in some programs, a series of actions. In some programs, such as Fireworks 8, the command is called Undo. In other programs, such as Photoshop CS2, it is called Step Backward. You can use the Redo or Step Forward command to reverse the results of an undo action. These options are available as commands on the Edit menu, or may also be buttons on the Main or Standard toolbar. (You may notice that the command name changes, depending on the action to undo or redo.) The first time you use the command, the most recent action is reversed. Repeat the command to reverse the action prior to that, and so on.

> **Extra for Experts**
>
> Some programs have a History panel that lists recently performed actions. You can undo and redo a series of actions using the History panel. To open the History panel, click Window on the Menu bar and then click History. Drag the Undo marker up the list to undo actions or down the list to redo actions.

S TEP-BY-STEP 1.7

1. Click the **Rectangle tool** in the toolbox. (You may find this tool on a toolbar hidden beneath another basic shapes tool.)

2. Position the mouse pointer in the lower-left part of the drawing area, and then drag up and to the right to draw a rectangle. Release the mouse button when you are finished.

3. Click the **Rounded Rectangle tool** in the toolbar. (You may find this tool on a toolbar hidden beneath another basic shapes tool.)

STEP-BY-STEP 1.7 Continued

4. Position the mouse pointer in the lower-right part of the drawing area, and then drag up and to the left to draw a rectangle with rounded corners. Release the mouse button when you are finished.

5. Click **Edit** on the Menu bar, and then click the command to reverse the action. For example, click **Undo Shape Tool**, or click **Step Backward**. The most recent action—drawing the rounded rectangle— is reversed. Notice that the rectangle is removed from the drawing.

6. Click **Edit** on the Menu bar, and then click the command to reverse the action again. The next most recent action—drawing the first rectangle—is reversed. It, too, is removed from the drawing.

7. Click **Edit** on the Menu bar, and then click the command to redo the action you just reversed. For example, click **Redo Shape Tool** or click **Step Forward**. The command reverses the most recent Undo action. In this case, it replaces the first rectangle. Deselect the rectangle, if necessary.

8. Save the changes and leave **Drawing** open to use in the next exercise.

Select Stroke and Fill Options

As mentioned earlier, when you draw a shape, it uses the current stroke and fill settings, or attributes. The options available for modifying stroke and fill depend on the graphics program you are using. Typically, you can change the thickness, style, and color of a stroke, and you can change the color or pattern of a fill.

Stroke thickness, which is sometimes called weight or tip size, is usually measured in *points*, although in some programs it is measured in pixels. There are 72 points in an inch. Some programs let you select the size from a menu or change the current value using a slider or increment arrows. The higher the point value, the heavier the stroke.

Stroke style may be specified by type, category, or effect. For example, you may be able to choose a solid line, a dotted line, or a stroke that looks as if it were created using a heavy watercolor brush, a graphite pencil, or a textured airbrush. See Figure 1-8 for examples. Changes to stroke style and weight can modify the impact of an object by softening its edges or adding emphasis. If you are using Photoshop, you may not have options for modifying strokes when you are using Shape layers mode. You can adjust the weight of lines drawn with the Line tool, however.

Note
To apply strokes and fills with Photoshop, you must draw in Paths mode. Select the path in the Paths palette, then click the Stroke path button to apply the current stroke settings using the selected tool (such as Pencil or Brush) or the Fill path button to apply the current fill settings.

FIGURE 1-8
Different strokes and fills

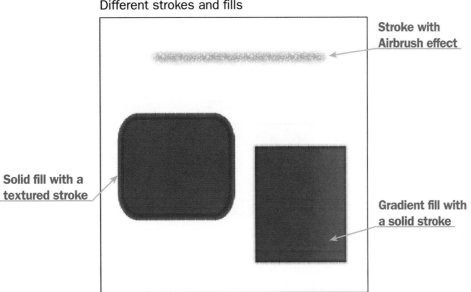

Stroke with
Airbrush effect

Solid fill with a
textured stroke

Gradient fill with
a solid stroke

In most programs, you can access stroke and fill options from the toolbox, from menu commands, or from dialog boxes. Some programs have *panels*, (called palettes in Adobe Photoshop), which are elements similar to dialog boxes that you can keep open on your screen while you work. You might find options for changing the Stroke and Fill in the Properties panel. In some programs, the options are available on a toolbar. To draw a new object using specific stroke and fill options, select the options before you draw. You can also change the options for existing objects by selecting the object or its layer, and then selecting the stroke or fill options you want to apply.

To select a stroke color, you usually 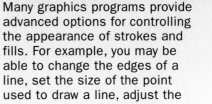 need to select a stroke color tool on the toolbar, the toolbox, or in a panel and then choose the desired color from a color palette. Most color palettes are a series of colored boxes that are often called swatches. You click the swatch containing the color you want to use. Some also have color bars in a particular color scheme, as well as No Color options, buttons for accessing additional options, and a text box where you can key the

Extra for Experts

Many graphics programs provide advanced options for controlling the appearance of strokes and fills. For example, you may be able to change the edges of a line, set the size of the point used to draw a line, adjust the percentage of texture applied to a fill, and even set a position for a stroke in relation to a vector path.

hexadecimal code for a particular color, as shown in Figure 1-9. Hexadecimal codes are standard alphanumeric values used to identify colors based on their components of red, green, and blue. (Lesson 5 includes more information about working with color.) After you select a stroke color, it becomes the default color, so all new objects you draw display that stroke color.

FIGURE 1-9
Color palette

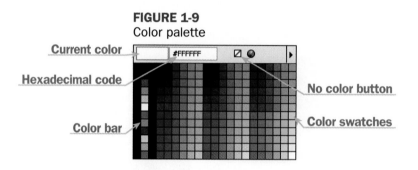

Current color

Hexadecimal code

Color bar

No color button

Color swatches

An object's fill can also be modified by style or color. Most graphics programs offer many fill options, such as solids, textures, blurs, gradients, patterns, and so on. You can also apply a fill color from a color palette in the same way you apply a stroke color. Select the fill color tool on the toolbar and then select the desired fill from the color palette.

STEP-BY-STEP 1.8

1. Click the tool for drawing straight lines in the toolbox.

2. Click the tool for selecting the stroke color. A color palette or dialog box may open.

3. Click a magenta (dark pink) swatch on the color palette (such as hexadecimal **#FF00FF**). The color palette may close after you select the color, or you may have to click **OK** to close the dialog box.

4. Change the stroke weight or size to **16** by selecting this value from a list or keying the value in the appropriate box. (The option name varies depending on your program. You might have a Line Size box, a Tip Size box, a Stroke Weight box, or some other variation that indicates the option to change the stroke weight. The option might be in the Stroke or Properties panel, in a dialog box that you access using menu commands, or from the Stroke Color palette.)

5. Change the stroke to a basic, solid, soft rounded style. If your program does not offer a basic, soft rounded style, select something similar, or leave the default setting.

6. Position the mouse pointer on the left side of the drawing area above the ellipse, press and hold **Shift**, and then click and drag across to the right to draw a straight horizontal line. Release the mouse button when you are finished.

7. Click the **Selection tool** in the toolbox.

8. Select the ellipse in the drawing area so you can change the stroke or fill.

Extra for Experts

In some programs, when you open the color palette the mouse pointer changes to an eyedropper. You can use the eyedropper to pick up any color currently displayed on your screen—even colors that are outside the color palette! For example, click the taskbar or click a color already in the drawing. Any color you click with the eyedropper becomes the current color.

STEP-BY-STEP 1.8 Continued

9. Click the tool in the toolbox that selects the fill, and then click a bright blue box (such as hexadecimal code **#0000FF**) in the color palette. The fill in the ellipse changes to blue. If you are using Photoshop, double-click the shape layer's thumbnail in the Layers palette, select the color in the Color Picker, and then click **OK**. The drawing should look similar to Figure 1-10.

FIGURE 1-10
Drawing with modified stroke and fill

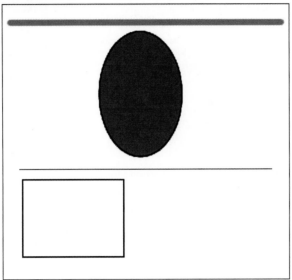

10. Save the changes and leave **Drawing** open to use in the next exercise.

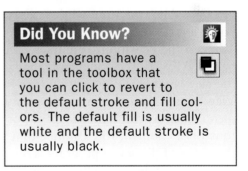

> **Did You Know?**
>
> Most programs have a tool in the toolbox that you can click to revert to the default stroke and fill colors. The default fill is usually white and the default stroke is usually black.

Change the View

While you are working in your graphics program, you may want to change the view to get a different look at your drawing. The *view* is the way your file is displayed on the screen. Most graphics programs let you display your drawing in different view modes such as normal or standard, full screen, or preview, as well as enable you to *zoom* or *pan* on the drawing area. Zooming adjusts the size of the drawing on the screen by a percentage of its actual size, while panning scrolls the drawing area up, down, left, and right in the document window.

You can also choose to show or hide the elements you need to accomplish a specific task. Most graphics programs have a toolbox, menu bar, toolbars, and panels, as well as a grid, guides and rulers, which can help you align and position objects in the drawing area. Some programs also have properties boxes and help panes. When everything is displayed, as in Figure 1-11, there's not much room on the screen for the drawing!

FIGURE 1-11
Drawing in Standard mode, with many screen elements displayed

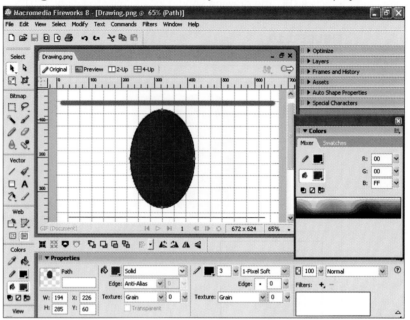

As you become more familiar with the options in your graphics program, you can decide which features you want to keep open and available while you work. You can then customize your screen to suit your work habits. Most of the commands that you use to change the view and display screen elements are located on the View menu. Other commands may be on a different menu, such as the Window menu, or available as buttons on a toolbar. You'll notice that many commands that control the way a program is displayed are *toggles*, which means they are either on or off. Each time you select the command, it switches from on to off, or off to on. When a command is on, it usually has a check mark beside it on the menu.

Keep in mind that the command names and locations depend on the specific graphics program you are using. For example, one program may have toolbar buttons for changing the view mode, while another may have only menu commands. Likewise, one program may have a Full Screen mode option for displaying only the drawing area with no other screen elements, while another program may offer a Full Screen with Menus command that displays the Menu bar as well as the drawing area. Some programs let you collapse elements, such as panels, so that you can see more of the drawing area. These elements can be expanded whenever you need to access the options contained within them.

 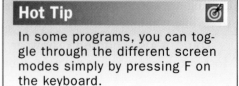

S TEP-BY-STEP 1.9

1. Change to **Full Screen with Menus** mode. You may do this by clicking a tool in the toolbox or, in some cases, a command on the View menu. This expands the area of the document window by hiding the program and document title bars. It leaves the Menu bar displayed, so you can still use it to access commands. If your program does not have a Full Screen with Menus mode, just change to Full Screen mode as directed in step 2.

> **Hot Tip**
>
> If you do not see the Full Screen options in the View menu, look for a View section in your toolbox.

2. Change to **Full Screen** mode, if this option is available as a tool in your graphics program. Full Screen mode expands the document window even more by hiding the Menu bar, too. If the option is not available, skip to step 3.

3. Click the tool or command that restores the standard or default view.

4. Choose the command to toggle the rulers off or on. In most programs you will find the Rulers command on the **View** menu. If the rulers were not displayed before, this action toggles them on; if they were displayed, it toggles them off.

5. Choose the command to toggle the drawing area grid off or on. This command is also usually on the View menu or on a Grid submenu.

6. Repeat steps 4 and 5 until the rulers and the grid are not displayed. In other words, toggle the rulers and grid off.

7. Choose the command to toggle the toolbox or Tools panel off or on. This command is usually on the Window menu, but it may be on the View menu.

> **Hot Tip**
>
> In most programs, an option to show or hide different panels, such as Properties, can be found on the Window menu.

8. Practice toggling different elements on and off to change the view. For example, show and hide the toolbars, and explore the different panels available in your program. Try collapsing and expanding panels using the arrows on the panels if this feature is available. When you are finished, be sure that the Tools panel, or toolbox, is displayed in Standard mode.

9. Save the changes and leave **Drawing** open to use in the next exercise.

> **Hot Tip**
>
> In most programs, elements such as panels have handles — called Grippers — you can use to drag the item to a different location on the screen. For example, you can move the toolbox to the bottom of the screen or drag a panel closer to the drawing area, making it a floating panel or toolbar rather than one that is docked at the edge of the screen.

Change the Zoom

When you need to get a closer look at a drawing, zoom in. As mentioned earlier, zooming increases or decreases the magnification of the drawing on your screen by a percentage of its original size. For example, zoom in to 200% to display the drawing at twice its actual size, or zoom out to 50% to display it at half its actual size. Zooming in gives you a closer look and makes it easier to see and work with a particular area, while zooming out makes the drawing look smaller and gives you an over-all view of its entire composition.

In most programs you can use commands on the View menu to zoom in, zoom out, or select a magnification percentage from a list. You can also simply click the Zoom tool and then click in the drawing area. Some programs have both a Zoom In tool and a Zoom Out tool, whereas other programs have only a single Zoom tool that zooms in by default. In that case, to zoom out, click the Zoom tool, press Alt, and then click the draw-ing area. Your graphics program may offer other options for zooming. For example, some programs have options to automatically adjust the zoom so all objects fit in the document window or only the selec-tion fits in the document window, and some programs have a Zoom box on the Status bar that you can click to select from a list of magnification percentages.

> **Extra for Experts**
>
> Most programs have shortcuts you can use to quickly adjust the zoom. For example, double-click the Zoom tool to restore 100% magnification, or double-click the Hand tool to fit all objects in the window.

S TEP-BY-STEP 1.10

1. Click **View** on the Menu bar, and then click the command to **Zoom In**. The magnification is increased and you get a closer look at the drawing.

2. Click **View** on the Menu bar, and then click the command to **Zoom Out**. The magnification is decreased, giving you a wider view of the drawing.

3. Click the tool for zooming in in the toolbox, and then click on the magenta horizontal line in the draw-ing area. The display zooms in on the line.

4. Click the tool for zooming out in the toolbox, and click on the magenta line again. The display zooms out. (If your program has only one Zoom tool, click it and press and hold **Alt** while you click in the drawing area.) Now, try zooming to a specific magnification.

5. Locate and click the Magnification menu in your program window. It may be on the status bar, at the bottom of the drawing area, or on the View menu.

6. On the Magnification menu, click **200%**. The drawing is displayed at twice its actual size. Depending on the size of your monitor, and the other elements that you have displayed, you probably can see only a small portion of the drawing, as shown in Figure 1-12.

STEP-BY-STEP 1.10 Continued

FIGURE 1-12
Drawing magnified to 200%

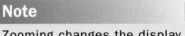

7. Save the changes and leave **Drawing** open to use in the next exercise.

Pan around a Drawing

Pan in the document window to shift the display so you can see a different part of the drawing area. Panning is particularly useful in large drawings or when you are zoomed in to a high magnification. In both circumstances, panning lets you scroll to move the parts of a drawing that were outside the document window into the document window. In most programs, you can pan by using the scroll bars to shift the display up, down, left, or right. Some programs have a tool for panning, called the Hand tool. You use it to drag the drawing area around within the document window.

> **Note** ☑
>
> Zooming changes the display size, not the actual image size. You can change the height and/or width of an image to make it larger or smaller. Look on the Modify menu or in a panel such as Info or Properties for the Image Size command.

STEP-BY-STEP 1.11

1. Click the **Hand tool** in the toolbox. Notice that the mouse pointer changes to resemble a hand. If your program doesn't have a Hand tool, use the scroll bars to complete the steps in this exercise.

2. Position the mouse pointer over the ellipse in the document window, and then drag the object down and to the left. The display pans to reveal the upper-right section of the drawing area, including the magenta line. Notice that the zoom magnification remains the same — 200%.

3. Drag the ellipse up and to the right. This pans to show the lower-left section of the drawing area, including the horizontal line and the rectangle. Release the mouse button when you are finished panning.

<u>**STEP-BY-STEP 1.11 Continued**</u>

4. Adjust the zoom so all objects fit in the drawing area. (Some programs have a Fit All option available from the View menu.) Leave **Drawing** open to use in the next exercise. (You do not need to save because you did not make any changes to the file.)

Modify the Drawing Area

As mentioned earlier, the drawing area — or canvas — is created using default settings for size, resolution, and background color when you create a new file. You can select different settings when you first create the file, or you can change settings at any time. In most programs, the size defaults to pixels, but you can use inches or centimeters (or another measurement system your program offers), if you prefer. However, you may have to select the measurement unit each time you modify the size as, in many programs, it will default back to pixels. Note that changing the size of the drawing area does not change the size of the existing drawing. This means that reducing the size of the drawing area may crop off part of the drawing, while enlarging the drawing area may leave too much blank space around the drawing.

Depending on your graphics program, you may be able to change all of the drawing area settings in a single dialog box, or you may need to use different dialog boxes for each setting. Commands for changing drawing area settings are usually found on the File or Modify menu, or in the Properties panel or dialog box.

Hot Tip

In addition to changing the size of the drawing area, some programs have options for changing its color, which is changing the background color for the entire image, and for trimming it, which automatically removes excess white space around the edges.

Important

Most programs have a default resolution of 96 pixels per inch, although some may be higher or lower. When creating new graphics files for the lessons in this Unit, you should use a resolution of 96 pixels per inch unless otherwise noted.

S**TEP-BY-STEP 1.12**

1. Locate and select the command for changing the size of the drawing area. For example, you may need to click Modify on the Menu bar, click Canvas, and then click Canvas Size; or click File, and then click Document Setup; or you may find the Canvas Size command in the Image menu. For some users, there may be a button such as Canvas Size in a Properties panel. The Canvas Size (or similar) dialog box is displayed.

2. Click the drop-down arrow in the width unit of measure box and click **Inches**. You should change the unit of measure before you set the new size.

3. Click the **Width** box and key **8**. (You may need to select the current value before keying to replace it with the new value.) This sets the width of the drawing area to 8 inches.

STEP-BY-STEP 1.12 Continued

4. Click the drop-down arrow in the height unit of measure box and click **Inches**. Click the **Height** box and key **8**. (Again, you may need to select the current value before replacing it.) This sets the height of the drawing area to 8 inches.

5. Click the **OK** button in the dialog box. The size of the drawing area is adjusted to 8 inches by 8 inches. Notice that there is more room around the edges of the objects in the drawing. The drawing area should look similar to the one in Figure 1-13. If parts of the drawing no longer display within the drawing area, try increasing the size of the drawing area to 9 inches by 9 inches.

FIGURE 1-13
Modified drawing area

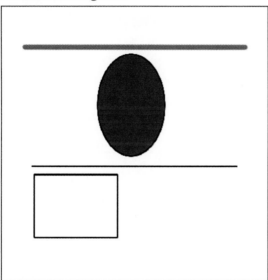

6. Save the changes and leave **Drawing** open to use in the next exercise.

Note

Your program may revert back to the default measurement unit of pixels, even if you select Inches when sizing the drawing area.

Print a Drawing

To prepare a hard copy of a drawing, you use the Print command. Some programs have a Print button on the Main or Standard toolbar that you can click to quickly print the file using the default settings. To change the settings, use the Print command on the File menu, which opens a Print dialog box similar to the one shown in Figure 1-14. In the Print dialog box, you can select options such as how many copies to print, what pages or other parts of the file to print, and which printer to use.

FIGURE 1-14
Print dialog box

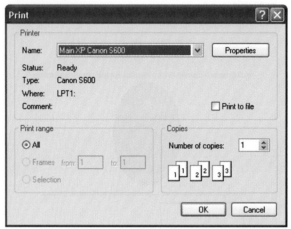

Printing a drawing is useful if you need to show it to someone for approval or if you want to check it for errors. However, keep in mind that graphics are often created for use in other programs or publications, not to stand on their own. While printing a drawing shows you how it will look on paper, it does not show you how it will look integrated into a presentation, newsletter, or Web page — or how it will look when animated.

> **Note** ✓
>
> Before printing, make sure that the printer you want to use is correctly attached to your computer or network, that it is on, and that the paper is loaded correctly.

S TEP-BY-STEP 1.13

1. Click **File** on the Menu bar, and then click **Print**. The Print dialog box opens.

2. Click the printer **Name** drop-down arrow and select the printer you want to use, if necessary.

3. Click in the **Number of copies** box and key **2** or use the up arrow to change the value. (You may have to select and replace the current value.) This sets the program to print two copies of the current file.

4. The default setting to print the entire drawing is selected. You can also select to print only selected objects or specific parts of the drawing. In this case, the default setting is correct.

STEP-BY-STEP 1.13 Continued

5. Click the **OK** button in the dialog box, or click **Cancel** if your instructor asks you not to print. The selected printer should print two copies of the file.

6. Save and close the **Drawing** file. Close your graphics program.

>
> **Important**
>
> Some graphics programs are not compatible with all types of printers, which means the file may not print at all. In the worst case, the printer and the program freeze because they are unable to process the necessary commands. If you have trouble printing, consult your instructor or your graphics program's online technical support files.

SUMMARY

In this lesson, you learned:

- You can create new graphics files or open existing graphics files.

- When you save a new file, you give it a name and a storage location. You should save frequently to avoid losing work.

- You can draw basic shapes such as ovals, rectangles, and lines using the drawing tools.

- You can change the color or style of strokes and fills in selected shapes or before you draw a new shape.

- You can use different view modes to change the way a file is displayed.

- You can toggle elements on or off depending on whether you want them displayed on the screen. You can also move elements on the screen, and, in some cases, collapse them to make more of the drawing area visible.

- You can zoom in on an object to get a closer look, zoom out to get an overall look at the entire drawing, or pan to shift the display to show areas outside the document window.

- You can modify the size, color, and resolution settings of the drawing area when you first create a new file or at any time.

- You can print an image to see how it will look on paper.

VOCABULARY *Review*

Define the following terms:

Active	Layer	Selection handles
Bitmap	Objects	Stroke
Default	Pan	Toggle
Drawing area	Panels	Vector
Fill	Pixels	View
Graphics	Points	Zoom
Hexadecimal code	Resolution	

REVIEW *Questions*

TRUE / FALSE

Circle T if the statement is true or F if the statement is false.

T   F   1. Some graphics programs start with a new blank file already open.

T   F   2. Use the Save As command to save a file for the first time.

T   F   3. Shapes are drawn using the current stroke and fill settings.

T   F   4. The Hand tool is used to select objects in a drawing.

T   F   5. Undo can reverse only the most recent action.

T   F   6. Vector graphics files are usually larger than bitmap graphics files.

T   F   7. Stroke thickness is usually measured in inches.

T   F   8. You can select more than one drawing object at a time.

T   F   9. Zoom in to get a closer look at a particular part of an image.

T   F   10. You must always specify settings in a Print dialog box before printing a file.

WRITTEN QUESTIONS

Write a brief answer to each of the following questions.

1. What are some of the common drawing tools?

2. What action might cause a bitmap image to lose definition?

3. What are some methods for selecting a stroke or fill color?

4. How can you tell if a screen element is toggled on?

5. If you want to display a drawing at 500 times its actual size, what should the zoom magnification be set to?

FILL IN THE BLANK

Complete the following sentences by writing the correct word or words in the blanks provided.

1. Some programs refer to the drawing area as the _____ or stage.

2. Although more than one file may be open at the same time, only one can be _____.

3. Use the _____ drawing tool to draw a multisided shape.

4. The _____ is the line used to draw a shape.

5. The small rectangles around the edge of a shape indicate that the shape is _____.

6. If you are unhappy with the results of your drawing, click the _____ button.

7. _____ graphics use pixels to define an image.

8. _____ in the document window to shift the display so you can see a different part of the drawing area.

9. Commands for showing and hiding panels are usually found on the _____ menu.

10. If you know it, you can key the _____ code for a particular color into the color palette text box in order to select that color.

PROJECTS

PROJECT 1-1

1. Create a new graphics file using the default drawing area settings.

2. Save the document as **Face**.

3. Change the size of the drawing area to 8 inches by 8 inches.

4. Use the Vector drawing tools to draw a face with the following stroke and fill settings. (If you are using Photoshop, use Paths mode so that you can apply fills and strokes. You may want to place each object on a separate layer.)
   A. Use the **Ellipse** tool with a 3-point black stroke and a white fill for the head.
   B. Use the **Polygon** tool with a 3-point black stroke for the eyes.
   C. Use the **Line** tool with a 2-point black stroke for the nose.
   D. Use a Freeform or Vector Path tool with a 6-point red stroke to draw a mouth.
   E. Fill the eyes with brown.
   F. Use a Freeform or Vector Path tool with a 20-point, airbrush-type stroke in brown to draw hair.

5. Print one copy of the file.

6. Save and close the **Face** file, but leave your graphics program open to use in Project 1-2.

PROJECT 1-2

1. Open **Project1-2** from the Data files for this lesson.

2. Save the file as **Revised Face**.

3. Zoom in on the eye on the right.

4. Select the eye on the right and change the fill color to green.

5. Pan over to the eye on the left.

6. Change the fill color of the eye on the left to yellow.

7. Zoom out so you can see the entire drawing.

8. Delete the nose.

9. Undo the deletion.

10. Print one copy of the file.

11. Save and close the **Revised Face** file, but leave your graphics program open to use in Project 1-3.

PROJECT 1-3

1. Open **Project1-3** from the Data files for this lesson.

2. Save the file as **Mouse**.

3. Select both ears and the nose and change the fill to pink.

4. Select both eyes and change the fill to blue.

5. Select the mouth and change the stroke to 10-point red. In Photoshop, change just the color to red.

6. Decrease the size of the drawing area to 6 inches by 6 inches.

6. Print one copy of the file.

7. Save and close the **Mouse** file. Close your graphics program.

 WEB PROJECT

Since primitive humans first drew pictures on the walls of caves, people have been using graphics to communicate and to express themselves creatively. Choose a time period in history and use the Internet to research graphics in that period. For example, you may choose the Renaissance and research how the artist Michelangelo painted the Sistine Chapel, or you may explore how Native Americans used pictures to tell stories as well as for decoration, or you may want to look into the impact digital graphics have had on modern society.

Use the information you gather in your research to write a report or essay that you can share with the class. Illustrate the report with an image that might have been created by people living during the period of your research.

 TEAMWORK PROJECT

As a group, compile a list of the different types of graphics programs that are available, including information about the features of each program, the system requirements, and the price. You may want to record the information in a database program or a spreadsheet. You can find the information on the Internet, in a software magazine, or by visiting or contacting a store that sells software. Once you compile the information, rate the programs in terms of value. Consider such factors as the cost, the number of features, the types of files you can create, whether you would need to purchase additional hardware to use the program, and whether the program is easily available in stores or on the Internet. When you are finished, share the results with your classmates.

CRITICAL*Thinking*

Many businesses use pictures as part of logos on letterhead stationery, clothing, and Web pages. Use your graphics program to create a drawing that you might use as part of a logo for a business. For example, a realtor might use a drawing of a house, a day-care provider might use a drawing of building blocks, and a landscaper might use a drawing of trees or flowers. Try to use as many drawing tools as you can, as well as different stroke and fill options. When you are finished, save the file, print it, and share it with your classmates.

IMPORTING AND EXPORTING GRAPHICS

OBJECTIVES

Upon completion of this lesson, you should be able to:

- Scan images.
- Acquire images from a digital camera.
- Import files.
- Open and save different file formats.
- Acquire clip art.
- Optimize and export images.

Estimated Time: 1.5 hours

VOCABULARY

Clip art

Color depth

Color palette

Compatible file format

Device driver

Dithering

Download

Export

File format

Import

Key term

Loss setting

Native file format

Optimize

Scanner

Search site

Smoothing

TWAIN

Websafe colors

Wizard

You can acquire graphics files in a number of ways without having to draw original artwork. You can use *clip art* files, which are images already saved in a graphics file format. You can scan printed material, capture original photographs with a digital camera, or even draw on a graphics tablet. You can insert the images into other documents or files, or *import* them for use in your graphics program. Importing makes a file available for editing. For example, you can import a photograph from a digital camera and then crop it, add vector shapes, and insert text, or you can download a clip art drawing from the Internet and change its background color.

Before you can use any hardware device to acquire pictures, the device must be correctly attached to your computer—or your computer network—and installed. Attaching the device usually means physically connecting the cables from the device to your computer, although some devices, such as internal modems, connect to slots inside the computer itself. Some other devices might involve optical or other wireless connections.

Installing the device also means installing the software that comes with the device and making sure the device driver works. The *device driver* is a software program that enables your computer to communicate with the hardware device. The driver usually comes on a CD with the device, or you can download it from the manufacturer's Web site. Your operating system may include drivers for common devices. When you set up and install new hardware, make sure you read and follow all instructions, or consult a professional.

Once you finish editing your graphics files, you can save them in a different file format or *export* them for use in other programs. Exporting stores the file so that it can be opened and used by other types of computer programs. That way, you can easily use the graphics to illustrate Web pages, presentations, or other documents. In this lesson, you will learn how to acquire graphics from different sources and how to import and export graphics using your graphics program.

Scan Images

When you have a printed image that you want to convert into a graphics file, use a scanner. A *scanner* is a hardware device that uses light to capture a digital version of a picture, which is then stored as a graphics file on your computer. Like any hardware device, the scanner must be correctly connected and installed on your computer to work.

Most scanners come with software that lets you select where you want to store the imported images and also determines the file format. However, because so many programs support scanning and *TWAIN*, which is the software language that is used to control scanners, you can probably import the image directly into the program of your choice. For example, you can scan an image into your graphics program so you can edit it, or you can scan an image into your desktop publishing program so you can include it in a publication.

Most programs let you preview a picture before you scan it. This is useful for making sure you have the printed page positioned correctly and have selected the options you need.

> **Note**
>
> You must consider a number of things when you import graphics images, including the quality of the image, its composition, and its subject content. If the image needs modification, make sure you can make the necessary changes using the tools you have available. Otherwise, you may want to look for a different image.

> **Note**
>
> Keep copyright laws in mind when selecting images for scanning. Make sure you have the owner's or artist's permission to use the image before you insert it into a document or file. Refer to the Computer Ethics special feature on page 44 for more information on copyright laws.

Scan an Image into Your Graphics Program

To scan an image directly into your graphics program, place the printed picture in the scanner and click the Scan command. The location of the Scan command depends on your program. Look for it on the File menu or the Insert menu if there is one. In some programs, a submenu offers you a choice of scanning the image or selecting the specific scanning device you want to use. In most cases, you then select options in a Scan dialog box. The options offered depend on the type of scanner you are using and your graphics program, but usually include settings for scanning in color, black and white, or grayscale, as well as for scanning text. When the scan is complete, the image is displayed as a new, unnamed file in the program window.

> **Did You Know?**
>
> Most images that you acquire will be bitmaps, not vectors. Some graphics programs, including Macromedia Freehand and Adobe Illustrator, do not offer features for editing bitmaps. However, you can import and open bitmaps in all graphics programs. You will learn more about working with bitmaps in Lesson 3.

STEP-BY-STEP 2.1

1. Make sure your scanner is correctly installed for use with your computer.

2. Launch your graphics program.

3. Insert a printed picture into the scanner. Make sure it is correctly positioned on the glass, and close the scanner cover.

4. Click **File** on the Menu bar, and then click **Scan**. If the Scan command is not on the File menu, look for it on the other main menus or on a submenu such as Import. If you still don't see it, your program may use the Import command instead, or the command may be located on a submenu. For example, you may have to click **Insert** on the Menu bar, click **Picture**, and then click **Scan**, or you may have to click **File** on the Menu bar, click **Import**, and then click **From Scanner**.

> **Note**
>
> If your graphics program does not have a Scan command, it may not support acquiring an image directly from a scanner. In that case, you might have to use a different program to scan the image, as described in the next exercise.

5. Click the command to start the scan. For example, in Fireworks, click the **TWAIN Acquire** command on the submenu and then click the name of the specific scanning device you want to use. In Photoshop, just click the name of the specific scanning device. Again, the specific command depends on the program you are using. It may simply say TWAIN or TWAIN_32, or there may not be a

STEP-BY-STEP 2.1 Continued

submenu at all. A Scan dialog box may display on your screen, as shown in Figure 2-1. If the Scan dialog box on your computer is different from the one in Figure 2-1, you are probably using a different graphics program, a different scanner, or both. However, the basic options should be similar.

FIGURE 2-1
Typical Scan dialog box

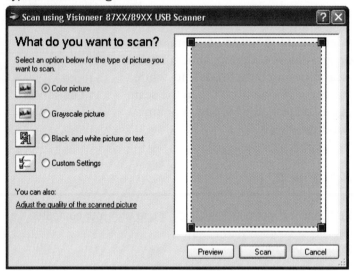

6. Click the options you want to use, and then click the **Scan** button in the dialog box. The scanner acquires the image and displays it in the drawing area.

7. Save the new image file as **Scanpic**, and close the file. Close your graphics program. You do not need it in the next exercise.

Scan an Image into a Document File

The steps for scanning directly into a document vary depending on the program you are using. In most cases, however, you select the Scan command from the Insert menu.

STEP-BY-STEP 2.2

1. Launch the program you are using to create the document. For example, if you are creating a slide show with Microsoft PowerPoint, launch Microsoft PowerPoint.

2. Save the new document with an appropriate name.

3. Position the insertion point where you want to insert the scanned image.

4. Click **Insert** on the Menu bar, and then click **Picture**. In most cases, a submenu displays.

5. Click **From Scanner** on the submenu. A Scan dialog box may open so you can select the options you want to use.

STEP-BY-STEP 2.2 Continued

6. Select options, and then click the **Insert** button. The image is scanned and then inserted in the file at the insertion point location.

7. Save changes to the file and close it, along with the program you were using.

Acquire Images from a Digital Camera

> ### Did You Know?
>
> If you have a graphics tablet, you can use it to draw or trace artwork or other images into a graphics file. A graphics tablet is a hardware device that lets you use a pen-like instrument called a stylus to write or draw on a flat surface. The input is digitized and saved in a graphics file format.

Digital cameras make it easy to take original photographs that you can transfer as files to your computer. Once you acquire the pictures, you can edit them or use them as is. The steps for acquiring pictures from a camera depend on the type of camera and the software you use. In most cases, the photographs are stored as files in the camera's internal memory or on a storage device attached to the camera, such as a disk, memory stick, or memory card. Usually, cameras store pictures in JPEG format, but some high-end cameras use TIFF. JPEG compresses the pictures, so they take up less space on the storage device than TIFF files, but some quality may be lost in the compression process.

Digital cameras have many of the same features as 35-millimeter "point and shoot" cameras, including zoom, auto-focus, and automatic flash. Digital camera resolutions range from 640 × 480 pixels to upwards of 1600 × 1200 pixels. You can get lenses you must focus manually, lenses that support digital zoom, and even cameras that let you use the lenses from your standard 35-millimeter camera. Of course, the more features a digital camera supports, the more the camera costs. Another consideration for choosing a digital cameral includes the type of interface used to connect the camera to the computer. Most digital cameras come with cables for connecting to USB, serial, or other external ports on your computer. In some cases—as with Flash cards—you may be able to insert the camera's storage device directly into a memory slot in the computer.

Most cameras come with software that automatically transfers the picture files from the camera to your computer. You can also acquire images from a digital camera by copying the files to your hard drive. When a digital camera is correctly connected to a computer, most operating systems read the camera as just another disk drive. That makes it easy to use the Copy and Paste (or Move) commands to transfer the files from the camera to your hard disk. Then, you can use the Open command in your graphics program to open the file. This is convenient if you know you want to use the image as it is, without making changes to it in your graphics program.

S TEP-BY-STEP 2.3

1. Make sure your camera is correctly installed for use with your computer.

2. Open the **My Computer** window from the desktop or the Start menu. My Computer displays the storage devices installed on your computer system, including the camera, as shown in Figure 2-2.

FIGURE 2-2
Digital camera listed as a storage device in My Computer

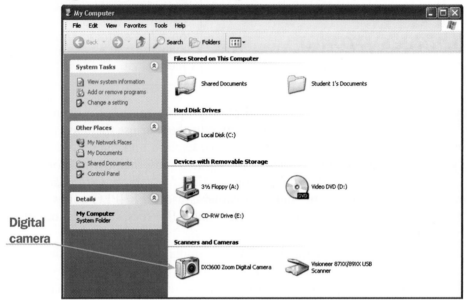

3. Double-click the icon representing the camera. A window displaying the contents of the camera opens. If necessary, double-click the specific location where the files are stored, such as internal memory or a storage device.

4. Click the file you want to copy to select it.

5. Click **Edit** on the window's Menu bar, and then click **Copy**.

6. Open the **My Documents** window, or the window that contains the folder where you want to store the image file.

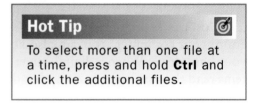

Hot Tip

To select more than one file at a time, press and hold **Ctrl** and click the additional files.

7. Click the **My Pictures** folder icon, or the icon representing the folder where you want to store the image file.

8. Click the **Edit** menu on the window's Menu bar, and then click **Paste**. Your operating system copies the image file(s) into the selected folder.

9. Close all open windows.

Import Files

Most graphics programs let you import files from any storage device attached to your computer, including hard drives, network drives, removable drives, and connected devices such as digital cameras. To import files, you usually create a new blank file, select a command such as Import or Place from the File menu, and then define the area in the new file where you want the imported data displayed. In this exercise, you import a file from a digital camera. The steps will be similar for importing from any storage device. If your program does not support importing files, you may be able to open the files directly using the Open command on the File menu, as described in the following section.

STEP-BY-STEP 2.4

1. Make sure your camera is correctly installed for use with your computer.

2. Launch your graphics program.

3. Create a new, blank, graphics file using the default drawing area settings. Most programs require that you import an image into an existing file.

4. Click **File** on the Menu bar, and then click a command such as **Import**. A dialog box similar to the one shown in Figure 2-3 opens.

FIGURE 2-3
Import dialog box

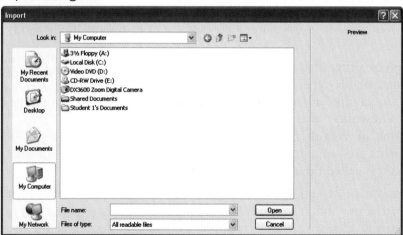

5. In the **Look in** list, open the location representing your digital camera's storage media, or the location where the file to import is stored.

6. Click the name of the file you want to import, and then click the command to import the file, usually **Open**. Your program may automatically import the picture and display it in the drawing area, or the insertion pointer may be displayed in an otherwise blank drawing area. If so, you must define the area where you want the image displayed.

STEP-BY-STEP 2.4 Continued

7. If necessary, drag the insertion pointer from the upper-left corner to the lower-right corner of the drawing area as shown in Figure 2-4. When you release the mouse button, the imported image is displayed in the drawing area you have specified.

FIGURE 2-4
Drag insertion pointer to define import area

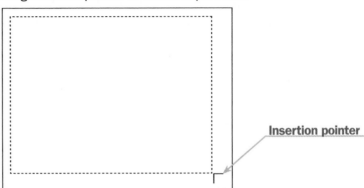

Insertion pointer

8. Save the file as **Camerapic**, and close it. Leave your graphics program open to use in the next exercise.

> **Did You Know?**
>
> Some programs make it easy to view stored images using a Filmstrip or Slide Show view. In Filmstrip view, thumbnail-sized pictures display across the bottom of the window, with a preview of the selected picture in the center of the window. In Slide Show view, pictures fill the entire display screen and may advance automatically at timed intervals.

Open and Save Different File Formats

Most graphics programs are associated with a default file format, or file type. The *file format* is the way the data in a file is stored. For example, Macromedia's Fireworks uses Portable Network Graphics (.png) as its default file format. (Common graphics file formats are listed in Table 1-1 in Lesson 1.) Sometimes, the default file format for a particular program is called the *native file format*.

Most programs also let you open files that have been saved in a *compatible file format*. A compatible format is one that a program can open, read, and save, even if it is not the default. Sometimes compatible files are referred to simply as readable files. Once the file is open, you can also choose to save it in your program's native file format.

Open Different File Formats

You can easily open compatible files in your graphics program using the Open command. In the Open dialog box, click the *Files of type* list to display compatible file types. Most graphics programs list many different types of graphics files, as well as options for displaying all compatible files or all files, whether they are compatible or not. The list usually includes the name of the file format, as well as the file extensions associated with that format. After you have selected the desired file type, you can locate and open the file you need.

> **Note** ☑
>
> If you try to open a non-compatible file, your program will not know how to read and display the data. As a result, your program will display a warning message instead of opening the file. To resolve this problem, you can try opening the file in its original program and saving it in a format that is compatible with your program.

S TEP-BY-STEP 2.5

1. Launch your graphics program if it is not already open.

2. Click **File** on the Menu bar, and then click **Open**.

3. Use the **Look in** list to navigate to the Data files folder.

4. Click the drop-down arrow in the **Files of type** box. This displays a list of compatible file types, similar to the one shown in Figure 2-5.

FIGURE 2-5
Files of type list in Open dialog box

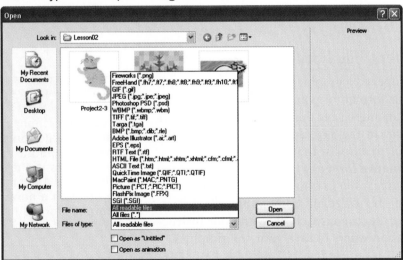

5. Click **BMP**. The *Files of type* list closes and only files in BMP—bitmap—format are displayed in the Open dialog box.

STEP-BY-STEP 2.5 Continued

6. Click the **Files of type** drop-down arrow again, and then click **GIF**. Now, only Graphics Interchange Format files are displayed.

7. Click the GIF-formatted file named **Step2-5**, and then click the **Open** button in the dialog box. The file opens in your graphics program, as shown in Figure 2-6. Leave **Step2-5** open to use in the next exercise.

FIGURE 2-6
GIF file open in graphics program window

Save a Different File Format

If you have opened a graphics file in a format that is not the native file format for your program, you can use the Save As command to save that file in your program's native file format. In the Save As dialog box, click the *Save as type* list to display the compatible file types. Your program's native format is usually at the top of the list. When you save a file in your program's native format, you leave the original, compatible file intact. Before beginning this exercise, check with your instructor for directions on where to save your solution files.

> **Hot Tip**
>
> If you make changes to a file in a different file format, use the Save command to quickly save the changes in the same format, or the Save As command to save the file with a new name, in a different storage location, or in a different format.

STEP-BY-STEP 2.6

1. Click **File** on the Menu bar, and then click **Save As**. The Save As dialog box opens.

2. Key the filename **Flake** in the *File name* box.

STEP-BY-STEP 2.6 Continued

3. Click the drop-down arrow in the **Save as type** or **Format** box. This displays a list of compatible file types, similar to the one shown in Figure 2-7.

FIGURE 2-7
Save as type list in Save As dialog box

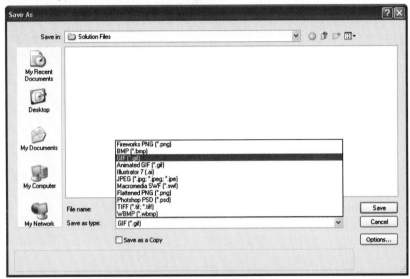

4. Click your program's default file format. Usually, the default format is at the top of the list.

5. Select the location where you want to save the file from the *Save in* list, and then click the **Save** button. If a dialog box displays options for the selected file format, click **OK** to select the default options. Now there are two versions of the file: **Step2-5** in GIF format, and **Flake** in your program's default file format.

6. Close the **Flake** file as well as your graphics program. You do not need it in the next exercise.

Acquire Clip Art

Many programs come with clip art collections, or you can buy clip art on a disk or CD. You can also download some clip art from the Internet. If you want to edit or modify a clip-art image, you can open the file in your graphics program. If you want to use the image as is, simply insert it directly into the file of your choice. For example, you can insert clip art into a report, Web page, or presentation file.

Did You Know?

Not all clip-art files are graphics. Some are animations, movies, or sounds that you can use to enhance your documents.

Insert Clip Art into a Document File

The steps for inserting clip art into a document vary depending on the program you are using. In most cases, however, you select the Clip Art command from the Insert menu. A dialog box, panel, or separate program window opens to provide access to the program's clip-art files. You may select a category to see the pictures stored for that category, or search for specific subjects using a search box. Some programs allow you to choose what type of pictures to find, such as photographs or drawn clip art pictures. You may need to scroll through pictures to find one you want. Once you have found what you want, you can click on the image to select it and then select the command to insert it into the current document. Alternately, some programs have an option for inserting a specific image file, which is useful if you know the filename and storage location for an image you want to use.

 Computer Ethics

COPYRIGHT LAWS

Although many sources allow you to download or scan images for your personal use, in other cases acquiring images without permission is illegal. Copyright laws protect artists and photographers just as they protect authors. In addition, even original photographs may cause problems if they include other people or other people's property in the picture without their permission. You may need to have people who appear in your photographs sign a "release," allowing you to use the picture, particularly if it will appear in a publication or on a Web site. For images from other sources, sometimes you can obtain permission to use them by writing or e-mailing the owner. In still other cases, you may be asked to pay a fee. Even when you obtain permission, you should always cite the source of the image. You can do this by adding a caption to the image or by creating a list of sources similar to a bibliography. You should include the name of the artist, the title of the image, the source where you obtained the image, the copyright date (which is the date the image was originally published), and the date you downloaded or acquired the image.

STEP-BY-STEP 2.7

1. Launch the program you are using to create the document. For example, if you are creating a newsletter with Microsoft Publisher, launch Microsoft Publisher.

2. Create a new blank document and save the document with an appropriate name.

3. Position the insertion point where you want to insert the image.

4. Click **Insert** on the Menu bar, and then click **Picture**. In most cases, a submenu opens.

5. Click **Clip Art** on the submenu to display the dialog box or panel that gives you access to clip-art images.

6. Select a category to see the images stored in that category, or key a word or phrase that describes the subject of images you want to find in a search box.

7. Click the image you want, and then, if necessary, click the **Insert** button. The image is inserted in the file at the insertion point location.

8. Save changes to the file and close it, along with the program you were using.

> **Hot Tip**
>
> One of the easiest ways to insert a clip-art picture is to use the Clipboard. Right-click the image and click Copy, then right-click the file where you want to insert the image and click Paste.

Download Images from the Internet

You can find many Web sites that provide free clip art for all occasions. You simply visit the site, locate the image you want, and then *download* it. Downloading copies the file from the Web site to your computer.

To find a list of clip-art sites, use your favorite search site and search for the key term "clip art." A *search site* is a Web site that helps you locate a Web page even if you don't know the page's address. A *key term* is a word or phrase that you believe identifies the Web site. After you search for a key term, the search site lists Web addresses of sites that match your term. Click on the Web address or the site name to jump directly to that site.

If you know the address of a site, you can also key the address directly in your browser's Address bar. Then press Enter or click a button such as Go to jump to that site.

Although some clip-art sites ask you to register by entering your name and e-mail address, many sites do not. You can simply download any file you want to use. Some sites have download procedures for copying clip-art files to your hard disk, or you can use your browser's Save As command to save the image as a graphics file on your computer.

You must have access to the Internet to locate and download clip-art files. That means your computer must be connected to the Internet and you must have an account with an Internet Service Provider (ISP).

> **Net Tip**
>
> It is important to know the source of any file you download from the Internet. Some files may be copyrighted material that you need permission to use, whereas some files may have viruses that could infect your computer and other computers on the same network. For that reason, it is a good idea only to download files from sources you know and trust to be virus free.

STEP-BY-STEP 2.8

1. Sign in to your Internet Service Provider (ISP) account if necessary and launch your Internet browser.

2. Go to your favorite search site, or key **www.google.com** in your browser's Address bar and press **Enter** or click the **Go** button.

3. Key **clip art** in the search box and then press **Enter**, or click the **Search** button. A list of clip-art sites is displayed on your screen. You should be able to tell from the descriptions whether these sites charge a fee for using the clip-art images or provide free access.

4. Click the link to the **Clipart Connection** Web site. (You may have to scroll down to find this link.) If the site is not listed on your search results page, key **www.clipartconnection.com** in your browser's Address bar and press **Enter** or click the **Go** button.

5. Click the **Animals** link in the column labeled **Clipart** to display a page of clip-art images of animals, and then scroll down to view the last row. It should look similar to Figure 2-8.

FIGURE 2-8
Free clip-art Web site

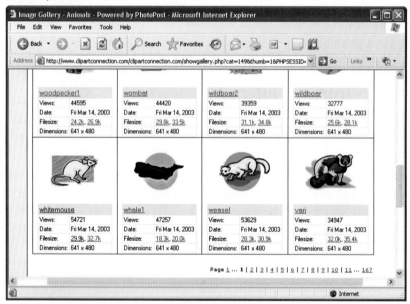

STEP-BY-STEP 2.8 Continued

6. Right-click the picture of the white mouse on the left end of the first row, and then click **Save Picture As** on the shortcut menu. (If you cannot locate the image, select a different one.) The Save Picture dialog box opens, as shown in Figure 2-9. Don't worry if the dialog box on your computer looks different from the one in the illustration.

FIGURE 2-9
Save Picture dialog box

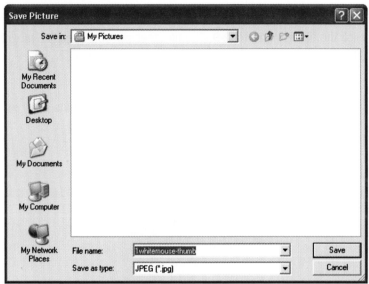

7. Key the filename **Mouse.jpg**. (You must key the file extension to save the picture properly.)

8. If necessary, click the **Save as type** drop-down arrow and then click **JPEG (*.jpg)**.

9. From the Save in list, select the location where you want to save the file, and then click the **Save** button in the Save Picture dialog box. The file is saved in JPEG file format.

10. Log off from the Internet if necessary, and close your browser.

Open Clip Art in Your Graphics Program

Use the Open command on the File menu to open a clip-art image in your graphics program. The steps are the same as for opening any compatible file type.

STEP-BY-STEP 2.9

1. Launch your graphics program.

2. Click **File** on the Menu bar, and then click **Open**. The Open dialog box displays. Depending on your graphics program, the Open dialog box may list all graphics files or only those in the native file format.

STEP-BY-STEP 2.9 Continued

3. If necessary, navigate to the location where you stored the Mouse.jpg file that you downloaded from the Internet in the previous exercise.

4. Click the drop-down arrow in the *Files of type* box to display the list of compatible file types.

5. Click **JPEG**, the file type you used to save the file you downloaded from the Internet in the previous exercise. Now, the Open dialog box displays only JPEG files, including the Mouse.jpg file.

6. Click the **Mouse.jpg** file to select it, and then click the **Open** button. If you do not have the downloaded file, click the file named **Step2-9**. The file opens in your graphics program window, as shown in Figure 2-10.

FIGURE 2-10
Downloaded picture open in graphics program

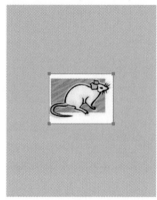

7. Click **File** on the Menu bar, and then click **Save As**. The Save As dialog box opens, and you can save the file in your program's native file format.

8. Key the filename **Mouse2** in the File name box.

9. Click the drop-down arrow in the **Save as type** box, and then click your program's native file format. Select the location where you want to save the file from the Save in list, and then click the **Save** button. If an Options dialog box displays, click **OK** to save the file using the default options. Leave **Mouse2** open to use in the next exercise.

Optimize and Export Images

When you have finished working with a file and want to make it available for use in a different program, you export it. Exporting converts a copy of the file to a different format, while leaving the original file intact. There are many reasons to export files to a different format. For example, if you plan to insert the file on a Web page, you want to use a small file that is supported by most Web browsers, such as GIF. If an image has solid colors, or very few colors, GIF is also appropriate. If you plan to insert the file in a newsletter that will be printed, you want to use a file type such as TIFF, which reproduces well on paper. Color photos usually are best saved as JPEG, but some grayscale and black and white photos can be saved as GIF without loss of quality. (Refer to Lesson 1, Table 1-1, for a description of common graphics file formats.)

The quickest method of exporting a graphics file is to use the Save As command to select a different file format and then save the file. However, if possible, before you export a graphic you should *optimize* it for the export file format. Optimizing involves selecting options for the best combination of file size and quality, depending on the export format you select. The methods for optimizing and exporting files vary greatly depending on your graphics program.

In some programs, you may be able to select from a list of preset optimization options for different file types, or to select a file type and then select specific settings in a dialog box or panel. Some programs let you select certain optimization settings in an Options dialog box when you use the Save As command, and some let you combine the export and optimization process. For example, your program may have an Export Wizard that automatically selects the best file format and optimization setting based on how you plan to use the image, or a feature such as Image Preview or Save for Web that lets you preview the effects of selected optimization options before you actually export the file.

> **Note**
>
> In some programs, you can optimize files for specific purposes, such as for use on the World Wide Web. In those programs, you access optimization options by clicking File on the Menu bar and then clicking a command such as Save for Web.

Export a File without Optimizing

In most programs, you can export a file without selecting optimization settings, or by accepting default settings, by using the Save As command. This is a good method to use if you know the program you want to export the file to, but are not sure how to set the specific file formatting options.

STEP-BY-STEP 2.10

1. Click **File** on the Menu bar, and then click **Save As**. The Save As dialog box opens.

2. Key the filename **Mouse3** in the File name box.

3. Click the **Save as type** drop-down arrow and select **Photoshop PSD**. (If you are using Photoshop as your graphics program, select a different file type, such as PNG.)

4. From the Save in list, select the location where you want to store the exported file, and then click the **Save** button. If an Options dialog box displays, click **OK** to export using the default settings. The **Mouse3** file is exported in the new file format. In some programs, such as Fireworks, the Mouse2 file remains open in your graphics program. In other programs, such as Photoshop, the Mouse2 file closes and the Mouse3 file remains open. Leave the file open to use in the next exercise.

About Optimizing a File

In general, the goal of optimizing is to keep the file size as small as possible while maintaining the highest possible quality. The optimization options vary, however, depending on the export file type.

If you are working with 8-bit graphics file formats such as GIF, TIFF, BMP, PICT, or PNG, the optimization options include color palette, color depth, dither, and loss settings. A *color palette* is a set of up to 256 colors that may be used in a file. Most programs have a number of built-in palettes suitable for different types of files, and you may be able to customize the palettes, import palettes from other programs, or create your own palettes.

Table 2-1 describes some common color palettes. Note that some palettes use *websafe colors*, which are colors that are displayed the same way in all Web browsers. Although many browsers display more colors than are included in websafe palettes, many designers prefer to use a websafe palette to ensure that all visitors to a Web page see the same colors in images.

TABLE 2-1
Common color palettes

PALETTE NAME	DESCRIPTION
Adaptive	A custom palette that includes the actual colors that are in the file. Usually produces a high-quality image. An adaptive palette is a good choice for preserving colors if you convert a file to GIF.
WebSnap Adaptive	An adaptive palette that converts actual colors to websafe colors.
Web 216	A palette of 216 websafe colors. These colors look the same regardless of computer platform.
Exact	A palette that contains the exact colors used in the image. It can contain no more than 256 colors and automatically converts to an adaptive palette when more than 256 colors are present.
System	Palettes of 256 colors that are defined by the current computer system.
Grayscale	A palette of up to 256 shades of gray. If you select this palette, the image is converted to grayscale.
Black & White	A two-color palette consisting of black and white.
Uniform	A palette based on the RGB (red, green, blue) color system.
Custom	A palette that has been modified or imported from another source.

Color depth refers to the number of colors in an image or on a screen. The depth of an image is usually measured by the number of colors in the image. The depth of a screen is usually measured in bits per pixel. The higher the color depth in an image, the larger the file size is, but the better the quality as well. If you reduce the color depth in order to reduce the file size, the image will probably lose quality.

Dithering is a process a program uses to approximate colors that are not part of its color palette. That means that the colors displayed may be similar to those in the original image, but not exactly the same. Dithering usually increases file size, but it can come in handy in certain situations. For example, use dithering to offset the way some monitors display gradients as separate bands of color instead of as a gradual change.

The *loss setting* is used to control compression. Increase the loss setting to allow more compression, which results in a smaller file but lower quality.

If you select the JPEG file type, you should set the quality and *smoothing* options. Smoothing is the degree of sharpness in edges. When you increase the smoothing setting, you decrease the sharpness, which results in a smaller file, but a less focused image. When you compress a JPEG file, some quality is lost. Set the quality percentage higher to maintain quality and minimize compression.

Note

Optimization settings are applied to the exported file, not to the original file.

Preview and Export a File

Although you can follow some basic rules to optimize your files, you must also use some trial and error. Most graphics programs provide preview features to determine whether the settings you select compromise the quality of the image. In addition, the programs usually tell you the file size, and some even give you an estimate of the download time, which is important if you plan to use the image on a Web page.

When you select the preview feature, your graphics program may automatically suggest a format for exporting the image. If you are happy with the settings, you can export the image. You can also try different file formats, and then change the settings to achieve the results you want. If your program has a split screen preview feature, you can even compare the same file with different settings. This method gives you a great deal of control over the results of the export process.

Did You Know?

In some programs, features in the Preview window let you select additional options such as cropping the image for export, selecting only a portion of the file for export, and removing unused colors from the exported file.

STEP-BY-STEP 2.11

1. Click **File** on the Menu bar, and then click a command such as Image Preview or Save for Web. The file is displayed in a Preview window. It should look similar to the one shown in Figure 2-11. If necessary, adjust the magnification so you can see the entire image. Notice the information at the top of the window: file size, download time, and file type. Make a note of this information so you can compare it to the values after you change the settings.

FIGURE 2-11
Preview window

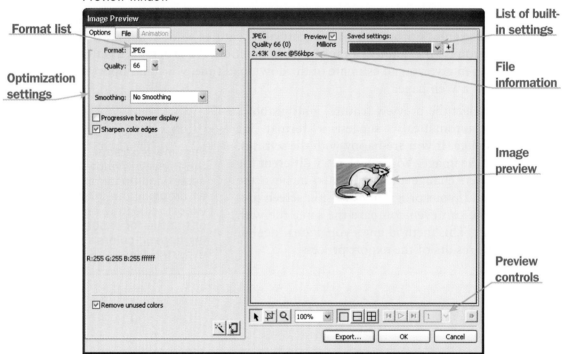

2. Click the **Saved settings** or **Built-in settings** list and select **GIF Adaptive 256**, or another GIF format that uses the Adaptive palette. Note the file size and download time compared to the original values.

3. Click the **Format** list and select **TIFF 8** (or PNG 8 if TIFF is not available). The file size and download time increase slightly because you have changed from a GIF file to a TIFF file, increasing the quality of the image.

4. Click the option to allow dithering. The file size increases again.

5. If your program has a split screen preview mode, click the button to display two preview windows within the dialog box.

STEP-BY-STEP 2.11 Continued

6. Click the **Saved settings** or **Built-in settings** list for the bottom image and select **JPEG - Smaller File** (or **JPEG low**). In Figure 2-12, you can see that the size of the file on the bottom is much smaller than the TIFF file on the top. If you have a high-quality monitor you will see that the JPEG image is also less defined.

FIGURE 2-12
Preview of both JPEG and TIFF files

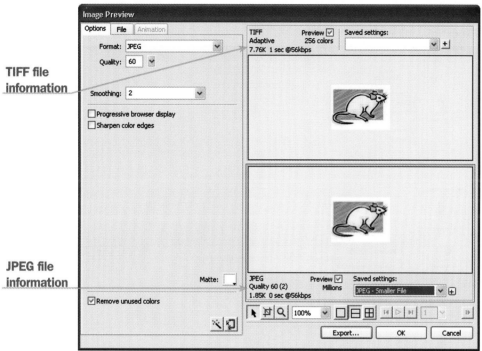

TIFF file
information

JPEG file
information

7. Click the **Saved settings** or **Built-in settings** list for the bottom image again and select **GIF Adaptive 256**, or another GIF format that uses the Adaptive palette. The quality improves and the file size and download time change.

8. Make sure that the bottom image is still selected, click the **Loss** box, key the value **25** or select **25** from the drop-down list, and then deselect the option to allow dithering. The quality does not change much, but the file size decreases.

STEP-BY-STEP 2.11 Continued

9. Click the **Export** or **Save** button in the dialog box. A dialog box such as Export or Save Optimized As may open, as shown in Figure 2-13. This dialog box allows you to key a filename and select a storage location for the new file.

> **Hot Tip**
>
> Click the OK button in the Image Preview window to save the optimization settings without exporting the file.

FIGURE 2-13
Export dialog box

10. Key the filename **Mouse4** in the File name box.

11. From the Save in list, select the location where you want to store the exported file, and then click the **Export** button. The file is exported to the specified location and saved with the new name in the new format. The Mouse2 (or Mouse3) file remains open in your graphics program. Leave **Mouse2** (or **Mouse3**) open to use in the next exercise.

> **Note**
>
> Once you select optimization settings, you can export the image again without going through the Image Preview window. Simply select the **Export** command from the **File** menu to open the Export dialog box, then name and export the file.

Use an Export Wizard

Not all graphics programs offer an Export Wizard, but if yours does, you may find it a quick and easy way to export files. A *wizard* is a series of pages or dialog boxes that step you through a process that may otherwise be confusing or complicated. An Export Wizard provides prompts that help you select the appropriate file type based on the image quality and file size you need.

STEP-BY-STEP 2.12

1. Click **File** on the Menu bar, and then click **Export Wizard**. The first page of the Export Wizard is displayed on your screen, as shown in Figure 2-14. The default option is to use the Wizard to select a file format. There may be other options available, as well. If your program does not offer an Export Wizard, skip this exercise, or click **Save As** on the **File** menu and then go to step 6.

FIGURE 2-14
First page of Export Wizard

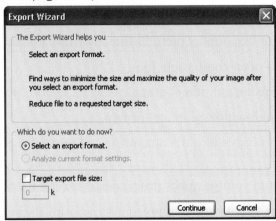

2. Click the **Continue** button. The second page of the Export Wizard opens. This page lists destination options, including a Web page, a desktop publishing program, and an image-editing program. Ordinarily you would select the option that best describes how you plan to use the exported image.

3. For the purpose of this exercise, click the option button for **A desktop publishing application**, and then click the **Continue** button. The Format Selected page of the Wizard is displayed on your screen. Because you specified the option for *A desktop publishing application*, the Wizard recommends using TIFF format.

4. Click the **Exit** button. The Wizard closes and the Image Preview dialog box opens. The options in the Image Preview dialog box depend on the selected file format. In this case, because the TIFF format is selected, there are no additional options.

5. Click the **Export** button to display the Export dialog box.

6. Key the filename **Mouse5** in the File name box. If you are using the Save As command in place of the Wizard, click the **Save as type** list and select **TIFF**.

7. From the Save in list, select the location where you want to store the exported file, and then click the **Export** button. The Mouse5 file is exported to the specified location in the TIFF format. The **Mouse2** file remains open in your graphics program.

> **Note** ☑
>
> As you may have noticed, you now have five copies of the same image, each in a different file format. Because each file is in a different format and is associated with a different file extension, you did not have to change the filename. However, having multiple files with the same name, even if they are in different formats, can get confusing.

8. Close the **Mouse2** file, saving all changes, and close your graphics program.

SUMMARY

In this lesson, you learned:

- You can import graphics images from a variety of sources, including scanners, digital cameras, and the Internet.

- In order to import graphics using a hardware device, you must make sure the device is correctly attached and installed to work with your computer.

- You can scan images directly into a graphics program or into a document file.

- You can use your operating system to copy files from a digital camera to your computer.

- Most graphics programs can import pictures directly from a digital camera.

- Graphics programs can open compatible files.

- You can save a file opened in a different graphics format in your program's native file format.

- Many Web sites let you download clip art for free.

- You can insert clip-art pictures into document files, or you can open them in your graphics program for editing.

- You can export files from your graphics program so you can use them in other programs.

- When you export a file, you have the opportunity to optimize the file by selecting options for the export file format.

VOCABULARY *Review*

Define the following terms:

Clip art	Export	Scanner
Color depth	File format	Search site
Color palette	Import	Smoothing
Compatible file format	Key term	TWAIN
Device driver	Loss setting	Websafe colors
Dithering	Native file format	Wizard
Download	Optimize	

REVIEW *Questions*

TRUE / FALSE

Circle T if the statement is true or F if the statement is false.

T   F   1. One way to acquire a graphics image is to draw it yourself.

T   F   2. A scanner uses light to capture a digital version of a printed picture.

T   F   3. TWIX is the software language used to control scanners.

T   F   4. Most computers can read a digital camera just like another disk drive if it is attached correctly to the computer.

T   F   5. Most graphics programs can open files saved in compatible file formats.

T   F   6. Before you can insert clip art into a document, you must open it in your graphics program.

T   F   7. Use the Save Picture As command to download clip art.

T   F   8. When you export a file to a different format, the original file remains unchanged.

T   F   9. Some graphics programs have an Export Wizard that prompts you through the process of exporting a file.

T   F   10. Dithering usually increases file size.

WRITTEN QUESTIONS

Write a brief answer to each of the following questions.

1. What are some of the different methods you can use to acquire graphics images?

2. What are some reasons for optimizing a file before exporting?

3. How might you find clip-art pictures on the Internet?

4. Why might you want to scan a picture into your graphics program instead of directly into a document file?

5. What operating system commands can you use to transfer files from a digital camera to your computer?

FILL IN THE BLANK

Complete the following sentences by writing the correct word or words in the blanks provided.

1. If a program supports the _____ software language, you can use it to import pictures from a scanner.

2. To open a file in a different program, _____ it from your graphics program.

3. _____ colors are displayed the same way in all Web browsers.

4. The default file format for a particular program may be referred to as the _____ file format.

5. A(n) _____ format is one that a program can open, read, and save, even if it is not the default.

6. A(n) _____ helps you locate a Web page, even if you don't know the page's address.

7. Use your browser's _____ command to save a clip-art image from the Web as a graphics file on your computer.

8. Increase the _____ setting to allow more compression, which results in a smaller file but lower quality.

9. If a graphics file retains its resolution no matter what type of screen it is displayed on, it is suitable for use on a(n) _____.

10. A(n) _____ is a series of pages or dialog boxes that step you through a process that might otherwise be confusing or complicated.

PROJECTS

PROJECT 2-1

1. Using a pen and piece of paper, draw a picture of a flower. Think about how the page will fit in the scanner before beginning, and how large the picture should be to display onscreen.

2. Scan the picture into your graphics program, making sure it is correctly positioned.

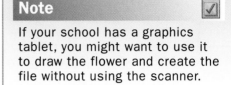

Note ☑

If your school has a graphics tablet, you might want to use it to draw the flower and create the file without using the scanner.

3. Save the file in your program's native file format as **Flower**.

4. Use the drawing tools to draw a 8-point green oval with no fill around the flower. If you are using Photoshop, you should draw the oval using Paths mode and then apply a green stroke using the pencil.

5. Print one copy of the file.

6. Save and close the **Flower** file, but leave your graphics program open to use in Project 2-2.

PROJECT 2-2

1. Use a digital camera to take a picture of someone in your class.

2. In your graphics program, create a new graphics file using the default drawing area settings.

3. Import the picture from the camera into the graphics file.

4. Save the file as **Photo**.

5. Using the drawing tools, draw a star using a bright yellow 10-point stroke and no fill around the head of the person in the photo. Be sure to select **None** for the fill setting. If you are using Photoshop, draw the star shape in Paths mode and then apply a yellow stroke.

6. Export (or save) the file in TIFF format and save it as **Modified Photo**.

7. Close the Photo file without saving changes.

8. Open the **Modified Photo** file in your graphics program. Notice that it includes the star shape.

9. Print one copy of the file.

10. Close the **Modified Photo** file without saving changes, but leave your graphics program open to use in Project 2-3.

PROJECT 2-3

1. Using your graphics program, open **Project2-3.bmp** from the Data files or use the Internet to locate and download a clip art image of a cat.

2. Save the file as **Cat** in your program's native file format.

3. Set the size of the drawing area to 5 inches by 5 inches.

4. Use the drawing tools to draw a rectangle around the clip-art image using no fill and a **black, 30**-point, **airbrush textured** line (or a textured format available in your program). If you are using Photoshop, draw the shape in Paths mode and then apply a **black** stroke with a mode such as **Soft Light**.

5. Export the file in **GIF Adaptive 256** format with the name **Revised Cat**.

6. Close the **Cat** file without saving changes.

7. Open the **Revised Cat** file in your graphics program. Notice that it includes the rectangle shape.

8. Print one copy of the file.

9. Close the **Revised Cat** file without saving changes, and then close your graphics program.

 WEB PROJECT

Consider the qualities you should look for when you evaluate a graphics image you might want to import and use. Using the Internet, research fundamental concepts of graphic design, including composition and lighting, as well as how to identify the point of interest and the attributes that determine prominence and support the subject. Look up the rules of composition, including the rule of thirds and the golden section/rectangle. When you have completed your research, locate at least three images that illustrate the concepts, and present them to your class.

 TEAMWORK PROJECT

Discuss with your classmates the type of hardware devices you can use to acquire graphics images, such as digital cameras, scanners, or graphics tablets. Select one type of device, and then create a report comparing features and prices. You may research the topic on the Internet, at a local retail store, or using magazines. Which features do the more expensive devices offer that the low-end models do not? Which features do you think are the most important, and which do you think you could do without? Which device do you think represents the best value? Present your report to your class.

CRITICAL *Thinking*

The way you acquire a graphics image may impact the way it looks in your graphics program, and the way it looks as part of a finished project. For example, a scanned image may not display the way you expect if you want to use it in a computer presentation or slide show, or a photo may not print accurately.

Import a picture into your graphics program using any of the methods discussed in this lesson. You might use clip art, a scanned image, a digital photo, or even a picture you draw using a graphics tablet. Save the picture in your program's native file format, and try printing it from your graphics program.

Decide whether the image looks best printed or onscreen. If you think the picture looks best printed, print it and then use a word processing program or pencil and paper to write a short story about the picture and use the printed picture as an illustration. If you think the picture looks best onscreen, export it so you can insert it in the word processing program or a presentation graphics program and display the story with the picture onscreen. Share your story with your classmates.

MODIFYING GRAPHICS

Graphics are modified to improve, enhance, or correct flaws in the images. You can modify original artwork that you create using the drawing tools in your graphics program, or you can modify images that you import from other sources. You can modify portions of an image or the entire image to achieve the desired results.

Even people who lack innate artistic talent can create wonderful graphics by making use of pattern, color, texture, and spatial relationships within an image. When you modify an image, you should keep in mind the basic principles of design to create an image that conveys the appropriate message, fits the purpose for which you are using it, and is pleasing to the eye. These principles include:

■ *proportion* - which describes the size and location of one object in relation to other objects in the image;

■ *balance* - which refers to the visual weight of objects and the way they are arranged; and

■ *contrast* - which refers to the juxtaposition of different elements to create visual interest.

You should also consider using *variety* to create visual interest by incorporating different elements in an image and *emphasis*, which is used to highlight or focus attention on a particular aspect of an image.

In this lesson, you learn how to use your graphics program to modify bitmap and vector graphics, keeping these principles in mind as you make adjustments.

Work with Bitmap Images

When you click a bitmap object using a selection tool, the entire object is selected just like a vector object. Most programs display a bounding box to indicate that an object is selected. A *bounding box* is a rectangular shape with selection handles displayed around the object. Once the object is selected, you can make basic changes, such as moving it or resizing it. However, because a bitmap is made of dots—or pixels—you can make some changes to the image by changing the dots themselves. For example, you can change the colors of bitmaps by changing the colors of the dots. You can even erase the dots to remove parts of the image.

Some programs designate certain tools specifically for creating and modifying bitmap images. For example, you may use the Brush or Pencil tool to paint bitmaps, the Marquee or Lasso tool to select pixels in a bitmap image, and the Brush or the Paint Bucket to change the color of selected pixels.

Most graphics programs offer additional tools you can use to make subtle changes or add effects to bitmaps. For example, you might be able to smudge the color or make the image look out of focus. Table 3-1 describes some common tools used for working with bitmaps. Keep in mind that different programs may have different names for the tools, but in most cases the function is the same.

TABLE 3-1
Tools used to work with bitmaps

ICON	TOOL NAME	DESCRIPTION
	Marquee	Used to select a rectangular area in a bitmap.
	Oval Marquee	Used to select an oval area in a bitmap.
	Lasso	Used to select a freeform area.
	Polygon Lasso	Used to select a straight-sided freeform area.
	Magic Wand	Used to select pixels based on color.
	Brush	Used to create a new bitmap object, or to apply the current stroke style and color to selected pixels in a bitmap.
	Pencil	Used to draw a new bitmap object.
	Paint Bucket	Used to fill selected areas with color.
	Eraser	Used to remove pixels from a bitmap image.

Vector illustration programs, such as Macromedia Freehand and Adobe Illustrator, do not support editing bitmap images. Therefore, in those programs the tools described in this table are used to create and modify vector graphics. You can usually open bitmaps and make basic changes such as resizing in vector programs, but you must use a program such as Macromedia Fireworks or Adobe Photoshop to access full-featured

Note

Although in some graphics programs you actually have to change to bitmap mode to use the bitmap tools, most programs that support both types of graphics let you work with either bitmap or vector tools interchangeably.

bitmap editing tools. When completing the exercises in this lesson, you should use a program such as Macromedia Fireworks or Adobe Photoshop, which provides tools for working with both bitmaps and vectors, or a program such as Paint, which is a Microsoft Windows accessory program that allows basic bitmap editing.

Select Pixels

When you want to work with just a portion of a bitmap image, you select the portion. Use either the Marquee tool or the Lasso tool to drag an outline around the area you want to select, or use the Magic Wand tool to select pixels based on color.

Drag the Marquee tool to select a rectangular area. Drag the Lasso tool to select a freeform area. When you release the mouse button after using either of these tools, a dashed line defines the area, and all the pixels in that area are selected. In some programs, the line flashes or looks like marching ants so that it is clearly visible in the image.

> **Hot Tip**
>
> As with other selection tools, you can select more than one area—overlapping or not—by selecting one, pressing and holding Shift, then selecting others.

Some programs offer variations of these tools for selecting special shapes. An Oval Marquee tool, for example, selects an oval area. A Polygon Lasso tool lets you draw a straight-sided polygon to define a selection. To use the Polygon Lasso, you click at each point where you want a side of the shape to begin or end, then double-click to complete the shape.

With the Magic Wand tool, you click a pixel to select all adjacent pixels of the same or similar color. You set the tolerance level property to control the Magic Wand. The lower the tolerance level, the more closely matched adjacent colors must be to be included in the selection. For example, if you select the Magic Wand tool and set the tolerance level to 0, when you click a pixel only adjacent colors that are exactly the same tone are selected. If you set the tolerance level to 50 or higher, you can select a wider range of tones.

Once an area is selected, you use other tools to modify it. To cancel a selection, press Escape (Esc), click anywhere outside the selection, or use the Deselect command, which you will usually find on the Select or Edit menu. You can move a selection marquee by dragging it or by pressing the arrow keys on your keyboard, and you can add to the selected area by holding down Shift and using any bitmap selection tool to define another area overlapping the first. When you release the mouse button, the overlapping areas combine into one.

S TEP-BY-STEP 3.1

1. Launch your graphics program, and open **Step3-1** from the Data files for this lesson.

2. Save the file as **Trees**.

3. Zoom in to **200%** magnification, or even larger if necessary. When selecting pixels, zooming in on the image makes it easier to select the area you want.

> **Note**
>
> If you find you cannot edit the file, you are probably using a vector graphics only program. Try using a program that provides tools for editing bitmap graphics.

STEP-BY-STEP 3.1 Continued

4. Click the **Marquee tool** in the toolbox, and then click and drag a rectangle around the tree on the right. The dashed line indicates the selected area, which includes some of the background, as shown in Figure 3-1.

FIGURE 3-1
Use Marquee tool to select rectangular area of pixels

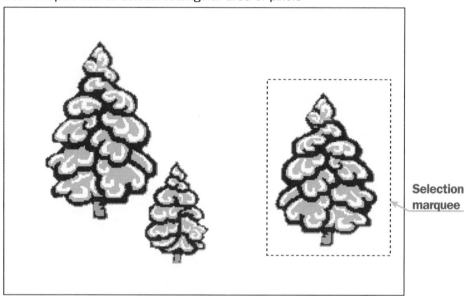

Selection marquee

5. Click outside the selection to deselect the area, and then click the **Lasso tool** in the toolbox.

6. Position the tip of the Lasso pointer along the edge of the middle tree. Click and drag around the outline of the tree to select it. Try to stay as close as possible to the outline of the tree.

7. Press **Esc** or click outside the selection to deselect the area, and then click the **Magic Wand tool** in the toolbox.

8. Click the brown trunk of the tree on the left. All adjacent brown pixels are selected.

9. Press and hold **Shift** on your keyboard, click the brown trunk of the middle tree, and then click the trunk of the tree on the right. Now, all three brown tree trunks are included in the selection, as shown in Figure 3-2.

STEP-BY-STEP 3.1 Continued

FIGURE 3-2
Use Magic Wand tool to select pixels based on color

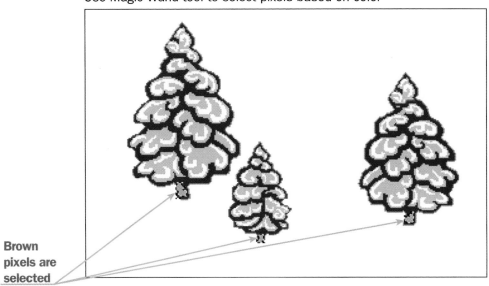

**Brown
pixels are
selected**

10. Leave the **Trees** file open with the trunks selected for the next exercise.

Use the Brush, Pencil, and Eraser

You can use the Pencil tool to draw freeform lines in a bitmap image using the current stroke color. The Brush tool is used to apply the current stroke style and color to selected pixels in a bitmap image. And the Eraser tool lets you erase pixels from a bitmap image. Simply drag the eraser across the area you want to remove.

If no area is selected, you can use the brush, pencil, and eraser anywhere in the drawing area. However, if an area is selected, these tools will affect only pixels within the selection.

> **Hot Tip**
>
> Change the size and shape properties of the Eraser to control the amount and shape of the pixels you erase.

STEP-BY-STEP 3.2

1. With the trunks still selected, click the **Brush tool** in the toolbox. You will use the brush to change the color of the selected area.

2. Click the stroke color palette and select a red (such as hexadecimal code **#FF0000**), and then set the stroke style to a **10**-point **Soft Line**. The stroke style settings are usually found in a panel such as Properties, or on an options menu. If you are using Photoshop, set the foreground color to **red**.

3. Click and drag the mouse pointer across the selected areas to change the pixels to red. Notice that only the pixels within the selection are modified. If you drag outside the selection, no change is made.

STEP-BY-STEP 3.2 Continued

4. Press **Esc** to deselect the areas. If you are using Photoshop, click the **Marquee tool** and then click anywhere outside the selection.

5. Click the **Pencil tool** in the toolbox, and then change the stroke (or foreground color) to black (**#000000**). Click and drag the mouse pointer to draw a diagonal line through the tree on the right. This colors a black line of pixels as you drag. Notice that because no area is selected, you can draw anywhere in the image.

6. Click the **Marquee tool** in the toolbox, and select an area from the right of the middle tree to the right edge of the image. Include the tree on the right and the background. You may need to zoom out so you can see the whole drawing area.

7. Click the **Eraser tool** in the toolbox, and then click and drag within the selected area. As you drag the tool, you erase the pixels, revealing the drawing area behind the image. Thoroughly erase all of the pixels within the selected area. When you are finished, the image should look similar to Figure 3-3.

FIGURE 3-3
Modified bitmap file

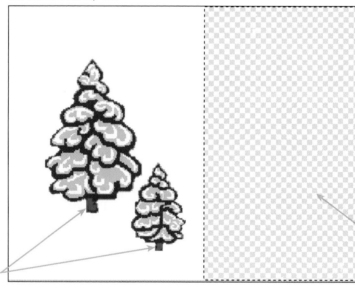

Pixels inside the marquee have been erased

Tree trunks are now red

8. Press **Esc** to cancel the selection, or click the **Marquee tool** and click outside the selection.

9. Save the changes and leave the **Trees** file open for the next exercise.

Use the Paint Bucket

The Paint Bucket tool applies the current fill color to pixels within a set color tolerance range. As with the Magic Wand tool, the lower the tolerance level, the more closely matched adjacent colors must be to be affected.

Extra for Experts

Some graphics programs also have a Gradient tool that you can use to fill an area with a gradient color. Gradient color shades gradually from a dark hue to a light hue. You can use the Paint Bucket and Gradient tools to fill vector shapes as well as bitmaps.

S TEP-BY-STEP 3.3

1. Click the **Paint Bucket tool** in the toolbox.

2. Select a dark brown fill such as hexadecimal code **#663300**.

3. Position the Paint Bucket mouse pointer so that the tip of the paint pouring out of the bucket is touching anywhere within the red trunk area of the tree on the left (zoom in if necessary), and then click the mouse button. The pixel on which you clicked and all the adjacent red pixels change to brown. If more than the trunk area changes color, the tolerance level may be set too high. Try changing it to a value lower than 50 so that only pixels of a similar color are affected.

4. Move the mouse pointer so it touches the red trunk area of the tree on the right, and click the mouse button to change the red pixels to brown.

   Now, you will change the fill color of the background.

5. Select a lighter blue from the fill color palette, such as hexadecimal code **#00CCFF**, click the **Paint Bucket tool** if it is not already selected, and then click anywhere on the white background. The current fill color is applied to the background.

6. Click with the **Paint Bucket tool** on the blank drawing area to fill it as well. The image should look similar to Figure 3-4. If white spots show up within the blue background fill, you did not erase all of the white pixels in the previous exercise. Use the **Brush** to paint them with the light blue.

FIGURE 3-4
Fill a background in a bitmap image

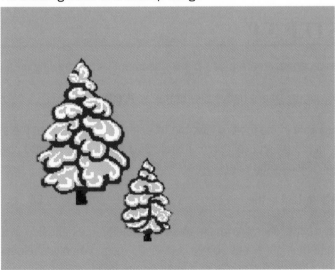

7. Save the changes and close the **Trees** file. Leave your graphics program open for the next exercise.

Reshape Vector Paths

Vector graphics are defined by points, which are positioned along the lines and curves that comprise the shape. You can change the shape by moving the points. Simply select the object with the Subselection tool, and then drag any point to a new location. In most programs, you can add, delete, and move points as well.

The tools for shaping vector paths vary, depending on your program. For example, some graphics programs have a Redraw Path tool that you use to extend or redraw existing vector paths. Select the tool, and then position the mouse pointer over the path to change. When the mouse pointer changes to the Redraw Path pointer, drag to extend or redraw the existing path.

A few programs offer tools that let you change the shape of a vector regardless of where the points are located. Points are moved, removed, or added as necessary. Select an object, and then select the Freeform tool. The mouse pointer changes to indicate the current action. Position the pointer on the selected path to pull or near the path to push. The path is modified based on the current size of the pointer, which you can change in the Properties panel or dialog box.

The Reshape Area tool lets you move all selected paths within an area defined by a circle attached to the pointer. Select the path and then select the Reshape area tool. Position the pointer over the selected path. When you drag, the portion of the path that falls within the pointer's circle moves. The portion outside the circle remains unchanged. As with the Freeform tool, change the size of the pointer in the Properties panel or dialog box.

Not all programs have the specific tools named in the following exercise. Experiment with the tools you have available to achieve the result shown in Figure 3-5.

STEP-BY-STEP 3.4

1. In your graphics program, create a new blank document with a drawing area of **8** inches by **8** inches.

2. Save the file in your program's native file format as **Profile**.

3. Select the **Ellipse tool** in the toolbox. Set the fill color to **white** and set the stroke to a **black**, **5**-point **Hard Line**, and then draw an oval approximately 350 pixels wide by 500 pixels high in the middle of the drawing area. (Display the rulers, if necessary.) This shape will be a head.

4. Select the **Freeform tool** in the toolbox, and set the Size property to **50**.

5. Move the pointer so it is directly over the middle handle on the right side of the shape, and then drag diagonally down to the right about 50 pixels (or 0.25 inch). When you release the mouse button, the path is reshaped, creating the profile of a nose on the head.

6. Select the **Reshape Area tool**, and set the Size property to **50**.

STEP-BY-STEP 3.4 Continued

7. Move the pointer so it is about halfway between the nose and the bottom of the head outside of the shape, then press and hold the mouse button. A circle appears around the mouse pointer, indicating the area that will be redrawn. Drag to the left about 50 pixels (or 0.25 inch). Again, when you release the mouse button, the path is reshaped, this time creating the profile of an open mouth. With PhotoShop, you may have to add one or more anchor points to define the path you want to reshape.

8. Click the **Subselection tool** in the toolbox. Notice that the vector points that make the shape are displayed instead of selection handles.

9. Drag the vector point at the top of the head straight down about 100 pixels (or 1.5 inches). When you release the mouse button, the path is redrawn, creating a flatter head.

10. Select the **Ellipse tool** and draw a small oval for an eye near the top right of the head, then deselect all shapes. The image should look similar to the one in Figure 3-5.

> **Note**
>
> When you use the Subselection tool, your program may display a message telling you that a selected shape must be ungrouped before you can edit its points. Click OK to continue.

FIGURE 3-5
Reshape vector paths

11. Save the changes and close the **Profile** file. Leave your graphics program open for the next exercise.

Position and Align Objects

When you create a graphics image, arrangement of the objects in the drawing area is important. The way you position objects in the foreground, middle distance, and background of an image can focus a viewer's attention on a particular part of the image, as well as give the image depth, perspective, and visual appeal. (Some programs have a Move tool specifically for this purpose.) When combined with different-sized objects, position can even give an image a three-dimensional effect.

You do not have to place each object in the perfect spot when you first create an image, because you can easily reposition objects after drawing them. The easiest way to position an object is to select it and then drag it to a new location. You can usually also use the arrow keys on the keyboard to move an object in small increments, such as 1 point for each press of the key. You may find the grid and rulers helpful for positioning objects. With the grid displayed, you can easily see whether objects are even or offset horizontally and vertically, and how much white space—the area between objects—there is.

In some programs, if you want to position the object in a precise location, you can set horizontal (X) and vertical (Y) *coordinates*. The coordinates are specific points laid out in an invisible grid in the drawing area. The grid starts in the top left corner, with coordinates of 0, 0. As you move an object to the right, the X coordinate increases. As you move down, the Y coordinate increases. You can view and/or control object coordinates using a panel, toolbar, or palette such as Info, Properties, or Transform. By default, the upper-left corner of the object is located at the coordinates displayed in the panel. You enter the coordinates based on the current unit of measure. By default, most programs use pixels, but you can usually change to inches or centimeters. The command for changing the unit of measure varies, depending on your program. It may be on the Options drop-down menu in the Info panel or in the Preferences dialog box. (To open the Options drop-down menu in a panel, click the Options menu button in the upper-right corner.)

You can also usually *align* and *distribute* objects in an image. When the snap to grid option is toggled on, the objects automatically align with the nearest gridline. You can also align an object to adjust its position horizontally and vertically relative to the top, bottom, left, and right of the drawing area or to the currently selected area. Distributing objects adjusts the space between them. Alignment and distribution options are usually available on a panel or palette, and may also be on a menu.

STEP-BY-STEP 3.5

1. Open **Step3-5** from the Data files for this lesson.

2. Save the file as **Apples**.

3. Select the small green apple.

4. Move the selection pointer over the object, drag the object up and to the left to position it to the left of the large yellow apple, and then release the mouse button.

   Now, you will move an object by entering X and Y coordinates.

5. Select the large yellow apple.

6. Open the panel or dialog box that contains the coordinate settings.

STEP-BY-STEP 3.5 Continued

7. Click in the X box and key **500** using pixels as the unit of measure. Click in the Y box and key **250**, and then press **Enter**. The selected apple moves so its upper-left corner is at the specified coordinates.

   Now, position the third apple by using the Align options.

8. Select the red apple. Open the panel, menu, or dialog box that contains the alignment options.

9. Select the option to align the object with the drawing area (**To Canvas**), select the option that aligns the object in the horizontal center, and then select the option that aligns the object in the vertical center. The apple moves to the center of the drawing area.

   Finally, put the finishing touches on the positions of the three objects by distributing them horizontally. (If a distribution option is not available in your program, skip to step 12.)

10. With the red apple still selected, press and hold **Shift**, click the green apple, and then click the yellow apple. All three objects are now selected.

Hot Tip

The steps for changing the unit of measure depend on your graphics program. In Fireworks, for example, select the unit on the Options menu in the Info panel.

Note

The position of coordinates is affected by the size and resolution of the drawing area and the specific program you are using. If at the end of the steps your results are not the same as those in the illustrations, you may be using a different program, a different resolution, or a different-sized drawing area. To make your image match the solution, drag the objects or adjust the coordinates as necessary.

11. In the Align panel, click the tool that distributes the selected objects by the bottom edge. The objects shift so they are evenly distributed vertically from the top of the drawing area to the bottom. The file should look similar to Figure 3-6. (If necessary, drag the apples into position as shown.)

FIGURE 3-6
Objects positioned in the drawing area

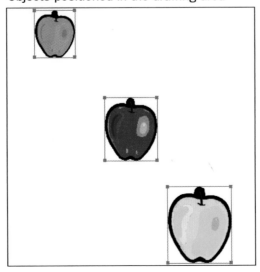

12. Save the changes and leave the **Apples** file open for the next exercise.

Group and Stack Objects

As you have learned, you can select more than one item at a time so that you can modify all objects at one time. In some programs, you can also *group* multiple objects. Grouped objects can be selected and modified as one unit. For example, if you create a group of three rectangles, you can change the fill color of all three objects at once. Group objects when you want the items to remain as one. That way, you don't have to worry about selecting all items each time you want to make changes.

To create a group, simply select the objects you want to include and then click the Group command on a menu such as Modify. Selection handles surround the entire group, rather than the individual objects in the group. Use the Ungroup command on the same menu to turn off grouping so you can work with the individual objects again.

Hot Tip

You can quickly access most of the commands covered in this lesson by right-clicking to display a menu with frequently used commands.

Most graphics programs also provide a tool with a name such as Subselection or Group Selection that allows you to select one or more items in a group without ungrouping all objects. You can then easily edit a portion of the group.

As you draw objects, they *stack* in the drawing area, even if they do not actually overlap each other. The first object you create is at the bottom or back of the stack, and the last object you create is at the top or front of the stack. You will sometimes need to rearrange the stacking order of objects to make sure that an object displays properly or to create overlapping effects. Stacking only affects objects on the same layer. If your program places objects on individual layers, you control the stacking by arranging the layers.

To rearrange the stacking order, select the object you need to change and then click the Arrange command on a menu such as Modify. Most programs give you four options for adjusting stacking order: Send to Back, Send Backward, Bring Forward, and Bring to Front. Send to Back moves an object behind all other objects, while Bring to Front positions an object in front of all other objects. Send Backward and Bring Forward move objects forward or backward one position at a time.

Extra for Experts

Do not confuse the stacking order with layers. Some programs have a Layers feature you can use to separate an image into individual transparent planes. Layers are used for creating complex images, animations, and certain special effects.

STEP-BY-STEP 3.6

1. Select all three objects if they are not already selected.

2. Select the command to group the objects. The three objects are now grouped together to make up a single object. Notice that the selection handles are displayed on the corners of the entire group. Changes that you make now will affect the entire group.

Try changing the alignment.

STEP-BY-STEP 3.6 Continued

3. If the Align panel is not open, open it. Make sure the option to align objects to the drawing area (canvas) is selected, and then click the tool that aligns the selected object at the left edge. The entire group moves to the left of the drawing area, as shown in Figure 3-7.

FIGURE 3-7
The grouped objects are left-aligned

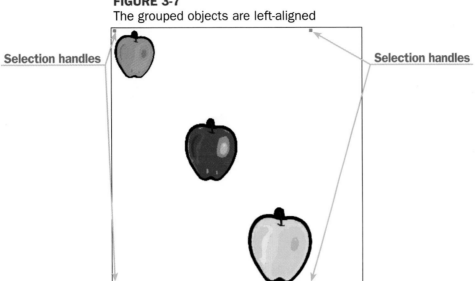

Selection handles   Selection handles

Now, ungroup the objects so you can change the stacking order.

4. Select the command to ungroup the objects. The three objects are ungrouped, although all three remain selected.

5. Click anywhere outside the selected objects to deselect them, and then select the small green apple on the left.

6. Set the X coordinate for the selected object to **200** and set the Y coordinate to **300** or drag the object over the red apple. Notice that even though you are dragging the green apple, it is stacked behind the red apple.

7. With the green apple still selected, click the **Arrange** command and then click **Bring Forward**. The object moves forward in front of the red apple.

8. Select the yellow apple on the right. Set the X coordinate to **300** and the Y coordinate to **225**, or drag the object so that it overlaps the red apple.

STEP-BY-STEP 3.6 Continued

9. With the yellow apple on the right still selected, click the **Arrange** command, and then click **Send to Back** on the submenu. The selected apple moves behind the other objects. When you deselect all objects, the image should look similar to Figure 3-8.

FIGURE 3-8
Modified image includes stacked objects

10. Save the changes and leave the **Apples** file open for the next exercise.

> **Hot Tip**
>
> Some programs have a Select Behind tool that you can use to select an object stacked behind another object.

Scale Objects

When you want to resize an object to make it larger or smaller, you can *scale* the object. To scale means simply to change an object's size.

Some programs allow you to simply drag a selection handle to scale an object. Other programs offer a Scale tool or Scale command for this purpose. (You may find the Scale command on the Transform menu, which is usually on the Modify or Edit menu.) When you select the Scale tool, *transform* handles may be displayed around the selected object. Transform is a term used to describe changes to the characteristics of an object or selection. You drag the transform handles to change the height, the width, or both dimensions at once. Most programs also allow you to scale an object precisely by specifying height and width in a panel or dialog box using pixels, inches, or centimeters as the unit of measure.

STEP-BY-STEP 3.7

1. Select the large, yellow apple.

2. Click the **Scale tool** in the toolbox, or select the **Scale** command. A bounding box with transform handles may display around the object.

3. Position the mouse pointer over the bottom center transform handle. When the pointer is positioned correctly, it looks like a vertical double-headed arrow with a horizontal line in the middle.

4. Drag the handle down halfway to the bottom of the drawing area. When you release the mouse button, the object is resized, as shown in Figure 3-9. Notice that since you changed the height but not the width, the apple looks distorted and out of proportion.

FIGURE 3-9
Height of the object has been increased

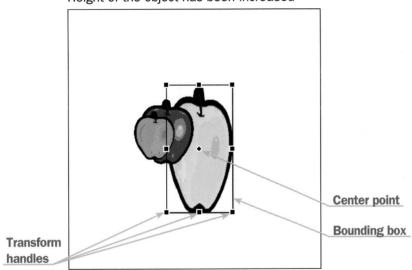

Center point

Bounding box

Transform
handles

5. Switch to the **Pointer tool** and then select the red apple in the middle.

6. Click the **Scale tool** in the toolbox to display the transform handles around the selected object. Position the mouse pointer over the handle in the upper-left corner and then drag diagonally approximately 100 pixels up and to the left. When you release the mouse button, the object is resized. This time, you changed both the height and width so the apple does not look distorted.

> **Hot Tip**
>
> Press and hold **Shift** while you drag a corner handle to maintain the original proportions of an object while scaling.

Now group the objects and scale the entire group at the same time.

7. Using the **Pointer tool**, select all three objects in the image. You may press and hold **Shift** and click the objects with the selection tool, or use the tool to drag a selection rectangle around the objects. Sometimes, when selecting stacked objects it may be easier to drag the selection tool than to click each object.

STEP-BY-STEP 3.7 Continued

8. Select the command to group the objects.

This time, set precise dimensions for scaling the entire group.

9. In the panel or dialog box that allows you to specify an object's size, select to use **pixels** as the unit of measure, if necessary. For example, in Fireworks, select pixels from the Options menu in the Info panel, click in the Width box and key **350**, click in the Height box and key **350**, and then press **Enter**. The object is scaled to the specified dimensions, as shown in Figure 3-10.

FIGURE 3-10
Scaled group

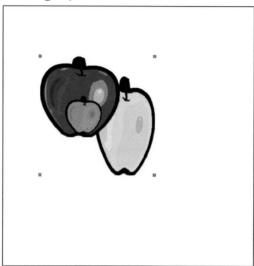

10. Save the changes and leave the **Apples** file open for the next exercise.

Rotate and Flip Objects

Two other methods of transforming an object are rotating and flipping. When you rotate an object, it pivots around an axis of rotation, sometimes called the point of origin. To *rotate* an object, select any transformation tool or the Rotate command and then move the mouse pointer near the object outside the bounding box. When the pointer changes to a rotation pointer, drag in any direction to rotate the object. Alternatively, some programs have a Rotate tool. Click the tool, and then drag a corner handle to rotate the object. Some programs also have menu commands that let you rotate by 180 degrees or by 90-degree increments, and some programs let you enter a specific value for the rotation.

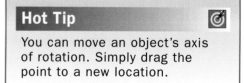

Hot Tip

You can move an object's axis of rotation. Simply drag the point to a new location.

You can *flip* an object horizontally or vertically to reverse the image from left to right or top to bottom. Most programs have Flip Horizontal and Flip Vertical commands, but some programs use a Reflect tool for flipping. When you use a Reflect tool you set a specific axis across which to flip the object. The default axis is 90 degrees, which flips the object to create a mirror image.

S TEP-BY-STEP 3.8

1. Select the grouped object, if it is not already selected.

2. Click the **Scale tool** or select the **Rotate** command to display transformation handles. Your program might have a Rotate tool that displays rotation handles.

3. Move the mouse pointer to an area outside the edge of the object until it changes to the rotation pointer. If your program has rotation handles, move the mouse pointer to touch a rotation handle. Drag counterclockwise—to the left—until the top right transformation handle is positioned straight up, as shown in Figure 3-11. Release the mouse button to complete the rotation.

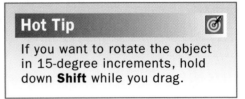

Hot Tip

If you want to rotate the object in 15-degree increments, hold down **Shift** while you drag.

FIGURE 3-11
Drag selected object to rotate it around its axis

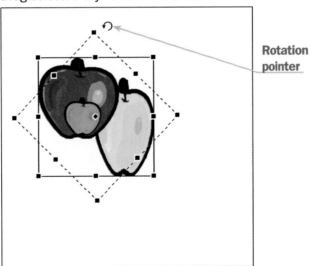

Rotation pointer

4. With the group still selected, click the command to flip the object horizontally, left to right.

STEP-BY-STEP 3.8 Continued

5. Use the align commands to align the object in the center of the drawing area, both horizontally and vertically. The image should look similar to the one in Figure 3-12.

FIGURE 3-12
Apples have been rotated, flipped, and positioned

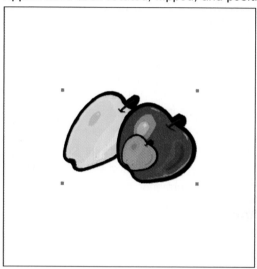

6. Save the changes and leave the **Apples** file open for the next exercise.

Copy Objects

When you want to duplicate a vector object or a complete bitmap object, you can use commands such as Copy and Paste or Duplicate. In some programs, the Copy and Paste commands create a new object directly on top of the original object, while in other programs the pasted object appears in the center of the drawing area. The Duplicate command creates a new object overlapping the original object. No matter what means you use to copy an object, you can move the copy to any location in the drawing area.

There are variations of the Copy, Cut, and Paste commands in most programs. For example, Paste Special lets you paste an item with a link to the original object. Some graphics programs have Paste in Front or Paste in Back commands. These commands paste the copied object directly on top of or behind the original object. Other variations include Paste as Mask, Paste Inside, and Paste Attributes, which lets you copy just the formatting from one object to another.

In programs that support bitmap editing, you can also use the Copy and Paste commands to create a bitmap object from selected pixels. Simply select the pixel area, click Copy on the Edit menu, and then click

Extra for Experts

The Copy, Cut, and Paste commands are used in all Windows programs to copy and move text as well as objects from one location to another. The item that is cut or copied is placed on the Clipboard, a temporary storage area in your computer's memory. When you select the Paste command, the item is inserted at the current location.

Paste on the Edit menu. The selected area becomes an object that you can select and modify as a complete unit. Most programs also have tools for duplicating an area of selected pixels without creating an object. Duplicating pixels is a great way to touch up photographs because you replace the pixels you don't like with copies of pixels you do like.

S TEP-BY-STEP 3.9

1. Ungroup the objects and then select only the small green apple.

2. Click **Edit** on the Menu bar, and then click **Copy**. The object is copied to the Clipboard.

3. Click **Edit** on the Menu bar, and then click **Paste**. A copy of the object is pasted into the graphics file. Don't worry if nothing seems to have happened! The new object may be positioned directly over the original object.

4. With the new object selected, click the command to flip the object horizontally, left to right. Drag the flipped object to the left of the original green apple.

5. Select the yellow apple.

6. Click **Edit** on the Menu bar, and then click **Duplicate**. A duplicate of the object is inserted overlapping the original. The duplicate object is selected.

Note

If you are using a program that does not have a Duplicate command, use the Copy and Paste commands instead.

7. Click the command to flip the object horizontally left to right, and then drag the duplicate up and to the right, behind the red apple.

Now, try copying more than one object at a time.

8. Select both green apples. You could group the two together, but since you don't plan on modifying them as a unit all the time, you can just work with the two selected objects.

9. Click **Edit** on the Menu bar, and then click **Duplicate**. Duplicates of both objects are created, overlapping the originals. Both new duplicates are selected.

STEP-BY-STEP 3.9 Continued

10. Drag the objects down and to the right, and then deselect all objects. The image should look similar to Figure 3-13.

FIGURE 3-13
Image includes copies of the original objects

11. Save the changes and close the **Apples** file. Leave your graphics program open to use in the next exercise.

Skew and Distort Objects

Sometimes you might want objects in an image to look distorted or slanted. You can *skew* an object to slant it along its horizontal or vertical axis. Most graphics programs supply a Skew tool or Skew command that you can use to display transform handles. Drag a center side handle to skew the object vertically, or drag a center top or bottom handle to skew the object horizontally. Drag a corner handle to skew it both vertically and horizontally at the same time, and to achieve perspective in the image.

When you *distort* an object, you change its height and/or width without maintaining the original proportions. Click the Distort tool or select the Distort command to display transform handles, then use the handles to move the sides or corners of the object to change its size and proportions. Use distorting to achieve a three-dimensional effect.

Note

If you are using a graphics program that does not have Skew and Distort tools, you may be able to achieve the same results simply by moving the vector points as described earlier in this lesson. Ask your instructor for information on how to proceed.

S TEP-BY-STEP 3.10

1. Open **Step3-10** from the Data files for this lesson.

2. Save the file as **Road**.

3. Select the object, and then click the **Skew tool** in the toolbox or select the **Skew** command. (You may find the Skew tool on a hidden toolbar beneath a tool such as the Scale tool.) The transform handles display around the object.

4. Move the mouse pointer so it is touching the lower-left handle, then drag the handle out to the lower-left corner of the drawing area. In most programs both the left and right lower corners of the object move, as shown in Figure 3-14. If both handles do not move in the program you are using, repeat the step to drag the right handle to the lower-right corner. Release the mouse button to complete the transformation.

FIGURE 3-14
Skewing an object

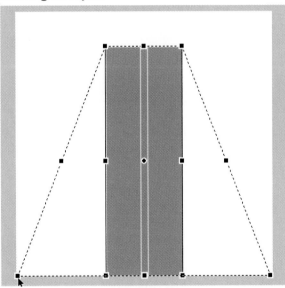

5. Move the mouse pointer so it is touching the upper-left handle, then drag the handle in so that it is just to the left of the center handle. If both handles do not move, repeat the step to drag the right corner to the center. Notice how skewing the object has made it look as if it is a road disappearing into the distance. Apply the transformation, if necessary.

Now, use the Distort tool to add a three-dimensional effect to the image.

6. Click the **Distort tool** in the toolbox or select the **Distort** command, then drag the bottom center handle to the right. Release the mouse button when the handle you are dragging is positioned in the lower-right corner of the drawing area. Don't worry about the part of the object that is hidden from view outside the drawing area.

STEP-BY-STEP 3.10 Continued

7. Drag the top center handle to the upper-left corner of the drawing area. Release the mouse button or press **Enter** to complete the transformation. When you deselect the object, the image should look similar to Figure 3-15.

FIGURE 3-15
Modified image has depth and perspective

8. Save the changes and close the **Road** file. Leave your graphics program open to use in the next exercise.

Crop an Image

When you want to remove portions of an image, you crop it. Cropping cuts out the portions of a file that you don't want. To crop an image in most graphics programs, you use the Crop tool to define a rectangular bounding box in the image. Double-clicking in the box, or pressing Enter, retains the content inside the rectangle while removing the content outside the rectangle. The drawing area is resized to fit the area within the box. In some programs, you can specify dimensions for the area you want to crop in a dialog box or panel.

Hot Tip

Some programs have commands for cropping or trimming the drawing area itself. Use such a command to automatically delete extra space around the image.

S TEP-BY-STEP 3.11

1. Open **Step3-11** from the Data files for this lesson.

2. Save the file in your program's native file format as **Harbor**.

3. Click the **Crop tool** in the toolbox, move the mouse pointer to the upper-right corner of the image, and then drag down and to the right to draw a rectangle that includes the full width and top half of the image, as shown in Figure 3-16.

FIGURE 3-16
Drag to define the area to crop

Content inside the box is kept

Cropping pointer

Content outside the box is removed

4. Release the mouse button when you have completed the rectangle. You can drag the handles on the bounding box to adjust the size of the crop area if necessary.

5. When you are satisfied with the area you have defined for cropping, double-click within the bounding box, or press **Enter**. The image is cropped, and the drawing area is resized.

> **Note** ☑️
>
> In some programs, when you click the Crop tool, crop handles may display around the edges of the image. Simply drag the crop handles to define the area you want to crop.

STEP-BY-STEP 3.11 Continued

6. Click **View** on the Menu bar, and then click **Fit All** to increase the magnification. The image should look similar to Figure 3-17.

FIGURE 3-17
Cropped image

7. Save the changes and close the **Harbor** file. Close your graphics program.

SUMMARY

In this lesson, you learned:

■ Some programs have graphics tools designed specifically for working with bitmap images.

■ You can select and modify areas of pixels in a bitmap image.

■ There are tools you can use to reshape vector paths.

■ You can move objects around in an image.

■ Most graphics programs have tools for aligning and distributing objects in an image.

■ You can group multiple objects together so that you can modify them as one unit.

■ Objects stack from back to front as you create them in a drawing; you can rearrange stacking order to change the way objects overlap.

■ There are many ways to transform an object, including scaling, skewing, distorting, flipping, and rotating.

■ You can create exact duplicates of vector and bitmap objects.

■ Cropping lets you remove parts of an image you don't want.

Extra for Experts

In a file that contains multiple objects, you can crop a single bitmap object, or selected pixels in the bitmap, while leaving the other objects in the drawing area intact. Simply select the object or pixels you want to crop, then click Crop Selected Bitmap on the Edit menu. Adjust the bounding box as desired, and then double-click within the bounding box to complete the procedure.

VOCABULARY *Review*

Define the following terms:

Align	Distribute	Scale
Bounding box	Flip	Skew
Coordinates	Group	Stack
Crop	Rotate	Transform
Distort		

REVIEW *Questions*

TRUE / FALSE

Circle T if the statement is true or F if the statement is false.

T F 1. Use the Magic Wand tool to transform an object.

T F 2. Double-click a selected object to cancel the selection.

T F 3. You can position an object by selecting it and then dragging it to a new location.

T F 4. The upper-left corner of the drawing area has the coordinates of 0, 0.

T F 5. If an area is selected, the Eraser removes pixels within the selection only.

T F 6. Send an object to the back if you want all other objects stacked behind it.

T F 7. Use the Paint Bucket to change the fill color of pixels in a bitmap image.

T F 8. Most graphics programs use points as the default unit of measure.

T F 9. When you use the Duplicate command, you cannot move the duplicate to a different position.

T F 10. When you crop an image, you remove content you do not want.

WRITTEN QUESTIONS

Write a brief answer to each of the following questions.

1. What are some of the tools you can use to modify bitmap images?

2. How does the tolerance setting affect the Magic Wand and the Paint Bucket?

3. What effect can you achieve by skewing an object along both its horizontal and vertical axes?

4. What are three methods you can use to position an object in the drawing area?

5. What are three methods you can use to select a portion of a bitmap image?

FILL IN THE BLANK

Complete the following sentences by writing the correct word or words in the blanks provided.

1. A(n) _____ box is a rectangular shape with selection handles that display around a selected object.

2. The area between objects is called _____.

3. Use the _____ tool to draw freeform lines in a bitmap image using the current stroke color.

4. The _____ coordinate increases when you move an object to the right in the drawing area.

5. _____ multiple objects to work with them as one unit.

6. To _____ means to change an object's size.

7. To maintain an object's _____, change both the height and width by the same amount.

8. To position an object along the bottom of the drawing area, you should _____ it with the bottom edge.

9. When you _____ an object, it pivots around a center point.

10. Flip an image _____ to reverse it from right to left.

PROJECTS

PROJECT 3-1

1. Open **Project3-1** from the Data files for this lesson.

2. Save the file as **Balloons**.

3. Use the **Marquee tool** to select the balloon on the bottom.

4. Flip the selection horizontally.

5. Use the **Magic Wand tool** to select the purple areas in the balloon on the upper-left, including the tail of the balloon. You may need to adjust the tolerance level to include all of the purple pixels in the selection.

6. Use the **Brush tool** to change the color of this balloon from purple to pink.

7. Use the **Lasso tool** to select the balloon on the upper-right.

8. Use the **Eraser tool** to delete the selected balloon.

9. Use the **Paint Bucket tool** to change the background color to light blue, including the area you erased.

10. Print one copy of the file.

11. Save and close the **Balloons** file, but leave your graphics program open to use in Project 3-2.

PROJECT 3-2

1. Open **Project3-2** from the Data files for this lesson.

2. Save the file in your program's native file format as **Robin**.

3. Crop the photo to a square approximately **310** by **300** pixels with the bird in the center.

4. Resize the drawing area to **5** inches by **5** inches.

5. Select the image object, open the Align panel, and select the options for aligning with the upper-left corner of the drawing area.

6. Use the **Copy** and **Paste** commands (or **Duplicate Layer** command) to create three copies of the object, and align one in each corner of the drawing area using the steps below:
   A. With the object selected, copy and paste the object.
   B. Align the object with the upper-right corner.
   C. Paste the object again, and then align the object with the lower-right corner.
   D. Paste the object again, and then align the object with the lower-left corner.

7. Paste the object one more time. This time, scale the object to **600** pixels wide by **600** pixels high, and align it in the center both horizontally and vertically.

8. Set the stacking order so the four smaller objects are in front of the larger object.

9. Use the **Marquee tool** to select the entire drawing area. Then, using the steps below, fill the selection with a gray color that you pick up from the snow in the image:
   A. Click the **Paint Bucket tool**.
   B. Open the fill color palette, and then move the mouse pointer (it is shaped like an eye-dropper) over the snow in the background until the color you want to use is displayed in the fill color palette. Click the mouse pointer to pick up the color and make it current.
   C. Click anywhere in the selection.

10. If necessary, change the stacking order of the selected area to send it to the back, behind the images of the bird.

11. Print one copy of the file.

12. Save and close the **Robin** file, but leave your graphics program open to use in Project 3-3.

PROJECT 3-3

1. Create a new file in your graphics program and save it as **House**.

2. Use the drawing tools to draw a picture that includes a house, a street, and at least one tree.

3. Use the skills you have learned in this lesson to integrate the objects together into a unified image. For example, define the foreground, middle ground, and background of the image by scaling and positioning objects appropriately. Stack, skew, and distort objects to create depth and perspective. Use fill and stroke properties to define shapes.

4. When you are satisfied with the drawing, save the file.

5. Print one copy of the file.

6. Save and close the **House** file, but leave your graphics program open to use in Project 3-4.

PROJECT 3-4

1. Create a new blank document in your graphics program and save it as **Arrow**.

2. Display the grid and the rulers

3. Use the **Polygon tool** to draw a triangle with a white fill and a **4-point black** stroke. Size the triangle approximately **220** pixels wide by **220** pixels high, and position it in the center of the drawing area with one angle pointing straight up.

4. Select the triangle with the **Subselection tool** to show the vector points.

5. Drag the point at the tip of the lower left of the triangle diagonally down and to the left to the corner of the next grid line.

6. Drag the point at the tip of the lower right of the triangle diagonally up and to the right to the corner of the next grid line.

7. Select the **Freeform tool** and change the size to **75**.

8. Position the pointer inside the triangle. Create a semicircular bulge pushing out in the middle of the line on the right side of the triangle by using the **Freeform pointer** to push the middle of the line up and to the right.

9. Use the same tool to create a semicircular bulge pushing in at the middle of the other two lines.

10. Print one copy of the file.

11. Save and close the **Arrow** file, and close your graphics program.

 WEB PROJECT

M.C. Escher was an artist known for his use of perspective and proportion to achieve optical illusions in his images. Use the Internet to research Escher and to locate some of his artwork that you can download. Write an essay explaining how Escher uses the basic principles of design, and why his images are so unique. Can you identify tools available in your graphics program such as duplicating and flipping that could help you achieve Escher-like images? Try your hand at creating such an image, then print it, and share it with your classmates.

 TEAMWORK PROJECT

Discuss with your classmates the basic principles of design and how you can use them to achieve different effects in an image. Gather some pictures such as posters, book covers, and magazine illustrations. Have each person in the team look for a specific design principle, such as proportion, balance, and contrast. Determine whether the artist made use of variety and emphasis. Discuss whether you think the image works, or if it could be improved by applying a transformation, such as changing the scale or the color. Rank the images on how many principles of design each one uses, and then share your results with the class.

CRITICAL *Thinking*

Look up a definition of the word *perspective* in a standard dictionary or in an art dictionary, if available. Look at different images to determine how the artist uses perspective. When you believe you have an understanding of how perspective can enhance an image, create a new file and use basic shapes to draw an image that uses perspective. It may be realistic, abstract, or stylized. Make use of the drawing and editing tools for both vectors and bitmaps to transform and modify the shapes in your drawing. Use color, alignment, and positioning as well as distortion and skewing. When you are finished, save the file, print it, and share it with your classmates.

ADDING TEXT TO GRAPHICS

OBJECTIVES

Upon completion of this lesson, you should be able to:

- Create a text object.
- Check spelling.
- Apply character formatting.
- Set text direction and alignment.
- Apply fills and strokes to text.
- Import text.
- Transform a text block.
- Convert text to vector graphics.

Estimated Time: 1.5 hours

VOCABULARY

Baseline

Expandable text block

Fixed-width text block

Font

Font size

Font style

Insertion point

Justified

Kerning

Leading

Orientation

Text block

Text flow

Wrap

Text may be incorporated in a graphics file as shapes that make up part of the image itself or, more traditionally, as words in captions, headlines, titles, and so on. For example, you may want to use the letter *M* as the focal point for a logo for a gift shop named *Marigolds*, or you may want to include the shop's address and store hours in an image to be used as a print advertisement.

Most graphics programs include tools for entering and editing text in much the same way as in a word processing or desktop publishing program. You can change character formatting, adjust spacing and alignment, and even check your spelling for errors. You can also convert text characters into shapes that you can modify using the tools you use to modify other vector objects. By combining the features of desktop publishing with graphics effects such as fills, strokes, and transformations, you can create exciting text objects that enhance your images and provide useful information. In this lesson, you learn how to create and modify text objects in a graphics file.

Create a Text Object

To enter text in a graphics file, you use a tool with a name such as Text or Type to create a *text block*, and then key the text using your computer keyboard. An *insertion point* within the block indicates where characters appear when keyed. The text is entered using the current formatting options set in your program, including the fill color, which determines the text color.

A selected text block has a bounding box and handles, similar to other selected objects in a graphics file. As you will learn, you can resize, move, duplicate, and otherwise modify a text block using many of the same commands you use to modify other graphics objects.

Most graphics programs let you create either a fixed-width text block of a certain size or an expandable text block with a size determined by the number of characters it contains. After you key text in a text block, you can edit it just as in a word processing program.

Create a Fixed-Width Text Block

In a *fixed-width text block*, you specify the block size before you begin keying the text. As you key text, it *wraps* within the block, which means that when text reaches the end of one line within the block, it moves automatically to the beginning of the next line. You can resize the block, if necessary, to adjust how the text fits in the block or how the block fits into the image as a whole. To create a fixed-width text block, select the text tool and then drag the pointer to define the size of the block.

S TEP-BY-STEP 4.1

1. Launch your graphics program and open **Step4-1** from the Data files for this lesson.

2. Save the file in your program's native file format as **Dance**.

3. Set the fill (or foreground) color to black. Text color is determined by the current fill color.

4. Click the **Text tool** in the toolbox, and then drag in the lower-left corner of the drawing area to draw a fixed-width text block that is approximately **166** pixels wide by **50** pixels high. If the unit of measure in your graphics program is set to inches, the block should be about **1.7** inches wide by **0.5** inches high. (In some programs the measurement may not show until after you release the mouse, but you can use the rulers as a guide or make adjustments to the values after you have created the block.) Notice that when you release the mouse pointer, a bounding box defines the area of the text block and an insertion point is flashing in the block. Text will be inserted to the left of the insertion point.

> **Hot Tip**
>
> You can set a precise size for the text block by entering specific dimensions the same way you enter dimensions for other graphics objects. In most graphics programs, that means keying the height and width in the Info panel, Size dialog box, or Properties panel. If you use one of these panels to set the width and height, you will need to click in the text box to move the cursor back inside for keying text.

> **Note**
>
> You may find it helpful to display the ruler.

STEP-BY-STEP 4.1 Continued

5. If necessary, change the font to **Arial**, the font size to **12**, and the alignment to **Left**. Deselect all font styles, such as bold and italics. (You will learn more about text formatting options later in this lesson.)

6. Using your keyboard, key the text **Backstage Dance Studio 622A Chestnut Street Cleveland Heights, OH 44118**. Do not press Enter to start new lines in the address—the text should wrap within the text block. It should look similar to the text block in Figure 4-1. However, if the text does not wrap into three lines as shown in the figure, you may have to resize the text block. Drag the right edge to the right to increase the block width to make enough space on the third line.

FIGURE 4-1
Text wraps within a fixed-width text block

Backstage Dance Studio
622A Chestnut Street
Cleveland Heights, OH 44118

7. Click the **Selection tool** in the toolbox, and click anywhere outside the text block to deselect the text block.

8. Save the changes and leave **Dance** open to use in the next exercise.

Create an Expandable Text Block

Most graphics programs also let you create expandable or auto-sizing text blocks. In an *expandable text block*, text is entered on a single line, which increases in width to accommodate as many characters as you enter. To create an expandable text block, select the Text tool, click in the drawing area where you want to position the block, and start keying text.

Did You Know?

In some programs, you can tell whether the insertion point is active in a text block by looking for a shape in the upper-right corner of the bounding box in place of a sizing handle. The shape may be a small square (usually in a fixed-width block) or a small circle (in an expandable block). Double-click the shape to switch from one type of block to the other.

S TEP-BY-STEP 4.2

1. Click the **Text tool** in the toolbox, and then click in the white background at the top of the drawing area (refer to Figures 4-2 and 4-3 for positioning). Do not hold down the mouse button or drag after clicking. An expandable text block is created at the spot where you clicked, as shown in Figure 4-2.

FIGURE 4-2
Expandable text block

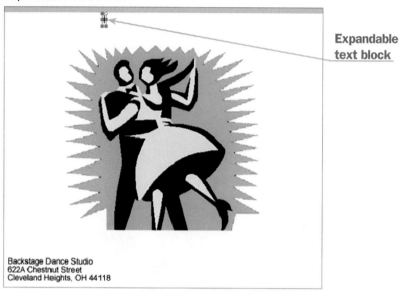

**Expandable
text block**

Backstage Dance Studio
622A Chestnut Street
Cleveland Heights, OH 44118

2. Key the text **Backstage Dance Studio**. Notice that as you key, the text block expands horizontally so that all of the characters display on one line. The file should look similar to Figure 4-3.

FIGURE 4-3
All text displays on one line in an expandable text block

Backstage Dance Studio
622A Chestnut Street
Cleveland Heights, OH 44118

3. Save the changes and leave **Dance** open to use in the next exercise.

Edit Text

In most graphics programs, you use the same standard text-editing commands as in other programs to move the insertion point within a text block and to make changes to the text. To position the insertion point in the text so you can make changes, double-click where you want to place the insertion point, or click the Text tool and then click where you want to position the insertion point. Table 4-1 describes some of the common keystrokes used to work with text.

> **Note** ☑️
>
> When you work with text, the mouse pointer usually looks like an I-beam. It may have a plus sign or arrow attached to it when you are inserting new text.

TABLE 4-1
Common text-editing keystrokes

PRESS THIS KEY	TO DO THIS
Up Arrow	Move insertion point up one line.
Down Arrow	Move insertion point down one line.
Left Arrow	Move insertion point one character to the left.
Right Arrow	Move insertion point one character to the right.
Backspace	Delete the character to the left of the insertion point.
Delete	Delete the character to the right of the insertion point.
Enter	Start a new paragraph.
Insert	Toggle between inserting and overwriting characters.

Use the same methods to select a text block that you use to select other graphics objects. To select an entire block, use the Pointer or Selection tool to click the text block. To select multiple objects, including text blocks, select the first, then press and hold Shift while you select additional objects.

You can use standard text selection methods to select text within the block. For example, with the mouse, click and drag across the text to select, or with the keyboard, position the insertion point at the beginning of the text to select, press and hold Shift, then press arrow keys to define the selection.

STEP-BY-STEP 4.3

1. Click the **Selection tool** in the toolbox and then double-click in the fixed-width text block. (If you are using Photoshop, click the **Type tool** and click in the block.)

2. Use the arrow keys to position the insertion point at the beginning of the word *Street* in the second line of text.

3. Press **Delete** six times to delete the word *Street*.

4. Key **Avenue** to replace the word *Street*.

5. Save the changes and leave **Dance** open to use in the next exercise.

Check Spelling

There is nothing like a spelling mistake to ruin a perfectly good graphics file. Luckily, many graphics programs include a spell checking feature you can use to make sure all words in your files are spelled correctly. You can check the spelling in one or more selected text blocks, or in an entire file. If no blocks are selected, the spelling checker checks all text in the file. When the checker identifies a misspelled word, it highlights it. You can choose to change the spelling or ignore the error. Some programs have additional options, such as ignoring or fixing all occurrences of the same error, or adding the highlighted word to the spelling checker's dictionary.

Of course, even the best spelling checker won't catch all spelling errors. For example, if you key the word *hole* when you mean to key *whole*, the spelling checker will not identify the mistake. The only way to be certain your text is correct is to proofread it carefully.

> **Note**
>
> Some programs will prompt you to select a language or dictionary before beginning the spell check procedure. Simply click the option you want to use and then click OK.

STEP-BY-STEP 4.4

1. Click the **Text tool**, and then click in the upper-left of the image to create an expandable text block.

2. In the text block, key the following text, including the spelling errors: **Acceptional training in all types of dance including Balet**, **Ballroom**, **Hip-Hop**, and **Tap.** (If the text is too long to fit across the width of the canvas, select a smaller type size.)

3. Click the command to start the spelling checker in your program. It may appear on a menu such as Text, Edit, or Tools.

4. The spelling checker should highlight the word *Acceptional* in the text block and display a dialog box similar to the one in Figure 4-4.

STEP-BY-STEP 4.4 Continued

FIGURE 4-4
Check Spelling dialog box

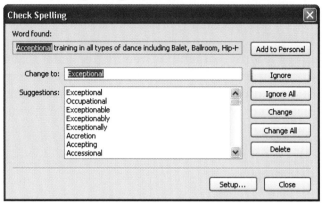

5. Click the correctly spelled word **Exceptional** in the dialog box, and then click the **Change** button.

6. The spelling checker should highlight the word *Balet*. Click the correctly spelled word **Ballet**, and then click the **Change** button.

7. Close any additional dialog boxes that display to complete the spell check.

8. Save the changes and leave **Dance** open to use in the next exercise.

Apply Character Formatting

Character formatting determines the appearance and spacing of text characters. Character formatting options in a graphics program are generally similar to those in word processing or desktop publishing programs. For example, you can change the design, size, and style of text, and you can adjust spacing between characters as well as between lines of text.

You can select character formatting options before you key new text, or you can apply formatting to existing text. In most programs, text formatting options are available on a menu such as Format or Text or in a panel with a name such as Character or Text. In some programs, such as Macromedia's Fireworks, you can select text formatting options directly in the text object's Properties panel or dialog box.

To format an entire text block, select the block and then select the formatting options. Alternatively, select just the text you want to format, and then select the formatting options.

Apply Font Formatting

You can change the look of text using font formatting. A *font* is the design of a set of characters, including letters, numbers, and symbols. You have three main font formatting options: you can change the font itself, the font size, and the font style.

There are two basic types of fonts: serif fonts and sans serif fonts. *Serif fonts* have short lines and curlicues at the ends of the lines that make up each character. Serif fonts are generally easy to read and are often used for lengthy paragraphs, reports, or letters. Some common serif fonts include Times New Roman, Garamond, and Century. *Sans serif fonts* have straight lines without serifs (curlicues) and are often used for headlines and titles. Some common sans serif fonts are Arial, Impact, and Tahoma. Other types of fonts include script fonts, which imitate handwriting, and symbol fonts, which include sets of symbols that you can insert as characters into text. Figure 4-5 shows examples of different fonts.

FIGURE 4-5
Sample fonts

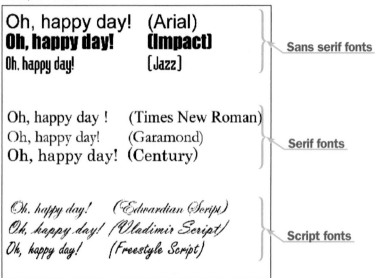

Your graphics program probably comes with some built-in fonts, and you may have other fonts available on your computer as well. You can buy and install font sets you need, or download them from the Internet.

Your graphics program uses a default font, such as Arial, for text objects, or it uses the most recently selected font. To choose a new font, locate your program's font list on a menu or in a panel or palette. For example, in Fireworks, the options are in the Properties panel, and in Photoshop they are in the Character palette. In most cases, the fonts are listed in alphabetical order in the font list, and you can sometimes see a preview of a font when you select it in the list.

Text objects also have a *font size* that you can change when formatting text. Font sizes are measured in points according to the height of an uppercase letter in the font set. There are 72 points in an inch. Select a new font size by locating your program's font size list on a menu or panel. You can choose one of the sizes on the list or key a size in the font size box. When changing font size, keep in mind the importance of the text in your image. If you want the text to dominate a large image, use a large font size. If the text has to fit in a small corner of the image, use a small font size.

Font style is the slant and weight of characters in a font set, such as bold and italic. Some programs also offer underlining as a font style. Font styles are used to call attention to the text. Bold is usually used to highlight text and make it stand out, whereas italic is usually used for subtle emphasis. Some programs allow you to apply font styles to any font, whereas others may limit the styles that can be applied to specific fonts.

S TEP-BY-STEP 4.5

1. Select the expandable text block containing the text *Backstage Dance Studio*. To format all text in a block, you select the entire block. If you are using Photoshop, select the layer. Remember, in most programs, when an object is selected, it has a bounding box and selection handles around it.

2. Click the **Font** list, and then click the font named **Impact**. If Impact is not available on your computer system, select a different sans serif font.

3. Select the current value in the **Font Size** list, key **16** and then press **Enter**. Now, the text in the text block is formatted in 16-point Impact.

   Now, try formatting only a portion of text in a block.

4. Click the **Text tool**, and then click and drag across the text *Backstage Dance Studio* in the fixed-width text block in the lower-left corner of the image to select it.

5. Click the **Font** list, and select **Impact**. Then click the **Font Size** list, select **14**, and then click outside the list. The selected text is formatted in 14-point Impact, while the rest of the text in the text block remains unchanged.

6. Using the Selection tool, select the expandable text block listing the types of dance training.

7. Change the font to **14**-point **Garamond**. (If the font size is too large to fit across the canvas, select a smaller font size.)

8. Apply **Italic** and **Underline** font styles, if available. You can use buttons or options in a panel or palette or on a menu to apply these styles.

9. Use the align commands on a menu or in a panel to center both expandable text blocks horizontally in relation to the drawing area.

STEP-BY-STEP 4.5 Continued

10. Deselect all text blocks. The image should look similar to the one in Figure 4-6.

FIGURE 4-6
Font formatting changes the look of the image

11. Save the changes and leave **Dance** open to use in the next exercise.

Set Kerning and Leading

Kerning controls the space between pairs of characters. Usually spacing is controlled by the font set, but sometimes when certain characters—such as T and A, or Y and O—are next to each other, you can clearly see uneven spacing. If the spacing within a word is uneven, the reader's eye hesitates, making it harder to read the text. Good kerning spaces characters so that each word is viewed by the reader as a single unit. Pay particular attention to kerning when using large font sizes, in text keyed in all uppercase letters, and when using light-colored characters on a darker background. These situations tend to make spacing problems stand out more.

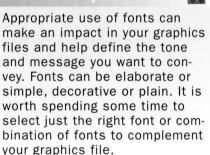

Extra for Experts

Appropriate use of fonts can make an impact in your graphics files and help define the tone and message you want to convey. Fonts can be elaborate or simple, decorative or plain. It is worth spending some time to select just the right font or combination of fonts to complement your graphics file.

In most programs, you key the kerning setting in a box in the Property panel, the Character panel, or a character formatting dialog box. Kerning is measured as a percentage of the default—or normal—spacing. The normal spacing setting is usually 0. To increase the spacing, increase the kerning setting. To decrease the spacing, decrease the setting. Some graphics programs have an automatic kerning feature you can turn on to automatically adjust the kerning for the best appearance. Turn the automatic kerning feature off if you want to be able to control the kerning manually.

Did You Know?

Many fonts are designed to automatically reduce the amount of space between certain letter pairs to maintain the appearance of even spacing.

Leading (pronounced to rhyme with wedding) is the amount of space between the baseline—bottom—of one line of text and the *baseline* of the next line. Leading is usually determined by the font. For example, if leading is set to 120% of the font size, and the font size is 10 points, the leading is 12 points. In most programs, you key the leading setting in a box in the Property panel, in the Paragraph panel, or in a paragraph formatting dialog box. Leading may be measured in pixels, points, or as a percentage. In most programs, you can select the leading unit you want to use.

If there is too much or too little space between lines, the reader's eye has trouble following from one line to the next. In general, space between lines should be greater than the space between words, but some situations, such as short lines of text, call for tighter leading. Tighter leading can also help make lines of text fit within a specified area.

STEP-BY-STEP 4.6

1. Select the fixed-width text block in the lower-left corner of the image. (In some programs, such as Photoshop, you must select the text.)

2. Click in the **Leading** box and select the current value, key **110**, and then press **Enter**. This sets the leading to 110%, which should move the lines further apart. Look for the Leading box in the Character panel, the Spacing panel, the Properties panel, or in a dialog box with a similar name. If you are unable to set leading to a percent value, you may be able to key or select a value less than the default leading value, such as 12 pt.

   Notice that the characters *t* and *y* at the beginning of the word *types* in the expandable text box near the top of the image are so close together that they appear to touch.

3. Click the **Text tool**, and select the **t** and **y** characters. (Your program may require you to click between the characters to change kerning.)

4. Click in the **Kerning** box and select the current value, key **5**, and then press **Enter**. (Or select a value from the kerning box's drop-down list that results in an obvious increase in the space between the characters.) This increases the kerning setting to 5% of normal, which increases the space between the two characters, making the word easier to read.

STEP-BY-STEP 4.6 Continued

5. Deselect all text blocks. The image should look similar to the one in Figure 4-7.

FIGURE 4-7
Kerning and leading have been adjusted

Kerning
has increased

Leading
has increased

6. Save the changes and leave **Dance** open to use in the next exercise.

Set Text Direction and Alignment

You can control the position of text within a block using alignment and direction options. Setting alignment and direction can help integrate the text into a graphics image, as well as enhance visual interest. As with character formatting, you can set the alignment and direction options before you key text or for existing text blocks. The commands are usually found on the Text or Format menu or in the Paragraph or Properties panel. You may be able to click a button to apply the option, or you may have to select it from a menu.

In most graphics programs, you set text direction and alignment at the same time. Direction options include both *orientation* and *text flow*. Orientation controls whether the text is displayed horizontally across the width of the block or vertically from the top to the bottom of the block. Text flow determines whether text can be read from left to right or right to left. It is usually used when you work with languages that flow right to left, such as Arabic or Hebrew.

Alignment controls the position of text in relation to the edges of the text block. Horizontally oriented text can be aligned with either the left or right edge, centered between the left and right edges, or *justified*—which means the space between words is adjusted so that the text aligns with both the left and right edges. Vertically aligned text can be aligned with the top or bottom edge of the text block, centered between the top and bottom edges, or justified between the top and bottom edges. Do not confuse text alignment within a text block with the alignment of an object in the drawing area. You can also align the text block to the drawing area using tools in a panel such as Align, just as you align other objects. Figure 4-8 shows examples of text formatting with different alignments and orientations.

FIGURE 4-8
Text with different alignments and orientations

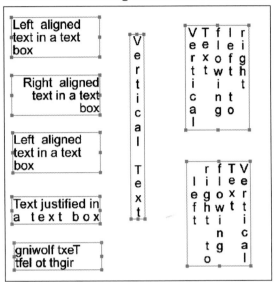

Some programs offer special alignment options such as Stretch alignment or Justify All Lines. Stretch alignment automatically stretches text to fill the width of a text block by adjusting character width. This may make the characters thicker or thinner, but does not change the spacing between them. Justify All Lines justifies every line in a text block, even short lines such as those that might appear at the end of a paragraph. Table 4-2 shows typical alignment options.

TABLE 4-2
Alignment Options

BUTTON	COMMAND	RESULT
	Left alignment	Text aligns with the left margin in the text block.
	Center alignment (horizontal orientation)	Text is centered horizontally between the left and right margins in the text block.
	Center alignment (vertical orientation)	Text is centered vertically between the top and bottom margins in the text block.
	Right alignment	Text aligns with the right margin in the text block.
	Justified alignment (horizontal)	Spacing is adjusted so that text aligns along both the left and right margins.
	Justified alignment (vertical)	Spacing is adjusted so that text aligns along both the top and bottom margins.

TABLE 4-2 Continued
Alignment Options

BUTTON	COMMAND	RESULT
⌶	Stretched alignment (horizontal orientation)	Character width is adjusted so that text aligns along both the left and right margins.
|A|	Stretched alignment (vertical orientation)	Character height is adjusted so that the text aligns along both the top and bottom margins.
	Top alignment	Text aligns with the top margin.
	Bottom alignment	Text aligns with the bottom margin.
Ab cd	Set text Orientation	Display a menu or orientation options

S TEP-BY-STEP 4.7

1. Select the fixed-width text block in the lower corner of the image.

2. Click the **Right alignment** button. (You will usually find this button in a panel such as Properties, or on an Options toolbar. Alternatively, you may select the command from a menu.) The text aligns to the right of the text block.

3. Drag the text block to the right side of the image. (In some programs, such as Photoshop, you may have to first select the command to transform the object.)

4. Select the expandable text block listing the types of dance training.

5. Click the **Center alignment** button to center the text within the text block. Then use the Align panel to align the text block at the top and horizontal center in relation to the drawing area.

6. Select the expandable text block at the top of the image, containing the text *Backstage Dance Studio*. You may have to first use the Select Behind tool or send the other text block to the back.

7. Change the orientation to **Vertical left to right**, and then drag the text block to position it as shown in Figure 4-9.

STEP-BY-STEP 4.7 Continued

FIGURE 4-9
Modify text alignment and direction

8. Save the changes and leave **Dance** open to use in the next exercise.

Apply Fills and Strokes to Text

Text objects have both a fill and a stroke just like any other drawing object. By default, a text object's stroke is transparent. You can change the color and appearance of text by modifying both fill and stroke options. Stroke options can usually be applied only to an entire text block, but solid fills—as opposed to textured or gradient fills—can be applied to an entire text block or to selected text within a block.

To apply a stroke or fill to text, select the text or the text block, then select the stroke or fill options you want to apply. You can also select the options before you key new text. Besides changing the color of the fill and the stroke, you can often change stroke options such as stroke weight, stroke style, and the position of the stroke relative to the path (outside the path, inside the path, or centered on the path). Depending on your program, the options may be available directly from the toolbox, in panels, or in dialog boxes.

> **Extra for Experts**
>
> Most graphics programs also allow you to specify how much space to leave before and after a paragraph of text, as well as set an indent for the first line of a paragraph. Some programs may also let you set margins within a text block, adjust the baseline shift to move characters above or below the baseline, and scale the width or height of characters as a percentage of their original size.

S TEP-BY-STEP 4.8

1. Select the text *Backstage Dance Studio* in the fixed-width text block in the lower-right corner of the image.

2. Click the tool in the toolbox that selects the fill and use the eyedropper pointer to pick up the color **orange** used in the image (or key the hexadecimal value **#FFA64D**). The color of the selected text changes to orange.

3. Select the vertically oriented text block.

4. Change the fill color to the same orange, and then click the tool that selects the stroke and click the color **black**. (If you are using a program that does not support applying strokes to text, just change the color to orange.) The text color changes to orange, and a black stroke displays around the text fill. Deselect the text block. The image should look similar to Figure 4-10.

FIGURE 4-10
Black stroke applied to orange text

5. Save the changes and close the **Dance** file. Leave your graphics program open to use in the next exercise.

> **Note**
>
> If your file does not look the same as the one in the figure, your graphics program may be set to apply the stroke differently. In the figure, the stroke is applied outside the text lines.

Import Text

If the text you want to use in a graphics file is already entered in a different file, you can import it into your graphics program. To import an entire text file into a text block in your graphics file, make the graphics file active and then choose the Import command. Locate and select the text file and then click the appropriate button in the Import dialog box. You will probably have to change the *Files of type* list to display all files in order to locate text files in the Import dialog box. You may also have to drag an insertion pointer to define the location and size of the text block you want to create, or just click in the drawing area to insert a default text block. (For more information on importing, refer to Lesson 2.) In most cases, the formatting from the original file will not be imported into the graphics file.

The type of text files that you can import depends on your graphics program. Some programs may let you import only plain text files whereas some will let you import Rich Text Format (.rtf) files as well.

S TEP-BY-STEP 4.9

1. Open **Step4-9a** from the Data files for this lesson.

2. Save the file in your program's native format as **Sweet**.

3. Import the text file **Step4-9b** into the **Sweet** graphics file. There are a number of ways this could be done, depending upon your program. Possible steps are:

    a. Click **File** on the Menu bar and click **Import**.

    b. Change the *Files of type* list to **All files**, locate and select **Step4-9b**, and then click **Open**.

    c. Drag the insertion pointer to define an import area the width of the drawing area, approximately **380** pixels – or **4.0** inches – wide. The height should adjust automatically. If you do not define an import area, scale the text block to approximately **385** pixels by **110** pixels (**4.0** inches by **1.0** inches).

4. Align the text block with the top left of the drawing area.

5. Click the **Center alignment** button to center the text in the text block, and then apply the **Bold** font style to all text in the text block.

6. Use the alignment options to align the text block with the drawing area vertically with the bottom edge and horizontally in the center.

> ### Did You Know?
>
> If you cannot import the text file, you can import text using the Copy and Paste commands. Open the text file in Notepad or another text processing program. Select and copy the text, and then paste the selection into a text block in the graphics file. Scale the text block to approximately 385 pixels by 110 pixels (4.0 inches by 1.0 inches), align it with the top left of the drawing area, and set the font color to black.

STEP-BY-STEP 4.9 Continued

7. Deselect the text block. At 150% magnification, the file should look similar to the one in Figure 4-11. If necessary, adjust the font formatting (font and font size) as well as leading and alignment to make your image match the one in the figure.

FIGURE 4-11
Import text from other files

8. Save the changes and leave **Sweet** open to use in the next exercise.

Transform a Text Block

You can transform a text block using the same methods you use to transform other graphics objects. In most programs, that means you can scale, skew, distort, rotate, and flip the entire text block. Transformations on text blocks can create interesting effects, including perspective and depth. Simply select the text block, and then apply the transformation.

Note

Some programs, such as Photoshop offer a tool for warping text blocks in place of the distort feature. You may find you achieve better results using the warp transformation instead of skewing or distorting.

STEP-BY-STEP 4.10

1. Select the text block, click the **Scale tool**, and drag a handle up to increase the height of the object to approximately 190 pixels, or 2.0 inches. Because you are increasing the height without increasing the width, the characters may seem a bit distorted.

2. Click the tool or menu command that allows you to skew an object, and drag the top-right handle down, along the right side, at least halfway to the center handle. This creates the appearance of depth; the text seems to be moving into the distance on the right side of the image. (If your program does not support this feature, you may just angle the text from bottom left to top right.)

STEP-BY-STEP 4.10 Continued

3. Left align the text within the text block.

4. Click the tool in the toolbox that selects the stroke and click a **light gray** color (**#CCCCCC**). The color is applied around the text, making it stand out a bit from the background image. (If your program does not support this feature, skip to step 5.)

5. Click anywhere outside the text block to deselect it. The image should look similar to Figure 4-12.

FIGURE 4-12
Transform text block to create interesting effects

6. Save changes and close the **Sweet** file. Leave your graphics program open to use in the next exercise.

Convert Text to Vector Graphics

When text is in a text block, you can edit and format the text, and you can transform the entire text block object. If you want to be able to modify and transform the text characters themselves, you can convert the text to vectors. Remember, vector graphics are defined by lines and curves that can be modified in many ways. Converting text to vectors is useful for incorporating the shape of a character into a drawing or larger image. Once the text is converted, you can use all the vector editing tools in your graphics program to modify the shape itself. Keep in mind, however, that you can't edit text that has been converted.

> **Note** ☑
>
> If you convert text to a shape and then change your mind, use the Undo command to revert back to text.

The command to convert text to vector graphics depends on your graphics program. It may be similar to Convert to Paths or Convert to Shape, and it will probably be on a Text menu.

S TEP-BY-STEP 4.11

1. Create a new file in your graphics program. Set the drawing area to **720** pixels by **720** pixels (**7.5** inches by **7.5** inches) with a white background. Save the file in your program's native file format as **Sams**.

2. Click the **Text tool**, and then set the font to **72**-point **Times New Roman**, **Left** aligned, with a regular (no bold or italics) font style. Set the fill color to **bright blue**.

3. Click anywhere in the drawing area, and then key the letter **S**.

4. Click the command to convert the text block to a vector shape. The bounding box is replaced by selection handles.

5. Scale the shape to approximately **96** pixels by **96** pixels (**1.0** inches by **1.0** inches), and then rotate it about an eighth of a turn to the left (**–40** degrees). You may use a feature such as numeric transform to rotate by a specific value, or display a panel, such as Info, which displays the rotation value as you perform the action. Refer to Figure 4-13 to see the position of

> **Note** ☑
>
> Your program may automatically adjust the dimensions of the character shape slightly to maintain proportion.

the shape after rotation. Position the shape by setting the X coordinate to **175** pixels (**1.8** inches) and the Y coordinate to **144** pixels (**1.5** inches). The file should look similar to Figure 4-13.

FIGURE 4-13
Letter S as a vector shape

6. Deselect the shape, then select the **Text tool** and change the fill color to **red**. Using the same font settings as for the letter S, key the letter **A** anywhere in the drawing area.

STEP-BY-STEP 4.11 Continued

7. Convert the *A* to a vector shape, then scale it to approximately **96** pixels by **96** pixels (**1.0** inch by **1.0** inch). Rotate the shape slightly to the right (about **15** degrees), then position it by setting the X coordinate to **285** pixels (**3.0** inches) and the Y coordinate to **167** pixels (**1.7** inches). (Again, use a feature such as numeric transform to rotate by a specific value, or display a panel, such as Info, which displays the rotation value as you perform the action.)

8. Repeat the process to insert an **M** with a **green** fill. Convert it to a vector, scale it to approximately **96** pixels by **96** pixels (**1.0** inch by **1.0** inch), and rotate it about an eighth of a turn (**–40** degrees) to the left. Position it by setting the X coordinate to **385** pixels (**4.0** inches) and the Y coordinate to **140** pixels (**1.5** inches).

9. Repeat the process again to insert an apostrophe with an **orange** fill, convert it to a vector, scale it to approximately **25** pixels by **50** pixels (**0.3** inch by **0.5** inch), and position it by setting the X coordinate at **508** pixels (**5.3** inches) and the Y coordinate at **144** pixels (**1.5** inches).

10. Repeat the process one more time to insert an S with a **purple** fill, convert it to a vector, and scale it to approximately **96** pixels by **96** pixels (**1.0** inch by **1.0** inch). Instead of rotating this shape, flip it horizontally so that it appears to be written backwards. Position it by setting the X coordinate to **530** pixels (**5.5** inches) and the Y coordinate to **175** pixels (**1.8** inches).

11. Select all of the shapes in the file and group them together. Then use the Align panel to center the group horizontally in the drawing area. When you deselect the group, the file should look similar to Figure 4-14. If necessary, ungroup the objects and adjust the position and rotation of the shapes.

FIGURE 4-14
Modified shapes combine to spell a word

12. Save and close the **Sams** file. Close your graphics program.

SUMMARY

In this lesson, you learned:

- You can create text block objects in a graphics file to hold regular text characters.
- There are two types of text blocks: expandable and fixed width.
- You can enter and edit text using basic word processing commands.
- Many graphics programs have spelling checkers that you can use to locate and correct spelling errors.
- You can apply font formatting to text in a text block.
- Adjusting kerning and leading settings can make text easier to read and help fit it within a defined space.
- Changing text alignment and orientation can help integrate text into a graphics image.
- Fill color determines the text color, but you can also apply stroke color to text.
- You can import text from another file into your graphics file.
- You can transform text by skewing, distorting, rotating, or flipping it.
- You can convert text objects to vector graphics to make possible other modifications to the object.

VOCABULARY *Review*

Define the following terms:

Baseline	Font style	Orientation
Expandable text block	Insertion point	Text block
Fixed-width text block	Justified	Text flow
Font	Kerning	Wrap
Font size	Leading	

REVIEW *Questions*

TRUE / FALSE

Circle T if the statement is true or F if the statement is false.

T   F   1. Font sizes are measured in pixels.

T   F   2. Font color is determined by the current fill color.

T F 3. A good spelling checker will catch all spelling errors so you don't have to proofread.

T F 4. Press Enter to start a new line in a text block.

T F 5. In an expandable text block, text wraps to fit within the size of the block.

T F 6. In a fixed-width text block, text is entered on a single line.

T F 7. Leading controls the amount of space at the beginning of a line of text.

T F 8. You cannot edit text characters that you have converted to vector shapes.

T F 9. Press the Insert key to toggle between inserting and overwriting characters.

T F 10. Usually, existing formatting is lost when you import text into a graphics file.

WRITTEN QUESTIONS

Write a brief answer to each of the following questions.

1. What are three reasons for incorporating text in a graphics file?

2. What is the difference between an expandable text block and a fixed-width text block?

3. Name at least three ways to format fonts.

4. What are two reasons for adjusting leading?

5. What are two methods of importing text into a graphics file?

FILL IN THE BLANK

Complete the following sentences by writing the correct word or words in the blanks provided.

1. _____ controls whether the text is displayed horizontally across the width of the block or vertically from the top to the bottom of the block.

2. A(n) _____ within a text block indicates where characters display when keyed.

3. _____ controls the space between pairs of characters.

4. Press _____ to remove the character to the right of the insertion point.

5. A(n) _____ is the design of a set of characters.

6. The bottom of a line of text is called the _____.

7. In a fixed-width text block, text _____ from the end of one line to the beginning of the next.

8. Use the _____ feature to proofread text in a graphics file.

9. _____ fonts have short lines and curlicues at the ends of the lines that make up each character.

10. _____ is the slant or weight of characters in a font set.

PROJECTS

PROJECT 4-1

1. Create a new graphics file with an **8** inch by **8** inch drawing area with a **light gray** background (hexadecimal code **#999999**) and save the file as **Story**.

2. Create a fixed-width text block that is approximately as wide as the drawing area and **195** pixels (**2** inches) high.

4. Select a sans serif font such as **Arial**, set the font size to **42** points, the font color to **black**, and the font style to **Bold**.

5. Key the following text:

    On a dark and stormy night, a long time ago, a little boy walked alone through the forest... (If the text is too large to fit within the text block, change to a smaller font size, such as 30 pts.)

6. Check the spelling in the text block and correct errors as necessary.

7. If possible, stretch align the text to fill the width of the block.

8. Skew and distort the text block, following the directions below, so that it appears to be receding into the distance (if you are using Photoshop, you may achieve better results using the Warp transformation tool):
    A. Select the **Skew tool.**
    B. Drag a top corner handle in toward the center handle.

    C. Select the **Distort tool**.

    D. Drag the top center handle up to the top of the drawing area, and the bottom center handle down to the bottom of the drawing area.

9. Center the text block in relation to the drawing area horizontally and vertically.

10. Print one copy of the file.

11. Save and close the **Story** file, but leave your graphics program open to use in Project 4-2.

PROJECT 4-2

1. Open **Project4-2** from the Data files for this lesson.

2. Save the file in your program's native file format as **Birds**.

3. Select the **Text tool**, set the fill color to **red**, and then create a text block and key the character **R** in a sans serif font such as **Comic Sans MS**.

4. Convert the text to a vector shape, and resize it to about **96** pixels square.

5. Position the shape to the left of the center image, centered vertically.

6. Duplicate the shape three times, and position each one on the blank area on each side of the center image.

7. If the tools are available, modify each character shape by applying different stroke formatting. Use the following as guidelines:

    A. Around one shape, apply a **22**-point **Air Brush, Textured, black** stroke.

    B. Around the second, apply a **25**-point **blue Highlighter** stroke.

    C. Around the third, apply an **18**-point **yellow, Crayon** stroke with a **Rake** texture.

    D. Around the fourth, apply a **20**-point **green, Oil** stroke with a **Textured Bristle** effect.

8. Use the Text tool to create an expandable-width text block and then use a 72-point black, bold, sans serif font such as Comic Sans MS to key the text **Spring?** (You may need to use a smaller font size.)

9. Change the orientation of the text block to vertical, so the text reads from top to bottom.

10. Drag the text block to position it to the right of the bird in the central picture.

11. Print one copy of the file.

12. Save and close the **Birds** file, but leave your graphics program open to use in Project 4-3.

PROJECT 4-3

1. Open **Project4-3a** from the Data files for this lesson.

2. Save the file in your program's native file format as **Winter**.

3. Import the file **Project4-3b** into the **Winter** file, in a text block as wide as the drawing area.

4. Format the text as follows:
   A. Select a **18**-point serif font such as **Century Schoolbook, Times New Roman,** or **Sylfaen.**
   B. Apply a **blue** fill color and a **black** stroke.
   C. Center the text in the text block.
   D. Align the text block to the bottom of the drawing area, centered horizontally.

5. Create a new text block at the top of the image and key the text **Haiku** in a **36**-point sans serif font, such as **Tahoma.** Center the text horizontally within the block.

6. Format the text in the reverse colors that you used for the imported text (blue stroke, black fill).

7. Center the text block horizontally, and align it with the top of the drawing area.

8. Print one copy of the file.

9. Save and close the **Winter** file, and close your graphics program.

 WEB PROJECT

For a report about ancient Egypt, you need information about hieroglyphics, the characters the Egyptians used for writing. You also want to include hieroglyphics in your report. Use the Internet to see if you can find general information about hieroglyphics as well as an actual hieroglyphics font set. Once you locate the font set, find out whether you can download it for free or if there is a charge.

 TEAMWORK PROJECT

Discuss with your classmates different logos used by professional sports teams or companies. Think of a few logos that incorporate text, and consider the qualities that make them memorable. For example, the color and font of the Coca-Cola logo are easy to identify.

Together with your teammates, think of a club or team at your school or a business in your community that could use a logo, and then use your graphics program to design one that uses both shapes and text. Make use of the skills you have learned in this lesson as well as in previous lessons. Select font formatting that suits the logo, including a font set and font size. Select stroke and fill settings that make the object easy to read and identify. Layer basic shapes behind the text to create a background, and convert text characters into vectors so you can position and transform them independently. When you are finished, print the logo and compare it to the images created by other teams.

CRITICAL *Thinking*

Use your graphics program to combine text and graphics to design a monogram for yourself that you could use on stationery or a bookplate, which is a label you place in a book to identify it as belonging to you. If you want to modify the characters independently, key each one in its own text block and then convert them to vector shapes. Use the available tools to modify and transform the text. You can try changing the stacking order to overlap text and shapes, using different stroke and fill options to enhance the text characters, and rotating or flipping the objects to make them more interesting. When you are finished, save the file, print it, and share it with your classmates.

CREATING SPECIAL EFFECTS

OBJECTIVES

Upon completion of this lesson, you should be able to:

- Work with color.
- Apply color effects.
- Apply color correction effects.
- Apply special effects.
- Save custom effects.
- Edit and remove effects.
- Create masks.

Estimated Time: 2 hours

VOCABULARY

Bevel

Brightness

CMY

Color system

Contrast

Emboss

Glow

Hue

Mask

Opacity

RGB

Saturation

Shadow

Spot color

Style

Value

You can use different effects to improve your graphics images and to create illusions. Color, for example, can convey a mood, change the perception of space and size, focus attention, add emphasis, and even improve image quality. Shadow effects may make an object appear to have three dimensions; an emboss effect may make an object appear to sink into the drawing area; and a blur effect may make an object appear to be far off in the distance. In addition, many effects are achieved by incorporating scale. Most graphics programs include features for creating these common effects. In this lesson, you learn to work with color and to apply special effects to bitmap and vector graphics.

Work with Color

Color affects the way people view an image more than any other graphics effect. Color, also called *hue*, is usually the first thing viewers see and to which they respond. Understanding the way viewers react to color and incorporating standard color techniques in your graphics can help you create appealing and informative images.

You have already learned how to apply color to fills and strokes simply by selecting a swatch from a color palette. Most programs also have tools for creating custom colors. You can create a custom color by selecting a color from a color bar or specifying color values in a color mixer panel, palette, or dialog box.

The color mixer panel or palette allows you to mix custom colors based on the current *color system*. A color system defines standard colors. It may also be called a *color model*. Color systems are available for graphics to be displayed on a computer screen (such as on a Web page) and for printed graphics. A graphics program usually has a default color system that you can change at any time.

Use a Color Bar

A color bar displays a spectrum of colors across a rectangle from left to right. Toward the top of the color bar, colors are lighter because they are mixed with white. Toward the bottom of the bar, colors are darker because they are mixed with black.

You can make any color the current stroke or fill color simply by clicking it on the color bar. If your program has a color bar, it's usually found in a color mixer panel or dialog box similar to the one in Figure 5-1. This may be the same location that displays the current color system and values. If this panel does not appear by default in your program, you can usually activate it from the Window menu.

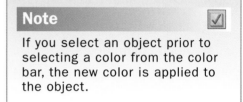

Note ☑

If you select an object prior to selecting a color from the color bar, the new color is applied to the object.

FIGURE 5-1
Color mixer panel

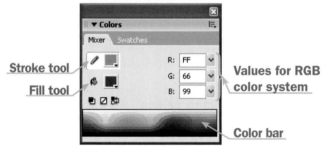

Stroke tool

Fill tool

Values for RGB color system

Color bar

 Historically Speaking

THE COLOR WHEEL

For ages, artists and scientists alike have used color wheels to display and classify color. A typical color wheel has twelve gradations of color ranging from red to violet. The primary colors are red, yellow, and blue. Secondary colors are created by combining the primary colors: red mixed with yellow makes orange; yellow mixed with blue makes green; and blue mixed with red makes violet. Intermediate colors are created by combining a primary color with the secondary color adjacent to it on the color wheel. For example, blue-green is an intermediate color. "Cool" colors range from green to violet, while "warm" colors range from red to yellow. Analogous colors are next to each other on the color wheel, while complementary colors are opposite each other.

STEP-BY-STEP 5.1

1. Launch your graphics program and create a new document, setting the drawing area to **8** inches by **8** inches, with a **white** background. If necessary, set the resolution to **96** pixels/inch. Save the file as **Ladies.**

2. Select the **Rectangle tool** and set the stroke to **4**-point **black**. Open the color mixer panel or dialog box if it is not already open. (If you are using Photoshop, you should work in Paths mode and create a new path for each new shape. Don't forget to apply a stroke to the shapes.)

3. Click the **Fill tool**. You may click the tool in the color mixer panel or in the toolbox. In the color bar, click somewhere in the **yellow** section to set the fill color to yellow.

   > **Note**
   >
   > Notice that when you select a color, the color's values display in the current color system boxes.

4. In the drawing area, draw a rectangle approximately **5** inches (**480** pixels) wide by **5.5** inches (**528** pixels) high.

5. Select the **Polygon tool** and set options to draw a triangle.

6. In the middle of the yellow rectangle, draw a triangle approximately **2.5** inches (**240** pixels) wide by **2.0** inches (**192** pixels) high, with one angle pointing straight up and the triangle base parallel to the bottom of the drawing area.

7. Select the **Ellipse tool**. Draw a circle about **1** inch (**96** pixels) in diameter sitting on the top angle of the triangle.

   > **Note**
   >
   > You may not be able to change the ruler or grid units to inches, but you may be able to change the unit of measure. For example, in Fireworks, display the Info panel, click the Options menu button, and then click Inches. The dimensions in the Properties and Info panels will display in inches.

STEP-BY-STEP 5.1 Continued

8. Select the **Rectangle tool** and draw a rectangle about **.25** inches (**29** pixels) wide by **1.5** inches (**144** pixels) high extending down from the base of the triangle, about **.5** inches (**48** pixels) in from the left angle. Duplicate the rectangle and position the duplicate to the left of the original. The drawing should look similar to the one in Figure 5-2.

FIGURE 5-2
Shapes are all the same color

9. Select the triangle shape in the drawing area. In the color bar, click somewhere in the **pink** section. The shape fills with pink. (If you are using Photoshop, click the **Fill path with foreground color** button in the Paths palette.)

10. Select the circle, then press and hold **Shift** and click to select the rectangles.

STEP-BY-STEP 5.1 Continued

11. In the color bar, click somewhere in the **purple** section to fill the selected shapes with purple. When you deselect all objects, the image should look similar to the one in Figure 5-3.

FIGURE 5-3
Shapes with custom fill colors

12. Save the changes and leave **Ladies** open to use in the next exercise.

Use a Color System

The two main color systems for use in graphics programs are the RGB model and the CMY (or CMYK) model. Graphics programs may use one of these systems as the default for new drawings, or you may be able to select the system when you start a new drawing. You can change the color system at any time using a menu or pop-up list accessed from the color mixer panel or dialog box.

The *RGB* system creates colors by combining different values of red, green, and blue. These are the basic colors of light in the spectrum we can see. This model mixes colors in the same way that colors of light are mixed. For this reason, the RGB model is most often used when graphics are to be displayed on devices that use light to display colors, such as computer monitors.

The *CMY* (or *CMYK*) system creates colors by combining percentages of cyan, magenta, and yellow. These colors are the colors of ink—often called *process colors*—used in four-color printing. The CMY system is used most often for drawings that are to be printed, either on a local printer or by a printing press.

The CMY system is called CMYK when black is added to the mix. In theory, combining full percentages

Extra for Experts

RGB colors are *additive colors*, because if you add full amounts of all three you get white (all colors are reflected). CMY colors are *subtractive colors* because they absorb light. As light passes through a color and is absorbed, that color is subtracted from the reflection that comes back to your eye.

of cyan, magenta, and yellow results in black, but for the best-quality output, black is added as a separate color. Having black available also makes it possible to mix more subtle colors.

In four-color printing, all colors are mixed from the four basic process colors. Sometimes, a designer may want to use a specific color of ink rather than have colors created by mixing. The designer can select a *spot color* from a color system such as the Pantone Matching System for a specific color. Use spot colors when it is necessary to have an exact color (such as a client's logo color) or when printing with only one or two colors.

In addition to RGB and CMY, most graphics programs include other color systems such as HSL (Hue, Saturation, Lightness) and Grayscale, which uses percentages of black to create shades of gray. Most programs also include a color system with a name such as Hexadecimal or Web Safe RGB. This color system allows you to key hexadecimal values to mix colors that will display the same way on all computer systems. Use this color system when preparing graphics for Web pages. In this type of system, which is used throughout this book, the colors are expressed in an alphanumeric form where the first two digits are the red value, the second two are the green value, and the last two digits are the blue value.

> **Note** ☑
> Different programs may use slightly different names for the same systems, such as HSB (Hue, Saturation, Brightness) instead of HSL.

To create a color using any color system, insert or adjust values or percentages for each color in the color mixer panel. Some programs allow you to drag sliders to adjust values, or you may need to key values. Units used for values differ by program. For example, RGB values usually range from 0 to 255, but CMY values may use percentages.

One way to find out the value of a color you are using is to select the object that has the color and then look at the values in the color mixer panel or dialog box. In some programs, the color values are listed in the Properties and Info panels as well. If you change the color system while the color is selected, some programs automatically adjust the values for the new system. Figure 5-4 shows the values for the same color in RGB hexadecimal and in CMY.

FIGURE 5-4
Same color defined with two different color systems: RGB hexadecimal (left) and CMY (right).

RGB hexadecimal values

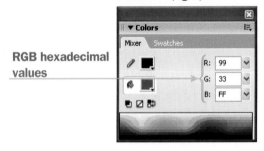
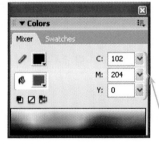

CMY color values

If you create a drawing using the RGB model, you can be fairly certain that your finished drawing will look the same when displayed on your screen, because your monitor uses RGB to display colors. But for a CMY graphic, where the color system used on screen (RGB) is different from the color system used to print (CMY), it can be a bit difficult to make sure that the image will appear on the printed image the same way as it appears on the screen. Some programs have features for converting RGB colors to CMY colors so you can successfully print the image the way you designed it. But sometimes the only way to tell for sure is to print and view the pages.

Of course, other factors affect the way the colors appear on your computer screen and in print, including the specific printer model, the specific monitor model, the file type, and the software program. You can take steps to ensure that the image people see is as close as possible to the one you created. For example, you can optimize the colors for the export file type. You may also be able to calibrate your monitor and apply color management systems so what you see on your monitor more closely matches the final printed output.

> **Net Tip**
>
> Look on the Web to find color system tables listing values for the entire range of colors. Such a table can save you time in experimenting with color values to find the one you want.

S TEP-BY-STEP 5.2

1. Select the triangle in the drawing area.

2. Switch to the hexadecimal or Web-safe color model if necessary. The available color systems may be listed on an options menu in a panel or dialog box such as Info, or Color Mixer.

> **Hot Tip**
>
> To open a panel's Options menu, click the drop-down arrow in the panel's upper-right corner. In a dialog box, look for a command or option button.

3. Double-click the **R** box and key **FF**, double-click the **G** box and key **33**, and then double-click the **B** box and key **33**. (Notice that the color of the triangle changes as each value is entered.) Press **Enter** to apply the color. #FF3333 is the hexadecimal code for an orange-red.

   Now, try applying a fill using CMY values.

4. Select the circle and then switch to the CMY or CMYK color model.

> **Hot Tip**
>
> You may be able to drag sliders to quickly select these values, or key the value in the first box and then press Tab to move quickly to the next box.

STEP-BY-STEP 5.2 Continued

5. Double-click the **C** box and key **200**, double-click the **M** box and key **200**, and then double-click the **Y** box and key **0**. If your program has a K box, set its value to **0**. If your program uses percentages for CMY colors, set C to **80%**, M to **20%**, and Y (and K) to **0%**. Press **Enter** to apply the color. The image should look similar to the one in Figure 5-5.

FIGURE 5-5
Image with modified fill colors

6. Save the changes and leave **Ladies** open to use in the next exercise.

Apply Color Effects

In addition to applying solid colors to fills and strokes, most programs provide options for creating color effects such as *textures*, *gradients*, and *patterns*. Textures can be applied to fills or strokes to make an object look as if it is painted on a textured surface. Patterns are bitmap graphics applied as a fill. Gradients are a type of pattern that blends colors to create different effects. These effects can give objects a three-dimensional look as well as add impact to an image.

Color effects can be selected before you draw new objects, or you can apply them to existing objects. The methods for accessing the color effects options vary depending on the program you are using. In most programs, you can access built-in textures, patterns, and gradient styles from a menu on the Properties panel, from the Stroke or Fill Options dialog box, or from the Filters or Effects menu on your program's main menu bar. Often, you can see a preview of the texture or pattern before you select it. If necessary, consult your program's Help system or ask your instructor for more information on locating the color effects options in your program.

Apply Textures

To apply a texture, select the object you want to format or tool you plan to use to create the object, and then select the texture for either the stroke or fill from a pop-up list or menu. In some programs, you can control the amount of texture applied by setting a percentage. Increase the percentage to make the texture appear heavier; decrease the percentage to make the texture appear lighter.

> **Hot Tip**
>
> Consider the stroke style and weight when you apply a texture. For example, if the stroke is not heavy or thick enough, you may not be able to see the texture, and some stroke styles may interfere with the selected texture.

STEP-BY-STEP 5.3

1. Select the circle if necessary. If you are using Photoshop, use the **Magic Wand** to select the fill in the circle.

2. Open the menu listing the available fill textures and select a texture similar to **Sandpaper**. If your program has an option to control the amount of texture, set it to **100%**.

3. Select the large, yellow rectangle shape and change the stroke weight to **15**. If you are using Photoshop, select the **Magic Wand** to select the stroke.

4. Open the menu listing the available stroke textures and apply a texture similar to **Grass**. If available, set the amount of text to **100%**. The image should look similar to the one in Figure 5-6.

FIGURE 5-6
Image with textures

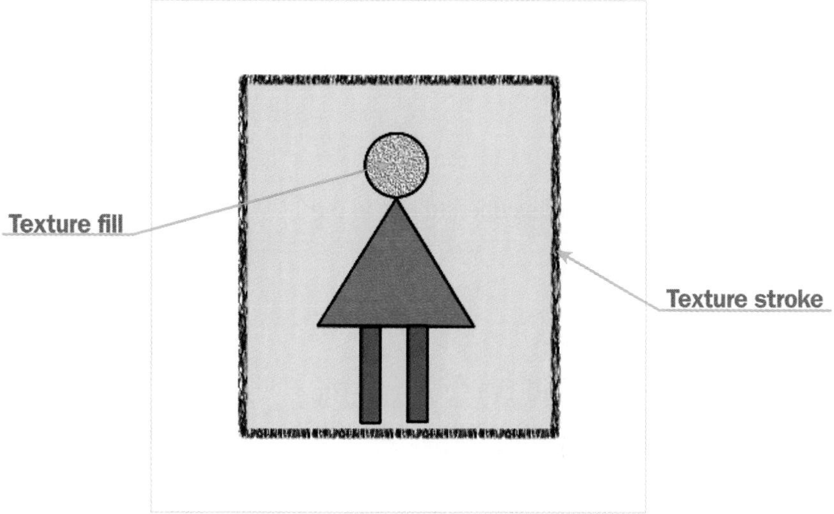

Texture fill

Texture stroke

5. Save the changes and leave **Ladies** open to use in the next exercise.

Apply Patterns

In some programs, you may be able to select a pattern directly from a list or pop-up menu, but in most programs, the list of patterns is not available until you select Pattern as the fill type or category. Then, the default pattern or the most recently selected pattern becomes active. It is displayed on the Fill Color tool and is applied to any selected object. Click the Fill Color tool or use the Fill Options dialog box or panel to display a list of built-in patterns.

S TEP-BY-STEP 5.4

1. Select the triangle.

2. Open the menu listing the available fill categories and select **Pattern**. If you are using a program that does not require you to select the category first, skip this step.

3. Open the list of available patterns and select one similar to **Berber**. With all objects deselected, the image should look similar to the one in Figure 5-7.

FIGURE 5-7
Image with a pattern fill

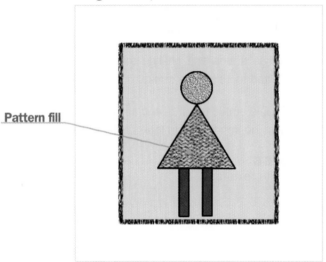

4. Save the changes and leave **Ladies** open to use in the next exercise.

Apply Gradients

By default, most gradients blend two colors—the current fill color and black. When you apply a gradient, you usually start by selecting a fill color. Then, you select the gradient pattern type, such as *linear*, which blends the colors horizontally across the object, or *radial*, which blends the colors out from the center of the object, from the Fill category or type list.

> **Extra for Experts**
>
> In some programs you can transform patterns and gradients. Handles are displayed within a selected object filled with a pattern or gradient. Drag the handles to transform the fill.

When you select a gradient fill, the gradient becomes the active fill and is displayed on the Fill Color tool in the toolbox. If an object is selected, the gradient fill is automatically applied to the selected object. When a gradient fill is selected, any new object you draw has the gradient fill. In some programs, you can apply the fill to an object using a Gradient tool. Click the Gradient tool in the toolbox, and then drag in the object to apply the gradient.

You can edit a gradient by changing the pattern or by changing the colors. In most programs, if you click the Fill Color tool when a gradient fill is active, an Edit Gradient dialog box similar to the one in Figure 5-8 appears in place of the usual swatches palette. To change a color in the gradient, click one of the gradient pointers to select it and then choose a new color. A preview area shows the result. You can also move gradient pointers to adjust the amount of that color in the gradient.

FIGURE 5-8
Options for editing a gradient fill

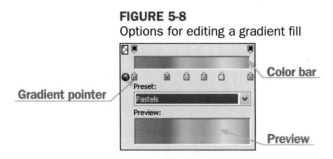

S TEP-BY-STEP 5.5

1. Select the large, yellow rectangle. (If you are using Photoshop, use the **Magic Wand** to select the yellow fill.)

2. Open the menu listing the available fill categories and select the **Radial** gradient pattern type.

3. Open the dialog box or panel that lists options for editing the gradient colors. For example, click the **Fill Color tool**.

STEP-BY-STEP 5.5 Continued

4. Change the black used in the gradient to red. For example, click the gradient pointer representing black at one end of the color bar and then click **red** on the swatches palette. Press **Enter** to apply the change, if necessary, or drag from the middle of the rectangle to the edge using the Gradient pointer. The file should look similar to the one in Figure 5-9.

> **Hot Tip**
>
> Some programs have preset gradient color schemes you can select from a drop-down list in the Edit Gradient dialog box.

FIGURE 5-9
Image with color effects

5. Save the changes and leave **Ladies** open to use in the next exercise.

Apply Color Correction Effects

Most graphics programs have tools for applying color correction effects to vector objects and bitmap images. For example, you can usually adjust the value, contrast, brightness, saturation, and opacity. *Value*, which is sometimes called lightness, is the range from black to white. Value can be measured by the level of *brightness*. When you increase the brightness, you add white to a hue; when you decrease the brightness you add black. *Contrast* refers to the degree of separation between the values of different parts of an image. *Saturation* measures the intensity of color, and *opacity* measures the level of transparency.

> **Note**
>
> Not all graphics programs have the same color controls, or call them by the same names. For example, some programs may use the term *tint* in place of brightness; *transparency* in place of opacity; or *luminosity* in place of lightness. Some vector editing programs may not have color correction effects at all.

You can use color effects in your images to imitate the real effects of light. For example, objects in the distance often appear fuzzy and have a cool tone, such as blue or violet. Objects up close are usually sharp, and have a warm tone, such as red, yellow, or orange. Saturation plays a role in the perception of distance, whereas brightness affects the perception of size. Closer objects appear highly saturated, whereas far-off objects appear pale. Objects filled with a bright color, such as yellow, look larger than objects filled with a dark color, such as navy blue—even if the objects are exactly the same size.

You can use these concepts to add dimension to an image and to separate foreground objects from background objects. You can also use them to make it easier for someone with a color deficit condition to see and interpret your images. You can help a person who has trouble seeing and differentiating between colors by increasing the contrast, increasing the lightness differences between foreground and background colors, and by avoiding using colors of similar lightness or saturation next to each other.

The commands for applying color effects are found in different places, depending on the program you are using. Some programs have an Adjust Color menu that you access from the Filters pop-up menu in the Properties panel or in the Menu bar. Click to open the Filters menu, then click Adjust Color to display a menu of color effects options. In other programs, you may find the color correction options on a submenu such as Adjust, which is accessed from the Image menu; or Colors, which is accessed from the Xtras menu. In any case, you may have to look around a bit, consult your program's Help system, or ask your instructor for more information.

To apply a color correction effect, first select the object to enhance, and then select the color effect. Usually, you set the level of the effect by changing the position of a slider in a dialog box, or by entering a specific value.

Hot Tip
Although you can apply color effects to vectors and to bitmaps, some color effects are particularly suited to bitmaps. For example, adjusting the contrast in a black and white photo can improve the image quality, while adding a sepia tone can make a photo look old. You can combine different color correction effects to achieve different results.

Set Hue, Saturation, and Lightness

Hue, as mentioned earlier, is another word for color. When you pick a color from a color palette, you pick a hue. You can modify the color by adjusting the saturation, which sets the color intensity, and the lightness, which controls how much light appears to be reflected from a surface. In some programs, you can also modify the hue based on the current color system. Many programs group these options together in the same dialog box or panel, as shown in Figure 5-10. In other programs, you may have to set each one individually. By default, these options are set to 0, which is normal, but you can increase or decrease the settings to achieve the effect you want. Most programs provide a preview area so you can view the results of making a change before you actually apply the change.

FIGURE 5-10
Hue/Saturation dialog box

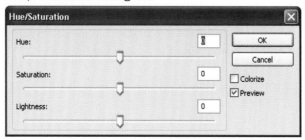

S TEP-BY-STEP 5.6

1. Use the **Save As** command to save the **Ladies** file with the name **Hue**.

2. Select the large rectangle and change the stroke to **4**-point **black**, with no texture. (To apply no texture you may have to set the texture value to **0%**. If your program does not allow you to edit the stroke, leave it as is.) Change the fill to a solid blue (hexadecimal **#0000FF**).

3. Select the triangle, the circle, and the two small rectangles, and change the fill from Radial to a **Solid** blue (hexadecimal **#0000FF**) with no pattern or texture. Now, all five shapes in the drawing should have the same stroke (4-point black) and fill (solid blue).

4. Select the large rectangle (or its fill). Open the menu that lists color correction options and select the option for adjusting the hue and saturation. If your program has separate dialog boxes for each option, start with Hue.

> **Note** ☑
>
> Some programs may display a dialog box asking permission to convert the image to a bitmap. Click OK to convert the image and continue.

5. Set the Hue level to **15**. Set the Saturation level to **30**. Set the Lightness level to **35**. You may set the levels by dragging a slider or by keying the value in a box.

6. Click the **OK** button or press **Enter** to apply the effects. Deselect the shape. The image should look similar to the one in Figure 5-11.

FIGURE 5-11
The color of the large rectangle has been modified

7. Select the triangle and set the Hue level to **–10**, the Saturation level to **–25**, and the lightness level to **–30**. Click the **OK** button or press **Enter** when you are finished.

STEP-BY-STEP 5.6 Continued

8. Select the circle and the two small rectangles and set the Hue to **25**, the Saturation to **30**, and the Lightness level to **45**. Click the **OK** button or press **Enter** when you are finished. the image should look similar to the one in Figure 5-12.

FIGURE 5-12
Shapes with the same color but different HSL values

9. Save the changes and leave **Hue** open to use in the next exercise.

Set Opacity

Opacity controls the amount of transparency in a color. It is measured as a percentage, with 100% being completely opaque and 0% being completely transparent. Decreasing the opacity is useful if you want the viewer to be able to see an object that is layered behind another object. Opacity controls may be found on the same menu or in the same dialog box as other color correction options, or it may be an option in the Properties panel.

STEP-BY-STEP 5.7

1. Select the **Ellipse tool**. Set the fill color to **red** and the stroke to **6**-point **black**. If necessary, remove all textures and patterns.

2. Draw a circle the height and width of the drawing area—**8** inches (768 pixels) in diameter. The circle is stacked on top of the other shapes, covering them completely.

STEP-BY-STEP 5.7 Continued

3. Locate and open the Opacity control and set the opacity level to **50%**. This makes the object 50% transparent, so you can see through it, as shown in Figure 5-13.

FIGURE 5-13
Decreasing the opacity makes the object semitransparent

4. Save the changes and close **Hue**. Leave your graphics program open to use in the next exercise.

Adjust Brightness and Contrast

You change the brightness and contrast of colors to change how much white or black is added. Increasing the brightness adds white, while decreasing the brightness adds black. You can change the brightness and contrast of an image to correct photographs or other bitmap images that are too dark or too light. You can also use these settings to adjust the color of vector graphics. Most programs combine the Brightness and Contrast settings in the same dialog box.

Extra for Experts

Some programs have a *colorize* option that you select to add color to a grayscale image or to change an RGB image to a two-tone image.

STEP-BY-STEP 5.8

1. Open **Step5-8** from the Data files for this lesson.

2. Save the file in your program's native file format as **Husky**.

3. Select the image and then open the menu that lists color correction options and select the option for adjusting the brightness and contrast. If your program has separate options for each, select the option for brightness.

STEP-BY-STEP 5.8 Continued

4. Increase the brightness to **30**, and then click the **OK** button or press **Enter** to apply the modification. Increasing the brightness adds white to the image. Now adjust the contrast.

5. Select the brightness and contrast option again (or just the contrast option) and set the contrast to **5**. Increasing the contrast adjusts the shades of gray in relation to each other. Click **OK** or press **Enter**. The image should look similar to the one in Figure 5-14.

FIGURE 5-14
Adjusting brightness and contrast makes details stand out.

6. Save the changes and close **Husky**. Leave your graphics program open to use in the next exercise.

Apply Special Effects

You can enhance graphics objects by applying effects such as shadows, glows, bevels, and embossing. Effects can be applied to vector objects, bitmap images, or text objects. Some can be applied to selected pixels in a bitmap as well. In most cases, you can combine effects to achieve different results. For example, you may add both a shadow and a glow to a vector object.

Hot Tip
Some programs have built-in commands for quickly applying commonly used effects such as fades, sepia tones, and grayscales.

To apply an effect, simply select the object to enhance, and then select the command to apply the effect. As with color correction effects, the location of the commands for applying special effects varies depending on the program you are using. Some may be on the same pop-up Effects or Filters menu as are the color correction effects, while some may be on a submenu accessed from the Filters menu or the Command menu. Again, look around to find the options, consult your program's Help system, or ask your instructor for more information.

If settings or options control the way the effect is applied, a dialog box appears and you can make selections. For example, you can adjust the position of a shadow or the shape of a bevel. In addition, some effects are enhanced by hiding—or *knocking out*—the shape itself. Hiding the object that has an emboss effect makes the effect much more dramatic.

Keep in mind that not all programs offer the same effects. For example, your program may have a feature for applying shadows but not glows, or for applying drop shadows but not inner shadows.

Apply Bevels and Embossings

Use an *embossed* effect to make an object appear to be pressed into the drawing area. Most programs also let you apply a raised emboss to make an object appear to rise out of the drawing area. *Bevels* also give an object a raised appearance. You can apply an inner bevel, which adds the effect within the edges of the object, or an outer bevel, which adds the effect outside the edges. You can usually adjust the position, sharpness, and width of bevels and embossing. You may also be able to change the bevel shape.

STEP-BY-STEP 5.9

1. Create a new graphics file, with a **white** drawing area, sized to **5** inches wide by **4** inches high. The resolution should be **96** pixels/inch. Save the file as **Card**.

2. Select the **Text tool**, and then set the font to **black**, **14**-point **Arial**. Set the orientation to horizontal, if necessary, and deselect all font styles, such as Italic and Underline. Click anywhere in the drawing area and then key the letter **W**.

3. Convert the letter to a shape and resize it to **2.0** inches (**192** pixels) square. Position it approximately **1** inch (**96** pixels) from the top of the drawing area, centered horizontally in the drawing area.

4. With the W shape selected, open the menu that lists the special effects, select the option for applying an emboss, and then select to apply an **Inset Emboss**. (If your program asks you if it is OK to rasterize the shape, click **OK** to continue.)

5. Set the width to **5**, and if necessary set the contrast to **75%**, the softness to **2**, and the angle to **135**.

6. If available, click the option to hide or deselect the option to show the object.

7. Import the file **Step5-9a** to the lower-left corner of the drawing area.

8. With the imported picture of the car selected, apply the **Outer Bevel** option from the appropriate menu.

STEP-BY-STEP 5.9 Continued

9. Set the bevel color to **dark gray** (hexadecimal code **#666666**), the bevel width to **5**, the contrast to **75%**, the softness to **3**, and the angle to **120**. If there is an option for a bevel edge shape, select **Flat**. When you deselect the object, the file should look similar to Figure 5-15.

FIGURE 5-15
Emboss effect draws attention to the shape, and bevel makes the picture stand out

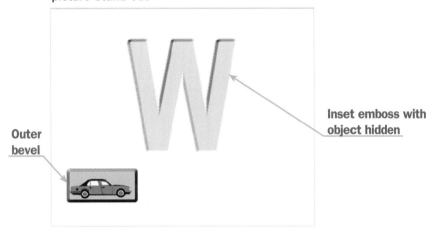

Inset emboss with object hidden

Outer bevel

10. Save the changes and leave **Card** open to use in the next exercise.

Apply Shadows and Glows

Shadows and *glows* are effects that let you add depth, dimension, and highlights to objects. Drop shadows add shading along two sides of the outer edge of an object. Inner shadows add the shading inside the edges. Glows apply a halo of color around all edges, and inner glows apply the halo inside the edges. You can usually adjust the position, color, and size of shadows and glows, and you may also be able to adjust other settings such as the sharpness and transparency.

STEP-BY-STEP 5.10

1. Select the W shape, open the menu that lists special effects options and select to apply a **Glow**.

2. Apply a light gray (hexadecimal **#CCCCCC**) glow. If available, set the width to **5**, the opacity to **75%**, the softness to **12**, and the offset to **0**.

3. Import the file **Step5-9b** to the lower-right corner of the drawing area.

STEP-BY-STEP 5.10 Continued

4. With the imported picture of the van selected, open the menu that lists special effects options and select to apply a **Drop Shadow**.

5. Position the shadow to the lower-right part of the object. If available, set the distance to **20**, the opacity to **65%**, and the softness to **4**. When you deselect the object, the image should look similar to Figure 5-16.

FIGURE 5-16
Glow effect highlights the shape and drop shadow highlights the bitmap picture

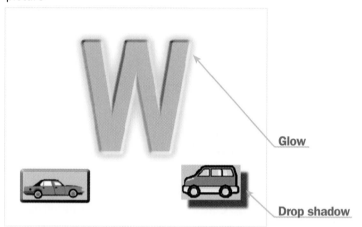

Glow

Drop shadow

6. Save the changes and leave **Card** open to use in the next exercise.

Use Sharpen and Blur

Use the sharpen and blur effects to adjust the focus or sharpness of an image. The sharpen effect brings a blurred image into focus, and the blur effect lessens the focus. Most programs offer different levels for each effect, similar to high, medium, and low settings. These effects are most often used on bitmap images, although they can be applied to vector objects and text as well.

> **Hot Tip**
>
> Sometimes the order in which you apply effects makes a difference in the result. For example, if you apply a glow and then apply an emboss, the effect is not the same as first applying an emboss and then applying a glow. Some programs let you reorder effects by changing their position in a list.

STEP-BY-STEP 5.11

1. Select the picture of the car.

2. Open the menu that lists special effects options and select to apply the lowest level blur effect available.

3. Select the picture of the van.

STEP-BY-STEP 5.11 Continued

4. Open the menu that lists special effects options and select to apply a middle-level sharpen effect.

Blurring gives one picture a softer look, while sharpening makes the other look crisp and clear.

5. Save the changes and leave **Card** open to use in the next exercise.

Save Custom Effects

To achieve a particular effect, you may have to adjust multiple settings and even use multiple effects. Once you have the effect just right, you can save it so the next time you want to use it, you don't have to start from scratch. The method for saving a custom effect varies from program to program, but usually you simply save the applied effects as a *style*, which is a collection of saved formatting settings.

To save formatting settings as a style, you apply the settings to an object and then select the New Style or Save as Style command to open the New Style dialog box. This command is usually available on the Special Effects menu or in the Styles panel or palette. In the New Style dialog box, you enter a name for the style. You may also be able to select or change the formatting settings. Once you save the style, it is displayed in the Styles panel along with default styles available in your program. To apply the style to other objects, select the object you wish to format and then click the style in the Styles panel.

> **Did You Know?**
>
> Using styles is a good way to ensure consistency in your files. You can save formatting settings such as strokes and fills as styles so you can quickly apply the same options to other shapes. Some programs even come with built-in styles to save you the trouble of creating them.

STEP-BY-STEP 5.12

1. Select the bitmap picture of the car. You will save the effects applied to this object as a style so you can apply them quickly to other objects.

2. Select the command to create a new style. If necessary, open the Styles panel or dialog box to locate the New Styles button, or select the command from the Options submenu on the special effects pop-up menu. A New Style dialog box displays.

3. Key the name **Bevel Blur** in the box for the style Name, and then click the **OK** button. The style is added to the list of styles.

4. Select the picture of the van.

5. Open the Styles panel or dialog box if it is not already open, and click the **Bevel Blur** style in the Styles list. The effects are applied to the selected object.

6. Save the changes and leave **Card** open to use in the next exercise.

Edit and Remove Effects

Y̦ou can edit an effect that has been applied to an object to adjust its settings. For example, you can change the position of a drop shadow, or the shape of a bevel. Most programs have a panel or list that shows effects that have been applied to an object. To edit an effect, select the object and then select the effect in the appropriate panel or list. Depending on your program, you can simply adjust settings to the selected effect, or you may have to click a button or double-click the effect to open a settings panel to edit the effect.

The quickest way to remove an effect is to use the Undo command as soon as you realize you are unhappy with the result. Many programs also have a command for turning off or deleting effects. Simply select the effect in the list of effects, and then click the appropriate button or menu command. For example, in Fireworks click the check mark to the left of an effect to turn it off. The check mark changes to an X. Click the X to turn the effect back on. To delete an effect, select it and then click the minus sign above the effects list.

S TEP-BY-STEP 5.13

1. Select the **W** shape and choose to edit the Inset Emboss. (For example, in Fireworks, select the **Edit and arrange live filters** button next to the Inset Emboss effect in the list.)

2. Change the angle from *135* degrees to **175** degrees, and change the width to **10**. Apply the changes.

3. Select the picture of the car, and remove the Blur effect. (For example, in Fireworks, click the Blur effect in the list of effects and click the minus sign button to delete the effect.)

4. Select the picture of the van and remove the Blur effect. When all objects are deselected, the image should look similar to the one in Figure 5-17.

FIGURE 5-17
Completed Card file

5. Save the changes and close **Card**. Leave your graphics program open to use in the next exercise.

Create Masks

The *mask* effect hides or accentuates a specific portion of an image. There are two basic types of masks: vector masks and bitmap masks. The commands for creating masks may be found on a menu such as Modify, Object, or Edit, or in a panel such as the Layers panel. Not all programs offer both types of masks.

Vector Masks

When you create a vector mask, you use a vector graphic to define the shape of the mask. You can use any vector object, such as a rectangle, polygon, or ellipse. Vector masks are also called *clipping masks* in some programs.

To create a vector mask, you first draw the vector object—called the mask object—and position it on top of the object you want to show through the mask. You may then use commands such as Cut and Paste as Mask, Clipping Path, or Paste Inside to create the mask. Only the area within the vector object's path is displayed, and the area outside the path is masked, or hidden.

In some programs, you can adjust properties for the mask to change the way it is displayed. For example, you may be able to show the stroke and fill used to draw the mask object. To show the stroke and fill of the mask object, you must usually select the mask object in a panel such as the Layer panel, and then select an option in a Properties panel to show fill and stroke.

STEP-BY-STEP 5.14

1. Open **Step5-14** from the Data files for this lesson.

2. Save the file in your program's native file format as **Bikes**.

3. Select the **Ellipse tool**—the stroke and fill do not matter—and drag to draw an oval approximately **2.0** inches (**192** pixels) wide by **3.0** inches (**288** pixels) high that covers the upper body and head of the person on the left in the picture. (If you are using Photoshop, you may have to create a layer from the background, and then use the **Elliptical Marquee tool** to select the oval shapes.)

STEP-BY-STEP 5.14 Continued

4. Duplicate the oval shape and position it over the upper body and head of the person on the right. When you release the mouse button, your drawing should look similar to Figure 5-18.

FIGURE 5-18
Draw the shapes to use as a mask

5. Select both oval shapes, and then select the command to create a vector mask. For example, click the **Edit** menu, click the **Cut** command, select the image in the file, click the **Edit** menu, and then click the **Paste as Mask** command. The image should look similar to Figure 5-19. All content inside the oval shapes is revealed and the content outside the shapes is masked.

FIGURE 5-19
Completed mask

6. Save the changes and close **Bikes**. Leave your graphics program open to use in the next exercise.

Bitmap Masks

Bitmap masks are sometimes called *layer masks* because they overlap and obscure underlying pixels. You can create a bitmap mask using a method similar to creating a vector mask. Simply paste a bitmap object as the mask instead of a vector object.

You can also create an empty mask to either reveal all or hide all the underlying objects. You then use bitmap tools to modify the mask to change the way the underlying object is viewed. For instance, you can use the Paint Bucket tool to add a fill to the mask or even erase parts of the mask to reveal the underlying object.

STEP-BY-STEP 5.15

1. Open **Step5-15** from the Data files for this lesson.

2. Save the file as **Beach** in your program's native file format.

3. Select the image, and then select the command to create an empty mask. For example, click **Modify**, click **Mask**, and then click **Reveal All**.

> **Note**
>
> If you create a mask to reveal all, you cannot see it in the file. If you create one to hide all, it displays the current background or drawing area color.

Now, apply a grayscale gradient fill to the mask to make the image look as if the fog is rolling in.

4. Click the **Gradient tool** in the toolbox. This tool may be on the menu hidden beneath the Paint Bucket tool.

5. Select a black to white linear gradient fill. Depending on your program, you may be able to select the colors directly from the fill color palette, or you may have to use a Gradient dialog box or panel.

6. Drag the Paint Bucket or Gradient mouse pointer from the upper-left corner of the image diagonally across to the lower-right corner. When you release the mouse button, the gradient is applied. It should look similar to Figure 5-20. The gradient may display a checkboard pattern on screen but will not show in print or in image preview.

FIGURE 5-20
Bitmap mask

7. Save the changes and close **Beach**. Close your graphics program.

SUMMARY

In this lesson, you learned:

■ You can mix custom colors using a color bar or by entering color system values.

■ You can use color to create illusions of distance, depth, and scale.

■ You can use color effects to add texture, patterns, and gradients to fills and strokes.

■ Color correction effects make it possible to enhance and improve vector and bitmap images.

■ Special effects make it easy to highlight objects as well as add interest and depth to an image.

■ You can save special effects as styles to use again.

■ If you are unhappy with an effect, you can edit or remove it.

■ Masks let you hide or emphasize portions of an image.

VOCABULARY *Review*

Define the following terms:

Bevel	Glow	Saturation
Brightness	Hue	Shadow
CMY	Mask	Spot color
Color system	Opacity	Style
Contrast	RGB	Value
Emboss		

REVIEW *Questions*

TRUE / FALSE

Circle T if the statement is true or F if the statement is false.

T F 1. Toward the bottom of a color bar, colors are darker because they are mixed with white.

T F 2. The two main color systems for use in graphics programs are the RGB model and the WHY (or WHYK) model.

T F 3. Use spot colors when it is necessary to have an exact color, such as a client's logo color.

T F 4. Patterns are bitmap graphics applied as a fill.

T F 5. A radial gradient blends colors out from the center of an object.

T F 6. When you decrease the brightness, you add white to a hue; when you increase the brightness you add black.

T F 7. To help a person who has trouble seeing and differentiating between colors, increase the contrast in an image.

T F 8. Knocking out a shape is the same as deleting it.

T F 9. Drop shadows add shading along the inside edges of an object.

T F 10. You can only create masks for vector objects.

WRITTEN QUESTIONS

Write a brief answer to each of the following questions.

1. Why is the CMY color system sometimes called CMYK?

2. What are at least three factors that affect the way colors appear on a computer screen?

3. What are at least three ways you can use color effects in your images to imitate the real effects of light?

4. What are three types of special effects and how do they change an object?

5. Why should you consider the stroke style and weight before applying a texture?

FILL IN THE BLANK

Complete the following sentences by writing the correct word or words in the blanks provided.

1. Color is sometimes called _____.

2. A(n) _____ displays a spectrum of colors across a rectangle from left to right.

3. The _____ color system is most often used when graphics are to be displayed on a computer monitor.

4. The _____ color system is used most often for drawings that are to be printed.

5. Use a(n) _____ gradient to blend colors horizontally across an object.

6. _____ is the range from black to white.

7. _____ controls the amount of transparency in a color.

8. A(n) _____ effect makes an object appear to be pressed into the drawing area.

9. Apply a(n) inner _____ to create a halo effect inside the edges of an object.

10. If you want to use custom effects over and over for different objects, you can save them as a(n) _____.

PROJECTS

PROJECT 5-1

1. Launch your graphics program and open **Project5-1** from the Data files for this lesson.

2. Save the file in your program's native file format as **Yacht**.

3. Select the **Text tool** and set the font to **52**-point, **Arial**, **black**, and **Bold**. Create an expandable text object in the area above the ship and key **Style**. Center the object horizontally.

4. Convert the text object to a shape. Select the entire text object if necessary and then click the **Fill Color** button and change the fill color of the text to hexadecimal code **#456B59**, which is a sea green. You will have to use a color system that accepts hexadecimal values.

5. Apply a **Raised Emboss** effect to the text object, setting the width to **10** if the option is available in your program.

6. Select the bitmap image.

7. Change the image to grayscale. You may do this by changing the saturation setting to **–100** (as low as possible), or by selecting a command to convert the image to **grayscale**. (For example, click **Commands** on the Menu bar, click **Creative**, and then click **Convert to Grayscale**.)

8. Set the brightness to **20** and the contrast to **–10**.

9. Print one copy of the image.

10. Save the changes and close **Yacht**, but leave your graphics program open to use in Project 5-2.

PROJECT 5-2

1. Open **Project5-2** from the Data files for this lesson.

2. Save the file in your program's native file format as **Jazz**.

3. Select the **Rounded Rectangle tool**. Set the fill color to **No Fill** and the stroke color to **black**.

4. Draw a rounded rectangle around the saxophone player in middle of the image (approximately **1.5** inches (**355** pixels) wide by **3.0** inches (**690** pixels) high, or large enough to fit around the figure).

5. Modify the stroke settings to **Soft Rounded**, about **10** pixels thick.

6. Create a vector mask using the rounded rectangle shape. (If necessary, cut the shape to the Clipboard, select the image, and then paste the shape as a mask.)

7. If possible in your program, select the mask object and choose to show the mask's fill and stroke. (*Hint:* Look for a *Show fill and stroke* check box in the Properties panel.)

8. Print one copy of the image.

9. Save the changes and close **Jazz**, but leave your graphics program open to use in Project 5-3.

PROJECT 5-3

1. Create a new graphics document, setting the drawing area to **7** inches square with a **white** background. Set the resolution to **96** pixels/inch. Save the file as **Head**.

2. Select the **Ellipse tool** and set the fill color to **white** and the stroke to 8-point, **Hard Line**, **black**. Draw a circle approximately **3.5** inches (**336** pixels) in diameter for a head, and then draw two ovals—at least **.5** inches (**48** pixels) wide—for eyes.

3. Use the **Line tool** to draw a nose and the **Vector Path tool** to draw a mouth.

4. Select the oval that comprises the outline of the head, and apply a solid brown fill (hexadecimal code **#996633**).

5. Apply a fill texture similar to piano keys, if available in your program, or select an uneven grid.

6. Increase the stroke weight to **25** points. Apply a **grid stroke** texture, and set the amount of texture to **100%**.

7. Select both eyes and apply a solid **navy blue** fill (hexadecimal code **#000080**), and then apply a grid fill texture.

8. Select and group all objects in the image and align the group in the center of the drawing area, horizontally and vertically.

9. Select the **Rectangle tool,** set the stroke to a **Soft Rounded** stroke with a weight of **8**, and set the fill to a pattern similar to **tweed**. If tweed is not available in your program, select a geometric pattern that uses brown, black, and white.

10. Draw a square approximately **5.0** inches (**480** pixels) on each side and layer it behind the group. Center it in the drawing area, horizontally and vertically.

11. Print one copy of the image.

12. Save the changes and close both **Head** and your graphics program.

 ## WEB PROJECT

Use the Internet to look up color value codes for different color systems. You might try searching for *hexadecimal color codes* or *CMY color codes*. Can you find a site that has both? Try entering codes in your graphics program's color mixer to see if the results are what you expect.

 ## TEAMWORK PROJECT

Discuss with your classmates the different ways color and effects can be used to enhance graphics used for different purposes. For example, consider how you might change the color and effects you use for the same image on a Web page and in a printed brochure. Then, use your graphics program to design an image that you could use to illustrate a class project. For example, you might design an image of a plant or animal to illustrate a science project, or a scene from a book to illustrate a literature project.

Save two versions of the file—one that you could use on a class Web site and one that you could use on a printed report cover. Change the colors and effects in each file based on its purpose. For example, use the RGB color system for the Web image, and the CMY color system for the printed file. When you are finished, compare the images onscreen and in print.

CRITICAL *Thinking*

For a Social Studies project on geography, you have been asked to prepare a photograph for use in a travel brochure. Locate a photograph of a scenic view that you can import into your graphics program. For example, take a picture with a digital camera, scan a picture from a book or magazine, or locate a picture on the Internet. Examine the picture to determine whether parts of it might benefit from color correction effects. For example, is it too bright or too dark? Could the contrast be improved? Would it look better in black and white or in a sepia tone? Perhaps you should add a bitmap mask to filter the image. Save different versions of the file testing different color correction effects. When you are finished, compare the different files on the computer screen and in print.

GRAPHICS

REVIEW *Questions*

TRUE / FALSE

Circle T if the statement is true or F if the statement is false.

T F 1. Vector files are usually smaller than bitmap files.

T F 2. Bitmap images retain definition even when they are resized.

T F 3. Most graphics programs let you open files that have been saved in a compatible file format.

T F 4. Color photos usually are best saved in the JPEG file format.

T F 5. You can modify a vector shape by moving the pixels.

T F 6. Emphasis is one of the basic principles of design.

T F 7. Text color is determined by the current stroke color.

T F 8. Although you can modify and transform the converted shape, you cannot edit text that has been converted to vectors.

T F 9. If you create a drawing using the CMY model, you can be fairly certain that your finished drawing will look the same when displayed on your screen.

T F 10. Bitmap masks are sometimes called pixel masks.

MATCHING

Match the correct term in Column 1 to its description in Column 2.

Column 1

___ 1. Balance

___ 2. Device driver

___ 3. Font style

___ 4. Glow

___ 5. Leading

___ 6. Loss

___ 7. Pattern

___ 8. Proportion

___ 9. PNG

___ 10. Resolution

Column 2

A. The quality or sharpness of an image, usually measured in pixels per inch or per centimeter.

B. The native file format for Macromedia Fireworks graphics files.

C. A software program that enables your computer to communicate with the hardware device.

D. The setting used to control compression.

E. The size and location of one object in relation to other objects in an image.

F. The visual weight of objects and the way they are arranged.

G. The slant and weight of characters in a font set.

H. The space between lines of text.

I. Bitmap graphics applied as a fill.

J. A halo of color applied around all edges of an object.

FILL IN THE BLANK

Complete the following sentences by writing the correct word or words in the blanks provided.

1. The _____ is the line used to draw a shape.

2. _____ in to increase the magnification of the image on your screen.

3. _____ a file before exporting to make the file size as small as possible, while maintaining the highest possible quality.

4. _____ colors are colors that are displayed the same way in all Web browsers.

5. When using the Magic Wand tool, increase the _____ level to select a wider range of tones.

6. _____ an object to slant it along its horizontal or vertical axis.

7. In a(n) _____ text block, text is entered on a single line, which increases in width to accommodate as many characters as you enter.

8. Good _____ spaces characters so that each word is viewed by the reader as a single unit.

9. Text _____ determines whether text can be read from left to right or right to left.

10. Modify the _____ level to adjust the intensity of a color.

PROJECTS

PROJECT U1-1

In this project you will design a graphic that you can use on an award certificate.

1. Launch your graphics program and create a new graphics document. Set the drawing area to 8 inches square, with a **white** background. Save the file as **Award**.

2. Select the tool for drawing five-pointed stars. Your program may have a **Star tool**, or it may have a **Polystar tool** that you can set for drawing a five-pointed star. Alternatively, you may use the **Line tool** to hand draw the star.

3. Set the fill color to **blue** (hexadecimal **#0000FF**). Set the stroke color to **yellow** (hexadecimal **#FFFF00**). Set the stroke weight to **14** points.

4. Drag to draw the star approximately **4** inches wide by **4** inches high, in the middle of the drawing area, with one point straight up.

5. Apply a texture such as **Grass** to the fill, with the texture amount set to **50%**

6. Apply a **Drop Shadow** effect to the shape. If options are available, set the distance to **50**, the opacity to **75%**, the softness to **8**, and the angle to **325**. If you cannot apply a drop shadow in your program, use a different effect, such as **Diffuse Glow**.

7. Align the shape in the center of the drawing area, horizontally and vertically.

8. Select the **Text tool** and set the font to **54-point Times New Roman, black**. Click in the middle of the star shape, and then key the number **1**.

9. Convert the text object to a vector shape and scale it to **1** inch wide by **1** inch high.

10. Apply a **Raised Emboss** effect. If options are available, set the width to **30**, the contrast to **80%**, the softness to **2**, and the angle to **130**.

11. Align the shape in the center of the drawing area, horizontally and vertically, and make sure it is stacked in front of the star.

12. Select the **Ellipse tool** and draw a circle approximately **7** inches in diameter.

13. Apply a **Radial Gradient** fill to the circle, set with **blue** on the outside, then **yellow**, and then **blue** again on the inside. You may be able to select **Blue Yellow Blue** from a list of Gradient Presets, or you may be able to use the Gradient pointers to select the colors from a color palette.

14. Center the shape horizontally and vertically in the drawing area, and stack it behind the other shapes.

15. Print one copy of the Award file.

16. Save changes and close the **Award** file. Keep your graphics program open to use in Project 2.

PROJECT U1-2

You plan to e-mail a photo to a friend, highlighting the saxophone players. But first, you must crop the image and correct the color.

1. Open **Project2** from the Data files. Save the file in your program's native file format as **Band**.

2. Select the **Crop tool**, and crop off approximately **1** inch from the left edge and **0.5** inch from the top of the image.

3. Correct the color by decreasing the brightness to **−30**, and increasing the contrast to **5**.

4. Select the **Ellipse tool** and draw a circle around the saxophonist on the left. Use **No Fill** and a **Hard 6**-point **white** line.

5. Select the **Line tool** (or the tool for drawing arrows) and draw an arrow pointing from right to left at the musician.

6. Select the **Text tool**, and set the font to 18-point **Arial, bold, white**.

7. On the bottom half of the image, create a fixed-width text block approximately **2** inches wide by .5 inches high, and key **See, I told you he was there!**

8. Center the text in the block, and center the block horizontally in the drawing area.

9. Print one copy of the file.

10. Save changes to the file.

11. Optimize the file using the **JPEG - Better Quality** setting if it is available, or manually set the optimization to a **JPEG** file format with an **80** quality setting and no Smoothing.

12. Export the file with the name **Band2**.

13. Save and close the **Band** file, and close your graphics program.

SIMULATION

You are the assistant manager of the Lighthouse View Inn, a Bed and Breakfast located on the coast of Maine. The owner would like the inn to attract a wider range of clients from across the country and around the world, and has asked you to design new graphics for use in printed and electronic media.

Before starting to work in your graphics program, take time to plan the project completely. Working alone or with a partner, review the following steps and then create a schedule for completing the jobs. Set up a timeline with appropriate milestones. Establish criteria that you believe should be met for each stage of the project, and create a rubric that you can use to gauge your accomplishments.

JOB U1-1

Lighthouse View Inn needs a new logo to use on business cards, stationery, brochures, advertisements, and Web sites. In this Job, you will use your graphics program to design a logo that incorporates text, vector shapes, and bitmap graphics.

1. Launch your graphics program and open the BMP format image **Job1** from the Data files.

2. Use the **Oval Marquee** or **Lasso tool** to select an elliptical area within the image around the house and lighthouse. If possible, scale the selection to **145** pixels wide by **190** pixels high (**1.5** inches wide by **2.0** inches high), including some of the gulls with the selection.

3. Cut the selection to the Clipboard and close the Job1 file without saving changes.

4. Create a new blank file in your graphics program, sizing the drawing area to **7** inches by **7** inches. Use a transparent background and the default resolution.

5. Save the file as **Inn**.

6. Paste the selection from the Clipboard into the Inn file.

7. Align it in the center of the drawing area horizontally and vertically.

8. Change the color in the image to **Grayscale** (set the Saturation to **–100**).

9. Use the **Text tool** to key the letter **V** in a **56**-point serif font in **black**. Convert the text to a vector path, and scale it to about **48** pixels wide by **48** pixels high (**0.5** inches wide by **0.5** inches high). Position the shape about **400** pixels from the top of the drawing area, and center it horizontally in the drawing area.

10. Apply a **Glow effect** to the letter. Set the width of the Glow to **1**, the Opacity to **55**, the Blur (or Softness) to **4**, and the Offset to **0**. Set the Color to **blue** (hexadecimal code **#0066FF**). (You may have to change the color back to **RGB** for the blue to display.)

11. Save the Glow effect as a style named **Inn Glow**.

12. Use the **Text tool** to enter the letter **L** in the same **56**-point serif font in **black**. Convert the text to a vector path, scale it to about **29** pixels wide by **29** pixels high (**0.25** inches wide by **0.25** inches high), and position it about **400** pixels from the top of the drawing area, to the left of the letter *V*.

13. Repeat step 12 to add the letter **I** to the image, positioning it to the right of the letter *V*.

14. Apply the **Inn Glow** effect to both the *L* and the *I*.

15. Select and group all four objects in the image, and then apply the **Inn Glow** style to the group.

16. Trim the drawing area to fit closely around the group. At this point, ask a classmate to review the image onscreen and to offer suggestions for improvement.

17. When you have incorporated suggested changes, optimize the image for export as a **GIF Websnap 128** file. If possible, select to use an **Alpha** transparency. Save the exported file as **Inn2**.

18. Print the **Inn** file, and then save it and close it, but leave your graphics program open to use in Job 2.

19. Ask a classmate to review the printed image and to offer comments and suggestions. If necessary, go back to modify the image file to incorporate any suggestions you think will improve the image.

JOB U1-2

The owner of the Inn wants new business cards using the new logo and a new company slogan. In this Job, you will design a prototype for the business card.

1. Create a new blank file in your graphics program, sizing the drawing area to **3.5** inches by **2** inches, a standard size for business cards. Use a **white** background and set the resolution to **96**.

2. Save the file as **Inn Card**.

3. Use the **Rectangle tool** to draw a rectangle using no fill and a **black 1**-point **Hard** line stroke. Size the rectangle about **317** pixels by **173** pixels (**3.3** inches wide by **1.8** inches high) and center it horizontally and vertically in the drawing area.

4. Import the GIF file **Job2** from the Data files. (This is a version of the **Inn2** file you created in Job 1.) Size the image to approximately **96** pixels wide by **125** pixels high (**1.0** inch wide by **1.3** inches high), and align it in the upper-left corner of the drawing area.

5. Create a text block aligned in the upper-right corner of the rectangle and key the text **Employee Name** using a **14**-point sans serif font, such as **Lucida Console**, in **blue** (hexadecimal code **#0066FF**). Start a new line in the block and key the text **Employee Title** using the same font in **12** points and **black**.

6. Create another text block aligned in the lower-right corner of the rectangle. Use the same font in **black** sized to **10** points, and key the text line by line as follows:
   56778 Ocean Drive
   Wells, Maine 04090
   Tel. (207) 555-5555
   Fax (207) 555-5556
   email employee@lvi.net

7. Create a final text block approximately 200 pixels wide by 40 pixels high (2.0 inches wide by .5 inches high). Using a serif font such as **Book Antiqua** in **black**, sized to **18** points, key **Lighthouse View Inn**. Start a new line, change to **12** points, and key **"Your Home Away From Home"**. If necessary, increase the width of the text block so that the text does not wrap, or use a smaller font size.

8. Position the text block in the vertical center of the drawing area, to the right of the imported image, or between the other two text blocks.

9. Select all three text blocks and set the text alignment to **Right**. Then, select each text box individually and adjust the leading to make the text easier to read and attractive. For example, increase the leading in the top and bottom text blocks, and decrease it in the middle.

10. Check the spelling in the file.

11. Select all objects in the file and group them.

12. Print the image. Ask a classmate to review the printed image. If necessary, go back to the file and make changes or improvements.

13. Save changes and close the **Inn Card** file. Leave your graphics program open to use in Job 3.

JOB U1-3

The owner of the Inn has asked you to gather a selection of pictures that could be used to illustrate aspects of Maine that might appeal to tourists from around the world. She needs four pictures, but she has asked you to provide at least eight from which she can choose. They can be photos or drawings, but she wants to see them both on screen and in print, as they will be used for a variety of purposes. In this Job, you research Maine using available resources, including the Internet, books, magazines, and CD-ROMs, to find the pictures. You then optimize the pictures for viewing onscreen and for printing. Before selecting a picture, you should consider its composition and format as well as its content. Think about how the pictures may be used and whether you will need to obtain permission to use them.

First, plan your research by considering accessible sources and the amount of time you have. Decide how to organize the pictures once you locate them, including naming them, storing them, and printing them. Make a schedule to ensure you complete the job on time. (This should be part of the timeline with milestones that you established at the beginning of these projects.)

When you are ready, locate as many pictures as you can on the Internet. You can use a search engine or go directly to a Web site such as www.state.me.us or www.visitmaine.com. Download the pictures, saving them with unique names such as *Maine1*, *Maine2*, and so on. Record all source information for the downloaded photos in a word processing or text file, or by hand. Include the address of the Web site; the photographer's name, if available; the date of the download; and the date the site was last updated, if available.

Next, try to locate information in a book or magazine. Try looking for pictures in travel magazines, geography books, or an encyclopedia. If you find any pictures, scan them into your graphics programs. Continue the same naming scheme that you used for the downloaded pictures. Record all source information for the pictures, including the publication name, the article name, the artist or photographer, the publisher, the date, and the page number.

Finally, try using a CD-ROM to locate pictures of Maine. You may have access to an encyclopedia on CD, such as Microsoft's Encarta, or you may have a travel or geography CD. If you find any pictures, save them on your computer using the name *Maine* and the next consecutive number. Again, don't forget to record all source information for the pictures.

When you are finished locating at least eight pictures, optimize them for viewing onscreen and for printing. Share them with your classmates and discuss whether they are appropriate for use in a marketing campaign. Select pictures better suited for use on a Web site and those better suited for other media, such as brochures, direct marketing flyers, posters, and presentations.

If possible, store the pictures in a database that you create with a database program or spreadsheet program. You can set up the database to include a preview of the picture or a link to the actual picture file. You can include information such as the source where you located the picture, information about the content of the picture, and how you anticipate using the picture. Then write a brief report explaining which pictures you would recommend for each use, and why. If possible, insert the pictures into your report. E-mail the report and the database to your instructor or to a classmate, asking for an opinion on the selected pictures.

ANIMATION AND VIDEO

Unit 2

Estimated Time for Unit: 9 hours

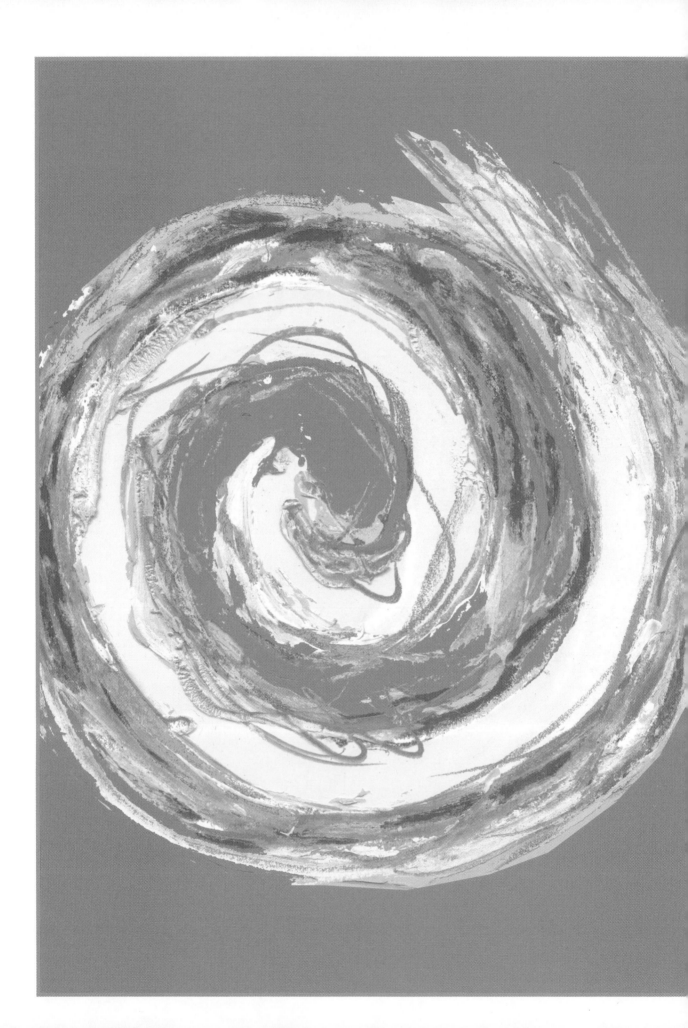

CREATING ANIMATIONS

OBJECTIVES

Upon completion of this lesson, you should be able to:

- Create, save, and close an animation file.
- Open an existing animation file.
- Set document properties.
- Insert content on the Stage.
- Create frame-by-frame animation.
- Preview and print an animation.
- Create motion animation.
- View multiple frames.
- Test an animation.

Estimated Time: 1.5 hours

VOCABULARY

.fla

.swf

Animation

Document properties

Ease

Frame

Frame rate

Frame-by-frame
  animation

Intermediate frames

Keyframe

Layer

Library

Loop

Movie

Onion skin

Pasteboard

Playhead

Timeline

Tweened animation

Work area

Animated graphics—that is, graphics combined with motion—are a key element of most Web sites and are frequently used in presentation graphics programs to enhance on-screen presentations. Also called *animations* or *movies*, these graphics take many forms, including animated text, games, flashing advertisements, lively cartoon characters, product demonstrations, or even how-to tutorials. They add action and excitement, and capture a viewer's attention in a way that static graphics cannot.

Some basic graphics programs let you create simple animations such as blinking or spinning logos. Using a more specialized animation program, such as Macromedia's Flash 8, you can create sophisticated animations that combine a variety of objects and effects, such as sounds, video, text, and even interactivity.

In this lesson, you learn the basic skills you will need to create an animation. You learn how to create and save an animation document and set document properties. You also learn to import graphics to use in the animation, control the motion of objects in an animation, and, finally, preview the animation on-screen.

Create, Save, and Close an Animation File

To create an animation, you must create and save an animation file, or document. The animation file is the file in which you store the content that comprises the animation. If you use Flash 8, the animation file has an *.fla* file extension. As with all computer programs, once you create an animation file, you must save it so that you can use it again in the future.

Create an Animation File

When you start your animation program, it may display a new, blank document, or it may display a Start page, which is a page from which you can select to create a new document or open an existing document. You can also create a new document at any time using the New command on the File menu, or the New button on the Main toolbar.

When you select the New command, the program creates a new blank file similar to Figure 6-1. The appearance of the screen depends on the program you are using as well as the default options set for your computer, so don't worry if your screen doesn't look exactly the same as the one in the illustration. For example, the toolbar may not display, and you may have additional panels open on the screen. In addition to the standard screen elements such as a document window, menu bar, toolbars, and scroll bars, most animation programs include a Stage, which is the area where you place the content for the animation; a *Timeline,* which you use to organize and control content over time; and a *work area* or *pasteboard,* which is the gray area around the Stage that you use to store content that you do not want to display in the completed animation. In addition, your program may display panels, which are small floating windows that you can open, close, expand, and collapse. The Tools panel displays by default. It provides the tools you use to draw and format objects just like the Toolbox in a graphics program, as covered in Unit 1. Another panel that displays by default is the Property Inspector. The Property Inspector provides access to the settings you use to control aspects of the selected object, such as its size or position. You can customize the display to show or hide the elements you need, and to zoom in or out on the Stage.

FIGURE 6-1
Typical animation program window

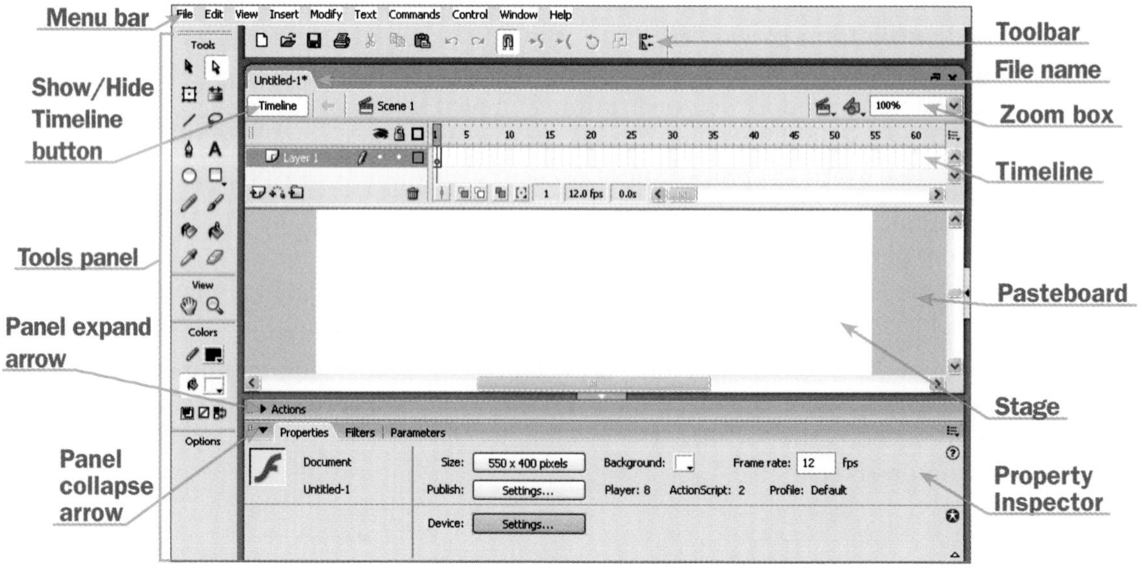

New files usually have a generic name, such as Untitled, and are numbered consecutively. So, the first file you create is Untitled-1, the second is Untitled-2, and so on. You customize the name of the file when you save it. Most animation programs let you have more than one file open at a time, although only one can be active.

S TEP-BY-STEP 6.1

1. Launch your animation program.

2. Click **File** on the Menu bar, and then click **New**. A New Document dialog box displays.

3. Click the **OK** button in the dialog box to create a new document.

4. Click **Window** on the Menu bar, and then click **Tools**. When you are not working with the drawing tools, you can close the Tools panel to make more room on-screen for the Stage, Timeline, and other panels.

5. Click the **Collapse** arrow in the Property Inspector panel to collapse the panel. The collapsed panel takes up less room on-screen, but is still available for quick access. If other panels are open on your screen, collapse them as well.

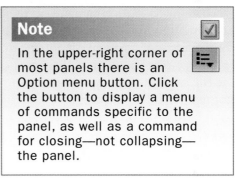

Note

In the upper-right corner of most panels there is an Option menu button. Click the button to display a menu of commands specific to the panel, as well as a command for closing—not collapsing—the panel.

6. Click the **Show/Hide Timeline** button, or click **Window** on the Menu bar, and then click **Timeline**. The Timeline is hidden. When you are working with content on the Stage, you can hide the Timeline to make even more room on-screen.

7. Click **View** on the Menu bar and then click **Zoom Out** to get a wider view of the Stage, as shown in Figure 6-2.

FIGURE 6-2
Customize the display

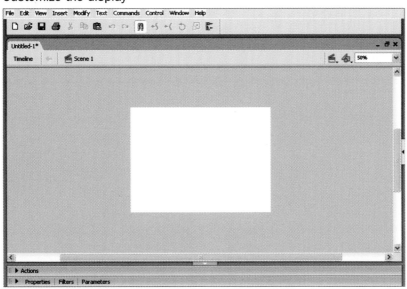

STEP-BY-STEP 6.1 Continued

8. Click **View** on the Menu bar, click **Magnification**, and then click **100%** to show the Stage at its actual size. Notice that in addition to percentages, the Magnification submenu includes other options such as Fit in Window, which automatically adjusts the magnification so that you can see the entire Stage, and Show All, which automatically adjusts the magnification so that you can see all content on the Stage.

9. Click the **Expand** arrow in the Property Inspector. Click the **Show/Hide Timeline** button, or click **Window** on the Menu bar, and then click **Timeline**.

10. Click **Window** on the Menu bar, and then click **Tools**. This returns the window to the default configuration. Leave the animation file open to use in the next exercise.

> ### Hot Tip
> Most programs have a Magnification drop-down list box somewhere near the Stage. In Flash, it is on the Edit toolbar above the upper-right corner of the Stage. Enter a magnification in the box, or click the drop-down arrow to display a list of magnification options.

Save an Animation File

Use the Save As command on the File menu to save an animation file for the first time. When you save a file for the first time, you give it a name and select a storage location. You should use filenames that help identify the file contents, and, of course, you must follow standard filename rules. That means you cannot use the following characters in the filename: /, \, >, <, *, ?, ", !, :, ;. You can save a file on a local hard disk, on a network drive, or on removable media, such as a floppy disk, a flash drive, a DVD, or a CD.

Once you have saved a file for the first time, you can quickly save changes by clicking the Save button on the Main toolbar, or by using the Save command on the File menu. Saving changes ensures that you don't lose your work if there's a problem with your computer or the software. Whenever you choose to save, the existing file will be overwritten with the current file. To keep the original file unchanged, you can use the Save As command to save an altered file with a new name or in a new location.

> ### Important
> You should save your files frequently. Until you save, your work is at risk of being lost if there is a mechanical problem with the computer or a power failure. To keep your work safe, you must save it.

S TEP-BY-STEP 6.2

1. Click **File** on the Menu bar, and then click **Save As**. The Save As dialog box opens, as shown in Figure 6-3.

FIGURE 6-3
Save As dialog box

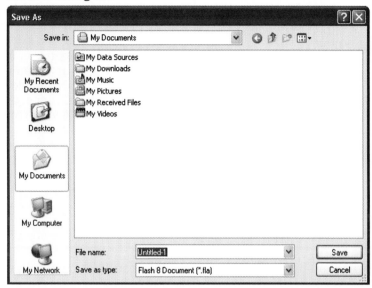

2. In the *File name* box, with the default name already selected, key **Motion**. This will be the name of the new file.

3. From the **Save in** list, select the location where you want to store the file.

4. Click the **Save** button in the dialog box. The file is saved with the new name in the selected storage location. Leave the **Motion** file open to use in the next exercise.

Close an Animation File

When you have finished using the file, you should close it using either the Close com- mand on the File menu or the Document Close button. After you close a file, the animation program remains open so that you can continue using it.

If you have not saved the file before issuing a Close command, the program displays a dialog box asking if you want to save. Click the Yes button to save the changes and close the file. Click the No button to close the file without saving the changes. Click the Cancel button to close the dialog box and continue working in the file. If you close the file without saving, all changes that you made since the last time you saved the file will be lost.

STEP-BY-STEP 6.3

1. Click **File** on the Menu bar.

2. Click **Close**. The **Motion** file closes. Leave your animation program open to use in the next exercise.

Open an Existing Animation File

T o work again with a file you have closed, you must open it in your animation program. You can use the Open button on the Main toolbar or the Open command from the File menu to display the Open dialog box. From the Open dialog box you can locate and select the file you want to open.

Hot Tip

Most programs also have commands for opening recently used file. For example, in Flash 8, you can open recent items from the Start page or from the File menu. From the Start page, simply click the file name under the heading *Open a Recent Item*. From the File menu, click Open Recent and then click the filename.

STEP-BY-STEP 6.4

1. Click **File** on the Menu bar, and then click **Open**. The Open dialog box displays the list of files in the folder, as shown in Figure 6-4. (Don't worry if your Open dialog box does not look exactly the same as the one in the figure. Your program may be set to display the filenames differently.)

FIGURE 6-4
Open dialog box

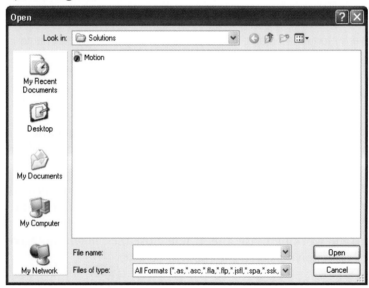

2. If the Motion file is not listed in the dialog box, click the **Look in** list drop-down arrow and then select the location where the file is stored.

STEP-BY-STEP 6.4 Continued

3. In the list of files, click **Motion**.

4. Click the **Open** button in the dialog box. The file opens in the program window. Leave the **Motion** file open to use in the next exercise.

Set Document Properties

When you create an animation document, you should set *document properties*. Document properties are the settings that determine the dimensions and color of the Stage as well as the speed at which the animation plays. In some programs, the default Stage size is 550×400 pixels (px). The minimum size is 18×18 px; the maximum size is 2880×2880 px. If you prefer to work in inches, millimeters, points, or centimeters, you can change the ruler units. The speed at which an animation plays is determined by the *frame rate*. Frame rate is measured in frames per second (fps). A *frame* is a single image in the sequence of images that comprise an animation. The default frame rate is 12. Set a lower rate to slow down the animation, or a faster frame rate to speed up the animation. The default background color is white, but you can select any color from the Background color palette by clicking the Background color button and then clicking a color swatch. You can also enter a title and description of the file, if you want.

You can set document properties using the Property Inspector or the Document Properties dialog box. You can change the properties at any time.

S TEP-BY-STEP 6.5

1. Click **Modify** on the Menu bar, and then click **Document**. The Document Properties dialog box displays, as shown in Figure 6-5.

FIGURE 6-5
Document Properties dialog box

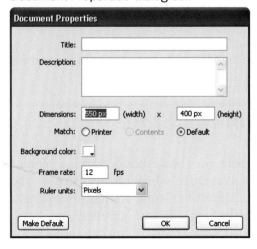

STEP-BY-STEP 6.5 Continued

2. Click the **Ruler units** drop-down arrow and then click **Inches** to change the ruler unit to inches.

3. Double-click in the **Dimensions (width)** box, and then key **8** to set the width of the Stage to 8 inches.

4. Double-click in the **Dimensions (height)** box, and then key **8** to set the height of the Stage to 8 inches.

5. Click the **Background color** button to display the color palette, and then click a **yellow** swatch.

6. Click the **OK** button in the dialog box. The Stage size adjusts to its new dimensions and background color, as shown in Figure 6-6.

FIGURE 6-6
Set properties to change the Stage size and color

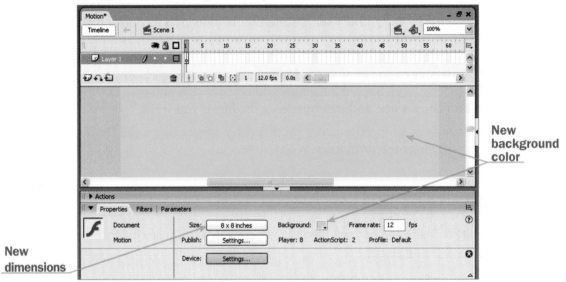

7. In the Property Inspector, click the **Background color** button, and then click the **white** color swatch on the palette.

8. Save changes and leave the **Motion** file open to use in the next exercise.

Insert Content on the Stage

A new animation document contains a blank Stage, a blank *keyframe*, and a single *layer*, called Layer 1. A keyframe is a frame in which change occurs. The change may be the insertion of new content, or the modification of existing content. A layer is an invisible sheet used to separate and organize content on the Stage. To insert content, you can use the drawing tools to draw objects as you would in a graphics program, or you can import existing objects, such as graphics files. For example, you might want to import a drawing of a logo that you created in a graphics program into an animation program so that you can make it spin, increase in size, or even fade in or out, or you might want to import a picture to use as a background for an animation. You can only insert content in a keyframe.

Using multiple layers helps you keep content organized on the Stage. For example, if you import an image to use as a background, you can place it on a layer named Background to keep it separate from the object you plan to animate.

Draw Content

Use the drawing tools in the Tools panel to draw basic shapes such as ovals, rectangles, lines, and stars. To draw a basic shape, click the Stroke Color button to select a stroke color, click the Fill Color button to select a fill color, and then select the shape tool. Click and drag on the Stage to draw the shape. For more information on using drawing tools, refer to Unit 1.

Most animation programs have features to help you size and position objects on the Stage, such as rulers and a grid. Use the commands on the View menu to display these features.

> **Important**
>
> In most programs, including Flash, shapes are drawn with a separate stroke and fill, and overlapping shapes intersect and segment one another. You may be able to select a different drawing model, such as Object Drawing in Flash, which groups the stroke and fill so that overlapping objects do not intersect and segment.

S TEP-BY-STEP 6.6

1. Click the **Collapse** arrow in the Property Inspector to collapse the panel, and then adjust the zoom magnification to **Fit in Window**.

2. Click **View** on the Menu bar and then click **Rulers** to display the horizontal and vertical rulers. The measurement unit is the same as the unit you select in the Document Properties dialog box.

3. Click the **Stroke color** button in the Tools panel, and then click a **black swatch** on the color palette.

4. Click the **Fill color** button in the Tools panel, and then click a **red swatch** on the color palette.

STEP-BY-STEP 6.6 Continued

5. Click the **Oval Tool** in the Tools panel, click in the upper-left corner of the Stage, and then click and drag down and to the right to draw a circle approximately 2.0 inches in diameter. Release the mouse button when the circle is finished. It should look similar to Figure 6-7.

FIGURE 6-7
Draw content on the Stage

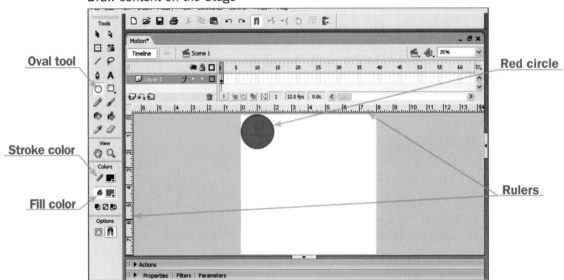

6. Save the changes and leave **Motion** open to use in the next exercise.

> **Hot Tip**
>
> Press and hold **Shift** while you drag to draw a perfect circle.

Create and Rename Layers

As mentioned earlier, by default an animation file has a single layer—Layer 1, so all content is entered on Layer 1. You can create multiple layers to keep content separate. This is useful for organizing and controlling objects in an animation. For example, you may want to animate one object to move across the Stage left to right and a different object across the Stage to move right to left. If both objects are on the same layer, they may interfere with each other. If you place each object on its own layer, you can easily work with them individually.

You use the Layers panel on the left side of the Timeline to create and control layers. Click a layer name to make it current. Click the Insert Layer button to create a new layer above the current layer. Double-click a layer name to rename it. Click the Delete Layer button to delete the current layer.

Generally, the content of layers higher in the Timeline displays in front of the content on layers lower in the list. Drag a layer up or down the list to change its position. You can also hide and lock individual layers. Locking a layer keeps you from making changes to the content on that layer. Hiding a layer hides the content on that layer so you can work with the content on a different layer without distraction.

> **Note**
>
> To view items that do not display within the Timeline panel, drag the bottom border of the panel up or down to resize it, or use the scroll bars.

Click in the Lock/Unlock Layer column to the right of a layer name to lock or unlock the layer. A lock icon indicates the layer is locked. Click in the Show/Hide Layer column to show or hide the layer. An X indicates the layer is hidden.

STEP-BY-STEP 6.7

1. Double-click the name **Layer 1** in the Layers panel, key **Red Ball**, and then press **Enter**. This renames the layer.

2. Click the **Insert Layer** button to create a new layer named *Layer 2*.

3. Double-click the name **Layer 2**, key **Background**, and then press **Enter**.

4. Drag the **Background** layer down in the list so it is below the *Red Ball* layer.

5. Click in the **Lock/Unlock Layer** column to the right of the *Red Ball* layer to lock the layer.

6. Click in the **Show/Hide Layer** column to the right of the *Red Ball* layer to hide the layer. Notice that the content no longer displays on the Stage. The Timeline should look similar to Figure 6-8.

FIGURE 6-8
Manage layers

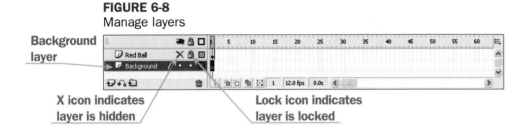

7. Save the changes and leave **Motion** open to use in the next exercise.

Import Content

In most animation programs you can use the Import command on the File menu to import content directly to the Stage, or to the file's *library*. The library is a folder in which you organize and store objects that you use in an animation. Once an object is stored in the library, you can insert it into an animation as often as you want. If an object is stored in a file's library, display the library panel, and then drag the item from the panel to the Stage. You can rename items in a library without affecting the original file, if you want.

STEP-BY-STEP 6.8

1. Click **Background** in the Layers panel to be sure the *Background* layer is active. Click **File** on the Menu bar, click **Import**, and then click **Import to Library**. The Import to Library dialog box opens so that you can select the file to import. If your program does not have an option to import to the library, select **Import**, and skip to step 7.

STEP-BY-STEP 6.8 Continued

2. Navigate to the data files folder, select **Step6-8.jpg**, and click **Open**. (If a dialog box prompts you for import settings, choose to import the graphic as a single flattened bitmap, and then click **OK**.)

3. Click **Window** on the Menu bar, and then click **Library**. The Library panel opens as shown in Figure 6-9. The name and type of the imported file display in the library list, and a preview of the object displays in the preview area. (If the Library panel is open, clicking Library on the Window menu closes it. Select the command again to open it.)

FIGURE 6-9
Library panel

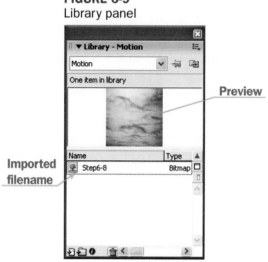

Preview

Imported filename

4. Right-click the filename **Step6-8** in the library list and click **Rename** on the shortcut menu. Key **Sky** and then press **Enter** to rename the object in the library. This does not affect the original file, only the object stored in the library.

5. Drag the graphic from the Library panel to the Stage. You may drag the object name or the preview image.

6. Close the Library panel.

7. Click the **Free Transform Tool** in the Tools panel. Handles display around the imported image so you can scale the object.

STEP-BY-STEP 6.8 Continued

8. Drag the handles to scale the object so it is the same size as the Stage (8.0 inches by 8.0 inches) and then drag the object to position it so it is aligned with the Stage, as shown in Figure 6-10.

FIGURE 6-10
Imported image on the Stage

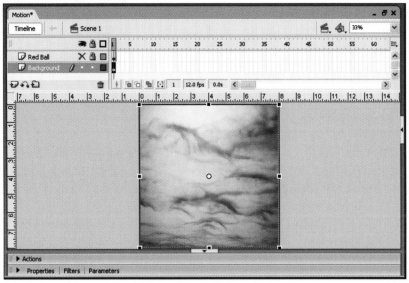

9. Save the changes and leave **Motion** open to use in the next exercise.

Create Frame-by-Frame Animation

To create an animation, you enter content in a series of frames, and then display the frames in sequence. Recall that a frame is a single image in the sequence of images that comprise an animation. If the content changes from frame to frame, it simulates motion over time. In *frame-by-frame animation*, you manually change the content on frames in a sequence. This type of animation is suited for complex animations that have subtle changes, such as a change in facial expression.

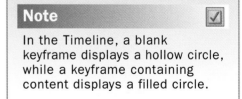

Note

In the Timeline, a blank keyframe displays a hollow circle, while a keyframe containing content displays a filled circle.

Most animation programs have two types of frames: regular frames, which display existing content, and keyframes, in which change occurs. To create frame-by-frame animation, you insert a keyframe and change the content in every frame of the Timeline.

When you insert a frame or keyframe, your program automatically inserts the content from the previous keyframe into the new frame, unless you specifically insert a blank keyframe. Insert a regular frame to extend the animation sequence without a change, or insert a keyframe if you want to make a change in the content.

Use commands on the Insert menu to insert a frame or a keyframe, or right-click the Timeline and use the commands on the shortcut menu. You can also delete a frame, or clear content from a keyframe.

Extra for Experts

Frame rate and the number of frames in a file determine the play time of the animations. If your animation file is set to display 12 fps, inserting a keyframe and changing the content every 12 frames results in a change in the action every second. A file with 60 frames results in a 5-second movie.

STEP-BY-STEP 6.9

1. Click the **Selection Tool** in the Tools panel. Click the **X** in the Show/Hide Layer column to the right of the *Red Ball* layer, and then click the **Lock** icon in the Lock/Unlock Layer column. Click in the Show/Hide Layer column to the right of the *Background* layer to hide the Sky image.

2. Right-click **frame 5** on the *Red Ball* layer of the Timeline and then click **Insert Keyframe** on the shortcut menu. Your program inserts a new keyframe in frame 5, and enters the content from the previous keyframe—the red circle object. The object is selected. The Sky image on the *Background* layer does not display.

3. Drag the object to the lower-left corner of the Stage, as shown in Figure 6-11.

FIGURE 6-11
Move the object in the keyframe

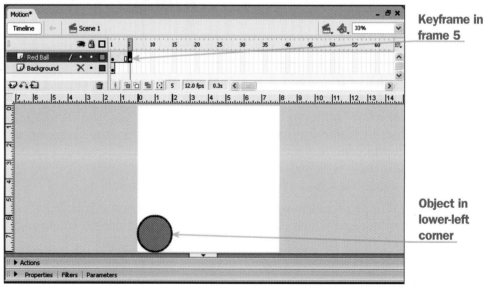

4. Click **frame 1** on the *Red Ball* layer. Notice that the circle object is still in its original position.

5. Right-click **frame 10** on the *Red Ball* layer of the Timeline and then click **Insert Keyframe** on the shortcut menu to insert another keyframe.

STEP-BY-STEP 6.9 Continued

6. Drag the circle object to the lower-right corner of the Stage.

7. Insert a keyframe in frame 15 of the *Red Ball* layer, and then drag the circle object to the upper-right corner of the Stage.

8. Insert a keyframe in frame 20 of the *Red Ball* layer and then drag the circle back to the upper-left corner of the Stage.

9. Insert a keyframe in frame 25 of the *Red Ball* layer. Click **Modify** on the Menu bar, click **Align**, and then click **To Stage**. Click **Modify** on the Menu bar again, click **Align**, and then click **Horizontal Center**. Click **Modify** on the Menu bar again, click **Align**, and then click **Vertical Center**. This aligns the red circle in the center of the Stage.

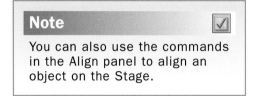

Note ✓

You can also use the commands in the Align panel to align an object on the Stage.

10. Display the *Background* layer. Right-click **frame 25** of the *Background* layer and then click **Insert Frame** on the shortcut menu. This inserts a regular frame and extends the content on the *Background* layer to the end of the animation sequence. The Stage and Timeline should look similar to Figure 6-12.

FIGURE 6-12
Frame-by-frame animation

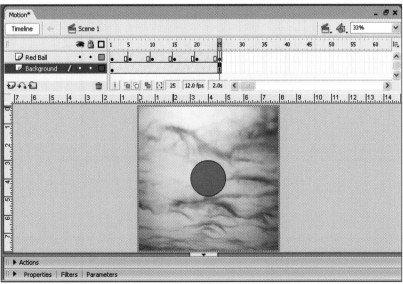

11. Save the changes and leave **Motion** open to use in the next exercise.

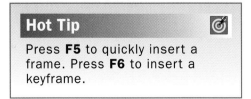

Hot Tip ◎

Press **F5** to quickly insert a frame. Press **F6** to insert a keyframe.

Preview and Print an Animation

You can preview an animation on the Stage at any time during its creation. You can drag the *playhead*—the vertical red marker above the Timeline—to see how the animation progresses. (Drag the playhead toward frame 1 to rewind the movie.) You can also use commands on the Control menu or buttons on the Controller toolbar to play or rewind the movie. It is important to preview the animation as you work so that you can identify and correct problems.

Another way to preview your work is to print it. You can print a single frame of an animation, or all frames. Select the options in the Page Setup dialog box, and then use the Print dialog box to select the number of copies. Page setup options include page margins, orientation, whether to print a single frame or all frames, and how to size and arrange the frames on the printed page. In order to print an animation, you must have a printer correctly installed and set up for use with your computer.

STEP-BY-STEP 6.10

1. Click **Control** on the Menu bar and then click **Play**. The animation plays from the beginning. Note that at each keyframe, the object moves to a different location on the Stage.

2. Click **File** on the Menu bar and then click **Page Setup**. The Page Setup dialog box displays, as shown in Figure 6-13.

FIGURE 6-13
Page Setup dialog box

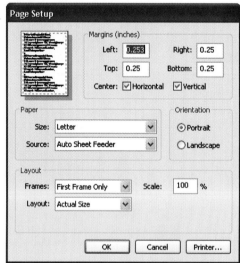

3. Click the **Frames** drop-down arrow, and then click **All frames**.

4. Click the **Layout** drop-down arrow, and then click **Storyboard - boxes**.

STEP-BY-STEP 6.10 Continued

5. Double-click in the **Frames** box and key **5** to print 5 frames across the page, and then click the **OK** button in the dialog box.

6. Click **File** on the Menu bar and then click **Print**. Click the **OK** button in the dialog box to print the animation. (If you do not have a printer correctly installed and set up for use with your computer, an error message displays. Click OK to continue without printing the animation.)

7. Save the changes and leave **Motion** open to use in the next exercise.

Create Motion Animation

When an animation does not require subtle changes, you may be able to use motion, or *tweened animation*. In a tweened animation, you specify a beginning keyframe and an ending keyframe, and your program automatically fills in the frames between, called the *intermediate frames*, to create the appearance of motion or change over time. You can use a motion tween to move an object, change its size or scale, rotate an object, or even change its color.

To create a motion tween, first specify the beginning and ending keyframes. Next, select an intermediate frame and select the command to create the motion tween. This command may be on the Insert > Timeline submenu, or you may be able to select it from a drop-down list in the Property Inspector. You may also right-click an intermediate frame and select it from the shortcut menu. You may also have to set tween properties in the Property Inspector to control the tween. For example, select the Scale option if you are tweening the size of an object, or deselect it if you want the size to remain constant. Other properties include *Ease*, which is the rate at which changes occur during a tween, and Rotate, which controls the direction and number of times an object rotates during the tween. Ease in by entering a negative value to begin the change slowly and accelerate. Ease out by entering a positive value to begin the change quickly and decelerate.

STEP-BY-STEP 6.11

1. Click the **Background** layer to select it, if necessary, and then click the **Insert Layer** button to insert a new layer. Rename the new layer **Blue Square**.

2. Hide the *Background* layer and the *Red Ball* layer.

3. Click **frame 1** on the *Blue Square* layer to select it. Click the **Fill color** button in the Tools panel and click a **blue** color swatch.

STEP-BY-STEP 6.11 Continued

4. Click the **Rectangle Tool** in the Tools panel, then click in the upper-right corner of the Stage and drag down and to the left to draw a square approximately 2.0 inches wide by 2.0 inches high. When you release the mouse button the Stage should look similar to Figure 6-14.

FIGURE 6-14
Draw a blue square

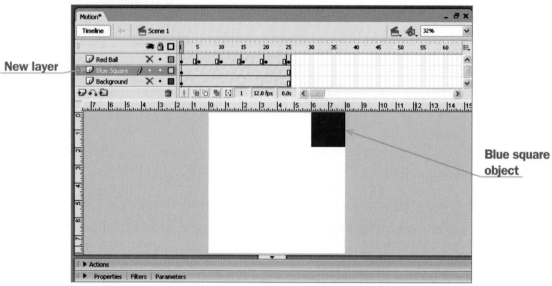

5. Right-click **frame 10** on the *Blue Square* layer and click **Insert Keyframe**. Click the **Selection Tool** in the Tools panel, and then drag the blue square object to the lower-left corner of the Stage.

6. Right-click **frame 5** on the *Blue Square* layer then click **Create Motion Tween**. In the Timeline, your program may insert an arrow between the beginning keyframe in frame 1 and the ending keyframe in frame 10, and change the color of the intermediate frames to blue.

7. Expand the Property Inspector, and then click to deselect the **Scale** check box.

STEP-BY-STEP 6.11 Continued

8. Double-click the **Ease** box in the Property Inspector and key **25**. Your screen should look similar to Figure 6-15.

FIGURE 6-15
Create a motion tween animation

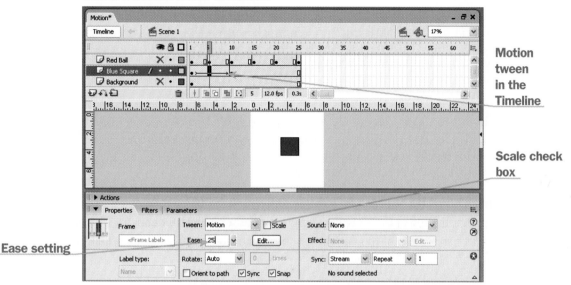

9. Insert a new keyframe on frame 20 of the *Blue Square* layer, and then drag the blue square back to the upper-right corner of the Stage. Right-click **frame 15** on the *Blue Square* layer and then click **Create Motion Tween**. Click to deselect the **Scale** check box in the Property Inspector, and set the Ease to **25**.

10. Right-click **frame 25** on the *Blue Square* layer and insert a new keyframe.

11. Click the blue square object to select it. Double-click in the **W** box in the Property Inspector, key **5** and then press **Enter**. The width of the selected object changes to 5.0 inches, and the height may automatically change as well. If the height does not change, click in the **H** box in the Property Inspector, key **5**, and then press **Enter** to change the height to 5.0 inches. Align the object in the horizontal and vertical center of the Stage.

12. Right-click **frame 23** of the *Blue Square* layer and create a motion tween. Leave the **Scale** check box in the Property Inspector selected.

13. Show all layers, then rewind and preview the animation. (You may want to collapse the Property Inspector or hide the Timeline to make more space available for viewing the Stage.) Notice that while the object animated with frame-by-frame animation jumps from spot to spot, the object animated with tweens moves smoothly across the Stage.

14. Save the changes and leave **Motion** open to use in the next exercise.

View Multiple Frames

Most animation programs offer an *onion skin* feature that enables you to view the contents of multiple frames on-screen at once. When you do so, you can check an object's motion and determine whether you may need to make slight changes to the position of an object in a particular frame. In this way, the onion skin functions as a static preview of a portion of your animation.

To turn on onion skinning, click the Onion Skin button below the Timeline. By default, markers on the Timeline define the length the onion skin displays, which includes the content of two frames on either side of the current frame. You can drag the markers to increase or decrease the length of the display.

STEP-BY-STEP 6.12

1. Hide the *Background* layer and the *Red Ball* layer so you can better see the onion skin content on the *Blue Square* layer. Collapse the Property Inspector.

2. Click **frame 10** on the *Blue Square* layer, and then click the **Onion Skin** button. The onion skin markers display at the top of the Timeline and the content of frames 8 through 12 display on the Stage. Notice that the content of the current frame—frame 10—is more opaque than the content of the other frames, as shown in Figure 6-16.

FIGURE 6-16
Onion skins display multiple frames in a tween

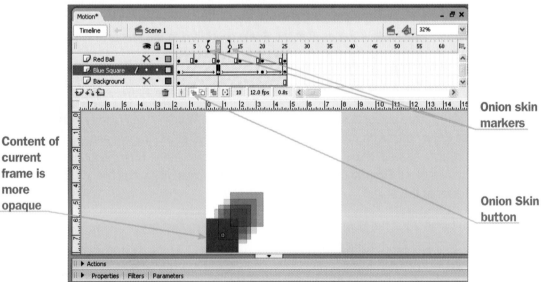

Content of current frame is more opaque

Onion skin markers

Onion Skin button

3. Drag the left onion skin marker to frame 5 to increase the length of the display to include frames 5 through 12.

4. Click the **Onion Skin** button below the Timeline to turn off the feature. Show all layers.

5. Save the changes and leave **Motion** open to use in the next exercise.

Test an Animation

When you have neared completion of an animation, you should test it to see how it will look to someone viewing it on the Web or in a presentation. Most animation programs let you test a movie in a player window, or in your Web browser. For example, Flash 8 includes the Flash Player program, which is used to display many Web-based animations. In Flash, you can test a movie by generating a Flash Player file and playing it in the Flash Player window. When you test a movie, Flash saves the animation file in Flash Player file format with an *.swf* file extension.

To test the animation, select the Test Movie command from the Control menu. By default, the animation plays in a continuous *loop*, which means it plays over and over without stopping. You can use the commands on the Control menu in the Flash Player window to deselect the Loop option, and to play or rewind the animation. Use the program close button to close the Flash Player window when you have finished viewing the animation.

STEP-BY-STEP 6.13

1. Click **Control** on the Menu bar and then click **Test Movie**. The animation plays in a loop in a Flash Player window.

2. Click **Control** on the Flash Player window Menu bar and then click **Loop** to deselect the Loop option. The animation stops playing at the end. It should look similar to Figure 6-17.

FIGURE 6-17
Test an animation in a player window

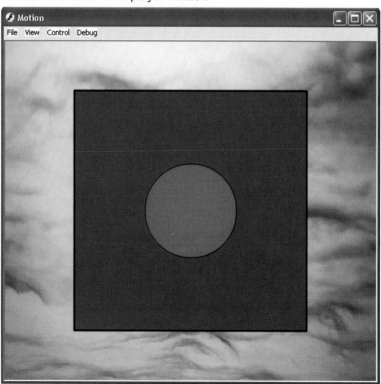

STEP-BY-STEP 6.13 Continued

3. Click **Control** on the Flash Player window Menu bar and then click **Rewind**. Click **Control** again, and then click **Play**. The animation plays one time.

4. Click the **Close** button in the Flash Player window to close the Flash Player and return to your animation program.

5. Save and close the **Motion** file. Close your animation program.

SUMMARY

In this lesson, you learned:

- To create an animation you must create and save an animation file.

- Animation programs have special screen elements such as the Stage, where you place content; the Timeline, which you use to organize and control content over time; and panels, which are small floating windows that you can open, close, expand, and collapse.

- You can customize the screen to display the elements you need.

- You can set document properties to determine the dimensions, color, and frame rate of an animation document.

- By default, all content is inserted on the same layer, but you can add layers to help keep content separate.

- You can draw content using the drawing tools, or import existing graphics for use in an animation.

- If an object is stored in the library, you can insert it many times into an animation.

- In frame-by-frame animation, you manually change the content on frames in a sequence.

- You can insert a keyframe on the Timeline at the location where you want a change to occur.

- You can preview an animation on the Stage, and you can print one or more frames of an animation.

- In tweened animation, your program automatically fills in the frames between a beginning keyframe and an ending keyframe to create the appearance of motion or change over time.

- To use the onion skin feature to view multiple frames on the Stage at the same time.

- To test an animation to see how it will look to someone viewing it on the Web.

VOCABULARY *Review*

Define the following terms:

.fla	Frame-by-frame animation	Onion skin
.swf	Intermediate frames	Pasteboard
Animation	Keyframe	Playhead
Document properties	Layer	Timeline
Ease	Library	Tweened animation
Frame	Loop	Work area
Frame rate	Movie	

REVIEW *Questions*

TRUE / FALSE

Circle T if the statement is true or F if the statement is false.

T   F   1. Place content that you want displayed in an animation on the pasteboard.

T   F   2. You can hide the Timeline to make more space available on-screen.

T   F   3. By default, the Stage is measured in centimeters.

T   F   4. Drawing tools in an animation program are similar to those in a graphics program.

T   F   5. The content of layers higher in the layer list appears in front of the content on layers lower in the list.

T   F   6. When you rename a file you have imported into the library, the original file is renamed as well.

T   F   7. When you insert a frame or keyframe, your program automatically inserts the content from the previous keyframe into the new frame.

T   F   8. Lock a layer so that you cannot see its content on the Stage.

T   F   9. Set a motion tween to Ease in to begin the change slowly and accelerate.

T   F   10. Use the onion skin feature to add and remove layers in an animation file.

WRITTEN QUESTIONS

Write a brief answer to each of the following questions.

1. What are three ways animations are used on a Web page?

2. What is the difference between a frame and a keyframe?

3. What is the different between frame-by-frame animation and motion tween animation?

4. What are two methods of entering content on the Stage?

5. What are two ways to preview an animation?

FILL IN THE BLANK

Complete the following sentences by writing the correct word or words in the blanks provided.

1. The _____ is the area where you place the content for an animation.

2. _____ are small floating windows that you can open, close, expand, and collapse.

3. The _____ determines the speed at which an animation plays.

4. A(n) _____ is a single image in the sequence of images that comprise an animation.

5. A(n) _____ is an invisible sheet used to separate and organize content.

6. The _____ is a folder in which you organize and store objects that you use in an animation.

7. Insert a(n) _____ if you want to make a change in the content of an animation.

8. In a(n) _____ animation, you specify a beginning keyframe and an ending keyframe, and your program automatically fills in the frames between.

9. _____ is the rate at which changes occur during a tween.

10. Use the _____ feature to view multiple frames on the Stage at the same time.

PROJECTS

PROJECT 6-1

Create an animation in which six colored balls drop down from the top of the Stage and form a pyramid.

1. Create a new animation file and save the file as **Pyramid**.

2. Set document properties to size the Stage to **6.0** inches wide by **5.0** inches high with a **light blue** background (hexadecimal **#0099FF**).

3. Rename *Layer 1* to **Ball 1**.

4. Set the stroke color to **black**, and the fill color to **red**, and then use the **Oval Tool** to draw a circle approximately **.5** inches in diameter in the upper-left corner of the Stage.

5. Right-click **frame 20** and click **Insert Keyframe**. Drag the circle down to the bottom of the Stage, positioned about **2.15** inches from the left edge.

6. Right-click **frame 10** and click **Create Motion Tween**. In the Property Inspector, deselect the **Scale** check box and set the Ease to **25**. Insert a frame in frame 70 to extend the animation. Preview the animation.

7. Insert a new layer and name it **Ball 2**. Select **frame 10** of the *Ball 2* layer and insert a keyframe.

8. Change the fill color to **yellow**, make sure frame 10 of the *Ball 2* layer is active, and then use the **Oval Tool** to draw a circle about **.5** inches in diameter in the upper-left corner of the Stage.

9. Right-click **frame 30** of the *Ball 2* layer and insert a keyframe. Drag the circle down to the bottom of the Stage, positioned about **.15** inches to the right of the red ball, or centered horizontally.

10. Right-click **frame 20** and select **Create Motion Tween**. In the Property Inspector, deselect the **Scale** check box and set the Ease to **25**. Preview the animation.

11. Insert a new layer and name it **Ball 3**. Select **frame 20** of the *Ball 3* layer and insert a keyframe.

12. Change the fill color to **green**, make sure frame 20 of the *Ball 3* layer is active, and then use the **Oval Tool** to draw a circle about **.5** inches in diameter in the upper-left corner of the Stage.

13. Right-click **frame 40** of the *Ball 3* layer and insert a keyframe. Drag the circle down to the bottom of the Stage, positioned about **.14** inches to the right of the yellow ball.

14. Right-click **frame 30** and click **Create Motion Tween**. In the Property Inspector, deselect the **Scale** check box and set the Ease to **25**. Preview the animation.

15. Insert a new layer and name it **Ball 4**. Select **frame 30** of the *Ball 4* layer and insert a keyframe.

16. Change the fill color to **pink**, make sure frame 30 of the *Ball 4* layer is active, and then use the **Oval Tool** to draw a circle about .5 inches in diameter in the upper-left corner of the Stage. Right-click **frame 50** of the *Ball 4* layer and insert a keyframe. Drag the circle down so it is positioned above and between the red and yellow balls.

17. Right-click **frame 40** and select Create Motion Tween. In the Property Inspector, deselect the **Scale** check box and set the Ease to **25**. Preview the animation.

18. Insert a new layer and name it **Ball 5**. Select **frame 40** of the *Ball 5* layer and insert a keyframe.

19. Change the fill color to **purple**, make sure frame 40 of the *Ball 5* layer is active, and then use the **Oval Tool** to draw a circle about .5 inches in diameter in the upper-left corner of the Stage. Insert a keyframe in frame 60 of the *Ball 5* layer and then position the circle to the right of the pink ball, above and between the yellow and green balls.

20. Right-click **frame 50** and create a motion tween, deselecting the **Scale** check box and setting the Ease to **25**. Preview the animation.

21. Insert a new layer and name it **Ball 6**. Insert a keyframe in frame 50 and use the **Oval Tool** to draw an orange ball, .5 inches in diameter in the upper-left corner of the Stage. Insert a keyframe in frame 70 of the *Ball 6* layer and then position the circle at the top of the pyramid.

22. Right-click **frame 60** and create a motion tween, deselecting the **Scale** check box and setting the Ease to **25**. Preview the animation.

23. Print all frames of the animation using a *Storyboard - boxes* layout, and five frames on each row.

24. Test the animation to see how it would look to someone viewing it on the Web.

25. Save all changes, and close the **Pyramid** file. Leave your animation program open to use in the next project.

PROJECT 6-2

Create an animation in which an imported graphic of a star increases in size, shrinks and rotates to the top of the Stage, and then blinks.

1. Create a new animation file and save it as **Night**.

2. Set document properties to size the Stage to **4.0** inches wide by **6.0** inches high. Using a tall, narrow Stage would be appropriates for a side panel on a Web page. Set the background color to **black**.

3. Rename *Layer 1* to be **Star**. Import the file **Project6-2.gif** into the library. If necessary, select the option to import it as a flattened graphic. Display the Library panel and rename the imported file **Star**.

4. Insert the **Star** graphic on the Stage. Scale the graphic to approximately .25 inches by .25 inches and then align it to the center of the Stage horizontally and vertically. To scale the graphic, select it, and then either set the dimensions in the Property Inspector, or click the **Free Transform Tool** and drag the sizing handles.

5. Insert a keyframe in frame 20. Right-click **frame 10** and create a motion tween. Keep the **Scale** check box selected in the Property Inspector, and set the Ease to **35**.

6. Select the graphic on frame 20 and scale it to approximately **2.0** inches by **2.0** inches and realign it to the center of the Stage. Preview the animation.

7. Insert a keyframe in frame 21 and then insert another keyframe in frame 30. Right-click **frame 25** and create a motion tween.

8. Click the **Rotate** drop-down arrow in the Property Inspector and select **CW**, which stands for clockwise. Select this option to rotate an object to the right; select **CCW** (counter-clockwise) to rotate an object to the left.

9. Double-click in the **Times** box, and key **8**, to set the object to rotate 8 times.

10. Keep the **Scale** check box selected in the Property Inspector, and set the Ease to **35**.

11. Select the object in frame 30 and scale it to **1.0** inch square. Position it at the top of the Stage, aligned horizontally. Preview the animation.

12. Insert keyframes in frames 31 through 46.

13. Select the object on frame 32 and delete it. Select the object on frame 33 and delete it. Leave the object on frames 34 and 35, but delete if from frames 36 and 37. Leave the object on frames 38 and 39 but delete it from frames 40 and 41. Leave it on frames 42 and 43, but delete it on frames 44 and 45.

14. Insert a frame on frame 50 to extend the animation. Preview the animation.

15. Print all frames of the animation using a *Storyboard - boxes* layout, and five frames on each row.

16. Test the animation to see how it would look to someone viewing it on the Web.

17. Save all changes, and close the **Night** file. Leave your animation program open to use in the next project.

PROJECT 6-3

Create an animation combining drawing objects and an imported graphic.

1. Create a new animation file and save it as **Star**.

2. Set document properties to size the Stage to **6.0** inches wide by **6.0** inches high. Set the background color to **red**.

3. Rename *Layer 1* to be **Oval1**.

4. Select the **Oval Tool** and set both the stroke and fill colors to **black**. Use the Oval Tool to draw a shape approximately **4.0** inches wide by **2.5** inches high. Select both the stroke and fill and align the shape in the center of the Stage horizontally and vertically.

5. Select **frame 15** and insert a keyframe. Select **frame 30** and insert a keyframe.

6. Select **frame 10** and create a motion tween. Select **frame 15** and scale the shape to **2.0** inches wide by **1.25** inches high. Align it in the top-left corner of the Stage. Select **frame 10** and set tween properties to scale the shape and rotate it clockwise **2** times. Set the Ease to **25**.

7. Select **frame 20** and create a motion tween. Set tween properties to scale the shape and rotate it clockwise **2** times. Set the Ease to **25**.

8. Insert a new layer and name it **Oval2**.

9. Select the **Oval tool** and set both the stroke and fill colors to **black**. Use the Oval Tool to draw a shape approximately **4.0** inches wide by **2.5** inches high. Select both the stroke and fill and align the shape in the center of the Stage horizontally and vertically.

10. Select **frame 15** and insert a keyframe. Select **frame 30** and insert a keyframe.

11. Select **frame 10** and create a motion tween. Select **frame 15** and scale the shape to **2.0** inches wide by **1.25** inches high. Align it in the top-right corner of the Stage. Select **frame 10** and set tween properties to scale the shape and rotate it counterclockwise **2** times. Set the Ease to **25**.

12. Select **frame 20** and create a motion tween. Set tween properties to scale the shape and rotate it counterclockwise **2** times. Set the Ease to **25**. Preview the animation.

13. Insert a new layer and name it **Star**. Import the file **Project6-3.gif** into the library. If necessary, select the option to import it as a flattened graphic. Display the Library panel and rename the imported file **Star**.

14. Insert the **Star** graphic in frame 1 of the *Star* layer. Align it to the center of the Stage horizontally and vertically.

15. Insert a keyframe in frame 3, and then every three frames up to frame 30 (frames 3, 6, 9, 12, 15, 18, 21, 24, 27, and 30).

16. Delete the Star object from the keyframe in frames 3, 9, 15, 21, and 27.

17. Print all frames of the animation using a *Storyboard - Grid* layout, and five frames on each row.

18. Test the animation to see how it would look to someone viewing it on the Web.

19. Save all changes, and close the **Star** file. Close your animation program.

 WEB PROJECT

Almost all Web sites use animations created with an animation program similar to the one you are using. Use the Internet to explore different Web sites to locate and identify different ways that animation is used. For example, you might find advertisements that blink to capture your attention, logos that spin, and even interactive games, such as Tic-Tac-Toe. Consider looking at the daily newspaper in print, and then at the paper's home page on the Web. Are there animations on the Web page? Do they enhance the content in a way that the printed page does not? Compile a list of the Web sites you visit and the types of animation that displays. Include whether you think the effect works better than a static graphic image.

 TEAMWORK PROJECT

Animation draws from many different disciplines. It requires art for content, language for storytelling, and science for technology. As a group, use sources such as the Internet or your library to locate information about animation, and then pick one aspect that interests you most. For example, you might pick the history of animation, how science and technology have influenced animation, how animation is used to tell stories or promote ideas, or you might focus on one particular animator. Research your selected topic on the Internet and then prepare a report or presentation that you can share with your classmates. If you want, use your animation program to create an animation to illustrate the report. Remember to cite your sources.

CRITICAL *Thinking*

Consider how a business that uses graphics to advertise in a magazine or newspaper might use animation to add motion to make the graphics stand out on the World Wide Web. For example, in a magazine an airline company might depict a plane on the runway or suspended in the air, but using animation, you could make the plane fly across the sky. An international banking company might use a picture of a globe in print, but on the Web the globe could spin and rotate. Look through magazines for ideas, and then use your animation program to create an animation. You can draw original artwork, or import graphics from a graphics program. (You might be able to scan a printed image into your graphics program, and then import it into your animations program!) Use the skills you learned in the lesson to create the layers you need to organize your content, and then create frame-by-frame or tweened animation. Preview the animation as you work, and test it when it is complete. When you are finished, save the file, print it, and share it with your classmates.

ENHANCING ANIMATIONS

Once you have mastered the basics of creating an animation file, you can enhance it to make it more professional. For example, to control the movement of objects on the Stage you can animate objects along a precise path. You can modify the color of an object to make it fade in or out. You can add different types of media, such as sound and text objects as well as elements that enable the viewer to interact with the animation as it plays in a Web browser. For instance, you can insert buttons that viewers can click to stop or replay the animation. These elements make the finished product more interesting, and provide the viewer with a satisfying experience.

Enhance Tween Animation

Basic motion and shape tweening lets you quickly animate an object to move on the Stage. Most animation programs also provide features that let you use tweens to move an object along a specific path and to change the color of an object.

Animate Objects Along a Path

When you want one or more objects to move precisely, you can use *path animation*, which is a feature available in most animation programs that forces objects to move along a specific path. The path may be a straight or curved line or the outside of a closed shape. It cannot have breaks or gaps and it cannot intersect or overlap itself. Path animation helps insure consistency in your animation file by keeping all objects moving the same way.

In most animation programs you create a *motion guide* layer on which you draw the path; objects tweened on layers linked to the motion guide will follow the path. When you create the motion tween, you set properties to align or *snap* the object to the path in each keyframe. For example, you snap the object to the beginning of the path in the first keyframe, and the end of the path in the ending keyframe. Your program fills in the intermediate frames by moving the object along the path.

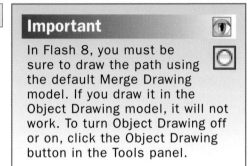

Important

In Flash 8, you must be sure to draw the path using the default Merge Drawing model. If you draw it in the Object Drawing model, it will not work. To turn Object Drawing off or on, click the Object Drawing button in the Tools panel.

STEP-BY-STEP 7.1

1. Start your animation program and create a new document. Save the document as **Beads**. Set the Stage dimensions to **6.0** inches by **7.0** inches. Display the rulers.

2. Rename *Layer 1* to **Blue**. Click the tool for drawing ovals and circles. (If you are using Flash 8, make sure that the Object Drawing model is off.) Set the fill color to blue and the stroke color to **black**, and then draw a circle approximately **1.0** inch in diameter on the Stage.

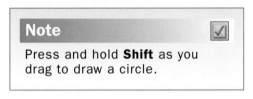

Note

Press and hold **Shift** as you drag to draw a circle.

3. Insert a keyframe in frame 10 and create a motion tween between frames 1 and 10. If available, select the option to snap the object to a guide and deselect the option to scale the object. Set the Ease value to **25**.

4. Select the command to insert a motion guide layer. For example, in Flash, click the **Add Motion Guide** button below the Layers panel in the Timeline. In most programs, the new layer is named *Guide: Blue,* (or *Guide: [linked layer name]*) indicating that it is a motion guide for the Blue layer. The Timeline and Stage should look similar to Figure 7-1.

STEP-BY-STEP 7.1 Continued

FIGURE 7-1
Motion guide layer

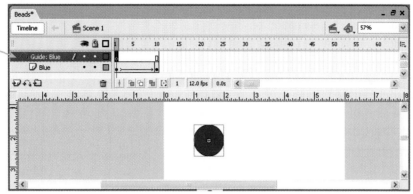

Motion guide layer

5. Hide the *Blue* layer and then select the tool for drawing smooth, curved, freeform lines. For example, in Flash, select the **Pencil Tool** with the **Smooth** modifier (make sure that Object Drawing is turned off).

6. Hide panels and adjust the zoom to make as much of the Stage visible as possible. In frame 1 of the motion guide layer, draw a U shape starting about **2.0** inches down from the top of the Stage, and about **1.5** inches in from the left, and ending about **2.0** inches from the top and **1.5** inches from the right.

7. Display the *Blue* layer. If necessary, click the **Selection Tool** in the Tools panel and then drag the circle to the top-left end of the U shape. Release the shape when its center point snaps to the beginning of the line. Your document should look similar to Figure 7-2.

FIGURE 7-2
Snap an object to the motion path

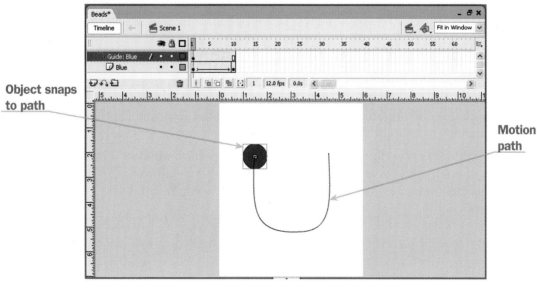

Object snaps to path

Motion path

STEP-BY-STEP 7.1 Continued

8. Select frame **10** of the *Blue* layer. Drag the circle to the top-right end of the U shape. Release the shape when its center point snaps to the end of the line.

9. Rewind and preview the animation on the Stage. The circle should move along the U shape from left to right.

10. Insert a frame in frame 20 of the *Blue* layer and in frame 20 of the motion guide layer to extend the content to the end of animation, then select the *Blue* layer and insert a new layer (a regular layer, not a motion guide). Note that the new layer is automatically linked to the *Guide: Blue* motion guide layer because you inserted it between the existing linked layer and the guide.

Hot Tip

If the shape does not stay aligned with the path, there may be a break or gap in the shape you drew in step 6. Delete the shape from frame 1 of the guide layer and try again, using a heavier stroke. If you drew the shapes with Object Drawing on, you must delete the guide layer and the circle and start again, being sure to turn Object Drawing off.

11. Rename the new layer **Red** and insert a keyframe in frame 10. Change the fill color to **red** and draw a circle about **1.0** inch in diameter.

12. Insert a keyframe in frame 20 of the *Red* layer, and then create a motion tween between frames 10 and 20. Set tween properties to snap the object to a path without scaling, and set the Ease to **25**. In frame 10, move the circle to snap to the upper-left end of the path; in frame 20 move it to snap to the path about .75 inches below the blue circle. Preview the animation, both circles should follow the path in sequence, like beads on a string.

Hot Tip

Hide the motion guide layer when you do not want the path to display in the completed animation.

13. Save the changes and leave **Beads** open to use in the next exercise.

Change the Color of an Object

In most animation programs, you can change the color of an object over time by setting properties to change the color effects during a tween. Called *color tweening*, you can use this feature to gradually change the brightness, tint, or *alpha* settings of an object. The alpha setting controls the transparency of the color. You use the alpha setting to make an object fade in or out.

Usually, the color effects settings are available in a properties panel or a color panel. Select the style or type of color effect you want to apply, and then set a value for the effect. For example, to make an object transparent, select the object, select the Alpha color style, and then set the Alpha amount to 0%.

STEP-BY-STEP 7.2

1. Select frame **1** of the *Blue* layer, and then select the circle object on the Stage. (Zoom in to get a closer look, if you want.)

2. Select the option to change the Alpha color effect, and then set the Alpha amount to **0%**. On the Stage, the object becomes transparent, as shown in Figure 7-3.

FIGURE 7-3
Make an object transparent

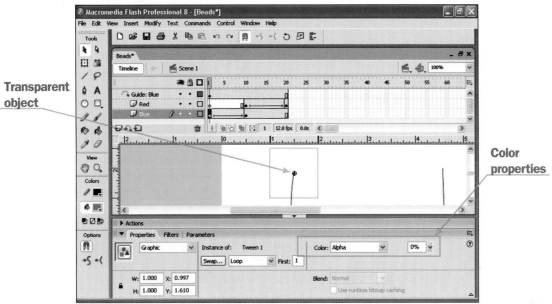

3. Select the circle object on frame 10 of the *Blue* layer. Select the option to change the Alpha color effect, and then set the Alpha amount to **100%**. On the Stage, the object becomes opaque.

4. Preview the animation. The blue circle should fade in as it moves around the path.

5. Save the changes and leave **Beads** open to use in the next exercise.

Edit a Frame or Frame Series

As you may have noticed, creating an animation can involve a lot of repetitive work. Many animations use similar sequences over and over to create the desired effect. To save time and insure consistency, most animation programs have commands for editing a frame or frame series so that you can quickly move, copy, or even reverse existing animations in the Timeline.

> **Note**
>
> Remember to adjust the number of frames in a layer when you insert or delete frames from other layers. Otherwise, the animation may end at different times in different layers.

Most programs have menu commands that you use to edit frames in the Timeline. For example, in Flash 8, you can select Timeline on the Edit menu to display a submenu of commands such as Cut Frames, Copy Frames, and Paste Frames. You can also right-click the selection in the Timeline and select the command from a shortcut menu. Sometimes, you may be able to drag the selection to a new location in the Timeline. When you move or copy a motion sequence, you must include both the first and last keyframes in the selection. Also, when you paste a selection into the Timeline, it overwrites any existing content. If necessary, insert blank frames or layers before selecting the Paste Frames command.

> **Important**
>
> Do not confuse the commands for editing frames with the commands for editing the content on a frame. For example, the Copy, Cut, and Paste commands on the Edit menu in most programs are for copying and moving content. To copy or move frames, you must use the Copy Frames, Cut Frames, and Paste Frames commands.

Table 7-1 lists some of the most common methods for editing frames.

TABLE 7-1
Editing frames

TO	DO THIS
Change the duration of an animation sequence	Drag the ending keyframe on the Timeline.
Select multiple frames	Click the first frame, press and hold Shift, and click the last frame.
Move selected frames	Drag the frames on the Timeline; or click Edit > Timeline > Cut Frames > click to choose a destination frame on the Timeline, and click Edit > Timeline > Paste Frames.
Copy selected frames	Press and hold Alt and then drag the frames on the Timeline; or click Edit, Timeline, Copy Frames, click to choose a destination frame on the Timeline, and click Edit > Timeline > Paste Frames.
Reverse select frames	Select frames to reverse and then click Modify > Timeline > Reverse Frames.
Insert blank frames	Select the frame(s) where you want to insert blanks, and use the command for inserting frames in your animation program.

Copy Frames

When you want to duplicate an animation, copy the selected frame or a series of frames to the Clipboard, and then paste the selection into a different location on the Timeline. Copying frames is useful even when you do not want an exact replica of an existing sequence, because you can edit the copied frames to create variation.

STEP-BY-STEP 7.3

1. Insert a new layer above the *Red* layer. Rename the layer **Blue2**. This layer also is linked to the motion guide.

2. Select frames **1** through **10** of the *Blue* layer and then select the command to copy the selected frames. For example, click frame **1**, press and hold **Shift**, and then click frame **10**. Right-click the selection and click **Copy Frames** on the shortcut menu. This copies the frames to the Clipboard so you can paste them into the new layer.

3. Select frame **21** of the *Blue2* layer and then select the command to paste the frames. For example, right-click frame **21** and then click Paste Frames on the shortcut menu. The copied frames display on the Blue 2 layer in the Timeline, as shown in Figure 7-4.

FIGURE 7-4
Copy a frame sequence

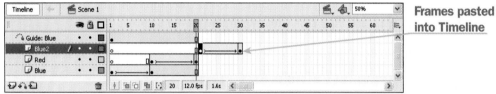

Frames pasted
into Timeline

4. Insert frames in frame 40 of all layers to extend the content to the end of animation.

5. Select frame **30** of the *Blue2* layer—the ending keyframe—and move the blue circle shape so it snaps to the path about .75 inches below the red circle.

6. Select the circle on frame 21 of the *Blue2* layer, and remove the color effect. For example, select **None** from the Color style list in the Property Inspector. Preview the animation. Now, three beads move along the string.

7. Save the changes and leave **Beads** open to use in the next exercise.

Move Frames

If you decide a frame or frame series would work better in a different location on the Timeline, you can use the Cut Frames command to remove a selected frame or frame sequence from its current location, and then paste the frames in the new location. In this exercise, copy the frames from the Red layer, and then move them to a different location.

STEP-BY-STEP 7.4

1. Select the **Blue2** layer and insert a new layer. Rename the layer **Red2**. Select frames **1** through **30** in the *Red2* layer and then select the command to remove the frames. For example, right-click the selection and click **Remove Frames**.

2. Select frames **10** through **20** of the *Red* layer, and then select the command to copy the frames.

3. Select frame **1** of the *Red2* layer and then select the command to paste the frames.

4. Select frames **1** through **11** of the *Red2* layer and then select the command to cut the frames. For example, click frame **1**, press and hold **Shift** and then click frame **11**. Right-click the selection and click **Cut Frames** on the shortcut menu.

5. Select frame **30** of the *Red2* layer and then select the command to paste the frames. For example, right-click frame **30** and then click **Paste Frames** on the shortcut menu. The frames move to the new location on the Timeline. Select frame 12 and clear the keyframe of all content. For example, right-click frame **12** and then click **Clear Keyframe** on the shortcut menu.

6. Select frame **40**—the ending keyframe—and move the red circle shape so it snaps to the path about **.75** inches to the left of the second blue circle. The document should look similar to Figure 7-5.

FIGURE 7-5
Move a frame sequence

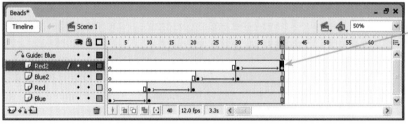

Frames moved in the Timeline

7. Preview the animation. Now, four beads move along the string.

8. Save the changes and leave **Beads** open to use in the next exercise.

Reverse Frames

An interesting effect that you can use to enhance an animation is to reverse a frame sequence to make it play backwards. This can be particularly effective when you combine it with copying frames.

S TEP-BY-STEP 7.5

In this exercise, you copy the entire animation sequence, and then reverse the copy so that the beads slide on to the string, and then off the string.

1. Select all frames in the *Blue*, *Red*, *Blue2*, and *Red2* layers. For example, click frame **1** of the *Red2* layer, press and hold **Shift**, and then click frame **40** of the *Blue* layer. Select the command to copy the selection to the Clipboard.

2. Select frames **41** through **80** in the *Blue*, *Red*, *Blue2*, and *Red2* layers. This is where you want to paste the copied frames. (If you do not select the destination location, your program may insert new layers to paste the copied frames.)

3. Select the command to paste the frames.

4. Select the copied frames—frames **41** through **80** in the *Blue*, *Red*, *Blue2*, and *Red2* layers—if they are not already selected, and then select the command to reverse the frames. For example, right-click the selection and then click **Reverse Frames**.

5. Insert a frame in frame 80 of the Guide: *Blue* layer to extend the content on the guide layer to the end of animation.

6. Preview the animation. The beads should slide on and then off the string.

7. Save the changes and close the **Beads** file. Close your animation program.

Use Sound

W hen you add sound to an animation, you introduce a new sensation, adding more life and excitement to what might otherwise be a one-dimensional experience. Instead of simply looking at the screen, the viewer hears the animation. In general, animation programs support two types of sounds: *streaming sound* which is synchronized with the animation, and *event sound*, which plays independently from the animation. Streaming sounds are often used to coordinate sound with action, such as playing music with an animation sequence, while event sounds are often used to highlight an action or event, such as the click of a button, or the end of a sequence. Event sounds must download completely before they play, so if they are large, they may cause a noticeable delay in an animation. Streaming sounds start to play as soon as enough data has downloaded.

To make sound available for use in an animation it must be stored in a sound file. Most programs can use sound files in at least two formats: **WAV** (pronounced wave) and **MP3**. Wave files can have the highest sound quality. However, the higher the quality, the larger the sound file.

To make a sound file smaller, you can record waves at a lower quality setting, or use recording or conversion software that uses *compression* techniques, which remove frequencies and masked elements that humans can't hear, to make the file smaller. Compression is the process of reducing the space required to store data by efficiently encoding the content.

You may be able to record the sound file yourself, or you may acquire it by importing it from another source. In addition, to play sound your computer must have a *sound card* and speakers. A sound card is a hardware device that lets your computer control and output sound.

Record a Sound File

To record your own sound files you must have the proper hardware and software. Most operating systems include at least a basic utility for recording sound, such as Sound Recorder, which comes with Windows, and most sound cards support recording. You can record or capture sounds from a variety of sources. For example, you can record your voice or other live sounds via a microphone connected to your computer's sound card. Or, you can connect a device such as a CD player or MP3 player to the sound card to record CD audio or other pre-recorded material. Be aware that most pre-recorded music files are protected by copyright laws, so you may use them only for personal use. If you want to publish a commercial animation on your Web site or create professional presentations and movies, you must use original recordings or obtain permission to use the music from its creator and publisher.

When you want to record a sound file, install the sound card and device drivers, and attach your microphone, or other device, to your sound card via the appropriate cable or cables. Next, set up the sound-recording software for use. This usually involves selecting the correct *input source*, which is the device you are using to acquire the sound, and adjusting the input volume. Some programs, including Sound Recorder, may prompt you through the setup procedure. When you are ready, click the program's Record button to begin recording the sound. When you are finished, click the Stop button to stop recording. Use the Rewind button to return to the beginning of the file, and the Play button to listen to the recording. As with any file, you must use the Save As command to save the sound file to disk to make it available for future use.

It is a good idea to plan ahead before recording a sound file to be sure you are prepared. If you are going to speak, write a script and practice reading it before you record the file. If you are going to use other media to create the sound, such as an instrument, be sure the item is available, and that you have rehearsed before recording. Of course, you can always delete the sound file and try again, but good preparation will save you time and effort.

> **Hot Tip**
>
> When setting up software to record from a CD player, select the CD Audio input source to make recordings via your computer's internal CD drive. Select **Line In** to use an external CD player that is connected to the computer via the line-in jack.

S TEP-BY-STEP 7.6

In this exercise, you record up and then down a musical scale—Do Re Mi Fa So La Ti Do Ti La So Fa Mi Re Do. You may do this using an instrument or your voice. You should practice the scale and be prepared to record it before beginning the exercise.

1. Use your operating system controls to make sure the right recording device—the microphone, in this case—is specified as the source and to adjust the volume of that device. For example, in Windows XP, click **Start**, and then click **Control Panel**. Click **Sounds, Speech, and Audio Devices** and then click **Sounds and Audio Devices**. Click the **Audio** tab. Click **Volume** in the Sound Recording section of the dialog box, make the appropriate changes in the Recording Control dialog box, and then close all open windows.

> **Note**
>
> Steps 1 and 2 may vary depending on the version of Windows you are using. For example, in Windows 2000, you may have to click Start>Settings>Control Panel to display the Control Panel, and then click Sounds and Multimedia to open the Recording Control dialog box.

STEP-BY-STEP 7.6 Continued

2. Start the sound-recording program. For example, in Windows XP, click **Start**, **All Programs**, **Accessories**, **Entertainment**, and then click **Sound Recorder**. The Sound Recorder window should look similar to Figure 7-6.

FIGURE 7-6
Sound Recorder

3. Click the program's **Record** button.

4. Silently count to three and then begin playing or singing the musical scale.

5. When you are finished, click the program's **Stop** button to stop recording.

6. Click the program's **Rewind** button, and then click the **Play** button to play back your recording. If you are not satisfied, create a new file without saving the changes, and try again.

7. Save the file as **Scale** and leave it open to use in the next exercise.

Edit a Sound File

When you play or record a sound file, the sound is represented visually in the program by a *waveform*, which is a graph that shows *amplitude* over time. Amplitude is a measure of volume, or loudness. Usually, the program window also shows the total length—or playing time—of the file in seconds, and the current position of the playhead in seconds. For example, in Sound Recorder, the waveform displays as shown in Figure 7-7.

FIGURE 7-7
A waveform in Sound Recorder

You can use sound-editing software to manipulate the waveform to change a sound file. For example, you can cut off a portion of the file to make it shorter, or add an effect such as echo. You can even rearrange the waveform to change the order in which the sound plays. Sound-editing capabilities vary from program to program. With Sound Recorder in Windows you can make basic changes to a wave file, while more sophisticated sound-editing programs, including those that are part of video-editing programs, enable you to edit individual channels or make corrections such as muting static in a selected section of the waveform. (You learn about working with sound in video programs in Lesson 10.) Some animation programs also have tools for making basic edits to a waveform.

To make basic edits to a sound file, you select the portion of the waveform you want to change, and then select the editing commands. To select on the waveform, you usually position two sliders—one at the beginning of the selection and one at the end. But in some programs, including Sound Recorder, you position the playhead to select all data to its left (before it) or to its right (after it). You may also be able to copy, cut, and paste selections.

> **Note**
>
> Sound-editing programs typically can edit sounds only in the WAV format or another format called *RAW*. That's because compressed formats such as MP3 eliminate some of the sound data necessary for editing.

STEP-BY-STEP 7.7

In this exercise, you delete the silence at the beginning of the Scale file.

1. With the **Scale** file open, select the silent portion at the beginning of the file. For example, in Sound Recorder, position the playhead at the point in the waveform just before the sound of the scale begins. You can do this by playing the file and watching the position value. When the sound starts, click the **Stop** button, and then drag the playhead back to a position a few hundredths of a second earlier. If you are using a program that lets you use two sliders, position the beginning slider at the beginning of the waveform, and then drag the ending slider to the point just before the sound of the scale begins.

2. Choose the command for deleting the content before the current position of the playhead, or for deleting the selection. For example, in Sound Recorder, click **Edit** on the Menu bar, and then click **Delete Before Current Position**. If necessary, click **OK** to confirm the deletion.

3. If there is any silence at the end of the file, delete it as well. For example, in Sound Recorder, position the playhead at the point where the scale ends, click **Edit** on the Menu bar, and then click **Delete After Current Position**. Click **OK** to confirm the deletion.

4. Play the file to hear the impact of the change, and then save the changes.

5. Add an echo effect to the sound file. For example, in Sound Recorder, position the playhead at the beginning of the sound file, click **Effects** on the Menu bar, and then click **Add Echo**.

6. Play the file to hear the impact of the change.

7. Close the file without saving the echo effect change. Close your sound-editing program.

Import and Add Sound in Animations

To add sound in most animation programs, you import the sound file into the program and then insert it into the animation Timeline. For example, in Flash 8 you use the Import command on the File menu to import the sound file into the document's library. You can then easily drag the sound file into any keyframe. Usually, you must insert each sound on a separate layer for them to play correctly.

Once the sound file is inserted, select properties in a panel such as the Property Inspector to control the sound. For example, select whether you want the sound to be streaming or event, and whether you want a *sound fade*, which is a change in the sound over time, such as increasing in volume in the left speaker while decreasing in volume in the right speaker. If the sound is an event, you can also specify how many times it should loop.

> **Note** ☑
>
> If you have QuickTime 4 (or a later version) installed on your computer, you can import sound file formats supported by QuickTime, such as AU, AIFF, or sound-only QuickTime movies.

When you create or choose the sounds to include in your animation, keep the intended purpose of the animation in mind. For example, if the animation is for a Web site, you need to keep the overall file size small for faster downloads. Thus, you should use more compact MP3 files and loop a shorter sound segment. On the other hand, if you plan to include the animation in a presentation that you will deliver in an auditorium equipped with a high-quality audio system, use the highest quality sound file possible.

STEP-BY-STEP 7.8

1. Launch your animation program and open the file **Step7-8a** from the data files. This is a variation of the Beads file you created earlier in this lesson.

2. Save the file as **Beads2**.

3. Import the **Scale** sound file into the document's library, or import **Step7-8b**. For example, click **File** on the Menu bar, click **Import**, and then click **Import to Library**. Locate and select the sound file, and then click **Open**.

4. Display the Library, if necessary. If you imported the sound file Step7-8b, rename it **Scale** in the Library. The sound file displays at the top of the list in the Library panel, with the waveform in the preview area. It should look similar to Figure 7-8.

FIGURE 7-8
Sound file in the library

STEP-BY-STEP 7.8 Continued

5. Select the *Guide: Blue motion guide* layer and insert a new layer. Rename the new layer **Sound**. (Notice that the layer is not linked to the motion guide, because you inserted it above the guide layer.)

Hot Tip

In Flash, click the **Play** button in the preview area to preview a sound file in the Library panel.

6. Select frame **1** of the *Sound* layer, and then drag the **Scale** sound file from the Library to the Stage. Release the file anywhere on the Stage. Close the Library. Notice the waveform in the Timeline, as shown in Figure 7-9.

FIGURE 7-9
Sound file in the Timeline

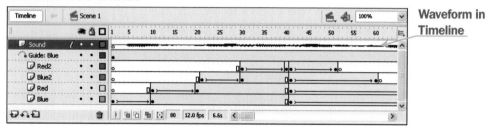

Waveform in Timeline

7. Select frame **1** of the *Sound* layer, and then set properties to make the sound stream. For example, in Flash, select the **Stream** setting from the Sync drop-down list in the Property Inspector.

8. Preview the animation on the Stage. The sound plays with the Timeline, ending at the last frame.

9. Save the changes and leave **Beads2** open to use in the next exercise.

Note ☑

To keep a streaming sound from ending abruptly, make sure the animation Timeline extends at least as long as the complete sound file.

Work with Text

Add text to an animation to display information or to enhance an image. You insert text by drawing a text block with the Text Tool, and keying the text just as you would in a word processing program. You can apply typical font formatting such as fonts, font styles, and font colors, as well paragraph formatting such as alignment. Once you insert a text block, you can animate it using the same techniques you use to animate other graphical objects. For example, you can cause it to increase in size, rotate, or move across the Stage.

Create a Text Block

To add a text block to an animation, select the Text Tool and then use the same basic process as when adding any object. Create a layer to hold the text, choose the Text Tool from the toolbox, specify text settings, and then click and key the text. You can select the formatting properties before you key the text or after. Most programs have two types of text blocks fixed-width and expandable. (For more information on working with text, refer to Lesson 4.)

S TEP-BY-STEP 7.9

1. Select the *Guide: Blue* layer and insert a new layer. Rename the new layer **Text**.

2. Select frame **1** of the *Text* layer.

3. Click the tool for inserting a text block. For example, in Flash, click the **Text Tool**.

4. Set properties for a **36** point **black**, **Arial** font, aligned left within the text block.

5. Click on the Stage above the motion path and key **BEADS**.

6. Select the text block, and position it about **.5** inches from the top of the Stage, centered horizontally. The Stage should look similar to Figure 7-10.

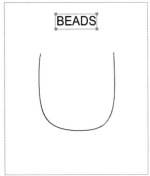

FIGURE 7-10
Text block on the Stage

7. Preview the animation. The text block displays without changing through the entire animation.

8. Save the changes and leave **Beads2** open to use in the next exercise.

Animate a Text Block

To animate a text block, use the same techniques you used to animate other objects. You can scale, move, rotate, and otherwise transform an object using either frame-by-frame or tweened animation. You can tween a text block along a path or change its color using color tweening.

S TEP-BY-STEP 7.10

1. Insert a keyframe in frame 20 of the *Text* layer and create a motion tween between frame 1 and 20. Set tween properties so the object does not scale or rotate. Set the Ease to **25**.

2. Select the text block on frame 1 of the *Text* layer, and set properties to change the Alpha color setting to **0%**.

3. Select the text block on frame 20 of the *Text* layer and set properties to change the Alpha color setting to **100%**.

STEP-BY-STEP 7.10 Continued

4. Insert a keyframe in frame 80 of the *Text* layer and create a motion tween between frame 20 and frame 80.

5. Select the text block on frame 80 and scale it to approximately **3.5** inches wide and **1.22** inches high. Reposition it so it is still aligned in the horizontal center of the Stage.

6. Set tween properties to scale the object and rotate it **4** times clockwise. Set the Ease to **25**.

7. Preview the animation on the Stage.

8. Save the changes and close the **Beads2** file. Keep your animation program open to use in the next exercise.

Create Symbols

Animation files tend to include a lot of objects such as graphics and sounds that make a file large. When a viewer plays an animation, the larger the file, the longer it takes to download and start playing. If an animation takes too long to play, viewers may get bored, and move on to faster, more interesting animations. Oneway animation programs such as Flash have addressed the issue of file size is to use *symbols*. A symbol is a reusable object stored in a document's Library. The symbol is stored only once but you can insert *instances* of the symbol as many times as you want. An instance is simply one occurrence of a symbol. Symbols impact file size, because no matter how many instances there are in an animation, the symbol is stored only once. They impact download speed because no matter how many instances there are, the symbol only has to download once.

Animation programs generally support different types of symbols. For example, in Flash you can create *graphic symbols*, *button symbols*, and *movie clip symbols*. Graphic symbols are usually static images comprised of drawing objects, groups, or imported graphics. Buttons are symbols that viewers can click to interact with the animation. Movie clips are symbols comprised of a frame sequence. You can create new symbols, or convert existing content into a symbol. In either case, you usually select the type of symbol and give it a name in a dialog box similar to the one shown in Figure 7-11.

FIGURE 7-11
Create a symbol

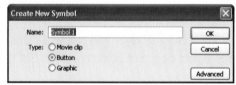

Create Graphic Symbols

You can create a graphic symbol from a static object such as a shape or an imported graphic. Most animation programs let you convert an object already on the Stage into a symbol. You can also create a new symbol using symbol-editing mode.

STEP-BY-STEP 7.11

1. Open the animation file **Step7-11** from the data files for this lesson, and save it as **Beads3**. Notice it already contains four regular layers all linked to a motion guide. Hide the motion guide layer.

2. Select frame **1** of the *Bead1* layer. Use the **Oval Tool** to draw a circle with a **white** fill and a **black** stroke, approximately **1.0** inch in diameter.

3. Select the shape—both the stroke and the fill—and select the command to convert it to a symbol. For example, in Flash select **Modify** on the Menu bar and then click **Convert to Symbol**. The Convert to Symbol dialog box displays.

4. Name the symbol **Bead**, and select the option to create a graphic symbol. Click **OK** to create the symbol and close the dialog box.

5. Display the Library panel. The **Bead** graphic symbol should be stored in the Library. The circle on the Stage is now an instance of the symbol.

6. Delete the instance of the Bead symbol from the Stage. Notice that the symbol remains stored in the Library.

7. Drag an instance of the **Bead** symbol to the Stage. Select the instance and set color properties to apply a **100% blue** tint. For example, in Flash, in the Property Inspector click the **Color Styles** drop-down arrow and click **Tint**, select **blue** from the color palette, key **100%** in the Tint Amount box, and then press **Enter**. The instance on the Stage is now blue, but the Bead symbol in the Library is still white with a black stroke, as shown in Figure 7-12.

FIGURE 7-12
Modify an instance

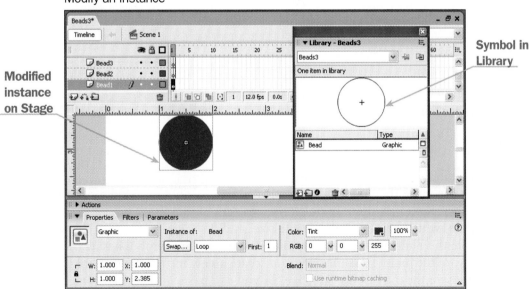

8. Select frame **1** of the *Bead2* layer and drag an instance of the **Bead** symbol from the Library to the Stage. Set color properties to apply a **100% red** tint.

STEP-BY-STEP 7.11 Continued

9. On frame 1 of the *Bead3* layer, insert another instance of the **Bead** symbol and apply a **100% yellow** tint. Insert another instance of the symbol on frame 1 of the *Bead4* layer and apply a **100% green** tint. Close the Library.

10. In each of the four *Bead* layers, insert a keyframe in frame 15 and create a motion tween. Set properties so the object does not scale or rotate. Set the Ease to **25**.

11. Display the motion guide layer and in each starting keyframe of each layer, snap the current instance to the left end of the path. The objects should overlap so that when you are finished you see only the green instance. In each ending keyframe, snap the instance in a line along the path, as shown in Figure 7-13.

FIGURE 7-13
Tween instances along a path

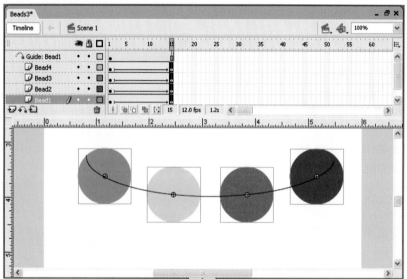

12. Preview the animation and then save the changes. Leave **Beads3** open to use in the next exercise.

Create a Movie Clip

> **Note** ☑
>
> When you edit a symbol, all instances based on the symbol change as well. However, you can edit an instance to change only the single occurrence.

Movie clip symbols can store an animation sequence that you plan to use more than once in a document. An instance of a movie clip takes up only one keyframe on the main Timeline, which helps reduce the file size, and can also help keep the Timeline neat and organized. A movie clip symbol has its own Timeline that is independent from the main Timeline. You can create a new movie clip symbol by inserting content and animation in the movie clip Timeline, or you can paste an existing frame sequence into a movie clip timeline.

Once you insert a movie clip in the main Timeline, you cannot preview it on the Stage using the Play command. To view it, you must open it in symbol-editing mode, or use the Test Movie or Test Scene command. The clip will play in a continuous loop.

STEP-BY-STEP 7.12

1. Select all frames in the document, including the guide layer and cut the selected frames to the Clipboard.

2. Select the command to create a new movie clip symbol. For example, click **Insert** on the Menu bar and then click **New Symbol**. The Create New Symbol dialog box displays.

3. Name the symbol **Bead Clip** and select the **Movie Clip** symbol type. Click **OK** to close the dialog box and create the symbol. The movie clip symbol Timeline displays in symbol-editing mode, as shown in Figure 7-14.

FIGURE 7-14
A movie clip symbol Timeline

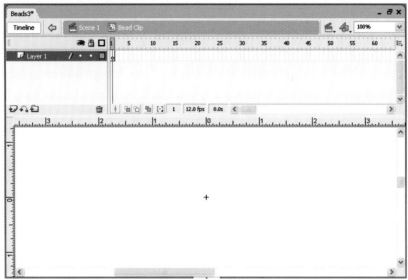

4. Select frame **1** and paste the frames from the Clipboard. (You may have to re-link the layers to the motion guide. If so, drag each one above the guide layer and release it, and then drag it back down to its previous position below the guide layer.)

5. Preview the movie clip in symbol-editing mode, and then select the command to exit symbol-editing mode. For example, in Flash, select **Edit** on the Menu bar, and then click **Edit Document**.

6. In the main Timeline, delete all layers except the *Bead1* layer. Rename the *Bead1* layer to **Movie Clip**, and then remove frames 2 through 15 so that only the blank keyframe in frame 1 remains.

7. Display the Library panel if necessary, and drag an instance of the **Bead Clip** symbol to the upper-left corner of the Stage.

8. Select the **Test Movie** command to preview the animation in the Flash Player window. Notice that the motion guide layer does not display, and that the animation loops continuously. Close the Flash Player window.

STEP-BY-STEP 7.12 Continued

9. Insert a second instance of the **Bead Clip** symbol on frame 1 of the *Movie Clip* layer. Position it approximately **1.0** inch below the first instance.

10. Insert a third instance of the **Bead Clip** symbol, positioned approximately **1.0** below the second instance.

11. Select the **Test Movie** command to preview the animation. Close the Flash Player window.

12. Save the changes and leave **Beads3** open to use in the next exercise.

Create Buttons

To make an animation more engaging for the viewer, you can introduce *interactive* controls such as buttons. Interactive controls allow the viewer to communicate with the animation by selecting an option that causes an action. For example, the viewer can click a button to replay an animation, or to stop a sound.

When you create a button, you specify four button states in the Button symbol Timeline:

■ Up, which is how the button looks whenever the mouse pointer is not on it.

■ Over, which is how the button responds to a *rollover*. A rollover is the action of moving the mouse pointer over the button.

■ Down, which is how the button looks when the viewer clicks on it.

■ Hit, which is the size of the area onscreen that will respond to a rollover or click.

Some programs require that you create the button graphics for each rollover state in a separate graphics application and then import them into the animation program. In other animation programs, such as Flash, you can convert an existing object into the Up state of a button, and then create the other states in the button's Timeline. You can also create a new button symbol and create the button content from scratch, or duplicate an existing button and modify it. Buttons can be comprised of almost any object, including a shape, an imported graphic, or a text block. You can even combine objects, such as a text block and a shape. To test the button on the Stage, you may have to enable a command, such as Enable Simple Buttons.

STEP-BY-STEP 7.13

1. In the **Beads3** file, insert a new layer. Rename the new layer **Replay Button**.

2. Select the command to create a new symbol. Name the symbol **Replay**, and select the **Button** symbol type. Click **OK** to create the symbol and close the dialog box. The button symbol Timeline displays in symbol-editing mode, as shown in Figure 7-15.

STEP-BY-STEP 7.13 Continued

FIGURE 7-15
The Button symbol Timeline

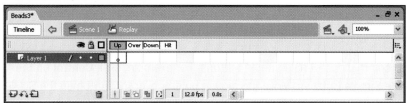

3. With the **Up** frame selected, use the **Rectangle Tool** to draw a rectangle with a **white** fill and a **black** stroke approximately **1.25** inches wide by **.5** inches high. (You may want to start the shape on the crosshair in the middle of the drawing area.)

4. Select the tool for creating a text block. Set properties to use **24** point **black Arial**, centered, then click on the left edge of the rectangle shape and key **Replay**. Click the **Selection Tool** and drag the text block to center it over the rectangle.

5. Click in the **Over** frame on the Timeline and insert a keyframe. Select the fill of the rectangle and change the color to **red**.

6. Click in the **Down** frame on the Timeline and insert a keyframe. Select the fill of the rectangle and change the color to **green**, then select the text in the text block and apply the **Bold** font style.

7. Click in the **Hit** frame on the Timeline and insert a keyframe. You do not have to modify the Hit state unless you want the area that responds to a click or rollover to be different from the area defined by the button itself. The symbol should look similar to Figure 7-16.

FIGURE 7-16
Define four button states in symbol-editing mode

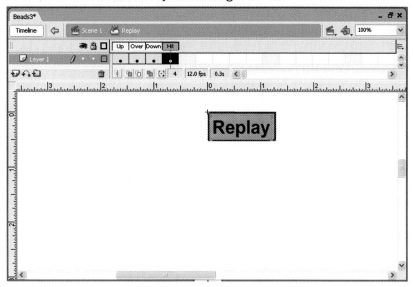

STEP-BY-STEP 7.13 Continued

8. Select the command to exit symbol-editing mode.

9. Drag an instance of the **Replay** button from the Library to frame 1 of the *Replay Button* layer. Position it in the lower-right corner of the Stage.

10. Select the command to enable simple buttons. For example, click **Control** on the Menu bar and then click **Enable Simple Buttons**. Move the mouse pointer over the button on the Stage. It should change to the Over state, with a red fill. Press and hold the button. It should change to green with bold text.

11. Save the changes and leave **Beads3** open to use in the next exercise.

Use Actions

Insert *actions* in an animation to control the flow of an animation. An action is a set of instructions that causes an event. An action may be very simple, such as Stop or Play, or it may be a complex formula that responds to conditions and other variables. Some programs require that you use an object-oriented programming language such as JavaScript to write *script statements*, which are coded instructions. Some programs come with built-in actions, and others, such as Flash do both. For example, if you have experience with object-oriented programming, you can use Flash's *ActionScript* language to write statements. If you do not know how to write statements, you can use a feature called *Script Assist* to select from a menu of basic actions. Some actions may require you to enter parameters, which are variables that control how the action will perform.

Usually, actions in an animation are linked to an event, such as a mouse click, or to a keyframe. For example, if you link a Stop action to a keyframe, when the playhead reaches that keyframe, the action occurs, stopping the animation. If you link a Stop action to a button, when the user clicks the button, the animation stops.

In most animation programs, to insert an action you select the object that you want to trigger the action, such as an instance of a button, or a keyframe, and then use the Actions panel or dialog box to locate and insert the script statement and the required parameters. In Flash, you can turn on Script Assist, and then double-click the Action to apply in the Actions panel, as shown in Figure 7-17.

FIGURE 7-17
The Flash Actions panel

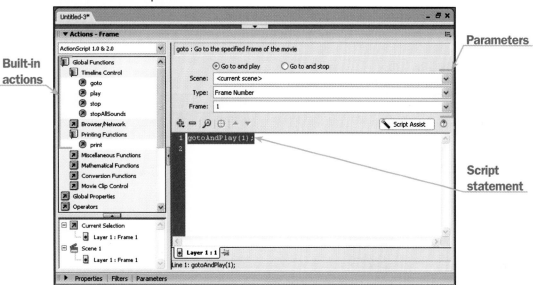

Add an Action to a Keyframe

When you want an action to occur when an animation reaches a particular keyframe, you assign the action to the keyframe. A lowercase *a* displays in the keyframe on the Timeline to indicate that it contains an action. Assigning a Stop action to a keyframe is very common, because it allows you to stop a movie clip or animation from looping continuously during playback.

> **Note**
>
> Actions follow the instructions in a script statement precisely, so you must be sure to use the correct format and parameters. If an action does not work the way you expect, you probably have to check the statement to be sure the correct frames and actions are included in the proper order.

*S*TEP-BY-STEP 7.14

1. Display the Library panel if necessary and then double-click the **Bead Clip** movie clip symbol to open it in symbol-editing mode.

2. Select the guide layer and insert a new layer. Rename the new layer **Stop Action**.

3. Insert a keyframe in frame 15 of the *Stop Action* layer. Select the command to display the Actions panel, pane, or dialog box. For example, in Flash click **Window** on the Menu bar and then click **Actions**, or just click the **Actions** panel expand arrow. (In Flash, the Actions panel displays above the Property Inspector panel by default.)

4. Display the category of actions that includes basic Timeline controls, and insert the action to stop playing the animation at the selected keyframe. In Flash, click the **Script Assist** button to turn on Script Assist, and then double-click **Stop** in the list of Timeline Controls.

STEP-BY-STEP 7.14 Continued

5. Close the scripting pane or Actions panel. Frame 15 of the *Stop Action* layer should indicate that it contains an action, similar to Figure 7-18.

FIGURE 7-18
A keyframe containing an action

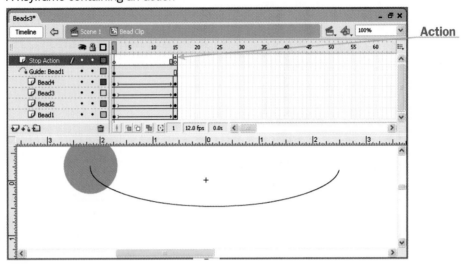

6. Exit symbol-editing mode.

7. Select the command to test the movie. Now, the animation should no longer play in a continuous loop, but should stop playing when it reaches the keyframe that contains the Stop action, in this case, the last frame of the Bead Clip movie clip symbol.

8. Close the Flash Player window.

9. Save the changes and leave **Beads3** open to use in the next exercise.

Add an Action to a Button

When you want an action to occur when the viewer clicks or rolls the mouse pointer over a button, you assign the action to the instance of the button. For example, you can assign a print action to a button so a viewer can print the current screen display, or you can assign a *go to* action to direct a viewer to a Web site. You can also use a *go to* action to replay an animation from the beginning.

> **Note** ☑
>
> To control the playback—rewind, replay, stop, and play—of a movie clip, insert the button with actions assigned to it in the movie clip Timeline, not the main Timeline.

STEP-BY-STEP 7.15

1. Select the *Replay Button* layer and insert a new layer. Rename the new layer **Stop**.

2. Insert a keyframe in frame 5 and insert a Stop action in the keyframe. This stop action insures that the animation will not play in a continuous loop.

3. Select frame **5** of the *Replay Button* layer and insert a keyframe. This extends the animation to frame 5.

4. Select the **Replay** button instance on frame 5 of the *Replay Button* layer. (You may have to disable the command to enable simple buttons before selecting the object on the Stage.) Select the command to display the Actions panel, pane, or dialog box.

5. Display the category of actions that includes basic Timeline controls, and insert a *go to* action. (The action probably defaults to *Go to and play*, with an option for changing it to *Go to and stop*.) Verify that the parameters specify to *Go to and play* frame number 1 of the current scene. If necessary, enter the parameters in the script statement.

6. Close the scripting pane or Actions panel.

7. Select frame **1** of the *Movie Clip* layer and move the keyframe from frame 1 to frame 2. Because the action is set to *Go to and play* frame 1, it may skip the movie clip instance unless the instance is in frame 2.

8. Insert a keyframe in frame 5 of the *Movie Clip* layer to extend the animation.

9. Select the command to test the movie. The animation should play to the end of the movie clip, and then stop.

10. Click the **Replay** button. The animation should replay. Close the Flash Player window.

11. Save the changes and close the **Beads3** file. Close your animation program.

SUMMARY

In this lesson, you learned:

- You can animate an object along a path to insure consistency and keep all objects moving the same way.

- You can use color tweening to gradually change the color of an object over time, or to make the object fade in or out.

- Editing a frame or frame series can save time and insure consistency because you can copy, move, or reverse the frames in the animation.

- Most animation programs support streaming sounds, which are synchronized to the Timeline, and event sounds, which play independently from the animation.

■ You can record your own sound files if you have a microphone and sound-recording software.

■ Sound files have waveforms that you can edit in sound-editing software to change the way the sound file plays.

■ Most animation programs are compatible with WAV and MP3 format sound files.

■ Text objects can be created to provide information, or to create interesting animation effects.

■ You can animate a text object using the same techniques you use to animate other objects.

■ Most animation programs use symbols to help create smaller files and faster downloads.

■ A symbol is stored only once, but you can insert as many instances of the symbol as you want.

■ Graphic symbols are usually static images, movie clip symbols store an animation sequence, and button symbols let a viewer interact with an animation.

■ You can assign actions to keyframes or buttons to control the flow of an animation.

VOCABULARY *Review*

Define the following terms:

Actions	Input source	Script statements
ActionScript	Instance	Snap
Alpha	Interactive	Sound card
Amplitude	Motion guide	Sound fade
Button symbol	Movie clip symbol	Streaming sound
Color tweening	MP3	Symbol
Compression	Path animation	WAV
Event sound	Rollover	Waveform
Graphic symbol	Script Assist	

REVIEW *Questions*

TRUE / FALSE

Circle T if the statement is true or F if the statement is false.

T   F   1. Use path animation to force objects to move along a specific path.

T   F   2. The alpha setting controls the amount of tint in a color.

T   F   3. You cannot edit copied frames.

T   F   4. To play sound, your computer must have a microphone.

T   F   5. Amplitude is a measure of volume or loudness.

T   F   6. You can animate a text block using the same techniques you use to animate other objects.

T   F   7. You can only insert one instance of a symbol in an animation.

T   F   8. Movie clips are symbols comprised of a static image.

T   F   9. You must know how to write script statements to use actions.

T   F   10. You cannot add an action to an instance of a button symbol.

WRITTEN QUESTIONS

Write a brief answer to each of the following questions.

1. Name at least two ways you can save time and insure consistency when creating an animation.

2. How does large file size impact an animation, and what is one way to minimize file size?

3. Name at least two sources you can use to acquire sound files.

4. Name at least one action and explain how it can be used in an animation.

5. What are two things to consider when you select a sound file for an animation? Why?

FILL IN THE BLANK

Complete the following sentences by writing the correct word or words in the blanks provided.

1. To make an object transparent, set the _____ amount to 0%.

2. _____ sound is synchronized with the Timeline.

3. _____ sound plays independently from the Timeline.

4. Sound files formatted in the _____ file format usually have the highest sound quality.

5. A(n) _____ is a graph that depicts a sound file.

6. A(n) _____ is a reusable object stored in a document's Library.

7. _____ controls allow a viewer to communicate with an animation.

8. The _____ state of a button defines how the button looks when the viewer clicks on it.

9. The _____ state of a button defines the size of the area onscreen that will respond to a rollover or click.

10. A(n) _____ is a set of instructions that cause an event.

PROJECTS

PROJECT 7-1

Create an animation for a professional dog trainer, using graphics, sound, and text.

1. Launch your animation program, and create a new document. Save it as **Train**. Set document properties to size the Stage to **8 inches** square, and apply a **pale yellow** background.

2. Rename *Layer 1* to **Spiral** and then import the graphics file **Project7-1a** to frame 1 of the *Spiral* layer.

3. Convert the graphics image on the Stage to a graphics symbol. Name the symbol **Bone**.

4. Select the instance of the Bone symbol on the Stage and resize it to approximately **1.0** inch wide. The height should adjust automatically.

5. Insert a keyframe in frame 35 and then create a motion tween. Select the **Snap** option and set the Ease to **20**.

6. Insert a motion guide layer. Select the tool for drawing smooth, freeform curves. On frame 1 of the guide layer draw a spiral with three layers starting in the center of the Stage and ending in the upper-right corner.

7. On frame 1 of the *Spiral* layer, snap the instance to the outer end of the path, in the upper-right corner of the Stage.

8. On frame 35, scale the instance to **5.0** inches wide, and then snap it to the inner end of the path, near the center of the Stage.

9. Hide the guide layer and preview the animation.

10. Select the guide layer and insert a new layer. Rename the new layer **Text1**. Select the **Text Tool** and set properties for **32** point **blue Arial,** aligned left. Click in the upper-left corner of the Stage and key **Need professional help?**

11. Insert a keyframe in frame 17 of the *Text1* layer and create a motion tween. Deselect the scale property and set the Ease to **20.**

12. Select the text block on frame 1 and set the Alpha amount to **0%.** Select the text block on frame 17 and set the Alpha amount to **100%.**

13. Select frames **1** through **17** on the *Text1* layer and copy them to the Clipboard. Select frame **18** on the *Text1* layer and paste the frames. Select frames 35 through 51 and remove the frames.

14. Select frames **18** through **34** and reverse the frames. Remove frames 35 through 50 so the animation ends in frame 35. Preview the animation.

15. Insert a new layer and rename the new layer **Text2**. Insert a keyframe on frame 17.

16. Insert a text block on frame 17 in the same location as the text block on the *Text1* layer, using the same text properties, and key **Call Jack the Dog Trainer!** If necessary, adjust the position so the two blocks are in the same location on the Stage.

17. Insert a keyframe in frame 35 of the *Text2* layer and create a motion tween. Deselect the **Scale** property and set the Ease to **20.** Select the text block on frame 17 and set the Alpha amount to **0%.** Select the text block on frame 35 and set the Alpha amount to **100%.**

18. Preview the animation.

19. Insert a new layer and rename it **Sound.** Import the sound file **Project7-1b** to the Library, and rename it **Bark.**

20. Drag the **Bark** sound file from the Library to frame 1 of the *Sound* layer.

21. Preview the animation.

22. Save the changes and close the **Train** animation file. Leave your animation program open to use in the next exercise.

PROJECT 7-2

Create an animated logo for a company, named Voice Integration Protocols, that provides Internet telephone services. Use a movie clip, and actions.

1. Open **Project7-2** from the data files and save the file as **VIP.**

2. Rename *Layer 1,* **Logo** and insert an instance of the **Logo1** graphics symbol from the Library to the Stage.

3. Insert a keyframe in frame 35 and create a motion tween. Set properties to scale the object and rotate it clockwise four times. Set the Ease to **20.**

4. Select frame **1** and scale the instance to **1.0** inch wide. Align it in the upper-left corner of the Stage and set the Alpha amount to **0%.**

5. Select frame **35** and scale the instance to **4.0** inches wide, if necessary. Align it in the middle of the Stage and set the Alpha amount to **100%**. Preview the animation.

6. Insert a new layer and rename it **Text**. Select the **Text Tool** and select properties for a **44** point **black, bold Arial**. Click anywhere on the Stage and key **V.I.P.**

7. Insert a keyframe in frame **35** and create a motion tween. Set properties to scale the object and rotate it counterclockwise four times. Set the Ease to **20**.

8. Select frame **1** and scale the instance to **.5** inches wide. Align it in the upper-right corner of the Stage and set the Alpha amount to **0%**.

9. Select frame **35** and scale the instance to **3.0** inches wide. Align it in the middle of the Stage and set the Alpha amount to **100%**. Preview the animation.

10. Select all frames in the Timeline and cut them to the Clipboard. Create a new movie clip symbol named **Logo Clip** and paste the frames from the Clipboard into the movie clip Timeline.

11. Select the *Text* layer in the movie clip Timeline and insert a new layer. Rename the layer **Stop Action**.

12. Insert a keyframe in frame **35** and then insert a Stop action in the keyframe, and then exit symbol-editing mode.

13. Delete the *Text* layer from the main Timeline and rename the *Logo* layer to **Movie Clip**. Insert a keyframe in frame 2 of the *Movie Clip* layer, and then insert an instance of the **Logo Clip** movie clip symbol on that keyframe. Align it with the top of the Stage, centered horizontally.

14. Insert a new layer and rename it **Stop**. Insert a keyframe on frame 35 and insert a Stop action in the keyframe.

15. Use the **Test Movie** command to test the animation in the Flash Player window, and then close the Flash Player window.

16. Save the changes and leave the **VIP** file open if you are going to complete Project 7-3. Leave your animation program open to use in the next project.

PROJECT 7-3

Enhance the VIP animated logo using buttons, actions, and sound.

1. Continue using the **VIP** file you created in Project 7-2. (If you did not complete Project 7-2, open **Project7-3a** from the data files.) Save the file as **VIP2**.

2. Insert a new layer and rename it **Sound**. Insert a keyframe in frame 5 of the *Sound* layer.

3. Import the **Project7-3b** sound file into the Library, and rename it **Ring**. Drag the **Ring** sound file from the Library to frame 5 of the *Sound* layer.

4. Select frame 5 of the *Sound* layer and set the sound properties so that the sound repeats two times.

5. Insert a new layer in the main Timeline and rename it **Replay Button**. Create a new button symbol named **Replay**.

6. In the *Up* state keyframe, insert an instance of the **Logo1** graphic symbol. Scale it to approximately **1.0** inch wide, and center it horizontally and vertically on the cross-hair.

7. Insert a keyframe in the *Over* frame. Select the **Text Tool** and set properties for **18** point, **bold, black Arial**. Click on the Stage and key **Replay**. Center the text block over the Logo1 instance.

8. Insert a keyframe in the *Down* frame. Increase the size of the font to **22** points, and re-align the text block to center it over the Logo1 instance.

9. Insert a keyframe in the *Hit* frame, and then exit symbol-editing mode.

10. Select frame **1** of the *Replay Button* layer and then insert an instance of the Replay button symbol in the lower-right corner of the Stage.

11. Select the instance of the Replay button on the Stage, and then insert a *go to* action with parameters set to *Go to and play* frame 1 of the current scene.

12. Insert a keyframe on frame 35 of the *Replay Button* layer.

13. Use the **Test Movie** command to test the animation in the Flash Player window. Test the Replay button, and then close the Flash Player window.

14. Save the changes and close the **VIP2** file. Close your animation program.

 WEB PROJECT

Although many sound recordings are protected by copyright laws, there are Web sites that provide access to free sound files. Use the Internet to search for free sounds and music that you could use in animations. Remember, the files should be in WAV or MP3 format, and they should not be too large. Keep a list of the Web sites that you might want to access again, and the types of sounds they have. Note the qualities that would make them suitable or unsuitable for use in an animation. For example, could you use them as streaming sounds or as event sounds? Would they enhance other content, or detract from it? With your instructor's permission, download one or two sound files and test them in your animation program or in your sound-recording software.

 TEAMWORK PROJECT

Animation can make almost any topic fun and interesting. As a group, make a list of mathematical concepts you have learned about this year or last. These might include math, geometry, or algebra. Select one concept that you agree you could illustrate using animation, such as how to find the area of a rectangle. Plan the animation by sketching content and flow on paper, and then use your animation program to create the animation. Include text and graphics. If you want, include sound, such as voice over explaining the concept, or music as a background. When the animation is complete, print it, and then present it to your classmates.

CRITICAL *Thinking*

Think about banner advertisements that display on Web pages. Many use animation to make text move or flash, and they may include buttons to link a viewer to a Web site, or to let a viewer stop, pause, or replay the animation. Select a group, team, or organization and then use Flash to create an animated logo that could display on a banner advertisement. Set the dimensions of the Stage to match the shape of a banner advertisement, and then use original artwork or imported graphics for the content. The logo should include both graphics and text. Try to include the skills you learned in this lesson, including motion paths, color tweens, sound, text, symbols, and actions. Preview the animation as you work, and test it when it is complete. When you are finished, save the file, print it, and share it with your classmates.

PUBLISHING AN ANIMATION

Creating and playing animations on your computer may be fun, but the goal is to make them available for others to use and view in different environments. You may want to display an animation on a Web page as an advertisement, attention-grabber, or entertainment. You may want to use an animation as an illustration for a Web cast, an online meeting, or a slideshow presentation. You may even want to make an animation available in graphics format for individuals to view on their computers, even if they do not have an animation program installed. To make an animation available to others, you *publish* it. Publish means to create a version of the file that you can deliver in the selected environment. For example, you can publish the animation file for use on the Web by creating a version that can be stored on a Web server.

Before publishing, you should prepare the animation file by analyzing its performance to identify frames that may be too large to download smoothly and quickly. You can then take steps to optimize the file to improve performance. In this lesson you learn how to analyze and optimize an animation, and how to publish it for different methods of delivery.

Analyze an Animation File

On the Web, you usually deliver an animation through a streaming connection, which means the animation starts playing before it finishes downloading. In other situations, such as in a presentation, the entire animation downloads before it begins to play. In either case, if a download takes too long, you may lose the attention of viewers who do not want to wait. Most programs include a feature that you can use to analyze the download performance of an animation to identify frames that may take too long to download. For example, Flash includes the Bandwidth Profiler. If you use a program that does not have an analysis tool, you can learn the factors that impact performance and take steps to create animations that play at an optimum download speed.

Performance may be impacted by the way you create the animation as well as the viewer's hardware, software, and connection settings. You can control the way you create the animation, but there is some guesswork involved in anticipating who will view your animation and what type of computer system they are using. Specifically, factors impacting performance include the following:

- The *bandwidth* or *connection speed* is the speed at which a network or modem transfers data. This speed varies depending on a computer's network connection or modem, so you must try to anticipate the users who will view your animation and the network connections they have.

- The *playback rate* is how quickly the computer plays the frames of the movie. This is the *frames per second* (fps) rate that you set in the Document Properties dialog box.

- The *streaming rate* is how quickly the network or modem can download frames of the animation. Streaming rate depends on two factors: the connection speed and the content on each frame. Streaming rate can vary even within an animation because some frames contain more content than others.

Extra for Experts

Download rate usually isn't quite as high as connection speed because the network connection typically requires 10% to 30% of overhead. So, a 33.6 Kbps connection may only be able to transfer about 24 kilobits to your computer per second. At that connection speed, if each frame of an animation includes 1 KB of data, the streaming rate is about 3 frames per second.

Analyze Frame and File Size

The first step in optimizing an animation file is to analyze the total file size as well as the size of each frame. Most programs let you generate and print a *size report*, which is a text file that includes the size of each frame in an animation as well as a running total file size for the entire animation.

To generate a size report, select an option in a dialog box that allows you to customize the export or publishing process. For example, in Flash you can use the Export Movie command or the Publish Settings command to generate an .swf Flash Player file. Once you generate a size report, you can open it in any text editor, such as Windows Notepad, or in a word processing program.

You can also use a program's analysis feature to display a visual representation or graph of how much data is on each frame in an animation. This feature may be available when you test an animation, such as in the Flash Player window. Usually, the graph also indicates whether a frame meets the *bandwidth target*, which is the maximum frame size for optimum download performance. For example, in Flash, the Bandwidth Profiler displays a horizontal red line at the bandwidth target. If a frame extends above the bandwidth target, it is likely to cause the download to pause.

STEP-BY-STEP 8.1

1. Launch your animation program, and open **Step8-1** from the Data files for this lesson. Save the file as **Beads4**. This file is similar to files you worked with in Lesson 7.

2. Use the command for exporting the movie. For example, in Flash, click **File** on the Menu bar, point to **Export**, and then click **Export Movie**. The Export Movie dialog box displays.

3. Key **Beads4 Analysis** in the *File name* box, and then make sure the default file format displays in the *Save as type* box. For example, in Flash, select **Flash Movie (*.swf)**. Click **Save**. An export options dialog box displays, similar to the one in Figure 8-1.

FIGURE 8-1
An export options dialog box

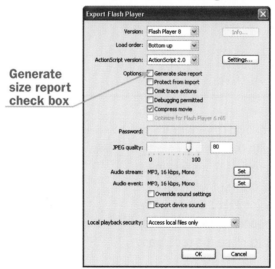

Generate
size report
check box

4. Select the option to generate a size report if necessary and then click the **OK** button. Your program exports the file with the name **Beads4 Analysis.swf**, and generates a text file with the name **Beads4 Analysis Report.txt**. The files are stored in the same location as the Beads4.fla file.

5. Open the report file in a text editor or word processing program. For example, use Windows to navigate to the folder where the **Beads4 Analysis Report.txt** file is stored, and then double-click the file name. Or, use Windows to start the Notepad text editor program, and then use the **File > Open** command to open the file. The file should look similar to Figure 8-2.

STEP-BY-STEP 8.1 Continued

FIGURE 8-2
An analysis report in Notepad

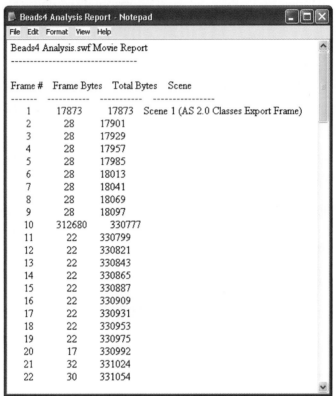

6. Scroll down the window to read all the data in the report to familiarize yourself with the way the report is organized and to see if there are files that seem much larger than others. Click **File** on the Menu bar, and then click **Print**. Click the **OK** (or **Print**) button in the Print dialog box to print the report. Click **File** on the Menu bar, and then click **Exit** to close the report and the text editor program.

7. In the **Beads4** file in your animation program, choose the command for testing the animation. In Flash, click **Control** on the Menu bar, and then click **Test Movie**.

Hot Tip

In Flash 8, once you generate a size report you can display it in the Output panel. In the Flash window, click Window on the Menu bar and then click Output. This panel may open automatically once you generate the report. You can close it or collapse it so it does not block the screen.

8. In the testing window, select the command to display the bandwidth profile. For example, in Flash, click **View** on the Menu bar and then click **Bandwidth Profiler**. The graph should look similar to Figure 8-3. If necessary, click **View** on the Menu bar and then click **Frame by Frame Graph** to select it.

STEP-BY-STEP 8.1 Continued

FIGURE 8-3
Bandwidth Profiler

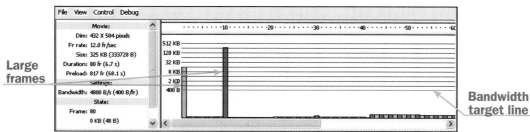

Large frames

Bandwidth target line

9. Locate the bandwidth target. (In Flash, it is a horizontal red line.) Note the frames that extend higher than the bandwidth target. These are frames that may delay the download. (You may need to increase the width of your window or scroll to the right to see all of the frames.)

10. Click the bar of the first frame to select it. Note the size of the frame, which is listed in the bottom section of the left frame of the Profiler. The file size should match that shown for frame 1 in your report printout. Leave the testing window for **Beads4** open to use in the next exercise.

> **Extra for Experts**
>
> You may be able to customize the bandwidth display for different connection speeds. For example, in Flash, in the Flash Player window click View, click Download Settings, and then click a connection speed. Changing the speed changes the bandwidth target so you can see how the animation will download under different circumstances. This is useful to ensure that the animation will perform well under a range of circumstances.

Check Playback and Streaming Rate

When you play back an animation file, if the playback speed of the first frame exceeds the downloading speed of the second frame, there will be a pause. In other words, if the playback ever catches up with the streaming, there is a pause. There is always an initial delay while the first frame (or, for some streaming players, the first several seconds of frames) downloads. Then, frame 1 starts playing while frame 2 downloads. By the time frame 2 finishes playing, frame 3 should have finished downloading and frame 4 should have started downloading. If frame 2 is not fully downloaded before frame 1 finished playing, there is a pause until frame 2 finishes downloading.

Most animation programs provide a tool for testing the download performance in real time. These tools simulate the time it takes for an animation to download and begin streaming, as well as the playback rate. You can watch the simulation to determine if you need to optimize any frames. In Flash 8, for example, you use the Simulate Download command with the Bandwidth Profiler.

STEP-BY-STEP 8.2

1. Choose the command that allows you to set the connection speed for the animation. In Flash, click **View** on the Menu bar, point to **Download Settings**, and then click **28.8** if this speed is not already selected. This is a fairly slow download speed. Notice that the bandwidth target is lower now that the speed is slower.

2. Choose the command that shows how the animation streams and plays. In Flash, click **View** on the Menu bar, and then click **Simulate Download**. The file downloads at the selected speed. (You may be able to view the download progress in the left pane of the profiler.) When the first frame download completes, a playhead moves across the top of the graph to indicate the streaming process, as shown in Figure 8-4. The green bar indicates the progress of the download and the playhead indicates what you are currently viewing. You may notice pauses before frames that extend far above the bandwidth target.

FIGURE 8-4
Playhead and streaming progress

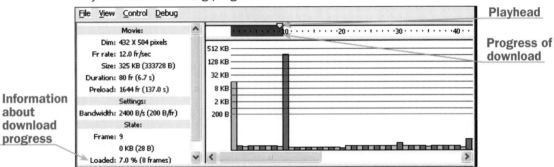

3. Change the connection speed to a faster settings, such as **T1**. Notice that the bandwidth target moves up from its previous position.

4. Select the command to simulate the download. Notice that there is only a slight pause at the beginning while frame 10 downloads.

5. Set the connection speed back to its default setting, usually 56 K.

6. Close the testing window. Leave the **Beads4** file open to use in the next exercise.

> **Note**
>
> The music may end before the animation is complete. If you believe viewers will be using a slow download speed, you could set the music to repeat, or optimize the file as described in the next exercise.

Optimize an Animation File

Once you have identified frames that may cause a pause during playback, you can optimize your animation file to improve performance. The goal of optimization is to reduce the file size of the entire animation file, as well as of individual frames, to insure a fast and smooth download and playback.

When you identify a frame that may cause problems, you should consider why it is so large, and what you might do to make it smaller. Content such as graphics objects, text, and sound increase the size of a frame. If you can simplify a frame, you may be able to make it smaller. For example, you may be able to move some content to a different frame, use instances instead of graphics, or even delete unnecessary objects. You may also be able to compress objects, such as sound files or graphics.

> **Note**
>
> When you compress text and shapes, no information is removed, so the quality remains unchanged. When you compress images and sound files, however, you may have to sacrifice quality to achieve a smaller file.

STEP-BY-STEP 8.3

You know from your report and from viewing the bandwidth profiler that frames 1 and 10 are the ones that cause a delay in the playback. You can reduce the size of these frames by deleting unnecessary graphics.

1. In the **Beads4** file, delete the *Background* layer. This layer contains graphics objects in frames 1 and 10 that significantly impact the frame size. Because the objects do not add much to the animation, you can delete them, making the frames smaller.

2. Test the movie with the bandwidth profile displayed. Notice that frame 10 is now well below the bandwidth target, and frame 1 is smaller as well.

Now, you reduce the size of frame 1 even more by moving and compressing the sound file.

3. Select frame 1 of the *Sound* layer, and then click and drag the keyframe to move the sound object to frame 2. By moving the sound to frame 2, you increase the size of frame 2, but decrease the size of frame 1.

4. Display the Library panel and select the **Scale** sound file. Display the file's Properties dialog box. For example, in Flash, right-click the file and then click Properties. The dialog box should look similar to Figure 8-5.

STEP-BY-STEP 8.3 Continued

FIGURE 8-5
Sound Properties dialog box

5. Click the **Compression** drop-down arrow, and then click **MP3**.

6. Click the **Bit rate** drop-down arrow, and then click **8 Kbps**. Click the **Quality** drop-down arrow, and then click **Medium**. Click the **OK** button to save the settings and close the dialog box.

7. Test the movie with the bandwidth profile displayed. Compare the current size of frames 1, 2, and 10 to the report you printed earlier in this lesson. You have managed to reduce some frame sizes, and distribute some of the size from frame 1 to other frames, which will improve performance. Notice that the music and the animation are also back in synchronization with each other.

8. Close the testing window. Save and close the **Beads4** file, and leave your animation program open to use in the next exercise.

Publish an Animation

When you are ready to distribute your animation, you publish it. By publishing, you generate a new file in a format suitable for the environment in which it will be viewed. For example, if you plan to distribute the animation on the Web, you publish it in HTML format. If you plan to distribute it on a CD or DVD, you publish is as an executable, standalone file. Other common published formats for animation include graphics such as jpg, gif, and png.

Publishing is a two-step process. First, you select *publish settings*, which are properties that control the way the file is published, and then you publish the file. You select publish settings in the Publish Settings dialog box, which you access from the File menu. Depending on your program, there is at least one tab—Formats—in the dialog box, on which you select the format you want to use to publish the animation, as shown in Figure 8-6.

FIGURE 8-6
Publish Settings dialog box

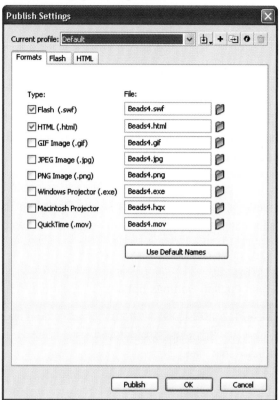

After you select the format, you select settings for the particular format, and publish the file. The published file is stored with the same name and in the same folder as the original animation file, with the appropriate file extension. You can use Windows to copy the file to a Web server or to a CD for distribution. When you save the file, the publish settings are saved as well.

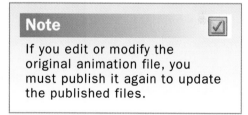

Note

If you edit or modify the original animation file, you must publish it again to update the published files.

Publish for Web Delivery

One of the most common ways to distribute an animation is over the Web. To view the animation, the user must have the necessary software, called a *player*. A *standalone player*, such as Flash Player, can be installed on any computer to play animations without requiring a Web browser or access to the Internet. A browser *plug-in* is a player that is loaded into a Web browser program so it can play an animation on a Web page when a user requests it. Most animation programs distribute their players free of charge over the Internet or on the CD-ROM that contains the program.

STEP-BY-STEP 8.4

1. Open **Step8-4** from the Data files for this lesson and save it as **Web Beads**. This file is also a version of a file you worked with in Lesson 7.

2. Select the command to display the publish settings information. For example, in Flash, click **File** on the Menu bar, and then click **Publish Settings**. The Publish Settings dialog box opens.

3. Click the format for publishing on the Web. For example, in Flash, select both the **Flash** and **HTML** check boxes, if necessary. These are the default publish formats for Flash animations, and they both must be selected to publish a file for the Web.

4. Within the dialog box, there is a tab for each type of file you select to be published. Click the tab for the first selected format. For example, in Flash, click the **Flash** tab. The tab displays options for the selected format, as shown in Figure 8-7. Many of the options are designed to optimize the published animation.

FIGURE 8-7
Flash Publish Settings options

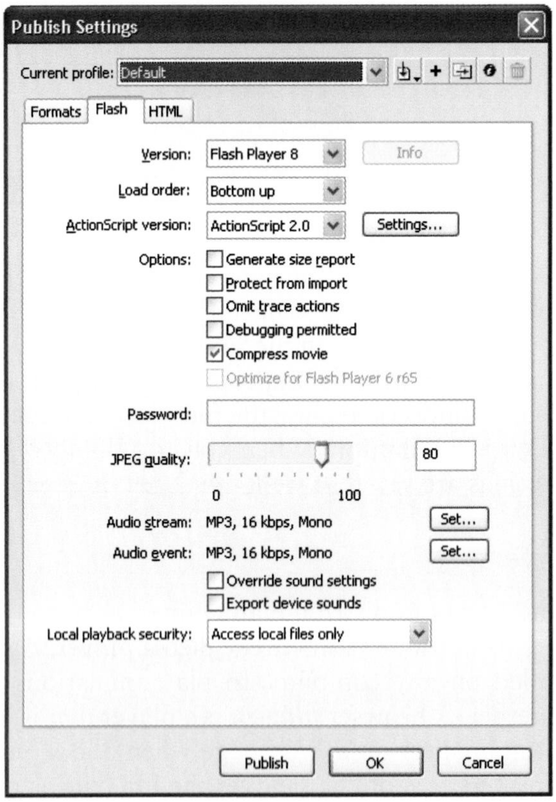

5. Click the tab for any other selected formats. For example, click the **HTML** tab to view the options for publishing HTML files, as shown in Figure 8-8. Review the default options. Many of the options control how the animation displays in HTML format on the Web page.

STEP-BY-STEP 8.4 Continued

FIGURE 8-8
HTML Publish Settings options

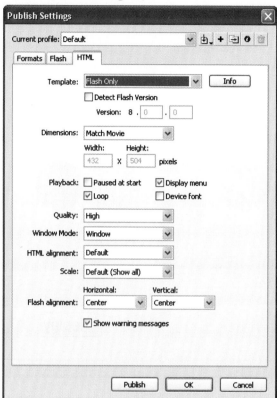

6. Click the **Publish** button to generate the two published files, and then click the **OK** button to close the Publish Settings dialog box.

7. Using Windows, navigate to the folder in which you store the files for this exercise. Double-click the **Web Beads.swf** file. If you have Flash Player installed, the file opens and plays in the Flash Player window.

8. Close the player window.

9. Using Windows, locate and then double-click the **Web Beads.html** file. The file opens and plays in your default Web browser, as shown in Figure 8-9.

STEP-BY-STEP 8.4 Continued

FIGURE 8-9
Animation playing in Internet Explorer

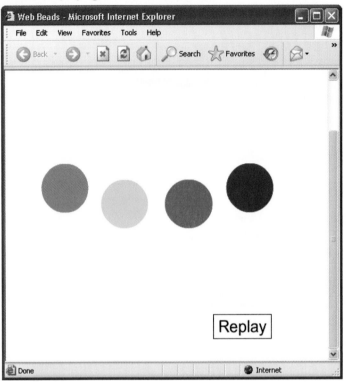

10. Test the Replay button and then close the Web browser.

11. Save the changes to **Web Beads** and then close the file. Leave your animation program open to use in the next exercise.

Publish an Animated GIF File

Publish to an Animated GIF format when you want to capture the images on each frame of your animation in the published file. Animated GIF files are comprised of a series of images, and are often used to display animations on Web pages or on any document that may be viewed onscreen. Select the GIF format in the Publish Settings dialog box, and then select the Animated option button. Select other options as desired and then publish the file. You may view the file in any program that supports animated GIFs.

STEP-BY-STEP 8.5

1. Open **Step8-5** from the Data files for this lesson and save it as **AGIF Beads**.

2. Click **File** on the Menu bar, and then click **Publish Settings**.

3. On the Formats tab, deselect the **Flash** and **HTML** check boxes, if necessary. (When you deselect Flash, HTML may automatically be deselected as well.) Click the **GIF Image** check box.

STEP-BY-STEP 8.5 Continued

4. Click the **GIF** tab, and then click the **Animated** option button in the *Playback* section of the dialog box. Make sure the **Loop continuously** option button is also selected, as shown in Figure 8-10.

FIGURE 8-10
GIF tab of Publish Settings dialog box

5. Click the **Publish** button, and then click the **OK** button to close the dialog box.

6. Using Windows, navigate to the folder in which you store the files for this exercise. Double-click the **AGIF Beads.gif** file. An animated GIF-compatible program such as Windows Picture and Fax Viewer should launch and play the file in a continuous loop.

7. Close the program window.

8. Save changes and close the **AGIF Beads** file. Leave the animation program open for the next exercise.

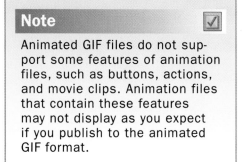

Note

Animated GIF files do not support some features of animation files, such as buttons, actions, and movie clips. Animation files that contain these features may not display as you expect if you publish to the animated GIF format.

Publish a Static Graphics File

Publish to a static graphic format when you want to capture an image of the first frame of one of your animation files. You can then open it in a graphics program for editing, or insert it in any compatible program. For example, you could insert it into a newsletter or report. Select either the GIF, JPEG, or PNG format in the Publish Settings dialog box, and then select the options as desired. Publish the file, and then view it in any graphics program.

S TEP-BY-STEP 8.6

1. Open **Step8-6** from the Data files for this lesson and save it as **JPG Beads**.

2. Click **File** from the Menu bar, and then click **Publish Settings**.

3. On the Formats tab, deselect the **Flash** and **HTML** check boxes, if necessary. Click the **JPEG Image** check box.

4. Click the **JPEG** tab. Notice that the only option that can be changed is Quality, as shown in Figure 8-11. Drag the Quality slider left to decrease the quality, which reduces the file size. Drag right to improve the quality and increase file size. The default value is usually the optimum balance of quality and file size.

FIGURE 8-11
JPEG tab of Publish Settings dialog box

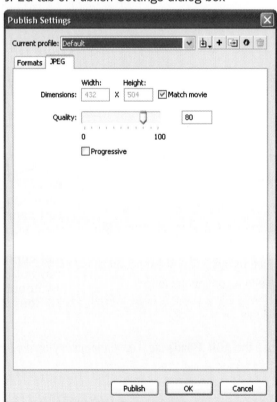

STEP-BY-STEP 8.6 Continued

5. Click the **Publish** button to publish the first frame of the animation in jpg format, and then click the **OK** button to close the dialog box.

6. Using Windows, navigate to the folder in which you store the files for this exercise. Double-click the **JPG Beads.jpg** file to open it in a compatible graphics program. You will see only the first frame of your animation.

7. Close the program window.

8. Save the changes and close **JPG Beads**. Leave the animation program open for the next exercise.

Publish an Animation to an Executable File

Publish an executable version of an animation when you want to be able to play the file on a computer that does not have a player installed. The executable file is published as an application file, or *projector*, which includes the data and a built-in player so the animation can be displayed anywhere, on any computer. Usually, you can select either a Windows projector, for use on systems running Windows, or a Macintosh projector, for use on Apple Macintosh systems.

STEP-BY-STEP 8.7

1. Open **Step8-7** from the Data files for this lesson and save it as **Projector Beads**.

2. Open the **Publish Settings** dialog box.

3. On the Formats tab, click the **Windows Projector** check box to select it. Deselect all other check boxes. There are no format options for a projector file.

4. Click the **Publish** button, and then click the **OK** button.

5. Using Windows, navigate to the folder in which you store the files for this exercise. Double-click the **Projector Beads** application file (.exe). It opens in a Flash Player window, or in the player window for the animation program you are using.

6. Close the program window.

7. Save the changes and close **Projector Beads**. Close your animation program.

SUMMARY

In this lesson, you learned:

■ You can analyze an animation file to see how it will perform when published.

■ The file size and frame size may effect the download and playback speed of an animation file.

- You can generate a file size report to see the total file size and the size of individual frames.
- You can display a bandwidth profile to see if frames meet the bandwidth target, and to simulate the download at different speeds.
- Optimize a file by creating smaller frames and distributing content to different frames to improve download and playback performance.
- Publish an animation so you can distribute it to viewers. You may publish to the Web, as an animated graphics file, as a static graphics file, or as an executable projector.

VOCABULARY*Review*

Define the following terms:

Bandwidth	Player	Publish settings
Bandwidth target	Plug-in	Size report
Connection speed	Projector	Standalone player
Playback rate	Publish	Streaming rate

REVIEW*Questions*

TRUE/FALSE

Circle T if the statement is true or F if the statement is false.

T F 1. Streaming rate can vary within an animation because some frames contain more content than others.

T F 2. In Flash, a horizontal purple line indicates the bandwidth target.

T F 3. To move the bandwidth target down, decrease the connection speed.

T F 4. When you play back an animation file, if the playback speed of the first frame exceeds the downloading speed of the second frame, there will be a pause.

T F 5. The goal of optimization is to improve the color display in an animation file.

T F 6. Publish an animated .jpg file to include all frames from the animation.

T F 7. Use instances instead of graphics to reduce frame size.

T F 8. Projector settings are the properties that control the way a file is published.

T   F   9. Published files are stored with the same name and in the same folder as the original animation file.

T   F   10. Most animation programs distribute their players free of charge over the Internet or on the CD-ROM that contains the program.

WRITTEN QUESTIONS

Write a brief answer to each of the following questions.

1. Name at least three ways to optimize an animation file.

2. Explain why a frame with a lot of content might cause problems during downloading.

3. Name at least two tools most animation programs provide for analyzing a file.

4. Explain the steps that go into publishing a file.

5. Explain why you might want to publish an executable file.

FILL IN THE BLANK

Complete the following sentences by writing the correct word or words in the blanks provided.

1. The _____ is the speed at which a network or modem transfers data.

2. The _____ rate is how quickly the computer plays the frames of the movie.

3. The _____ rate is how quickly the network or modem can download frames of the animation.

4. Generate a(n) _____ report to see the size of each frame in an animation as well as a running total file size for the entire animation.

5. The bandwidth _____ is the maximum frame size for optimum download performance.

6. A(n) _____ player such as Flash Player can be installed on any computer to play animations without requiring a Web browser or access to the Internet.

7. A published _____ includes the animation file data and a built-in player so the animation can be displayed anywhere, on any computer.

8. Publish to a(n) _____ format when you want to capture the images on each frame of your animation in the published file.

9. A browser _____ is a player that is loaded into a Web browser program so it can play an animation on a Web page when a user requests it.

10. Once you have identified frames that may cause a pause during playback, you can _____ your animation file to improve performance.

PROJECTS

PROJECT 8-1

Analyze, optimize, and then publish an animation for the Web.

1. Launch your animation program, and open **Project8-1** from the Data files. Save the file as **Web VIP**.

2. Generate a file size report by exporting the animation to a file named **VIP Analysis** and selecting the option to generate the size report in the Export options dialog box.

3. Open the **VIP Analysis Report** in a text editor such as Notepad and print it. Close the text editor.

4. In your animation program, test the **Web VIP** file using a bandwidth profiler to identify any frames that may be too large. Close the test player window.

5. In your animation program, move the sound from frame 2 of the *Sound1* layer to frame 5 of the same layer.

6. Display the Library panel and display the Properties dialog box for the **Ring 1** sound file. Compress the file to **MP3** format, and set the bit rate to **8 kbps** and the quality to **medium**. Click the **OK** button to close the dialog box.

7. Test the movie again to see how the changes impact the bandwidth profile. Compare the results to the printed file size report.

8. Simulate the download at the default speed and at **DSL** speed. Select the default speed again, and then close the bandwidth profile graph.

9. Close the testing window.

10. Display the Publish Settings dialog box and select the formats for publishing to the Web. Click **Publish** to publish the files, and then click **OK** to close the Publish Settings dialog box.

11. Use Windows to navigate to the folder where the published files are stored, and then double-click the **Web VIP.html** file to open it in your browser. Test the **Replay** button.

12. Close your browser.

13. Save changes to the **Web VIP** file and close it. Leave your animation program open to use in the next project.

PROJECT 8-2

Analyze, optimize, and then publish an animation as a standalone, executable file.

1. Launch your animation program, and open **Project8-2** from the Data files. Save the file as **Train Projector**.

2. Generate a file size report by exporting the animation to a file named **Train Analysis** and selecting the option to generate the size report in the Export options dialog box.

3. Open the **Train Analysis Report** in a text editor such as Notepad and print it. Close the text editor.

4. In your animation program, test the **Train Projector** file using a bandwidth profiler to identify any frames that may be too large. Close the test player window.

5. In your animation program, move the text block from frame 1 of the *Text1* layer to frame 2. Move the sound from frame 1 of the *Sound* layer to frame 5 of the same layer.

6. Display the Library panel and display the Properties dialog box for the **Bark** sound file. Compress the file to **MP3** format, and set the bit rate to **8 kbps** and the quality to **medium**. Click the **OK** button.

7. Test the movie again to see how the changes impact the bandwidth profile. Compare the results to the printed file size report.

8. Simulate the download at the default speed, at a slower speed, and at **DSL** speed. Select the default speed again, and then close the bandwidth profile graph.

9. Close the testing window.

10. Display the Publish Settings dialog box and select the formats for publishing a standalone **Windows Projector**. Click **Publish** to publish the file, and then click **OK** to close the Publish Settings dialog box.

11. Use Windows to navigate to the folder where the published file is stored, and then double-click the **Train Projector** application file to open it.

12. Close the program window.

13. Save changes to the **Train Projector** file and close it. Leave your animation program open to use in the next project.

PROJECT 8-3

Analyze, optimize, and then publish as a graphic image for use in a handout.

1. Launch your animation program, and open **Project8-3** from the Data files. Save the file as **Pyramid Picture**.

2. Generate a file size report by exporting the animation to a file named **Pyramid Analysis** and selecting the option to generate the size report in the Export options dialog box.

3. Open the **Pyramid Analysis Report** in a text editor such as Notepad and print it. Close the text editor.

4. In your animation program, test the **Pyramid Picture** file using a bandwidth profiler to identify any frames that may be too large. Close the test player window.

5. In your animation program, delete the *Background* layer.

6. Display the Library panel and display the Properties dialog box for the **Bounce** sound file. Compress the file to **MP3** format, and set the bit rate to **8 kbps** and the quality to **medium**. Click the **OK** button.

7. Test the movie again to see how the changes impact the bandwidth profile. Compare the results to the printed file size report.

8. Simulate the download at the default speed, at a slower speed, and at **DSL** speed. Select the default speed again, and then close the bandwidth profile graph.

9. Close the testing window.

10. Select frame 80. Display the Publish Settings dialog box and select the formats for publishing a **JPEG** image file. Click **Publish** to publish the file, and then click **OK** to close the Publish Settings dialog box.

11. Use Windows to navigate to the folder where the published file is stored, and then double-click the **Pyramid Picture.jpg** image file to open it.

12. Close the program window.

13. Save changes to the **Pyramid Picture** file and close it. Close your animation program.

 ## WEB PROJECT

Animation programs such as Flash provide the tools you need to create sophisticated animations. However, you can create animations without using technology. Use the Internet to research ways to create animation without a computer program. For example, look up flip books, thaumatropes, and zoetropes. Select one method, and locate instructions for using it. Print the instructions, and then use the method to create an animation. Try duplicating the results using your animation program. When you are finished, write a report comparing the two methods. Are there similarities? Are there differences? Which method is easier? Which produces a better result? Present your report to your classmates.

 TEAMWORK PROJECT

Using an animation to illustrate a science experiment or project brings the results to life in a way that a static graph or image cannot. As a team, complete an experiment as assigned by your Science instructor, and then use your animation program to create an animation file illustrating the results. For example, you can use an animation to illustrate change over time, or to compare trial groups with a constant. Use the skills you have learned about animation to include graphics, sound, and motion. Test the animation file, analyze, and optimize for optimum performance. Publish it as a projector and copy it to a CD so your instructor can review it on any computer. Present it to your class.

CRITICAL *Thinking*

Animation is basically a way to tell a story using a sequence of pictures. Write an original story or select a story that you have read in class, and then use your animation program to illustrate the story. Start by drawing a storyboard to map out the flow of the story. Select the objects you want to include. You may use original drawings or imported graphics. Decide if you want to include sound and, if so, select or record the sound files. When you have finished planning the project, begin the animation. Make use of symbols, including movie clips, if necessary. Use layers to keep your project organized. As you work, test the animation. Ask a classmate to review it and make suggestions. When you are satisfied with your work, analyze the file and optimize it as necessary. Publish the file for viewing on the Web and as a standalone projector.

WORKING WITH VIDEO

OBJECTIVES

Upon completion of this lesson, you should be able to:

- Work with digital video.
- Set up a video project.
- Capture video from a digital camcorder.
- Open and save an existing video project.
- Import video and graphics files.
- Create and preview a video sequence.
- Edit a video sequence.

Estimated time: 2 hours

VOCABULARY

24p
Aspect ratio
Assets
Audio track
Bins
Capture
Codec
Digital video recorder
Digital video
Firewire
Footage
High Definition (HD) video
IEEE 1394
iLink
In point
Interlaced video
Lossless
Lossy
Non-linear editing
NTSC (National Television Systems Committee)
Out point
PAL (phase alternating line)
Progressive video
Project
Sequence
Source clip
Static motion video
Streaming video
Timebase
Video conferencing
Video track
Voice over
Web-based motion video
Webcam
Workspace

Animations are great for creating the illusion of motion on your computer screen, but when you want real, live action, you use video. *Digital video* is video in which all of the information representing images has been digitized, so that you can edit and display it on a computer. Using a video editing software program, you can turn digital video footage into movies that entertain or inform. In today's multimedia world, there are numerous opportunities to use video for business, or just for fun. For example, in business, you can use video as part of a marketing campaign, as a training tool, to provide information on a variety of topics, or as part of a live broadcast such as a conference or lecture. At home, you can add music and titles to your home movies, edit out the boring parts, and create a memorable record of a vacation, special occasion, or big game.

In this lesson, you learn key concepts about digital video, such as the different types of video available and how to determine video quality. You then learn how to set up a video project, acquire video from a variety of sources, and perform basic edits. Finally, you learn to preview the video.

Programs that you use to edit digital video are usually *non-linear editing* (NLE) programs, which means they can randomly access the video scenes and clips in any order. Some offer sophisticated editing features, and some are quite basic. All the step-by-step exercises in Lessons 9 through 11 use Adobe Premiere Pro 2.0, a video program that is available for both PC and Mac systems. Where necessary, alternate instructions for Adobe Premiere Elements 2.0 are provided. If you are working on a Mac, you can also use Apple's Final Cut Pro to edit high-quality videos. For simple video editing at home or school, you can use Microsoft Windows MovieMaker, which comes with the Windows operating system, or Apple's iMovie which comes with Mac computers. Although these programs use the same concepts as Premiere Pro, they may not include all of the features covered in this unit, some of the features may be named differently, and the screen interface may look different.

> **Important**
>
> Most video-editing programs let you edit and preview video clips, but not play completed video files. To play video files you use a media player such as Apple QuickTime or Windows Media Player.

About Digital Video

Like an animation, digital video presents moving pictures organized into frames. Unlike an animation, frames of video data don't contain text, shapes, or images. Instead, the entire frame is a single bitmapped image.

The two basic types of digital video are static and Web-based. *Static motion video* refers to images that are recorded and saved as a file for playback. *Web-based motion video*, which is sometimes called *streaming video,* refers to video images captured in real time and transmitted over an Internet connection, such as is done with video conferencing or webcams. *Video conferencing* is a meeting set up and transmitted on the Internet using video and audio. A *webcam* is a video camera attached to a computer that transmits the video to a Web page.

To record digital video *footage*, which is raw, unedited material, you need a *digital video recorder*, which is usually a digital camcorder. You may also use a digital camera with a video recording feature, a webcam, or even your cellular telephone, if it is equipped with a video feature. The video is captured to a storage device such as a cassette tape, memory card, or a DVD.

Once you record video, you import the content for use in a video program, where you can assemble it into a professional quality movie, which is sometimes called a project. You can distribute the movie as a computer file, on a CD or DVD, or on the Internet. You can also use the video in other applications. For example, you can import it into an animation or a presentation program, or place it on a Web site.

To import the video to your video program, connect the camcorder to your computer using cables, and then use the features of your video program to capture selected clips. Most camcorders transfer video from tapes using an *IEEE 1394* connection. IEEE 1394, which is a two-way digital connection that transfers data at up to 400 megabits per second, may also be called *Firewire* or *iLink*. During the capture, the video is saved as a digital video file on your computer.

> **Note**
>
> Digital video technology is evolving rapidly, with new, higher-quality cameras and storage devices becoming available all the time. Digital8 camcorders that use 8-mm cassette tapes are giving way to Mini DV camcorders that use smaller Mini DV cassette tapes. However, DVD camcorders that record directly on to DVDs are becoming more affordable every day.

Table 9-1 describes some common video file formats.

TABLE 9-1
Common video file formats

FORMAT	DESCRIPTION
DV	Most digital video camcorders capture video in DV format, which offers extremely high-quality resolution.
Audio Video Interleaved (AVI)	Most digital video files that you capture from a camcorder to a PC are stored in AVI format.
MPEG1	Often used in digital cameras and camcorders to capture small video clips. It is the compression format used to create video CDs and is commonly used for posting clips on the Internet.
MPEG2	Used for commercially produced DVD movies and home movies stored on DVD discs. It is also the form of compression used to deliver digital satellite broadcasts.
MPEG4	Used for streaming and downloadable Web content and is also used by some portable video recorders.
Windows Media Video (WMV)	Microsoft Corporation's proprietary video format. It is compatible with Windows Movie Maker and Windows Media Player.
QuickTime (MOV)	Developed by Apple, it is used for video displayed on both Windows and Macintosh computers.

Because digital video is stored in digital format, the quality never degrades no matter how much you edit the content. Resolution is usually measured in lines, with 500 lines considered high quality. You may also hear video referred to as either progressive or interlaced. *Progressive video* draws each line of an image on the screen progressively from the top to the bottom, while *interlaced video* alternates between drawing the even numbered lines and the odd numbered lines on the screen. Progressive video is generally considered to be higher quality because it provides an increased vertical resolution, no flickering, and easier compression. When you see a lowercase letter *i* following a resolution value, it indicates that the video is interlaced; when the value is followed by a lowercase *p*, it is progressive.

> **Note** ☑
>
> If you do not have a camcorder, you can still create digital videos using existing video files and still images.

Digital video is usually interlaced, using either the *NTSC* (National Television Systems Committee), the standard television format used primarily in the United States, or *PAL* (phase alternating line), the standard television format used primarily in Europe. *High definition (HD) video*, however, is progressive. For example, *24p* is an HD format that runs 24 progressive frames per second. HD video camcorders may become more readily available as the standard becomes more popular. HD is delivered in a wide screen format—16:9 *aspect ratio* rather than the standard 4:3—with a resolution of about 720 lines, so the quality is significantly better than standard resolutions. (Aspect ratio is the ratio of the width of an image to the height of an image.)

Other factors that impact the quality of digital video include:

- **Frame size.** This setting is measured in pixels and determines the size the video will display on screen. Common sized include 320 by 240, 640 by 480, and 720 by 480. A larger frame size results in a larger, more detailed onscreen display. It also results in a larger video file which requires more storage space, more memory for processing, and more time for downloading.

- **Frame rate.** As in an animation, frame rate controls how fast the video plays and is measured in frames per second (fps). Typically frame rates range from 23 to 30 fps. At less than 15 fps, the video becomes "jumpy."

- **Color depth.** This setting controls the number of bits of data the computer assigns to each pixel of the frame. Usually, you can select from a variety of options ranging from 256 shades of gray to millions of colors.

- **Compression.** Because digital video files may be quite large, most video file formats use some type of *codec*, which stands for compressor/decompressor, and is a system for compressing a large amount of data into a smaller file. The file can be opened and decompressed to deliver the original content. Some codecs are called *lossy*, because they cause a loss of quality by actually removing pieces of data. Codecs that do not cause a loss of quality are called *lossless*.

 Communication Skills

VIDEO TIPS

In order to create an effective video, you must start with quality footage. Even without a lot of experience, you can record professional quality video by keeping a few basic rules in mind.

- Think small. You'll find that when you import the video into your program, shorter clips are easier to work with and make the final video better and more professional.
- Be quiet. Remember, you are recording sound as well as video. Everything you say will be captured.
- Keep the camera still and let the action move. You will record more effective footage if you let the action happen in front of the camera, rather than trying to move the camera to capture the action. When you do have to move the camera, be slow and steady. Try not to jerk from one shot to the next.
- Limit the zoom. Zooming in and out during a shot can detract from the action. Set up the zoom before you start recording, or use the zoom slowly for effect during the shot.
- Start early; end late. Leave extra footage at the beginning and end of each scene so you don't miss any action on either side. You can always edit out the parts you don't need.
- Check your equipment. Charge your camera's battery and make sure you have enough storage space before you begin. Have an extra tape or disc on hand, and a spare battery or an AC power adapter if possible.
- Plan ahead. Map out your storyboard—a series of sketches or drawings that roughly depict the scenes and shots you want to include—ahead of time so you are sure to record all of the scenes you want and need.

Set Up a Video Project

Although a completed video program consists of a *sequence*, or series, of frames, each sequence may be comprised of many *assets*. Assets are digital content such as video clips, text, drawings, sounds, and still images. In most video programs, to keep all of these assets organized and available for use in a video program, you create a *project*. A project is a file that stores the sequences you assemble, references to the assets that are associated with the sequences, and instructions for how to assemble and display the video. Note that the assets themselves are not stored in the project file but in their original storage location.

Create a New Project

Usually, when you start a video program a Welcome screen or dialog box prompts you to either create a new project or open an existing project. If you select to create a new project, the New Project dialog box displays. You key a file name and select a storage location. In some programs, including Premiere Pro, you also specify project settings.

Usually, there are general settings, such as the methods for processing the video, the *timebase*, which specifies the time divisions your program uses to calculate the time position of an edit, and playing back the video. Capture settings control how the program interacts with the camera device. The video rendering settings control the frame size, picture quality, compression settings, and aspect ratios used to play back video. Finally, the default sequence specifies the number of video tracks and the number and type of audio tracks in each sequence. A *video track* is the video portion of the recorded video, and an *audio track* is the audio portion. In most programs, the settings impact all items in the project, and cannot be changed.

> **Note**
>
> Many programs, including Adobe Premiere Pro 2.0, create folders in the selected storage location in which to store supporting files such as preview files and source file references. The folders are used for all projects stored in the same location.

Most programs include preset project settings based on a video standard, frame size, and sound quality, so you can simply pick the one that matches the type of video you want to create. After you select project settings, your program creates the project and displays it onscreen.

> **Note**
>
> All the step-by-steps in this lesson are based on the steps required when using Adobe Premiere Pro 2.0.

S TEP-BY-STEP 9.1

1. Launch your video program. A Welcome screen or dialog box displays, offering you a choice of creating a new project, opening an existing project, getting help, or exiting the program. Click the option for creating a new project. A New Project dialog box displays. It should look similar to Figure 9-1.

FIGURE 9-1
New Project dialog box

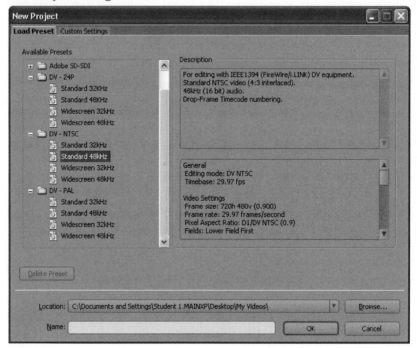

2. In the *Name* text box, key **First Video**.

3. Click **Browse**, select a storage location, and then click **OK**.

4. Select the **DV—NTSC Standard 32kHz** preset, if necessary.

5. Click the **OK** button. Your program creates the project and displays the default application window. Leave your program open to use in the next exercise.

Manage the Workspace

At first glance, the video program window may appear crowded and confusing. Most programs organize the window into an arrangement of panels or panes called the *workspace*.

Each panel has a tab that displays the panel name. In some programs each panel has a close button, while in other panels there may be a collapse arrow you can use to collapse the panel instead of closing it. Panels may also have menu buttons that you click to display a menu or related commands. You can open, close, move, and resize panels at any time using many of the same techniques you use in your graphics or animation program. For example, click the close button to close the panel, or drag a panel border to resize the panel. Drag the panel handle to move the panel, or make it float in the window. Your program probably comes with a few built-in workspaces designed for specific tasks, such as editing or applying effects. For example, when Adobe Premiere Pro starts, the Editing workspace displays, as shown in Figure 9-2. Table 9-2 describes the elements of the Editing workspace. Refer to Figure 9-2 to locate each element. If you are using Premiere Elements, your workspace may not have as many panels as Premiere Pro, the panels may be arranged differently onscreen, and some of the panels may have different names. For example, the Project panel is named *Media* in Premiere Elements, and instead of both a Source Monitor and a Program Monitor, there is one panel named *Monitor* which is used in Clip mode to display clips like the Source Monitor or in Timeline mode to display a sequence like the Program Monitor.

FIGURE 9-2
Adobe Premiere Pro 2.0

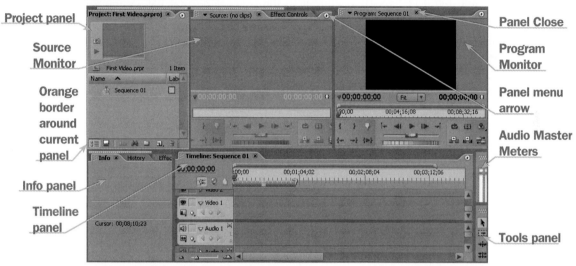

TABLE 9-2
Editing workspace elements

ELEMENT	DESCRIPTION
Project panel	Displays the project name and lists assets in the project. You can use the tools in the panel to organize the clips. (Called Media in Premiere Elements.)
Source Monitor	Displays and plays back the current clip. This may be grouped with the Effect Controls and Audio Mixer panels. (Called Monitor in Clip mode in Premiere Elements.)
Program Monitor	Displays and plays back a sequence of clips. (Called Monitor in Timeline mode in Premiere Elements.)
Timeline panel	Displays the sequence timeline where you assemble and rearrange a sequence.
Info panel	Displays information about the current or selected item. This is usually grouped with the Effects and History panels. (Does not display by default in Premiere Elements. The Properties panel displays similar information.)
Audio Master Meters	Used to monitor audio tracks. (Does not display by default in Premiere Elements.)
Tools panel	Displays tools for editing a sequence in the Timeline. (Not available in Premiere Elements. Some tools display on the Timeline tab.)

STEP-BY-STEP 9.2

1. Click anywhere in the Source Monitor or Monitor, if you are using Premiere Elements to select it. A border outlines the current panel.

2. Drag the bottom border down to increase the height of the panel. Notice that the height of other panels in the top portion of the screen increases as well, and that the Timeline panel height in the lower section of the screen decreases.

3. Click the **Info** tab if necessary to bring it to the front. If you are using Premiere Elements, click **Window** on the Menu bar and then click **Info** to display the Info panel. Click the **Close** button on the Info panel. The panel closes. In Premiere Pro the Effects or History panel, which are grouped with the Info panel, displays.

4. Click the menu arrow in the Project panel (the Media panel in Premiere Elements) to display a shortcut menu of related commands, as shown in Figure 9-3.

FIGURE 9-3
Display a panel menu

5. On the shortcut menu, point to **View** to display a submenu or view options for the Project panel.

   A checkmark next to an option on the menu indicates that it is selected. For example, in Premiere Pro, there should be a check mark next to Preview Area, because the Preview Area at the top of the panel displays by default. In Premiere Elements, the Preview Area does not display by default, so there is no checkmark.

6. Click **Preview Area** to toggle the option off or on.

7. Click the **Close** button in the Program Monitor to close the panel. The Source Monitor panel expands to fill the space, as shown in Figure 9-4. If you are using Premiere Elements, click the collapse arrow in the Effects and Transitions panel, and then click the expand arrow to restore it to its original size.

STEP-BY-STEP 9.2 Continued

FIGURE 9-4
Customize the workspace

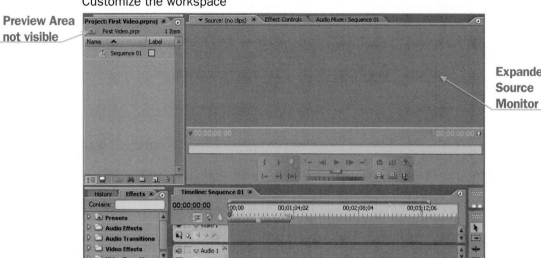

8. Click the menu arrow in the Project panel, point to **View** on the shortcut menu, and then, if there is no arrow next to the Preview Area command, click **Preview Area** to display the preview area at the top of the Project panel again.

9. Click **Window** on the Menu bar, point to **Workspace**, and then click the command to display the default editing workspace. If you are using Premiere Pro, click **Editing**. If you are using Premiere Elements, click **Edit**. The program reverts to the default Editing Workspace arrangement. Leave your video program open to use in the next exercise.

Capture Video from a Digital Camcorder

After you have set up your video project, you can import, or *capture*, the source video footage from a camcorder into the video-editing program. Usually, you import the video as clips, or individual video files. Although you can import one long video clip, it is easier to work with the clips and assemble a sequence if each clip is a short, manageable size. Once you capture the clip, it displays in the Project panel or a similar location in the workspace. A clip in the Project panel is called a *source clip*, because it is the original clip, with no edits or changes. You may preview it in the Project panel, or open it in the Source Monitor, which has a larger preview area.

> **Note** ☑
>
> If you import one long clip, you can use selected portions of it to assemble a sequence, or split it into multiple clips. Selecting a portion of a clip is covered later in this lesson.

To import the video, you must first correctly set up the camera for use with your computer. This may involve installing device drivers, but usually just means attaching the Firewire cable from the camera to the Firewire port on the computer.

Capture Video

Most video programs have a capture mode in which input from the digital camera is played in a window on the computer screen. You can usually play, rewind, pause, and stop the video using either the controls on the camera or the controls in the capture window. You use the controls to locate the start of the video you want to capture, and then click the Record button. When you are finished recording, click the Stop button.

Most programs prompt you to name the clip file. You may also be able to key additional information such as a description of the clip or the name of a scene. This can be helpful when you are ready to arrange your clips into a sequence. Your program saves the clip as a video file in the same storage location as the current project file, and adds a reference, or link, from the clip file to the project. You can repeat the process to capture as many clips as you want; each time you start and stop recording, you create a new clip. Once you capture a clip, it is available in your video program so you can preview and edit it.

Note

Refer to the user's manual that came with your camera for complete instructions on how to connect the camera to the computer for transferring video.

Important

If you move or rename the source file stored on your computer, your project may have trouble locating it. Many programs, including Premiere Pro, display a dialog box asking you to locate and select the source file so that it can reestablish the link.

STEP-BY-STEP 9.3

To complete this exercise, you need a digital video camera that you have already used to record footage, and a computer with a Firewire connection. If you don't have the required hardware and software, you can skip this exercise and the next, and go on to Step-by-Step 9.5.

1. To capture video from a camcorder using Premiere Pro, click **File** on the Menu bar, and then click **Capture**. A Capture dialog box or panel similar to the one in Figure 9-5 displays.

STEP-BY-STEP 9.3 Continued

FIGURE 9-5
Capture panel

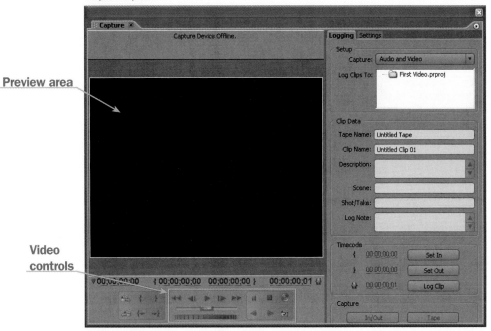

Preview area

Video controls

2. Correctly connect your camera to your computer. Set the camera to playback mode and turn it on. The current video frame should display in both the preview area of the Capture dialog box and on the camera's preview screen.

3. Use the controls on the camera or in the Capture dialog box to locate the first frame that you want to record—or the frame *before* the first frame you want to record.

4. Click the **Record** button at the bottom of the Capture dialog box to begin recording. Notice that the number of frames captured, and the duration of the clip displays in the panel.

5. Let the video record for at least ten seconds, but no more than 30 seconds, and then press **Esc** on your keyboard, or click the **Stop** button at the bottom of the Capture dialog box. The video should stop recording. A dialog box such as Save Captured Clip should display.

6. In the *Clip Name* box, key **Clip1**, and then click the **OK** button. The captured video file is saved in the same location as the project file, and a link to the clip is added to the project.

STEP-BY-STEP 9.3 Continued

7. Close the Capture dialog box. The clip name displays in the Project panel, and information about the clip displays in the Info panel, as shown in Figure 9-6. Leave the project file open to use in the next exercise.

FIGURE 9-6
Captured clip in the Project panel

Use the Source Monitor

In most programs you can preview and work with source clips in a panel similar to the Source Monitor before you assemble the clips into a sequence. (In Premiere Elements, you can click the Clip button near the top of the Monitor panel to make sure it is in Clip mode.) Table 9-3 describes the components of the Source Monitor. Take a moment to refer to Figure 9-7 to locate each component.

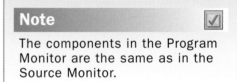

Note ☑

The components in the Program Monitor are the same as in the Source Monitor.

FIGURE 9-7
Source Monitor

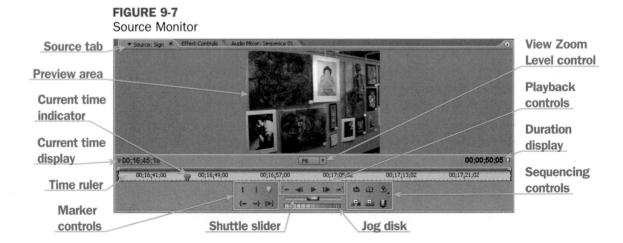

TABLE 9-3
Source Monitor panel components

COMPONENT	DESCRIPTION
Source tab	Displays the name of the source clip.
Time ruler	Measures the sequence time horizontally, using the settings specified in the project's timebase.
Current time indicator	Sets the current frame. Drag to position the time indicator to select or mark a frame.
Current time display	Shows the timecode for the current frame.
Duration display	Shows the total duration—or length—of the clip.
Preview area	Displays the clip.
Zoom control	Displays a menu of zoom settings.
Shuttle slider	Drag the shuttle slider to play the clip while adjusting the speed. The speed increases as you move further from the center.
Jog disk	Drag the jog disk to navigate to nearby frames.
Playback controls	Use to play, stop, step forward, and step back within the clip.
Marker tools	Use to set markers and points to identify frames on the time ruler.
Sequencing controls	Use to control how clips are added to a sequence.

S TEP-BY-STEP 9.4

1. Double-click the clip name in the Project panel. It opens in the Source Monitor so you can preview and edit it.

2. Click the button to preview the clip. In Premiere Pro, click the **Play/Stop Toggle** button in the Source Monitor. In Premiere Elements, click the **Play/Pause Toggle** button in the Monitor. Notice the current time displays at the left end of the time ruler and the current time indicator moves from left to right as the clip plays.

> **Hot Tip**
> Use ScreenTips to identify the names of tools in any panel.

> **Hot Tip**
> You can also drag the clip to the Source Monitor panel.

3. Click the toggle button to stop the clip.

4. Click the **Step Back** button a few times to move back through the frames in the clip.

5. Click the **View Zoom Level** drop down arrow and then click **25%** on the menu to change the zoom.

6. Click the **View Zoom Level** drop down arrow again, and then click **Fit**.

STEP-BY-STEP 9.4 Continued

7. Drag the **Shuttle** slider all the way to the right to play the clip at high speed. Note that when you release the slider, it returns to the middle position.

8. Drag the **Jog** disk slowly to the left to move the current time indicator. If you are using Premiere Elements, skip this step.

9. Click **File** on the Menu bar, and then click **Save** to save to project file.

10. Click **File** on the Menu bar, and then click **Close** to close the file. The Welcome screen displays. Leave your video program open to use in the next exercise.

Open and Save an Existing Video Project

As with other types of application programs, you can open an existing video project file so you can work with it again. You can save changes to the file, or you can save the file with a new name or in a new location. To open an existing file, click Open Project on the Welcome screen to open an existing project file, or click the name of the file in the list of Recent Projects. Alternatively, you can use the File > Open command. Use the File > Save As command to save the file with a new name or in a different location. Keep in mind that the project must be able to locate and open any video source files to which it is linked. If it cannot, it will display a dialog box asking you to locate them.

> **Note**
>
> If you are using Premiere Pro, the data files for this lesson have a .prproj file extension. The files for Premiere Elements have a .prel file extension.

STEP-BY-STEP 9.5

1. On the Welcome screen, click **Open Project** to display the Open Project dialog box.

2. Navigate to the location where the data files for this lesson are stored and click **Step9-5** to select it. Click the **Open** button to load the project into your program.

3. Click **File** on the Menu bar and then click **Save As** to display the Save As dialog box.

4. In the *File name* text box, key **Art Show**.

5. From the **Save in** list, select the location where you want to store the files for this lesson.

6. Click the **Save** button. Leave the **Art Show** file open to use in the next exercise.

Import Video and Graphics Files

If you already have a source video file stored on your computer, you can import it into a project file. You can also import graphics images, such as photos stored in JPEG format, which can be used to create interesting effects, such as a video collage or a transition, or audio files which can be used to create sound tracks or *voice overs*. A voice over is a technique in which the voice of the narrator plays on an audio track while the video track simultaneous displays something other than the narrator speaking. Most programs can import a wide variety of video formats, including .avi, .mov, and mpg, and many audio formats, including .aiff and .wav.

When you import a video clip or still image, the source file—which is the original file stored on your computer or other storage device—is not moved or changed in any way; your video program simply stores a reference to the source file in the project file. For this reason, you should not rename or move the source file once you have imported it, or your program may have trouble locating it. Imported files are listed in the Project panel, where you can manage and organize them.

Import Files

The process of importing a file into your project is much like importing a file into an animation or graphics program. In most programs, you use the Import or the Add Media command on the File menu to locate and select the source file.

STEP-BY-STEP 9.6

Before beginning this exercise, use Windows to copy the video source files **Step9-6a**, **Step9-6b**, and **Step9-6c** and the graphics source file **Step9-6d** from the data files for this lesson to the folder where you will store the solution files for this lesson.

1. Select the command to import a video file. If you are using Premiere Pro, click **File** on the Menu bar, and then click **Import**. If you are using Premiere Elements, click **File** on the Menu bar, click **Add Media**, and then click **From Files or Folders**. A dialog box, with a name such as *Import*, displays.

2. Locate and select the video file **Step9-6a** that you copied to the solution files for this lesson, and then click **Open**. Your program imports the video clip into the project file, using the same name as the source file.

3. Select the command to import a file, and then locate and select the video file **Step9-6b**. Click **Open** to import the file.

4. Import the video file **Step9-6c**.

STEP-BY-STEP 9.6 Continued

5. Use the same command to import the graphics file **Step9-6d**. The image is added to the Project panel list. Notice that the icon next to the clip name is different from the video clips, indicating that the clip is a graphic image. Your Project panel should look similar to Figure 9-8.

FIGURE 9-8
Imported clips in the Project panel

Imported clips

6. Save the changes and leave **Art Show** open to use in the next exercise.

Use the Project Panel

You can use the Project panel to manage clips. For example, you can rename the clips, group them into folders (which are called *bins* in some programs, including Premiere Pro), change the order of clips, and even delete clips. To make it easier to work with the clips, you can expand the size of the panel, and change the view.

STEP-BY-STEP 9.7

> **Did You Know?**
>
> In Premiere Pro, clip types are labeled with colors to help you identify them in larger projects. The labels display in the Project panel in a column to the right of the clip name. For example, video clips are light green, and still images are purple. When a clip is placed in the timeline, its name is shaded with the label color as well.

1. Drag the right border of the Project panel to the right until you see a column named *Media Start* in Premiere Pro, or *Comment* in Premiere Elements.

2. In the Project or Media panel, right-click the **Step9-6a** clip name, and then click **Rename**. Key **Sign**, and then press **Enter** to rename the clip. This does not rename the source video file, only the reference to the clip in the project file.

3. In the Project or Media panel, rename the *Step9-6b* file to **Interview1**.

4. Rename *Step9-6c* to **Interview2**, and rename *Step9-6d* to **Metro Photo**. The panel should look similar to Figure 9-9.

STEP-BY-STEP 9.7 Continued

FIGURE 9-9
Renamed clips in expanded panel

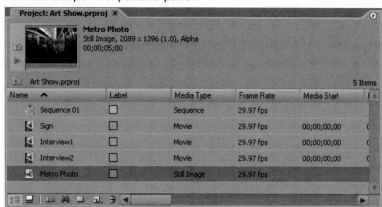

5. Click the **Icon** button at the bottom of the Project panel to change to Icon View.

6. Click and drag the **Metro Photo** clip one spot to the left, and drop it between *Interview1* and *Interview2*. The panel should look similar to Figure 9-10.

FIGURE 9-10
Project panel in Icon view

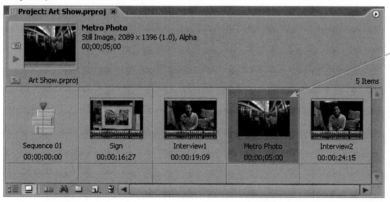

7. Click the **Bin** or **Folder** button, and then key **Images** and press **Enter** to create a new folder/bin.

8. Right-click the **Metro Photo** clip (you may have to scroll up in the panel, or expand the height of the panel to locate it) and then click **Duplicate**.

9. Drag the **Metro Photo Copy** clip on to the **Images** bin/folder, and then release the mouse button. This moves the clip into the **Images** bin.

10. Click the **List** button at the bottom of the panel to change to List View.

STEP-BY-STEP 9.7 Continued

11. Click the expand arrow next to the **Images** bin/folder to expand it so you can see its contents. The panel should look similar to Figure 9-11.

FIGURE 9-11
Organize items in folders/bins

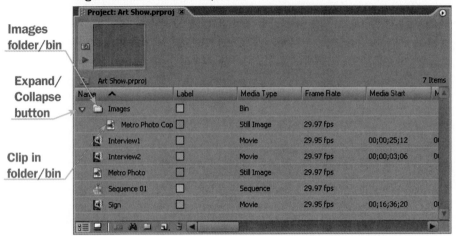

12. Right-click the **Images** bin/folder icon and then click **Clear**, or click the **Clear** button at the bottom of the Project panel, to delete the bin/folder and its contents.

13. Drag the right border of the Project panel back to its original position.

14. Save the changes and leave **Art Show** open to use in the next exercise.

Create and Preview a Video Sequence

To create a video, assemble clips into a sequence in the Timeline. You can easily drag a clip to the timeline from either the Project (Media) panel or the Source Monitor (Monitor). You can also use only a portion of the clip, if you want, by using the controls in the Source Monitor (Monitor) to specify the portion, and then dragging it to the Timeline. Once the clips are in the Timeline, you can rearrange them. The final video plays the clips in the order in which they are assembled.

Using the Timeline

The Timeline displays a sequence graphically by showing clips, transitions between clips, and effects that you add to the sequence. A sequence must contain at least one video track, but it can have multiple video and audio tracks that run parallel to each other. For example, you can use two video tracks to superimpose one image over another in the final video, and you can use multiple audio tracks if you want to mix audio during the video. You can also insert audio only, video only, or both. You use the tools in the Timeline panel to organize each sequence. Table 9-4 describes the components of the Timeline panel. Take a moment to review these, referring to Figure 9-12 to locate each component.

FIGURE 9-12
Timeline panel

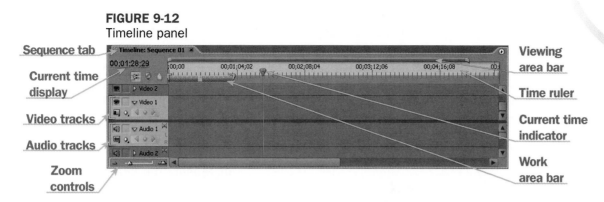

TABLE 9-4
Timeline panel components workspace elements

COMPONENT	DESCRIPTION
Sequence tab	Displays the sequence name. (Not available in Premiere Elements.)
Time ruler	Measures the sequence time horizontally, using the project's timebase. Markers and other points also display on the time ruler.
Current time indicator	Sets the current frame in the sequence.
Current time display	Shows the timecode for the current frame.
Viewing area bar	Used to shift the view of contents in the Timeline (like a scroll bar).
Work area bar	Indicates the portion of a sequence selected for preview or export.
Zoom controls	Used to adjust the magnification of the time ruler display. (Displays at the top of the Timeline in Premiere Elements.)
Video tracks	Displays all video tracks in the sequence.
Audio tracks	Displays all audio tracks in the sequence.

Inserting Clips

To add a clip to a Timeline sequence, drag it from either the Project (Media) panel or the Source Monitor (Monitor) and drop it on the appropriate track in the Timeline. You may want to expand the width of the Timeline panel, or close some other panels you are not using to get a wider view of the Timeline. If you want to change the clip in any way, you should open it in the Source Monitor (Monitor) before placing it in the Timeline. For example, from the Source Monitor (Monitor) you can select to include the video track, the audio track, or both tracks.

> **Note**
>
> In some programs, including Premiere Pro, a project may have more than one sequence. They may display as separate tabs in the Timeline panel, or you can drag each tab into a separate Timeline panel.

In most programs, you can choose to either replace, or overlay, existing clips that are already in the Timeline, or insert the new clips before or after existing clips. You can also leave gaps between clips, but they result in gaps in the video. To insure that there are no gaps, most programs have a snap feature you can use to snap the start of one clip to the end of the previous clip. Usually, snap is active by default.

Extra for Experts

When you insert a clip into the timeline, you actually create an instance, similar to the instances you use in animations. The original clip remains unchanged, and you can insert as many instances of a single clip as you want, without increasing the final file size.

S TEP-BY-STEP 9.8

1. If necessary, close the Info, History, and Effects panels so the Timeline expands to fill the space.

2. Make sure the current time indicator is all the way at the left end of the time ruler, and then place the **Interview2** clip on the Timeline. To do this, click the **Interview2** clip in the Project panel, drag it on to the *Video 1* track in the Timeline panel, and then release the mouse button. By default, both the video and the audio are placed in the Timeline, which should look similar to Figure 9-13.

FIGURE 9-13
Clip in the Timeline

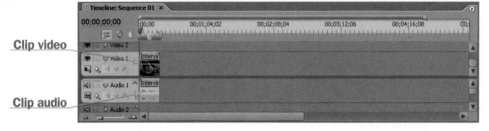

3. Double-click the **Interview1** clip. It displays in the Source Monitor or Monitor.

4. Click the **Toggle Take Audio and Video** button until it displays just a sound icon. This sets the program to take just the audio from the clip and displays only the sound waveform in the panel.

5. Drag the clip from the preview area in the Source Monitor (Monitor) to the *Audio 1* track in the Timeline so it abuts the **Interview2** clip. The Timeline should look similar to Figure 9-14.

Note ☑

By default, in Premiere Pro, the three audio tracks in the Timeline are formatted for stereo. If a clip is not in stereo, it cannot be placed on a stereo track, so your program automatically creates a mono audio track—the *Audio 4* track—where it can place the clip.

STEP-BY-STEP 9.8 Continued

FIGURE 9-14
Two clips in the Timeline

Audio waveform in Source Monitor

Toggle Take Audio/Video

Audio only clip

6. Place the **Metro Photo** clip in the *Video1* track of the timeline, abutting the **Interview2** clip, and above the **Interview1** audio clip. It will not extend as long as the Interview1 audio clip. (Notice in Premiere Pro, that the name is shaded purple—the still image label color.)

7. Save the changes to **Art Show** and leave it open to use in the next exercise.

Use a Portion of a Clip

If you want to use only a portion of a clip in a sequence, you specify the portion by using the controls in the Source Monitor or Monitor to place a marker at the *in point*, which is the starting frame, and another marker at the *out point*, which is the ending frame. In most programs, to set an in point, you position the current time indicator on the time ruler at the location where you want the clip to start, and then you click the Set In Point button. Likewise, to set an out point, you position the current time indicator and click the Set Out Point button.

Note ☑

In some programs, such as Premiere Pro, you can click the Insert button in the Source Monitor to place a clip on the Timeline. It is inserted at the location of the current time indicator. Click the Overlay button to place the clip on the Timeline, replacing the clip to the right of the current time indicator.

Did You Know?

Not all video clips have separate audio and video tracks. Some have both audio and video on the same track. When you insert a clip with only a single track in the timeline, it is placed on the video track.

When you place the clip in the Timeline, only the portion between the in point and the out point is used. Setting in and out points does not change the source clip; it simply specifies the portion of the clip to use. You can use a different portion of the same clip by setting new in and out points, and dragging that clip to the Timeline.

STEP-BY-STEP 9.9

1. Double-click the **Sign** clip to open it in the Source Monitor or Monitor.

2. Preview the clip.

3. Drag the current time indicator (in the Source Monitor or Monitor) along the time ruler to **00;00;16;00**.

4. Click the **Set In Point** button to set the in point. Notice that the area after the in point on the time ruler becomes shaded.

5. Position the current time indicator at **00;00;32;26**, which is the last frame that displays the drawing, and click the **Set Out Point** button. Now, the area between the points is shaded.

6. If available, click the **Play In to Out** button to preview the selected portion of the clip.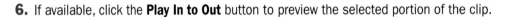

7. Click the **Toggle Take Audio and Video** button until it displays just a video icon to take just the video from the clip.

8. Drag the current time indicator in the Timeline all the way to the left, to the beginning of the sequence, if necessary. If you are using Premiere Elements, click **Clip** at the top of the Monitor to display the cip again.

9. Drag the clip from the Source Monitor (Monitor) preview area to the *Video 1* track of the Timeline to the right of the **Metro Photo** clip. It should look similar to Figure 9-15. (If you do not reposition the current time indicator, you may have to drag the clips to position them correctly, or use the **Undo** command to reverse the previous action, and try again.)

Note

You can split a clip that has been placed on the Timeline into two or more clips, if you want. Click the Razor Tool in the Tools panel and then click on the clip where you want to create the split. Or, position the current time indicator where you want to create the split, click Sequence on the menu bar, and then click Razor at Current Time Indicator.

Hot Tip

Use the Step Forward and Step Back buttons to position the current time indicator precisely. Each time you click a button, the current time indicator moves slightly, and the current time display adjusts.

STEP-BY-STEP 9.9 Continued

FIGURE 9-15
Audio, video, and image clips in the Timeline

Still image clip

Selected clip portion in Source Monitor

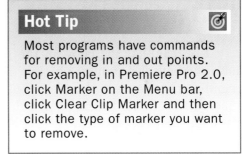

10. Save the changes and leave **Art Show** open to use in the next exercise.

Preview the Video

At any time, you can preview the sequence in the Program Monitor or similar panel. (In Premiere Elements, you can click the Timeline button in the Monitor to change to Timeline mode.) You can play it from beginning to end, or position the current time indi-

> **Hot Tip**
>
> Most programs have commands for removing in and out points. For example, in Premiere Pro 2.0, click Marker on the Menu bar, click Clear Clip Marker and then click the type of marker you want to remove.

cator at a point where you want to start. You can also use the controls in the Program Monitor to step back and forward or to stop the video at any time. You may want to expand the Program Monitor panel, or close panels you are not using to increase the size of the preview area. You can also render the sequence before previewing. Rendering converts all content to bitmapped format and creates a temporary file that your program uses to display the preview. Rendering may take a few minutes, or even longer, depending on your computer and the size of the file. You do not have to render to file to preview it.

STEP-BY-STEP 9.10

1. If you would like, increase the size of the Program Monitor (Monitor) panel in order to increase the size of the preview area. If you are using Premiere Elements, click **Timeline** at the top of the Monitor.

2. Click the button to preview the video. In Premiere Pro, click **Play/Stop Toggle** and in Premiere Elements, click **Play/Pause Toggle**. The sequence starts playing from the position of the current time indicator.

3. Watch the preview for problems, or things you might want to change (you learn about editing in the next exercise).

4. Save the changes and leave **Art Show** open for the next exercise.

> **Extra for Experts**
>
> If you would like, you can render the video. In Premiere Pro, click Sequence on the Menu bar and then click Render Work Area. In Premiere Elements, click Timeline on the Menu bar and then click Render Work Area. Your program probably displays a dialog box showing the progress of the rendering while it renders the sequence and creates the preview file. When the rendering is complete, the preview plays.

Edit a Sequence

Y̶ou can edit the clips on the timeline to improve or modify the sequence. If you are unhappy with the changes, you can use the Undo command. Many programs also have a command that lets you revert to a previously saved version of a project file. Before you edit a clip you must select it in the Timeline. As with most objects, the easiest way to select a clip is to click it.

Some programs let you adjust the length of a clip already on the timeline by trimming the edges of the clip. (In some programs, it is called a Ripple Trim.) In effect, trimming sets a new in point or a new out point. Drag the left edge of the clip with the Trim In pointer to set a new in point, and the right edge of the clip with the Trim Out pointer to set a new out point. As you drag, a ScreenTip displays the number of seconds you are trimming.

If a clip abuts another clip, it may be hard to position the Trim tools to make the change. You can temporarily move the clip to a different location on the Timeline to have better access to it. Clips can easily be rearranged on the timeline, usually by simply dragging them around. You can also zoom in on the Timeline to get a closer look.

> **Note**
>
> To delete a clip from a sequence, select it and press the Delete key, or right-click it click Clear on the shortcut menu.

STEP-BY-STEP 9.11

1. Click and drag the **Interview1** audio clip to the right along the *Audio 1* track so there is a large gap between it and the **Interview2** clip.

The end of the Interview2 audio and the beginning of the Interview1 audio repeat the same dialog "...fish eye lens." You can trim the in point of the Interview1 audio clip to remove the repetition.

STEP-BY-STEP 9.11 Continued

2. Zoom in on the **Interview1** audio clip. Position the mouse pointer over the left edge of the **Interview1** audio clip until it resembles a square bracket with a double-headed arrow through it. This is the Trim In pointer.

3. Drag the edge of the clip slowly and carefully to the right to trim **3** seconds (**00;00;03;00**) from the clip. This should remove the repetitive dialog so the first dialog on the track is *The drawing itself....* If necessary, use the **Undo** command to reverse the action and try again. Note that once you start trimming you can see the seconds trimmed in the Program Monitor and in a screen tip. If necessary, zoom in more, which may make it easier to trim small amounts.

4. When you are satisfied that you have trimmed out the unnecessary dialog, drag the audio clip on the timeline and drop it under the **Sign** video clip. This leaves a gap between the **Interview1** audio and the **Interview2** audio, corresponding to the still image on the video track, as shown in Figure 9-16.

FIGURE 9-16
The edited sequence

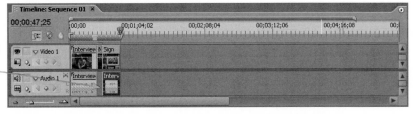

Gap between audio clips

5. Preview the entire sequence to see how the edits affect the video.

6. Drag the **Interview1** audio clip to the left on the Timeline so that it abuts the end of the **Interview2** clip. This eliminates the gap in the audio track. Preview the sequence again.

7. Save the changes and close the **Art Show** project file. Close your video program.

SUMMARY

In this lesson, you learned:

- Digital video is video in which all of the information representing images has been digitized so that you can edit and display it on a computer.

- There are two basic types of digital video: static motion video in which images are recorded and saved as a file for playback and Web-based motion video—or streaming video—in which video images are captured in and transmitted real time over an Internet connection.

- To record digital video footage you need a digital video recorder such as a camcorder.

- You can capture video clips from a camcorder to video-editing software, or you can import video files. You can also import static images and audio files.

- To connect a digital camcorder to a computer you use an IEEE 1394 connection, often called Firewire or iLink.

- The quality of digital video depends on the resolution, as well as other factors such as frame size, frame rate, color depth, and compression.

- Most video file formats use some type of codec, which stands for compressor/decompressor.

- Most video-editing programs store video clips and other assets in a project file.

- You can assemble clips and other assets into a sequence to create a movie.

- You can select a portion of a clip to use in a sequence by setting the clip's in and out points.

- You can preview a sequence in your video-editing program.

- You can edit a sequence in different ways, including rearranging the clips, trimming clips, and even deleting clips.

VOCABULARY *Review*

Define the following terms:

24p	IEEE 1394	Project
Aspect ratio	iLink	Sequence
Assets	In point	Source clip
Audio track	Interlaced video	Static motion video
Bins	Lossless	Streaming video
Capture	Lossy	Timebase
Codec	Non-linear editing	Video conferencing
Digital video recorder	NTSC (National Television	Video track
Digital video	Systems Committee)	Voice over
Firewire	Out point	Web-based motion video
Footage	PAL (phase alternating line)	Webcam
High Definition (HD) video	Progressive video	Workspace

REVIEW *Questions*

TRUE / FALSE

Circle T if the statement is true and F if the statement is false.

T F   1. Because digital video is stored in digital format, the quality never degrades no matter how much you edit the content.

T F   2. It is easier to work with one long video clip rather than lots of short clips.

T F   3. You can only import video files into a video program.

T   F   4. When you trim a clip in your video program, the original file is not affected.

T   F   5. You cannot rearrange clips once they are inserted in a sequence.

T   F   6. Leaving gaps between clips in the Timeline results in gaps in the video.

T   F   7. When assembling a sequence, you can select to insert only the audio from a clip, only the video, or the audio and the video.

T   F   8. 24p is a high-definition format that runs 24 progressive frames per second.

T   F   9. The color depth setting controls the amount of brightness and contrast in a video.

T   F   10. When you delete a clip from a project, the source file is deleted as well.

WRITTEN QUESTIONS

Write a brief answer to each of the following questions.

1. What types of assets can you use in a video sequence?

2. Explain the difference between static motion video and Web-based motion video.

3. What are three ways to distribute a movie you create using digital video?

4. Name at least three devices you can use to record digital video.

5. Name at least three factors that impact the quality of digital video.

FILL IN THE BLANK

Complete the following sentences by writing the correct word or words in the blanks provided.

1. An IEEE 1394 connection is commonly known as either iLink or _____.

2. In Adobe Premiere Pro 2.0, a(n) _____ border displays around the current panel.

3. You position the current _____ indicator to set the current frame in the Source Monitor, the Program Monitor, or the Timeline.

4. Set a(n) _____ point to mark the starting frame of a portion of a clip.

5. Set a(n) _____ point to mark the ending frame of a portion of a clip.

6. When you _____ a sequence to preview it, the content is converted to bitmapped format, and your program creates a temporary preview file.

7. A(n) _____ is a video camera attached to a computer that transmits the video to a Web page.

8. A codec that loses quality by removing pieces of data during compression is called _____.

9. Most video programs organize the window into an arrangement of panels or panes called the _____.

10. An original clip imported into a project with no edits or changes is called the _____ clip.

PROJECTS

PROJECT 9-1

Before beginning this project, copy the video source files **Project9-1a**, **Project9-1b**, **Project9-1c**, and **Project9-1d** from the data files for this lesson to the folder where you store the solutions files.

1. Launch your video-editing program, and create a new project file named **Dogs Life**. If necessary, select the **DV-NTSC Standard 32kHz** preset.

2. Import the following video files into the project:
   Project9-1a
   Project9-1b
   Project9-1c
   Project9-1d

3. Rename the clips as follows:
   A. *Project9-1a* to **Wake Up**
   B. *Project9-1b* to **Meal Time**
   C. *Project9-1c* to **Feed Me**
   D. *Project9-1d* to **Dessert**

4. Place the **Wake Up** clip at the beginning of the *Video 1* track in the Timeline.

5. Place the **Feed Me** clip to the right of the **Wake Up** clip in the Timeline.

6. Open the **Meal Time** clip in the Source Monitor or Monitor and set the in point at the beginning of the clip and the out point at **00;00;02;00**, or **2** seconds into the video. Insert the trimmed clip on the Timeline to the right of the **Feed Me** clip.

7. Set new in and out points on the **Meal Time** clip as follows:
   A. Set the in point at **00;00;07;00**.
   B. Set the end point at **00;00;12;00**.

8. Insert the new trimmed clip on the Timeline to the right of the previous **Meal Time** clip.

9. Open the **Dessert** clip in the Source Monitor or Monitor. Set an in point at **00;00;35;00** and set an out point **00;00;46;00**.

10. Insert the clip on the Timeline to the right of the previous **Meal Time** clip.

11. Preview the entire sequence. Notice the difference in quality between the first clip—**Wake Up**—and the other clips.

12. Delete the **Wake Up** clip from the Timeline, and then delete it from the Project (Media) panel.

13. Move the remaining clips to the left to the beginning of the Timeline.

14. Preview the sequence again.

15. Save the **Dogs Life** project file and close it. Leave your video program open to use in the next project.

PROJECT 9-2

Before beginning this project, copy the video source files **Project9-2a, Project9-2b, Project9-2c,** and **Project9-2d,** and the audio source file **Project 9-2e** from the data files for this lesson to the folder where you store the solutions files.

1. Create a new project file named **Dogs Walk**. If necessary, select the **DV-NTSC Standard 32kHz** preset.

2. Import the following video files into the project:
   Project9-2a
   Project9-2b
   Project9-2c
   Project9-2d

3. Import the **Project9-2e** audio file into the project.

4. Rename the clips as follows:
   A. *Project9-2a* to **Walk1**
   B. *Project9-2b* to **Walk2**
   C. *Project9-2c* to **Walk3**
   D. *Project9-2d* to **Walk4**
   E. *Project9-2e* to **Music**

5. Place both the audio and video tracks of the **Walk1** clip at the beginning of the Timeline.

6. Preview the sequence. If necessary, trim static from the end of the Walk1 clip. (If you zoom in on the Timeline you can see the static on the *Audio 1* track.)

7. Insert the video only of the **Walk2**, **Walk3**, and **Walk4** clips into the Timeline.

8. Open the **Music** clip in the Source Monitor or Monitor.

9. Select the first **37.28** seconds of the clip and then place it into the *Audio 1* track, to the right of the **Walk1** clip. If necessary, trim the **Music** clip so its end corresponds to the end of the **Walk4** clip.

10. Preview the sequence.

11. Save the **Dogs Walk** project file and close it. Leave your video-editing program open for the next project.

PROJECT 9-3

Before beginning this project, copy the video source files **Project9-3a**, **Project9-3b**, **Project9-3c**, **Project9-3d**, **Project9-3e**, and **Project9-3f** and the audio file **Project9-3g** from the data files for this lesson to the folder where you store the solutions files.

1. Create a new project file named **Dogs Life2**. If necessary, select the **DV-NTSC Standard 32kHz** preset.

2. Import the following video files into the project:
   Project9-3a
   Project9-3b
   Project9-3c
   Project9-3d
   Project9-3e
   Project9-3f

3. Import the **Project9-3g** audio file into the project.

4. Rename the clips as follows:
   A. *Project9-3a* to **Eating**
   B. *Project9-3b* to **Barking**
   C. *Project9-3c* to **Walk3**
   D. *Project9-3d* to **Walk2**
   E. *Project9-3e* to **Walk1**
   F. *Project9-3f* to **Leaving**
   G. *Project9-3g* to **Music**

5. Place both the audio and video tracks of the **Eating** clip at the beginning of the Timeline. Preview the sequence and trim off any static at the end of the clip.

6. Insert the video only of the **Leaving**, **Walk1**, **Walk2**, and **Walk3** clips into the Timeline.

7. Insert both the audio and video tracks of the **Barking** clip after the **Walk3** clip.

8. Determine how much audio you need to fill the gap on the audio track between the **Eating** clip and the **Barking** clip. (*Hint:* In Premiere Pro, select the **Leaving**, **Walk1**, **Walk2**, and **Walk3** clips by holding the **Shift** key and clicking on each one. When they are all selected, the Info panel will display the total duration of the items selected. If necessary, click **Window** on the Menu bar, and then click **Info** to display the Info panel.)

9. Open the **Music** clip in the Source Monitor.

10. Select any portion of the clip equal to the duration time you need to fill the gap, and then place the clip in the gap in the Timeline.

11. Preview the sequence. If necessary trim clips to eliminate static and gaps.

12. Make adjustments or edits if necessary, and then save the **Dogs Life2** project file and close it. Close your video-editing program.

 WEB PROJECT

The cost of a digital camcorder is dropping quickly as the technology becomes more commonplace. In addition, new features are being added to camcorders to make them easier to use and more sophisticated. Use the Internet to research digital camcorders to make a recommendation to your school about which product to purchase. Because there are so many products available, you might want to start by deciding which features you want the cameras to include—asking yourself what elements would be the most useful in a school setting—and selecting a price range. Record the information in a word processing document or a spreadsheet so you can compare it easily. Also look for reviews and customer opinions. When you have gathered all of the data, select the product that you would recommend. Write a report of at least 500 words about the product and why you recommend it. Support your decision using the data from your research. Present the report to your classmates.

 TEAMWORK PROJECT

Video is an excellent medium for recording a live event. With digital video, you can go back and add someone's thoughts about the event, narration, or opinion, and assemble it into a movie. As a team, select an upcoming event at your school or in your community that you could record on video. For example, you might choose a big game, a theater production, a lab experiment, or a special assembly. Before the event, assign roles to each team member, such as director, photographer, producer, and script writer. Get together and plan the specific action you want to record, so that you don't miss anything. (You could record the entire event, but that would use a lot of resources, and would probably be too much content to use in a movie sequence.) Use a camcorder to record at least five minutes of the event, being sure to record the action you agreed on, as well as other action that may occur spontaneously. You might also use a digital camera to take still pictures. Record one or more interviews with someone who participated in or observed the event.

Review the raw footage, and then select and capture the clips you want into your video program. Assemble the clips into a sequence, and preview it. Make any edits or adjustments, and preview it again. Ask classmates to preview it and make suggestions for how you might improve it, and then incorporate the improvements into the video. Present the video to your class.

CRITICAL*Thinking*

You can use video to illustrate and present a story or poem. Write an original poem, or select a poem written by someone else. Use a video camcorder to record yourself reading the poem. Use the camcorder, a digital camera, or both to capture images that illustrate the poem. If you do not have the equipment to record original footage, locate video and image clips that you can use royalty free on the Internet, or stored on your computer or network. Capture or import the clips into your video program and assemble them into a sequence that effectively presents the poem. Preview the sequence as you work, and ask classmates to preview it. Improve and enhance the sequence using editing methods, or even by adding new or different material. When you are satisfied with your work, present it to the class.

ENHANCING VIDEO

One of the benefits of digital video is that you can easily dress it up by applying changes to the actual bitmap images using techniques similar to those you use to enhance graphics and animations. You can add transitions to control changes between the end of one clip and the beginning of the next, you can apply effects such as blurs and color changes, and you can add text such as titles and credits. You can also change the length and/or speed of a clip, which can make the video play in slow or fast motion, and you can even reverse the frames to play the clip backwards.

In this exercise you learn how to create transitions between clips, apply effects, add titles, and adjust the speed and length of a clip.

Add Transitions

Usually, when you assemble clips in the Timeline one clip starts immediately after the previous clip ends, which may result in a choppy video. You can smooth out the flow between clips and make a video more interesting by adding transitions. In a video, a *transition* is the frames that are used to phase out one scene (or clip) and phase in the next. Some transitions are subtle, such as a *cross dissolve*, which fades out the previous clip while fading in the next. Some are more involved, such as a *slide,* which sets one clip to slide off one edge of the frame while the next clip slides in from the opposite side, or a *peel*, which gives the appearance of "peeling away" one clip to reveal another clip underneath. Most programs come with built-in transitions that you can apply to your video, or you may be able to select from a list of transitions. In Adobe Premiere Pro, the built-in video transitions are listed in the Effects panel, in a bin (folder) named

Video Transitions. Within the bin, the transitions are organized into categories such as Dissolve, Slide, and Wipe, as shown in Figure 10-1. In Adobe Premiere Elements, the built-in video transitions are listed in the Effects and Transitions panel under the heading Video Transitions. To apply a transition, you drag it to the Timeline.

FIGURE 10-1
Video Transitions

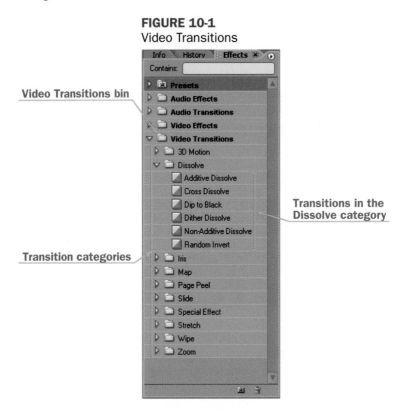

Video Transitions bin

Transitions in the Dissolve category

Transition categories

A transition may be *double-sided*, which means it involves the end of one clip and the beginning of the next, or *single-sided*, which means it involves only the beginning or end of one clip. In most programs, transitions obscure about 1 second of video content, so you usually do not want the transition to occur during an important part of the video. This means that when you capture, import, or select portions of clips, you should make sure to include handles at the beginning and end of the clip. A *handle* is extra frames before the in point or after the out point of a clip. If the transition occurs during the handle, it will not obscure important video content.

When you drag a transition to the Timeline, you can select to position it based on the *cut line* between clips, which is the break where one clip ends and the next begins. In Premiere Pro, you can identify the position relative to the cut line by looking at the mouse pointer. Table 10-1 describes the three options available for positioning transitions.

Note ☑

If the handle is too short to cover the length of a transition, your program may display an alert warning you that it will repeat frames to create the transition. This may not be a problem, depending on the content of the video, or you may want to choose a different transition.

Did You Know?

Sometimes, the handle before the in point is called the head material, and the handle after the out point is called the tail material.

TABLE 10-1
Transition position options

MOUSE POINTER	POSITION	DESCRIPTION
	Center	Centers the transition on the cut line between two clips so it obscures an equal number of frames at the end of the first clip and the beginning of the second clip.
	End	Aligns the transition to end at the end of a clip. This may be used to transition out of the video in a single-sided transition, or to obscure frames at the end of the first clip only in a double-sided transition.
	Start	Aligns the transition to start at the beginning of a clip. This may be used to transition in to the video in a single-sided transition, or to obscure frames at the beginning of the second clip in a double-sided transition.

For some double-sided transitions, such as a peel, you should overlap the beginning of one clip with the end of the previous clip. To overlap clips, you use multiple video tracks in the Timeline. The video in the higher track always plays over the video in the lower track. For example, place clip 1 on video track 2, and then place clip 2 on video track 1. Position the clips so the end of clip 1 overlaps the beginning of clip 2, and position the transition to end at the end of clip 1, so it overlaps the beginning of clip 2 (see Figure 10-2).

> **Note**
>
> Some transitions have settings that you can change in a dialog box or panel such as the Effect Controls or Properties panel.

> **Hot Tip**
>
> Zoom in the Timeline to get a closer look when working with transitions.

S TEP-BY-STEP 10.1

Before beginning the exercise, use Windows to copy the source video files **Step10-1a**, **Step10-1b**, and **Step10-1c** from the folder where the Data files for this lesson are stored into the folder where you will store the solution files.

1. Launch your video editing program and create a new project. If necessary, select the **DV-NTSC Standard 32kHz** preset. Save the project as **Realtor**.

2. Import the source files **Step10-1a**, **Step10-1b**, and **Step10-1c** from your solutions folder into the project.

3. Rename the clips as follows:
   A. *Step10-1a* to **House1**
   B. *Step10-1b* to **House2**
   C. *Step10-1c* to **House3**

> **Note**
>
> All the step-by-steps in this lesson use Adobe Premiere Pro 2.0, a video program that is available for both PC and Mac systems. Alternate steps for Adobe Premiere Elements 2.0 are provided as necessary.

STEP-BY-STEP 10.1 Continued

4. Zoom in on the Timeline, and then drag the **House1** clip to the Timeline, and drop it at the beginning of the *Video 2* track (the clips do not have separate audio tracks).

5. Drag the **House2** clip to the Timeline, and drop it on the *Video 1* track so that it starts about 1 second before the end of the *House1* clip, as shown in Figure 10-2.

Hot Tip

Position the current time indicator at the location where you want to place a clip before you place the clip on the Timeline, so that the clip snaps into place. You can position the indicator precisely by using the Step Forward and Step Back controls in the Program Monitor or Monitor panel.

FIGURE 10-2
Overlap clips in the Timeline

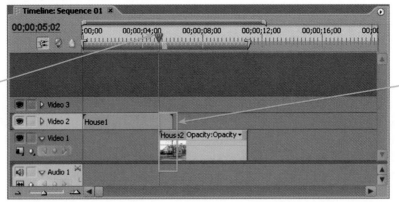

6. Drag the **House3** clip to the Timeline and drop it on the *Video 1* track so it abuts the end of the *House2* clip.

7. Display the list of available video transitions. If you are using Premiere Pro, display the Effects panel and click the expand arrow to the left of the Video Transitions bin. If you are using Premiere Elements, display the Effects and Transitions panel and scroll down to locate the video transitions. (You may want to expand the panel itself by dragging its top border up.)

8. Expand the **Page Peel** category. (If your program does not have peel effects, select a different category).

Note

In Premiere Pro, the Effects panel is grouped with the Info panel. Click the Effects panel tab to move it to the front of the group, or select Window > Effects to display the Effects panel.

Note

In Premiere Elements, click the Transitions button at the top of the Effects and Transitions panel to hide effects and display transitions.

STEP-BY-STEP 10.1 Continued

9. Click and drag the **Center Peel** transition to the Timeline, and drop it when it is aligned with the cut at the end of the *House1* clip (in the *Video 2* track). (If your program does not have Center Peel, select a similar transition.)

10. Drag the current time indicator in the timeline, or click the **Play** button in the Program Monitor. If you stop the clip with the current time display at 5:10, the Timeline and the Program Monitor should look similar to Figure 10-3.

FIGURE 10-3
Preview a peel transition

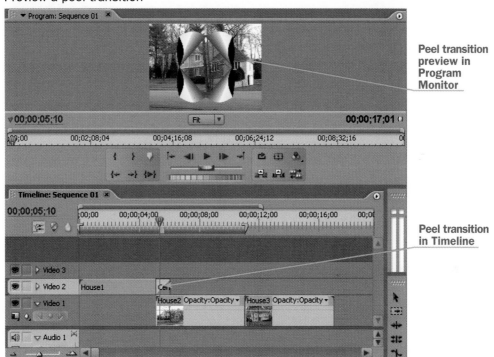

Peel transition preview in Program Monitor

Peel transition in Timeline

11. Expand the **Dissolve** video transition category, and then drag the **Cross Dissolve** transition to the Timeline. Drop it when it is centered over the cut between the House2 and House3 clips. Your program may display an alert that there is insufficient media. Click **OK** to create the transition using copied frames.

STEP-BY-STEP 10.1 Continued

12. Preview the transition. If you stop the clip with the current time display at 10:25, the Timeline and the Program Monitor should look similar to Figure 10-4.

FIGURE 10-4
Preview a dissolve transition

13. Save the changes to **Realtor**, and leave it open to use in the next exercise.

Add Effects

Video effects are changes that add a special visual or audio characteristic to your video. They do not add new content to the video. Instead, they change how the video is rendered. Many video effects are similar to effects that you add to graphics or animations. For example, you can change the contrast or brightness of video clips, apply a blur, or rotate or resize a clip. Some effects act like transitions because they affect only the beginning or end of a clip, but others affect the entire clip. For example, a Fast Blur In creates a transition-like effect of a blurred image coming into focus.

Apply Effects

You can apply an effect to any clip in a sequence, and you can apply more than one effect to a clip. Most programs come with a wide selection of video and audio effects, organized into categories such as Adjust, Distort, Stylize, and so on. Usually, there is a category

---

Extra for Experts

Adobe Premiere has a companion product called Adobe After Effects that provides additional video effects for the serious video editor.

of built-in effects called something like Presets, which includes common effects with the most typical settings. To apply an effect, you drag it to the Timeline and drop it on the clip you want to modify.

S TEP-BY-STEP 10.2

1. Display the panels you need for applying effects or transitions. In Premiere Pro, click **Window** on the Menu bar, point to **Workspace**, and then click **Effects** to display the Effects panel and the Effect Controls panel. In Premiere Elements, make sure the Effects and Transitions panel is displayed.

2. In the Effects (or Effects and Transitions) panel, expand the **Presets** category and then expand the **Blurs** category.

3. Drag the **Fast Blur In** effect to the Timeline and drop it on the **House1** clip.

4. Preview the sequence to see how the effect changes the clip. It should start blurred, and come into focus over the course of the first second of the clip. If you stop the clip when the current time display is at :20, the screen should look similar to Figure 10-5. (If a Timeline displays on the right side of the Effect Controls panel, click the **Show/Hide Timeline View** toggle to hide it.)

FIGURE 10-5
Preview a blur effect

Effect Controls panel

Blur effect preview in Program Monitor

Show/Hide Timeline View toggle

Fast Blur In effect

STEP-BY-STEP 10.2 Continued

5. Expand the **Video Effects** category and then expand the **Stylize** category. Drag the **Replicate** effect to the Timeline and drop it on the **House3** clip, in the *Video 1* track. The Replicate effect replicates the video so you see multiple columns and rows of the image in the same frame, as shown in Figure 10-6.

FIGURE 10-6
Apply a replicate effect

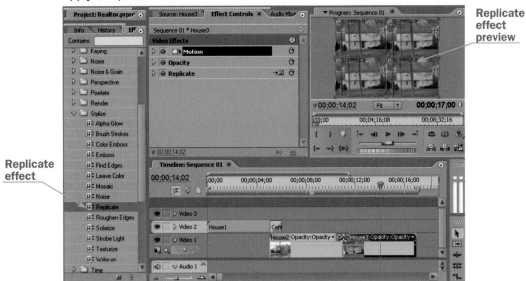

6. Preview the sequence. Save the changes and leave **Realtor** open to use in the next exercise.

Customize Effects

Usually when you apply a video effect, it uses default settings. You can modify the settings to customize the effect. For example, you may be able to change the width of a bevel or increase the amount of brightness. In Premiere Pro, you adjust settings in the Effect Controls panel, or by using a settings dialog box you access from the Effect Controls panel. In Premiere Elements, you use the Properties panel.

You may notice effects that you did not apply attached to a clip. Most programs automatically apply certain effects to all clips that you add to the Timeline. (These may be called Fixed effects.) Generally, they affect a clip's position, scale, movement, opacity, and audio volume. You can usually adjust the fixed effect settings, if necessary, but you cannot remove them.

S TEP-BY-STEP 10.3

1. In the Timeline, click the **House1** clip to select it. The effects applied to the clip display in the appropriate panel. In Premiere Pro, they display in the Effect Controls panel, as shown in Figure 10-7. In Elements, they display in the Properties panel.

FIGURE 10-7
Effects in Effect Controls panel

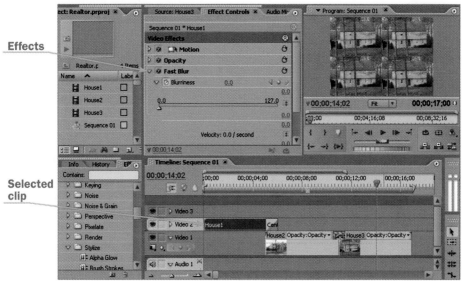

2. Position the current time indicator about 2 seconds into the **House3** clip (about **13:09** or **13:10**), and then select the command to split the clip using the Razor tool. In Premiere Pro, click **Sequence** on the Menu bar, and then click **Razor at Current Time Indicator.** In Premiere Elements, click **Timeline** on the Menu bar, and then click **Split Clip**.

3. Select the second **House3** clip in the Timeline to display its effects in the appropriate panel, and then click the **Setup** icon to the right of the Replicate effect name to display the Replicate Settings dialog box, shown in Figure 10-8.

FIGURE 10-8
Replicate Settings dialog box

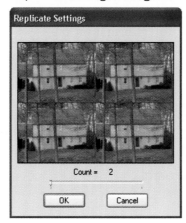

STEP-BY-STEP 10.3 Continued

4. Drag the **Count** slider to the right to set the count to **4**. This will replicate the image into four rows and four columns. Click **OK** to apply the setting.

5. Preview the sequence. The first **House3** clip should display two columns and two rows of images, and the second **House3** clip should display four columns and four rows.

> **Note**
>
> The options in an effects settings dialog box depend on the effect. The more complicated the effect, the more settings there are to adjust.

6. Save the changes to **Realtor** and leave it open to use in the next exercise.

Add Titles

You can incorporate text and graphics in your videos by creating titles. *Titles* are simply text or graphics that you create and add like a clip to a video sequence. Typically, titles are used to display information at the beginning of a video, such as the movie name, and at the end of the video, such as credits. You can also insert titles at any point in a sequence. For example, you might want to name each scene, or identify content, such as the name of a person. By default, a title is usually still, which means it is a static image, but you may create a moving title that is animated so the content moves.

Create a Still Title

To create a *still title*, you usually select the command to create the title and then key a title name to start a utility such as Titler that you use to select formatting, key the title text, or insert drawing objects. To key the text, select a tool such as Text, or Type, and then key the text in a text block. You can select formatting such as font, font styles, and alignment. In most programs you can save time by selecting from a list of text or title styles that already have formatting settings built in. You can also format the entire text block. For example, you can center it in the frame.

Depending on your program, you may also be able to set properties to scale the font, transform text and objects, and apply effects such as shadows, fills, and strokes. (These features are similar to those you use to create and format text objects in graphics and animations programs. Refer to Lesson 4 for information on working with text in a graphics program, or Lesson 7 for information on working with text in an animation program.)

Usually, the title is saved automatically when you close the Titler feature, or when you save the project file. In most programs it is added to the list of available clips. You can open the title to edit it, or to copy it to create a new title using the same settings.

> **Extra for Experts**
>
> In some programs, you can create a title based on a template, which is a model that includes font formatting as well as graphics objects designed for a particular use. For example, Premiere Pro comes with templates for different types of businesses, weddings, sports videos, education, and more. If one of the templates suits your needs, select it and then replace the sample text with your own text to create the title.

S TEP-BY-STEP 10.4

1. Click **Title** on the Menu bar, click **New Title**, and then click **Default Still**. In the Title *Name* text box, key **Intro**, and then click **OK**. The Titler panel displays. By default, it is grouped with the Titler Styles panel.

In some programs, the Title Properties panel also displays, as shown in Figure 10-9. If the current video frame displays in the Titler panel, select the command to hide it. In Premiere Pro, clear the **Show Video** check box. In Premiere Elements, click **Title** on the Menu bar, click **View**, and then click **Show Video**.

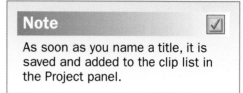

Note

As soon as you name a title, it is saved and added to the clip list in the Project panel.

FIGURE 10-9
Premiere Pro's Titler panel

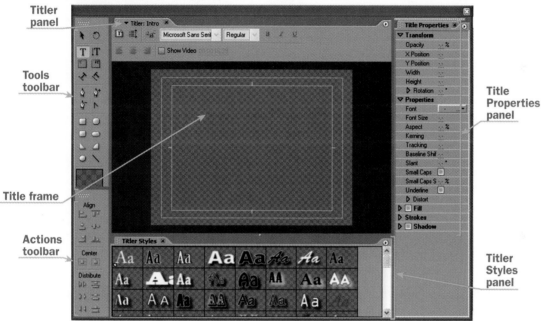

Titler panel

Tools toolbar

Title frame

Actions toolbar

Title Properties panel

Titler Styles panel

2. Click the **Type Tool.** Scroll down in the Titler Styles panel and then click the **CaslonPro Slant Blue 70** style (a sans serif font in blue with a white glow). If your program does not have the CaslonPro Slant Blue 70 style, select a different style, or set font options to create a similar effect.

3. With the Type Tool active, click in the upper-left corner of the frame in the Titler panel and key **Is house hunting**.

4. Select the command to decrease the font size by **50%**. In Premiere Pro, in the Title Properties panel, click the **Font size** value, key **50**, and then press **Enter**. In Premiere Elements, click the **Size** value on the toolbar near the top of the Titler panel, key **35** (50% of 70), and then press **Enter**. If available, click to clear the **Small Caps** check box.

5. Click in the text block to make it active and position the insertion point at the end of the line. Press **Enter** to start a new line and key **giving you**. Press **Enter** and key **blurred vision?**

STEP-BY-STEP 10.4 Continued

6. Center the text in the text block using the Center align button on the Titler panel toolbar at the top of the panel.

7. Center the text block in the title panel horizontally and vertically. For example, click the **Vertical Center** button and then click the **Horizontal Center** button. The screen should look similar to Figure 10-10.

FIGURE 10-10
Title text

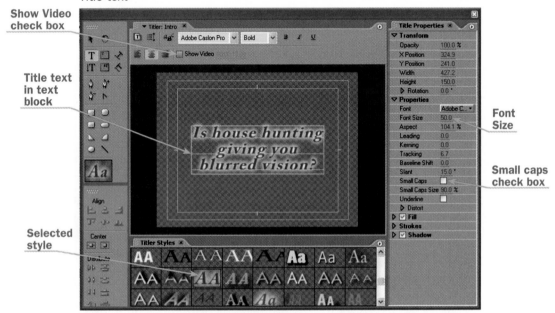

8. Save the title by restoring the default workspace or closing the Titler panel. Note that the **Intro** clip is listed with the other clips in the project.

9. Double-click the title clip name **Intro** in the Project or Media panel to open the title in the Titler panel for editing.

10. Click the **New Title Based on Current Title** button, key **Middle** in the new Title *Name* text box, and click **OK**. (If the caption is not available, close the **Intro** title, and create a new title named **Middle**. Repeat steps 2 through 4 above to select formatting options.)

11. Replace the word *blurred* on line 3 with the word **double**.

12. Restore the default workspace or close the Titler panel. The title is added to the list of clips.

13. Save the **Realtor** project file and leave it open to use in the next exercise.

Add a Title to a Sequence

Once you create a title, your program adds it to the list of clips so you can insert it into a sequence. You can simply drag it into the Timeline to position it just like you do any clip. You can trim a title to make it longer or shorter. You can even enhance a title clip using transitions and effects. A title may display over the video—so you see the video in the background—or it may display over a blank screen so it does not obscure the video content. If you want the title to display over the video, insert it in a video track over the video clip. For example, if the video is in video track 1, place the title clip in video track 2, positioned over the video.

STEP-BY-STEP 10.5

1. Drag the **Intro** title to the *Video 3* track and overlay it directly above the **House1** clip, which is in the *Video 2* track.

2. Trim two seconds off the end of the title clip so that it is only three seconds long. (Use the Trim Out tool to move the out point of the clip two seconds to the left.)

3. Drag the **Middle** title to the *Video 3* track and position it so it begins after the Center Peel transition, above the **House2** clip.

4. Preview the sequence. The titles should display over the video. If you stop the video with the current time display at **8:00**, the screen should look similar to Figure 10-11.

FIGURE 10-11
Titles in the sequence

5. Save the changes and leave **Realtor** open to use in the next exercise.

Create a Moving Title

In most programs you can animate titles to make them roll or crawl. A *roll* is an effect that causes lines of text to move vertically through the frame. A *crawl* causes a single line of text to move horizontally across the frame. When you create a new title, select the option to create either the default Roll title or the default Crawl title. Usually, you can apply the animation to an existing title by clicking the Roll/Crawl Options button in the Titler panel and then selecting the settings to apply. Instead of creating a still image title, the program creates a clip in which the text moves.

STEP-BY-STEP 10.6

1. Click **Title** on the Menu bar, click **New Title**, and then click **Default Roll**. Key **Close** in the *Name* text box and then click **OK**. This creates a new roll title named Close.

2. Select to use the same font style you used for the other two titles, then click in the upper-left corner of the frame and key **Call Clearview Realty**. Reduce the font size by **50%**, if necessary, and center the text block horizontally. If available, clear the **Small Caps** check box.

3. Create a new text block below the first, reduce the font size by **50%**, if necessary, and key **555-555-5555**. Center the text block horizontally.

4. Create a third text block, reduce the font size by **50%**, if necessary, and key **Bring Your Dreams**. Then create a fourth text block, reduce the font size to **50%**, if necessary, and key **Into Focus**. Center both blocks horizontally. The title should look similar to Figure 10-12. If necessary, click the **Selection Tool** and drag the blocks into position.

FIGURE 10-12
Text for the Roll title

STEP-BY-STEP 10.6 Continued

5. Click the **Roll/Crawl Options** button to display the Roll/Crawl Options dialog box, shown in Figure 10-13.

FIGURE 10-13
Text for the Roll title

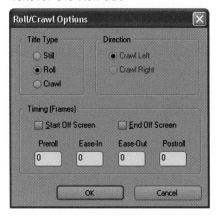

6. Select the option to start the animation off the screen. For example, select the **Start Off Screen** check box in the Timing (Frames) section. Click **OK** to apply the change.

7. Restore the default workspace, or close the Titler panel.

8. Drag the **Close** title to the Timeline and drop it on the *Video 3* track so it abuts the end of the **Middle** title.

9. Preview the sequence. The **Close** title text should scroll up from the bottom of the frame.

10. Save the changes and leave the **Realtor** project open to use in the next exercise.

Adjust Clip Speed and Duration

The default speed and duration of a clip is controlled by the source file, but you can modify the settings if you want. Modifying these settings is useful for creating effects such as slow or fast motion in a video, or for adjusting a clip to fill a set amount of time in a sequence. Usually, speed is set as a percentage of the original speed, so when it plays normally, the speed setting is 100%. Speed and duration are linked, which means that if you change one setting, the other is automatically adjusted. For example, if you change the speed to 200% to cause it to play at twice the original speed, the duration is cut in half. You can unlink the settings if you want to change one without affecting the other. In most programs you can also select to play a clip in reverse.

Most programs have a dialog box where you can set the speed and duration settings. In Premiere Pro, select Clip on the Menu bar and then click Speed/Duration to display the Speed/Duration dialog box. In Premiere Elements, select Clip on the Menu bar and then click Time Stretch.

STEP-BY-STEP 10.7

1. Select the **Close** title in the Timeline, and then select the command to display the dialog box where you can adjust the speed and duration settings. In Premiere Pro, click **Clip** on the Menu bar, and then click **Speed/Duration**. In Premiere Elements, click **Clip** on the Menu bar and then click **Time Stretch**. The dialog box should look similar to Figure 10-14.

FIGURE 10-14
Clip Speed/Duration dialog box

2. Change the Duration to **5:26**—this should extend the title clip through the end of the **House3** video. Notice that the Speed automatically decreases as you enter the duration value. Click **OK** to apply the change.

3. Preview the sequence. Now, the **Close** title extends to the end of the video. (If necessary trim the **Close** title so it displays through the last frame of the video.)

4. Select the **Close** title, if necessary, and display the dialog box where you can set speed and duration, again.

5. If available, click the **Reverse Speed** check box to play the clip in reverse, and then click **OK**. (This option may not be available in Premiere Elements. If you are using Premiere Elements, skip to Step 8.)

6. Preview the sequence. The **Close** title plays in reverse, scrolling off the bottom of the frame.

7. Use the **Undo** command to reverse the previous action, or deselect the option to play the clip in reverse.

8. Save the changes to the **Realtor** project and then close it. Close your video-editing program.

SUMMARY

In this lesson, you learned:

■ You can greatly enhance the quality of your video by adding video effects, transitions, and titles.

■ Just like trimming and sequencing your clips on the timeline, video effects and transitions do not change the original source clips. Instead, they can be viewed as instructions for how to process the original clips to produce the final video.

■ One of the benefits of digital video is that you can easily dress it up by applying changes to the actual bitmap images.

■ You can smooth out the flow between clips and make a video more interesting by adding transitions.

■ When you capture, import, or select portions of clips, you should make sure to include handles at the beginning and end of the clip to use for transitions.

■ You can position a transition centered over a cut line, or at the beginning or end of a clip. You can even overlap clips on multiple video tracks to make some transitions more effective.

■ Video effects do not add new content to the video, but they change how the video is rendered.

■ You can apply an effect to any clip, and you can apply more than one effect to a clip.

■ You can modify effect settings to customize the effect.

■ You can create titles to add text and graphics objects to a video.

■ You can create a still title or one that rolls or crawls through the frame.

■ Creating and formatting titles is similar to working with text in a graphics or animation program.

■ You can position a title so that it overlays the video.

■ Clip speed and duration are usually linked, so if you change one, the other one adjusts automatically.

■ By changing clip speed and duration you can create slow motion or fast motion effects.

■ Most programs have an option that lets you play a clip in reverse.

VOCABULARY *Review*

Define the following terms:

Crawl	Peel	Still title
Cross dissolve	Roll	Titles
Cut line	Single-sided transition	Transition
Double-sided transition	Slide	Video effects
Handle		

REVIEW *Questions*

TRUE / FALSE

Circle T if the statement is true and F if the statement is false.

T   F   1. You must never overlap clips in different video tracks.

T   F   2. Video effects add graphics symbols to video frames.

T   F   3. You can apply more than one video effect to a clip.

T   F   4. You can modify settings to customize a video effect.

T   F   5. Titles are usually only used at the end of a video.

T   F   6. You cannot change the speed of a clip without changing its duration.

T   F   7. In most programs, transitions obscure some video content.

T   F   8. Most programs automatically apply certain effects to all clips that are added to the Timeline.

T   F   9. You cannot edit a title once it has been added to a sequence.

T   F   10. Titles can be displayed over the video so you see the video in the background.

WRITTEN QUESTIONS

Write a brief answer to each of the following questions.

1. Why is it important to include handles on clips?

2. What is the difference between a still title and an animated title?

3. What type of effects can you create by changing the clip speed or duration?

4. What are two reasons for adding transitions to a video?

5. Give examples of at least three types of video effects.

FILL IN THE BLANK

Complete the following sentences by writing the correct word or words in the blanks provided.

1. A(n) _____-sided transition involves the end of one clip and the beginning of the next.

2. A(n) _____-sided transition involves only the beginning or end of one clip.

3. A(n) _____ is an extra frame (or frames) before the in point or after the out point of a clip.

4. The _____ line is the break between clips.

5. A(n) _____ is an effect that causes lines of text to move vertically through a video frame.

6. A(n) _____ is an effect that causes a single line of text to move horizontally across a video frame.

7. A(n)_____ title is a static image that does not move.

8. To quickly select formatting settings for title text, select a text or title _____.

9. To play a clip backwards, select the option to _____ the speed.

10. Usually, clip speed is set as a(n) _____ of the original speed.

PROJECTS

PROJECT 10-1

Before beginning the exercise, copy the source video files **Project10-1a, Project10-1b,** and **Project10-1c** from the folder where the Data files for this lesson are stored into the folder where you will store the solution files.

1. Launch your video editing program and create a new project. If necessary, select the **DV-NTSC Standard 32kHz** present. Save the project as **Day Out 1**.

2. Import the source files **Project10-1a, Project10-1b,** and **Project10-1c** from your solutions folder into the project.

3. Rename the clips as follows:

   Project10-1a to **Walk1**

   Project10-1b to **Walk2**

   Project10-1c to **Walk3**

4. Zoom in on the Timeline. Drag the **Walk1** clip to the Timeline and then drop it at the beginning of the *Video 2* track. Note that the clips do not have separate audio tracks.

5. Drag the **Walk2** clip to the Timeline and drop it on the *Video 1* track so that it starts about 5 seconds in from the beginning of the Timeline, which is about 1 second before the end of the **Walk1** clip.

6. Drag the **Walk3** clip to the Timeline and drop it on the *Video 1* track so it abuts the end of the **Walk2** clip.

7. In the panel that lists video transitions, expand the **Video Transitions** category and then click to expand the **Wipe** category.

8. Click and drag the **Band Wipe** transition to the Timeline, and drop it when it is aligned with the cut at the end of the **Walk1** clip, in the *Video 2* track.

9. Click and drag the **Gradient Wipe** transition to the Timeline, and drop it when it is centered over the cut line between the **Walk2** and **Walk3** clips. A Gradient Wipe Settings dialog box may display. Click **OK** to accept the default values. Your program may display an alert that there is insufficient media. Click **OK** to create the transition using copied frames.

10. Preview the sequence to see the transitions.

11. Save the changes to the **Day Out 1** project and then close it. Leave your video-editing program open to use in the next exercise.

PROJECT 10-2

Before beginning the exercise, copy the source audio file **Project10-2b** from the folder where the Data files for this lesson are stored into the folder where you will store the solution files.

1. Open the project file **Project10-2a** from the Data files for this lesson and save it as **Day Out 2**.

2. Display the panel that lists video effects, and then click to expand the **Presets** category.

3. Expand the **Solarizes** category.

4. Drag the **Solarize In** effect to the Timeline and drop it on the **Walk1** clip.

5. Drag the **Solarize Out** effect to the Timeline and drop it on the **Walk3** clip.

6. Preview the sequence to see the effects.

7. Import the sound file **Project10-2b** from the Data files into the **Day Out 2** project, and rename it **Music**.

8. Overlay the **Music** clip on the *Audio 1* track at the beginning of the timeline.

9. Preview the sequence to see the effects.

10. Use the Trim Out tool to trim the end of the **Music** clip by about 10:24 so it ends at the same time as the video (15:27).

11. Preview the sequence.

12. Save the changes to the **Day Out 2** project and close it. Leave your video editing program open to use in the next exercise.

PROJECT 10-3

1. Open the project file **Project10-3** from the Data files for this lesson and save it as **Day Out 3**.

2. Create a new still title named **Open** by doing the following:
   A. Click **Title** on the Menu bar.
   B. Click **New Title**.
   C. Click **Default Still**.
   D. In the Title *Name* text box, key **Open**.
   E. Click **OK**.

3. Scroll down in the Titler Styles panel and select a title style that has a serif font in white with a red glow (Caslon Red 84). If your program does not have the Caslon Red 84 style, select a different style, or set font options to create a similar effect.

4. Click in the upper-left corner of the frame in the Titler panel and key **A Dog's**, press **Enter** and key **Day Out**.

5. Center the text block horizontally and vertically.

6. Create a new title based on the **Open** title and name it **Trail Text**. To do this, do the following:
   A. Click the **New Title Based on Current Title** button.
   B. In the Title *Name* text box, key **Trail Text**.
   C. Click **OK**.

7. Replace the text on the first line with the text **On the** and replace the text on the second line with the text **Trail**.

8. Center the text in the text block and center the text block horizontally and vertically in the frame. Restore the default workspace, or close the Titler panel.

9. Make sure the current time indicator is at the beginning of the Timeline, and then insert the **Open** title on the *Video 1* track at the beginning of the Timeline. In Premiere Pro, to insert the title instead of overlaying, press and hold **Ctrl** while you drag it to the Timeline. In Premiere Elements, you may have to insert the clip at the beginning of the *Video 2* track first, and then move it to the *Video 1* track.

10. Move the **Music** clip on *Audio 1* track to the left, so it starts about 2 seconds into the sequence.

11. Place the **Trail Text** title on the *Video 2* track abutting the end of the **Band Wipe** transition (above the **Walk2** clip which is in the *Video 1* track).

12. Trim about 3 seconds off the **Trail Text** title so it only plays for 2 seconds.

13. Create a new title based on the Roll default and name it **Close**.
    A. Click **Title** on the Menu bar.
    B. Click **New Title**.
    C. Click **Default Roll**.
    D. In the Title *Name* text box, key **Close**.
    E. Click **OK**.

14. Select a title style that has a serif font in white, such as **GaramondPro OffWhite 28**. If your program does not have the Garamond Pro OffWhite 28 style, select a different style, or set font options to create a similar effect.

15. Click in the upper-left corner of the frame and key **Produced by**. Create a new text block below the first text block and key your own name. Create a new text block below the second text block and key today's date.

16. If the text is too large to fit across the panel, change the font size of each text block to approximately **70%**. (Depending upon the length of your name, you may need to use a smaller percentage.) Align the middle text block in the vertical center of the frame. Position the top block about halfway between the top of the frame and the middle block, and position the bottom block about halfway between the middle block and the bottom of the frame. Center all blocks horizontally.

17. Set the Roll options to start the roll off the screen, then restore the default workspace or close the Titler feature.

18. Place the **Close** title on the *Video 1* track so it abuts the end of the **Walk3** clip.

19. Trim out the **Music** clip so it ends at about **28:12**. If you cannot trim out the clip all the way to 28:12, trim it as far as you can.

20. Edit the duration of the **Close** title so it extends as long as the **Music** clip, but keep the speed at **100%**. (If the **Music** clip ends at 28:12, the duration of the **Close** title clip should be 7:15.)

21. Preview the sequence.

22. Save the changes and close the **Day Out 3** project. Close your video-editing program.

 WEB PROJECT

What types of jobs are there that use video-editing and production skills? Use the Internet to research the industry to learn about employment opportunities. Find out what type of education is required for the jobs, and how much experience is necessary. Look up starting salary or hourly pay, as well. Record the information that you locate in a word processing document or spreadsheet. Write a report of at least 700 words about the job possibilities, citing your research. You might compare different jobs, or focus on one job. Present the report to your class.

TEAMWORK PROJECT

As you know from watching television commercials, even a 20-second video can convey an effective message. However, the commercial you think is effective may not seem very good to your grandparents. That's because different advertisements target different audiences.

As a team, discuss the type of content that might affect who responds to an advertisement. For example, music, actors, location, humor, and clothing are all selected because they appeal to a specific audience. Select at least three video advertisements that you can analyze. You might be able to record them from TV or locate them on the Internet. (Many Web sites play video advertisements. Try looking on television station Web sites or movie studio Web sites.) Assign team members a content category, and then watch the videos and track the content that you think is geared to a specific audience. Record your observations by taking notes, or by entering information in a spreadsheet or a word processing document. When you have completed the analysis, develop an audience profile for each advertisement, which means write down the characteristics of the target audience, and explain why the advertisement would appeal to this audience. Characteristics might include age group, gender, educational level, and ethnic background. Include specific examples from the videos.

Consider how you might change the advertisement to appeal to a different audience. Write a new script and use a video camera to record the footage you need to produce the new advertisement. Capture the footage into your video editing program and assemble the advertisement. Preview it for you class, and see if they can identify the new target audience.

CRITICAL *Thinking*

One of the most interesting things about digital video is that you can use non-linear editing techniques. Recall that non-linear editing means that you can use any part of the video in any order. That means that theoretically you can create many different movies using the same original source clip. Think about what type of source video you might be able to use to create different movies. Does it have to be long? Does it have to be varied? What type of content would be best? Use a digital video camcorder to record at least two minutes of video. It may be a continuous scene, or you may record different, shorter scenes that add up to two minutes. Capture the video into your video editing program and then see how many different sequences you can create using the same source. Use transitions, effects, and titles to enhance your videos. Let your classmates preview the sequences and provide feedback on how you might improve, or suggestions for other sequences you might create. Improve the sequences, and then invite your classmates to preview them all. Vote on which sequence is the best.

PUBLISHING VIDEO

OBJECTIVES

Upon completion of this lesson, you should be able to:

- Understand Video Exporting.
- Export to a movie file.
- Play a movie file.
- Publish for the Web.
- Preview a DVD.
- Export to a DVD.
- Export to a DVD-compatible file.
- Publish to a CD-compatible file.
- Export a still image.

Estimated Time: 1.5 hours

VOCABULARY

AutoPlay DVD

CD burner

Data rate

DVD burner

Progressive download

Sample

Sample rate

Streaming video server

SVCD

VCD

Your video-editing program gives you the tools you need to develop, edit, and enhance video projects, but you cannot use it to display the completed videos for all to see. For that, you must export the video out of the video-editing program in a format that other applications can display.

- You can export a video as a movie file so others can view it on a computer using a player program such as Windows Media Player or QuickTime Player.

- You can export a video file so you can import it into a different program, such as a presentation or animation program.

- You can publish a video on a DVD so others can view it on a computer or television using a DVD player.

- You can export to a streaming video file so you can distribute it via the Internet.

- You can export video frames to still images that you can use in other videos or in documentation such as a brochure or poster.

- You can even export the file back to videotape.

In this lesson you learn how to export video in different formats so you can publish and distribute it.

Understand Video Exporting

When you export a video file, your video-editing program renders the video frames, compresses them, and then writes them as the new file. In most programs, you may select to export a single frame, one or more clips, or the entire sequence. The command for exporting is usually found on the File menu, and a submenu offers a choice of export types, such as exporting to a movie file, to a DVD, or to an audio-only file. Depending on many different factors including the number of frames, the frame size, the frame rate, and the selected codec, exporting may take a long time.

Before you export a video from your video-editing program, you should consider what you plan to do with the exported file, because that will help determine the export method and file format you should use. For example, if you plan to incorporate the video into a file created with another program, such as an animation or a presentation, you must make sure the exported file is compatible with the other program. If you plan to distribute the completed video, you need to consider the delivery method. Will you use a DVD or CD? Do you want to stream it on the Web? With most video-editing programs, you can select from a list of formats designed for a specific purpose or delivery method. The following are some of the most common delivery methods.

- To distribute the video on a DVD, you will probably use the MPEG-2 format, which is the industry standard for commercial DVDs. In addition, most video-editing programs have a command that lets you burn the video directly to a DVD, using standard formatting options.

- To deliver the video on a CD-ROM, you will probably use the MPEG-1 format, which is the industry standard for video CDs. Some video CDs use MPEG-2. Usually, you will export the file and then use a CD-burner program to copy it to the CD.

- To deliver the video over the Internet, you would select a format that is optimized for progressive download or for streaming, and is compatible with common Web media players, such as Macromedia Flash Video, Microsoft Windows Media, RealNetworks RealMedia, or Apple QuickTime. *Progressive download* means that the video begins to play before it is completely downloaded. Streaming video is delivered without downloading the file to a disk.

- To create an all-purpose movie file that you can use in other programs, you may simply use a common video format such as AVI or QuickTime that can be used by many programs across many platforms.

With most video-editing programs, you can customize video export settings to optimize the file. The available settings depend on the selected preset, or the type of file you select to create. Table 11-1 describes some of the common video export settings.

> **Note**
>
> Some codecs and file types do not support certain video features, such as transitions, effects, and titles. For example, titles are not exported when you export to an MPEG format.

TABLE 11-1
Common video export settings

SETTING	DESCRIPTION
Compressor	You can select the specific codec to use to compress the file. If you plan to use the video in a different program, you should select a compatible codec.
Color depth	Depending on the selected codec, you may be able to specify an 8-bit (256-color) palette for matching the colors on a Web page or in a presentation.
Frame size	You can specify the frame size in pixels of the exported video (some codecs only support specific frame sizes). Also, you should select 4:3 Aspect to constrain the frame size to the 4:3 aspect ratio used by conventional television. Keep in mind that increasing the frame size displays more detail but creates a larger file.
Frame rate	You can choose the number of frames per second (some codecs only support a specific set of frame rates). Keep in mind that a higher frame rate may result in a smoother playback, but it also creates a larger file.
Quality	Depending on the codec and file type, you may be able to set the picture quality. Lowering the picture quality may reduce the file size.
Data rate	The **data rate** controls the amount of video information that must be processed each second during playback. Depending on the codec, you may be able to set a maximum data rate.

Other factors to consider include file size and quality. The highest quality video files are very large, and even when compressed they will require significant computer resources to display properly. Consider that an .avi formatted video file less than *50 seconds* long may be nearly *200 MB* in size! A standard CD only stores up to 700 MB of data. Keep in mind, however, that when you select options that reduce the file size, you usually sacrifice quality. For example, you can reduce the frame size to create a smaller file, but then the video displays onscreen in a smaller window. This may not be an issue if you deliver it over the Web or as part of a presentation file, but it will be if you plan to show the video as a standalone program on a television or computer monitor. Likewise, you can lower the resolution or frame rate, but both options will result in poorer quality.

Finally, another consideration should be the audience's hardware and software. For example, if you are distributing the video on a CD, you may want to reduce the data rate so that even someone using an older, single- or double-speed CD-ROM drive can view a smooth video. You may also want to select a format that is compatible with many programs and platforms, such as Window Media or QuickTime.

> **Hot Tip**
>
> Try to export to a frame size and frame rate that are the same or smaller than the project settings you've used to edit the video. If you choose something larger, the rendered video often has a blocky, "pixilated" look.

Export to a Movie File

You can export a video from your video editing program to a movie file to play it in a media player program such as Windows Media Player, RealNetworks RealPlayer, or QuickTime Player. You can also use the movie file in a file that you create with another, compatible program such as an animation or presentation program.

Export a Movie File

The command to export a movie file is usually on the File > Export submenu. Once you select to export to a movie file, a dialog box such as Export Movie displays, so you can name the export file and select a storage location. From this dialog box, you can export the video using the default settings, which are usually based on the settings you select when you create the project file, or you can open a dialog box where you can modify the settings. The settings are generally divided into four categories:

- *General* settings include options such as the codec file type and the frame range. There may be other general settings, such as whether to export audio, and whether to embed the exported file in a project file.

- *Video* settings include the options described in the previous section.

- *Keyframe and rendering settings* include options for optimizing the export for progressive or interlaced video and for still images.

- *Audio* settings include options such as the audio codec file type, the sample rate, type, and the number of audio channels to include in the exported file. An audio *sample* is the smallest unit of a digitized sound, typically an 8- or 16-bit value that represents the audio signal at a particular moment. The *sample rate* is the number of samples per second used to represent the sound. A higher rate increases the audio quality and the file size; lower sample rates decrease quality and file size.

> **Note**
>
> In the following exercise, you export a movie file to play in Apple's QuickTime player. If you do not have the QuickTime player installed, ask your instructor if you should download it (it is available for free). If you only have Windows Media Player available on your system, you will have to export to an AVI file format. The video settings options will not be the same, and the resulting movie file will be significantly larger than the QuickTime file.

> **Note**
>
> All the step-by-steps in this lesson use Adobe Premiere Pro 2.0, a video program that is available for both Microsoft Windows and Apple Macintosh systems. If you have a different video-editing program, you may have to adapt the instructions to complete the exercises.

STEP-BY-STEP 11.1

In this exercise you will export a video to a movie file. Before beginning this exercise, copy the video source files Step11-1b, Step11-1c, and Step11-1d from your Data files folder to your Solution files folder.

1. Start your video-editing program and open the project **Step11-1a** from the Data files for this lesson. If necessary, locate and identify the source files as follows:

CLIP NAME	SOURCE VIDEO FILE NAME
House1	Step11-1b
House2	Step11-1c
House3	Step11-1d

2. Save the project as **CVRealty**.

3. Select the Timeline, click **File** on the Menu bar, point to **Export**, and then click **Movie**. A dialog box such as **Export Movie** opens, which allows you to export the sequence to a movie file. It should look similar to Figure 11-1.

FIGURE 11-1
Export Movie dialog box

4. Click **Settings** to display a dialog box where you can customize the settings.

5. Click the **File Type** drop-down arrow and then click **QuickTime**.

STEP-BY-STEP 11.1 Continued

6. Verify that the range settings include the entire sequence (or Timeline), and that the options to export the video and audio are both selected. If there is an option to add the exported file to the project, deselect it. The dialog box should look similar to Figure 11-2.

FIGURE 11-2
General settings in the Export Movie Settings dialog box

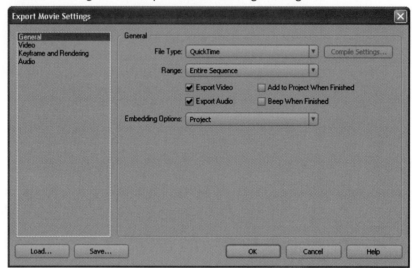

7. Click **Video** in the list on the left side of the dialog box to change to the Video settings page.

8. Click the **Compressor** drop-down arrow and then click **Indeo® video 5.1**, if it is available. Alternatively, select a similar compressor, such as **Intel Indeo Video 4.4**.

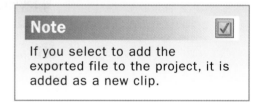

Note

If you select to add the exported file to the project, it is added as a new clip.

9. Click the **Frame Rate** drop-down arrow and then click **23.976**.

10. Drag the Quality slider to **50%**, or key **50** in the Quality text box. The dialog box should look similar to Figure 11-3.

STEP-BY-STEP 11.1 Continued

FIGURE 11-3
Video settings in the Export Movie Settings dialog box

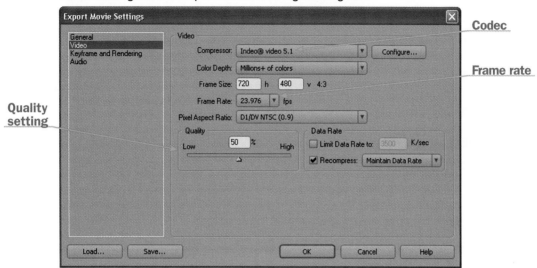

11. Click **OK** to close the Export Movie Settings dialog box and return to the Export Movie dialog box.

12. If necessary, navigate to the folder where you store the solutions for this lesson. In the *File name* box, replace the default name by keying **CVMovie.mov**. Click **Save** to export the file. This may take a few minutes during which time a progress dialog box displays. When the export is complete, the **CVRealty** project remains open in your video-editing program. Minimize your program, but leave it open to use in later exercises.

Hot Tip

Consult your program's Help system for information about specific export settings.

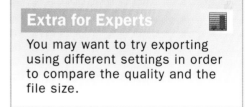

Extra for Experts

You may want to try exporting using different settings in order to compare the quality and the file size.

Play a Movie File

To play the movie file, open it in a media player, such as Windows Media Player or the QuickTime player. To open the movie in your system's default media player, use Windows to open the folder where the movie file is stored, and then double-click the file icon. To open it in a different media player, right-click the file icon, point to Open With, and then click the media player you want to use.

STEP-BY-STEP 11.2

1. Use Windows to locate and open the folder where you have stored the solution files for this lesson.

2. Double-click the **CVMovie.mov** file icon. The video file opens in the QuickTime player. (If you do not have QuickTime installed, a message may display prompting you to download the free QuickTime player program. Ask your instructor for permission, and if it is approved, follow the prompts to download the program.)

> **Note** ☑
>
> QuickTime may open with its first screen as an upgrade screen. You should choose not to upgrade to Pro.

3. Click **Play** to play the video. The final frame should look similar to Figure 11-4.

FIGURE 11-4
CVMovie.mov file in the QuickTime player

4. Close the QuickTime player, and then restore your video-editing program window. Leave it open to use in the next exercise.

Publish for the Web

To prepare a video file for distribution over the Internet, you must export it to a format that is optimized for streaming or progressive downloading. You can then distribute it by storing it on a *streaming video server*, which is a computer on the Internet configured to deliver video files by streaming or progressive downloading. There are a number of such formats, including Flash Video, QuickTime, RealMedia, and Windows Media.

Some video-editing programs come with a feature that lets you select a file format and then select a built-in style or preset that applies typical export settings for that format. In Adobe Premiere Pro, the feature is the Adobe Media Encoder. You may be able to customize certain settings within the preset before exporting the file, if you want. Other programs, such as Adobe Premiere Elements, have commands for selecting an Internet-compatible format directly on the Export menu. You may then be able to open an Export Settings dialog box in which you can customize the settings. Depending on the format you select, you may be able to preview the video on your computer in a media player.

STEP-BY-STEP 11.3

In this exercise you will export a sequence from your video-editing program to a Web-compatible format.

1. Click **File** on the Menu bar, point to **Export**, and then click **Adobe Media Encoder**. If Adobe Media Encoder is not available, select an option such as **Windows Media**, and then skip to step 3.

2. Click the **Format** drop-down arrow and then click **Windows Media** if necessary.

Did You Know?

In the Adobe Media Encoder Export Settings dialog box, when you click the Format drop-down arrow the list of available formats is usually divided by a horizontal line. The formats above the line are usually used to export files for distribution on DVDs or CDs; the formats below the line are usually used to export files for distribution on the Web or for movie files.

STEP-BY-STEP 11.3 Continued

3. Verify that the *Range* settings include the **Entire Sequence**. Click the **Preset** drop-down arrow and then click **WM9 NTSC streaming**. This is the preset to export a file optimized to stream in Windows Media Player 9 in NTSC format. Your program loads the settings associated with the preset, as shown in Figure 11-5. If you are using Premiere Elements, click the **Advanced** button to display the Export Settings dialog box.

FIGURE 11-5
WM9 NTSC streaming preset in the Export Settings dialog box

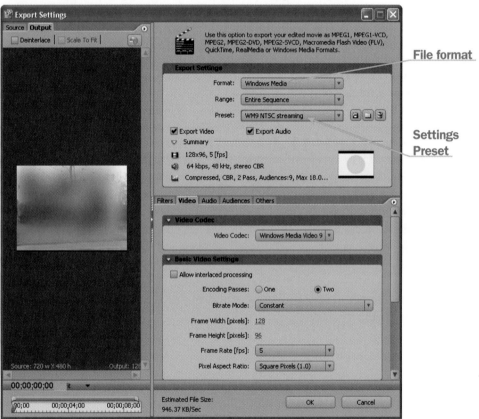

4. Deselect the option to export the audio (because there is no audio in the sequence, you do not have to export it). Notice that as soon as you change a setting, the *Preset* box displays *Custom* instead of the preset you selected in step 3.

5. If available, select to use only one encoding pass instead of two. (Two passes may increase the quality of the exported file, but it takes twice as long to process.) You may want to look over some of the other available settings, but do not change any more at this time.

6. Click **OK** or **Save** to apply the settings and close the dialog box. (If you are using Elements, a dialog box may prompt you to name the preset. Key **wma no audio**, and then click **OK** twice.) A dialog box in which you select a storage location and name the export file displays.

STEP-BY-STEP 11.3 Continued

7. If necessary, navigate to the folder where you store the solutions for this lesson. Click in the *File name* text box and replace the default name by keying **CVStream.wmv**. Click **Save** to export the file. This may take a few minutes, during which time a progress dialog box displays. When the export is complete, the **CVRealty** project remains open in your video-editing program. Minimize your program, but leave it open.

8. Use Windows to locate and open the folder where you have stored the solution files for this lesson.

9. Double-click the **CVStream.wmv** file icon. The video file opens in Windows Media Player and begins to play. If you do not have Windows Media Player installed, right-click the icon, point to **Open With**, and select a media player that you have available.

10. Close Windows Media Player and then restore your video-editing program window. Leave it open to use in the next exercise.

Publish to a DVD

When you want to distribute your video on a disk, you can burn it on a DVD. Some programs—including Premiere Pro—have a feature that lets you export and burn the DVD directly. Your audience can then play the disc using a DVD player connected to a monitor or television.

A standard DVD stores 5.2 gigabytes of data, which is enough to play more than two hours of video. The standard DVD frame size is 740 by 480 pixels, and the frame rate is usually 29.97 frames per second, which aligns with the standard television frame rate. The format for video stored on a DVD is MPEG-2. If your program does not support burning a video directly to a DVD, skip this section.

Preview a DVD

Some programs let you preview a DVD before you burn it on to a disc. The preview usually has video controls that you can use to play, pause, stop, fast forward, rewind, and step through the video. By default, most programs create an *AutoPlay DVD*, which starts playing the movie automatically, but you may be able to select to create a DVD that has menus that the viewer can use to start the video, or to select an option such as a scene or special feature. The menus link to markers in the video sequence; if there are no markers, your program will create them at logical spots, such as a cut line between clips. If you choose to create menus, you may have to select from a list of built-in menu templates. The templates are formatted with a layout, text, and graphics. When you preview a DVD formatted to use menus, you can usually test the menus in the preview window using the mouse. If your program does not support previewing a DVD, skip this section.

S TEP-BY-STEP 11.4

1. Click **Window** on the Menu bar and then click **DVD Layout** to display the DVD Layout panel, as shown in Figure 11-6.

FIGURE 11-6
DVD Layout panel

2. Click **Preview DVD** to display the Preview DVD window.

3. Click **Play/Pause Toggle** to preview the DVD. When the double vision title displays, click **Stop**. The preview should look similar to Figure 11-7.

STEP-BY-STEP 11.4 Continued

FIGURE 11-7
DVD preview

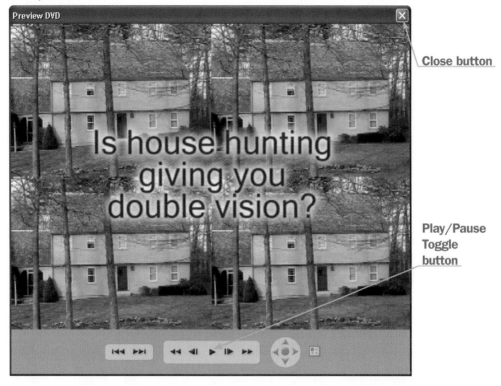

4. Click **Play/Pause Toggle** to resume playing the video. When it is finished, click the **Close** button in the upper-right corner of the window to close the preview. The DVD Layout panel displays.

5. Click **Change Template** to display the DVD Templates dialog box.

6. Click **Apply a Template for a DVD with Menus** option.

7. Select the first available template in the list, and then click **OK**.

8. You may see a Missing DVD Markers dialog box. If so, click **Yes** to automatically create DVD scene markers. Then you will see the Automatically Set DVD Scene Markers dialog box. Select **At Each Scene**, if necessary, and then click **OK**.

STEP-BY-STEP 11.4 Continued

9. Select the command to preview the DVD. The preview window displays the menu you selected. It should look similar to Figure 11-8, depending on the template you selected in step 7. Sound or music associated with the template may play, as well.

FIGURE 11-8
A DVD Main Menu

Play Movie link

Scene Selection link

Menu formatted with a template

10. Use the mouse to click the link to **Scene Selection**. The preview should display links to the clips in the video sequence, as shown in Figure 11-9.

STEP-BY-STEP 11.4 Continued

FIGURE 11-9
A DVD Scene Selection menu

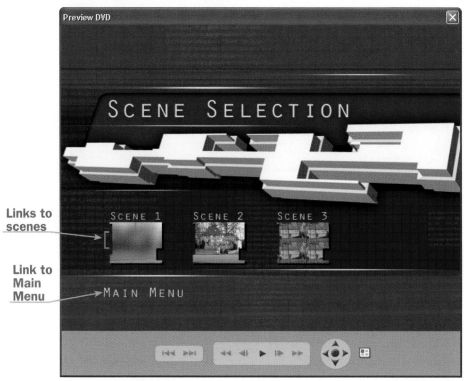

Links to scenes

Link to Main Menu

11. Click the link to the **Main Menu**, and then click the link to play the movie. When the movie is finished, close the preview window.

12. Click **Change Template**, click **Autoplay DVD with no Menus**, and then click **OK**.

13. Close the DVD Layout panel and leave the **CVRealty** project open to use in the next exercise.

Export to a DVD

If your program has a feature that lets you burn a video on a DVD, you must have a DVD burner correctly set up and installed for use with your computer. A *DVD burner* is a drive that writes data on to a DVD using a laser to burn the data on the disc. You must also have a blank, writable DVD.

When you select the command to export the video to a DVD, the program looks for and detects the necessary hardware, and loads the default preset for formatting the video for a DVD. It then displays a dialog box in which you can enter a name for the DVD and select options such

> **Note** ✓
>
> You may be able to burn the DVD directly from the DVD preview window. For example, in Adobe Premiere Pro, click Burn DVD to display the Burn DVD dialog box. Follow the steps in the next exercise to complete the process.

as the number of copies to make. You can also access a dialog box where you can modify the settings, if you want. If your program does not detect a DVD burner, you may be able to store the encoded files in a folder, which you can then take to a computer equipped with a DVD burner for processing.

STEP-BY-STEP 11.5

In this exercise you will export a video to a DVD from your video-editing program.

1. Make sure the Timeline is active, click **File** on the Menu bar, point to **Export**, and then click **Export to DVD**. Your program checks for an installed DVD burner, and then displays a dialog box similar to the one in Figure 11-10.

FIGURE 11-10
Burn DVD dialog box

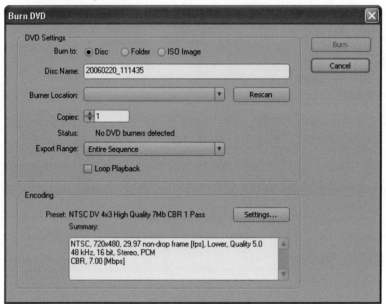

2. In the *Disc Name* text box, replace the default name with the name **CVDVD**. If you do not have a DVD burner, select the option to export to a folder (4.7 GB, if available), and key the folder name CVDVD. If necessary, browse to select to store the folder in the location where you store the solution files for this lesson.

3. If available, verify that the *Range* includes the **Entire Sequence**, and then click **Settings**. Set the Preset to **NTSC DV 16:9 High Quality 4 Mb VBR 2 Pass**. Click **OK** to return to the Burn DVD dialog box. If the Range and Settings options are not available, skip to step 4.

4. Make sure there is a blank, writable DVD in your DVD burner, and then click **Burn**. The process may take a while during which time a progress dialog box displays. When it is complete, click **Close** to close the progress dialog box. Your video-editing program remains open. Leave it open for the next exercise.

5. Insert the DVD in a DVD drive on your computer (or in a DVD player attached to a television monitor). The video should play automatically.

Export to a DVD-compatible File

If you do not have a DVD burner, you can export a video to a file formatted for a DVD so that you can transport it to a different computer or to a service bureau where it can be burned to a DVD. To export a DVD-compatible file, you select the command to export the file, select the format—MPEG-2—and then customize the settings. You may be able to preview the video file in a media player that supports MPEG-2 video. In Premiere Pro, you use the same Adobe Media Encoder feature to export a file for a DVD that you use to export a file into a Web-compatible format. In Premiere Elements, you select the MPEG format from the Export menu.

S TEP-BY-STEP 11.6

In this exercise, you export a sequence in a DVD-compatible format from your video-editing program.

1. Click **File** on the Menu bar, point to **Export**, and then click **Adobe Media Encoder**. If Adobe Media Encoder is not available, select an option such as **MPEG** and then skip to step 3.

2. Click the **Format** drop-down arrow and then click **MPEG2**.

> **Note** ☑
>
> If your program does not have a feature similar to the Adobe Media Encoder, the options for exporting a file for a DVD may be available directly from the File > Export submenu.

3. Verify that the *Range* settings include the **Entire Sequence**. Select the **NTSC MPEG-2 Generic** preset and deselect the Export Audio check box. If you are using Premiere Elements, click the **Advanced** button to display the Export Settings dialog box.

4. Set the Frame Rate to **23.976**, set the Bitrate Encoding to **VBR, 1 Pass**, and then click **OK** or **Save** to apply the settings and close the dialog box. (If you are using Elements, a dialog box may prompt you to name the preset. Key **mpg dvd**, and then click **OK** twice.) The Save File dialog box, in which you select a storage location and name the export file, displays.

> **Hot Tip** ◎
>
> You may need to scroll down in the Export Settings dialog box in order to see the Bitrate Setting options.

5. If necessary, navigate to the folder where you store the solutions for this lesson. Click in the *File name* text box if necessary and replace the default name by keying **CVMPG2**. Click **Save** to export the file. This may take a few minutes during which time a progress dialog box displays. When the export is complete, the **CVRealty** project remains open in your video-editing program. Minimize your program, but leave it open.

6. Use Windows to locate and open the folder where you have stored the solution files for this lesson.

STEP-BY-STEP 11.6 Continued

7. Double-click the **CVMPG2.m2v** file icon. The video file opens in Windows Media Player (or a different DVD player program) and begins to play. If it does not open, click **File** in the Windows Media Player window and then click **Open**, locate and select the **CVMPG2.m2v** file, and then click the **Open** button. A dialog box may display, informing you that even though the file extension is not recognized, Windows Media Player may be able to play the file. Click **Yes** to play the file.

8. Close Windows Media Player and then restore your video-editing program window. Leave it open to use in the next exercise.

> **Note**
>
> Premiere Pro might include an eXtensible Metadata Platform (XMP) file with an exported MPEG-1 or MPEG-2 file. The file has the same name as the MPEG file, with an .xmp file extension. Metadata is descriptive file information that can be searched and processed by a computer. You do not need it to play the video. Similarly, Elements may include an XMPSES file.

Publish to a CD-Compatible File

You can also export a video to a file formatted for a CD and then use a different program to burn it on to a disc. Usually, you select the command to export the file, select the file format, and then customize the settings. You may be able to preview the exported file in a media player that supports MPEG video. In Premiere Pro, you use the same Adobe Media Encoder feature to export a file for a CD that you use to export a file into a DVD or Web-compatible format. In Premiere Elements, you select MPEG from the Export menu, and then select a CD compatible format.

CDs that contain video content are often called *VCDs*. To burn a file to a CD, you must have a CD burner correctly set up and installed for use with your computer. A *CD burner* is a drive that writes data on to a CD using a laser to burn the data on the disc. You must also have a blank, writable CD, which may be called a CD-RW. A CD burner is generally less expensive than a DVD burner, and writable CDs are generally less expensive than writable DVDs. Your audience can play the disc using a CD player connected to a monitor or television. Note that most DVD players can read and play VCDs, but CD players cannot read and play DVDs.

A standard VCD stores about 700 megabytes of data, which is enough to play about an hour of video. The video file format is usually MPEG-1, and the resolution is usually 352 by 240 pixels for NTSC. The frame size and frame rate can vary, depending on the codec and the selected settings, but the file cannot exceed 700 MB if you want to fit it on the CD. Therefore, you may have to settle for a smaller frame size and slower frame rate if you want to try to preserve quality. A newer format, called *SVCD*, which stands for super video compact disc, uses the MPEG-2 format. It lets you store about the same amount of video on a CD, but the resolution—480 by 480 for NTSC—is better.

STEP-BY-STEP 11.7

In this exercise you will export a sequence from your video-editing program in a CD-compatible format.

1. Click **File** on the Menu bar, point to **Export**, and then click **Adobe Media Encoder**. If Adobe Media Encoder is not available, select an option such as **MPEG**.

2. Select an MPEG1-VCD-compatible format. In Premiere Pro, click the **Format** drop-down arrow and then click **MPEG1-VCD**. In Premiere Elements, click **BTSC VCD** in the Export MPEG dialog box.

3. Verify that the *Range* settings include the **Entire Sequence**. Select the **NTSC VCD Medium Quality Standard Bitrate** as the preset file type. The available presets depend on the selected file format. Your program loads the settings associated with the preset, as shown in Figure 11-11. If you are using Premiere Elements, click the **Advanced** button to display the Export Settings dialog box.

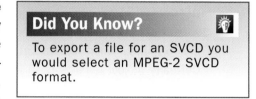

> ### Did You Know?
>
> To export a file for an SVCD you would select an MPEG-2 SVCD format.

FIGURE 11-11
Set options to export a file for a VCD

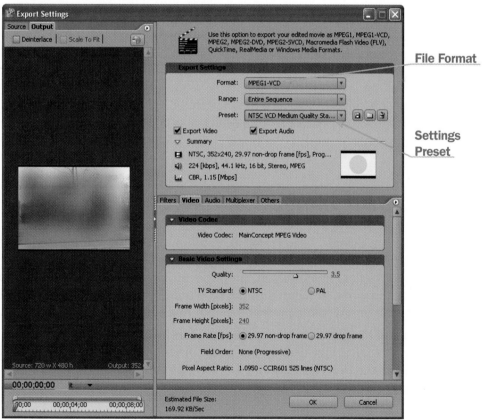

STEP-BY-STEP 11.7 Continued

4. Deselect the Export Audio check box, and then click **OK** or **Save** to apply the settings and close the dialog box. (If you are using Elements, a dialog box may prompt you to name the preset. Key **mpeg1 vcd**, and then click **OK** twice.) A Save File dialog box, in which you select a storage location and name the export file, displays.

5. If necessary, navigate to the folder where you store the solutions for this lesson. Click in the *File name* text box and replace the default name by keying **CVMPG1**. Click **Save** to export the file. This may take a few minutes, during which time a progress dialog box displays. When the export is complete, the **CVRealty** project remains open in your video-editing program. Minimize your program, but leave it open.

6. Use Windows to locate and open the folder where you have stored the solution files for this lesson.

7. Double-click the **CVMPG1.m1v** file icon. The video file opens in Windows Media Player. If necessary, click **Play**. If you do not have Windows Media Player installed, right-click the icon, click **Open With**, and select a compatible media player that you have available.

8. Close Windows Media Player and then restore your video-editing program window. Leave it open to use in the next exercise.

> **Note**
>
> *.m1v* is the file extension for MPEG-1 video formatted video files. The file icon may display as an MPEG file, and the File Save dialog box may indicate that the file type is MPEG, but the three-character file extension is .m1v.

> **Extra for Experts**
>
> You may be able to publish digital video back to a DV tape using a process that is the reverse of capturing video. Connect the camcorder to your computer via an IEEE 1394 port, set it to recording mode, and then select the command in your video-editing program to export to tape. Set options, and then select the command to record.

Export a Still Image

Y̶ou can export a single video frame as a still image stored in a graphics file format such as Windows Bitmap, GIF, or TIFF. You can then use the graphics file in the same ways you would use any graphics file. For example, you can import it into a graphics program for editing, use it in an animation, add it to a brochure in a desktop publishing program, use it to illustrate a report or to create a poster, insert it in a presentation, or even import it into a different video project.

To export a still image, select the frame you want to export and then select the command to export a frame. A dialog box displays so you can name the file and select a storage location. Before you export the file you may open a settings dialog box to select options such as the graphics file type.

STEP-BY-STEP 11.8

1. Position the current time indicator on the Timeline four seconds into the sequence in the **CVRealty** project. The frame should display the double vision title, with the four houses behind it.

2. Click **File** on the Menu bar, point to **Export**, and then click **Frame** to export a single frame. A dialog box displays so you can select a storage location and name the exported file.

3. Click **Settings** to display the Export Frame Settings dialog box in which you can customize the export settings. This dialog box is similar to the Export Movie Settings dialog box you have used in previous exercises.

4. Click the **File Type** drop-down arrow and then click **GIF**.

5. If available, deselect the option to add the exported file to the project, and then click **OK** to apply the settings and close the dialog box.

6. If necessary, navigate to the folder where you are storing the solutions for this lesson. Click in the *File name* text box and key **CVStill.gif** to replace the default file name, and then click **Save** to export the file. When the export is complete, the **CVRealty** project remains open in your video-editing program.

7. Close the **CVRealty** project and close your video-editing program.

8. Use Windows to locate and open the folder where you have stored the solution files for this lesson.

9. Double-click the **CVStill.gif** file icon. The graphics file opens in a compatible program, as shown in Figure 11-12.

FIGURE 11-12
Exported still image

10. Close the graphics program window.

SUMMARY

In this lesson, you learned:

■ In order to distribute video you create using a video-editing program, you must export the video in a format that other applications can display.

■ Before you export a video, you should consider what you plan to do with the exported file.

■ You can export a video as a movie file so that you can play it in a standalone media player or import it into a different program. Typically, movie files are exported in AVI or QuickTime format.

■ You can optimize an exported file for delivery over the Web. Some Web-compatible file types include Windows Media, Flash Video, QuickTime, and RealMedia.

■ You can export and publish a video file to a DVD or SVCD in MPEG-2 format, or to a VCD in MPEG-1 format.

■ You can export a single frame of a video as a graphics file.

■ To export a video, you usually select the type of export and then select the file type. You can usually use a preset list of the most common settings for that file type, including a codec, or you can customize settings.

■ Video files are generally quite large. If you select options that make the file smaller, you will probably sacrifice quality.

VOCABULARY *Review*

Define the following terms:

AutoPlay DVD	Progressive download	Streaming video server
CD burner	Sample	SVCD
Data rate	Sample rate	VCD
DVD burner		

REVIEW *Questions*

TRUE / FALSE

Circle T if the statement is true and F if the statement is false.

T F   1. You can only export an entire video sequence.

T F   2. Video is usually exported to a DVD in MPEG-2 format.

T F   3. Macromedia Flash Video is a Web-compatible video file type.

T   F   **4.** When you select options that reduce video file size, you usually sacrifice quality.

T   F   **5.** A standard DVD has enough capacity for more than two hours of video.

T   F   **6.** Most DVD players can read and play VCDs, but CD players cannot read and play DVDs.

T   F   **7.** You cannot export video from your computer to a digital video tape.

T   F   **8.** Exporting a video is usually very fast.

T   F   **9.** With most video-editing programs, you can customize video export settings to optimize the file.

T   F **10.** When you want to create a smaller video file you can increase the frame size.

WRITTEN QUESTIONS

Write a brief answer to each of the following questions.

1. List at least three ways you might use a video that you export to a movie file.

2. What are at least two important considerations when deciding whether to use a DVD or a CD for distributing video?

3. List at least three reasons you might want to export a video frame as a still image.

4. Name at least three video settings you may be able to customize.

5. What are at least three factors to consider when you are deciding how to export a video file?

FILL IN THE BLANK

Complete the following sentences by writing the correct word or words in the blanks provided.

1. Video is usually exported to a VCD in _____ format.

2. The _____ rate controls the amount of video information that must be processed each second during playback.

3. You can distribute a video over the Web by storing it on a streaming video _____, which is a computer on the Internet configured to deliver video files by streaming or progressive downloading.

4. The _____ format lets you store about the same amount of video as on a VCD, but the resolution is better.

5. A CD _____ is a drive that writes data on to a CD.

6. A(n) _____ download is when a video begins to play before it is completely downloaded.

7. When you want to create a movie file that you can use in many programs across many platforms you should select either the _____ format or the QuickTime format.

8. To improve the audio quality you can increase the _____ rate, but it will result in a larger file.

9. In Adobe Premiere Pro, you can use the Adobe Media _____ feature to export a file into a Web-compatible format.

10. When you export a video frame as a still image, your video-editing programs saves it in a(n) _____ file format such as GIF or TIFF.

PROJECTS

PROJECT 11-1

In this project you will open an existing video and then export it to a movie file. Once exported you will play the movie in QuickTime. Before beginning this exercise, copy the video source files **Project11-1b** and **Project11-1c** and the audio source file **Project 11-1d** from your Data files folder to your Solution files folder.

1. Start your video-editing program and open **Project11-1a** from the Data files for this lesson. If necessary, locate and identify the source files as follows:

CLIP NAME	SOURCE FILE NAME
Walk1	Project11-1b
Walk2	Project11-1c
Music	Prokect11-1d

2. Save the project as **WalkFinal**.

3. Edit the **Close** title to change the sample text *Student's Name* to your own name, and *Today's Date* to today's actual date, and then restore the default workspace or close the Titler. (For information on editing a title, refer to Lesson 10.)

4. Select the Timeline panel, click **File** on the Menu bar, point to **Export**, and then click **Movie**.

> **Note**
>
> If, when opening the Project11-1a file, you see dialog boxes requesting the location of "Rendered" files, simply click Skip in each dialog box until the project file opens.

5. Select the following general settings, leaving other settings unchanged:
   File Type: **QuickTime**
   Range: **Entire Sequence** (or **Timeline**)
   Export Video
   Export Audio
   Do not add to the project when finished.

6. Select the following video settings, leaving other settings unchanged:
   Compressor: **Indeo® video 5.1** or comparable.
   Quality: **50%**.

7. Name the exported file **WalkQT.mov**, and store it in the folder where you store solutions for this lesson.

8. When the export is complete, use Windows to locate the **WalkQT.mov** file and double-click the file icon to open the video in the QuickTime player.

9. Click **Play** to play the movie in the QuickTime player.

10. Close QuickTime. Leave the **WalkFinal** project open in your video-editing program to use in the next project.

PROJECT 11-2

In this project you will export the video sequence from the **WalkFinal** project to a file suitable for distribution on the Web. You will then use Windows Media Player to play the sequence.

1. Click **File** on the Menu bar, point to **Export**, and then click **Adobe Media Encoder**. If your program does not offer a feature such as Adobe Media Encoder, select an option such as **Windows Media** from the Export menu, click the **Advanced** button in the Export dialog box, and then skip step 2.

2. Select the following export settings, leaving other settings unchanged:
   Format: **Windows Media**
   Range: **Entire Sequence**
   Preset: **WM9 NTSC 256K download** (or select options for a Windows Media Player
   9-compatible file in NTSC format optimized for downloading at 256 Kbs).
   Export Video
   Export Audio

3. Change the number of Encoding Passes to **One**.

4. Name the exported file **WalkWM**, and store it in the folder where you store solutions for
   this lesson. (If necessary, name the preset **wma with audio**.)

5. When the export is complete, use Windows to locate **WalkWM.wmv** and double-click the
   file icon to open and play the video in the Windows Media Player.

6. Close the Windows Media Player. Leave the **WalkFinal** project open in your video-editing
   program to use in the next project.

PROJECT 11-3

In this project you will export the video sequence from the **WalkFinal** project to a file suitable
for distribution on an SVCD. You will then play the video sequence in Windows Media Player.

1. Click **File** on the Menu bar, point to **Export**, and then click **Adobe Media Encoder**. If your
   program does not offer a feature such as Adobe Media Encoder, select an option such as
   MPEG from the Export menu, select the **NTSC SVCD** format and then skip to step 4.

2. Select the following export settings, leaving other settings unchanged:
   Format: **MPEG2-SVCD**
   Range: **Entire Sequence**
   Preset: **NTSC SVCD High Quality Standard Bitrate CBR 1 Pass** (or select options for an
   SVCD-compatible file in NTSC format optimized for high quality).
   Export Video
   Export Audio

3. Set the Quality to 3.5, or about **70%**.

4. Name the exported file **WalkSVCD**, and store it in the folder where you store solutions for
   this lesson.

5. When the export is complete, use Windows to locate the **WalkSVCD.mpg** file and double-
   click the file icon to open and play the video in the Windows Media Player.

6. Close the Windows Media Player. Leave the **WalkFinal** project open in your video-editing
   program to use in the next project.

PROJECT 11-4

In this project you will select a single frame to export as a still image in a graphics file format suitable for using in a brochure. You will then open the exported file in a graphics program.

1. Position the current time indicator about 1 second in to the video sequence in the **WalkFinal** Timeline.

2. Click **File** on the Menu bar, point to **Export,** and then click **Frame.**

3. Select to export the frame in **TIFF** format.

4. Do not add the image to the project.

5. Name the exported file **WalkStill.tif,** and store it in the folder where you store solutions for this lesson.

6. When the export is complete, use Windows to locate the **WalkStill.tif** file and double-click the file icon to open it in a compatible graphics program.

7. Close the graphics program. Leave the **WalkFinal** project open in your video-editing program to use in the next project.

PROJECT 11-5

In this project you will preview the video sequence from the WalkFinal project as it would look on a DVD without menus. Then you will add a menu and preview the DVD again. After you preview the file, you will burn it to a DVD.

1. Click **Window** on the Menu bar, click **DVD Layout,** click **Preview DVD,** and then click **Play/Pause Toggle.**

2. When the video finishes playing, close the preview window.

3. Click **Change Template,** click the **Theme** drop-down arrow, and then click **Travel.** Click the **Winter** template and then click **OK.** If the Winter template is not available, select a different template such as **Countryside** or **Blue Sky.**

4. Click **Yes** in the Missing DVD Markers dialog box to create automatic markers. Then click **OK** in the Automatically Set DVD Scene Markers dialog box to establish markers **At Each Scene.**

5. Preview the DVD using the Scene Selection menu.
   A. Click **Preview DVD.**
   B. Click the text **Scene Selection** link.
   C. Click **Scene 1.**

6. When the video finishes playing, close the preview window.

7. Select to export the video directly to a DVD. Click **Burn DVD** in the DVD Layout panel, or click the Timeline, click **File** on the Menu bar, point to **Export,** and then click **Export to DVD.**

8. If you have a DVD burner, with your instructor's permission, burn the video to the DVD using the default settings. Alternatively, burn the video to a folder. In either case, name the disc/folder **A Dog's Day Out**.

9. When the DVD is complete, test it in a DVD player.

10. Save changes and close the **WalkFinal** project and close your video-editing program.

 WEB PROJECT

As video cell phones, Webcams, and digital camcorders become more popular, so do Web sites that offer video sharing services. Some of these sites provide free video clips that you can download to use on your own Web site, and some of them let you post videos so other people can see them. Some even have contests you can enter to have your videos judged. Use the Internet to research free video sharing sites. Pick at least three different sites and compare the services they offer. Record the information in a word-processing document or spreadsheet. Some things you might want to find out include: Do you have to register? Is there a fee? Can anyone access your videos or is it limited to your friends or buddy list? Is there a particular audience, such as teens, kids, adults, or can the audience be anyone? When you have compiled the information, make a decision about which site you would recommend using and write your recommendation in a 500-word report. Back up your decision using facts from your research. Present your findings to your class. With your parent's and instructor's permission, join a site and upload a video.

 TEAMWORK PROJECT

As a team, research the history of your local community. You can do this using books, the Internet, or by talking to people such as librarians in the community. Select a topic that you find interesting in your community and plan a video between two and five minutes in length. To get started, assign jobs to each member of the team. For example, someone might be the director, someone might be the writer, someone might the producer, and someone might be the "talent" or person who is recorded as part of the video. Decide how you can best capture the selected topic in video. You may want to record clips of interesting places, or interview interesting people. Remember, it is best to use short clips. Storyboard the video by writing down each scene you want to use. If you want to include narration, write a script for each scene as well, or select music you might want to include as an audio track. If you plan to interview people, decide what questions you want to ask to get them to say something interesting and relevant to the topic.

When you are ready, use a camcorder to record all of the scenes. It is OK to record more video than you will need—you can always select the specific clips you want to use. Capture the clips into your video-editing program and review them to make sure you have everything you put on your storyboard. If necessary, go back and record additional footage and capture it into your program. Assemble the clips into a sequence to create the movie. Incorporate transitions and effects if they will enhance the video. Use titles to include the title of the movie and the credits, and to name places or people you have in the clips. Preview the sequence as you work, and ask classmates for comments and suggestions. Make changes as necessary to improve the video.

When the video is complete, publish it so you can present it to your class. You may want to export it as a movie file that you can play on a computer, or you may want to burn it to a DVD or CD. If your class or school has a Web site, you may be able to make it available on a Web page.

CRITICAL *Thinking*

The size of exported video files can vary greatly depending on the file format and quality. In this exercise, assemble a sequence, no more than a minute in length, that you can use to test different export formats and settings. The goal will be to determine the best balance of file size and quality. To assemble the sequence, you can use clips from other projects, or record and capture new footage.

Set up the test as you would a science experiment. Do some research about the different file types and settings, and how they affect file size and quality. Come up with a hypothesis. Select a control and three or four variables to test. For example, you might decide you are only going to export in AVI format, but you will use different codecs or vary the frame rate or the frame size. You might decide you are only going to export in QuickTime format, but you will vary the quality setting or the audio settings. You can judge the exported files by file size and by quality, such as how fuzzy is the resolution, or how jumpy is the flow. Record the results in a table or a spreadsheet, and then write a report explaining your findings. Present the results to your class.

ANIMATION AND VIDEO

REVIEW *Questions*

TRUE / FALSE

Circle T if the statement is true or F if the statement is false.

T F   1.   A Timeline is the area on the screen where you preview an animation.

T F   2.   Frame rate is usually measured in frames per second (fps).

T F   3.   You can record sound files to use in other programs.

T F   4.   One way to keep an animation file from getting too large is to use symbols.

T F   5.   One of the most common ways to distribute an animation is on a CD.

T F   6.   If a download takes too long, you may lose the attention of viewers who do not want to wait.

T F   7.   Non-linear editing programs can randomly access video scenes and clips in any order.

T F   8.   Most video-editing programs only have one video track and one audio track.

T F   9.   You can create rolling titles to add to a video sequence.

T F   10.   Usually, the speed and duration of a video clip are linked, so if you change one setting the other is automatically adjusted as well.

MATCHING

Match the correct term in Column 1 to its description in Column 2.

Column 1		Column 2

    ___ 1. Alpha

    A. The setting that controls the rate at which changes occur during a tweened animation sequence.

    ___ 2. Footage

    ___ 3. Keyframe

    B. To create a version of a file that you can deliver in the selected environment.

    ___ 4. Handle

    C. A file comprised of a series of images that is often used to display animations on Web pages.

    ___ 5. Compression

    ___ 6. Animated GIF

    D. The setting that controls the transparency of an object.

    ___ 7. Sample

    E. Raw, unedited, video material.

    ___ 8. Ease

    F. A system for compressing a large amount of data into a smaller file.

    ___ 9. Codec

    ___ 10. Publish

    G. The smallest unit of a digitized sound.

    H. A frame in which a change occurs.

    I. Extra frames before the in point or after the out point of a video clip.

    J. The process of reducing the space required to store data by efficiently encoding the content.

FILL IN THE BLANK

Complete the following sentences by writing the correct word or words in the blanks provided.

1. In an animation program, a(n) _____ is an invisible sheet used to separate and organize content on the Stage.

2. In a(n) _____ animation, you specify a beginning keyframe and an ending keyframe, and your program automatically fills in the intermediate frames.

3. Use _____ animation to force an object to move along a specific line or curve.

4. The graph that visually represents a sound in a program is called a(n) _____.

5. The _____ is the speed at which a network or modem transfers data.

6. When you play back an animation file, if the playback speed of the first frame exceeds the downloading speed of the second frame, there will be a(n) _____.

7. Most video programs have a(n) _____ mode in which input from the digital camera is played in a window on the computer screen.

8. In a video, a(n) _____ is the frames that are used to phase out one scene (or clip) and phase in the next.

9. To distribute a video on a DVD, you usually export the file in the _____ format.

10. A DVD _____ is a drive that writes data on to a DVD using a laser.

PROJECTS

PROJECT U2-1

In this project, you create an animation for a Web site named **Rick's Kitchen** that offers recipes, cooking tips, and nutritional information.

1. Open your animation program and create a new document.

2. Save the file as **RKLogo1**.

3. Set Document Properties to change the ruler unit to **inches,** and then set the stage dimensions to **5.0** inches wide by **5.0** inches high. Set the Background color to **off white** (hexadecimal **#ECE9D8**).

4. Rename *Layer 1* to **Shape**.

5. Turn on object drawing, if necessary. In frame 1 of the *Shape* layer, draw a five-sided polygon with a black stroke and light blue fill (hexadecimal **#0099FF**) approximately **4.0** inches wide by **3.8** inches high, positioned with a point straight up. Center the shape on the stage horizontally and vertically.

6. Insert a keyframe in frame 10 of the *Shape* layer.

7. Create a motion tween between frames 1 and 10. Set options to scale the object and to rotate it clockwise **8** times. Set the Ease to **–25**.

8. In frame 10, resize the polygon to approximately **1.0** inch wide by **.95** inches high, and center it on the stage horizontally and vertically.

9. Insert a keyframe in frame 20 and create a motion tween between frames 10 and 20. Set options to scale the object and rotate it clockwise **8** times. Set the Ease to **25**.

10. In frame 20, resize the polygon to approximately **4.0** inches wide by **3.8** inches high. Center the polygon vertically and horizontally to the stage. Rewind and play the animation on the stage.

11. Insert a new layer and rename it **Hat**.

12. Import the graphics file **Project1** to the Library.

13. Open the Library panel and rename the graphics file to **Hat**.

14. Select frame 1 of the *Hat* layer, and then drag the **Hat** graphic from the Library to the stage.

15. Size the image to approximately .5 inches wide by .38 inches high and center it on the stage horizontally and vertically.

16. Insert a keyframe in frame 20 of the *Hat* layer and create a motion tween between frames 1 and 20. Set tween options to scale the object.

17. In frame 20 of the *Hat* layer, resize the **Hat** graphic to approximately **3.0** inches wide by **2.27** inches high, and center it on the stage.

18. Rewind and preview the animation on the stage.

19. Insert a new layer and rename it **Text**. Insert a keyframe in frame 20.

20. In frame 20 of the *Text* layer, create an expandable text block and, using a **48**-point sans serif font in **black**, key **Rick's**. Position the top of the text block about **1.5** inches from the top of the stage, centered horizontally.

21. Also in frame 20 of the *Text* layer, create another expandable text block using the same font settings and key **Kitchen**. Position the bottom of the text block about **0.5** inches from the bottom of the stage, centered horizontally.

22. Print all frames of the animation in the **Storyboard - Grid** format, with five frames across the page.

23. Rewind and play the animation on the stage.

24. Save the changes to the **RKLogo1** file and close it. Leave your animation program open to use in the next exercise.

PROJECT U2-2

In this project, continue to add actions and a button to the **RKLogo** animation, and publish it for the Web.

1. In your animation program, open the file **Project2a** from the Data files for this lesson and save it as **RKLogo2**.

2. Insert a new layer and name it **Sound**.

3. Import the sound file **Project2b** from the Data files for this lesson into the Library, and rename it **Applause**.

4. Insert the **Applause** sound in frame 1 of the *Sound* layer.

5. Insert a new layer and rename it **Stop**. Insert a keyframe in frame 20.

6. Insert a **Stop** action in frame 20 of the *Stop* layer.

7. Test the movie in the Flash Player. When it is finished, close the Flash Player window.

8. Create a new button symbol and name it **Replay**.

9. In the Up state keyframe of the button symbol **Timeline**, draw a circle with a **white** fill and a **black** stroke, about .75 inches in diameter, centered around the crosshair on the stage.

10. Create an expandable text block and, using a **14**-point **black** sans serif font, key **Replay**. Center the text block within the circle.

11. Insert a keyframe in the Over state and change the fill color of the circle to blue (hexadecimal **#0099FF**).

12. Insert a keyframe in the Down state and change the fill color of the circle to a darker blue (hexadecimal **#0000FF**) and the text color to **white**.

13. Insert a keyframe in the Hit state and then exit symbol-editing mode.

14. Insert a new layer and rename it **Button**.

15. Insert a keyframe in frame 20 of the *Button* layer.

16. Display the Library if necessary and drag an instance of the **Replay** button to the lower-right corner of the stage.

17. Select the **Replay** button instance and assign a **Goto and Play** action, set to go to and play the first frame of the current scene.

18. Test the animation in the Flash Player window, and test the **Replay** button.

19. Save the changes to the file, and then set publish settings to publish the animation in Flash and HTML format for the Web. Set the HTML dimensions to **75%**.

20. Publish the animation and then preview it in your Web browser. Test the **Replay** button.

21. Close your Web browser.

22. Save the changes to the **RKLogo2** file and close it. Close your animation program.

PROJECT U2-3

In this project, create a brief video that can play on the Rick's Kitchen Web site. Before beginning, copy the video source file **Project3** from the Data files for this lesson into your Solutions folder.

1. Start your video-editing program and create a new project. If necessary, select the the **DV - NTSC Standard 32kHz** preset. Save the project as **RKVideo**.

2. Import the video clip **Project3** from the Solutions folder into the project, and rename it **Rice**.

3. Preview it in the Source Monitor or Monitor.

4. Set an out point at **2:15** and then insert the selected portion of the clip in the *Video 1* track in the Timeline.

5. Set an in point at **5:05** and an out point at **7:05** and insert the selected portion of the clip in the *Video 1* track, abutting the end of the first clip.

6. Insert a cross-dissolve transition centered on the cut line between the two clips.

7. Create a new rolling title named **Open**. Select a font style that has orange text with a black shadow, such as **Tekton Bold Bronze 88**.

8. Decrease the font size by about **50%**, and key **Marlborough-Style Fried Rice: Friday on Rick's Kitchen.** Center the text block horizontally in the frame.

9. Set Roll/Crawl options so the text crawls left, starting and ending off the screen.

10. Save the title and then insert it at the start of the *Video 2* track of the Timeline. If necessary, trim the title so it is as long as the video (about 4.17 seconds).

11. Decrease the speed of the **Open** title clip by **50%**—without changing the duration.

12. Preview the video in the Program Monitor.

13. Export the video in a format suitable for streaming on the Web. Select a Windows Media-compatible format (such as **WM9 NTSC 256K download** in Adobe Premiere Pro, or **Cable Modem, DSL** in Adobe Premiere Elements). Save the file as **RKStream**.

14. When the export is finished, save the **RKVideo** project and close it. Close your video-editing program.

15. If possible, use Windows to locate the **RKStream** file and preview it in Windows Media Player. When it is finished, close Windows Media Player.

SIMULATION

The owner of the Lighthouse View Inn, a Bed and Breakfast located on the coast of Maine, is planning a marketing campaign to attract a wider range of clients. As the marketing assistant, you believe that a strong presence on the World Wide Web is vital to a successful marketing campaign. In the following tasks you will develop marketing content that can be used on the Inn's Web site, or placed as advertisements on other Web sites. You will first develop an animation of the Inn's logo, which you created in the Simulation in the Unit 1 Review. Then you will develop a short video depicting the beauty of Maine.

Before starting to work, read through each project completely. Take time to plan what you will need to accomplish the job, and how you will do it. Working alone or with a partner, review the steps and then create a schedule for completing the job. Set up a timeline with appropriate milestones. Establish criteria that you believe should be met for each stage of the project, and create a rubric that you can use to gauge your accomplishments.

JOB U2-1

1. Open your animation program and create a new document.

2. Save the file as **LVILogo**.

3. Set Document Properties to change the ruler unit to inches, and then set the stage dimensions to **5.0** inches wide by **5.0** inches high. Set the Background color to **white**.

4. Rename *Layer 1* to **Background**.

5. Import the graphics file **Job1a** to the Library and rename it **Logo**. Drag it from the library to frame 1 of the *Background* layer, resize it to approximately **1.5** inches wide by **2.0** inches high and center it horizontally and vertically on the stage.

6. Use the **Oval Tool** with **no fill** and a **4**-point **black** stroke to draw an oval approximately **1.6** inches wide by **2.1** inches high, and center it horizontally and vertically on the stage. It should appear to frame the image.

7. Group the oval and the graphic and then convert the object to a graphic symbol named **Background**.

8. Insert a keyframe in frame 10 and create a motion tween between frames 1 and 10. Deselect the **Scale** check box and set the Ease to **35**.

9. Select the instance on frame 1 and set the Color Alpha to 0. Play the animation on the stage. The picture should fade in. Insert a frame in frame 40 to extend the animation.

10. Insert a new layer and rename it **L**. Insert a keyframe in frame 10.

11. Select the **Text Tool** and set the font to a **48**-point serif font in bold blue (hexadecimal **#0066FF**) and then key an uppercase letter **L** in frame 10 of the *L* layer. Position the text block so its upper-left corner is about **1.75** inches from the left of the stage and about **3.0** inches from the top of the stage.

12. Insert a new layer and rename it **V**. Insert a keyframe in frame 10.

13. Select the **Text Tool** and key an uppercase letter **V** in frame 10 of the *L* layer, using the same font settings as in step 11.

14. Resize the text block so it is approximately **.75** inches wide by **1.0** inch high. Position it so its top is about **3.0** inches from the top of the stage, and center it horizontally on the stage.

15. Insert a new layer and rename it **I**. Insert a keyframe in frame 10. Use the same font settings as previously and key an uppercase letter **I**. Position the text block so its upper-right corner is about **1.75** inches from the right of the stage and about **3.0** inches from the top of the stage.

16. In the *L*, *V*, and *I* layers, insert a keyframe in frame 25.

17. Select the *I* layer and insert a motion guide. Insert a keyframe in frame 10.

18. Select the Pencil Tool with a smooth modifier, and draw a curved line that starts on the left side of the stage and follows the shape of the oval up and around, and then through the middle of the three letters. If necessary, insert a frame in frame 40 to extend the animation.

19. On the *I* layer, create a motion tween between frames 10 and 25. Deselect the **Scale** check box and set the Ease to **25**.

20. In frame 10 of the *I* layer, snap the **I** to the beginning of the motion path, and then set the Alpha color to **0%**. (If necessary, in frame 25, snap the letter to the line at its original position on the stage.) Then, if necessary, insert a frame in frame 40 to extend the animation.

21. Link the *L* and *V* layers to the *I motion guide* layer and insert motion tweens on each layer between frames 10 and 25. Deselect the **Scale** check box on each layer and set the Ease to **25**.

22. In frame 10 of the *V* layer, snap the **V** to the beginning of the motion path, and then set the Alpha color to **0%**. Repeat the step for the letter **L**. If necessary, insert a frame in frame 40 of each layer to extend the animation.

23. Rewind and play the animation on the stage.

24. Select the *I Guide* layer and insert a new layer. Rename the layer **Name**.

25. Insert an expandable text block and, using a **black, 32**-point sans serif font, key **Lighthouse View Inn**. Press **Enter** and key **Wells, Maine**. Center the text in the text block. Align the text block with the top of the stage, centered horizontally.

26. Insert a new layer and rename it **Contact**. Insert an expandable text block and, using the same font as in step 26, key **(207) 555-5555**. Press **Enter** and key **www.lvi.net**. Center the text in the text block. Align the text block with the bottom of the stage, centered horizontally.

27. Insert a new layer and rename it **Sound**. Import the sound file **Job1b** to the Library, and rename it **Gulls**. Insert it in frame 1 of the *Sound* layer.

28. Insert a new layer and rename it **Stop**. Insert a keyframe in frame 40 and insert a **Stop** action.

29. Test the movie in the Flash Player. When it is finished, close the Flash Player window.

30. Set publish settings to publish the animation for the Web, using the default Flash and HTML settings.

31. Publish the animation and preview it in your browser. Close your Web browser.

32. Save the changes to the **LVILogo** file and close it. Close your animation program.

JOB U2-2

In this job, you are going to create a short video that shows some attractions of Maine. You will export the video in a format suitable for streaming on the Web, and also to a movie file. You have three video clips available: **Job2a**, **Job2b**, and **Job2c**, and a still image, **Job2d**. You also have a sound file of chirping birds, **Job2e**. You may record your own video footage to include as well, or locate other still images. Before beginning, copy the video source files— **Job2a**, **Job2b**, and **Job2c**—the still image **Job2d**, and the sound file **Job2e** from the Data files to your Solutions folder.

Start by opening your video-editing program and creating a new project file. Save the project as **LVIVideo**. Import the clips and images from your Solutions folder, and review them so you know what you have to work with. Rename them using descriptive names. At this point, plan the video. Create an outline and a storyboard that illustrates the entire video. Decide how long you want the video to be, what order you want to show the clips, which portions of the clips you want to use, and so on. You may choose to include the audio only, video only, or both. You may want to record or locate a separate audio file that you could use. (You could even use the **Job1b.wav** file supplied for the previous exercise, but if you do, be aware it is not stereo, and can only be inserted on a mono audio track, which in Adobe Premiere Pro is usually track 4.) Consider whether you want to use any effects or transitions. Decide what type of titles to use and whether you want to try inserting graphics in a title. When you have completed the outline and the storyboard, ask a classmate to review them and to offer suggestions. Incorporate the suggestions into your work.

When you are satisfied with the plan, assemble the video. Insert the clips and images in the Timeline, and preview them. Rearrange them if necessary, or adjust the in and out points. Apply the effects and transitions that you planned in your storyboard. Create and insert titles, including ending credits with your name and the date, using rolling text. Preview the video as you work, and ask your classmates to preview it as well. Take their suggestions seriously, and use them to improve the project.

When the video is finished, export it in a format suitable for the Web, such as Windows Media Player, or QuickTime. Customize the settings to achieve a balance of file size and quality. Save the exported file as **LVIStream**. Export the video again as a movie file (named **LVIMovie.mov**) that can be played on different computers using different programs, such as QuickTime. Again, customize the settings to achieve a balance of file size and quality. Present the video to your class using a media player.

PRESENTATION SYSTEMS

Unit 3

Estimated Time for Unit: 9 hours

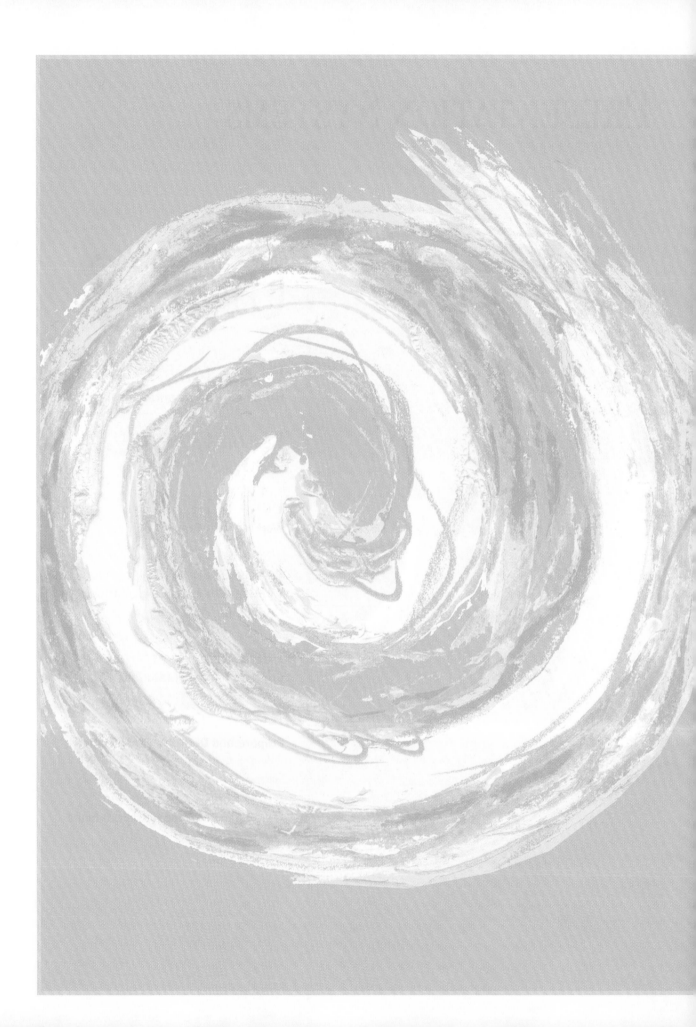

WORKING WITH PRESENTATIONS

Estimated Time: 1.5 hours

OBJECTIVES

Upon completion of this lesson, you should be able to:

- Open, save, and close a presentation.
- Identify parts of a presentation window.
- Adjust the view of the presentation as you work.
- Move from slide to slide in a presentation.
- Format the slide design using design templates and color schemes.
- Add slides to a presentation and apply a slide layout.
- Enter and edit slide text.
- Check for spelling errors.
- Set transitions between slides.
- Preview a presentation.

VOCABULARY

Blinds

Bullet

Color scheme

Design template

Fade

Notes pane

Placeholder

Presentation program

Primary level

Slide

Slide layout

Slide pane

Slide show

Subordinate level

Task pane

Thumbnails

Transitions

In this lesson, you will learn about *presentation programs*—programs you can use to create a professional slide presentation for a classroom, corporate training session, business seminar, or similar situation. The resulting presentation is designed to be displayed on a computer monitor or television screen connected to a computer, or projected on a screen using an overhead projector, 35-mm slide projector, or multimedia projector connected to your computer.

Most presentation programs also allow you to create a slide show that runs by itself and is displayed on a computer monitor or television screen. You may create a self-running slide show if you want to present product and/or sales information at your company's booth at a trade show or convention. The slide show can be set to run continuously or shown only when interested parties stop by your booth.

Presentation programs typically offer other presentation options as well. You may be able to use your program to deliver your presentation over the Internet or package your presentation into a self-running program that can be easily shared via e-mail, over a network, or on a CD-ROM.

Regardless of where and how you decide to use your presentation, you can print out accompanying handouts. These handouts allow your audience to follow along with your presentation and take notes. If a computer is not available, you can use the handouts alone as your visual aides.

There are several different presentation programs available, including Corel Presentations (part of WordPerfect Office), Lotus Freelance Graphics (part of Lotus SmartSuite), and Astound Presentation. But by far the most popular presentation program is Microsoft PowerPoint, which is part of the Microsoft Office suite of programs. Therefore, while the general concepts and tasks discussed in this lesson can be applied to any presentation program, the figures and steps are specific to Microsoft PowerPoint 2003.

Explore the Presentation Window and Close a File

You use your presentation program to create files in which you store your presentation content. Typically, presentations include text, graphics, animations, and objects such as charts or tables, organized on slides, which are displayed as a slide show. A *slide* is a single screen of information within a presentation. A *slide show* is the display of slides in consecutive order. Most of the commands for working with presentation files are the same, or similar to, the commands for working with files in other types of programs.

Most presentation programs start with a new, blank file similar to the one in Figure 12-1 open in the program window.

FIGURE 12-1
Typical presentation program window

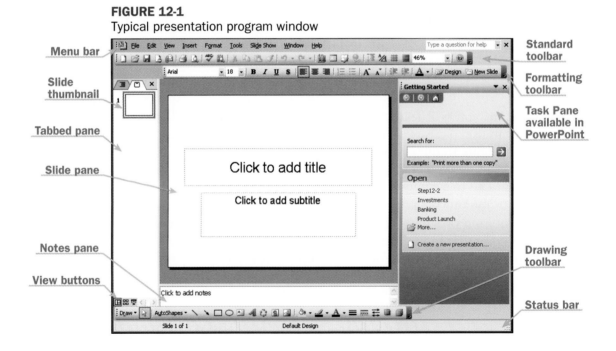

Notice that in addition to the standard screen elements such as a Menu bar, toolbars, and scroll bars, most presentation programs display elements designed specifically for developing presentations. For example, the main area of the window is the *slide pane*, where you view and edit slides. Below the slide pane is the *notes pane*, where you can key text notes about each slide. A tabbed pane along the left side of the window displays *thumbnails*, which are small pictures that represent larger slides. Usually, you can change the tabbed pane to show a presentation outline, which displays the text content of each slide. Your program probably also has a *task pane* on the right side of the window. The task pane provides quick access to frequently used commands and features. The appearance of the screen depends on the program you are using as well as the default options set for your computer, so don't worry if your screen doesn't look exactly the same as the one in the illustration.

When you have finished using a presentation file, you should close it. You can close a file by using the Close command on the File menu, or by clicking the Close Window or Document Close button on the document's Menu bar. After you close a file, the graphics program remains open so that you can continue using it.

> **Hot Tip**
>
> To change the width of any pane, drag its border.

> **Note**
>
> If you have not yet saved a presentation file, when you issue a close command the program displays a dialog box asking if you want to save. Click the Yes button to save the changes and close the file. Click the No button to close the file without saving the changes. Click the Cancel button to close the dialog box and continue working in the file. If you close the file without saving, all changes that you made since the last time you saved the file will be lost.

S TEP-BY-STEP 12.1

1. Launch your presentation program. Take a moment to locate the features in Figure 12-1 on your screen. (Your screen may not be exactly the same as the one in the figure, depending on your program, and whether or not screen elements have been customized.)

2. Click the **Outline** tab in the tabbed pane.

3. Click the **Close** button in the task pane. When the task pane closes, the slide pane expands to fill the area on the screen, as shown in Figure 12-2. If your program does not have a task pane, skip to step 5.

FIGURE 12-2
Close the task pane

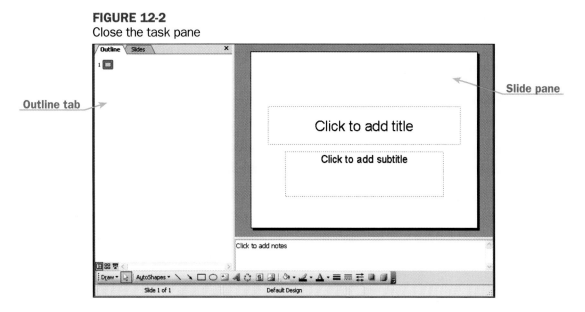

STEP-BY-STEP 12.1 Continued

4. Click **View** on the Menu bar, and then click **Task Pane** to display the task pane again.

5. Click the **Slides** tab in the tabbed pane.

6. Click the **Close Window** button at the right end of the Menu bar to close the blank presentation file. Leave your presentation program open to use in the next exercise.

Open and Save an Existing Presentation File

To work with an existing file that you have saved and closed, you must open it in your presentation program. You can use the Open button on the Standard toolbar or the Open command from the File menu to display the Open dialog box. You can use the Open dialog box to locate and select the file you want to open. Some programs, such as PowerPoint, list recently used files on the File menu and on the Getting Started task pane. Simply click a file name to open it.

You can use the Save As command on the File menu to save a presentation file for the first time, with a new name, or in a different storage location. Once you have saved a file for the first time, you can quickly save changes by clicking the Save button on the Main or Standard toolbar, or by using the Save command on the File menu.

Did You Know?

Some programs, such as PowerPoint, automatically save changes every 10 minutes, and store the changes in a file named AutoRecover that you may be able to use to restore data in the event of a computer failure. If you want PowerPoint to automatically save your changes more often, open the Tools menu and click Options. Click the Save tab, and key the number of minutes you want PowerPoint to wait between saves in the *Save AutoRecover info every XX minutes* box.

STEP-BY-STEP 12.2

1. Click **File** on the Menu bar and then click **Open**. The Open dialog box displays a list of files in the current folder.

2. Click the **Look in** list drop-down arrow and then select the location where the Data files for this lesson are stored.

3. In the list of files, click **Step12-2**.

4. Click the **Open** button in the dialog box. The file opens in the program window, as shown in Figure 12-3. This presentation file includes six slides, which you can see in the tabbed pane on the left. The current slide—which is Slide 1—has a blue rectangle around it, and displays in the slide pane.

STEP-BY-STEP 12.2 Continued

FIGURE 12-3
Open an existing presentation

5. Click **File** on the Menu bar, and then click **Save As**. The Save As dialog box opens.

6. In the File name text box, with the current file name already selected, key **Courses**. This will be the new name of the file.

7. From the Save in list, select the location where you want to store the file.

8. Click the **Save** button in the dialog box. The file is saved with the new name in the selected storage location. Leave the **Courses** file open to use in the next exercise.

Change the Presentation View

Every presentation program includes several ways in which you can view your work. The most common views are the following:

■ Normal view, which is usually the default view, displays one slide in the slide pane, and either the Slides tab or the Outline tab in the tabbed pane. Use the scroll bars in the slide pane or the tabbed pane to scroll through the presentation content. To make a slide current, click it in the tabbed pane.

In Normal view you can change the Zoom setting to adjust the magnification of the slide in the slide pane or the thumbnails in the tabbed pane, and you can display rulers and a grid to help you position content on the slide. To change to Normal view, click View on the Menu bar and then click Normal, or click the Normal View button.

■ Slide Sorter view displays thumbnails of all slides in the slide pane, which is the main area of the window, organized in columns and rows. You can easily reorganize the slides to change the order of the presentation. To select a slide in Slide Sorter view, simply click it in the slide pane.

In Slide Sorter view, like in Normal view, you can change the Zoom setting to adjust the magnification of the slides in the main window (slide pane). To change to Slide Sorter view, click View on the Menu bar and then click Slide Sorter, or click the Slide Sorter View button.

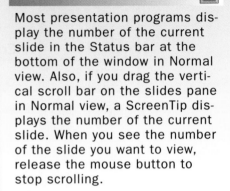

- Slide Show view displays a preview of the slide show on your computer screen. Each slide displays in full-screen size so you can clearly see how your slides will look during an actual presentation. Click the screen to move to the next slide, and, when you have reached the end of the slide show, to exit Slide Show view.

To change to Slide Show view, click View on the Menu bar and then click Slide Show. The slide show will begin with the first slide in your presentation. Or click the *Slide Show from current slide* button. The slide show begins with the current slide.

> **Note** ☑
>
> Most presentation programs display the number of the current slide in the Status bar at the bottom of the window in Normal view. Also, if you drag the vertical scroll bar on the slides pane in Normal view, a ScreenTip displays the number of the current slide. When you see the number of the slide you want to view, release the mouse button to stop scrolling.

STEP-BY-STEP 12.3

1. Click **View** on the Menu bar and then click **Slide Sorter**.

2. Click the **Zoom** drop-down arrow on the Standard toolbar, and then click **100%.** The presentation should look similar to Figure 12-4.

FIGURE 12-4
Slide Sorter view

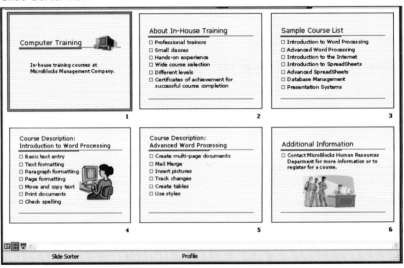

3. Click **Slide 6** to make it current.

4. Click **View** on the Menu bar and then click **Normal**. Slide 6 remains current, and displays in the slides pane.

STEP-BY-STEP 12.3 Continued

5. Click **Slide 4** on the Slides tab in the tabbed pane to make it current.

6. Click the **Outline** tab in the tabbed pane. Scroll up in the tabbed pane and then click the **Slide 2** icon to make it current. Your screen should look similar to Figure 12-5.

FIGURE 12-5
The Outline tab in Normal view

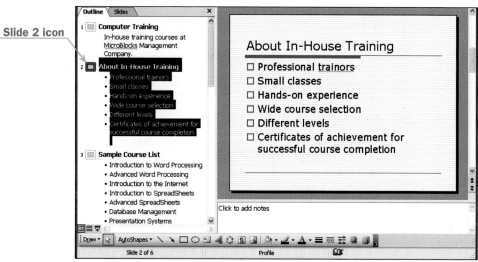

7. Click the **Slides** tab, and then click **Slide 1** to make it current.

8. Click **View** on the Menu bar and then click **Slide Show**. The first slide displays in full screen view, as shown in Figure 12-6.

FIGURE 12-6
Slide 1 in Slide Show view

STEP-BY-STEP 12.3 Continued

9. Click anywhere on the screen to progress to the next slide. Click the screen six more times to progress through the entire slide show and exit Slide Show view. Leave the **Courses** file open to use in the next exercise.

Format the Slide Design

The slide design determines the colors, fonts, and background graphics used on the slides in a presentation. You can modify a slide design by applying a design template or changing the color scheme. A *design template* is a set of built-in formats that you can apply in one step. Formatting with a design template is quick and easy, and it provides your presentation with a unified, professional look. A *color scheme* is a set of coordinated colors used for the background, titles and other text, shadows, fills, bullets (and other accents), and hyperlinks. Each design template offers more than one color scheme.

In most programs you select slide design elements in a dialog box or a task pane. For example, in PowerPoint, design templates and color schemes are available in the Slide Design task pane which you can open by selecting Slide Design from the Format menu, or by clicking the Slide Design button on the Formatting toolbar. You can apply a design template or color scheme to all slides in a presentation or to only selected slides. To apply a template or color scheme to all the slides in a presentation, simply click the desired thumbnail in the task pane. To apply a template or color scheme to selected slides, select the slides, and then rest the mouse pointer on the desired thumbnail to display a drop-down arrow. Click the drop-down arrow and then click Apply to Selected Slides.

Hot Tip

To select more than one slide in the tabbed pane in Normal view or in Slide Sorter view, select the first slide, hold down Ctrl, and click additional slides. Or, click the first slide of a group, hold down Shift, and click the last slide of the group to select all slides between the two slides.

Note

In PowerPoint, design templates in the task pane are organized into three groups: templates used in the current presentation, recently used templates, and an alphabetical list of all available templates.

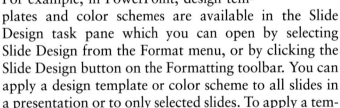
Design

Extra for Experts

To download additional templates for use in PowerPoint, scroll to the bottom of the Slide Design task pane and click the *Design Templates on Microsoft Office Online* thumbnail.

STEP-BY-STEP 12.4

1. Click **Format** on the Menu bar and then click **Slide Design**. The Slide Design task pane, or a similar dialog box, displays listing thumbnails for the available design templates.

2. Rest the mouse pointer over the first design template thumbnail. A ScreenTip displays its name. In some programs, such as PowerPoint, the ScreenTip may also display information about how the design is used in the current presentation, and a drop-down arrow may become available, as shown in Figure 12-7.

STEP-BY-STEP 12.4 Continued

FIGURE 12-7
Design templates in PowerPoint's Slide Design task pane

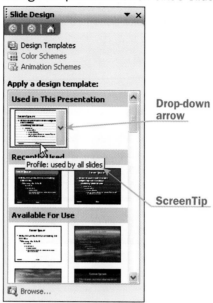

Drop-down arrow

ScreenTip

3. Locate and click the **Globe** design template. (If you don't have this design template available, select one that appears similar to the design shown in Figure 12-9.) The Globe design is applied to all slides in the presentation.

4. Make Slide 1 current, if necessary. Locate the **Radial** design template, and then rest the mouse pointer on its thumbnail. (If the Radial design template is not available in your program, select a different template.)

5. Select the command to apply the **Radial** design template to the current or selected slides only. For example, in PowerPoint, click the drop-down arrow on the **Radial** design template thumbnail, and then click **Apply to Selected Slides**. The Radial design template is applied to Slide 1 only.

> **Note** ☑
>
> If you are using PowerPoint but cannot locate the Globe or Radial templates, it is possible that some design templates are not installed. Locate and click the thumbnail labeled Additional Design Templates in the task pane to install them.

6. At the top of the Slide Design task pane, click the **Color Schemes** link to display the Color Schemes options in the task pane. If your program does not use task panes, look for a **Color Schemes** command on the **Format** menu.

STEP-BY-STEP 12.4 Continued

7. Scroll down if necessary to display the last color schemes, as shown in Figure 12-8.

FIGURE 12-8
Color Schemes in PowerPoint's Slide Design task pane

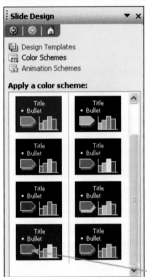

Last color scheme
in left column

8. Select the command to apply the last color scheme in the left column (the one with the blue background and the green arrow) to the current slide. For example, in PowerPoint, click the color scheme's drop-down arrow and then click **Apply to Selected Slides**. (If you do not have the color scheme option shown, select one that is similar.)

9. Save the changes and leave **Courses** open to use in the next exercise.

Add Slides to a Presentation

Y̶ou can easily add new slides to a presentation at any time simply by selecting the New Slide command on the Insert menu or by clicking the New Slide button. New slides are inserted after the current slide.

In most programs, new slides are created using a default *slide layout*. The slide layout determines the location of different types of content on the slide, such as text blocks and graphics objects. For example, in PowerPoint, the default slide layout includes one *placeholder* for a text title and another for a single column of bulleted text items. A placeholder is a box that

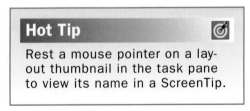

Hot Tip

Rest a mouse pointer on a layout thumbnail in the task pane to view its name in a ScreenTip.

defines a specific area on the slide. You may use the default slide layout, or select a different layout. You may also apply a different slide layout to an existing slide. Usually, you display a Slide Layout dialog box or task pane by selecting Slide Layout from the Format menu. In some programs, such as PowerPoint, the Slide Layout task pane displays automatically whenever you insert a new slide.

S TEP-BY-STEP 12.5

1. Click **Slide 5** in the Slides tab to make it current.

2. Click **Insert** on the Menu bar and then click **New Slide**. A new slide using the default layout is inserted after Slide 5, as shown in Figure 12-9. If you are using PowerPoint, the Slide Layout task pane probably displays automatically.

FIGURE 12-9
Insert a new slide

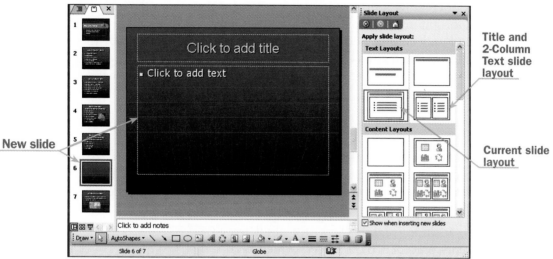

3. Click the layout that has placeholders for a title and two columns of text (called **Title and 2-Column Text** in PowerPoint) to change the slide layout. The new layout should look similar to the one shown in Figure 12-10.

FIGURE 12-10
Slide with Title and 2-Column Text slide layout

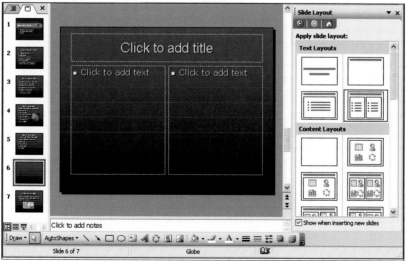

STEP-BY-STEP 12.5 Continued

4. Close the Slide Layout task pane, if necessary.

5. Save the changes to **Courses** and leave it open to use in the next exercise.

Work with Text

A large part of creating a presentation is working with text on the slides. Text usually conveys the most important information on the slide and must be presented in a way that is easy for viewers to read and understand. Add text using the placeholders provided by the layout you have chosen for that slide. After text has been entered, you can edit it as necessary. For example, you can insert and replace text, or delete text. You can also copy or move text from one location to another.

Enter Text

Once you select a slide layout that includes a text placeholder, you can easily add text. Most text placeholders contain messages such as *Click to add title*, or *Click to add text*. Simply click the message to activate the placeholder, and then begin keying the text. The text is automatically formatted with the font and font size specified by the current design template.

Many slides include placeholders for bulleted text—a list of items preceded by a *bullet*, which is a marker such as a dot, check mark, or asterisk. To add bulleted text to a slide, click the *Click to add text* message to open the placeholder and begin keying the first item in the bulleted list. Press Enter to add another item to the list. To create a *subordinate level*, which is a level that is indented under the *primary level*, or main level, press Tab at the beginning of the bullet item. Press Shift + Tab at the beginning of the bullet item to return to the primary level.

> **Hot Tip**
>
> You should try to create at least two bullet items for any level. Otherwise the list may look unorganized and be difficult to read.

Choose your words carefully when inserting slide text. You want to keep each line short and to the point so that people viewing the presentation can read it easily and understand the main concepts. Also, use parallel construction for bulleted items. That is, if one bullet item begins with a verb, the others should as well. Try to avoid crowding a slide with too much text. It is better to have more slides with less text on each one. This also enables you to use larger font sizes which are easier to read from a distance. More text may be permissible when a presentation is most likely to be viewed by an individual (up close to a screen), rather than delivered by a speaker who can discuss each point.

> **Note** ☑
>
> Some programs, such as PowerPoint, automatically reduce the font size of text to fit it all within a placeholder. This can result in inconsistent slide design, as well as small text that is difficult to read. If necessary, create a new slide to accommodate all of the text.

STEP-BY-STEP 12.6

1. On the new Slide 6, click the **Click to add title** placeholder.

2. Key **Benefits of In-House Training**.

3. Click the **Click to add text** placeholder on the left.

4. Key **Skills** and then press **Enter**.

5. Key **Advancement** and then press **Enter**.

6. Key **Growth**, press **Enter**, and then key **Development**. Do not press Enter at the end of the list or you will insert an extra bullet.

7. Click the **Click to add text** placeholder on the right.

8. Key **Challenges**, press **Enter**, key **Knowledge**, press **Enter**, key **Career**, press **Enter**, and then key **Improvement**. The slide should look similar to Figure 12-11.

FIGURE 12-11
Two bullet lists on a slide

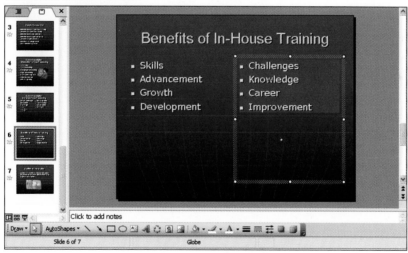

9. Save the changes and leave **Courses** open to use in the next exercise.

Edit Text

You can edit text directly on a slide or in the Outline tabbed pane in Normal view. Edit text using the same methods you would use in a word processing program. For example, to insert text, click to position the insertion point, and then key the new text. To replace text, select it and then key the replacement text. You can even use the Copy and Paste commands to copy text from one location to another and the Cut and Paste commands to move text to a new location.

STEP-BY-STEP 12.7

1. Make Slide 4 current. Double-click the word **Basic** at the beginning of the first bulleted item, and then press **Delete** to delete the selected word.

2. Press **Delete** again to delete the lowercase *t* at the beginning of the word *text*, and then key the uppercase letter **T**.

3. Select **Slide 5**. Click **Format** on the Menu bar and then click **Slide Layout**. In the Slide Layout task pane or similar dialog box, click the layout that has placeholders for a title and two columns of text (called **Title and 2-Column Text** in PowerPoint) to apply it to the current slide. Close the Slide Layout task pane, if necessary.

4. Click the **Outline** tab in the tabbed pane. Click and drag to select the last four bulleted items on Slide 5, as shown in Figure 12-12.

FIGURE 12-12
Edit text in the Outline tab

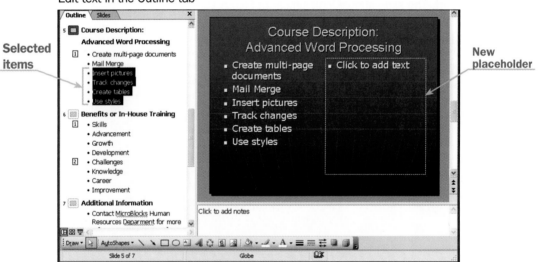

5. Select the command to cut the selection to the Clipboard. For example, click **Edit** on the Menu bar and then click **Cut**, or click the **Cut** button on the Standard toolbar.

6. In the slide pane, click the **Click to add text** placeholder on the right side of Slide 5, and then select the command to paste the selection from the Clipboard. For example, click **Edit** on the Menu bar and then click **Paste**, or click the **Paste** button on the Standard toolbar. The bulleted items are placed from the Clipboard to the column on the right. If there is an extra bullet at the end of the column, press **Backspace** twice to remove it.

7. In the Outline tab on Slide 5, click at the end of the last bulleted item in column 1—*Mail Merge*—and press **Enter** to start a new line. Press **Tab** to indent to a subordinate level.

8. Key **Letters** and press **Enter**. Key **Envelopes**, press **Enter**, and then key **Labels**. Notice that the text you key in the Outline tab also displays on the slide in the slide pane. The slide should look similar to the one in Figure 12-13.

STEP-BY-STEP 12.7 Continued

FIGURE 12-13
Key a multi-level bullet list

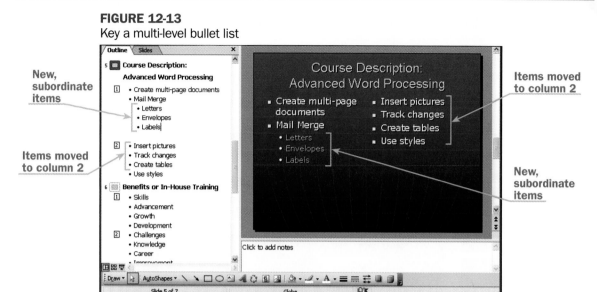

9. Save the changes and leave **Courses** open to use in the next exercise.

Check Spelling

One of the final steps in proofing any document, including a presentation file, is to check it for spelling errors. Most presentation programs have a spelling checker feature that you can use to locate and correct spelling errors. The command is usually on the Tools menu, or there may be a Spelling button on the Standard toolbar.

When the spelling checker finds an error, it highlights it and displays a Spelling dialog box. In most programs, you may select from the following options:

- Select a correction from the Suggestions list and click Change to change just this instance, or Change All to make the same correction throughout the presentation. Some programs may have a Correct button instead of a Change button.

- Key your correction in the *Change to* box and click Change to change just this instance, or Change All to make the same correction throughout the presentation.

- Click Ignore to ignore the word.

- Click Ignore All to ignore the word throughout the presentation.

- Click Add to add the word to the spelling dictionary.

- Click AutoCorrect to add the word to the AutoCorrect list, which looks for common spelling errors and corrects them as you key.

- Click Close to end the spelling check.

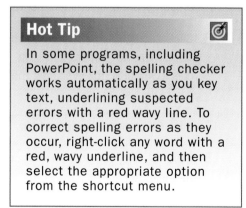

Hot Tip

In some programs, including PowerPoint, the spelling checker works automatically as you key text, underlining suspected errors with a red wavy line. To correct spelling errors as they occur, right-click any word with a red, wavy underline, and then select the appropriate option from the shortcut menu.

STEP-BY-STEP 12.8

1. Click the **Slides** tab in the tabbed pane and make Slide 1 current.

2. Click **Tools** on the Menu bar and then click **Spelling** to start the spelling checker. It stops at the word *MicroBlocks*, as shown in Figure 12-14.

FIGURE 12-14
Using a spelling checker

3. Click **Ignore All** to leave the spelling unchanged throughout the presentation and continue the spell check. It stops at the word *trainors*, highlighting the suggested correction: *trainers*.

4. Click **Change** to correct the error and continue the spell check. The next error is the spelling of *SpreadsSheets*.

5. Click **Change All** to correct the spelling throughout the presentation, and continue the spell check.

6. Click **Change** to correct the spelling of the word *Deparment* to *Department* and continue the spell check. A dialog box indicating that the spell check is complete displays.

7. Click **OK** to close the dialog box.

8. Save the changes and leave **Courses** open to use in the next exercise.

> **Important**
>
> Even if you use a spelling checker, you must still be sure to proofread your presentation text carefully. The spelling checker will not flag correctly spelled words that are used in error, such as the word *red* in place of *read*, or typographical errors such as *on* in place of *or*.

Set Transitions

One of the easiest ways to jazz up your presentation is to add *transitions*. Transitions are the effects used to advance from one slide to the next during a slide show. At a minimum, a transition is simply an automatic change, set to occur at a specific interval. But, a transition may also include special effects such as *blinds*, which give the illusion of window blinds opening over a slide, or a *fade*, in which the slide content is gradually revealed through black. Most presentation programs include a collection of built-in transitions that you can apply to a single slide, or to all slides in a file.

Usually, you select a transition in a dialog box or task pane, accessed by selecting the Slide Show command on the Menu bar and then clicking Slide Transition. You can also set transition properties, such as the speed and whether to advance the slides only on a mouse click or automatically. If you select automatically, you can also set a time interval. You may be able to add a sound to the transition, such as applause or a whoosh. You also have the opportunity to preview the transition on the current slide, or on all slides in the presentation.

Note	
To play sounds, your computer must have a sound card and speakers.	

S TEP-BY-STEP 12.9

1. Make Slide 1 current.

2. Click **Slide Show** on the Menu bar, and then click **Slide Transition**. The Slide Transition task pane, or a similar dialog box displays.

3. Click **Newsflash** (or a similar transition) in the *Apply to selected slides* list. (Scroll down to locate the effect; the list is alphabetical.) If the AutoPreview check box at the bottom of the task pane is selected, the transition displays in the slide pane.

4. Click the **Speed** drop-down arrow in the *Modify transition* section of the task pane (or locate a similar control), and click **Slow**. If the AutoPreview check box is selected, the transition displays in the slide pane.

5. Click the **Sound** drop-down arrow in the *Modify transition* section of the task pane (or locate a similar control), and click **Applause**. Again if the AutoPreview check box is selected, the transition displays in the slide pane. (If a message displays prompting you to install the Sound Effects feature, click Yes.)

STEP-BY-STEP 12.9 Continued

6. Click **Automatically after** in the *Advance slide* section of the task pane (or locate a similar control) and change the time value to **4** seconds (**00:04**). The options should look similar to those shown in Figure 12-15.

FIGURE 12-15
Set Slide Transition options

7. Click **Slide 2** in the Slides tab, press and hold **Shift**, and click **Slide 7**. This selects Slides 2 through 7.

8. Click **Strips Right-Up** in the *Apply to selected slides* list.

> **Hot Tip**
>
> To remove a transition from a slide, display the slide and then click No Transition from the *Apply to selected slides* list.

9. Select **Medium** from the *Speed* drop-down list in the *Modify transition* section of the task pane (or locate a similar control). Click **Automatically after** and change the time value to **4** seconds (**00:04**).

10. Save the changes and leave **Courses** open to use in the next exercise.

Preview a Presentation

To see how a presentation will look to an audience, preview it using Slide Show view. In Slide Show view you can see and hear the transitions, and determine whether the content is easy to read and understand in a real-life situation. You can take notes about the presentation so that you can make improvements, and you can ask colleagues or classmates to watch it and offer suggestions. In addition, you can practice your presentation skills by narrating the slide show just as you would if you were presenting it at a conference or meeting.

In many presentation programs, the slide show starts from the current slide, so make Slide 1 current before changing to Slide Show view if you want to start from the beginning. During the slide show, you can bypass automatically timed transition intervals by pressing Page Down, clicking the mouse button, or pressing the Spacebar to advance to the next slide, or by pressing Page Up to go back to the previous slide. Press Esc to end the slide show at any time.

S TEP-BY-STEP 12.10

1. Make Slide 1 current and then change to Slide Show view. The slide should display using the **Newsflash** transition, accompanied by the sound of applause. After four seconds, it should automatically advance to the second slide.

2. Click anywhere on the screen to advance to Slide 3.

3. Press **Page Down** to advance to Slide 4.

4. Press **Page Up** to go back to Slide 3.

5. Press Spacebar to display Slide 4, and then let the slide show advance automatically until the end.

6. Click the screen to exit Slide Show view.

7. Save the changes and close **Courses**. Close your presentation program.

SUMMARY

In this lesson, you learned:

- You use a presentation program to create a professional slide presentation.

- Most presentation programs start with a new, blank file open in the program window, but you can create a new file or open an existing file at any time.

- Most presentation programs have three views you can use for working with your presentation file: Normal view, Slide Sorter view, and Slide Show view.

- You can use a design template and color scheme to quickly format a presentation with a professional look that includes backgrounds, bullet styles, and fonts.

- You can enter and edit text directly on a slide or in the Outline tab using commands similar to those in a word processing program.

- Most presentation programs include a spelling checker feature that you use to locate and correct spelling errors.

- You can add transitions to jazz up the way the presentation advances from one slide to the next. Transitions may include special effects as well as sound.

- You can preview your presentation in Slide Show view to see how it will look to an audience in a real-life situation.

VOCABULARY *Review*

Define the following terms:

Blinds	Placeholder	Slide show
Bullet	Presentation program	Subordinate level
Color scheme	Primary level	Task pane
Design template	Slide	Thumbnails
Fade	Slide layout	Transitions
Notes pane	Slide pane	

REVIEW *Questions*

TRUE/FALSE

Circle T if the statement is true or F if the statement is false.

T   F   1. Most presentation programs start with a new blank file open in the program window.

T   F   2. Slide Sorter view is usually the default view.

T   F   3. If you apply a design template to one slide, you must apply it to all slides in the presentation.

T   F   4. New slides are inserted before the current slide.

T   F   5. New text is automatically formatted with the font and font size specified by the current design template.

T   F   6. Press Tab to add another item to a bulleted list.

T   F   7. Click Ignore All in a spelling dialog box to correct all occurrences of the same error.

T   F   8. Each slide in a presentation may have a different transition.

T   F   9. You can add sound to a transition.

T   F   10. A slide show always starts with slide 1.

WRITTEN QUESTIONS

Write a brief answer to each of the following questions.

1. Describe at least three ways you can display a presentation that you create with a presentation program.

2. Describe at least three ways you can make text on a slide easier to read.

3. What are at least three reasons for previewing a presentation?

4. What are the three common presentation program views?

5. What are three benefits to using a design template to format a presentation?

FILL IN THE BLANK

Complete the following sentences by writing the correct word or words in the blanks provided.

1. A(n) _____ is a single screen of information within a presentation.

2. Slide Sorter view displays _____ of all slides in the main window, organized in columns and rows.

3. A design _____ is a set of built-in formats that you can apply in one step.

4. A color _____ is a set of coordinated colors used for the background, titles and other text, shadows, fills, bullets (and other accents), and hyperlinks.

5. The slide _____ determines the location of different types of content on the slide, such as text blocks and graphics objects.

6. A(n) _____ is a marker such as a dot, check mark, or asterisk that may precede items in a list.

7. _____ are the effects used to advance from one slide to the next during a slide show.

8. In Slide Show view, press _____ to go back to the previous slide.

9. The main area of a presentation window in Normal view is called the slide _____.

10. You can edit text directly on a slide or in the _____ tab in the tabbed pane.

PROJECTS

PROJECT 12-1

1. If necessary, launch your presentation program, and then open **Project12-1** from the Data files.

2. Save the presentation as **Cloud9**.

3. Display the Outline tab and select the number 9 in the title on Slide 1. Replace it with the word **Nine**.

4. Select **Slide 2** and then display the Slide Layout task pane or dialog box. Change the layout to **Title and 2-Column Text** (or any layout that has placeholders for a title and two columns of text).

5. Move the last four bulleted items from the bottom of column 1 to column 2.

6. Select **Slide 5** and insert a new slide. Apply the **Title Slide** layout (or any layout that has placeholders for a title and a subtitle).

7. Click the title text placeholder and key **Contact Cloud Nine for a Free Consultation**.

8. Click the subtitle placeholder and key **555-555-5555**, press **Enter**, and then key **mail@cld9.net**.

9. Apply the **Clouds** design template (or one similar to it) to all slides in the presentation.

10. Change the color scheme on Slides 2 through 6 to a light blue background with white text.

11. Apply the **Checkerboard Across** transition (or one similar to it) to all slides using the following properties:
    A. **Slow** speed.
    B. No sound.
    C. Advance automatically after **5** seconds, or on a mouse click.

12. Check the spelling in the presentation and correct any errors.

13. Select **Slide 1**, if necessary, and then preview the presentation from the beginning in Slide Show view.

14. Save and close the **Cloud9** file, but leave your presentation software open to use in Project 12-2.

PROJECT 12-2

1. Open **Project12-2** from the Data files.

2. Save the presentation as **Service**.

3. Apply the **Teamwork** design template (or one similar to it) to all slides.

4. Change the color scheme on all slides to the one with a dark green background with a light green arrow.

5. Insert a new slide at the end of the presentation using the **Title Slide** layout (or any layout that has a placeholder for a title and a subtitle).

6. Key the title **For More Information**.

7. Copy the text *Standard Shipping Human Resources Department* from Slide 1 and paste it into the subtitle placeholder on Slide 6.

8. Change the color scheme on Slide 6 only to one with a beige background and a light brown arrow (or a similar color scheme).

9. Apply the **Wheel Clockwise, 4 Spokes** transition (or a similar transition) at **Slow** speed to all slides in the presentation, set to advance on a mouse click or automatically after 5 seconds.

10. For Slide 1 only, add the **Applause** sound to the slide transition.

11. Check the spelling in the presentation and correct any errors.

12. Preview the presentation in Slide Show view from the beginning.

13. Save and close the **Service** file. Leave your presentation software open to use in the next project.

PROJECT 12-3

1. Open **Project12-3** from the Data files.

2. Save the presentation as **Eagle**.

3. Apply the **Mountain Top** design template (or one similar to it) to all slides.

4. Change the color scheme on all slides to the one with a white background with a light blue arrow.

5. Insert a new slide at the end of the presentation using the **Title Slide** layout (or any layout that has a placeholder for a title and a subtitle).

6. Key the title **Let Us Plan Your Next Adventure**.

7. Key the subtitle **Call 555-555-5555 to get started today!**

8. Change the color scheme on Slide 1 only to one with a light blue background and an orange arrow (or a similar color scheme).

9. Change the slide layout on Slide 2 to one with placeholders for a title and two columns of text.

10. Cut the last four bulleted items from the left column and paste them into the right column. Delete the extra bullet, if necessary.

11. Change the slide layout on Slide 3 to one with placeholders for a title and two columns of text.

12. Cut the last four bulleted items from the left column and paste them into the right column. Delete the extra bullet, if necessary.

13. Apply the **Wedge** transition (or a similar transition) at **Slow** speed to all slides in the presentation, set to advance on a mouse click or automatically after **5** seconds.

14. Check the spelling in the presentation and correct any errors.

15. Preview the presentation in Slide Show view from the beginning.

16. Save and close the **Eagle** file. Close your presentation software.

 WEB PROJECT

Color, text formatting, design, and layout are some of the factors that contribute to the effectiveness of a slide presentation. Use the Internet to look up information about how to design a presentation. You should be able to find tips and suggestions about creating different types of presentations, such as how to use color in a marketing presentation, or the use of text in a scientific report. When you have completed your research, write a report of at least 500 words explaining what you have learned, and present it to the class.

 TEAMWORK PROJECT

With your classmates, discuss the elements that you need to make an effective presentation, such as content, color, and organization. Plan a presentation to illustrate a school project, such as a book report for language arts, a science experiment, a math concept, or a social studies project. Consider how you will display the presentation. Will it be on a computer or projected on a screen? Will it run standalone or will someone deliver it? When you are ready, draft an outline that includes the titles and text you will place on each slide, and specifies the order in which the slides will be presented. Then assign a few slides to each member of your team, who then will write the slide text and select a layout. Remember to keep your items short and to the point. When selecting a layout, imagine what other elements you may want on the slide to convey your message, such as clip art, a chart, or an animation. Share the slide information with the other members of your team, and provide feedback on the elements that work as well as where there might be improvement. Take turns entering the slide information into a new presentation. As a group, decide on the design template and color scheme to use and apply them to the presentation. Discuss whether to use transitions throughout and assign them as needed. Finally, proof the presentation for spelling errors. Present your finished product to the class and ask for comments.

CRITICAL *Thinking*

Consider how a company might use a presentation to provide employees with information. For example, how would they present information about benefits or new job opportunities? How about information on regulations and safety guidelines? Create a presentation that your school could use to present information about regulations and safety guidelines to students and teachers. Start by creating an outline that includes the titles and text you want on each slide, and selecting slide layouts. Enter the slides in a new presentation, and apply a design template and color scheme that you think reinforces the message of the presentation. Select and apply transitions and then preview the presentation. Make adjustments and improvements, and then show the presentation to your class.

ENHANCING A PRESENTATION

OBJECTIVES

Upon completion of this lesson, you should be able to:

- Create a new presentation.
- Delete, duplicate, and reorganize slides.
- Change font, font size, and other font attributes.
- Set text alignment.
- Format lists.
- Adjust line spacing.
- Work with design template colors.
- Change the slide background.
- Modify the slide masters.

Estimated Time: 2 hours

VOCABULARY

Content template

Fill effect

Footer

Hanging indent

Indent

Line spacing

List marker

Numbered list

Paragraph spacing

Slide master

Starting value

Symbol font

Title master

Once you have mastered the basics of working with a presentation file, you are ready to take the next step toward building presentations that capture the attention of your audience and communicate your message. Three of the most important elements of an effective presentation include text, color, and flow. In this lesson, you learn how to create and save a new presentation, reorganize the slides in a presentation, and apply formatting to text. You also learn how to work with bulleted and numbered lists, apply colors and backgrounds to slides, and make changes that affect all slides.

Create a New Presentation

Most presentation programs open with a new, blank presentation in the presentation window. You can create another blank presentation at any time. In some programs there is a feature that lets you create a new presentation that includes text and formatting designed for a particular type of presentation, such as for training or marketing. For example, in PowerPoint the AutoContent Wizard will prompt you through the steps for creating a particular type of presentation.

> **Important**
>
> Though the general concepts and tasks discussed in this lesson can be applied to any presentation program, the figures and steps are specific to Microsoft PowerPoint 2003.

Create a Blank Presentation File

As in other types of programs, you can use the New command on the File menu or the New button on the Standard toolbar to create a new, blank presentation file. Each new file includes a single blank slide formatted with the Title Slide (or similar) layout. You use a blank presentation when you want to create a presentation from scratch by entering your own content and applying your own formatting.

In some programs when you select the New command, a dialog box or task pane displays options for creating different types of presentations. You can click Blank presentation to create the new file.

> **Hot Tip**
>
> Select a design template when you create a new file to quickly format the presentation. New slides that you insert will have the design template formatted. For example, in PowerPoint, click From Design Template in the New Presentation task pane to display the Slide Design task pane. Click a template to apply it to the Title Slide in the blank presentation, and to all new slides that you insert.

S TEP-BY-STEP 13.1

1. Launch your presentation program. A new blank presentation displays.

2. Click the **Close Window** button to close the blank presentation.

3. Select the command to create a new blank presentation. For example, in PowerPoint, click **File** on the Menu bar and then click **New**. In the New Presentation Task Pane or dialog box, click **Blank presentation**. A second new blank presentation displays. It may be named *Presentation2*.

> **Note**
>
> In PowerPoint, the option for creating a Blank presentation is available in the New Presentation Task Pane and in the Getting Started Task Pane that displays when you first launch the program.

4. Close the blank presentation file and leave your presentation program open to use in the next exercise.

Create a Presentation from a Content Template

The organization, content, and formatting of a presentation should reflect the purpose and goal of the presentation. For example, a presentation for selling a product requires a different approach from a training presentation. When you know the purpose but you are not sure how you want to organize and format the presentation, you may benefit from using a *content template*. A content template is a presentation template that includes prompts, formatting, and slides organized for a specific presentation type. The prompts provide instructions and tips for creating the presentation. In some programs, you may also select how you plan to output the presentation because that may also affect the colors and layouts used in the finished product. You then modify placeholder text and graphics on each slide to personalize the presentation, add or delete slides as desired, and make other modifications to complete your presentation. Some content templates even include transitions.

S TEP-BY-STEP 13.2

1. Click **File** on the Menu bar and then click **New**.

2. Select the command to create a new presentation using a content template. For example, in PowerPoint, in the New Presentation Task Pane click **From AutoContent wizard**.

3. Follow the prompts to create a product or services overview. For example, in PowerPoint, click **Next**, and then click the **Sales/Marketing** button. In the list of presentation types, click **Product/Services Overview**, and then click **Next**.

4. If the option is available, select to output the presentation on your computer screen, and then click **Next**.

5. In the box available for keying a presentation title, key **Self-Service Window Treatments**. If available, select to include slide numbers on each slide, but do not include any other information. Click **Next** and then click **Finish** to create the presentation. The title that you keyed displays on the title slide, as shown in Figure 13-1. Your name may be entered as a subtitle.

FIGURE 13-1
A presentation created using a content template

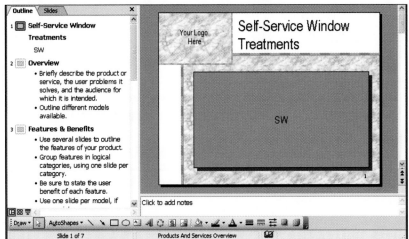

STEP-BY-STEP 13.2 Continued

6. Save the presentation file as **Drapes** and leave it open to use in the next exercise.

> **Note** ☑
>
> The prompts and the number of slides may vary depending on the type of presentation you select to create.

Customize Text Content

A presentation that you create using a content template includes a few slides, already formatted using a design template that is suitable for the type of presentation you are creating and the method of output you plan to use. Each slide has text placeholders that prompt you to insert appropriate information. The prompts may also provide tips and suggestions for determining how many slides you need, and how to organize your presentation. To customize the presentation you simply replace the text prompts with your own information. You may also change the slide layout and apply transitions, as you learned in Lesson 12.

STEP-BY-STEP 13.3

1. On the title slide, click the subtitle placeholder, if necessary, and then click and drag to select the subtitle text (this may be your name or initials) and then key **A Decorator Look at In-Stock Prices**.

2. Click **Slide 2** to make it current. Select the prompt text for the first bullet item and then key **Use our self-service products to select and order a variety of window treatments**.

3. Select the prompt text for the second bullet item and then key **We offer drapes, curtains, blinds, shutters, shades, and more.** The slide should look similar to Figure 13-2.

FIGURE 13-2
Customize text content

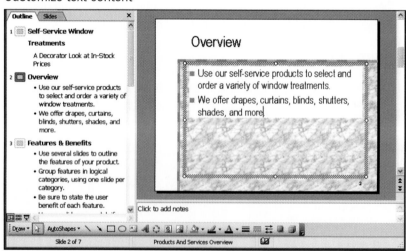

STEP-BY-STEP 13.3 Continued

4. Make Slide 3 current and replace the bulleted prompts with the following:

We provide easy to follow measuring instructions.

We offer a wide range of fabrics and materials.

We allow you to test samples in your home.

We can answer all of your questions before, during, and after you place an order.

5. Insert a new slide, click the placeholder for the title text, and key **Procedure**. Key the following bulleted items:

Meet with Window Consultant.

Select window treatment style and color.

Measure windows at home.

Record measurements on Self-Service Form.

Record selection on Self-Service Form.

Bring, mail, or e-mail form to service center.

Install window treatments.

Enjoy!

6. Make Slide 7 current and replace the sample title with **Sample Pricing (per Window)**. Select the command to display slide layout options if necessary. For example, in PowerPoint, click **Format** on the Menu bar and then click **Slide Layout**. Select the layout that has placeholders for a title and two columns of bulleted text, such as the **Title and 2-Column Text** layout in PowerPoint, and then close the task pane.

7. In column 1, replace the bulleted prompt with the following items:

Drapes: $33.95

Curtains: $27.95

Horizontal blinds: $32.95

Vertical blinds: $38.95

Shutters: $29.95

8. In column 2, key the following items:

Pleated shades: $25.95

Roman shades: $28.95

Bamboo rollups: $22.95

Valance: $15.95

9. Make Slide 8 current and replace the bulleted prompts with the following items:

Our self-service window treatments are available at all store locations.

You may also order online from your home computer.

10. Select the command to display slide transition options. For example, in PowerPoint, click **Slide Show** on the Menu bar and then click **Slide Transition**.

STEP-BY-STEP 13.3 Continued

11. Make Slide 1 current. Select to apply a transition such as **Blinds Horizontal** at **Slow** speed. Set the slides to advance on a mouse click, or automatically after **5** seconds (**00:05**). Apply this transition to all slides. Close the task pane, if necessary.

12. Check the spelling and correct all errors, and then preview the presentation in Slide Show View.

13. Save the changes and leave **Drapes** open to use in the next exercise.

Delete, Duplicate, and Reorganize Slides

To improve the flow and organization of a presentation, you may need to copy, move, and delete slides. Copying slides is useful if you like the layout of a particular slide, and want to quickly create a similar slide. Moving slides makes it easy to reorganize a presentation. And you can delete slides that you no longer need. These tasks are easily accomplished in Slide Sorter View because you can see the overall organization of the presentation on screen at once, but you can use Normal View if you prefer.

To delete a slide, make it current and then select Delete Slide from the Edit menu, or press Delete on the keyboard. To delete multiple slides, select them all and then select the delete command. Some programs may display a warning box; click Yes to delete the slides and continue. Some programs do not display a warning, so be sure you have the correct slide selected. Slides following the deleted slide(s) are automatically renumbered in the presentation.

To make an exact duplicate of a slide, select the original slide and then select the Duplicate command from the Edit menu. The duplicate slide is inserted after the original slide. To move a slide, click and drag it to a new location. As you drag, a thin vertical bar indicates where the slide will be inserted. When the bar is positioned at the location where you want to place the slide, release the mouse button. The slides are renumbered accordingly.

STEP-BY-STEP 13.4

1. Click **Slide 5** to make it current. Click **Edit** on the Menu bar and then click **Delete Slide**. The slide is removed from the presentation and the following slides are renumbered.

2. Change to **Slide Sorter View**. (In some programs a star icon displays to indicate there are transitions for each slide, and the advancement interval. This icon may also display in the tabbed pane in Normal view.) Make sure **Slide 5** is current, and then press **Delete** to delete the slide. Again, the following slides are renumbered.

3. Click and drag **Slide 5** to the end of the presentation. Release the mouse button when the black bar is to the right of Slide 6, as shown in Figure 13-3.

STEP-BY-STEP 13.4 Continued

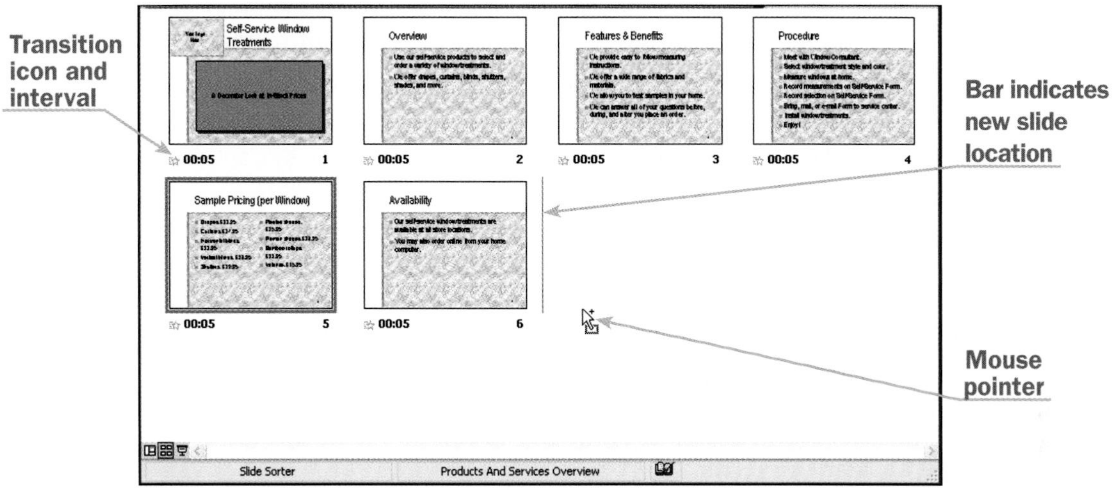

FIGURE 13-3
Drag to move a slide

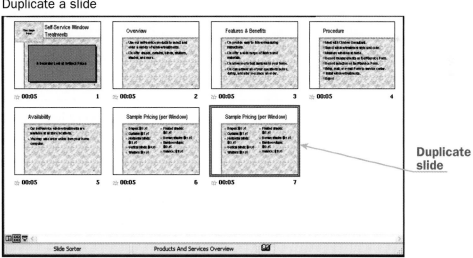

4. With the slide still selected, click **Edit** on the Menu bar and then click **Duplicate**. An exact copy of the slide displays after the original slide (Slide 6), as shown in Figure 13-4.

FIGURE 13-4
Duplicate a slide

5. Save the changes and leave **Drapes** open to use in the next exercise.

Change Font, Font Size, and Other Font Attributes

Although design templates include font formatting, you may want to apply your own, or modify the text on certain slides. You can format text on a slide using most of the same techniques you use to format text in a word-processing document. You can apply fonts, font sizes, font styles, and font colors. You may even be able to apply some font effects, such as shadows.

The easiest view for working with text is Normal View. To modify selected words or characters, simply select the text in the Outline tab or in the Slide pane, and then select the commands to make the change. To modify all text in a placeholder, select the placeholder itself. To select a placeholder, click within it to make it active, and then click its border. An active placeholder has diagonal hash marks as its border; a selected placeholder has a thick dotted line as its border.

In some programs, toolbar buttons make it easy to access common font formatting commands, or you may use a Font dialog box. For example, in PowerPoint, you can access the Font and Font Size boxes on the Formatting toolbar, as well as buttons for applying bold, italic, underline, and shadows. There are also buttons for increasing and decreasing the font size. When you click the Increase Font Size button, for example, the text is increased to the next font size shown on the Font Size list. This is a convenient method for changing font size when you are not sure of the exact size you need. Table 13-1 illustrates and describes some of the common text formatting toolbar buttons.

> **Hot Tip**
>
> Keep in mind that using more than two or three fonts on a slide may make the text more difficult to read and unattractive. In addition, using too many font styles—bold, italics, underlines—and effects such as shadows, can be confusing to the viewer.

TABLE 13-1
Common text formatting tools

ICON	TOOL NAME	DESCRIPTION
B	Bold	Applies the bold font style to selected or new text.
I	Italic	Applies the italic font style to selected or new text.
U	Underline	Applies a continuous underline to selected or new text.
S	Shadow	Applies the shadow font effect to selected or new text.
A▲	Increase Font Size	Increases the font size of selected text to the next larger standard size.
A▼	Decrease Font Size	Decreases the font size of selected text to the next smaller standard size.
A	Font Color	Displays a palette of color swatches from which you may select a font color.

Many programs have a toolbar button that you can use to copy text formatting. For example, in PowerPoint, you use the Format Painter button. Copying formatting may be useful for quickly applying consistent formatting on a slide, or throughout a presentation. First, click the formatted text, then click the button for copying formatting, and then click the text to format. To copy the formatting more than once in succession, click the formatted text, double-click the button for copying formatting, click the first text to format, click the next text to format, and so on. Click the button or press Esc when you are finished to turn the feature off.

STEP-BY-STEP 13.5

1. In the **Drapes** file, change to Normal View. On Slide 6 click on the placeholder on the right to select it. (Click the border, or click within the text, and then click the border.) Then press **Delete** twice. This deletes the text in the placeholder and then the placeholder itself.

2. Change the slide layout for Slide 6 to one that includes placeholders for a title and a column of text, such as the **Title and Text** layout in PowerPoint.

3. Make Slide 7 current, select the placeholder on the left and then press **Delete** twice. Change the slide layout to one that includes placeholders for a title and a column of text.

4. On Slide 6, double-click the word **Drapes** in the first bullet item to select it. Click the **Bold** button on the Formatting toolbar, and then click the **Italic** button.

5. With the word **Drapes** still selected, double-click the tool used for copying formatting, such as the **Format Painter** button. Click the word **Curtains** in the second bullet item. The bold and italic formatting from the word Drapes is copied to the word Curtains.

6. Continuing on Slide 6, click the words **Horizontal**, **blinds**, **Vertical**, **blinds**, and **Shutters**. On Slide 7 click the words **Pleated**, **shades**, **Roman**, **shades**, **Bamboo**, **rollups**, and **Valance** to copy the formatting to these words as well. Click the **Format Painter** button to turn the feature off. When you deselect the placeholder, Slide 7 should look similar to Figure 13-5.

FIGURE 13-5
Bold and italic applied to text

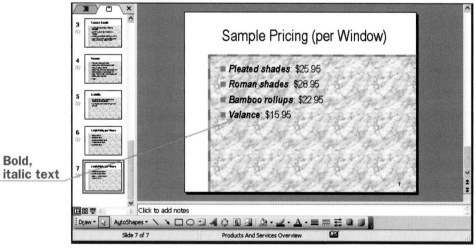

7. Make Slide 1 current and click to select the placeholder around the subtitle text.

8. Click the **Font** drop-down arrow on the Formatting toolbar, and then click **Arial Black**.

9. Click the **Font Size** drop-down arrow on the Formatting toolbar and then click **44**.

10. Click the **Shadow** button on the Formatting toolbar to apply a shadow effect.

STEP-BY-STEP 13.5 Continued

11. Select the placeholder around the title text and then click the **Font Color** drop-down arrow. Click the **Brown** swatch third from the left on the top row (the ScreenTip is *Follow Shadows Scheme Color*).

12. Click the **Bold** button on the Formatting toolbar, and then click outside the slide to deselect the place-holder. The slide should look similar to Figure 13-6.

FIGURE 13-6
Modify font formatting

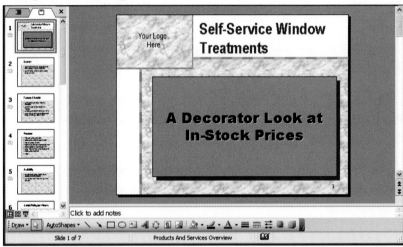

13. Save the changes and leave **Drapes** open to use in the next exercise.

Set Text Alignment

The current design template controls the way text aligns in slide placeholders. In many design templates, for example, title text is left-aligned (placed against the left margin), but in some designs title text is centered or right-aligned. You can change the alignment of text in any placeholder using the Alignment buttons on the Formatting toolbar. You can also justify text, which adds spaces between words to force the text to align against both the left and right margins.

> **Hot Tip**
>
> Some programs, such as PowerPoint, use a feature called AutoFit to automatically adjust the font size so that text fits within a placeholder. To turn off AutoFit, click Tools on the Menu bar, click AutoCorrect Options, and then click the AutoFormat As You Type tab. Click to clear the *AutoFit title text to place-holder* and then *AutoFit body text to placeholder* check boxes, and then click OK.

To align text, change to Normal View and then click anywhere in a bulleted item, slide title, or paragraph. You can also select an entire placeholder to change all the text inside. Then click the Align Left, Center, or Align Right button, located on the Formatting tool-bar. To justify text, select it and click Format, click Alignment, and click Justify.

S TEP-BY-STEP 13.6

1. On Slide 1, select the title text placeholder and then click the **Center** button on the Formatting toolbar. All text in the placeholder is center-aligned.

2. Select the subtitle text placeholder and then click the **Align Right** button on the Formatting toolbar. All text in the placeholder aligns with the right margin. The slide should look similar to Figure 13-7.

FIGURE 13-7
Modify text alignment

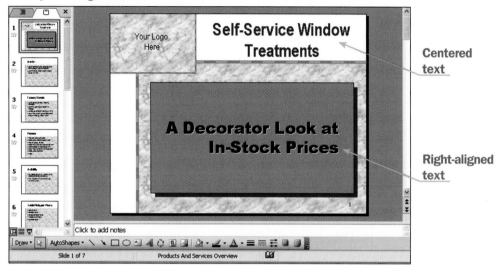

3. Save the changes and leave **Drapes** open to use in the next exercise.

Format Lists

In most presentation programs, you can create bulleted lists (lists or items preceded by a symbol) and ***numbered lists,*** which are lists in which each item is preceded by a number or letter, in consecutive order. Typically, bulleted lists are used when the order of items does not matter, such as to list agenda items, important talking points, and brief descriptions. Numbered lists are used when the order is important, such as in procedural steps or directions. The format of a list is determined by the current design template.

To apply default list formatting, select the text or the placeholder, and then click either the Numbering or Bullets button on the Formatting toolbar. You may customize a list to change the ***list marker,*** which is the symbol inserted to the left of items in a list. For example, you can select a different marker, change the color, or adjust the size. The marker size is usually measured as a percentage of the size of the text. You may also adjust the ***indent,*** which is the distance between the marker (or paragraph text) and the left margin.

Customize a Bulleted List

In a bulleted list, each item is preceded by a bullet symbol—the marker—specified by the current design template. You can select a different marker from a list of available symbols, change the bullet's size in relation to the text, and change the bullet color. You can change the bullet for a single item, or for all items within a placeholder.

In most programs you can customize a bulleted list. For example, in PowerPoint, to customize a bulleted list, select the item, items, or placeholder, and then select options on the Bulleted tab of the Bullets and Numbering dialog box, which is shown in Figure 13-8. Usually, you open this dialog box by clicking Bullets and Numbering on the Format menu.

FIGURE 13-8
Bulleted tab of the Bullets and Numbering dialog box

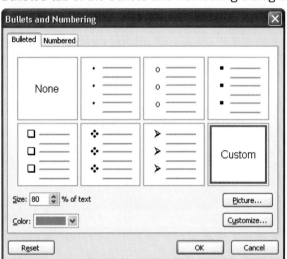

If you want to use a symbol that is not displayed in the built-in list, you can select one from an available *symbol font*, which is a font such as Monotype Sorts, Symbol, Webdings, Wingdings, and ZapfDingbats that includes symbol characters. To select a symbol to use as a bullet marker, click the Customize button in the Bullets and Numbering dialog box, select a symbol font from the Font drop-down list, click a symbol, and then click OK.

Hot Tip

In some programs you can select a clip art picture to use as a bullet marker. For example, in PowerPoint, click the Picture button in the Bullets and Numbering dialog box, select a picture, and then click OK. You can even import a picture such as a company logo. Click the Import button in the Picture Bullet dialog box. Navigate to the folder containing the file, select the file, click Add, and then click OK.

STEP-BY-STEP 13.7

1. Make Slide 3 current and select the placeholder around the bulleted list.

2. Select the command to open the Bullets and Numbering dialog box, and make sure the **Bulleted** tab is active.

3. Click a marker that looks like a right-pointing arrowhead. If there is no arrowhead marker available, select a different marker. If your program lets you customize the marker, use that option to select an arrowhead.

4. Change the color of the marker to **black**. For example, in PowerPoint, click the **Color** drop-down arrow and then click a **black** color swatch.

STEP-BY-STEP 13.7 Continued

5. Apply the change. For example, in PowerPoint, click **OK** in the dialog box. The slide should look similar to Figure 13-9.

FIGURE 13-9
Customized bulleted list

Black, arrowhead marker

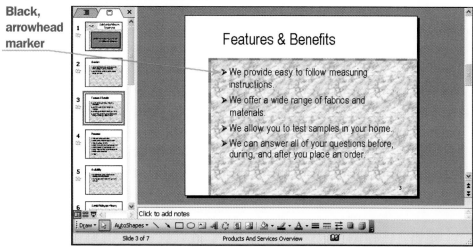

6. Save the changes and leave **Drapes** open to use in the next exercise.

Customize a Numbered List

Customizing a numbered list is similar to customizing a bulleted list. Select the item, items, or placeholder, and then select options to change the numbering style and options such as color and size. In PowerPoint, you select numbering options on the Numbered tab of the Bullets and Numbering dialog box shown in Figure 13-10. You can also change the *starting value* if you want the list to begin with a number other than 1. The starting value is the number used for the first item in the list.

FIGURE 13-10
Numbered tab of the Bullets and Numbering dialog box

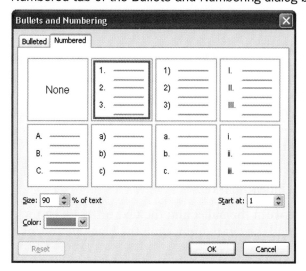

S TEP-BY-STEP 13.8

1. Make Slide 4 current and select the placeholder around the bulleted list.

2. Select the command to apply numbered list formatting to the selected items. For example, in PowerPoint, click the **Numbering** button on the Formatting toolbar to change the items to a numbered list.

3. Select the command to open the Bullets and Numbering dialog box, and make sure the **Numbered** tab is active.

4. Change the color of the number to **black**. For example, in PowerPoint, click the **Color** drop-down arrow and click a **black** color swatch.

5. Increase the size of the marker to **100%** of the text.

6. Apply the change. The slide should look similar to Figure 13-11.

FIGURE 13-11
Customized numbered list

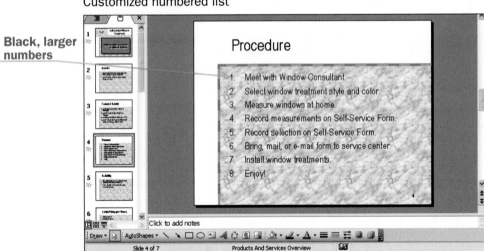

Black, larger numbers

7. Save the changes and leave **Drapes** open to use in the next exercise.

Adjust Indentation

In general, lists are formatted with a *hanging indent,* which means the beginning of the first line—the marker—is indented to one spot, and the beginning of the text lines are indented more. You can adjust the indent for all lines or for the first line only, and you can increase or decrease the amount of space between the marker and the text. In most programs, you adjust the indents by dragging the indent markers on the ruler. First, select the item or items to change—you cannot change the indents for an entire placeholder—and then do one of the following:

■ To adjust the position of the bullet or to add an indent to the first line of a paragraph only, drag the First Line Indent marker.

■ To adjust the distance between the bullet and the text or to adjust the distance between the lines in a paragraph and the left margin, drag the Hanging Indent marker.

■ To move the first line and the hanging indents together to maintain the relationship between the bullet and the text and to increase or decrease the paragraph's distance from the left margin, drag the Left Indent marker.

STEP-BY-STEP 13.9

1. Display the rulers, if necessary. (Click **View** on the Menu bar, and then click **Ruler**.)

2. Make Slide 4 current, if necessary, and then click and drag to select all items in the numbered list.

3. Drag the **Left Indent** marker (the rectangle below the triangle along the bottom edge of the horizontal ruler) to the 1.5-inch mark on the horizontal ruler. This moves the list marker and the text to the right, as shown in Figure 13-12.

FIGURE 13-12
Customize an indent

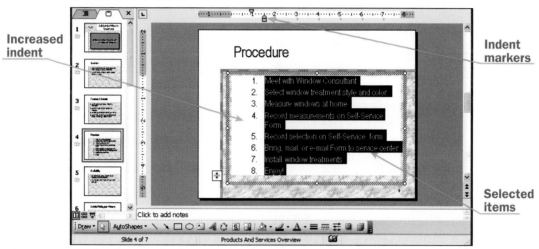

4. Make Slide 5 current, and then click and drag to select both items in the list.

5. Drag the Hanging Indent marker (the triangle above the rectangle along the bottom edge of the horizontal ruler) to the 1.0-inch mark on the horizontal ruler to increase the distance between the bullets and the text.

6. Save the changes and leave **Drapes** open to use in the next exercise.

Adjust Line Spacing

Line spacing is the amount of white space between the base of one line and the top of the next line. *Paragraph spacing* is the amount of white space before or after a paragraph. In both instances, if the space is too narrow or too wide, the text may be difficult to read, and look awkward on the slide. Use the options in your program's Line Spacing dialog box to adjust the space between lines and paragraphs. For example, to open the Line Spacing dialog box in PowerPoint, click Format on the Menu bar and then click Line Spacing. It should look similar to Figure 13-13. Usually, the space is measured in lines, with an option to use points if you prefer. You may even be able to preview the change to see if it improves the slide before you apply it.

FIGURE 13-13
Line Spacing dialog box

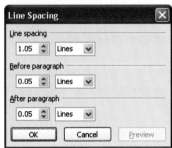

STEP-BY-STEP 13.10

1. Make Slide 3 current and select the placeholder around the bulleted list.

2. Select the command to display the Line Spacing dialog box. For example in PowerPoint, click **Format** on the Menu bar, and then click **Line Spacing**.

3. Decrease the *Line spacing* value to **.85 Lines**.

4. Increase the *Before paragraph* value to **0.5 Lines**.

5. Increase the *After paragraph* value to **0.5 Lines**.

6. If available, click the **Preview** button to see how the changes affect the slide. Notice that the program automatically adjusts the font size so that the text still fits within the placeholder. (Drag the dialog box out of the way, if necessary, to see the changes.)

7. Decrease the *Before paragraph* and *After paragraph* values to **0.3 Lines**, and then click the **Preview** button to view the change. Click **OK** to apply the change. The slide should look similar to Figure 13-14.

STEP-BY-STEP 13.10 Continued

FIGURE 13-14
Modify line and paragraph spacing

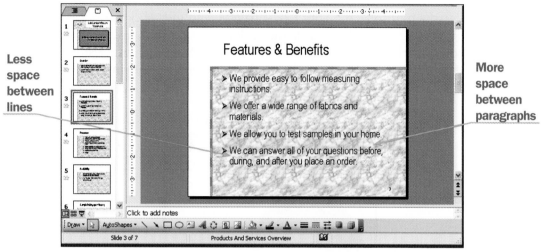

8. Save the changes and leave **Drapes** open to use in the next exercise.

Work with Design Template Colors

Color is a vital part of any presentation. The colors that you use affect both the appearance and the readability of the slide. For example, if there is not enough contrast between the background and the content, the slide will be difficult to read. Using a color for content that has a high contrast with the background makes the content appear to float over the slide instead of blending into it, so it is easier to read and makes a memorable impact. Colors can even affect a viewer's emotional reaction to a slide. For example, black may be depressing, whereas red may be too exciting.

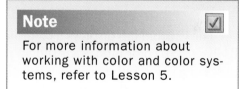

Note

For more information about working with color and color systems, refer to Lesson 5.

Most presentation design templates have preset color schemes that use a coordinated palette of eight colors to provide the optimum contrast and coordination among different elements on the slide. The colors usually affect the title and body text, slide background, bullets, object shadows and fills, and accents, such as list markers. When you open a color palette to format an element such as the font or a bullet marker, the colors in the color scheme display across the top line, and coordinating colors that are not part of the color scheme display across the second line. (You have used these palettes to select font and list marker colors.) The color marked as Automatic is the default scheme color for the selected element. You can click any color to apply it to the selection. Alternatively, you may add a standard or customized color to the color scheme palette, or change the colors in the color scheme completely.

Add a Color to a Color Scheme Palette

To add a color to a color scheme palette, select it in the Colors dialog box and then click OK. Usually, you can access the Colors dialog box by clicking More Colors at the bottom of the color palette you use to apply color to a particular element. For example in PowerPoint, click the Font Color drop-down arrow to display the Font Color palette, and then click More Colors, or display the Bullets and Numbering dialog box, click the Color drop down arrow, and then click More Colors. In most programs, the Colors dialog box has two tabs: Standard and Custom. The Standard tab displays a palette of selected colors from the RGB color model, as shown in Figure 13-15.

FIGURE 13-15
Standard tab of the Colors dialog box

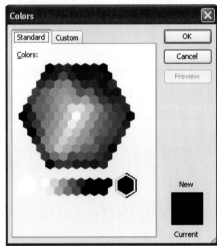

The Custom tab displays a color bar that you can use to select a custom color using either the RGB or HSL color models, as shown in Figure 13-16. Either click somewhere in the color palette to select a color and then adjust its value with the slider, or select the model from the drop-down list and then enter the color values in the appropriate boxes. Click OK to apply the color and add it to the color palette.

FIGURE 13-16
Custom tab of the Colors dialog box

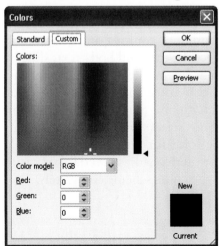

STEP-BY-STEP 13.11

1. Make Slide 1 current and select the title text placeholder.

2. Select the command to display the dialog box where you can set custom colors. For example, in PowerPoint, click the **Font Color** drop-down arrow on the Formatting toolbar, and then click **More Colors** to display the Colors dialog box. Make sure the **Custom** tab is active, and that **RGB** is selected as the Color model.

3. In the Red box, key **200**. In the Green box, key **100**. In the **Blue** box, key **20**. Click **OK** to apply the change to the selected text, and to add the color to the color palette.

4. Make Slide 2 current and select the title text placeholder.

5. Select the command to display the font color palette. For example, in PowerPoint click the **Font Color** drop-down arrow on the Formatting toolbar. The new, custom color should display at the left end of the second row of swatches, as shown in Figure 13-17.

FIGURE 13-17
Add a color to the color palette

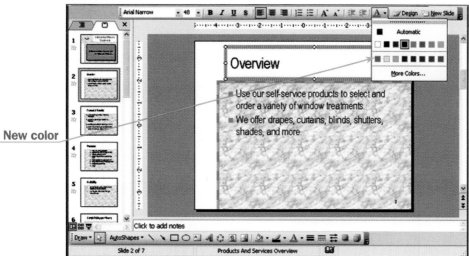

6. Click the new custom color swatch to apply the color to the selected text.

7. Save the changes and leave **Drapes** open to use in the next exercise.

Change the Colors in a Scheme

You can also modify the colors in a particular color scheme, which is useful if you want to change the color formatting on all slides formatted with that color scheme, or create a completely new color scheme to store with the current design template.

To change colors in the current color scheme, display the task pane or dialog box that lists the current color scheme, and then click the command to edit the scheme. For example, in PowerPoint, click Format on the Menu bar, click Slide Design, and then click the Color Schemes link at the top of the task pane to display the available color schemes. Click the scheme you want to edit, and then click the Edit Color Schemes link at the bottom of the task pane. A dialog box, such as the Edit Color Scheme dialog box, displays.

In PowerPoint, you can click the element you want to change and then click the Change Color button to open the Colors dialog box. Select or create a new color and then click OK to return to the Edit Color Scheme dialog box. You may click the Preview button to see how the new colors look on a slide, click the Add As Standard Scheme button to add the new color scheme to the list of schemes associated with the current design template, or click Apply to apply the changes. If you apply the changes without creating a new color scheme, the scheme is available for use with the current presentation file, but not with other files that use the same design template. Other programs offer similar features for changing the colors in a color scheme.

S TEP-BY-STEP 13.12

1. Make Slide 1 current, and then select the command to display the color schemes available for the current design template. For example, in PowerPoint, click **Format** on the Menu bar, click **Slide Design**, and then click **Color Schemes** in the Slide Design task pane.

2. Click the command to edit the color scheme. In PowerPoint, the command is **Edit Color Schemes** at the bottom of the task pane. A dialog box, such as the Edit Color Scheme dialog box shown in Figure 13-18, displays.

FIGURE 13-18
Edit Color Scheme dialog box

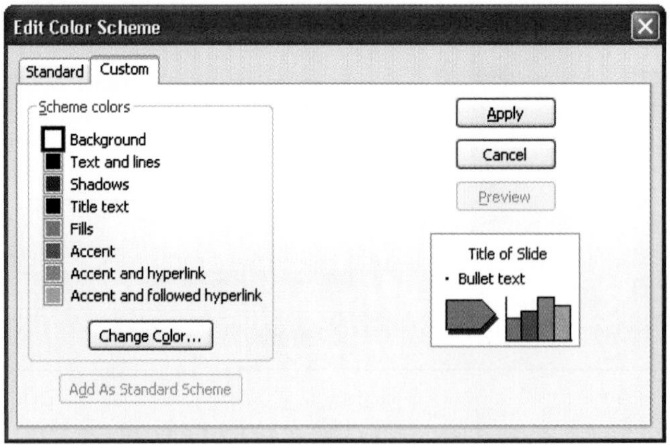

3. Select the option to change the background color. For example, in PowerPoint, click **Background**, if necessary, and then click the **Change Color** button. The Background Color dialog box—which is similar to the Colors dialog box—opens.

4. Change the color to black. In PowerPoint, for example, click the **black** color swatch, and then click **OK**. The background color changes to black.

5. Select the command to change the color used for shadows to a custom color. For example, in PowerPoint, still in the Edit Color Scheme dialog box, click **Shadows** and click the **Change Color** button. Click the **Custom** tab, if necessary, and make sure the **RGB** color model is selected.

STEP-BY-STEP 13.12 Continued

6. In the Red box, key **200**; in the Green box, key **100**; in the Blue box, key **20**; and then click **OK**. This changes the shadow color to the same custom orange you used for the title text previously in this lesson.

7. Apply the changes. For example, in PowerPoint, click the **Apply** button. The new background and shadow colors are applied throughout the presentation. Slide 1 should look similar to Figure 13-19.

FIGURE 13-19
Modified color scheme

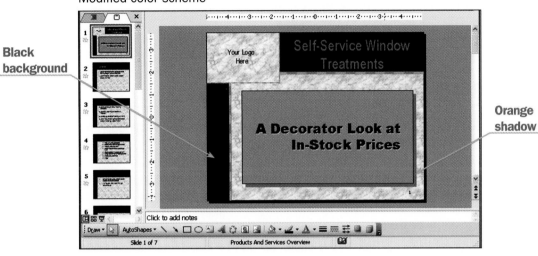

8. Save the changes and leave **Drapes** open to use in the next exercise.

Change the Slide Background

To modify the background of a single slide or selected slides, you can change the color or apply a *fill effect*. A fill effect is a pattern, gradient, picture, or texture that you apply to the fill of an object or the background of a slide. You can select a background color or fill effect from the Background dialog box, which you can usually open by selecting the Background command on the Format menu.

To apply a color, you usually click the color palette drop-down arrow in the Background dialog box and then click a color. To apply a fill effect, click Fill Effects on the color palette to open the Fill Effects dialog box. Select the options you want to use, and then click OK to return to the Background dialog box. The Fill Effects dialog box typically has four tabs that you can use to select different options, but your program may have different tabs, or different methods for changing the background.

- Gradient. Use the options on the Gradient tab to blend colors horizontally, vertically, diagonally, from the corners, or from the center. Some programs have preset gradient combinations, or you can select the colors you want to blend.

- Texture. On the Texture tab you can select from the list of available textures.

> **Hot Tip**
>
> To remove a background graphic that is part of the design template you selected, select *Omit background graphics from master* before clicking Apply to All or Apply in the Background dialog box.

■ Pattern. Click the Pattern tab to display a palette of pattern options. Select a color in the Foreground list and then a different color in the Background list, and click the desired pattern in the palette. For best results, use two colors that are fairly light so that the pattern background does not overwhelm the slide text.

■ Picture. On the Picture tab you may select a graphic as your slide background. This option is useful for adding a photograph or other graphic to the background of a slide. For example, you may want to use a company logo as a background, or a picture of a product.

Important

Fill effects may impact the viewers' ability to read text and graphics on a slide. Be careful not to select an effect that has colors similar to the colors you use for slide content, or that has a complicated pattern or texture that might distract the viewers' attention.

STEP-BY-STEP 13.13

1. Select **Slide 1**, if necessary, and then select the command to display the Background dialog box. For example, in PowerPoint, click **Format** on the Menu bar, and then click **Background**.

2. Select the command to display the Fill Effects dialog box. For example in PowerPoint, click the drop-down arrow for the current background color, and then click **Fill Effects** on the color palette.

3. Select the option to apply a texture such as Blue tissue paper. For example, in PowerPoint, click the **Texture** tab, and click the **Blue tissue paper** texture (the first thumbnail in the third row). If Blue tissue paper is not available, select a different texture.

4. Apply the change. If available, click the **Preview** button to see the new background on the current slide.

5. Select the command to apply a fill effect again, and this time select the option to apply a gradient. In PowerPoint, for example, display the Fill Effects dialog box again and click the **Gradient** tab.

6. If your program has the option, click the **Preset** option button, and then click **Parchment** in the *Preset colors* list. If the preset option is not available, select any similar gradient color scheme.

7. If available, click the **From corner** Shading style, or any similar style, and then apply the change.

8. If necessary, select the command to apply the change to the Background to the title slide only. For example, in PowerPoint, in the Background dialog box, click the **Apply** button. The title slide should look similar to Figure 13-20.

STEP-BY-STEP 13.13 Continued

FIGURE 13-20
Apply a gradient to the slide background

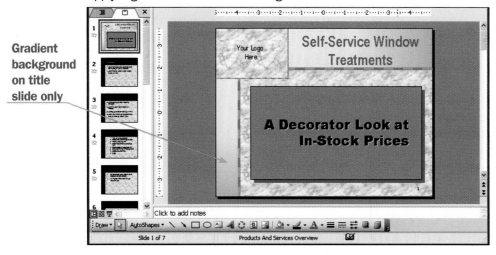

Gradient background on title slide only

9. Save the changes and leave **Drapes** open to use in the next exercise.

Modify the Slide Masters

When you want to make global changes to presentation slides, you can edit the *slide master*. The slide master is a template that stores certain layout and formatting characteristics for all slides formatted with a specific design template, except those slides formatted with the Title Slide layout. When you want the changes to affect title slides, you can edit the *title master*, which is a slide master specifically designed for title slides. Editing a slide master is a fast and easy method of ensuring that all slides have the same formatting. There is one slide master and one title master for each design template used in a presentation. So, if you use two design templates in a presentation, you will have two slide masters and two title masters.

Typically, you can edit the title style and the text style by modifying the font and paragraph formatting options. You can also resize and move the title and body area placeholders. You can resize placeholders by dragging one of the selection handles. Resizing a placeholder is useful when you want to use a larger font for text throughout the presentation, or make more or less room available for objects such as pictures. You can reposition a placeholder by dragging it to a different location on the slide. This is useful if you want to make a background graphic visible, or leave room for graphic content such as clip art on the slides.

> **Extra for Experts**
>
> In PowerPoint, if you want to change the footer for selected slides, change to Normal View and display the Header and Footer dialog box again. Make your changes and click Apply.

> **Note** ☑
>
> Some changes you make to the title style on the slide master also affect the title style on the title master. For example, if you change the title style on the slide master from 44 to 46 point, the title style on the title master changes proportionately, from 51 to 53 point. Therefore, it is a good idea to edit the slide master first, and then make any final adjustments to the title master.

In addition, you can add information to the *footer* of presentation slides. The footer is the area across the bottom of each slide. Most programs provide footer space for the date, the slide number, and customized text. You may also be able to insert graphics. You set footer options and key footer text in the Header and Footer dialog box.

To display a slide master in PowerPoint, make any slide except a title slide current, click View on the Menu bar, click Master, and click Slide Master. To display a title master, make the title slide current, click View on the Menu bar, click Master, and then click Slide Master. To display the Header and Footer dialog box, click View on the Menu bar, and then click Header and Footer.

Hot Tip

In PowerPoint, if you want the date in the footer to update automatically, select the *Update automatically* check box in the Header and Footer dialog box. Alternatively, select the Fixed check box to keep the date you key from updating.

STEP-BY-STEP 13.14

1. Make Slide 2 current, and then select the command to display the slide master. For example in PowerPoint, click **View** on the Menu bar, click **Master**, and then click **Slide Master**.

2. Select the placeholder around the title text. (You may not be able to see the text if it is formatted with the same color as the slide background.)

3. Change the font color to the custom color you added to the palette earlier in this lesson. For example, in PowerPoint, click the **Font Color** drop-down arrow on the Formatting toolbar, and click the custom color. It should be on the left end of the second row of color swatches. This changes the color for all title text.

4. Select the placeholder around the bulleted text, and then apply bold formatting to all text within the selected placeholder. Change the bullet list marker to the arrowhead you applied to Slide 3 earlier in this lesson.

5. Change the bullet marker color to black. This changes the bullet marker for all slides.

6. Select the command to display the Header and Footer options for the slide master. For example, in PowerPoint, click **View** on the Menu bar, and then click **Header and Footer**.

7. Select the option to display today's date. In PowerPoint, for example, select the **Date and time** check box, select the **Fixed** option, and then key today's date in the Fixed text box.

8. Select the option to hide slide numbers. For example, in PowerPoint, deselect the **Slide number** check box.

9. Add your name as a footer on all slides. In PowerPoint, for example, select the **Footer** check box, and then key your name in the text box.

10. Select the option to hide the header and footer information on the title slide. For example, in PowerPoint, select the **Don't show on title slide** check box. The Header and Footer dialog box should look similar to Figure 13-21.

STEP-BY-STEP 13.14 Continued

FIGURE 13-21
Header and Footer dialog box

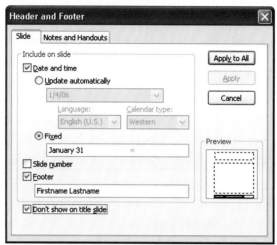

11. Apply the changes to all slides, and then change back to Normal View. For example in PowerPoint, click **View** on the Menu bar, and then click **Normal** or click **Close Master View** on the Slide Master View toolbar.

12. Select Slide 1 and then preview the presentation in Slide Show View.

13. Save the changes and close the **Drapes** file. Close your presentation program.

SUMMARY

In this lesson, you learned:

■ You can create a new, blank presentation when you want to enter your own content and apply your own formatting.

■ When you base a new presentation on a content template, it includes prompts, formatting, and slides organized for a specific presentation type.

■ You can duplicate, move, or delete slides as desired to improve the flow of your presentation.

■ Buttons on the Formatting toolbar allow you to change the font and font size of text, to add bold or italic, to change the color of text, and to adjust text alignment.

■ In some programs you can copy formatting.

■ You can align text on the left or right margins, centered, or justified.

■ You should use bulleted lists when the order of items does not matter, and numbered lists when the order is important.

■ You can customize a list by changing the marker or by adjusting the indent.

■ When you change the line spacing and the paragraph spacing you can make the text on a slide easier to read.

- It is important to make sure there is enough contrast between the background of a slide and the content on the slide.

- You can change the color of objects on a slide to another color in the color scheme, or you can add a color to the scheme or create your own colors.

- When changing the background of a slide, you can apply a flat color, gradient, pattern, texture, or picture. You can also remove the background graphic from the design template if you like.

- To make global changes to presentation slides, you can edit the slide master and the title master.

- You can insert footers on presentation slides.

VOCABULARY *Review*

Define the following terms:

Content template	Line spacing	Starting value
Fill effect	List marker	Symbol font
Footer	Numbered list	Title master
Hanging indent	Paragraph spacing	
Indent	Slide master	

REVIEW *Questions*

TRUE / FALSE

Circle T if the statement is true or F if the statement is false.

T   F   1. Prompts in a content template may provide tips for creating the presentation.

T   F   2. You cannot rearrange slides in a presentation.

T   F   3. You cannot duplicate slides in Normal View.

T   F   4. To modify all text in a placeholder, select the placeholder itself.

T   F   5. All text in a presentation is left-aligned.

T   F   6. Bullets are always the same size as the text.

T   F   7. All numbered lists start with number 1.

T   F   8. The amount of white space before or after a paragraph is called the marker.

T   F   9. Most presentation design templates have preset color schemes that use a coordinated palette of eight colors.

T   F   10. You can modify the colors in a color scheme.

WRITTEN QUESTIONS

Write a brief answer to each of the following questions.

1. Describe at least three benefits to using a content template to create a new presentation.

2. Explain why contrast is important for colors on a slide.

3. What are the four types of fill effects you can apply to a slide background?

4. Name at least four ways that you can change font formatting.

5. Describe the difference between a bulleted list and a numbered list and explain when you might use one or the other. Give examples of each.

FILL IN THE BLANK

Complete the following sentences by writing the correct word or words in the blanks provided.

1. When you know the purpose but you are not sure how you want to organize and format the presentation, you may benefit from using a _____ template.

2. A(n) _____ placeholder has diagonal hash marks as its border.

3. A(n) _____ placeholder has a thick dotted line as its border.

4. Click the _____ Font Size button to make the selected font larger.

5. _____ text to add spaces between words to force the text to align against both the left and right margins.

6. Typically, _____ lists are used when the order of items does not matter.

7. A list _____ is the symbol inserted to the left of items in a list.

8. Most lists have a(n) _____ indent, which means the beginning of the first line—the marker—is indented to one spot, and the beginning of the next lines are indented more.

9. _____ spacing is the amount of white space between the base of one line and the top of the next line.

10. The slide _____ is a template that stores certain layout and formatting characteristics for all slides formatted with a specific design template.

PROJECTS

PROJECT 13-1

1. Launch your presentation program and create a new presentation file based on a training content template for display on a computer screen. (If your program prompts you to install the template, ask your instructor for permission, and then install it.) Key the title **Kitchen Safety**, and include slide numbers.

2. Save the presentation as **Kitchen**.

3. On the title slide, replace the default subtitle text with the text **Food Science Lab Safety Regulations**.

4. Increase the font size of the subtitle to **40** points, and center it within the placeholder. Increase the font size of the title to **54** points and apply the Bold font style.

5. On Slide 2, replace the bullet item prompts with the following bulleted list:

   ■ **Kitchen safety is of primary importance.**

   ■ **No experiments will take place until all rules and regulations are understood.**

   ■ **All rules and regulations will be followed, with NO EXCEPTIONS.**

6. On Slide 3, replace the sample title with the title **Key Points**, and then replace the bullet item prompts with the following bulleted list:

   ■ **Cleanliness**

   ■ **Fire Safety**

   ■ **Food Handling**

   ■ **Respect**

7. Delete Slides 4 and 5. (In PowerPoint, these are Overview and Vocabulary.)

8. On the new Slide 4, key the title **Cleanliness** to replace any sample title. Replace the bullet item prompts with the following bulleted list:

   - **Work area must be sanitary.**
   - **Hair must be tied back or restrained by a hair net.**
   - **Hands must be washed with soap before, during, and after all experiments.**

9. On Slide 5, key the title **In Case of Fire** to replace any sample title. Replace the bullet item prompts with the following bulleted list:

   - **Report fire to instructor.**
   - **If possible, retrieve and use fire extinguisher.**
   - **If necessary, pull fire alarm.**
   - **Evacuate building in a calm, orderly, fashion.**

10. Change the bulleted list on Slide 5 to a numbered list.

11. Delete Slide 6.

12. Replace the title text on the new Slide 6 with the text **For More Information**. Replace the bullet item prompts with the following bulleted list:

    - **Contact your instructor.**
    - **Consult your training manual.**
    - **Consult the department's Web site.**

13. Move Slide 6 so it displays after the title slide.

14. Check the spelling and correct all errors. Preview the presentation in Slide Show View, clicking to advance the slides.

15. Save the changes and close **Kitchen**, but leave your presentation program open to use in Project 13-2.

PROJECT 13-2

1. Open **Project13-2** from the data files for this lesson.

2. Save the file as **Kitchen2**.

3. Select Slide 6, *In Case of Fire*, and duplicate it.

4. Select Slide 7 and replace the title with **In Case of Accident**. Edit the numbered items to create the following list:

   - **Report accident to instructor.**
   - **If possible, retrieve and use first aid kit.**
   - **If necessary, call 911.**
   - **If possible, assist in a calm, orderly fashion.**

5. On Slide 1, change the color of the title text to the red that is part of the color scheme palette.

6. On Slide 2, select the placeholder around the bulleted list and then customize the bullet marker to use a checked box symbol. For example, in PowerPoint use the following steps:
   A. Display the Bulleted tab of Bullets and Numbering dialog box.
   B. Click the **Customize** button.
   C. Click the **Font** drop-down arrow and select the **Wingdings** font.
   D. Locate and select the checked box.
   E. Click **OK**.
   F. Increase the size of the marker to **90%** of the text.
   G. Click **OK**.

7. Increase the spacing before and after the paragraphs to **0.5 Lines**.

8. On Slide 6, increase the size of the number markers to **90%** of the text, and change the color to **black**.

9. Copy the number list formatting from Slide 6 to Slide 7.

10. Preview the presentation in Slide Show View, clicking to advance the slides.

11. Save the changes and close the **Kitchen2** file, but leave your presentation program open to use in Project 13-3.

PROJECT 13-3

1. Open **Project13-3** from the data files for this lesson.

2. Save the file as **Kitchen3**.

3. Select the title slide and display the title slide master.

4. Select the subtitle placeholder on the title slide master, and drag it down about **1.0** inch, and to the left about **1.0** inch (use the rulers as a guide).

5. Click the **Bold** button on the Formatting toolbar to make all subtitle text on title slides bold.

6. Display Normal View. Select Slide 2, and then display the slide master.

7. Modify the background on the slide master to a gradient, such as the preset **Daybreak** gradient available in PowerPoint, using the **From title** Shading style. Apply the change to all slides.

8. Modify the title text style to 40-point **Arial Black**. Change the font color to **blue**. In PowerPoint, click the **blue** swatch on the left end of the color palette (the ScreenTip is *Follow Background Scheme Color*).

9. Select the bullet list placeholder and customize the bullet markers to the checked box Wingdings symbol you used in Project 13-2.

10. While still in Slide Master View, open the Header and Footer dialog box.

11. Select a fixed time and date display, and enter today's date. Deselect the **Slide number** check box.

12. Select the **Footer** option, and then key your name in the text box.

13. Apply the footer information to all slides. On the slide master, select the footer area place-holder, and change the font color to **black**. Select the date/time area placeholder and change the font color to **black**. Close Slide Master View.

14. Display the dialog box for editing the color scheme and select to edit the Shadows color. Change the color to a dark pink—RGB color Red **250**, Green **50**, and Blue **200**. Apply the change.

15. Preview the presentation in Slide Show View, clicking to advance the slides.

16. Save changes and close the **Kitchen3** file. Close your presentation program.

 WEB PROJECT

Whereas some presentations are designed to run unattended on a computer or TV monitor, many are designed to be presented with spoken commentary by a narrator. If you are going to deliver a successful presentation, you should understand the importance of public speaking. Use the Internet to research successful public speaking. You should be able to find Web sites that provide general public speaking information as well as tips and suggestions specifically for giving presentations. For example, the group called Toastmasters, which is dedicated to public speaking, has a Web site with lots of useful information. When you have completed your research, write a report of at least 500 words explaining what you have learned and why it is important. Supplement the written report by creating a presentation that you can present to your class with narration, practicing the speaking skills you have learned.

 TEAMWORK PROJECT

Assume you are a physician's assistant in a pediatrician's office. You want to create a presentation about safety that you can play on TV monitors installed in the waiting room. Working as a team, plan the content for the presentation. Consider the subject matter you want to include, and remember to plan for the specific audience of children in a doctor's office. For example, although you want to convey important safety information, you need to make the presentation fun and light-hearted so it appeals to children.

Create an outline that details the specific safety information you want to include. For example, you may want to include sports safety, such as bicycle helmets, or you may want to include health protection, such as washing hands. You can use your own experiences and knowledge, or you can research the topic in books, magazines, or on the Internet. You might even want to talk to the school nurse. When you have the text content ready, select a design template. You can modify it using a background and colors that appeal to your audience. Key the text for the presentation. Make sure the text is large because the televisions are mounted high on the wall. Keep the text simple and easy to read. Look for fun bullet markers to highlight your lists, and fun fonts that are also easy to read. Apply interesting transitions and sounds that hold your young audience's attention, and adjust the timing so slow readers can read each slide before the next one is presented. When the presentation is complete, check the spelling and correct errors. Test the presentation in Slide Show View, and make adjustments as necessary. Present it to your class.

CRITICAL *Thinking*

Many companies use presentations to announce important information, such as a new product, or the success of a particular department. How might a presentation used to announce information be different from a presentation selling a product or service, or a training presentation? Create a presentation that your school could use to announce a new class, club, or organization. Start by creating an outline that includes the titles and text you want on each slide. Decide if you want to use a content template, or start from scratch. If necessary, select a design template and a color scheme. You can modify the color scheme if you want. Enter the slide text using slide layouts that you think help present the information effectively. Select and apply transitions and then preview the presentation. Make adjustments and improvements, such as changing colors, customizing bullet markers, and adjust alignments and spacing. Don't forget to check your spelling. When the presentation is complete, show it to your class.

WORKING WITH GRAPHIC OBJECTS

OBJECTIVES

Upon completion of this lesson, you should be able to:

- Insert pictures from files on a slide.
- Insert clip art on a slide.
- Copy and paste pictures on a slide.
- Format pictures.
- Insert, modify, and format tables.
- Create and modify charts.
- Create diagrams.
- Use drawing objects to draw shapes and create text boxes.
- Manipulate objects on a slide.

Estimated Time: 2 hours

VOCABULARY

Cell

Chart

Column

Data series

Datasheet

Diagram

Legend

Merge

Row

Split

Table

Table borders

Text box

Titles

X-axis

Y-axis

Graphics are a critical component of any slide presentation. Graphics visually support the message of the presentation and help capture and maintain the attention of an audience. For example, you can use pictures to illustrate an idea, a table or chart to display data, or a cartoon to provide humor. Logos can be used to identify a brand, product, or company, and you can add original drawing objects to enhance a slide or highlight information on a slide.

In this lesson you learn how to make graphics objects part of your presentations. You learn how to insert graphics files and how to create original graphics objects using the drawing tools, tables, charts, and diagrams. You also learn how to format and manipulate objects on a slide.

Insert Pictures

Pictures, as you learned in Unit 1, are graphics images stored in a graphics file format. For example, many photographs are stored in JPEG (.jpg) format, and many drawings are stored in GIF (.gif) format. You can insert pictures on any slide in a presentation.

Note

For a refresher on different types of graphics files, refer to Lesson 1.

Most presentation programs have commands for inserting pictures from different sources, including clip art collections, graphics files stored anywhere on you computer or network, scanners, or digital cameras. Usually, you select a command, such as Insert > Picture, select the type of item you want to insert, browse to locate the item, and then click OK. You can usually use Copy and Paste commands to insert a picture file on a slide as well. Simply select the image in its original location and copy it to the Clipboard, then select the slide in your presentation program and paste the image.

Some slide layouts include a placeholder designed specifically for containing objects such as pictures, but you do not need a placeholder to insert a picture. Once a picture is inserted on a slide, you can move it by dragging it to a new location, or scale it by dragging a selection handle.

Important

Remember copyright laws when you acquire images for use in a presentation. Usually images are available free for personal use, but if you plan to distribute a presentation or use it in a professional setting, you must obtain permission from the owner or artist, and you must cite the source.

Insert Picture Files

If the image you want to use on a slide is already stored in a graphics file format, you can insert it by selecting the slide or placeholder and then selecting the command to insert a picture from a file. For example, in PowerPoint, click Insert on the Menu bar, click Picture on the Insert menu, and then click From File. Locate and select the file, and then click Insert.

Hot Tip

In PowerPoint, you can click the Insert Picture icon in an object placeholder to quickly open the Insert Picture dialog box.

STEP-BY-STEP 14.1

1. Launch your presentation program, and open **Step14-1a** from the Data files. Save the file as **Axis**.

2. With Slide 1 current, select the command to insert a picture file. For example, click **Insert** on the Menu bar, click **Picture**, and then click **From File**.

STEP-BY-STEP 14.1 Continued

3. Locate and select the graphics file **Step14-1b** in the Data files for this lesson and then click **Insert**. The file—the company's logo—is inserted in the middle of the slide, as shown in Figure 14-1. Selection handles display around the picture's borders. In some programs, a green rotation handle displays as well.

FIGURE 14-1
A graphics file inserted on a slide

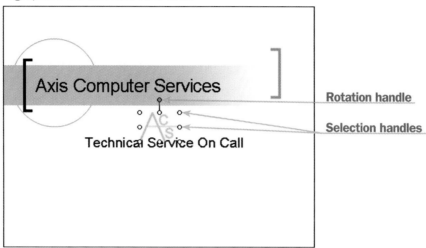
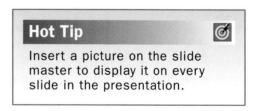

4. Position the mouse pointer over the picture so the mouse pointer resembles a 4-headed arrow—the move pointer—and then click and drag the picture to the lower-left corner of the slide, approximately 1.0 inch from the left edge and 0.5 inches from the bottom edge.

> **Hot Tip**
>
> Insert a picture on the slide master to display it on every slide in the presentation.

5. Click anywhere outside the picture to deselect it.

6. Save the changes and leave **Axis** open to use in the next exercise.

Insert Clip Art

Most presentation programs come with built-in collections of clip-art images or CDs containing clip-art files. They may also have tools that you can use to organize and locate clip-art files, and even to access clip-art Web sites. For example, PowerPoint has the Clip Art task pane and the Clip Organizer from which you can locate clip-art on your computer or access Microsoft's Clip Art and Media Home page.

To insert a clip-art image in most programs, select the slide or placeholder where you want the image to display, click Insert on the Menu bar, click Picture, and then click Clip Art. Use the available tools to locate and select the clip-art image. For example, in PowerPoint, enter a key term in the Search box, select the locations you want to search, and select the type of files you want to find. When the files display, click the one you want and then click the command to insert it on the slide.

STEP-BY-STEP 14.2

1. In the **Axis** presentation file, make Slide 2 current. Change the slide layout to one that has a bulleted list on the left, and a placeholder for an object such as clip art on the right. In PowerPoint, select the **Title, Text, and Clip Art** layout. If necessary, decrease the font size of the text in the bulleted list so it all fits in the placeholder.

2. Select the object placeholder, and then select the command to insert clip-art. For example, click **Insert** on the Menu bar, click **Picture**, and then click **Clip Art** or double-click the object placeholder. A task pane or dialog box displays clip art options.

3. In the Search box, key **Business.** If necessary, select to search in all locations for clip-art files, and then click the button to start searching. Your program displays the clips that match your criteria.

4. Select a picture of a man watering a money tree (see Figure 14-2), and then click **OK** to insert the picture in the placeholder. Close the task pane, if necessary. The slide should look similar to Figure 14-2. If you cannot locate the picture shown in Figure 14-2, select a similar picture, or cancel the dialog box and insert the picture file **Step14-1c**, using the steps described in the previous exercise.

FIGURE 14-2
Insert clip art

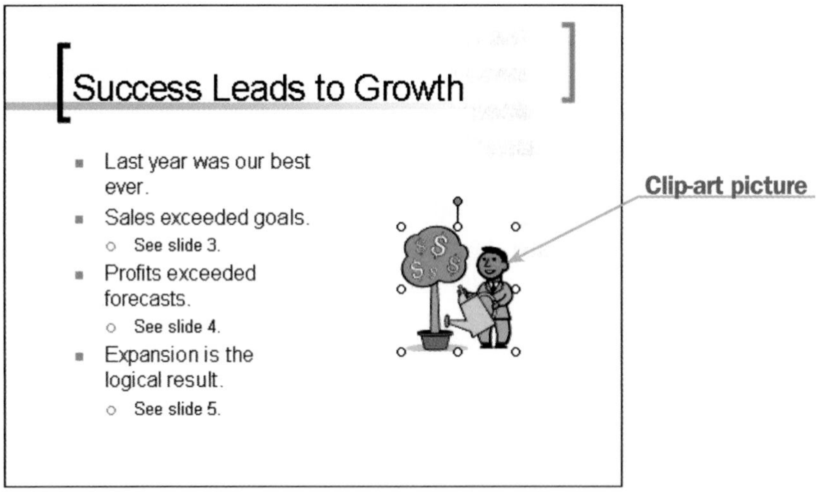

Success Leads to Growth

- Last year was our best ever.
- Sales exceeded goals.
  - See slide 3.
- Profits exceeded forecasts.
  - See slide 4.
- Expansion is the logical result.
  - See slide 5.

Clip-art picture

5. Position the insertion point over the selection handle in the upper-right corner of the picture so it resembles a diagonal double-headed arrow—the scale pointer. Click and drag up and to the right to increase the size of the image. Release the mouse button when the right edge of the picture is about 1.0 inch from the right edge of the slide.

6. Save the changes and leave **Axis** open to use in the next exercise.

> **Note**
>
> With most presentation programs, you can acquire images directly from a scanner or digital camera that is correctly connected and configured for use with your computer. For information on using a scanner or digital camera to acquire images, refer to Lesson 2.

Copy and Paste Pictures

If you have a picture that has already been inserted in a file, you can use the copy and paste commands to insert it on a slide. This is useful for inserting a picture that is in a document such as a word processing file, in a different presentation file, or even in the same presentation file on a different slide. You can even use the Copy and Paste commands to acquire images stored on the Internet.

To copy and paste a picture, open the file where the picture has already been inserted. Right-click the picture and click Copy on the shortcut menu. Switch to the presentation file, right-click the slide or placeholder where you want the picture to display, and click Paste on the shortcut menu.

STEP-BY-STEP 14.3

1. Display Slide 1 of the **Axis** file and right-click the logo picture. Click **Copy** on the shortcut menu.

2. Make Slide 3 current, right-click anywhere on the slide, and click **Paste** on the shortcut menu. The picture is pasted in the same place where it is positioned on Slide 1.

3. Save the changes and leave **Axis** open to use in the next exercise.

> **Extra for Experts**
>
> In some programs, you can compress the pictures in a presentation to make the presentation file smaller. Select the command to compress the pictures and select options such as whether to compress all pictures or selected pictures, what resolution to maintain, and whether to delete cropped areas. Click OK to apply the compression.

Format Pictures

Once you insert a picture on a slide, you can use your program's picture editing tools to format and modify the image. Click the object to select it and then select the formatting command you want to use. Most programs provide tools for cropping images, as well as for adjusting contrast and brightness and modifying colors. The changes you make to the image on the slide do not affect the original graphics file or copies of the file that may be inserted in other presentations or files.

The commands for formatting a picture are usually available in a dialog box with a name such as Format Picture, as shown in Figure 14-3, or on a toolbar. You may find these commands are similar to some of those you use in graphics and animation programs to format objects.

Note

If a picture requires a lot of formatting or editing, you should use a graphics program to make the modifications before inserting it in your presentation.

FIGURE 14-3
Format Picture dialog box

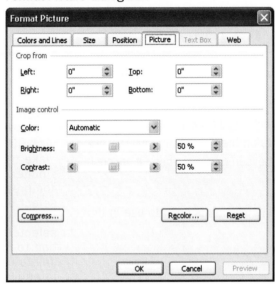

S TEP-BY-STEP 14.4

1. Click the picture on Slide 2 to select it. Select the command to display picture formatting options. For example, click **Format** on the Menu bar and then click **Picture**, or click the **Format Picture** button on the Picture toolbar.

2. Select the command to increase the brightness to **56%**, and then click **OK** to apply the change.

3. Save the changes and leave **Axis** open to use in the next exercise.

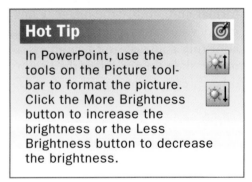

Hot Tip

In PowerPoint, use the tools on the Picture toolbar to format the picture. Click the More Brightness button to increase the brightness or the Less Brightness button to decrease the brightness.

Work with Tables

An effective way to organize content on a slide is to use a *table*. A table is a set of data arranged in *columns* and *rows*. A column is a vertical component of the table, and a row is the horizontal component. The rectangular area at the intersection of a column and a row is called a *cell*. You enter data in the cells. Tables make certain kinds of information easier to read. They are useful for presenting information in a grid format, such as an agenda, schedule, telephone list, or product specifications.

You can insert a table in an object placeholder or directly on any slide in a presentation. You may modify a table layout at any time by adding or deleting columns or rows, by resizing the entire table, or by changing a column width or row height. You can also *merge* cells, which means combining multiple cells to create one cell, or *split* a cell, which means dividing one cell to create multiple cells. You can format the data in a table, or you can format the table itself using color, fills, and alignments. Figure 14-4 shows a table on a slide.

FIGURE 14-4
A table on a slide

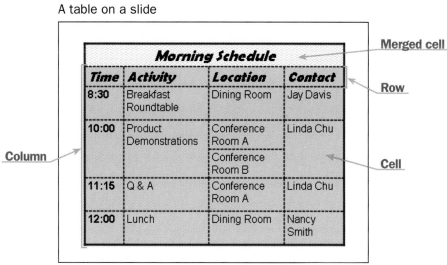

Insert a Table

To insert a table, select the object placeholder or the slide where you want the table to display, click Insert on the Menu bar, and then click Table. Alternatively, click the Insert Table button, which is available on the Standard toolbar in most presentation programs. You must then key the number of rows and columns that you want in the table, and click OK, or drag across a grid to specify the number of columns and rows.

An insertion point displays in the current, or active, cell. Key the data for that cell, and then press the Tab key or click the mouse pointer to make the next cell current.

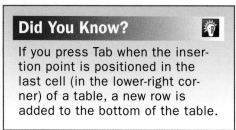

Did You Know?

If you press Tab when the insertion point is positioned in the last cell (in the lower-right corner) of a table, a new row is added to the bottom of the table.

S TEP-BY-STEP 14.5

1. In the **Axis** file, select **Slide 2** and then insert a new slide. Select a layout that includes a placeholder for a table, such as PowerPoint's **Title and Table**, or select a **Title Only** layout.

2. Click in the title text placeholder and key **Sales**.

3. Select the object placeholder, if necessary, and then select the command for inserting a table. (If your slide layout does not have an object placeholder, just select the command for inserting a table.) For example, in PowerPoint, click **Insert** on the Menu bar and then click **Table**, or double-click the table placeholder. In the *Number of columns* box, key **5**, in the *Number of rows* box, key **3**, and then click **OK** to create the table. The slide should look similar to Figure 14-5.

FIGURE 14-5
Insert a blank table with 5 columns and 3 rows

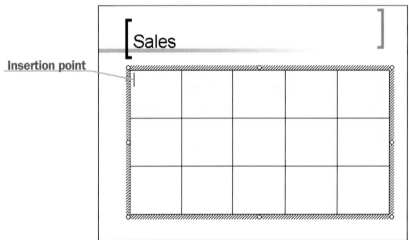

4. Press **Tab** to move the insertion point to the second cell, and then key **Quarter 1**. Press **Tab** and key **Quarter 2**. Press **Tab** and key **Quarter 3**. Press **Tab** and key **Quarter 4**.

5. Press **Tab** to move the insert point to the first cell in the second row, and then key **This Year**. Press **Tab** and key **$5,250**. Press **Tab** and key **$6,775**. Press **Tab** and key **$8,950**. Press **Tab** and key **$10,500**.

6. Press **Tab** and key **Last Year**. Press **Tab** and key **$4,445**. Press **Tab** and key **$4,700**. Press **Tab** and key **$4,950**. Press **Tab** and key **$5,100**. The slide should look similar to Figure 14-6.

STEP-BY-STEP 14.5 Continued

FIGURE 14-6
Key data in a table

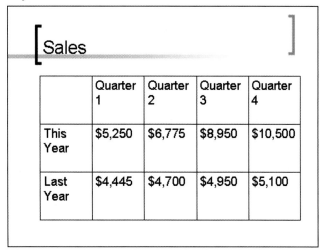

7. Save the changes and leave **Axis** open to use in the next exercise.

Modify a Table

There are many ways to modify the layout of a table. When you need more cells for displaying data, insert a new column or row. You can insert a column to the left or to the right of the column containing the active cell, and you can insert a row, above or below the row containing the active cell. To delete a column or row make a cell in it active and then select either the Delete Columns or Delete Rows command. Usually, the commands for inserting and deleting columns and rows are on a Table menu, which can be accessed from a toolbar that becomes available when the table is active, or from a shortcut menu.

You can resize an entire table by dragging a sizing handle, and you can adjust the width of columns and the height of rows by dragging the table borders.

Most programs have the ability to merge multiple cells or to split cells into multiple cells. To merge cells in PowerPoint, select the cells and then click the Merge Cells button on the Tables toolbar. To split a cell, make it active, click the Split Cells button, and then key the number of columns and/or rows that you want to create.

STEP-BY-STEP 14.6

1. Position the mouse pointer on the left border of the table so it changes to a double-line with arrows pointing left and right. Click and drag the border to the left about **0.25** inches, or just enough to increase the width of the first column so the text fits on a single line within the cells.

2. Position the mouse pointer on the border (the horizontal line) between rows 1 and 2 so it changes to a double-line with arrows pointing up and down. Click and drag the border up to just under the Quarter numbers.

3. Position the mouse pointer on the border between rows 2 and 3 and double-click. This is a shortcut method of automatically adjusting the row height to fit the data in the row. If it does not change the row height, drag the border to just under the numbers.

Hot Tip

Double-click a column border to automatically adjust the column width.

4. Position the mouse pointer on the bottom border of the table and double-click to automatically adjust the height of row 3. If the row height does not adjust automatically, drag the border to just under the numbers.

5. Click in any cell on the top row of the table, and then select the command to insert a row above. For example, in PowerPoint, display the Tables and Borders toolbar, if necessary. Then, click the **Table** button on the Tables and Borders toolbar and then click **Insert Rows Above**. Your program adds a row to the top of the table, with all cells selected.

Extra for Experts

To insert more than one column or row, in the existing table select the same number of columns or rows you want to insert, and then select the appropriate command. To delete multiple columns or rows, select them and then select the Delete command.

6. With all cells in the row still selected, select the command to merge the cells. For example, in PowerPoint, click the **Merge Cells** button on the Tables and Borders toolbar. Your program removes the borders between the selected cells, creating one cell the width of the table.

7. Click in the merged cell and key **Two-Year Comparison**. The table should look similar to Figure 14-7.

STEP-BY-STEP 14.6 Continued

FIGURE 14-7
Modified table

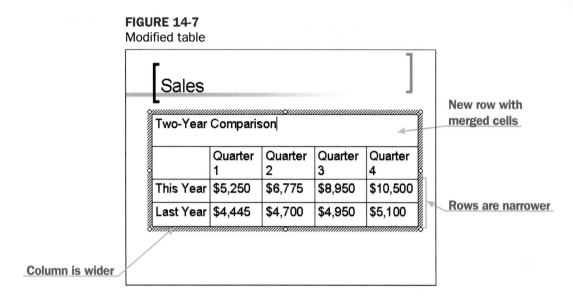

8. Save the changes and leave **Axis** open to use in the next exercise.

Format a Table

To format data in a table, select the cell (or multiple cells) or the text in the cell, and then use the tools on the Formatting toolbar, such as the Font, Font Size, Font Color, or alignment buttons. You can also format the table itself using tools on the Tables and Borders toolbar if one is available, or in a Format Table dialog box. For example, you can apply colors and styles to the *table borders*, which are the horizontal and vertical lines that define the columns and rows, and you can apply fill color or effects to the cells. In some programs, you can select a vertical alignment to position the text at the top, middle, or bottom of the cell. The commands for formatting the table itself are usually found on a table menu or toolbar.

STEP-BY-STEP 14.7

1. Click and drag to select the text in the top row of the table, and then change the font size to 36. For example, in PowerPoint click the **Font Size** drop-down arrow on the Formatting toolbar and click **36**.

2. Center the text horizontally in the cell. For example, in PowerPoint click the **Center** button on the Formatting toolbar. If available, click the **Center Vertically** button on the Tables and Borders toolbar to vertically center the text as well.

3. Click and drag to select the cells on the second row of the table, and then center the text horizontally.

4. Click and drag to select all cells containing dollar values, and then right-align the text. For example, in PowerPoint, click the **Align Right** button on the Formatting toolbar.

STEP-BY-STEP 14.7 Continued

5. Click the table placeholder to select the entire table. Select the command to display a Format Table dialog box. For example, in PowerPoint, click **Format** on the Menu bar and then click **Table**. If necessary, click the tab for formatting borders.

6. Click to display the Border color palette, and select the **khaki** color that is used for accents (third swatch from the right). Change the border width to **6** points. Apply the border to the outside of the table, leaving the default black border between cells within the table. (The method for applying the border may depend on your program. For example, you may be able to click a picture of an outside border, or you may have to individually click the top, bottom, left, and right borders. A preview should display the border formatting.)

7. Click **OK** to apply the border formatting.

8. With the entire table still selected, select the command to format the table again. If necessary, click the tab for formatting fills.

9. Change the fill color to light gray. For example, in PowerPoint, display the Fill Color palette and click the **light gray** swatch on the right. Click **OK** to apply the fill to all selected cells.

10. Click outside the table to deselect it. It should look similar to Figure 14-8.

FIGURE 14-8
Formatted table

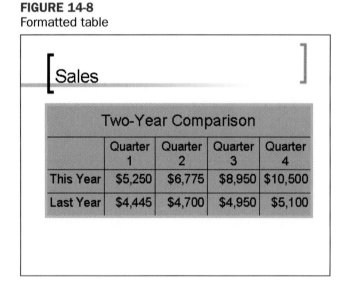

Two-Year Comparison			
	Quarter 1	Quarter 2	Quarter 3	Quarter 4
This Year	$5,250	$6,775	$8,950	$10,500
Last Year	$4,445	$4,700	$4,950	$5,100

11. Save the changes and leave **Axis** open to use in the next exercise.

Create a Chart

A table is useful for displaying data in columns and rows, but a *chart* may be a more effective method of illustrating data. A chart is a graphical representation of table data. Most presentation programs have tools for creating charts. Usually you key the data into a *datasheet*, which is a set of cells linked to a chart, and then select a chart type to use to display the data. You should consider the message you want to convey before you select a chart type, because different chart types are used for different purposes. The types of charts that you can create depend on your presentation program, but you may be able to preview the charts in a dialog box with a name such as Chart Types. Table 14-1 describes some common chart types.

TABLE 14-1
Common Chart Types

CHART TYPE	DESCRIPTION
Column	Shows data changes over a period of time or illustrates comparisons among items.
Bar	Illustrates comparisons among individual items.
Line	Displays trends over time or categories.
Pie	Shows the proportional size of items to a total value. Often used to show percentages of a whole.
XY (Scatter)	Shows the relationships among the numeric values in several data series, or plots two groups of numbers as one series of XY coordinates. Commonly used for scientific data.
Area	Displays trends in values over time or categories.

Insert a Chart

You can create a chart in an object placeholder or directly on a slide by selecting the Chart command on the Insert menu or by clicking the Insert Chart button on the Standard toolbar.

A sample datasheet displays over a sample column chart, as shown in Figure 14-9. Rows are labeled with numbers, and columns are labeled with letters. You identify a cell by referencing its column label and row number. For example, the cell in the upper-left corner is called cell A1, because it is at the intersection of column A and row 1.

FIGURE 14-9
Sample chart and datasheet

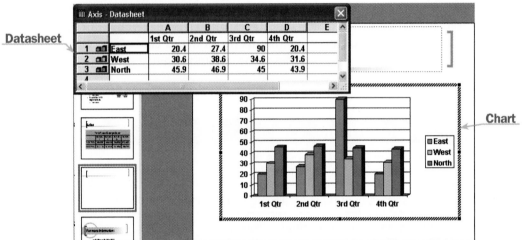

Click in any cell in the datasheet and key new data to replace the sample data. As you key new data, the sample chart updates automatically. The datasheet contains three rows and four columns of sample data. If necessary, you may add data in empty cells. Once you have finished keying the data, click outside the chart to insert it on the slide.

> **Important**
>
> When you work in the datasheet that contains sample data, you should remove columns and rows that you do not need, or they may display in your chart. To remove a row or column, right-click its label (such as 1, 2, 3 or A, B, C) and click Delete on the shortcut menu.

STEP-BY-STEP 14.8

1. Select **Slide 3** if necessary and then insert a new slide. Select a layout that includes a placeholder for a chart, such as **Title and Chart**, or select a **Title Only** layout.

2. Click in the title text placeholder and key **Sales Comparison**.

3. Select the object placeholder, if necessary, and then select the command for inserting a chart. For example, in PowerPoint, click **Insert** on the Menu bar and then click **Chart**, or double-click the chart placeholder. Your program creates a sample chart and datasheet.

4. In the datasheet, click the cell labeled *East*, if necessary, and key **This Year**. Press **Tab** and key **5250**. Press **Tab** and key **6775**. Press **Tab** and key **8950**. Press **Tab** and key **10500**. Notice that as you change the values the chart updates as well.

STEP-BY-STEP 14.8 Continued

5. Click the cell labeled *West* and key **Last Year**. Press **Tab** and key **4445**. Press **Tab** and key **4700**. Press **Tab** and key **4950**. Press **Tab** and key **5100**.

6. Click on the row 3 heading on the left side of the datasheet to select the entire row, and then press **Delete**. This deletes the row that you are not going to use. The slide should look similar to Figure 14-10.

FIGURE 14-10
The chart displays the data

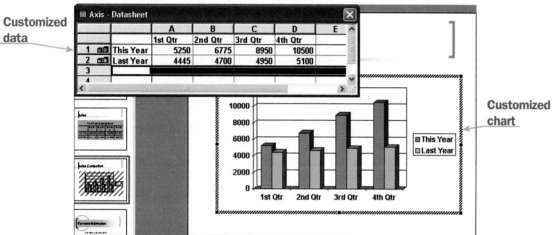

Customized data

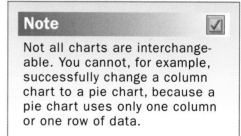

Customized chart

7. Click on the slide outside the chart placeholder. Save the changes and leave **Axis** open to use in the next exercise.

Modify and Format a Chart

In most programs, clicking a chart on a slide selects the slide object, but does not make it available for editing. When you want to edit the chart, you must double-click the object. Then, the datasheet displays and menus and toolbars specific to editing charts become available. You can edit and format the data in the datasheet or modify and format the chart.

The most important step in formatting a chart is selecting the chart type. To change the chart type, open the chart for editing and select the Chart Type command. This may be a button on a toolbar, or a command on a menu. Click the chart type you want to use, and, if necessary, click a chart sub-type, which is a variation of the selected type. Click OK to apply the new chart type to your existing data.

> **Note** ☑
>
> Not all charts are interchangeable. You cannot, for example, successfully change a column chart to a pie chart, because a pie chart uses only one column or one row of data.

You can usually create and modify elements in the chart using the chart options dialog box. For example, you may be able to insert or hide titles, a legend, and data labels. The *titles* are the text labels used to identify an entire chart, the *X-axis*, or the *Y-axis*. The X-axis is the category axis, and displays the categories in the chart, and the Y-axis is the value axis, and displays the values. A *legend* is the key that identifies each *data series* by color. A data series is one set of data displayed in the chart. A data label is the text that identifies the contents of a data series. There may be other options depending on the chart type. You can delete chart elements by clicking the element to select it and then pressing Delete.

You can usually apply formatting to different chart elements using commands on a shortcut menu. Right-click the element you want to format, then click Format *elementname* on the shortcut menu. For example, to format a chart title, right-click the title and click Format Chart Title on the shortcut menu. A dialog box displays formatting options for the specific element.

Many programs provide tools for formatting the data in the datasheet. For example, you may be able to select a Currency Style to automatically insert dollar signs and decimal points, a Percent Style to change a decimal number to a percentage, or a Comma Style to insert commas in the appropriate locations. Select the data you want to format, and then click the appropriate button on the Formatting toolbar or select a command such as Format > Number to display a dialog box in which you can select the formatting you want to use.

Hot Tip

Some programs have commands or buttons for angling text within a cell. This can be useful for fitting cells on a slide.

S TEP-BY-STEP 14.9

1. Double-click the chart on Slide 4 to make it available for editing.

2. In the datasheet, select all of the number values and then select the command to apply currency formatting. For example, in PowerPoint, click the **Currency Style** button on the Formatting toolbar. Notice that the values along the value axis (the left edge of the chart) change to currency format.

3. Close the datasheet. Select the command to change the chart type. For example, in PowerPoint, click **Chart** on the Menu bar and then click **Chart Type**. Select the **3-D Column** chart sub-type, if it is available in your program, and then click **OK**.

STEP-BY-STEP 14.9 Continued

4. Select the command to change the chart type again, select the **Clustered Column** with a **3-D** visual effect, and then click **OK**.

5. Select the command to change chart options. For example, in PowerPoint, click **Chart** on the Menu bar and then click **Chart Options**. On the tab for formatting the legend, select to position the legend at the bottom of the chart. Click **OK**.

6. On the chart, right-click anywhere on the value axis (the dollar values on the left side of the chart) and then click **Format Axis** on the shortcut menu to open a formatting dialog box.

7. On the tab for formatting numbers, set the decimal places to **0** and then click **OK**. Click anywhere outside the chart. The slide should look similar to Figure 14-11.

FIGURE 14-11
Modify and format the chart

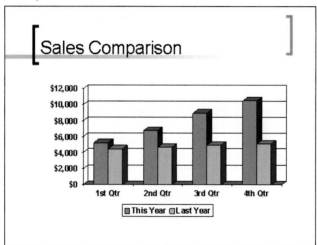

8. Save the changes and leave **Axis** open to use in the next exercise.

Create a Diagram

Many presentation programs let you create *diagrams*, which are a particular type of chart used to display conceptual information rather than data. Most diagrams use labeled shapes to illustrate relationships between groups, items, or processes. Table 14-2 describes common types of diagrams.

TABLE 14-2
Types of diagrams

DIAGRAM TYPE	DESCRIPTION
Organization	An organization diagram is also called a flow chart. It depicts a hierarchical relationship within a group. You might use an organization chart to show the relationship between managers and subordinates in a company division, or to depict a family tree.
Cycle	A cycle diagram is used to chart any kind of cyclical process, such as the life cycle of a tree or the design and production of a computer chip.
Radial	A radial diagram illustrates the relationship of several items to a single item. For example, use a Radial diagram to show how the phones in a particular department are connected to a single incoming phone line, or to illustrate how computer workstations are linked to a single hub or server.
Pyramid	A pyramid diagram illustrates the proportions of individual elements within a whole. For example, the Food Pyramid uses a pyramid diagram to show the proportionate amounts of each food group a person should consume in a single day.
Venn	A Venn diagram depicts items with overlapping characteristics, such as the secondary and tertiary colors in a color wheel that are comprised of two primary/secondary colors.
Target	A target diagram illustrates items that build on each other, such as the steps toward a specific goal. For example, you might use a target diagram to list the steps for following a recipe or building a house.

To create a diagram, select the placeholder or slide where you want the diagram to display, and then select the appropriate command on the Insert menu. For example, in PowerPoint, select the Insert > Diagram command, or click the Insert Diagram button. Click the type of diagram you want to create and then click OK. The default diagram displays text prompts that you can click to key your own labels. You may add, delete, and format shapes. The formatting options depend on the type of diagram, but usually you can change the fill color, and apply font formatting to the text. You may also be able to rearrange the shapes.

S TEP-BY-STEP 14.10

1. Select **Slide 4** if necessary and then insert a new slide. Select a layout that includes a placeholder for a diagram, such as **Title and Diagram or Organization Chart**, or select a **Title Only** layout.

2. Click in the title text placeholder and key **Organized for Growth**.

3. Select the object placeholder, if necessary, and then select the command for inserting a diagram. Select the option for creating an organization chart, and then click **OK**. Your program creates a blank diagram, as shown in Figure 14-12. (Close the task pane, if necessary.) It may also display a toolbar with commands specific to the selected diagram type.

FIGURE 14-12
Blank organization chart

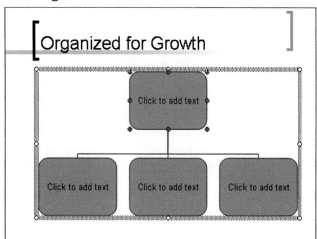

4. Click the shape at the top of the chart and key **President and CEO**. Click the shape on the left of the second row and key **V.P. Sales**. Click the shape in the middle of the second row and key **V.P. Marketing**. Click the shape on the right of the second row and key **V.P. Service**.

5. Click the *V.P. Sales* shape, and then click the command to insert a subordinate shape. For example, in PowerPoint, click the **Insert Shape** list arrow on the Organization Chart toolbar, and then click **Subordinate**. Your program inserts a new shape and automatically resizes the existing shapes so that they fit on the slide.

6. Click the new shape and key **Regional Manager**.

7. Click the *V.P. Service* shape, and then click the command to insert a subordinate shape. Click the new shape and key **Regional Manager**.

8. Click to select one *Regional Manager* shape, press and hold **Shift**, and then click the other *Regional Manager* shape. Select the command to format the shapes. For example, in PowerPoint, click **Format** on the Menu bar and then click **AutoShape**. A dialog box with formatting options displays.

STEP-BY-STEP 14.10 Continued

9. Click to open the Fill Color palette, and click the **khaki** color that is third from the right, then click **OK**.

10. Click to select the *President and CEO* shape. Change the fill color of the shape to **light gray**. Click and drag across the text in the shape and then change the font color to **white**. Click the **Bold** button on the Formatting toolbar.

11. Click outside the diagram. The slide should look similar to Figure 14-13.

FIGURE 14-13
Customized organization chart

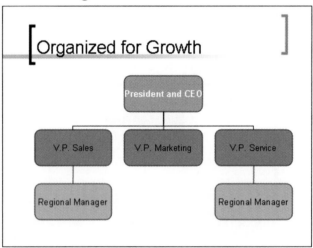

12. Save the changes and leave **Axis** open to use in the next exercise.

Work with Drawing Objects

You can create and format original drawings on a slide using your program's drawing tools. These tools are similar to the tools in a graphics or animation program. For example, you can use the Oval tool to draw a circle or an oval, the Rectangle tool to draw a rectangle or square, and the Line tool to draw straight lines or curves. You can also create *text box* objects. A text box is a rectangular object in which you key and format text. A text box is similar to a text block in a graphics or animation program.

> **Note** ☑
>
> The drawing tools in most presentation programs will be limited. If you want to use a complex or sophisticated drawing on a slide, you should create it in a graphics program first, and then insert it in your presentation program.

Draw Basic Shapes

Drawing with your presentation program's drawing tools is the same as drawing with a more sophisticated graphics or animation program's drawing tools. Select the tool on a toolbar or in a toolbox, and then click and drag to draw the shape. Press and hold Shift as you drag to constrain the shape. For example, click the Rectangle tool, and then click and drag to draw a rectangle; press and hold Shift while you drag to draw a square.

Shapes are drawn using the default color scheme formatting settings, but you can change the formatting to modify the shapes. Formatting options usually include Fill Color, Line Color and Line Style, and there may be options specific to the current object. For example, if you select an arrow shape, you may have options for formatting arrowheads. Depending on your program, you may be able to apply some effects, such as shadows or 3-D contouring, and you may be able to change attributes such as the stacking order or the alignment. Formatting options are usually available in a Format Shape dialog box, or you may be able to use buttons on the Drawing toolbar.

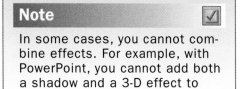

Hot Tip

You can also apply formatting to a placeholder on any slide.

Note

In some cases, you cannot combine effects. For example, with PowerPoint, you cannot add both a shadow and a 3-D effect to the same object.

S TEP-BY-STEP 14.11

1. Make slide 3—the table—current.

2. Click the **Oval** tool on your Drawing toolbar or toolbox, and then click and drag to draw an oval around the value *$10,500* in Quarter 4 of this year.

3. With the shape still selected, select the command to format it. For example, in PowerPoint, click **Format** on the Menu bar and then click **AutoShape**.

4. Display the fill color options, and select to apply no fill. For example, in PowerPoint, click the **Fill Color** palette button, and click **No Fill**. Change the line color to **red**, and increase the line weight to **2.5 pt**. Apply the formatting.

STEP-BY-STEP 14.11 Continued

5. Click outside the shape to deselect it. The slide should look similar to Figure 14-14.

FIGURE 14-14
Shapes drawn on a slide

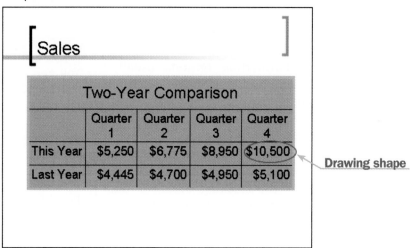

6. Save the changes and leave **Axis** open to use in the next exercise.

Create a Text Box

To create a text box, click the command to insert a text box, or click the Text Box tool on a toolbar or in a toolbox, and then click and drag to draw the object. An insertion point displays within the text box so you can key the text. Use the commands on the Formatting toolbar to format the text as you would format it in a text placeholder. (Refer to Lesson 13 for information on formatting text on a slide.) You can format the text box itself, as well.

STEP-BY-STEP 14.12

1. Select the command to insert a text box, and then click and drag in the area below the table to draw a text box approximately 3.5 inches wide and 0.5 inches high. Key **Values based on gross sales.**

2. Click the text box border to select the text box, and then select the command to format the text box. For example, in PowerPoint, click **Format** on the Menu bar and then click **Text Box.**

3. Click to display the Line Color palette, click a black color swatch, and then click **OK.** Drag the text box to center it horizontally on the slide (you may want to display the grid).

STEP-BY-STEP 14.12 Continued

4. Click outside the text box to deselect it. The slide should look similar to Figure 14-15.

FIGURE 14-15
A text box inserted

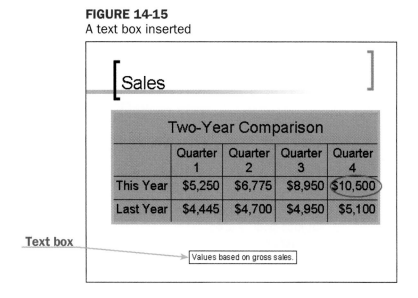

5. Save the changes and leave **Axis** open to use in the next exercise.

Insert Built-In Shapes

Some programs have a feature that you use to quickly insert built-in shapes, such as hearts, stars, or lightning bolts. For example, PowerPoint has a long list of AutoShapes that includes basic shapes, block arrows, stars, and banners.

To insert a built-in shape, select the command to display the shapes, click a category, if necessary, then click the shape you want to use. On the slide, click to insert a default-sized shape, or click and drag to insert the shape at a size you control.

STEP-BY-STEP 14.13

1. Make Slide 6 current. Select the command to display the built-in shapes available in your program. For example, in PowerPoint, click the **AutoShapes** button on the Drawing toolbar.

2. Click the category that contains commonly used shapes. For example, in PowerPoint, click **Basic Shapes**.

3. Click the lightning bolt shape. If a lightning bolt is not available in your program, select a different shape.

STEP-BY-STEP 14.13 Continued

4. Click on the slide to the right of the contact information. Your program inserts the shape, as shown in Figure 14.16.

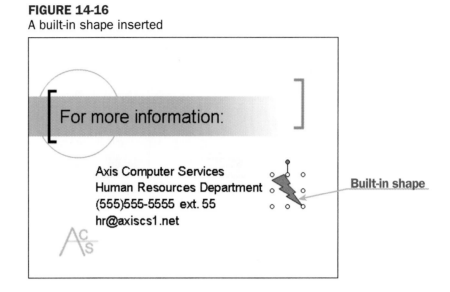

FIGURE 14-16
A built-in shape inserted

5. Save the changes and leave **Axis** open to use in the next exercise.

Manipulate Objects

Many tools are available for manipulating objects on a slide, and most are similar to the tools you learned about in Lesson 3, Modifying Graphics. You can scale, move, or delete any object. You can also group, rotate, align, and change the stacking order of objects. In many programs, you must use commands in a format dialog box to manipulate objects, but in some programs the options are available on a shortcut menu that you can access by right-clicking the object, or from a toolbar. For example, in PowerPoint, you can click Draw on the Drawing toolbar to display a shortcut menu of options for manipulating objects.

STEP-BY-STEP 14.14

1. With the lightning bolt still selected, select the command to align the lightning bolt in the center of the slide horizontally and vertically. For example, in PowerPoint, click the **Draw** button on the Drawing toolbar, click **Align or Distribute**, and then click **Relative to Slide**. Display the Align or Distribute menu again and click **Align Center**. Display the Align or Distribute menu again and click **Align Middle**.

2. Select the command to rotate the object, and then rotate it so the tip of the bolt is pointing to the upper-right corner of the slide. You may be able to drag a rotation handle, or you may enter a precise rotation value in a formatting dialog box.

STEP-BY-STEP 14.14 Continued

3. Resize the lightning bolt so it stretches diagonally across the slide. You may drag the sizing handles to resize the shape, or set the size to 7.25 inches high by 6.25 inches wide in a format dialog box. If necessary, realign the object with the center of the slide.

4. Select the command to change the stacking order to send the lightning bolt behind everything else on the slide. For example, in PowerPoint, click the **Draw** button on the Drawing toolbar, click **Order**, and then click **Send to Back**. The slide should look similar to Figure 14-17.

>
> **Hot Tip**
>
> Some programs let you adjust the shape of drawn objects. For example, in PowerPoint, you can drag the yellow adjustment handle to modify a shape such as the angle of an arrowhead, or the depth of a star's points.

FIGURE 14-17
Modify an object

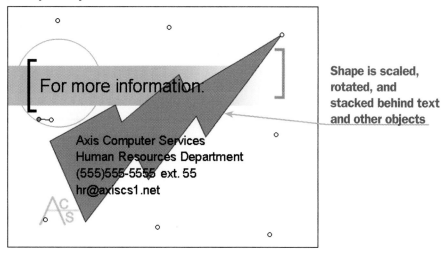

Shape is scaled, rotated, and stacked behind text and other objects

5. Check the spelling in the presentation and correct errors as necessary.

6. Make Slide 1 current and then preview the presentation in Slide Show View.

7. Save the changes and close the **Axis** file. Close your presentation program.

SUMMARY

In this lesson, you learned:

- Graphics such as pictures, tables, and charts can be used to illustrate a presentation.

- You can insert pictures from files, from a clip-art organizer, or by using the copy and paste commands. You may also be able to import pictures directly from a scanner or camera.

- Most programs provide tools for cropping images, as well as for adjusting contrast and brightness and modifying colors.

- A table is an effective way to organize content on a slide in columns and rows.

- You can modify a table by adding or deleting columns and rows. You can also merge and split cells.

- Use the font formatting commands to format text in a table. You can also format the table itself by applying colors and styles to borders and cells.

- A chart is good way to illustrate table data on a slide.

- You should select a chart type that suits the purpose of your data.

- You can usually create and modify chart elements such as titles, axis, the legend, and data series.

- Diagrams are a particular type of chart used to display conceptual information.

- An organization chart is useful for depicting hierarchical relationships.

- Most presentation programs have drawing tools similar to those in a graphics or animation program. You can draw basic shapes, text borders, and insert built-in shapes.

- You can move, scale, rotate, and align objects on a slide. You can even change the stacking order of overlapping objects.

VOCABULARY *Review*

Define the following terms:

Cell	Legend	Text box
Chart	Merge	Titles
Column	Row	X-axis
Data series	Split	Y-axis
Datasheet	Table	
Diagram	Table borders	

REVIEW *Questions*

TRUE / FALSE

Circle T if the statement is true or F if the statement is false.

T   F   1. You must insert pictures in an object placeholder.

T   F   2. You can locate clip art by searching for a key term.

T   F   3. Changes you make to a picture on a slide do not affect the original graphics file.

T   F   4. The rectangular area at the intersection of a column and a row is called a square.

T   F   5. You cannot add rows or columns to an existing table.

T   F   6. To quickly adjust row height, double-click the border between rows.

T   F   7. You cannot change the chart type.

T   F   8. A pie chart is often used to show percentages of a whole.

T   F   9. An XY (Scatter) chart is commonly used to show scientific data.

T   F 10. Another name for an organization chart is fixed chart.

WRITTEN QUESTIONS

Write a brief answer to each of the following questions.

1. Name at least three types of graphics objects you can use in a presentation.

2. Name at least three methods you can use to insert pictures on a slide.

3. Name at least three types of data you might present in a table.

4. Name at least three chart types, giving an example of how each one might be used.

5. Name at least four ways that you can manipulate objects on a slide.

FILL IN THE BLANK

Complete the following sentences by writing the correct word or words in the blanks provided.

1. A(n) _____ is the vertical component of a table.

2. A(n) _____ is the horizontal component of a table.

3. _____ multiple cells to combine them into one large cell.

4. Press the _____ key to move from one cell to the next.

5. Table _____ are the horizontal and vertical lines that define columns and rows.

6. A chart is a(n) _____ representation of table data.

7. A(n) _____ chart shows data changes over a period of time or illustrates comparisons among items.

8. The _____ axis displays the categories in the chart.

9. The _____ axis displays the values in the chart.

10. A(n) _____ diagram is used to illustrate the proportions of individual elements with a whole.

PROJECTS

PROJECT 14-1

1. Launch your presentation graphics program. Open **Project14-1a** from the Data files, and save the file as **Retreat**.

2. On Slide 1, insert the picture file **Project14-1b** from the Data files for this lesson.

3. Scale the picture to **6.5** inches high. The width should adjust automatically.

4. Center the picture horizontally and vertically on the slide. For example, in PowerPoint:
   A. Click the **Draw** button on the Drawing toolbar.
   B. Click **Align or Distribute** and select the **Relative to Slide** command, if necessary.
   C. Click the **Draw** button, click **Align or Distribute**, and then click **Align Center**.
   D. Click the **Draw** button, click **Align or Distribute**, and then click **Align Middle**.

5. Change the stacking order to send the picture to the back, behind other objects on the slide. For example, in PowerPoint:
   A. Click the **Draw** button on the Drawing toolbar.
   B. Click **Order** and then click **Send to Back**.

6. Make Slide 2 current and change the layout to one that has placeholders for a title, a column of text, and a clip-art picture, such as PowerPoint's **Title, Text and Clip Art** layout. If necessary, adjust the font size of the text so it all fits in the placeholder.

7. Locate and insert a clip-art picture related to travel, such as suitcases. (If you cannot locate an appropriate clip-art picture, insert the picture file **Project14-1c.**)

8. Apply a **6 point** border around the clip-art picture, using the blue color assigned to the background color scheme (on the left end of the color palette). To do this in PowerPoint:
   A. Click the **Line Color** list arrow on the Drawing toolbar and then click the **blue** color swatch.
   B. Click the **Line Style** button on the Drawing toolbar and then **6 pt solid**.

9. Select the picture on Slide 1 and copy it to the Clipboard. Make Slide 3 current and paste the picture.

10. Resize the picture to about **2.5** inches high (the width should adjust automatically) and drag it to position it in the upper-left corner of the slide.

11. Apply the **Wheel Clockwise, 2 Spokes** (or similar) transition at **Slow** speed. Set the slides to advance on a mouse click or automatically after 5 seconds (**00:05**). Apply this transition to all slides.

12. Preview the presentation in Slide Show View from the beginning.

13. Save the changes and close **Retreat**. Leave your presentation program open to use in the next project.

PROJECT 14-2

1. Open **Project14-2** from the Data files, and save the file as **Retreat2**.

2. Make Slide 2 current and insert a new slide. Select a layout with placeholders for a title and a table, or for a title only, such as PowerPoint's **Title and Table** or **Title Only** layout.

3. Insert a table with two columns and five rows.

4. Click the title placeholder and key **General Budget**.

5. Key the following table data:

Travel	$16,750
Lodging	$10,000
Meals	$3,000
Conference Facilities	$5,500
Conference Materials	$1,200

6. Add a new row to the bottom of the table. In the first cell, key **Miscellaneous**. In the second cell, key **$2,000**.

7. Move the entire table up a small amount on the slide so that it is about 3/8 of an inch from the bottom of the slide.

8. Center all text in the table vertically, and right-align all of the values in the second column.

9. Change the borders around the outside of the table to **6** point **dark blue**, and change the inside border to **dashed, 1** point **white**. For example, in PowerPoint:
   A. Select the table. Click the **Border Width** button on the Tables and Borders toolbar and then click **6 pt.**
   B. Click the **Border Color** button on the Tables and Borders toolbar and then click the **dark blue** swatch that is third from the right.
   C. Click the **Borders** button drop-down arrow and then click the **Outside Borders** button.
   D. Change the **Border Width** to **1 pt.**
   E. Change the **Border Color** to **White.**
   F. Change the **Border Style** to **dashed.**
   G. Click the **Borders** button drop-down arrow and then click the **Inside Borders** button.

10. Use the drawing tools to draw an oval around the highest cost in the table ($16,750). Set the shape to have **no fill** and a **3** point **yellow** line. For example, in PowerPoint:
    A. Click the **Oval** tool on the Drawing toolbar and then click and drag to draw the shape around the value on the slide.
    B. Click the **Fill Color** list arrow on the Drawing toolbar and then click **No Fill.**
    C. Click the **Line Style** button on the Drawing toolbar and then click **3 pt.**
    D. Click the **Line Color** list arrow on the Drawing toolbar and then click the **Yellow** color swatch.

11. Check the spelling in the presentation and correct all errors.

12. Preview the presentation in Slide Show View from the beginning.

13. Save the changes and close **Retreat2.** Leave your presentation program open to use in the next project.

PROJECT 14-3

1. Open **Project14-3** from the Data files, and save the file as **Retreat3.**

2. Make Slide 3 current and insert a new slide. Use a layout that has placeholders for a title and a chart, or for a title only, such as PowerPoint's **Title and Chart,** or **Title Only** layout.

3. Click the title placeholder and key **Breakdown of Expenses.**

4. Insert a new chart.

5. In the datasheet, click the cell in the first row, second column (labeled *1st Qtr in PowerPoint)* and key **Travel.** Press **Tab** and key **Lodging.** Press **Tab** and key **Meals.** Press **Tab** and key **Conference Facilities.** Press **Tab** and key **Conference Materials.** Press **Tab** and key **Miscellaneous.**

6. Click the cell in the second row, first column (labeled *East* in PowerPoint) and key **Expense**. Press **Tab** to move to the *Travel* column (make sure the datasheet is scrolled all the way to the left so that the *A* column, *Travel*, is selected) and key **16500**. Press **Tab** and key **10000**. Press **Tab** and key **3000**. Press **Tab** and key **5500**. Press **Tab** and key **1200**. Press **Tab** and key **2000**.

7. Click the row heading for row 2 and press **Delete**. Click the row heading for row 3 and press **Delete**. Close the datasheet.

8. Change the chart type to **Pie Chart**.

9. Modify the chart options so the data labels display the percentages, with leader lines. For example, in PowerPoint, follow these steps:
   A. Click **Chart** on the Menu bar and then click **Chart Options**.
   B. Click the **Data Labels** tab.
   C. Click to select the **Percentage** check box and the **Show leader lines** check box, and deselect all other check boxes if necessary.
   D. Click **OK**.

10. Format the plot area so it has no border. For example, in PowerPoint, follow these steps:
    A. Position the mouse pointer on the border around the pie chart so the ScreenTip displays *Plot Area*.
    B. Right-click and then click **Format Plot Area**.
    C. Select **None** in the Border section.
    D. Click **OK**.

11. Increase the size of the plot area by dragging one of its corner selection handles. If necessary, drag the data labels (the percentages) away from the chart so the leader lines display.

12. Click anywhere outside the chart to deselect it.

13. Check the spelling in the presentation and correct all errors.

14. Preview the presentation in Slide Show View from the beginning.

15. Save the changes and close **Retreat3**. Close your presentation program.

 WEB PROJECT

When you select pictures, it is important to select a file format that is suitable for the method you will use to display the presentation. Use the Internet to research which file formats are best for use in a presentation file, and why. Consider the different ways you might display the presentation—on a computer screen, using an overhead projector, on the Web—and how that might impact the file formats you should use. Is JPEG right for Web delivery? What about GIF? Organize your research and write a report explaining what you have learned. Illustrate the report with a table that lists the different file formats and the situation for which they might be used.

TEAMWORK PROJECT

For a social studies project, create a presentation about a place you would like to visit. As a team, select the location. It might be a foreign country, a city, a landmark, or even a local destination. Research the location using the Internet, books, and magazines. You might divide the research up according to topic. For example, one person might research historical information, another might research geographical information, a third might research important places to visit, and so on. Each person should collect enough information for at least two slides of bulleted items, and should plan how to use graphics to illustrate the slides. You might locate picture files that are part of a clip-art collection, or you might be able to download pictures from the Internet. You could also scan pictures from a book or magazine. You might want to create a table listing facts about the location, or use a chart or diagram. Or you might be able to create drawing objects. Don't forget to record all sources so you can cite them as part of the project.

When the research is complete, meet to organize the presentation. Write an outline for the presentation, and plan the slide layouts you will use. Decide which slides will have pictures and which will just have text. At this point, ask other classmates to review the outline and offer suggestions. Incorporate the suggestions and then create the presentation. Select a design template and enter the text and graphics. If necessary, insert text boxes on slides with graphics so you can cite the source of the picture. Check the spelling. Add slide transitions and preview the presentation. Make adjustments as necessary. Ask classmates to review the presentation and make suggestions, and then go back to incorporate their ideas. Finalize the presentation, and then present it to the class.

CRITICAL *Thinking*

Do you earn an allowance? Do you have a job? These are sources of income. Expenses are the items that you spend money on, such as snacks, movies, and clothes. Income and expense information is often displayed using tables, charts, and diagrams. To make a case for increasing your salary or allowance, create a presentation that compares your income with your expenses. Start by drafting an outline that you can use to organize the slides. Include facts about how you earn money and how you spend money. Try to emphasize reasons you deserve more. Ask a classmate to review the outline and offer suggestions that you can incorporate into your plan.

When you are ready, create the presentation and select a design template. Create the slides using the appropriate slide layouts. Use bulleted text items to explain how you use your money and why you deserve more. Use pictures to add humor to the slides. Use a table to list items you buy and what each item costs—a simple budget of sorts. Use a chart to compare your income with your expenses (column chart), to show a trend in your spending or saving habits (line chart), or to display the breakdown of total expenses into categories (pie chart). You might use a cycle diagram to show how the money flows in and out.

Check the spelling and apply transitions to the presentation. Ask a classmate to review it, and incorporate any suggestions. When it is complete, present it to the class.

WORKING WITH MOVIES, ANIMATION, AND SOUND

To add life to a presentation, you can embellish it with active multimedia content such as animations, video clips, and sound. Active content makes a presentation more interesting to the viewer and helps capture and maintain the audiences' attention. You can insert an animated GIF file or a video clip to help illustrate text or in place of static graphics. You can insert audio content to provide additional information through narration, set a mood with a song, or emphasize a point with a short, sudden sound such as a bell or whistle.

Another way to jazz up a presentation is by animating transitions between slides, and the static content on the slides. For example, you can set bulleted items to slide into place, or titles to spin.

In this lesson, you learn how to add movies and sound to slides, as well as how to animate text and graphics objects.

Work with Movies

In most presentation programs, you can insert *movie* files on any slide, and play them as part of the presentation. In a presentation, a movie is either an animated GIF file or a video clip file. You can insert movie files from many different sources. Usually, there are animated GIF files in the clip art collection that comes with the program. You can also insert any animated GIF file that is stored on your computer, a removable storage device, a network, or the Internet. For example, you can create your own animated GIFs using an animation program (see Lesson 8) and then insert them on a slide. Likewise, you can create your own video files using a video recorder, or insert video files stored on your computer, network, or the Internet.

It is important to consider the method you will use to deliver a presentation before you add active multimedia content. If the presentation is running in stand-alone mode in a crowded and noisy convention hall, will the audience be able to hear it? If you are narrating the presentation in person, will it conflict with the audio inserted on the slides? Will audio and video in the presentation distract the audience from your spoken narration? You should also know the system you will be using. For example, the computer must have the necessary hardware, including a sound card, speakers, and an enhanced video card.

Extra for Experts

If you are using PowerPoint, you should note that the program does not actually play multimedia files; it uses the Windows operating system and a version of Windows Media Player to play video and audio within a presentation. This may cause problems when you try to play a presentation that includes video and audio on different computers. If the computer you are using does not have the same or compatible software as the computer on which you created the presentation, the multimedia files may not play correctly, or at all. If a clip does not play as you expect, you may need to consult the Microsoft Web site for support.

Insert an Animated GIF

An animated GIF is a clip art drawing that has some element of animation in it. The files have a *.gif* file extension, just like a non-animated GIF graphics file, but when they play, something moves. Animated GIFs are frequently cartoons, or cartoon-like in nature, so they can be used to add humor or a light touch to a presentation.

You can insert any animated GIF file in an object placeholder, or directly on a slide using a command on the Insert menu. For example, in PowerPoint, click Insert on the Menu bar, click Movies and Sounds, and then click Movie from File. Change the file type to include all files, if necessary, locate and select the file to insert, and then click OK. To preview the animated GIF, change to Slide Show View.

Usually, the inserted animated GIF object displays in a small size. You can scale the object, or move it to a different location. You may even be able to format some aspects of the image, such as the color (refer to Lesson 14 for information on modifying pictures).

Did You Know?

In some programs, thumbnails of animated GIFs display an icon such as a star to indicate that the file is animated.

Note

Most presentation programs include animated GIFs in a clip art collection. To insert a clip art animated GIF, display the clip art collection dialog box or task pane, locate and select the desired clip, and select the command to insert it on the slide.

STEP-BY-STEP 15.1

1. Start your presentation program and open **Step15-1a** from the data files for this lesson. Save the file as **Pets**.

2. Make sure Slide 1 is current, and then select the command to insert an animated GIF file. For example, in PowerPoint, click **Insert** on the Menu bar, click **Movies and Sounds** and then click **Movie from File** to display the Insert Movie dialog box.

3. Locate and select the **Step15-1b.gif** animated GIF file in the data files for this lesson. (You may have to change the *Files of type* to **All Files**.) Click **OK**. The file is inserted in the middle of the slide, as shown in Figure 15-1. It looks like a regular, static, graphics picture.

FIGURE 15-1
Animated GIF file on a slide

Inserted GIF file

4. Scale the picture to about **1.5** inches high (the width should adjust automatically) and position it below the subtitle text box, centered horizontally.

5. Change to **Slide Show View** to preview the animation. The dog's tail should wag, and its mouth should open and close, as if it is barking. (The animation will loop by default.)

6. End the show. For example, in PowerPoint, right-click the screen and click **End Show** to exit Slide Show View.

7. Save the changes and leave **Pets** open to use in the next exercise.

Insert a Video File

Most presentations support live video files. For example, you might want to include a video clip of a company president's speech in a presentation for new employees, or you might want to include a clip of a demonstration in a presentation about a new product. The types of video files that you can insert depends

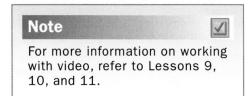

Note   ☑

For more information on working with video, refer to Lessons 9, 10, and 11.

on your presentation program, but most support Audio Video Interleave (.avi), and Motion Picture Experts Group (.mpg) files. However, the specific codecs—compression/decompression formats—used to encode the file may also affect whether or not a video clip will play in the presentation.

You can insert video in an object placeholder, or directly on a slide using the same command you use to insert an animated GIF. For example, in PowerPoint, you click Insert on the Menu bar, click Movies and Sounds, and then click Movie from File. You then locate and select the file and click OK.

> **Hot Tip**
>
> In PowerPoint, double-click a media clip placeholder to display movie clips stored in the clip art collection.

In most programs, after you have inserted the video clip, you then specify whether you want the video to play automatically when the slide displays, or on a mouse click. How you want the video to start depends on how you plan to display the presentation. If the presentation will run standalone, you may want it to play automatically, but if you plan to deliver the presentation yourself, you may want it to start on a mouse click. Also, if the video is set to start on a mouse click, you—or viewers—can skip it if you want. You can change this setting at any time.

When you insert the video, the first frame of the video displays on the slide. To preview the video, double-click it, or use Slide Show View. Like the animated GIF file, you can move or scale the object. Keep in mind, however, that if the resolution is not high enough, increasing the scale of the video may cause it to appear grainy or fuzzy.

Video files are usually linked to a presentation, not stored as part of the presentation file. That means the video file should be stored in the same location as the presentation file at all times, or *packaged* with the presentation, so the presentation program can locate it and play it. Packaging is a feature that lets you copy all required files and a *viewer* program to a CD so you can deliver the presentation on a different computer system. A viewer program lets you play a presentation even if the presentation program is not installed on the computer. You learn how to package a presentation for delivery in Lesson 17.

> **Hot Tip**
>
> Some programs have a command to automatically size a video for best playback. In PowerPoint, select the video object, click Format on the Menu bar, and then click Picture. In the dialog box, click the Size tab, click the *Best scale for slide show* check box, and then click OK.

STEP-BY-STEP 15.2

Before beginning this exercise, you should use Windows to locate **Step15-2.avi** in the data files, and copy it to the location where you will store the solution files for this lesson.

1. Make Slide 4 current.

2. Select the media clip placeholder, and select the command to insert a video file. For example, in PowerPoint, click **Insert** on the Menu bar, click **Movies and Sounds**, and then click **Movie from File**. The Insert Movie dialog box displays.

3. Locate and select the **Step15-2.avi** movie file that you copied to your Solutions folder for this lesson, and then click **OK**.

STEP-BY-STEP 15.2 Continued

4. Select the option to start the movie when clicked. The first frame of the video displays on the slide, as shown in Figure 15-2.

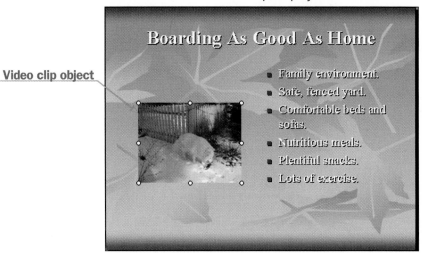

FIGURE 15-2
The first frame of a video clip displays on the slide

Video clip object

5. Double-click the video object. The video plays on the slide.

6. Save the changes and leave **Pets** open to use in the next exercise.

Set Movie Options

In most presentation programs you can control the way a video clip plays. Use the options in the Movie Options or a similar dialog box to set options such as whether the video should play once or loop repeatedly, whether you want to rewind the video when it is finished playing, and even to set the volume of the sound portion of the audio.

 Note

Video clips and animated GIFs are protected by copyright laws. Do not use files that are owned by someone else unless you obtain permission, and always cite your sources.

STEP-BY-STEP 15.3

1. Right-click the video object on Slide 4, and select the command to edit the movie clip. For example, in PowerPoint, click **Edit Movie Object** to display the Movie Options dialog box. It should look similar to Figure 15-3.

FIGURE 15-3
Movie Options dialog box

2. Select the option to zoom the movie to full screen if available, and then click **OK**.

3. Change to Slide Show View, and then click the video object on the screen. The video clip plays in full screen mode. Notice that it is a bit grainy because of the resolution. Also notice that when the clip ends, the last frame displays on the slide.

4. End the slide show and select the command to edit the movie clip again. Deselect the option to zoom the movie to full screen. Select the option to rewind the movie when it is done playing. Also, mute the sound. For example, in PowerPoint, click the **Sound volume** icon and then click **Mute**.

5. Click **OK** and then change to **Slide Show View**. Click the video object. The video plays at its default size, without any sound. At the end, it rewinds to the first frame.

6. Exit Slide Show View.

7. Save the changes and leave **Pets** open to use in the next exercise.

Work with Sound

You know that transitions and animations can include WAV formatted sounds, such as applause, whistles, and bells. When you want more sound, such as music or voice, you can insert a sound file as an object on a slide. You may use sound files that are included in the program's clip art collection, or you may use any sound file stored on your computer, a removable storage device, a network, or the Internet. You can even record your own sound file and then insert it on a slide (for more information on recording a sound file, refer to Lesson 8). Most presentation programs also let you record sounds and narration as part of a presentation. Most presentations support many sound file formats in addition to .wav. Some of the most common include Musical Instrument Digital Interface (.mid, .midi), MP3, and Windows Media Audio (.wma).

If the sound file is smaller than 100 KB, it will be embedded in the presentation, or stored as part of the presentation file itself. If it is larger than 100 KB it will be linked to the presentation file. That means the sound file should be stored in the same location as the presentation file at all times, or packaged with the presentation so the presentation program can locate it and play it. As mentioned earlier, you will learn how to package a presentation for delivery in Lesson 17.

As with video, when you select a sound file format, you should consider the size of the file, the sound quality, and whether the file will be able to play on the delivery method you plan to use. For example, WAV files are large, but can play on a wide variety of computers. MIDI, MP3, and WMA files offer good quality, but WMA files only play on Windows computers. MIDI and MP3 files play on a variety of platforms. Of course, you must have a sound card and speakers to play audio, and a microphone to record it.

Insert a Sound File

To insert a sound file as an object on a slide, select a command from the Insert menu. For example, in PowerPoint, click Insert on the Menu bar, click Movies and Sounds, and then click Sound from File. If necessary, select the specific file type, locate and select the file to insert, and then click OK. In most programs, you then specify if you want the sound to play automatically or on a mouse click. The sound object displays as an icon on the slide. Double-click the icon to preview the sound; click anywhere on the slide to stop the sound.

You can set sound options to control how the object plays. For example, you can loop the sound so it plays over and over until the slide changes, and you can hide the sound icon during a presentation. However, you should hide the icon only if you have set the sound to play automatically, because if the icon does not display during the presentation, you cannot click it to play the sound.

Note

Most presentation programs include sound files in a clip art collection. To insert a sound clip file, display the clip art collection task pane or dialog box, locate and select the desired clip, and select the command to insert it on the slide.

Important

When downloading a sound file from the Web, always make sure the clip is copyright-free or royalty-free or you have been given the specific right to use it for personal use. Some sites let you create your own music loops for downloading without requiring copyrights or permissions.

Extra for Experts

Some presentation programs let you link to one or more sound tracks on a CD-ROM. To link to a CD, insert the CD you want to use into its drive, and then select the command to play a CD Audio Track. For example, in PowerPoint, click Insert on the Menu bar, click Movies and Sounds, and then click Play CD Audio Track. Specify the tracks to play, and then click OK. Keep in mind that the CD must be in the computer whenever you deliver the presentation in order for the music to play.

STEP-BY-STEP 15.4

1. Make Slide 1 current.

2. Select the command to insert a sound file. For example, in PowerPoint, click **Insert** on the Menu bar, click **Movies and Sounds**, and then click **Sound from File**. The Insert Sound dialog box displays.

3. Locate and select the **Step15-4.wav** sound file, and click **OK**. Select to play the sound automatically. A sound icon displays on the slide, as shown in Figure 15-4.

FIGURE 15-4
A sound icon on a slide

Sound icon

4. Double-click the sound icon to hear the sound.

5. Change to Slide Show View to see how the animated GIF file looks while the sound plays.

6. Exit Slide Show View.

7. Right-click the sound icon on Slide 1 and then click the command to edit the sound object. The Sound Options dialog box (or one similar to it) displays. It should look similar to Figure 15-5.

Note ☑

Because the Step15-4.wav file is only 34 KB, it will automatically be embedded into the presentation. You do not need to copy it to the folder where you are saving your presentation.

FIGURE 15-5
Sound Options dialog box

STEP-BY-STEP 15.4 Continued

8. Select the options to loop the sound and to hide the icon during the slide show, and then click **OK**.

9. Change to **Slide Show View**. Now, the barking repeats as long as the slide displays, and you cannot see the sound icon.

10. Exit Slide Show View.

11. Save the changes and leave **Pets** open to use in the next exercise.

Record Sound on a Slide

Most presentation programs let you record sound directly into a presentation file. This is useful for adding your own sound effects, vocals, or voice over to accompany a single slide. A voice over is spoken text played while other content displays. You must have a microphone, and a sound card configured for use with your computer to record sound, and speakers to play the sound back.

Before recording sound, take some time to plan exactly what you are going to record, to practice, and to have everything you need ready and accessible. For example, if you plan to speak, write a script and practice reading it.

To start, select the command for recording sound. For example, in PowerPoint, click Insert on the Menu bar, click Movies and Sounds, and then click Record Sound. If you want, key a name for the sound file and then click the Record button to start recording. (If you do not key a name, a default name, such as Recorded Sound 1 is used.) Use your microphone to record the sound, and click the Stop button to stop recording when you are finished. Click the Play button to hear the sound before inserting it. Click **OK** to save the file as part of the presentation, and create a sound icon on the slide.

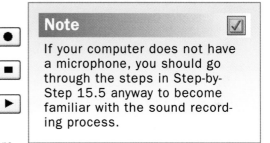

> **Note** ☑
>
> If your computer does not have a microphone, you should go through the steps in Step-by-Step 15.5 anyway to become familiar with the sound recording process.

STEP-BY-STEP 15.5

1. Practice reading out loud the following text to use as a voice over:

Choose Annie's for safe, worry-free care for your beloved pet.

2. When you are comfortable reading the text, select Slide 5 in the **Pets** file.

STEP-BY-STEP 15.5 Continued

3. Select the command for recording sound on a slide. For example, in PowerPoint, click **Insert** on the Menu bar, click **Movies and Sounds**, and then click **Record Sound**. The Record Sound dialog box should look similar to the one in Figure 15-6.

FIGURE 15-6
Record Sound dialog box

4. In the Name box, key **Annies** to replace the sample sound file name.

5. Click the **Record** button.

6. In a steady, normal tone, read the following text into the microphone:

Choose Annie's for safe, worry-free care for your beloved pet.

7. Click the **Stop** button. Click the **Play** button to preview the recording. If you are not happy with it, you can click **Cancel**, and start again.

8. When you are satisfied with the recording, click the **OK** button. A sound icon displays on the slide.

9. Drag the sound icon to the lower-right corner of the slide and then change to Slide Show View. On Slide 5, click the sound icon to play the voice over.

10. Exit Slide Show View. Save the changes and leave **Pets** open to use in the next exercise.

Animate Slide Objects

In most presentation programs you can animate text blocks and other objects on a slide. Just as transitions control the way an entire slide comes into view during a slide show, animations control the way the objects on the slide come into view, and sometimes move to a different location on the slide or exit the slide. You can set titles to fade in, or pictures to move from one side of a slide to another. Animations can be purely decorative, or they can enhance the delivery of a presentation. You can use animation effects to display a picture, and then display the text describing the picture, or you can set text to scroll up and off the slide like credits at the end of a movie.

Some presentation programs come with built-in *animation schemes*, which are collections of animation settings and transitions that you can apply to a single slide or all slides. To quickly animate a single slide, make it current and then select an animation scheme in a dialog box or task pane. You should be able to preview the scheme before you apply it. For example, in PowerPoint, click Slide Show on the Menu bar, and then click Animation Schemes to display the Animation Schemes task pane. Click the scheme you want to use, and watch how it affects the slide in the Slide pane. To apply the same scheme to all slides, click the Apply to All Slides button.

Often, the schemes will be organized into categories that define how much action or speed they apply. For example, animations in a *subtle* category may slowly fade in each element on a slide, whereas animations in an *exciting* category may quickly bounce each element into place, and then back out again. There may also be a section for recently used schemes at the top of the list.

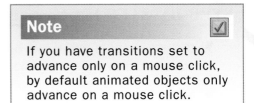

Note   ☑

If you have transitions set to advance only on a mouse click, by default animated objects only advance on a mouse click.

STEP-BY-STEP 15.6

1. Make Slide 2 current. Select the command to display the available animation schemes. For example, in PowerPoint, click **Slide Show** on the Menu bar, and then click **Animation Schemes**. In PowerPoint, the schemes display in a task pane, as shown in Figure 15-7.

FIGURE 15-7
Animation Schemes task pane

2. Select the **Elegant** animation scheme. In PowerPoint you will find this option in the Moderate category. If your program does not have an Elegant animation scheme, select a scheme that causes the title and then each bulleted item to display with a subtle scroll effect.

3. Select both Slides 3 and 4, and apply the **Elegant** animation scheme or the comparable one that is available in your presentation program.

4. Make Slide 5 current and apply the **Big title** animation scheme. In PowerPoint you will find it in the Exciting category. If your program does not have a Big title animation scheme, select a scheme that causes the title and each line of text to start out large and then shrink down to normal size.

5. Make Slide 1 current and change to Slide Show View. Click the screen to advance to Slide 2.

6. After the title displays on Slide 2, click the screen to display each bullet item. After the last bullet item, click the screen to advance to Slide 3.

STEP-BY-STEP 15.6 Continued

7. Click the screen to display each bullet item, and then to advance to Slide 4. Click the video object to play it, and then click the screen to display each bullet item and then to advance to Slide 5.

8. On Slide 5, click the screen to display the subtitle, and then to display the phone number. Click the sound icon to play the voice over.

9. Click the screen twice to end the slide show.

10. Save the changes and leave **Pets** open to use in the next exercise.

> **Hot Tip**
>
> To remove an animation scheme in PowerPoint, click No Animation in the Animation Schemes task pane.

Create Custom Animations

To apply different animation effects to elements on the same slide, you can create custom animations. With custom animations, you can control the speed and direction of the animation, as well as whether the animation should start only on a mouse click, or automatically at the same time as the previous animation, or after the previous animation. You can create custom animations for all types of objects, including text, graphics, video, and sound. You can even apply custom animations to slides already formatted with an animation scheme.

In most programs, custom animations are organized into four main groups:

- *Entrance effects* control how an element comes into view on the slide.

- *Emphasis effects* apply an animation after the object is displayed on the slide. They are frequently used for graphics objects such as pictures, charts, and tables, but can also be used for text objects.

- *Exit effects* control how an element is removed from the slide.

- *Motion Paths* allow you to specify a path along which an object will move.

In addition, sound objects have a Sound Actions category, and movie objects have a Movie Actions category. These provide additional options for animating these specific types of objects within a presentation.

In PowerPoint, once an object has been animated, a small numbered tag displays in its upper-left corner on the slide in Normal View. You can click the numbered tag to select an effect.

Apply Custom Animation Effects

To apply custom animations, select the command to display the dialog box or task pane. For example, in PowerPoint, click Slide Show on the Menu bar and then click Custom Animation to display the Custom Animation task pane. Select the object you want to animate in the Slide pane, then select the animation effect.

Once you select the effect, you can set the following options to control the start, direction, and speed.

■ *Start* determines whether the animation starts on a mouse click, at the same time as the previous animation, or after the previous animation.

■ *Direction* determines the side of the slide from which the animation begins.

■ *Speed* determines the speed at which the animation plays.

Some types of animations have different options. For example, if you select a spin emphasis effect, the spin amount is available in place of the direction setting.

You can select more than one effect for a single object. As you select effects for the objects on a slide, they display in the Custom Animation list in the order in which they will occur. To change the order, click an effect and drag it to a different location in the list, or use the Re-Order arrows that may be available.

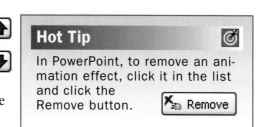

Hot Tip

In PowerPoint, to remove an animation effect, click it in the list and click the Remove button.

STEP-BY-STEP 15.7

1. Make Slide 1 current and select the command to make custom animation options available. For example, in PowerPoint, click **Slide Show** on the Menu bar and then click **Custom Animation**. In PowerPoint, the Custom Animation task pane displays.

   Notice that the sound object—called Media 4—already displays in the list. This is the sound file of the dog barking that you inserted earlier in this lesson. All sound and movie objects have custom animations that control whether they start automatically or on a mouse click.

2. Select the title text placeholder, and then select the command to add an entrance effect. For example, in PowerPoint's Custom Animation task pane, click the **Add Effect** button, and then click **Entrance**. A list of available animations displays.

STEP-BY-STEP 15.7 Continued

3. Click **Fly In** or a similarly named effect. The effect is applied to the text, and the item is added to the list of effects, as shown in Figure 15-8.

FIGURE 15-8
Custom animations

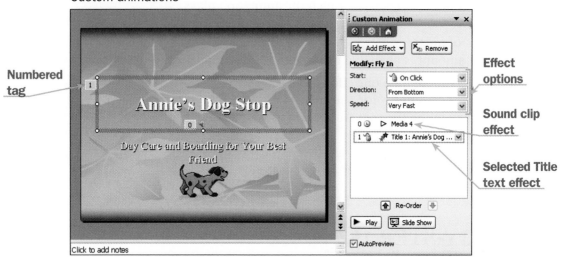

4. Select to start the effect with the previous action. For example, in PowerPoint click the **Start** drop-down arrow and then click **With Previous**. This changes the setting so that instead of waiting for a mouse click, the title flies in at the same time as the previous action—which is the sound file playing. (Notice that the sound file displays above the *Title 1* animation in the Effects list, which means it plays first.)

5. Set the direction to **From Left**. For example, in PowerPoint, click the **Direction** drop-down arrow and then click **From Left**.

6. Set the speed to **Fast**. For example, in PowerPoint, click the **Speed** drop-down arrow and then click **Fast**.

7. Select the subtitle place holder and select to add a fly-in entrance effect. Set the effect to start after the previous, from the left, at a fast speed. In PowerPoint, the Custom Animations task pane should look similar to Figure 15-9.

STEP-BY-STEP 15.7 Continued

FIGURE 15-9
Add animation effects

8. Change to Slide Show View to preview Slide 1. After the subtitle displays, end the slide show.

9. Save the changes and leave **Pets** open to use in the next exercise.

Set Effect Options

To further customize animations, most programs let you adjust, or fine-tune, such settings as when an effect starts. In PowerPoint some options are available on a shortcut menu that displays when you select an effect and then click the drop-down arrow next to its name in the list of effects. Other options are available in an effect options dialog box. Open the dialog box in PowerPoint by displaying the shortcut menu and then clicking Effect Options. The name of the dialog box depends on the current effect.

Usually, the effect options dialog box has two or three tabs. On one tab, you can set options such as the direction, add a sound to the animation, and select to hide or dim the object after the animation. On the second tab, you can adjust the timing of the effect to include a delay, modify the speed, and even repeat the animation multiple times. You can also set *triggers* which are controls that allow you to coordinate the start of one effect with the start of another on the same slide. The third tab depends on the type of object you are animating. For example, you can animate a chart as a single object, or you can animate individual chart elements one by one.

> **Note** ☑
>
> Step-by-Step 15.8 is specific to PowerPoint. If you're using a different program, ask you instructor how to locate the command for customizing effects options.

STEP-BY-STEP 15.8

1. Make Slide 2 current, and then click the numbered tag on the slide to the left of the first bullet item to select the animated text (see Figure 15-10).

FIGURE 15-10
Select an effect to make changes

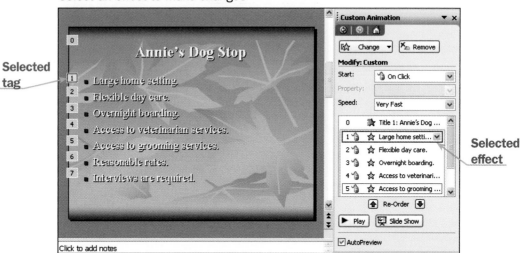

2. In the list of effects, click the drop-down arrow next to the item, and then click **Start After Previous** on the shortcut menu. Now, instead of waiting for a mouse click, the animation will begin as soon as the previous animation ends.

> **Note** ☑
>
> If there are too many items in the list of animations to fit in the task pane, a double arrow pointing down displays instead. Click it to display the hidden items.

3. Select the second bullet item and set it to start after the previous animation.

4. Set the remaining five bullet items to start after the previous animation.

5. Make Slide 3 current. Select the picture and then select to add the Spin Emphasis effect. For example, in PowerPoint, click the **Add Effect** button, click **Emphasis** and then click **Spin**. Set the effect to start with the previous effect, and leave the amount and speed at the default settings.

6. With the effect still selected, drag the effect up the list of effects so it comes after the title effect, or click the **Re-Order Up** button to move it up the list.

7. Set each bullet item to start automatically after the previous animation.

8. Make Slide 4 current. Move the video object up the list of effects so it is after the title. Change it to start automatically with the previous animation.

9. Select the bulleted text placeholder on the slide. Click the **Start** drop-down arrow and then click **With Previous**. This sets all items in the placeholder to display at the same time.

STEP-BY-STEP 15.8 Continued

10. Make Slide 5 current. Select the sound object (Media 3) and move it up to second on the effects list, after the title. Click its drop-down arrow and then click **Effect Options** to display the Play Sound dialog box. Click the **Timing** tab. It should look similar to Figure 15-11.

FIGURE 15-11
The Timing tab in the Play Sound dialog box

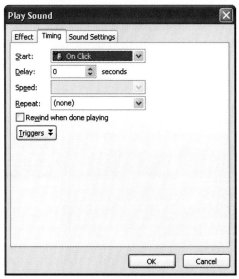

11. Set the sound to start with the previous animation. Key **1.5** in the *Delay* text box to set a 1.5 second delay. Click the **Sound Settings** tab, and select to hide the sound icon during the slide show. Click **OK**.

12. Set each subtitle text object to start after the previous animation.

13. Make Slide 1 current and change to **Slide Show View**. After the animations on each slide complete, click the screen to advance to the next slide. At the end of the slide show, click the screen twice to return to Normal View.

14. Save the changes and leave **Pets** open to use in the next exercise.

Create a Motion Path Animation

One of the most interesting ways to animate objects on a slide is to create a motion path. A motion path animation causes an object to move on the slide from one location to another. You can select from a palette of motion paths, or you can draw your own path. To apply a motion path, display the Custom Animation dialog box or task pane, select the object to animate, and then select the command to add a motion path. For example, in PowerPoint, click the Add Effects drop-down list and then click Motion Paths. Select from the built-in paths, or select to draw a custom path using standard Drawing tools. Some programs, offer a wide range of basic shapes, special shapes, and lines and curves.

In PowerPoint, once you add a path, it displays on the slide in Normal View as a line with red and green arrowheads. To adjust the length or shape of the path, select the line and drag either end to a different location.

STEP-BY-STEP 15.9

1. Make Slide 1 current, if necessary.

2. Select the picture and drag it to the left side of the slide.

3. Display the custom animation task pane or dialog box, if necessary, and select to add a motion path effect. For example, in PowerPoint, click the **Add Effect** button and then click **Motion Paths**.

4. Select the command to move the object along a straight line from left to right. In PowerPoint, this is the **Right** motion path command. The animation plays, and then the path displays on the slide, as shown in Figure 15-12.

FIGURE 15-12
A motion path effect

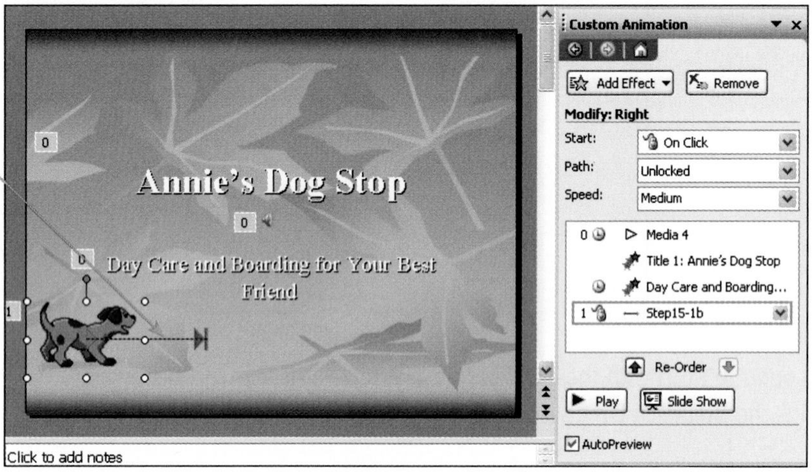

5. Click the motion path line to select it. Selection handles display on each end of the line. Drag the selection handle at the right end of the line about 1.5 inches to the right to the middle of the slide. When you release the mouse button, the motion path is extended.

6. Move the effect up the list one spot so it is under the title, and set it to start with the previous animation.

7. Change to **Slide Show View** to preview the animation. You may advance through all the slides, or end the slide show after Slide 1.

8. Save the changes and close **Pets**. Leave your animation program open to use in the next exercise.

Record Narration

If your presentation will be played as a self-running slide show at a kiosk, conference center, or other venue, or if you are not comfortable speaking during the presentation, you can record narration for the entire slide show. To record narration, select the command to display the Record Narration dialog box. For example, in PowerPoint, click Slide Show on the Menu bar, and then click Record Narration.

To prepare for the recording, you should practice reading your narration. Write it as a script, specifying what you plan to read for each slide, and then read it as many times as it takes until you are comfortable. Use a slow, steady speaking voice, and pronounce each word completely. Do not rush. For best results, read it and display the slides in the presentation at the same time so you can judge the timing.

Most programs give you the opportunity to set the *recording level*, which is a setting that controls the volume at which the narration is recorded. Depending on your program, you may be able to establish the proper recording level by clicking a command such as Set Microphone Level, and speaking some test phrases. In some programs, a slider adjusts automatically as you speak to set the recording level, but you can fine-tune the level by dragging the sliders manually. You may also be able to select a different sound quality. Keep in mind, however, that a higher sound quality increases the size of the presentation file.

Once you set the recording level you can begin recording the narration. Select the slide where you want the narration to begin, and then click OK. PowerPoint displays the slide, or prompts you to confirm the starting slide. Begin speaking into the microphone to record your narration. To move to the next slide, click on the slide or press Page Down. To pause the recording, right-click the slide and click Pause Narration on the shortcut menu. To resume recording, right-click the slide and click Resume Narration.

After the last slide, click the screen to stop the recording. You may then have the option of saving the *timings*. The timings are the intervals that control the length of time a slide is displayed before the transition to the next slide. Saving your timings at this point sets the intervals based on how long you took to record the narration for a slide, and when you advanced to the next slide. You learn to set customized timings in Lesson 17.

> **Note**
>
> By default, narration sound files are embedded in the presentation, which may result in a large file. Usually, you can choose to save the narration in a separate file and link it to the presentation, rather than embedding the data in the presentation file. Be aware, however, that the narration file would need to be packaged with the presentation and travel with it in order to be accessible on other systems.

> **Note**
>
> In most presentation programs, you can play only one sound at a time on a slide, so recorded narration plays instead of sound file objects.

STEP-BY-STEP 15.10

1. Practice reading the following text until you are comfortable with it:

> **Annie's Dog Stop is a full-service doggie day care and boarding facility. You can leave your dog, confident that he or she will be well cared for and well loved. Only friendly, socialized dogs come to Annie's for day care so everyone has a great time. When you leave your pet overnight, Annie's is just like home. No cages, crates, or kennels. Just a bed or sofa, with lots of people and pets for company. Choose Annie's for safe, worry-free care for your beloved pet.**

2. Open **Step15-10** from the data files and save it as **Pets2**.

STEP-BY-STEP 15.10 Continued

3. Make Slide 2 current, and then select the command to record narration. For example, in PowerPoint, select **Slide Show** on the Menu bar, and then click **Record Narration**. The Record Narration dialog box displays. It should look similar to Figure 15-13.

FIGURE 15-13
Record Narration dialog box

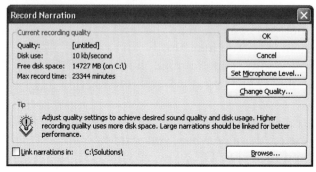

4. Click the command to set the microphone recording level. For example, in PowerPoint, click the **Set Microphone Level** button.

5. Read the sample phrase into the microphone. The green bars indicate that the microphone is picking up the sound correctly. If no green bars display, drag the slider to the right and read the phrase again.

6. When you are satisfied with the recording levels, click **OK** to close the dialog box, and then click **OK** again. A new Record dialog box may display, prompting you to select to begin recording with either the current slide or the first slide. Select the option to begin recording on the current slide.

7. After the title for Slide 2 displays read the following text:
Annie's Dog Stop is a full-service doggie day care and boarding facility. You can leave your dog, confident that he or she will be well cared for and well loved.

8. Click the screen to advance to Slide 3. After the title for Slide 3 displays, read the following text:
Only friendly, socialized dogs come to Annie's for day care so everyone has a great time.

9. Click the screen to advance to Slide 4. After the title for Slide 4 displays, read the following text:
When you leave your pet overnight, Annie's is just like home. No cages, crates, or kennels. Just a bed or sofa, with lots of people and pets for company.

10. Click the screen to advance to Slide 5. After the title for Slide 5 displays, read the following text:
Choose Annie's for safe, worry-free care for your beloved pet.

11. Click twice to end the presentation.

12. Click the **Save** button to save your slide timings. The slides display in Slide Sorter View.

STEP-BY-STEP 15.10 Continued

13. Make Slide 1 current, if necessary, and change to **Slide Show View** to preview the presentation. If you are not satisfied with the narration, use the **Undo** command to remove it, and then start again.

14. When you are satisfied, save changes and close **Pets2**. Close your presentation program.

SUMMARY

In this lesson, you learned:

■ To insert animated GIF files and movie clip files into a presentation.

■ Most programs include animation GIF files in a clip art collection, but you can also insert the files from other sources.

■ Most programs support AVI and MPG video files, but sometimes the specific codecs used to encode the file affect whether or not a video clip will play correctly in a presentation.

■ All video files and sound files larger than 100 KB are linked to a presentation, so they must be stored in a location where the presentation file can locate them when you deliver the presentation.

■ You can insert sound files in many different formats, including .wav, .midi, .mp3, and .wma.

■ You can record sound directly on a slide.

■ You can control the way objects move on a slide using animations.

■ An animation scheme quickly applies animations to the objects on a single slide, or all slides in a presentation.

■ You can create customized animations to apply different animation effects to elements on the same slide.

■ Custom animations can also control how and when sound plays on a slide.

■ You can record narration to accompany an entire presentation.

VOCABULARY*Review*

Define the following terms:

Animation scheme	Recording level	Trigger
Movie	Timings	Viewer
Package		

REVIEW *Questions*

TRUE/FALSE

Circle T if the statement is true or F if the statement is false.

T   F   1. In a presentation, a movie is either an animated GIF file or a video clip file.

T   F   2. Video files are usually stored as part of a presentation file.

T   F   3. If a sound file is larger than 100 KB it will be embedded in the presentation.

T   F   4. You cannot remove a sound recorded on a slide, so you must get it right the first time.

T   F   5. A small numbered tag displays in the upper-left corner of an animated object in Normal View.

T   F   6. You can only apply one animation effect to each object.

T   F   7. In PowerPoint, the name of the Effect Options dialog box changes depending on the current effect.

T   F   8. Select a higher sound quality to decrease the size of a presentation file.

T   F   9. There is no way to skip a video that is inserted in a presentation.

T   F   10. By default, the first frame of a video clip displays on the slide.

WRITTEN QUESTIONS

Write a brief answer to each of the following questions.

1. Name at least three things you should consider when selecting a sound file format for use in a presentation.

2. Why should you keep a sound icon displayed during a presentation if you have the sound set to play when clicked?

3. How can you prepare for recording narration?

4. Why should you store a video file in the same location as the presentation file?

5. Give at least two examples of how the method you use to deliver a presentation might affect the way you should use multimedia.

FILL IN THE BLANK

Complete the following sentences by writing the correct word or words in the blanks provided.

1. If the _____ of a video clip is not high enough, increasing the scale of the video object may cause the video to appear grainy or fuzzy.

2. Sounds in the _____ file format are usually used for transitions and animations.

3. If you not comfortable speaking during a presentation, you can record _____ for the entire slide show.

4. An animation _____ is a collection of animation settings and transitions that you can apply to a single slide or all slides.

5. To apply different animation effects to elements on the same slide, you can create _____ animations.

6. _____ effects are frequently used to animate graphics objects such as pictures, charts, and tables.

7. _____ are controls that allow you to coordinate the start of one effect with the start of another on the same slide.

8. A motion _____ animation causes an object to move on the slide from one location to another.

9. The recording _____ is a setting that controls the volume at which a narration is recorded.

10. _____ are the intervals that control the length of time a slide is displayed before the transition to the next slide.

PROJECTS

PROJECT 15-1

Before beginning this project, use Windows to copy the movie file **Project15-1d.avi** from the data files for this lesson to the location where you will store the solutions.

1. Launch your graphics program. Open the file **Project15-1a** from the data files for this lesson and save it as **Drive**.

2. Make Slide 1 current and select to insert a movie from a file. For example, in PowerPoint, click **Insert** on the Menu bar, click **Movies and Sounds**, and then click **Movie from File**.

3. Locate, select, and insert **Project15-1b.gif**, an animated GIF file, on the slide.

4. Scale the picture to approximately **1.0** inches high (the width should adjust automatically) and position it below the subtitle, centered horizontally on the slide.

5. Select to insert a sound from a file. For example, in PowerPoint, click **Insert** on the Menu bar, click **Movies and Sounds**, and then click **Sound from File**. Locate, select, and insert the **Project15-1c.wav** sound file. Set it to play automatically.

6. Display the Sound Options (or similarly named) dialog box. For example, in PowerPoint, right-click the sound icon and click **Edit Sound Object**. Select **Hide sound icon during slide show**. Click **OK**.

7. Preview Slide 1 in Slide Show View. In PowerPoint, right-click the screen and click **End Show** to exit Slide Show View.

8. Make Slide 4 current and select the media clip placeholder.

9. Select to insert a movie from a file, and then locate, select, and insert **Project15-1d.avi**, the movie file that you copied to your **Solutions** folder for this lesson.

10. Choose to play the movie when clicked.

11. Double-click the object on the slide to preview the video.

12. Select the command to edit the movie options. For example, in PowerPoint, right-click the object, and then click **Edit Movie Object**.

13. Set the movie to loop until stopped and rewind when done playing. Mute the volume.

14. Preview Slide 4 in Slide Show View. Click the movie clip to play it. When you are done, exit Slide Show View.

15. Make Slide 5 current. Practice reading the following sentence:
    At Safety First, we are committed to training safe, qualified, and exceptional drivers.

16. Select the command to record sound on the slide. For example, in PowerPoint, click **Insert** on the Menu bar, click **Movies and Sounds**, and then click **Record Sound**.

17. Click the **Record** button and read the following sentence into the microphone:
    At Safety First, we are committed to training safe, qualified, and exceptional drivers.

18. Click the **Play** button to preview the voice over. If you are satisfied, click **OK**. If not, click **Cancel** and record it again.

19. Drag the sound icon to the lower-right corner of the slide.

20. Make Slide 1 current and preview the entire slide show. Click the screen to advance from one slide to the next. On Slide 4 click the video object to play it. On Slide 5, click the sound icon to play the voice over. At the end of the slide show, exit Slide Show View.

21. Save the changes and close **Drive**. Leave your presentation program open to use in the next project.

PROJECT 15-2

1. Open **Project15-2** from the data files and save it as **Drive2**.

2. Make Slide 2 current and apply the **Spin** animation scheme or one similar to it.

3. Select Slides 3 and 4 and apply the **Zoom** animation scheme or one similar to it.

4. Make Slide 1 current and select the title text placeholder.

5. Add the **Diamond Entrance** effect or one similar to it. For example, in PowerPoint, click the **Add Effect** button, click **Entrance**, and then click **Diamond**.

6. Set the effect to start after the previous animation. Set the Direction to **Out**, and set the Speed to **Fast**.

7. Select the subtitle text placeholder and apply the **Diamond Entrance** effect or one similar to it. Set the effect to start after the previous effect. Set the Direction to **In** and set the Speed to **Fast**.

8. Make Slide 2 current and set each bulleted item to start after the previous animation.

9. Make Slide 3 current and set all bulleted items to display at the same time, with the previous animation. For example, in PowerPoint, click the bulleted text placeholder, click the **Start** drop-down arrow, and then click **With Previous**.

10. Select the picture and apply the **Grow/Shrink** emphasis effect (or one similar to it), set to start with the previous animation.

11. Make Slide 4 current. Move the video up in the effects list so it is after the title text, and set it to start after the previous animation.

12. Set the first bulleted item to start with the previous animation, and all other bulleted items to display at the same time as the previous animation.

13. Make Slide 5 current. Select the title text placeholder and add a **Fly In Entrance** effect (or one similar to it), set to start with the previous animation, fly in from the top, and at a very fast speed.

14. Select the subtitle text placeholder and add a **Fly In Entrance** effect, set to start with the previous animation, fly in from the bottom, and at a very fast speed.

15. Select the sound object and move the effect up so it is between the title effect and the subtitle effect. Display the Play Sound dialog box. For example, in PowerPoint, click the drop-down arrow next to the object in the Effects list, and then click **Effect Options**. On the Timing tab, set the sound to start with the previous animation. On the Sound Settings tab, set it to hide the icon during the slide show.

16. Make Slide 1 current and change to Slide Show View. Play through the entire presentation, clicking to advance the slides.

17. Save the changes and close **Drive2**. Leave your presentation program open to use in the next project.

PROJECT 15-3

1. Open **Project15-3** from the data files for this lesson and save it as **Drive3**.

2. Practice reading the following narration:
   Safety First is a first-class driver's training school. We offer comprehensive classroom and on-the-road instruction. Classroom training is geared to the appropriate age level. We guarantee success. Trust Safety First to teach your teen the rules of the road. At Safety First, we are committed to training safe, qualified, and exceptional drivers.

3. When you are comfortable reading the text, make Slide 2 current and select the command to record narration. For example, in PowerPoint, click **Slide Show** on the Menu bar and then click **Record Narration**.

4. Click the command to set the recording level. For example, in PowerPoint, click the **Set Microphone Level** button and read the sample phrase. Adjust the volume slider as necessary, and then click **OK**.

5. In PowerPoint, click **OK** to begin recording, and select to start the narration on the current slide. After the title on Slide 2 displays, read the following:
   Safety First is a first-class driver's training school. We offer comprehensive classroom and on-the-road instruction.

6. Click the screen to advance to the next slide. After the title on Slide 3 displays, read the following:
   Classroom training is geared to the appropriate age level. We guarantee success.

7. Click the screen to advance to the next slide. After the title on Slide 4 displays, read the following:
   Trust Safety First to teach your teen the rules of the road.

8. Click the screen to advance to the next slide. After the title on Slide 5 displays, read the following:
   At Safety First, we are committed to training safe, qualified, and exceptional drivers.

9. Click the screen twice to end the slide show, and then click **Save** to save your timings.

10. Make Slide 1 current and change to **Slide Show View**. Preview the entire presentation and then exit Slide Show View.

11. Save changes and close **Drive3**. Close your presentation program.

WEB PROJECT

Scientists frequently use slide presentations to educate and inform. One science topic that has been in the news lately is alternative energy sources. Select one type of alternative energy and research it on the Internet. Some possible topics include wind power, solar power, or hydrogen fuel cells, but there are many other possibilities as well. Look for background information such as why alternative energy is an issue right now, as well as current information about the specific type of energy and how it can be and is being used. Track down reasons both for and against the viability of the energy source, including statistics comparing it to traditional types of fuel, such as natural gas or oil. Keep track of your sources. When you have completed your research, design a presentation to inform your classmates about what you have learned.

Start by writing an outline and planning the content for each slide. Try to plan for graphics objects such as pictures, tables, or charts, as well as active content such as movies and sounds. For example, if you have the resources you can record video depicting how energy is used, or showing a classmate acting as an expert reading a statement for or against the energy source. When you are satisfied with your plan, ask a classmate to review it and make suggestions, and improve the plan by incorporating some of the ideas.

Create the presentation using a design template. Add transitions and animations to make the content come alive. Insert sound to complement the content. For example, record narration or voice overs. Check the spelling and correct errors. Ask a classmate to review the presentation and make suggestions, and then incorporate the suggestions to improve the presentation. When the presentation is complete, display it for your class.

 TEAMWORK PROJECT

Have you ever played an interactive computerized game in which a sound plays, or a picture changes when you click a certain spot on the screen? By adding sound to a presentation you can create such an effect that could be used to teach young children or to help anyone learning a new language. For example, you could create a presentation that includes pictures of animals, and record sound files that have the names of the animals. When a viewer clicks the sound icon next to the animal's picture, it plays the recording of the animal's name.

As a team, design a presentation that uses pictures and sound to teach vocabulary. Assign roles to each team member. For example, someone might be in charge of gathering the pictures, someone might be responsible for writing slide text, someone could be the quality control manager—responsible for making sure the spelling is correct and everything works properly— and someone might be the "talent" or person who records the sound files. Select a topic and decide how you will organize the slides. You should include instructions for using the presentation and at least ten vocabulary words. Locate pictures illustrating the vocabulary term, and then create the presentation. Design the presentation using colors and graphics that will appeal to your audience of students. You may want to use animations as well. Record the sound files and set options so they play when the sound icon is clicked. Review and test the presentation as a team, and decide how you can improve it, and then make the changes. Ask someone from a different team to test it and make suggestions as well. When it is complete, show it to your class. If your instructor agrees, invite some younger students to test it.

CRITICAL*Thinking*

A slide show can be a creative way to tell a story. You can combine pictures with text written on the slide, or added as narration. Write a short story. It can be fiction or non-fiction. It does not have to be very long but it should have all of the important parts of a story, such as characters, a beginning, a middle, an end, and a climax. When you finish writing the story, ask a classmate to read it and make suggestions, and then revise and improve it.

Use pictures to illustrate the story. You can draw the pictures and scan them into graphics files, locate appropriate clip art files, or create the pictures using a graphics program. Create a presentation and insert one picture on a slide. If you have a microphone, record narration of you reading the story. Practice reading it out loud before recording, and decide how much narration you want with each slide. If you do not have a microphone, key the text on the slides. Complete the presentation using transitions and animations.

Ask a classmate to review the presentation and make suggestions for improving it. Incorporate the suggestions into the presentation. Deliver the presentation to your class.

CREATING SUPPORT MATERIALS

When the time comes to deliver a presentation, you may not be able to use a computer and monitor. In that case, you can be prepared by having overhead transparencies of each slide that you can display using an overhead projector, or 35-mm slides so you can present the show using a standard slide projector. Although you may lose some of the animations and effects that you have used to enhance the content, you will still be able to display the presentation.

Whatever method you use to deliver the presentation, and no matter how exciting and engaging the slide show might be, your audience may forget it once the presentation ends. To reinforce the message of a presentation, you can create support materials that you can give to the viewers before, during, or after the presentation. Most presentation programs let you print a copy of each slide, which you can make available singly or in a packet. Or, you can create handouts to give to your audience. You can also key notes into your presentation to use as a script or just as reminders for when you deliver your presentation.

In this lesson you learn how to create support materials and how to generate overhead transparencies and 35-mm slides.

Use Notes Pages

The main reason for creating notes pages is to help you remember what to say while you deliver a presentation. You may create one notes page for each slide. Each page may include text as well as graphics. For example, you may key lists, paragraphs, or keywords, and you may insert supporting charts and tables, or even a photo or map. Even if your presentation is destined for the Web or a self-running show, you still may want to create notes. When you publish the presentation, you can choose to include the notes, which will then be available to help the viewer better understand the data presented on each slide.

Create Notes

In most presentation programs you can key notes directly into a notes pane in Normal view. Usually, the notes pane is quite small, but you can resize it by dragging the border that separates it from the Slide pane. Alternatively, your program may have a Notes Page View. In Notes Page View, a thumbnail of the slide displays in the top half of the page, and a placeholder where you can key text and insert objects displays in the bottom half of the page. You can scale and move both the slide thumbnail and the placeholder as necessary. For example, you can make the thumbnail smaller and increase the placeholder to include more notes on the page. You can scroll through the notes pages without returning to Normal View using the vertical scroll bar, the Next Slide or Previous Slide buttons in the vertical scroll bar, or the Page Up and Page Down keys.

Note

You can use standard text formatting commands to format notes text. To make all font formatting commands available, and to view the formatting on screen in Normal View, you may have to click the Show Formatting button on the Standard toolbar.

S TEP-BY-STEP 16.1

1. Launch your presentation program, and open **Step16-1** from the data files for this lesson.

2. Save the file as **Health**.

3. Click in the notes pane and key **Welcome audience**. It should look similar to Figure 16-1.

STEP-BY-STEP 16.1 Continued

FIGURE 16-1
Key notes directly into the notes pane

Text in
notes pane

4. Press **Enter** to start a new line in the notes pane, and then key **Introduce yourself and other staff members.**

5. Select the command to display Notes Page View. For example, in PowerPoint, click **View** on the Menu bar, and then click **Notes Page**. Click the **Zoom** drop-down arrow on the Standard toolbar and set the zoom to **75%** if necessary. Your screen should look similar to Figure 16-2.

> **Note**
>
> The amount of content that fits on your screen in Notes Page View depends on the size of your monitor. For example, if you are using a large monitor, you may be able to see the entire page on the screen.

FIGURE 16-2
Notes Page View

Slide
thumbnail

Note text

STEP-BY-STEP 16.1 Continued

6. Scroll to the next notes page. For example, press **Page Down**, or click the **Next Slide** button at the bottom of the vertical scroll bar.

7. Click the slide thumbnail to select it, and then press and hold **Shift**. Drag the handle in the lower-right corner of the thumbnail up and to the left to scale the picture. Release the mouse button when the picture is about 3.0 inches wide by 2.25 inches high. You can use the rulers to gauge the size of the object.

8. Click the text placeholder to select it and drag the top-middle handle up to increase the height of the placeholder to about 6.0 inches. With the placeholder still selected, click the Font Size drop-down arrow and then click **20**, and click the **Bullets** button on the Formatting toolbar. All text you key in the placeholder will display the new formatting.

9. Click the **Click to add text** prompt in the text placeholder and key the following bulleted items:
   ■ Planning and providing healthy meals is an important part of your job as a day care provider.
   ■ The children in your care depend on you to serve them nutritious food.
   ■ Although it might sometimes seem hard to plan good meals, once you learn a few simple guidelines, you'll find that it's not only just as easy as planning junky meals, it might even be cheaper!
   ■ I'm going to give you some ideas and suggestions that you will be able to use every day.
   ■ Please feel free to stop me and ask questions at any time.

10. Zoom out to **50%** magnification or a magnification that allows you to see the full page. Your screen should look similar to Figure 16-3.

FIGURE 16-3
Modified notes page

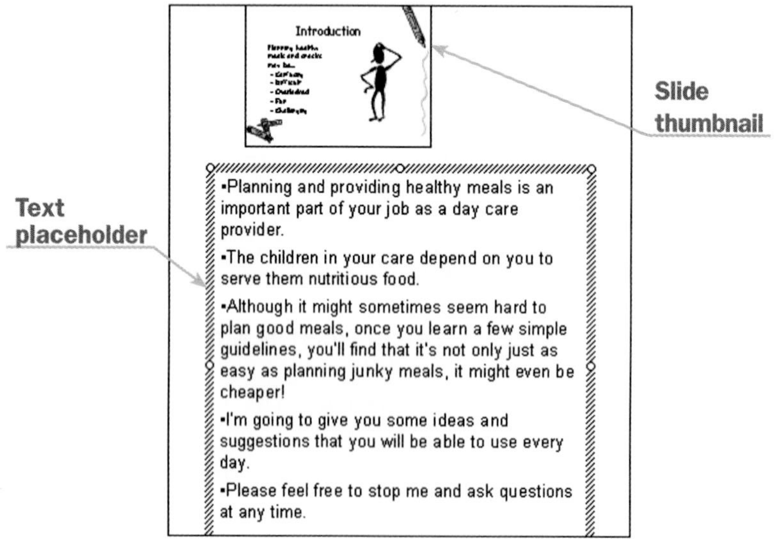

STEP-BY-STEP 16.1 Continued

11. Click the **Normal View** button to change to Normal View.

12. Save the changes to **Health** and leave it open to use in the next exercise.

Use the Notes Master

When you want changes to affect all notes pages in a presentation, edit and format the *notes master*. The notes master is a template that determines layout and formatting for all notes pages. Like the slide and title masters (refer to Lesson 13), the notes master displays placeholders for text and objects that appear on each page. You can change font formatting, scale, move, or delete the placeholders, or insert a graphic such as a company logo. You can use the Header and Footer dialog box to add a header or footer to the notes pages and you can even apply a color scheme that displays on notes pages, but does not affect the slides. (For more information on working with the Header and Footer dialog box, refer to Lesson 13.) Usually, to display the notes master, click Master on the View menu, and then click Notes Master. When you are finished making changes, click Close Master View.

Hot Tip

You can use your program's spelling checker to check the spelling in notes pages.

Important

Headers and footers you set up in Notes Master View also display on handouts. To create headers and footers for selected notes pages, select the desired slides in Normal or Slide Sorter view before displaying the notes master.

STEP-BY-STEP 16.2

1. Display the Notes Master for the **Health** presentation. For example, in PowerPoint, click **View** on the Menu bar, click **Master**, and then click **Notes Master**. The Notes Master slide should look similar to the one in Figure 16-4.

FIGURE 16-4
Notes Master view

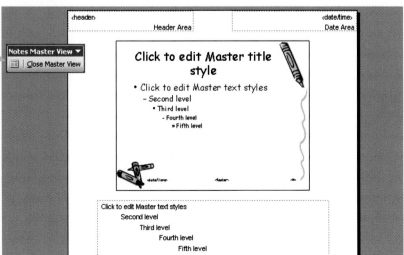

STEP-BY-STEP 16.2 Continued

2. Click to select the text placeholder and then change the font size to **16**. Click the **Bullets** button on the Formatting toolbar to apply bullet list formatting.

3. Display the Header and Footer dialog box. For example, in PowerPoint, click **View** on the Menu bar and then click **Header and Footer**. Make sure that the Notes and Handouts tab is active.

4. Select the option that lets you insert a fixed date and/or time and key today's date. For example, in PowerPoint, select the **Fixed** option button in the Date and Time area (if necessary), and then click in the Fixed text box and key today's date.

5. Select the option to display a header, and then key the header text **Prepared by** followed by your own name.

6. Select the options to display a page number and a footer. Key the footer text **Meal Planning for Family Day Care Providers**.

7. Apply the settings to all slides.

8. On the Notes Master slide, click to select the footer placeholder, and then drag the handle on the right side of the placeholder to the right about **0.5** inches to increase its width to **3.75** inches.

9. Close Notes Master View and display Slide 1 in Notes Pages View. Adjust the zoom to about **40%** or whatever size you need to see the entire page. It should look similar to Figure 16-5.

STEP-BY-STEP 16.2 Continued

FIGURE 16-5
Changes to the Notes Master affect the notes pages

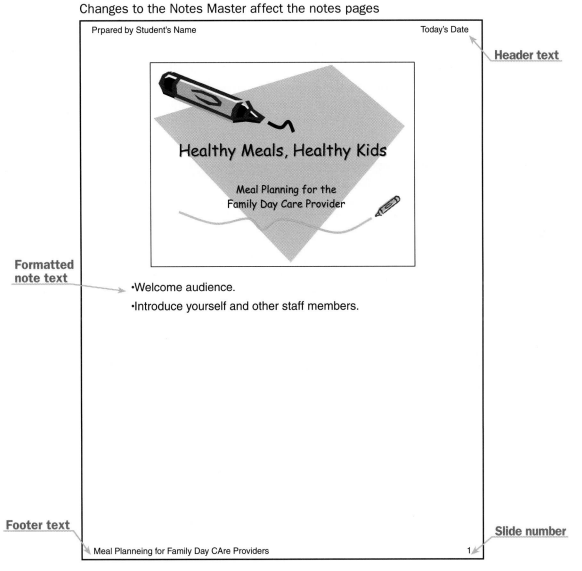

10. Save the changes and leave **Health** open to use in the next exercise.

Preview and Print Notes Pages

To refer to your notes easily during a presentation you will have to print the notes pages. By default, your program is probably set to print slides. You must select the option to print notes pages, as well as any other options you want, before you print. You can do this in the Print dialog box or in the Print Preview window. If you use the Print Preview window, you can preview the pages to make sure they are correct before you print them. In most programs, you can click the Print Preview button on the Standard toolbar to display the Print Preview window. Use the buttons and controls on the Print Preview toolbar to change the display and set options for printing. Table 16-1 illustrates and describes some common Print Preview tools.

TABLE 16-1
Common Print Preview tools

ICON	TOOL NAME	DESCRIPTION
	Next Page	Displays a preview of the next page or slide.
	Previous Page	Display a preview of the previous page or slide.
Print...	Print	Displays the Print dialog box.
Print What:	Print What	Displays a drop-down menu of elements and layouts that you can print, such as handouts, notes, or slides.
57%	Zoom	Lets you adjust the magnification of the preview on the screen.
A	Landscape	Changes the preview to Landscape orientation.
A	Portrait	Changes the preview to Portrait orientation.
Options ▾	Options	Displays a menu of options such as Header and Footer, which displays the Header and Footer dialog box, Color/Grayscale, which lets you select to print in color, black and white, or grayscale; Scale to Fit, which automatically adjusts the size of the data to fit the size of the page; and Frame Slides, which adds a border line frame around each page.

When you are ready to print the notes pages, click the Print button on the Print Preview toolbar or select Print from the File menu to display the Print dialog box. In the Print dialog box you can verify and change many of the options available in the Print Preview window. For example, you can verify that Notes Pages is selected in the Print What box, you can select whether to print in color, grayscale, or black and white, and you can choose to frame the pages with a border line. Other options let you select to print all notes pages, or only the notes for the current slide or a range of slides, and to specify how many copies of each page to print.

> **Note** ☑
>
> When you click the Print button on the Standard toolbar in Normal or Slide Sorter view, the Print dialog box does not display. Use this option to print only when you want to print using the current print settings.

S TEP-BY-STEP 16.3

1. Display the **Health** presentation file in Print Preview. For example, in PowerPoint, click the **Print Preview** button on the Standard toolbar, or click **File** on the Menu bar and then click **Print Preview**. Slide 1 displays in the Print Preview window.

2. Change the preview to display the notes pages. For example, in PowerPoint, click the **Print What** drop-down arrow and then click **Notes Pages**. If necessary, click the **Portrait** button on the Print Preview toolbar to change to Portrait orientation. The Print Preview window should look similar to Figure 16-6.

FIGURE 16-6
Notes page in Print Preview

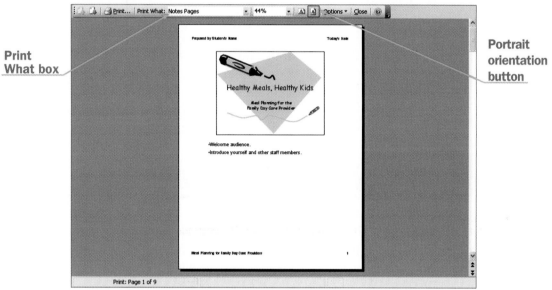

Print What box

Portrait orientation button

3. Click the **Next Page** button to display the notes page for Slide 2. Repeat this step to scroll through all notes pages in the presentation (there are nine—one for each slide).

STEP-BY-STEP 16.3 Continued

4. Click the **Print** button on the Print Preview toolbar. The Print dialog box displays, similar to that shown in Figure 16-7.

FIGURE 16-7
Print dialog box

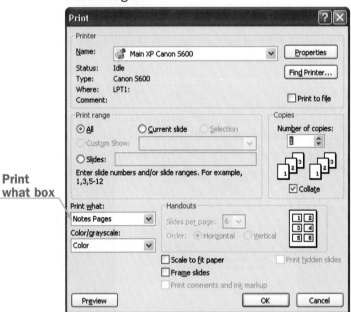

Print what box

5. Verify that the correct printer is selected, that the **All** button is selected in the *Print range* section, that **Notes Pages** displays in the *Print What* box, and that the *Number of copies* is set to **1**. Click the **Color/grayscale** drop-down arrow and click **Pure Black and White**. (You can save ink and print faster if you print in black and white.)

6. With your instructor's permission, click **OK** to print the notes pages. Alternatively, click **Cancel** to close the dialog box without printing.

7. Close Print Preview and change to Normal View.

8. Save the changes and leave **Health** open to use in the next exercise.

Prepare and Print Handouts

Whereas notes pages are designed for the person delivering the presentation, *handouts* are designed to be used by the audience. Handouts are printed pages that you can give to the audience before or after the presentation. They usually include a small thumbnail of each slide and space where viewers can handwrite their own notes. Usually, the default handout layout prints one slide on each handout page, but in most programs you can select to print 2, 3, 4, 6, or 9 slides per handout page. On the *3 slides per page* layout in Portrait orientation, blank lines display to the right of each slide thumbnail where the viewer can take notes. In Landscape orientation, the blank lines display below each thumbnail. You can also select to print only the presentation outline, without slide thumbnails. For the layouts that have 4, 6, or 9 slides per page, you can select either a *horizontal printing order* or a *vertical printing order*. In a horizontal printing order, which is the default, consecutive slides are printed across the page horizontally left to right, and then to the next line. In a vertical printing order, consecutive slides are printed from the top of the page to the bottom, and then to the top of the next column.

You select the handout layout—along with other options—in Print Preview, or in the Print dialog box. When you are ready to print, click the Print button on the Print Preview toolbar or select File on the Menu bar and click Print to display the Print dialog box. Select options, and then click OK.

> **Note**
>
> In most programs you must use the handout master to change the formatting of handout pages. You can select the layout to display, and then insert graphics, headers and footers, and apply a color scheme that will affect only the handout pages. You cannot, however, scale, move, or delete the slide placeholders. To display the handout master, click Master on the View menu, and then click Handout Master. When you are through making changes, click Close Master View.

STEP-BY-STEP 16.4

1. Change to Print Preview.

2. Display handouts with 1 slide per page. For example, in PowerPoint, click the **Print What** drop-down arrow and then click **Handouts (1 slide per page)**.

3. Change the display to handouts with 3 slides per page. The screen should look similar to Figure 16-8.

FIGURE 16-8
Handouts with 3 slides per page

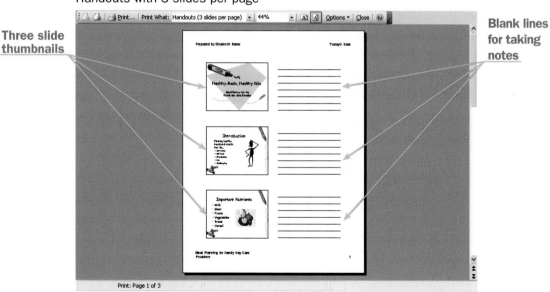

STEP-BY-STEP 16.4 Continued

4. Change the display to handouts with 9 slides per page. Change the orientation to Landscape, and then change to vertical printing order. For example, in PowerPoint, click the **Print What** drop-down arrow and then click **Handouts (9 slides per page)**. Click the **Landscape** button on the Print Preview toolbar. Click the **Options** drop-down arrow on the Print Preview toolbar, click **Printing Order**, and then click **Vertical**. The screen should look similar to Figure 16-9.

FIGURE 16-9
Handouts with 9 slides per page, in Landscape orientation, with a vertical printing order

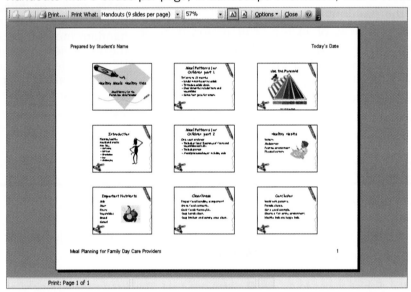

5. Click the **Print** button on the Print Preview toolbar to display the Print dialog box.

6. Verify that the correct printer is selected, that the **All** button is selected in the *Print range*, that **Handouts** displays in the *Print what* box, and that the *Number of copies* is set to **1**. Under *Handouts*, *Slides per page* should be set to **9**, and the **Vertical** option button should be selected. Click the **Color/grayscale** drop-down arrow and click **Pure Black and White**. (With your instructor's permission, you may print the handout in color.)

7. With your instructor's permission, click **OK** to print the handout. Alternatively, click **Cancel** to close the dialog box without printing.

8. Close Print Preview and change to Normal View.

9. Save the changes and leave **Health** open to use in the next exercise.

Export Support Materials

When you want more options for formatting and organizing your presentation as handouts, you can export the file to a different format so you can open it in a different program. Most presentation programs let you save a file in a variety of formats or even export it directly for use in a different program.

Save a Rich Text Format File

Use the *rich text format (.rtf)* to save all the text and most of the formatting in a file that you can open in a word processing program such as Microsoft Word or a desktop publishing program such as Microsoft Publisher. The text displays as an outline, with slide titles formatted as the highest heading level. You can then format and manipulate the presentation text to create more elaborate handouts, or to use the text in a report or other publication.

> **Extra for Experts**
>
> Although graphics objects are not saved in an .rtf file, you can open and save the file in a different program and then use the Copy and Paste commands to copy the graphics objects from the presentation file into the .rtf file. For example, open the .rtf file in Word, copy and paste the graphics, and then save the file in Word's .doc format.

S TEP-BY-STEP 16.5

1. Click **File** on the Menu bar and then click **Save As** to display the Save As dialog box.

2. In the *File name* text box, key **ExHealth** to replace the filename *Health*.

3. Click the **Save as type** drop-down arrow and then click the option for printing in .rtf format. It may be **Outline/RTF** or ***.rtf**. You may have to scroll to the bottom of the list to locate the format.

4. Click the **Save** button to save the file. The **Health** file remains open in your presentation program.

STEP-BY-STEP 16.5 Continued

5. Launch a word processing program such as Microsoft Word or Microsoft WordPad. Use the **File** > **Open** command to locate and open the **ExHealth.rtf** file. It should look similar to the one in Figure 16-10.

FIGURE 16-10
The ExHealth.rtf file open in Microsoft Word

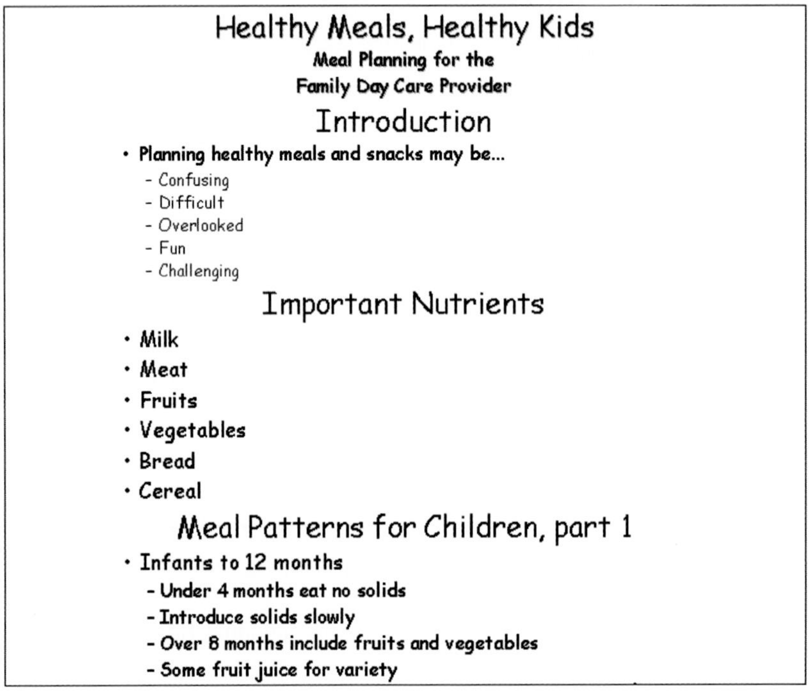

Healthy Meals, Healthy Kids
Meal Planning for the
Family Day Care Provider

Introduction
• Planning healthy meals and snacks may be...
  – Confusing
  – Difficult
  – Overlooked
  – Fun
  – Challenging

Important Nutrients
• Milk
• Meat
• Fruits
• Vegetables
• Bread
• Cereal

Meal Patterns for Children, part 1
• Infants to 12 months
  – Under 4 months eat no solids
  – Introduce solids slowly
  – Over 8 months include fruits and vegetables
  – Some fruit juice for variety

6. Close the **ExHealth.rtf** file and the word processing program. Leave **Health** open to use in the next exercise.

Export Support Materials

Some presentation programs have a command to export presentation notes, handouts, and outlines directly to a word processing file. For example, you can use PowerPoint's File > Send To > Microsoft Office Word command to export presentation data into a Microsoft Word file. Depending on the program and the available options, the exported file usually includes thumbnails of each slide and either blank lines where the audience can take notes, or the data from your own notes pages. You may also be able to export just the presentation outline. The advantage of creating handouts in this manner is that you can use the word processing program to apply more sophisticated formatting than what might be available in the presentation program. For example, in Word, the presentation data is formatted as a table, so you can add border lines, fills, and shading. If your program does not support this feature, skip to the next exercise.

Extra for Experts

You can also import an existing outline into a presentation to create slide text. The outline can be in a variety of file formats including HTML, text, Word, Lotus, or Excel. For example, in PowerPoint, click Insert on the Menu bar and then click Slides from Outline. Locate and select the file in which the outline is stored, and then click OK. Text formatted as a main heading (heading 1 in Word) becomes the slide titles, and subheadings become bulleted items.

STEP-BY-STEP 16.6

1. Select the command to export the presentation to a word processing program. For example, in PowerPoint, click **File** on the Menu bar, click **Send To**, and then click **Microsoft Office Word**. A dialog box of layout options displays, similar to the one in Figure 16-11.

FIGURE 16-11
Layout options for exporting to Microsoft Word

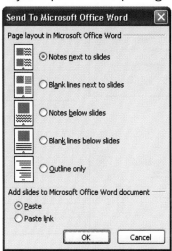

STEP-BY-STEP 16.6 Continued

2. Select the option to print blank lines next to the slide thumbnails. Verify that the **Paste** button is selected, and then click **OK**. Your program exports the presentation content to a new, unnamed file and displays it on-screen. (This may take a few moments.) It should look similar to Figure 16-12.

FIGURE 16-12
The exported file in Microsoft Word

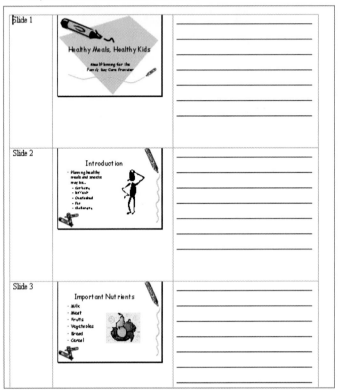

3. Save the file as **ExHealth2** and then close it. Close the word processing program. Leave **Health** open to use in the next exercise.

Extra for Experts

To link the presentation data to the Word file, click the Paste Link option button in the Send To Microsoft Office Word dialog box. If you change the data in the presentation file, the data in the Word file updates automatically.

Create Overheads and 35-mm Slides

If you plan to give your presentation before a live audience, you are not limited to displaying the slides on a television monitor, digital screen, or wall display. Most presentation programs let you generate overhead transparencies from your slides that you can display on a regular portable screen using an overhead projector. Or, you can have your presentation processed into slides and use a slide projector. It is useful to have at least one of these options available in case there is a problem with the computer equipment you plan to use to deliver the presentation, if there is no compatible computer available, or if something happens to damage the presentation file.

Both overhead transparencies and 35-mm slides are made by reproducing the slide image on *transparency film,* which is a thin film medium used to create a positive image that can be viewed or projected by transmitted light. Creating an appealing and effective presentation for delivery on 35-mm slides or overheads requires a different approach from creating a presentation for delivery on a monitor, and you should consider the presentation design including the color, layout, font formatting, and graphics. If you know you will be delivering your presentation using slides or overhead transparencies, you can incorporate these design elements into your presentation from the beginning. If you have created a presentation for delivery on a monitor, you should look carefully at the existing slides and make changes as necessary before creating the 35-mm slides or the transparencies. You may want to use the Save As command to save the file with a new name, so that you have one version for delivery on-screen, and one that you can modify for 35-mm slides or overheads.

Unlike a presentation viewed on a monitor or similar device, presentations that use overheads or 35-mm slides are projected onto a screen using a light, which will affect the way colors display and contrast. In addition, you should consider whether the shape, size, and style of fonts in the presentation make the text easy to read. Clear, sans serif fonts such as Arial and Tahoma, in a minimum 24-point size, generally display well when projected.

You may need to adjust the position of placeholders to ensure at least a half-inch margin all around the edge of the slide, so that frames or protectors do not overlap the slide content. You should also consider adding slide numbers to your presentation. They are invaluable, should you ever accidentally drop or mix up your overheads or 35-mm slides. (For information on adding slide numbers, refer to the *Modify the Slide Masters* section in Lesson 13.) Finally, you do not need to include transitions, animations, video, or sound in a presentation that will be used for creating overheads or 35-mm slides.

Create Overheads

Transparencies, which may also be called overheads, view-graphs, foils, and acetates, are placed on an overhead projector, which then displays the transparency's image on a screen or wall by projecting light. An added benefit to using overheads is that you may be able to write on them using an erasable marker.

To generate overhead transparencies with most presentation programs, you simply print the slides on transparency film, which can be purchased at most office supply stores, computer stores, or on the Internet. Make sure you select the correct transparency film for your printer. Using the wrong film can result in problems ranging from a smeared image to a jammed printer. To find out what film you should use, check the manufacturer's compatibility guide, making sure the product you select was designed to work with your printer or copier. You may also want to purchase transparency frames or protectors to protect your transparencies from scratches, dust, and so on.

Before printing the overheads, make any necessary changes to the design template or color scheme to display your slide content clearly on the transparencies. Typically, when you create overheads you should use a light background with dark text. Background patterns and designs may look grainy or interfere with the slide content. If necessary, print a test on the transparency film to see how it will look.

Hot Tip
Because transparency film tends to have a lot of static, you may find it helpful to load only one transparency into the printer's feed bed at a time, and print only the current slide by clicking the *Current slide* option in the *Print range* area of the Print dialog box.

You must then change the slide size so it is correct for overheads. Usually, you do this in the Page Setup dialog box. Click File on the Menu bar and then click Page Setup. Click the *Slides sized for* or similarly named drop-down arrow, and then click Overhead.

You may want to use Print Preview to check the slides before printing and to select additional options. When you are ready to print, load the transparency film in the printer, and click the Print button on the Print Preview tool box, or choose File > Print. Select options in the Print dialog box, and then click OK.

If you do not have transparency film, you can still work through the steps in the following exercise using plain paper.

Hot Tip

To maximize the size of the slide on the transparency, click the Options button on the Print Preview toolbar and click Scale to Fit Paper, or select the Scale to Fit Paper check box in the Print dialog box.

STEP-BY-STEP 16.7

1. Save the **Health** file with the name **HealthTR**.

2. Apply a basic template that has a white background, black text, and no graphics to all slides in the presentation. For example, in PowerPoint, apply the **Default Design** template.

3. Remove all transitions. For example, in PowerPoint, display the Slide Transition task pane or dialog box, and select **No Transition**. If necessary, remove the option to advance the slides automatically and then click **Apply to All Slides**.

4. Remove all animations. For example, in PowerPoint, display the Animation Schemes task pane or dialog box, select **No Animation**, and then click **Apply to All Slides**. If necessary, display the Custom Animation task pane or dialog box and remove any individual animations.

5. Display the Slide Master and then display the Header and Footer dialog box. Select to print slide numbers on all slides. For example, in PowerPoint, click **View** on the Menu bar, and then click **Header and Footer**. In the Header and Footer dialog box, click the **Slide number** check box, and then click **Apply to All**.

6. On the Slide Master, move the slide number placeholder up about 0.25 inches and to the left about 0.25 inches to be sure it is at least 0.5 inches away from the edges of the slide. Repeat this step on the Title Master, if necessary.

7. Close the Slide Master.

STEP-BY-STEP 16.7 Continued

8. Display the Page Setup dialog box. For example, in PowerPoint, click **File** on the Menu bar and then click **Page Setup**. The Page Setup dialog box should look similar to Figure 16-13.

FIGURE 16-13
The Page Setup dialog box

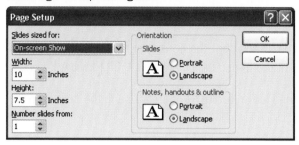

9. Select the option to size the slides for overheads. For example, in PowerPoint, click the **Slides sized for** drop-down arrow and then click **Overhead**. Click **OK** to apply the change.

10. Change to Print Preview. If necessary, select to display slides. For example, in PowerPoint, click the **Print What** drop-down arrow and then click **Slides**. Slide 1 should look similar to Figure 16-14.

FIGURE 16-14
Slide 1 prepared for overhead transparencies

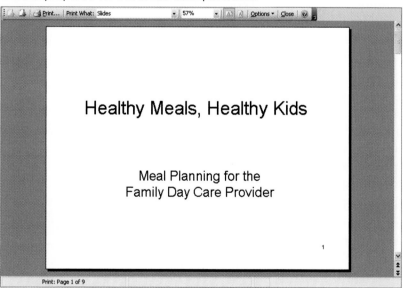

11. If necessary, select the option to print in Color and scale the content to fit the paper. For example, in PowerPoint, click the **Options** drop-down arrow, click **Color/Grayscale**, and then click **Color**. Click the **Options** drop-down arrow again, and then select **Scale to Fit Paper**.

STEP-BY-STEP 16.7 Continued

12. Scroll through the slides to make sure the content displays the way you want it on the overheads. If necessary, close Print Preview and make adjustments.

13. With your instructor's permission, load the transparency film in your printer, and then click the **Print** button on the Print Preview toolbar, or click **File** on the Menu bar and then click **Print** to display the Print dialog box.

14. In the Print dialog box, verify that the correct printer is selected, as well as all options you want to use. Click **OK** to print the transparencies. Close Print Preview, if necessary.

15. Save the changes and leave **HealthTR** open to use in the next exercise.

Create 35-mm Slides

To generate 35-mm slides, use your presentation program to create and save a file correctly formatted for 35-mm slides, and then send the file to a *service bureau* for processing. A service bureau is a company that takes the slide information and reproduces it on the 35-mm slides, for a fee. Although there are standard steps you can take to prepare your presentation file so that the 35-mm slides are created correctly, it is a good idea to check with the service bureau for specific instructions; each bureau may have different requirements regarding file size and graphics formats. For example, some may accept larger files than others, and some may recommend a certain file type for graphics.

> **Note** ☑
>
> If your presentation file exceeds the file size recommended by the service bureau, consider removing unneeded graphics, compressing them, or creating multiple files for processing.

As with overheads, you should take the time to modify your presentation design before creating the 35-mm slides. For example, you may want to change the color scheme to one that uses a dark background with light text, and check that the fonts are large and clear. As with overheads, background patterns and designs may not render well on a 35-mm slide. In addition, you may encounter problems if the slide background contains a semitransparent graphic, because not all printers handle transparency the same way.

To ensure that the 35-mm slides reproduce correctly, you must change the page setup for your presentation file to size the slides properly. By default, most presentation programs size slides for display on a monitor or screen. When you adjust the size for 35-mm slides, your program will change the *aspect ratio*—which is the ratio that compares the width of an image to the height of the image—to correctly format the slide content. If there is already content on the slides, you should check to be sure the formatting is acceptable. For example, you may have to adjust line breaks or margins. Most service bureaus recommend that you have a minimum 0.5-inch margin on all sides.

> **Note** ☑
>
> If you do not change the aspect ratio, you may end up with 35-mm slides that have black areas on the sides.

You should try to use common fonts that will be available at the service bureau for text, bullet markets, and other symbols. Usually, if the bureau does not have the font, it will substitute a similar font. To ensure that there are no font substitutions, you can embed Windows *TrueType fonts* in the presentation. A TrueType font reproduces the same when printed as when displayed on-screen. When you embed the fonts, they are stored in the file, creating a larger file size. To embed the fonts in the presentation file, display the Save As dialog box and select the command to display Save Options. Select the option to embed TrueType fonts. Then when you save the file, the embedded fonts will be saved also.

> **Note** ☑️
>
> You can also supply a font in a separate file so the service bureau can use it when generating the 35-mm slides. This is useful if you are using a proprietary font that you have purchased.

Finally, be aware that certain elements do not always reproduce the way you expect when transferred to a 35-mm slide, depending on the equipment used by the service bureau. For example, rotated text may display in a different color, or with a colored background, and grouped images, such as imported charts and tables, may have to be ungrouped before they can be reproduced. To ungroup an image, right-click it, click Grouping, and then click Ungroup. Always ask the service bureau exactly what you need to do to be sure the slides will display the way you want them.

Even if you do not plan to send the file to a service bureau to create 35-mm slides, you can work through the steps to prepare the presentation file.

STEP-BY-STEP 16.8

1. Click **File** on the Menu bar and then click **Save As** to display the Save As dialog box.

2. Display the Save Options. For example, in PowerPoint click the **Tools** arrow and click **Save Options**. The Save Options dialog box displays, as shown in Figure 16-15.

FIGURE 16-15
Save Options dialog box

STEP-BY-STEP 16.8 Continued

3. Select the option to embed the TrueType fonts. For example, in PowerPoint, select the **Embed TrueType fonts** check box, and select the **Embed all characters (best for editing by others)** option button. Click the **OK** button to close the dialog box.

4. Change the filename to **Health35**, and then click the **Save** button to save the file with the new name, and with the embedded fonts.

5. Change the color scheme for all slides to a green background with yellow title text.

6. Display the Page Setup dialog box and select the option to size the slides for 35-mm slides. For example, in PowerPoint, click the **Slides sized for** drop-down arrow and then click **35mm Slides**. Click **OK** to apply the change.

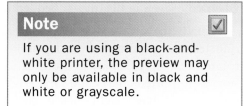

Note

If you are using a black-and-white printer, the preview may only be available in black and white or grayscale.

7. Change to Print Preview. Slide 1 should look similar to Figure 16-16. (If necessary, select to display slides, in color, and scaled to fit the paper.)

FIGURE 16-16
Slide 1 prepared for 35-mm slides

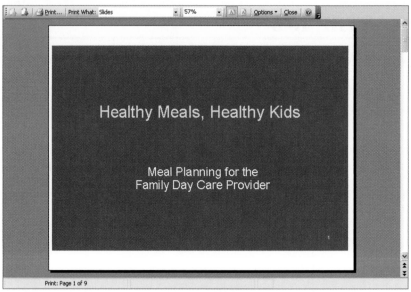

8. Scroll through the slides to make sure the content displays the way you want it on the 35-mm slides. If necessary, close Print Preview and make adjustments.

9. When you are satisfied with the presentation, save the changes and close **Health35**. It is now ready to submit to a service bureau for processing. Close your presentation program.

SUMMARY

In this lesson, you learned:

- Notes can help you remember what to say while you deliver a presentation.

- You can key one notes page for each slide in either the notes pane or in Notes Page View.

- You can use the Notes Master slide to make formatting and layout changes.

- Headers and footers that you add to the Notes Master also print on handouts.

- You can use Print Preview to preview slides, notes pages, and handouts before printing.

- You can also select options in the Print Preview window to control the way the pages print. For example, you can change the orientation, the printing order, and the color.

- You can select most of the same options in the Print dialog box that you can select in Print Preview.

- Print handouts to give to the audience before or after a presentation.

- Handouts include a thumbnail of each slide and space where viewers can handwrite their own notes.

- You can select from different handout layouts, including 1, 2, 3, 4, 6, or 9 slides per handout page, or an outline. The three slides per page layout includes blank lines where viewers can take notes.

- If you want to be able to edit or format the handouts in a different program, you can export the presentation file.

- You can save the file as a different file type, such as Rich Text Format (.rtf), so that you can open it in a word processing or desktop publishing program. RTF saves text and most formatting, but does not save graphics objects.

- Some presentation programs have commands that you can use to send the presentation directly to another program. For example, PowerPoint lets you send a presentation to a Word file.

- You can generate overhead transparencies or 35-mm slides from your presentation file so that you can deliver the presentation even if you do not have access to a compatible computer and monitor.

- There are unique design issues you should consider when you create a presentation for delivery on overheads or 35-mm slides, including the way colors and fonts project, and whether content will be covered by a frame or protector.

- To create overheads, print the slides on transparency film.

- To create 35-mm slides, you prepare the presentation file and then send it to a service bureau, which generates the slides for a fee.

VOCABULARY *Review*

Define the following terms:		
Aspect ratio	Notes master	Transparency film
Handouts	Rich Text Format (.rtf)	TrueType fonts
Horizontal printing order	Service bureau	Vertical printing order

REVIEW *Questions*

TRUE/FALSE

Circle T if the statement is true or F if the statement is false.

T F 1. The main purpose of notes pages is to give the audience a place to take notes during a presentation.

T F 2. The headers and footers you set up for notes pages also print on handouts.

T F 3. You must use Print Preview to select options for printing notes pages and handouts.

T F 4. Only the three slides per page handout layout includes blank lines where the viewer can take notes.

T F 5. Rich Text Format saves all text, formatting, and graphics so you can work with the file in a different program.

T F 6. Presentations that use overheads or 35-mm slides are projected onto a screen using a light.

T F 7. You may be able to write on overhead transparencies using an erasable marker.

T F 8. You must special order transparency film from a service bureau.

T F 9. When you design a presentation for overheads you should use a light background with dark text.

T F 10. When you design a presentation for 35-mm slides, you should use a dark background with light text.

WRITTEN QUESTIONS

Write a brief answer to each of the following questions.

1. Why is it a good idea to have either 35-mm slides or overheads available for delivering a presentation? Give at least two examples.

2. Name two problems that might occur if you use the wrong transparency film, and at least one way you can avoid the problems.

3. What is a good reason for printing notes or handouts in black and white?

4. What is the difference between printing the three slides per page handout layout in Landscape orientation and in Portrait orientation?

5. Why are there different design considerations for a presentation delivered on overheads or 35-mm slides? Name at least two things that might need to be changed.

FILL IN THE BLANK

Complete the following sentences by writing the correct word or words in the blanks provided.

1. When you want changes to affect all notes pages in a presentation, edit and format the Notes _____.

2. _____ are printed pages that you can give to the audience before or after the presentation.

3. In a(n) _____ printing order, consecutive slides are printed across the page horizontally left to right, and then to the next line.

4. In a(n) _____ printing order, consecutive slides are printed from the top of the page to the bottom, and then to the top of the next column.

5. _____ film is a thin film medium used to create a positive image that can be viewed or projected by transmitted light.

6. A(n) _____ bureau is a company that takes the slide information and reproduces it on the 35-mm slides for a fee.

7. When you adjust the size for 35-mm slides, your program will change the _____ ratio to correctly format the slide content.

8. A(n) _____ font reproduces the same when printed as when displayed on-screen.

9. In _____ Page view, a thumbnail of the slide displays in the top half of the page, and a placeholder where you can key text and insert objects displays in the bottom half of the page.

10. To automatically adjust the size of a slide for printing, select the _____ to Fit Paper option.

PROJECTS

PROJECT 16-1

1. Launch your presentation program, and open **Project16-1** from the data files.

2. Save the presentation as **Next1**.

3. In the notes pane for Slide 1, key the following two lines:
   Welcome audience.
   Introduce self and other staff members.

4. Change to Notes Page View.

5. Display the page for Slide 2. Click in the text placeholder and key the following lines:
   Explain that change is good.
   Students have worked hard for many years and are prepared for the next step.
   Explain that everyone is different, and that there is no "one size fits all" future.
   The choices are exciting.
   After all, you can always change your mind.

6. Display the Notes Master.

7. Select the text placeholder and change the formatting as follows:
   A. Increase the font size to **18** points.
   B. Apply bullet list formatting.

8. Add the following headers/footers to the notes and handout pages:
   A. Add a fixed date that displays today's date.
   B. Add header text that displays your name.
   C. Add footer text that displays the text **What's Next?**

9. Close the Notes Master.

10. Change to Print Preview and select to print the notes pages in Portrait orientation in black and white.

11. Preview all pages and then print them. Close Print Preview.

12. Save and close the **Next1** presentation, but leave your presentation program open to use in Project 16-2.

PROJECT 16-2

1. Open **Project16-2** from the data files and save the file as **Next2**.

2. Display the Handout Master.

3. Apply a color scheme with a light yellow background. For example, in PowerPoint, do the following:
   A. Display the Color Schemes task pane or dialog box.
   B. Click the scheme with a light yellow background.

4. Display the Header and Footer dialog box and make the following changes:
   A. Remove the page numbers.
   B. Edit the footer text to display **What's Next? Presentation Handouts**.
   C. If necessary, change the date to today's date.

5. Close the Handout Master and then change to Print Preview.

6. Select to print **Handouts (1 slide per page)**.

7. Set options to print in color.

8. Change the preview to print three slides per page in landscape orientation.

9. Print the handouts and then close Print Preview.

10. Save the changes and close the Next2 file. Leave your presentation program open to use in the next project.

PROJECT 16-3

1. Open **Project16-3** from the data files and save the file as **Next3**.

2. Apply the **Default Design** template to all slides in the presentation.

3. Remove all transitions from all slides. For example, in PowerPoint, do the following:
   A. Display the Slide Transition dialog box or task pane.
   B. Select **No Transition**.
   C. If necessary, remove the option to advance the slide automatically.
   D. Click **Apply to All Slides**.

4. Remove all animations from all slides. For example, in PowerPoint do the following:
   A. Display the Animation Schemes dialog box or task pane.
   B. Select **No Animation**.
   C. Click **Apply to All Slides**.
   D. If necessary, display the Custom Animation dialog box or task pane and remove individual animations.

5. Display the Page Setup dialog box and size the slides for an overhead presentation.

6. Display the Slide Master and then display the Header and Footer dialog box. Select to display slide numbers on all slides.

7. On the Slide Master, move the Page Number placeholder up and to the left to be sure it is at least 0.5 inches away from the edges of the slide. Repeat the step on the Title Master, if necessary, and then close Master View.

8. Change to Print Preview and select to print slides, in color, scaled to fit the paper.

9. Check all slides in Print Preview to make sure they are suitable for printing overheads.

10. If available, load transparency film in your printer. If not, use regular paper.

11. With your instructor's permission, print the slides. When the printing is complete, close Print Preview.

12. Save the changes to **Next3** and close it. Leave your presentation program open to use in the next project.

PROJECT 16-4

1. Open **Project 16-4** from the data files.

2. Display the Save As dialog box and select to embed TrueType fonts. For example, in PowerPoint do the following:
   A. Click **File** on the Menu bar and then click **Save As**.
   B. Click the **Tools** drop-down arrow and then click **Save Options**.
   C. Select the **Embed TrueType Fonts** check box and select the option to embed all characters.
   D. Click **OK**.

3. Save the file as **Next4**.

4. Apply the **Studio** design template or one that is similar to all slides in the presentation. Change the color scheme to one with a dark blue background.

5. Remove all transitions from all slides. For example, in PowerPoint do the following:
   A. Display the Slide Transition dialog box or task pane.
   B. Select **No Transition**.
   C. If necessary, remove the option to advance the slide automatically.
   D. Click **Apply to All Slides**.

6. Remove all animations from all slides.
   A. Display the Animation Schemes dialog box or task pane.
   B. Select **No Animation**.
   C. Click **Apply to All Slides**.
   D. If necessary, display the Custom Animation dialog box or task pane and remove individual animations.

7. Display the Page Setup dialog box and size the slides for 35-mm slides.

8. Display the Slide Master and then display the Header and Footer dialog box. Select to display slide numbers on all slides.

9. On the Slide Master, move the Page Number placeholder up to be sure it is at least 0.5 inches away from the bottom of the slide. Repeat the step on the Title Master, if necessary. Close Master View.

10. Change to Print Preview and select to print slides, in color, scaled to fit the paper.

11. Check all slides in print preview to make sure they are suitable for printing 35-mm slides, and then close Print Preview.

12. Save the changes to **Next4** and close it. Close your presentation program.

 WEB PROJECT

To generate 35-mm slides from a presentation file, you must send the file to a service bureau. Each bureau is a little bit different. For example, they have different requirements for submitting a file, they have different delivery procedures, and they charge different fees. In this project, use the Internet to research at least three different service bureaus. Find information that you can use to compare the companies and record the information in a spreadsheet or table.

Some of the information you should gather includes the following:

- Locate information about the file format required for submission.

- Find out if there are restrictions on the format of objects that might be part of the file, such as graphics and clip art.

- Ask about fonts and font substitutions.

- Find out if the bureau's equipment can successfully reproduce all colors, formatting, and objects.

- Find out if there is a maximum file size that the bureau can accept.

- Find out the type of submission method—online or by mail.

- Research the costs. Most companies charge per slide, but there may be a minimum cost, or additional costs for graphics, and other features, or for a rush delivery.

- Find out how long the process takes and how the slides will be returned to you.

When you have finished gathering, organizing, and analyzing the data, make an informed decision about which one you would recommend. Create a presentation or write a report of at least 200 words explaining your choice, using your data to back up and support your decision. Ask a classmate to review your work and make suggestions, and then use the suggestions to make improvements. Finally present your finished project to the class.

TEAMWORK PROJECT

No Child Left Behind is a federal program designed to improve schools throughout the United States. As a team, plan and create a presentation that describes how your school and school district has been affected by this program. Assign different tasks to each team member. For example, one person can be the project manager who assigns and delegates responsibilities. One person can be the designer, who designs the presentation and decides how it will be delivered. Someone can write the outline and plan the content for the presentation slides, and others can be reporters who research the topic within the school and the community. Good sources of information are school administrators, teachers, curriculum planners, school committee members, parents, and students. Ask what schools are doing, and how they might have changed since No Child Left Behind was enacted. Ask for statistics that indicate whether there have been improvements since changes took place so you can create tables or charts. Take pictures or videos or record interviews so you can include them in the presentation. (Remember to obtain permission to use someone's likeness or voice.)

When you have compiled all the information you need, meet as a team to review it and decide what to use and what to save for another project. Create the presentation using a design template, transitions, and animations. Add notes that you can use while delivering the presentation. Review it as a team, and decide how you can improve it, and then make the changes. Ask someone from a different team to review it and make suggestions as well. When it is complete, print the notes pages and handouts, and then deliver the presentation to your class. If your instructor agrees, invite some of the people you interviewed to come to the presentation.

CRITICAL*Thinking*

A well-organized and designed presentation can provide a convincing argument for almost anything. In this project, plan a presentation that you will deliver using overhead transparencies to convince the school board to provide or increase funding for a school activity. The activity might be a field trip, class project, club, organization, or team event. Start by creating a budget that illustrates how much the activity will cost, how much funding already exists, and how much more it will require. Next, write down why the activity is important. For example, explain who will benefit and in what ways. Gather pictures or videos that illustrate the activity, or the people who will benefit.

When you have completed your research and planning, organize the presentation. Select a design template suitable for overheads and decide how many slides you will need. Write the presentation outline. Design and create graphics such as tables and charts to illustrate your budget. As you work, key notes for the notes pages to help you remember the main points you want to emphasize when you deliver the presentation. Practice delivering the presentation using Slide Show View, and ask a classmate to review it. Use the classmate's suggestions to improve the presentation. When it is complete, print the notes pages and print handouts. If possible, print the overheads. Deliver the presentation to your class.

PREPARE AND DELIVER A PRESENTATION

OBJECTIVES

Upon completion of this lesson, you should be able to:

- Customize a presentation by hiding slides and creating custom shows.
- Insert hyperlinks in a presentation.
- Add action buttons to a presentation.
- Prepare a presentation by setting slide timings and selecting slide show options.
- Package a presentation.
- Deliver a live presentation.
- Deliver a self-running presentation.
- Publish a presentation to the Web.
- Broadcast a presentation.

Estimated Time: 1.5 hours

VOCABULARY

Action button

Broadcast

Custom show

Hyperlink base

Live presentation

Lobby page

Path

Presenter view

Primary monitor

Publish

Secondary monitor

Self-running presentation

Single file Web page

Slide show file

Web page title

The goal of creating an effective presentation is to deliver it to an audience. You have different options for delivering a presentation, including presenting it to a live audience, presenting it as a self-running show, publishing it to the Internet or a company intranet, and broadcasting it on a network. You can take steps to prepare a presentation for a particular audience and for a particular delivery method. For example, you can choose to include only certain slides so you can deliver it to a specific group of people who may not need to see the entire slide show. You can create action buttons so that someone viewing a self-running show can restart the presentation at any time. You can create hyperlinks to different programs and to supplemental material such as a company Web site. In other words, you can customize a presentation so that the audience has the best opportunity to understand the content and the message you want to convey.

In this lesson, you learn how to prepare a presentation for delivery. You learn to customize a presentation, insert hyperlinks, and create action buttons. You learn to deliver a presentation in front of a live audience, and how to take notes during a presentation. You also learn how to set up a self-running presentation, how to package a presentation so you can take it on the road, and how to deliver a presentation on the Internet.

Customize a Presentation

Most presentation programs let you tailor a presentation for a specific audience. For example, imagine you have created a presentation that explains every aspect of a company's benefits policy. A newly hired part-time employee does not need to see the same information that a newly hired, salaried manager needs to see. Instead of creating multiple presentations, you can customize one presentation for each different audience. One method of customizing a presentation is to simply hide the slides you don't want an audience to see. Another method is to create a custom show that uses only a subset of the slides within the complete presentation.

Hide Slides

To hide slides in a presentation, select the slide or slides you want to hide. Then click a command such as Hide Slide on the Slide Show menu. A hidden slide is not deleted. It displays in Normal View and in Slide Sorter View so you can edit it. It just does not play in Slide Show View. Hidden slides usually display a hidden slide icon in Normal and Slide Sorter Views. To unhide the slides, select the same command again.

> **Note**
>
> When you deliver a presentation to a live audience, you can select to display hidden slides if you want. See the section *Deliver a Live Presentation* later in this lesson for more information.

S TEP-BY-STEP 17.1

1. Open **Step 17-1** from the data files, and save the file as **Daycare**.

2. Select Slides 3 through 7.

3. Select the command to hide the slides. For example, in PowerPoint, click **Slide Show** on the Menu bar and then click **Hide Slide**. The slides are still visible in Normal View, but a hidden slide icon displays next to each hidden slide in the tabbed pane, as shown in Figure 17-1.

STEP-BY-STEP 17.1 Continued

FIGURE 17-1
Hidden slides display in Normal View

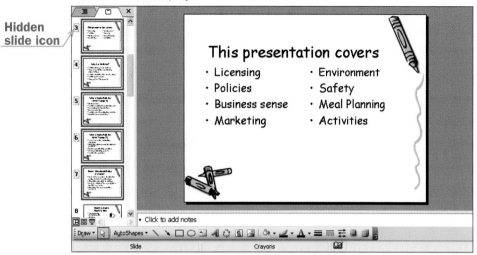

Hidden slide icon

This presentation covers
- Licensing
- Policies
- Business sense
- Marketing
- Environment
- Safety
- Meal Planning
- Activities

4. Make Slide 1 current and change to Slide Show View. Click the screen to advance through the slides. Notice that the five hidden slides do not display.

5. At the end of the slide show, return to Normal View. Select Slides 3 through 7 and select the command to unhide the slides. For example, in PowerPoint, click **Slide Show** on the Menu bar and then click **Hide Slide**. The hidden slide icon no longer displays.

6. Make Slide 1 current and change to Slide Show View. Click the screen to advance through the slides. This time, all slides display.

7. Save the changes and leave **Daycare** open to use in the next exercise.

Create a Custom Show

Another way to tailor a presentation to a specific audience is to create a *custom show*. A custom show is a presentation created from selected slides within a presentation. The custom show has its own name, but the slides remain stored in the original presentation. When you deliver the presentation, you can select to display either the entire presentation or the custom show. You may even have more than one custom show within a presentation.

To create a custom show, click a command such as Custom Shows on the Slide Show menu to display a dialog box in which you key a name for the show and select the slides to include. In most programs, you can also preview the show from the Custom Shows dialog box.

S TEP-BY-STEP 17.2

1. Select the command to create a custom show. For example, in PowerPoint, click **Slide Show** on the Menu bar and then click **Custom Shows**. The Custom Shows dialog box displays.

2. Select the command to define the custom show, which means to name it and select the slides to include. In PowerPoint you would click **New** to display the Define Custom Show dialog box, shown in Figure 17-2.

FIGURE 17-2
Define Custom Show dialog box

3. Name the custom show **Policies**. For example, key the name **Policies** in the *Slide show name* text box.

4. Add Slide 4 to the custom show. For example, click **Slide 4** in the *Slides in presentation* list, and then click the **Add** button. The slide becomes the first slide in the custom show.

5. Add Slide 5 to the custom show. For example, click **Slide 5** in the *Slides in presentation* list, and then click the **Add** button. Repeat the step to add Slides, 6, 7, and 8 to the custom show. The dialog box should look similar to Figure 17-3.

Hot Tip

You can select multiple slides to add to—but not remove from—the custom show at one time. To select multiple non-consecutive slides, press and hold Ctrl and then click each slide to select. To select consecutive slides, click the first slide, press and hold Shift, and click the last slide.

FIGURE 17-3
Slides added to the custom show

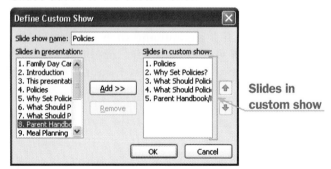

Slides in custom show

6. Click **OK** to close the dialog box. The **Policies** custom show is now listed in the Custom Shows dialog box.

STEP-BY-STEP 17.2 Continued

7. Create another new custom show and name it **Meals**.

8. Add slides 9, 10, 11, 12, 13, 14, 15, and 16 to the **Meals** custom show, and then click **OK**.

9. Preview the *Policies* custom show. For example, in PowerPoint select the **Policies** custom show in the Custom Shows dialog box and then click **Show**. The **Policies** custom show displays in Slide Show View. Click the screen to advance through the slides. At the end of the show, the **Daycare** presentation displays in Normal View.

> **Note**
>
> You can edit a custom show to add or remove slides. In PowerPoint, select the show in the Custom Shows dialog box and then click Edit. Add slides as desired. To remove a slide, click the slide in the *Slides in custom show* list, and then click Remove. To delete an entire custom show, click it in the Custom Shows dialog box, and then click Remove.

10. Preview the *Meals* custom show. For example, display the Custom Shows dialog box, select the **Meals** custom show and then click **Show**. Click the screen to advance through the slides in the **Meals** custom show.

11. Save the changes and leave **Daycare** open to use in the next exercise.

Use Hyperlinks

A hyperlink is text or an object that you click to display a destination location. The destination may be a different slide in the same presentation, a custom show, a different presentation file, a file in a different format such as a Microsoft Office Word document, a Microsoft Office Excel workbook, a Macromedia Flash 8 animation, an e-mail address, or a page on the Internet or on an intranet. Hyperlinks can be useful in a self-running presentation to direct a viewer to a company's Web site, or to enable a viewer to send an e-mail message to someone at the company. They can be useful in a live presentation so that you can jump to a specific slide whenever a particular issue or question is raised, to start a custom show, or to launch a program to display supporting data.

Create Hyperlinks

The steps for creating a hyperlink on a slide are similar no matter what the destination location. You select the text or object you want to use as the hyperlink, click the Insert Hyperlink button or command to display the Insert Hyperlink dialog box, locate and select the destination location, and then click OK to create the hyperlink.

Create a Hyperlink to a Slide in the Current Presentation or to a Custom Show

Select the text or object you want to use as the hyperlink, display the Insert Hyperlink dialog box, select the option to display slides in the current presentation, select the destination, and then click OK. For example, in PowerPoint, click the Insert Hyperlink button on the Standard toolbar and then click *Place in This Document* on the Link to bar to display a list of slide titles and custom shows in the current presentation. Click the destination slide or custom show. If you select a custom show, select the *Show and return* check box if you want your program to automatically return to the slide with the hyperlink after displaying the slides in the custom show. Click OK to create the hyperlink.

Create a Hyperlink to a Slide in Another Presentation

Select the text or object you want to use as the hyperlink, and then display the Insert Hyperlink dialog box. Select the option to display existing files, select the file, and then click OK. For example, in PowerPoint, click the Insert Hyperlink button on the Standard toolbar and then click *Existing File or Web Page* on the Link to bar. Browse to the location where the destination presentation file is stored and click the filename to select it. To link to a particular slide in the destination presentation, click Bookmark to open the Select Place in Document dialog box, click the destination slide, and then click OK. Click OK again to create the hyperlink.

Create a Hyperlink to an E-mail Address

To create a hyperlink that displays an e-mail message window pre-addressed to a particular e-mail address, simply key that address on a slide; your program should automatically create the hyperlink. Alternatively, select any text or object and then display the Insert Hyperlink dialog box, select the option to link to an e-mail address, specify the destination address, and then click OK. For example, in PowerPoint, click the Insert Hyperlink button on the Standard toolbar and then click *E-mail Address* on the Link to bar. Key the destination e-mail address in the *E-mail address* text box, or click an address in the *Recently used e-mail addresses* list. Key the text you want to display as the message subject in the *Subject* box, and then click OK.

Create a Hyperlink to a Web Page

Key the Web address on a slide; your program should automatically create the hyperlink. Alternatively, select the text or object you want to use as the hyperlink, display the Insert Hyperlink dialog box, specify the destination, and then click OK. For example, in PowerPoint, click the Insert Hyperlink button on the Standard toolbar and click *Existing File or Web Page* on the Link to bar. Key the address of the Web page in the *Address* text box, and then click OK.

Hot Tip

If you do not know the address of the destination Web page, click the Browsed Pages button in the Insert Hyperlink dialog box, and then click the page name. Or, click the Browse the Web button to launch your Web browser, and then browse to the destination Web page.

Create a Hyperlink to a Data File

Select the text or object you want to use as the hyperlink, display the Insert Hyperlink dialog box, locate and select the destination, and then click OK. For example, in PowerPoint, click the Insert Hyperlink button on the Standard toolbar and click *Existing File or Web Page* on the Link to bar. Browse to the folder where the data file is stored, and then click to select it. Click OK to create the hyperlink.

Hot Tip

To display a list of recently used files in the Insert Hyperlink dialog box, click the Recent Files button.

STEP-BY-STEP 17.3

1. Make Slide 3 of the **Daycare** presentation current and select the text *Policies*.

2. Select the command to display the Insert Hyperlink dialog box. For example, in PowerPoint, click the **Insert Hyperlink** button on the Standard toolbar. The dialog box should look similar to Figure 17-4.

FIGURE 17-4
Insert Hyperlink dialog box

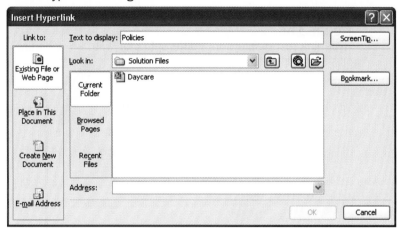

3. Select the command to display places in the current document. For example, in PowerPoint, click **Place in This Document** in the Link to bar.

4. Scroll down in the *Select a place in this document* list to locate the custom shows. Select the **Policies** custom show. Select the **Show and return** check box. The dialog box should look similar to Figure 17-5.

FIGURE 17-5
Select to link to a custom show

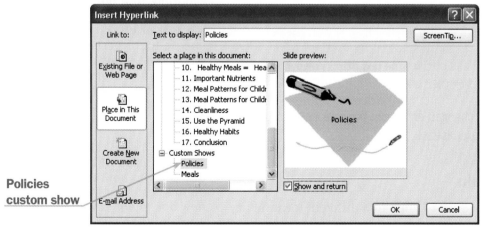

Policies
custom show

5. Click **OK** to create the hyperlink.

6. Select the text *Meal Planning* on Slide 3 and then display the Insert Hyperlink dialog box. If necessary, select the command to display places in the current document.

STEP-BY-STEP 17.3 Continued

7. In the *Select a place in this document* list, select the **Meals** custom show. Select the **Show and return** check box, and then click **OK**.

8. Select the text *Conclusion* on Slide 3 and then display the Insert Hyperlink dialog box. If necessary, select the command to display places in the current document. Select Slide **17**. **Conclusion** in the *Select a place in this document* list, and then click **OK**. When you deselect the text, Slide 3 should look similar to Figure 17-6.

FIGURE 17-6
Hyperlink text displays in a different color, with an underline

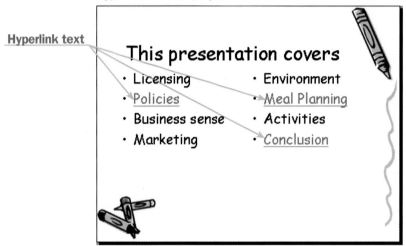

9. Make Slide 15 current and select the text *http://mypyramid.gov* in the text box at the bottom of the slide.

10. Display the Insert Hyperlink dialog box and select the command to display existing files or Web pages.

11. In the Address box, key the text **http://mypyramid.gov** and then click **OK**.

12. Save the changes and leave **Daycare** open to use in the next exercise.

Use Hyperlinks

To use a hyperlink to jump to a different location in a presentation, you must be viewing the presentation in Slide Show View. By default, hyperlink text is formatted in a particular color based on the current color scheme, with an underline. When you rest the mouse pointer on the hyperlink, it changes to resemble a hand with a pointing finger. Once a hyperlink has been clicked, it changes color.

Extra for Experts

In PowerPoint, you can create a hyperlink to a file and create the file at the same time. Select the text or object you want to use as the hyperlink, and then display the Insert Hyperlink dialog box. In the *Link to* bar, click Create New Document. Key the name of the new file in the *Name of new document* text box. Click Change and change to your hyperlink base folder and then click OK. Click either the *Edit the new document later* option button or the *Edit the new document now* option button, and then click OK to close the dialog box. If you selected to edit the new document now, the program launches and creates the file so you can begin to edit data.

When you select a different file or a slide in a different presentation as the hyperlink destination, that file must always be stored in exactly the same folder or your presentation program may not be able to locate it. This can be a problem if you use a different system when you deliver your presentation. To keep linked files organized, you can create a *hyperlink base*, which is a folder in which you store all hyperlink destination files. You identify the *path* to the hyperlink base in the presentation file so that your program always knows where to look to find the linked files. The path is the address of the folder, including the folder name and storage location. You can change the hyperlink base if you move the linked files, but without editing each hyperlink destination.

In most programs, you can create a hyperlink base by specifying the path to the folder where the linked files are stored in the Document Properties dialog box. For example, in PowerPoint, open the presentation file, click File on the Menu bar, and then click Properties. Locate the *Hyperlink base* text box, key the path to the folder, and then click OK. If you move the folder, you can edit the path to the hyperlink base.

STEP-BY-STEP 17.4

1. Make Slide 1 current and then change to Slide Show View. Click the screen to advance to Slide 3.

2. Click the **Meal Planning** hyperlink. The Meals custom show should display in Slide Show View. Click the screen six times to advance through the slides.

3. On the *Use the Pyramid* slide, click the hyperlink at the bottom of the slide. Your browser should launch and display the *USDA MyPyramid.gov* Web page. (You may have to log on to the Internet to access the Web page.)

4. Close your Web browser and click the screen to advance through the slides. After the last slide in the custom show, Slide 3 of the main show should display.

5. Click the **Policies** hyperlink to start the Policies custom show. Click the screen to advance. Again, after the last slide in the custom show, Slide 3 of the main show should display.

6. Click the **Conclusion** hyperlink. The last slide in the Daycare presentation should display. Click the screen twice to end the show.

STEP-BY-STEP 17.4 Continued

7. Display the file's Properties dialog box. For example, in PowerPoint, click **File** on the Menu bar, and then click **Properties**. The dialog box should look similar to the one in Figure 17-7.

FIGURE 17-7
Daycare Properties dialog box

Hyperlink base box

8. In the *Hyperlink base* text box, key the path to the location where you store the solution files for this lesson, and then click **OK**.

9. Save the changes and close **Daycare**. Leave your presentation program open to use in the next exercise.

Add Action Buttons

An *action button* is a graphics element that a viewer can click or roll over to cause an action to occur. The viewer might click an action button to return to the first slide in a presentation, to play a sound or video, or to launch a different program. Most programs come with built-in action buttons that you can insert on any slide. The buttons display icons that indicate the action that will occur. A button that links to Help might display an icon of a question mark and a button that links to the first slide in a presentation—Home—might display a house. Table 17-1 describes some common built-in action buttons.

TABLE 17-1
Common action buttons

BUTTON	NAME	DESCRIPTION
🏠	Home	Used to link to the first slide in a presentation or to a home page.
?	Help	Used to link to a Help program or help information.
ⓘ	Information	Used to link to supplemental information.
◁	Back or Previous	Used to link to the previous slide.
▷	Forward or Next	Used to link to the next slide.
◁|	Beginning	Used to link to the first slide in a presentation.
|▷	End	Used to link to the last slide in a presentation.
↩	Return	Used to link the previously displayed slide.
▯	Document	Used to link to a document or file outside the presentation.
◁⦂	Sound	Used to play a sound file.
▣	Movie	Used to play a movie file.
☐	Custom	Can be customized with any icon for any use.

To insert an action button, select the slide or slides on which you want the button to display. To display an action button on every slide in a presentation, insert it on the Slide Master. To display an action button on every title slide, insert it on the Title Master. Select the command to display a list of available action buttons. For example, in PowerPoint, click Slide Show on the Menu bar and then click Action Buttons to display the palette of available action buttons. Click the button you want to use, and then click and drag on the slide to draw the button. Your program then displays a dialog box in which you can edit the settings of the button. In PowerPoint this is the Action Settings dialog box.

In the settings dialog box, you can usually choose to make the action button a hyperlink or to run a program. You may be able to assign a sound to the action as well. For example, you can set the button to play a chime when you click it. Once you select the action, you use the drop-down list to select the hyperlink destination, the program to run, or the sound file to play. Default settings may be automatically entered for some buttons. For example, if you insert the Next Slide action button, the action to hyperlink to the next slide in the presentation is automatically entered. In most programs, you can specify action settings for a mouse click and for a mouse rollover.

S TEP-BY-STEP 17.5

1. Open **Step17-5** from the data files, and save the file as **Meals**.

2. Make Slide 9 current and then select the command to create an action button. For example, in PowerPoint, click **Slide Show** on the Menu bar and then click **Action Buttons**.

STEP-BY-STEP 17.5 Continued

3. Click the **Home** action button, or any button set to automatically link to the first slide in a presentation.

4. Click and drag in the lower-right corner of Slide 9 to draw a button approximately .75 inches square. (You can resize the button object later, if necessary.) When you release the mouse button in PowerPoint, the Action Settings dialog box displays, as shown in Figure 17-8. Notice that the button is already set to hyperlink to the first slide in the presentation when the button is clicked.

FIGURE 17-8
Action Settings dialog box

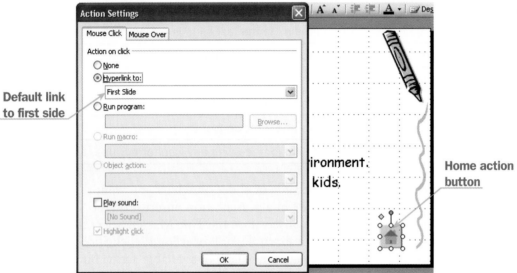

Default link to first side

Home action button

5. Click **OK** to close the dialog box.

6. Change to Slide Show View. After the content displays, click anywhere on the screen except on the action button. The show ends. Click the screen again to return to Normal View.

7. Change to Slide Show View. After the content displays, click the action button. The first slide in the presentation displays.

8. Make Slide 2 current. Display the slide master and then select the command to create an action button. Click the Beginning action button, or any button set to automatically link to the first slide in a presentation.

9. Click and drag in the lower-left corner of the slide master to draw a button approximately .75 inches square. (You can resize the button object later, if necessary.) When you release the mouse button, the Action Settings dialog box displays with the button already set to hyperlink to the first slide in the presentation when the button is clicked. Click **OK** to create the action button.

10. Repeat steps 8 and 9 to insert a **Back or Previous** button, a **Next or Forward** button, and an **End** button. The slide master should look similar to Figure 17-9.

STEP-BY-STEP 17.5 Continued

FIGURE 17-9
Action buttons on the slide master

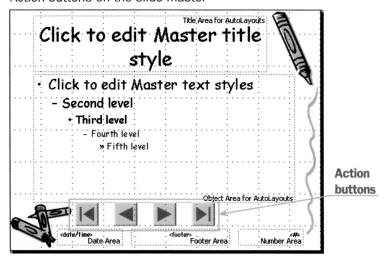

11. Close Slide Master View. The four buttons display on all slides except the two formatted in the Title slide layout.

12. Make Slide 1 current and display the Title Slide Master. Insert a **Back or Previous** action button in the lower-left corner, and a **Next or Forward** action button in lower-right corner. The slide master should look similar to Figure 17-10.

FIGURE 17-10
Action buttons on the title slide master

13. Close master View and change to Slide Show View. Use the action buttons to navigate among the slides in the presentation. When you are finished, return to Normal View.

14. Save the changes and close **Meals**. Leave your presentation program open to use in the next exercise.

Prepare a Presentation

Once you finish creating, enhancing, and improving the presentation content, you should take steps to prepare the presentation for delivery. Because you want to deliver a professional, high-quality presentation, you know that you should check the spelling on every slide, proofread data to make sure it is correct, and test the animations to make sure they progress the way you want. In addition, you can set slide timings, which are useful for controlling the pace of a presentation. You can also select slide show options to specify how you plan to deliver the presentation, and which slides you want to use.

Set Slide Timings

You can add automatic timings to a presentation when you want to control the pace of a self-running slide show. For instance, you can make sure a slide displays long enough for a viewer to read the content. You can also use automatic timings for a live presentation if you do not want to be forced to use buttons to advance the slides. To set automatic timings, rehearse the presentation, manually advancing each slide at the appropriate time. An onscreen timer shows the elapsed time. Your program tracks how long each slide displays, and then applies the timing to the presentation.

In most programs, to set slide timings you select a command such as Rehearse Timings on the Slide Show menu. The presentation displays in Slide Show View. You can read the information on the slide as if you are a viewer, or read your notes or a script as if you are delivering a live presentation. If you have animations set to advance on a mouse click, you can incorporate them into the timing. You can also simply watch the on-screen timer and advance the slides at a specific interval. When as much time as you believe is necessary has elapsed, advance to the next slide. Use the buttons on the Rehearsal toolbar to advance the slides, pause the timing, or repeat a slide to change the timing. After the last slide, you have the option of saving the timings. Click Yes to save the timings or click No if you want to start over.

S TEP-BY-STEP 17.6

1. Open **Step17-6** from the data files, and save the file as **Meals2**.

2. Select the command to set timings. For example, in PowerPoint, click **Slide Show** on the Menu bar and then click **Rehearse Timings**. The slide show starts, and the Rehearsal toolbar displays on the screen.

3. Read the title and subtitle on the first slide, and then click to advance to the next slide.

4. Click **Pause** on the Rehearsal toolbar to pause the slide show. Notice that the timer on the toolbar counts the elapsed time for the current slide and the elapsed time for the entire presentation, as shown in Figure 17-11.

STEP-BY-STEP 17.6 Continued

FIGURE 17-11
The Rehearsal toolbar

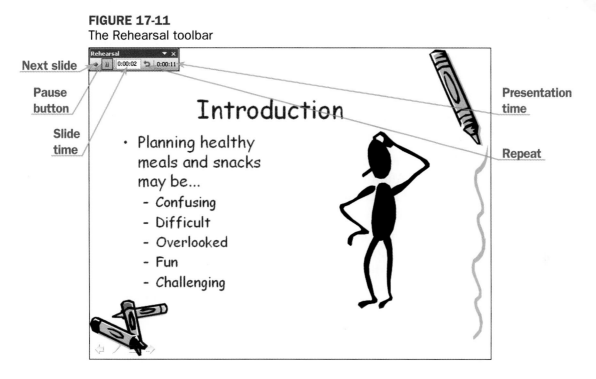

5. Click **Pause** on the Rehearsal toolbar to resume the show and read the text on the slide. When you have finished, click to advance to the next slide.

6. Continue through each slide in the slide show, reading all of the text and then advancing to the next slide. After the last slide, a dialog box displays the total length of the show and asks if you want to save the timings.

7. Click **Yes** to save the timings. The slide show displays in Slide Sorter View.

8. Preview the presentation in Slide Show View. The slides automatically advance at the pace set by the new timings.

9. Save the changes and leave **Meals2** open to use in the next exercise.

Select Slide Show Options

You can customize the delivery of a presentation by selecting slide show options. Slide show options let you specify a delivery method, and they let you include only specific slides or a custom show. You can also choose to turn off narration, slide timings, or animations, set the resolution to match the monitor on which the presentation will display, and even change the color of the pen you use to write on the slides during a presentation. (For information about writing on slides, see the section *Deliver a Live Presentation* later in this lesson.)

In some cases, such as when you want to prepare a self-running presentation, you must set slide show options to prepare the presentation. In other cases, slide show options are useful for customizing a presentation file for a particular delivery. For example, if you usually deliver an entire presentation to a live audience, you can customize it to deliver only a portion of the presentation as a self-running presentation.

To set slide show options, select the command to display the dialog box in which you select settings to set up the show. For example, in PowerPoint, click Slide Show on the Menu bar and then click Set Up Show. Select the type of show you want to run from the Show type options. There are usually three show types available:

■ Presented by a speaker (full screen): Select this type, the default, if you plan to deliver a live presentation.

■ Browsed by an individual (window): Select this type if you expect one person or a small group to view the presentation on a computer monitor at a set time and place. The Menu bar, scroll bars, and some toolbars display on the screen as well.

■ Browsed at a kiosk (full screen): Select this type if you want the presentation to run continuously in Slide Show View. Automatic timings, narration, action buttons, and hyperlinks function. Clicking the screen has no effect.

After you select the show type, select the slides you want to include in this presentation—all of them (the default), a range of slides, or just the slides in a custom show. Select additional options such as whether to use automatic timings, and whether to play narration or animations, and then click OK.

> **Extra for Experts**
>
> To improve the performance of your presentation on certain computers, you can select the *Use hardware graphics acceleration* check box in the Set Up Show dialog box.

S TEP-BY-STEP 17.7

1. Select the command to display the dialog box for setting up the slide show. For example, in PowerPoint, click **Slide Show** on the Menu bar and then click **Set Up Show**. A dialog box similar to the Set Up Show dialog box shown in Figure 17-12 displays.

FIGURE 17-12
The Set Up Show dialog box

2. Verify that the option for presenting the show by a speaker is selected.

STEP-BY-STEP 17.7 Continued

3. Select the option to display the show without animations.

4. Select the option to advance the slides manually.

5. Click **OK** to close the dialog box and apply the settings.

6. Change to Slide Show View. The automated timings are not in effect, and the fade in animations do not display.

7. Click the screen to advance through the presentation. When you are finished, end the show and return to Normal View.

8. Save the changes and close the **Meals2** file. Leave your presentation program open to use in the next exercise.

Package a Presentation

Most presentation programs let you package a presentation so that you can place all the necessary files together on CD in order to deliver the presentation at a different location using any computer system. Some programs let you include a viewer program in the package so that the presentation plays automatically when the CD is inserted in a drive, or so that you can display the presentation even if the presentation program is not installed on the delivery computer. For example, you can send the CD to a client, who can then view it on any computer that has a CD drive. You do not have to include the viewer if you plan to deliver the presentation live.

To package the presentation, open the presentation file you want to package and then select the command to display a dialog box where you can select options for packaging. To do this in PowerPoint, click File on the Menu bar and then click Package for CD to display the Package for CD dialog box. Key a name for the CD in the *Name the CD* text box. You may click the Options button to select options such as whether to include the viewer and whether to embed TrueType fonts. You may also be able to assign a password to the folder to control access to the files. You may click the Add Files button to include additional presentation files in the same package.

If your computer is equipped with a CD burner, which is a CD drive that lets you write data onto a CD, and if you have a blank, writable CD, you may copy the packaged presentation directly to the CD. Alternatively, you may copy the packaged presentation to a folder on your computer system or to a network. Others can then access the packaged system from the network, or you can move the entire folder to a removable device such as a CD, an external drive, or to a flash memory device so you can transport it.

Note ☑

With some versions of the Windows operating system, you may have to copy the files to a folder and then use a CD burning utility to copy the folder to a CD.

S TEP-BY-STEP 17.8

1. Open **Step17-8** from the Data files and save the file as **Annies**.

2. Select the command to package the presentation. For example, in PowerPoint, click **File** on the Menu bar and then click **Package for CD**. A dialog box similar to the one shown in Figure 17-13 displays.

FIGURE 17-13
The Package for CD dialog box

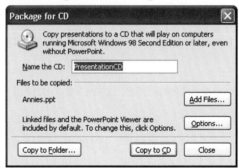

3. If there is a *Name the CD* text box, key **Annies Live**.

4. Select the command to display additional options—click **Options** in the dialog box shown—verify that the option to include the viewer is selected, and that the option to include linked files is selected.

5. Select the option to embed TrueType fonts and then click **OK**.

6. If you have a CD burner, insert a writable CD in the drive and then click the command to copy the files to the CD. Your program copies the presentation files to the CD and then displays a dialog box asking if you want to create another CD. Click **No**.

   If you do not have a CD burner, or if you are using a version of Windows that requires you to copy to a folder before copying to a CD, click the command to copy the files to a folder, browse to select the location where you want to store the folder, and then click **OK**.

7. Close the dialog box and remove the CD.

8. Insert the CD into a CD drive (either on your computer or on another). The viewer program should start automatically. (If necessary, click **Accept** to accept the program license.) The presentation should start and play through to the end, as in Slide Show View.

   If you copied the files to a folder, use Windows to navigate to the folder. Double-click the viewer program icon, select the **Annies** file, and then click **Open**. The file plays in the viewer window. Alternatively, use a CD burning program to copy the folder to a CD, and then try Step 8.

9. Save the changes to **Annies** and close it. Leave your presentation program open to use in the next exercise.

Deliver a Live Presentation

A *live presentation* is a presentation that you deliver in front of a live audience. Usually, you narrate the presentation live, and advance the slides manually. This gives you the opportunity to vary from a script to suit your audience. For example, if someone asks a question, you can take the time to answer without advancing to the next slide. If the audience already knows some of the information in the presentation, you can skip those slides. You may deliver the presentation using a computer connected to a large monitor or projector. You may also use 35-mm slides or overhead transparencies (refer to Lesson 16 for more information on 35-mm slides and overheads). Depending on the size of the room, you may need to have a microphone so that the audience can hear you.

> **Note**
>
> Follow the manufacturer's instructions to install and test the device before your audience arrives.

In any case, you must be prepared to speak clearly and intelligently about your subject. It is a good idea to practice more than once before you go live, and to make sure you have all the supporting documents you need on hand, such as printed speaker's notes, supplemental spreadsheets or reports, and reference documents. You should also print out enough handouts for the entire audience.

To start the presentation, open the presentation file and change to Slide Show View. If you are using a viewer instead of the presentation program, launch the viewer program, then select and run the presentation file. Most programs provide on-screen navigation tools that you can use to control the flow of the presentation. For example, click the Next Slide icon to advance to the next slide, or the Preview Slide icon to go back to the previous slide.

You may be able to display a shortcut menu of commands for accessing presentation features by right-clicking the screen or clicking the Slide icon in the lower left of the screen. For example, you should be able to select to show or hide the pointer. You may also be able to access your speaker's notes on the screen during a presentation, and to cause the screen to temporarily go blank.

> **Hot Tip**
>
> You may add to speaker notes during a presentation by displaying the speaker notes on-screen and then keying directly into the Notes text box.

Table 17-2 describes some of the slide show controls you can use while delivering a live presentation. Note that there may be more than one way to perform a task.

TABLE 17-2
Slide show controls

TO	DO THIS
Display the next slide	Press Spacebar, Page Down, the down arrow, Enter, or click anywhere on the screen or the Next Slide icon. Or right-click to access the shortcut menu and then click Next.
Display the previous slide	Press Backspace, the up arrow, or Page Up, or click the Previous Slide icon. Or right-click to access the shortcut menu and then click Previous.
Jump to specific slide	Key the slide number and press Enter. Or display the shortcut menu, click Go to Slide, and then click the slide to display. (Slide numbers of hidden slides display in parentheses.)
Blank the screen	Display the shortcut menu, click Screen, and then click Black Screen to show a black screen, or White Screen, to show a white screen. To return to the show, click the screen.
View speaker's notes	Display the shortcut menu, click Screen, and then click Speaker Notes. Click Close to close Speaker Notes.
Pause the show	Display the shortcut menu, and then click Pause.
End the show	Press Esc or display the shortcut menu, and then click End Show.

Use Pointer Options

In most programs the mouse pointer automatically displays during a slide show by default, but disappears after 15 seconds of inactivity. Usually, you can select to display the pointer all the time, or hide it. For example, to change the pointer options in PowerPoint, right-click the screen or click the Slide icon to display the shortcut menu, and then click Pointer Options. Alternatively, click the Pen icon to display the Pointer Options. Click Arrow Options and then click Automatic for the default option, Hidden to hide the arrow, or Visible to display the arrow.

You can use the mouse pointer to write on a slide during a slide show. This can be useful for circling items, or showing connections between items. Most programs offer a ballpoint pen option, and some programs also let you select a felt tip pen or highlighter. You can usually select the pen color as well. Marks are erased when you advance to the next slide, or when you use an eraser option. However, when the pen is active you cannot advance to the next slide by clicking the screen. Use a keyboard alternative, such as pressing Page Down, instead.

To write on a slide during a PowerPoint presentation, start the slide show, right-click the screen or click the Slide icon to display the shortcut menu, and then click Pointer Options. Click the type of pointer you want to use—either Ballpoint Pen, Felt Tip Pen, or Highlighter. Drag on the screen to draw on the slide. To change back to the regular pointer, select Arrow from the Pointer Options menu. To change the color of the pen, click Ink Color on the Pointer Options menu, and then click a color on the ink color palette.

> **Hot Tip**
>
> To quickly turn on the pen in PowerPoint, press Ctrl+P during the slide show. Press Ctrl+U to change to the Arrow pointer.

Use Two Monitors

When you are delivering a live presentation, you may want to connect a second monitor to your computer so you can display your notes or access other programs and files while the presentation displays. In some programs, using two monitors also gives you access to *presenter view*, which displays controls you can use to quickly navigate through the presentation, view your notes, and perform other tasks that help you deliver a live presentation.

To use two monitors, the computer must have Windows 98 or a later operating system. Once both monitors are installed, you must designate one as the *primary monitor*, which is the monitor you will use for your own tasks, and one as the *secondary monitor*, which is the monitor on which the audience will view the presentation. To do so, right-click the desktop, click Properties, and then click the Settings tab. Select the primary monitor and then click *Use this device as the primary monitor* (if needed). Select the secondary monitor and then click *Extend my Windows desktop onto this computer*. Click OK. You must then set up the show to run on the secondary monitor. Click Slide Show on the Menu bar and then click Set Up Show. Click the arrow on the *Display slide show on* list, and select the secondary monitor. To use presenter view, select the Show Presenter View check box, and then click OK.

STEP-BY-STEP 17.9

1. Set up your equipment as necessary to prepare for a live presentation. For example, attach your computer to a large monitor or screen, or to two monitors. Check your microphone to make sure it works.

2. Open **Step17-9** from the data files, and save the file as **Meals3**.

STEP-BY-STEP 17.9 Continued

3. Change to Slide Show View to start the show. If you have two monitors, display presenter's view on the primary monitor. If you are working with one monitor, display speaker's notes on screen. For example, in PowerPoint, right-click the screen, click **Screen**, and then click **Speaker Notes**. Your screen should look similar to Figure 17-14.

FIGURE 17-14
Display speaker notes during a slide show

4. Referring to the speaker notes, welcome the audience and introduce yourself and others.

5. Click the screen to advance to the next slide, and then click it to display the bulleted text. Refer to the speaker notes to discuss the importance of healthy meal planning for a day care provider.

6. Advance to the next slide and click to display each bulleted item. Referring to the speaker notes, ask the audience to offer suggestions of how to incorporate each item into a meal, or offer your own suggestions. When ready, click to advance to the next item.

7. Continue advancing through the presentation, talking and engaging the audience. When Slide 5, Meal Patterns for Children, part 2, displays, activate the highlighter pen. For example, in PowerPoint, right-click the screen, click **Pointer Options**, and then click **Highlighter**. Drag to highlight the text *including soda*. Your screen should look similar to Figure 17-15.

STEP-BY-STEP 17.9 Continued

FIGURE 17-15
Highlight text during a slide show

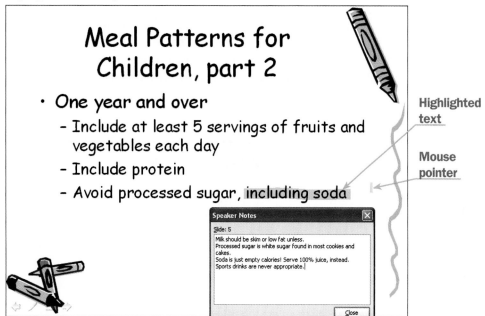

8. Turn off the highlighter. For example, in PowerPoint, right-click the screen, click **Pointer Options**, and then click **Arrow**.

9. Continue advancing through the presentation. At the last slide, thank the audience, and ask for questions.

10. End the show. If necessary, select to discard your on-screen annotations.

11. Save the changes and close **Meals3**. Leave your presentation program open to use in the next exercise.

Deliver a Self-Running Presentation

A *self-running presentation* plays automatically in an unattended situation. For example, you might use a self-running presentation at a kiosk or trade-show booth, for independent training sessions, or to send to a client. You may want a self-running presentation to be completely automated, so that the viewer cannot interact with the presentation at all. For a completely automated presentation, you should set automatic timings and record any narration that you think is necessary.

In some situations, you want the viewer to have control over the presentation. For example, you may want the viewer to advance the presentation at his or her own pace, by clicking the screen, or you may want to provide action buttons so the viewer can stop, start, or restart the presentation, or skip a slide, as necessary. This is useful at a trade-show or kiosk, where someone may walk up to the booth at any time.

When selecting slide show options for a self-running presentation, you usually can select to display the presentation in a window or sized to fill the screen. The window option is suitable for situations where you want the viewer to be able to control the flow of the presentation using the mouse. The full-screen option is suitable for situations where you want to provide a completely automated presentation, or if you only want to allow control via action buttons or hyperlinks. When you select this option, the presentation is set to loop continuously until the Esc key is pressed. You should use the File > Save As command to save the presentation as a *slide show file*. A slide show file opens in full-screen Slide Show View, not in a presentation program window. If you are using PowerPoint, a slide show file has a .pps file extension.

S TEP-BY-STEP 17.10

1. Open **Step17-10** from the data files and save it as **Meals4**.

2. Select the command to display the dialog box for setting up the slide show. For example, in PowerPoint, click **Slide Show** on the Menu bar and then click **Set Up Show**. A dialog box displays.

3. Under *Show type*, click the option for a full-screen self-running showing, such as **Browsed at a kiosk (full screen)**. Notice that once you select the kiosk option, the slide show is automatically set to loop continuously until the Esc key is pressed.

4. Under *Advance slides*, click to select the **Manually** option. Click **OK** to close the dialog box and apply the changes.

5. Change to Slide Show View. Click anywhere on the screen except on an action button. Nothing happens.

6. Click the **Next** action button to advance to the next slide.

7. Click the **End** action button to advance to the last slide.

8. Click the **Next** action button. The first slide displays because the presentation is set to loop continuously.

9. Press **Esc** to end the show.

10. Save the change and leave **Meals4** open to use in the next exercise.

Deliver an Online Presentation

The Internet or an intranet can be an exciting, cost-effective means for delivering a presentation. You can *broadcast* a live presentation, or make a presentation available on-demand, which means whenever it is convenient for the viewer. You can also *publish* a presentation to the Web, which means that you save the file in a Web-compatible format on a Web server so that viewers can access it using a Web browser.

Publish a Presentation

When you want to make a presentation available on a Web site, save it as a Web page or publish it to the Web. When you save a presentation as a *single file Web page*, it is stored in metafile hypertext markup language (MHTML) format with an .mht file extension. All supporting files such as graphics, sounds, and video are integrated into the same file; no supporting folder is required.

A presentation file displays the following elements on-screen in the browser window:

- The Outline, or navigation, frame displays along the left side of the window, and lists the slide numbers and titles of all slides in the presentation. Click a title to go to that slide.

- The Slide frame displays the slide.

- The controls along the bottom of the window let you show or hide the outline, expand or collapse the outline, show or hide the speaker notes, navigate through the slides, or change to Slide Show View.

You can preview a presentation as a Web page prior to publishing it so you can get an idea of how it will look to someone viewing it on the Web. That way, you can make changes before you publish it. Use the File > Web Page Preview command to open the presentation in your Web browser.

When you publish a file you can change and select options to control the Web page display. For example, you can set a *Web page title*, which is the text that displays in the Web browser title bar when the presentation displays, select the specific slides to publish, or even change the presentation colors. You can usually select whether to display the speaker notes. Speaker notes can be useful in a published presentation for making narration or commentary available to the viewer in case a computer does not have sound, or in case a viewer is hearing impaired.

> **Note**
>
> If you want to be able to edit a presentation file with an HTML editor, such as Microsoft FrontPage or Macromedia Dreamweaver, you can save it as a Web page in HTML format. Saving as a Web page creates a folder that contains an .htm file and all supporting files, such as images, sound files, and more.

When you are ready to publish a presentation, select the command to save the file as a Web page. For example, in PowerPoint, click File on the Menu bar, and then click Save as Web Page. Select the storage location you want to use. It should be on a local intranet or on a Web server so that viewers can access it online. Key a name in the File name text box. At this point, you can click Save to save the file as a Web page using the default options.

To optimize the presentation for the Web, click the Publish button to open the Publish as Web Page dialog box. In this dialog box you can select specific slides to publish, you can select the type of browsers you want to support, you can specify a storage location, and you can select whether to display speaker notes. You can also click the Web Options button to open the Web Options dialog box to select additional settings. For

> **Note**
>
> If you make changes to a presentation after publishing it, you must republish the data to update it on the Web site.

example, if you already have action buttons for navigating in your presentation, you can choose not to display navigation controls on the Web page. When you have finished selecting options, click OK to close each dialog box, and then click Publish to publish the Web page file.

STEP-BY-STEP 17.11

1. Select the command to preview the presentation in your Web browser. For example, in PowerPoint, click **File** on the Menu bar and then click **Web Page Preview**. It should look similar to Figure 17-16.

FIGURE 17-16
Presentation in Web Page Preview

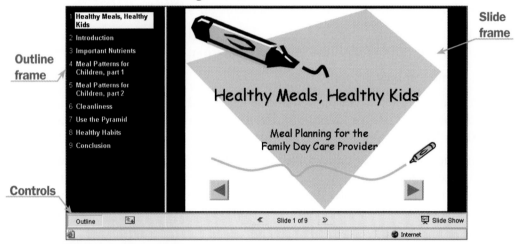

2. Click **Outline** to hide the outline.

3. Click the **Next** action button to advance to the next slide.

4. Close your Web browser.

5. Select the command to save the file as a Web page. For example, in PowerPoint, click **File** on the Menu bar and then click **Save as Web Page**. The Save As dialog box displays, with options already selected for saving a Web page.

6. Select the location where you want to store the published Web page.

7. Click the **Change Title** button, key **Day Care Provider Meal Planning**, and then click **OK**.

8. Click **Publish** to display the Publish as Web Page dialog box, and then click the **Web Options** button. A dialog box similar to the one in Figure 17-17 displays.

STEP-BY-STEP 17.11 Continued

FIGURE 17-17
Web Options dialog box

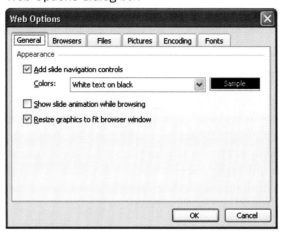

9. Deselect the option to add slide navigation controls—you have action buttons in the presentation already—and then click **OK**.

10. Select the option to open the published Web page in a browser, if necessary, and then click **Publish**. Your program publishes the file and displays the presentation in your browser. It should look similar to Figure 17-18.

Warning

If your computer is set to block certain content, an Information Bar may display, along with a dialog box asking if you want to display blocked content. Click **OK** to close the dialog box, then click the **Information Bar**. Click **Allow Blocked Content**, and then click **Yes** in the Security Warning dialog box to display the presentation in your browser.

FIGURE 17-18
The published presentation

STEP-BY-STEP 17.11 Continued

11. Use the action buttons to browse through the presentation. When you are finished, close your browser.

12. Save the changes and close **Meals4**. Close your presentation program.

Broadcast a Presentation

Another way to deliver your presentation using the Internet is to broadcast it. Broadcasting displays the presentation to an invited audience via the Internet or an intranet. This is useful for delivering a presentation to people who are in different locations, or who cannot all attend the same meeting at the same time. For example, you can use a presentation to pitch an idea to a potential client located in a different state, or to communicate with team members based at a different office building. The audience and the presenter must have access to the same shared computer or server in order to participate in the broadcast.

A broadcast is usually done live, and it can contain live video and sound, including narration from the presenter. Most programs also record the broadcast in a file that is stored on the Web server so it can be accessed and played on a Web browser at any time. To include live video you must have a video camera installed and set up for use with your computer. Also, to include live sound, you must have a microphone.

Hot Tip

Before starting the broadcast, you should send e-mail invitations to the audience members, informing them of the time and address of the broadcast.

When your equipment is set up and ready for use, you can start the broadcast. Display the presentation file and then select the command to start. For example, in PowerPoint, click Slide Show on the Menu bar, click Online Broadcast, and then click Start Live Broadcast Now. Your program prepares the presentation and displays a message when it is ready (this may take a few minutes). Click the command to start the broadcast. A dialog box displays where you can key a message to display on the *lobby page*, which is a Web page that displays

Important

If the Broadcast command does not display on your Slide Show menu, the feature may not be installed. With your instructor's permission, you may be able to download it from the Microsoft Office Online Web site.

in the user's browser window while he or she is waiting for the broadcast to begin. You can also select whether you plan to transmit live audio and video, live audio only, or none. Click Settings to open the Broadcast Settings dialog box, where you can select the folder where you want to store the broadcast recording. Click Select to return to the Broadcast Settings dialog box. Click OK to return to the Live Presentation Broadcast dialog box.

If you have not yet sent out invitations, or if you just want to send a reminder, click the Invite Audience button to create an e-mail message that automatically displays the address of the broadcast. Key a message and click Send. The recipient can simply click the link to the address in the message to access the broadcast.

Note

To broadcast a presentation to more than 10 people with PowerPoint, you need to use a Windows Media Server. If you don't have one, you may be able to contract with a Windows Media service provider for access.

When you are ready to begin the broadcast, click Start. The Broadcast Presentation dialog box opens. If you are transmitting live video and audio, the connections are tested. You can click Recheck Microphone to recheck the microphone before you begin transmitting; click Audience Message to recheck the message to the audience on the lobby page; or click Preview Lobby Page to display a preview of what the audience is currently seeing. When you are ready, click Start to begin the broadcast. The first slide displays. The broadcast ends when you end the slide show. You may have the option of replaying the recording or working in your presentation program.

> **Note**
>
> The presenter does not see the live video onscreen during the presentation. The audience sees the video in a frame on the left side of the browser window. The audience also sees a description of the broadcast in the Web browser, along with buttons for getting help, sending the presenter an e-mail message, and displaying any slides.

SUMMARY

In this lesson, you learned:

- You can hide slides you don't want displayed during a presentation.

- You can create custom shows using selected slides within a presentation.

- You can insert hyperlinks to a destination location, such as a different slide, a custom show, a Web page, a data file or document, or to an e-mail address.

- During a presentation, you can click the hyperlink to jump to the destination.

- Action buttons let you or a viewer navigate through a presentation. Most programs include built-in action buttons set to link to common destinations.

- You can set automatic timings to control the pace of a self-running slide show or if you do not want to be tied to the computer during a live presentation.

- You can set slide show options to customize the delivery of a presentation.

- When you need to deliver a presentation to a different computer, you can package it and burn it on a CD.

- When you deliver a live presentation, the audience is present in the room. It is important to be prepared to answer questions and vary from a set script.

- During a live presentation, you may want to use two monitors so you can access different content such as speaker's notes.

- You can write on the slides during a live presentation.

- You can set up a self-running presentation so viewers can see it even if there is no one available to present it.

- A self-running presentation may be completely automated, or the viewer may be able to control the flow of slides.

- Publish a presentation when you want to optimize it for delivery on a Web page. Viewers can access the presentation online using a Web browser.

- Broadcast a live presentation over the Internet or a company intranet to a group that cannot all be in the same place at the same time.

VOCABULARY *Review*

Define the following terms:		
Action button	Lobby page	Secondary monitor
Broadcast	Path	Self-running presentation
Custom show	Presenter view	Single file Web page
Hyperlink base	Primary monitor	Slide show file
Live presentation	Publish	Web page title

REVIEW *Questions*

TRUE / FALSE

Circle T if the statement is true or F if the statement is false.

T　F　1. When you hide a slide it is deleted from the presentation file.

T　F　2. You can use text or an object to create a hyperlink.

T　F　3. If you record slide timings, you must use them every time you deliver the presentation.

T　F　4. You can use the mouse pointer to write on a slide during a slide show.

T　F　5. You can attach two monitors to a computer for use during a live presentation.

T　F　6. Once you publish a presentation to the Web, you cannot edit or update the presentation file.

T　F　7. You can display speaker notes in a published presentation.

T　F　8. You must invite the audience to view a live presentation broadcast.

T　F　9. The presenter does not see the live video during a presentation broadcast.

T　F　10. There is no way to see a presentation broadcast once the live feed has ended.

WRITTEN QUESTIONS

Write a brief answer to each of the following questions.

1. Explain at least three ways to use a hyperlink in a presentation.

2. What are two reasons for setting automatic timings?

3. What are three benefits of delivering a live presentation?

4. Name at least two situations in which you might use a self-running presentation.

5. What are two reasons for using a presentation broadcast?

FILL IN THE BLANK

Complete the following sentences by writing the correct word or words in the blanks provided.

1. A(n) _____ show is a presentation created from selected slides within a presentation.

2. When you rest the mouse pointer on a(n) _____ it changes to resemble a hand with a pointing finger.

3. A hyperlink _____ is a folder in which you store all linked files.

4. An action _____ is a graphics element that a viewer can click or rollover to cause an action to occur.

5. _____ a presentation so that you can place all the necessary files together on CD in order to deliver the presentation at a different location using any computer system.

6. _____ view displays controls you can use to quickly navigate through a presentation, view your notes, and perform other tasks that help you deliver a live presentation.

7. The _____ monitor is the monitor you will use for your own tasks.

8. The _____ monitor is the monitor on which the audience will view the presentation.

9. You should use the File > Save As command to save a self-running presentation as a(n) _____ file so that it opens in full-screen Slide Show View, not in a presentation program window.

10. When you save a presentation as a(n) _____ file Web page, it is stored in metafile hypertext markup language (MHTML) format with an .mht file extension.

PROJECTS

PROJECT 17-1

1. Launch your presentation program and open **Project17-1** from the data files. Save the file as **Pets**.

2. Create a custom show.
   A. Name the show **Dogs**.
   B. Include Slides 3, 4, 5, and 6.
   C. Preview the custom show, clicking the screen to advance.

3. Create another custom show.
   A. Name the show **Cats**.
   B. Include Slides 7, 8, 9, and 10.
   C. Preview the custom show, clicking the screen to advance.

4. Make Slide 2 current and insert a hyperlink to the **Cats** custom show, setting the link to return to the original slide at the end of the show. To do this in PowerPoint:
   A. Select the text *Cats*.
   B. Click the **Insert Hyperlink** button.
   C. Click **Place in this Document**.
   D. Click the **Cats** custom show.
   E. Select the **Show and return** check box.
   F. Click **OK**.

5. On Slide 2, insert a hyperlink to the **Dogs** custom show, setting the link to return to the original slide at the end of the show. To do this in PowerPoint:
   A. Select the text *Dogs*.
   B. Click the **Insert Hyperlink** button.
   C. Click **Place in this Document**.
   D. Click the **Dogs** custom show.
   E. Select the **Show and return** check box.
   F. Click **OK**.

6. On Slide 2, insert an action button to the last slide in the presentation. To do this in PowerPoint:
   A. Click **Slide Show** on the Menu bar, click **Action Buttons**, and then click the **End** action button.
   B. Click and drag to draw a button in the lower, middle of the slide, about 1.0 inch square.
   C. Click **OK** in the Action Settings dialog box to accept the default hyperlink to the last slide.
   D. If necessary, adjust the position of the button to center it horizontally, approximately 1.0 inch from the bottom of the slide.

7. On Slide 11, insert a hyperlink to the Humane Society's Web site. To do this in PowerPoint:
   A. Select the web site address *http://www.hsus.org*.
   B. Click the **Insert Hyperlink** button.
   C. Click **Existing File or Web Page**.
   D. Key **http://www.hsus.org** in the Address text box.
   E. Click **OK**.

8. Make Slide 1 current and change to Slide Show View.

9. Click the screen to advance to Slide 2.

10. Click the **Cats** hyperlink and view the Cats custom show, then click the screen to advance through the custom show.

11. Click the **Dogs** hyperlink and view the Dogs custom show, then click the screen to advance through the custom show.

12. Click the **End** action button to go to the last slide in the presentation.

13. Click the hyperlink to the Humane Society Web site.

14. Close your browser.

15. End the slide show and return to Normal View.

16. Save the changes and then package the presentation for delivery on a CD.
   A. Name the CD **Choose a Pet**.
   B. Include the viewer program.
   C. Burn the package on a CD, or copy it to a folder on your computer.

17. Save and close the **Pets** presentation.

18. Test the CD (or use the files in the folder to start the viewer and display the presentation).

19. Close the viewer program but leave your presentation program open to use in the next project.

20. If possible deliver the presentation to a live audience.

PROJECT 17-2

1. Open **Project17-2** from the data files, and save the file as **Pets2**.

2. Rehearse and save timings for the entire presentation. To do this in PowerPoint:
   A. Click **Slide Show** on the Menu bar and then click **Rehearse Timings**.
   B. Once the text displays, read the title and subtitle, and then advance to the next slide.
   C. Repeat step B for all slides in the presentation.
   D. After the last slide, choose to save the timings.

3. Set up the presentation for use at a kiosk:
   A. Include all the slides.
   B. Use the timings.
   C. Use graphics acceleration if your computer has it.

4. Test the presentation in Slide Show View.

5. Package the presentation for delivery on a CD.
   A. Name the CD **Pet Show**.
   B. Include the viewer program.
   C. Burn the package on a CD, or copy it to a folder on your computer.

6. Save and close the **Pets2** presentation.

7. Test the CD (or use the files in the folder to start the viewer and display the presentation).

8. Close the viewer program, but leave your presentation program open to use in the next project.

PROJECT 17-3

1. Open **Project17-3** from the data files, and save the file as **Pets3**.

2. On the Slide Master, insert action buttons to navigate through the presentation. To do this in PowerPoint:
   A. Make Slide 2 current and then display the slide master.
   B. Click **Slide Show** on the Menu bar, click **Action Buttons**, and then click the **Beginning** action button.
   C. Click and drag to draw a button on the bottom of the slide, about .75 inch square.
   D. Click **OK** in the Action Settings dialog box to accept the default hyperlink to the last slide.
   E. Repeat steps B, C, and D to add a **Back or Previous** action button, a **Forward or Next** action button, and an **End** action button.
   F. Size and position the buttons in a row in the bottom right of the slide.
   G. Close master View.

3. On the Title Slide Master, insert the same action buttons to navigate through the presentation. To do this in PowerPoint:
   A. Make Slide 1 current and then display the Title Slide Master.
   B. Click **Slide Show** on the Menu bar, click **Action Buttons**, and then click the **Beginning** action button.
   C. Click and drag to draw a button on the bottom of the slide, about .75 inch square.
   D. Click **OK** in the Action Settings dialog box to accept the default hyperlink to the last slide.
   E. Repeat steps B, C, and D to add a **Back or Previous** action button, a **Forward or Next** action button, and an **End** action button.
   F. Size and position the buttons in a row in the bottom, right of the slide.
   G. Close master View.

4. Publish the complete presentation to the Web, without using the Web navigation tools. To do this in PowerPoint:
   A. Click **File** on the Menu bar and then click **Save as Web Page**.
   B. Select the storage location for the Web page.
   C. Click **Publish**.
   D. Click **Web Options**.
   E. Deselect the **Add slide navigation controls** check box.
   F. Click **OK**.
   G. Select to open the published page in your browser.
   H. Click **Publish**.

Warning
If your computer is set to block certain content, an Information Bar may display, along with a dialog box asking if you want to display blocked content. Click **OK** to close the dialog box, then click the **Information Bar**. Click **Allow Blocked Content**, and then click **Yes** in the Security Warning dialog box to display the presentation in your browser.

5. Use the action buttons to navigate through the presentation in your browser.

6. Close your browser.

7. Save and close **Pets3**, then close your presentation program.

 WEB PROJECT

Use the Web to research information about equipment you might need to deliver live presentations, or to broadcast a presentation live on the Internet. Research the cost of projectors, large monitors, video cameras, and microphones. You want to find out what types of equipment are available, whether the quality varies, where you can get the equipment, and how much it costs. You also need to know if it is compatible with your existing equipment. Record the information in a word processing document or a spreadsheet. When you have gathered the data, compare and analyze it to determine whether it would be worthwhile to invest in some or all of the equipment. Write your recommendation as a report and create a supporting presentation. Include references to the data that you collected. For example, create a table or a chart, or use hyperlinks to the Web sites where you found the information. Deliver the presentation live to your class.

 TEAMWORK PROJECT

New students at your school may feel lost and lonely trying to learn their way around. A presentation introducing the school could help them make friends and integrate into the student body more quickly. The presentation could be made available as a self-running slide show in the library or an administration office, or published to the school's Web site.

As a team, plan a presentation introducing your school. Think of the areas you want to cover, and then split the team up so that different people are responsible for collecting information about different aspects of school life. You may want to include information such as how the schedule works, where kids hang out, and how to locate the library, the gym, and the cafeteria. You may want to introduce the administration, including the principal, vice principal, and guidance counselors. You could list sports teams, clubs, and historical facts. Each group should write or gather the slide content for their area, including pictures, video, and sound you may want to add to the presentation. When the content is complete, meet and review it together, making suggestions for improvements, additions, or deletions.

Create the presentation selecting a suitable design template. Set the presentation up to be a self-running show, even including narration, if you want. Use hyperlinks and action buttons so viewers can navigate the presentation without assistance. Proofread and spell check the presentation, and preview it in Slide Show View. Make improvements and adjustments as necessary. When you are satisfied, package the presentation on a CD so it can be displayed on any computer. If possible, publish the presentation to the school Web site.

CRITICAL *Thinking*

For a history or social studies class, interview someone who is at least 60 years old about his or her life. For example, you may interview a relative, a friend, a teacher, or a coach. Find out as much as you can about the person. Ask the person about the changes that have occurred during his or her life, what was different when he or she was young, and what important events have taken place. Record the information by taking notes, or ask permission to record it using a tape recorder or a video camera. You can take still pictures of the person as well.

When you have gathered the information, organize it into a presentation that you can deliver to a live audience. Write the outline, select graphics and organize sound and video. Create the presentation selecting a suitable design template. Apply transitions and animations. Include hyperlinks, if you want. You might want to divide the presentation into custom shows about different aspects of the person's life. Add speaker notes as necessary to help you during the presentation delivery. Proofread and spell check the presentation, and preview it in Slide Show View. Ask a classmate to preview it and make suggestions. Make improvements and adjustments as necessary. When you are satisfied, print handouts to accompany the presentation and deliver it live to your classmates. With your instructor's permission, invite the subject of the interview to the presentation.

PRESENTATION SYSTEMS

REVIEW *Questions*

TRUE / FALSE

Circle T if the statement is true or F if the statement is false.

T   F   1. To preview a presentation on the screen, change to Slide Sorter View.

T   F   2. All text in a presentation must be in bullet list format.

T   F   3. When you duplicate a slide, it is inserted after the original slide.

T   F   4. Most presentation design templates have preset color schemes that use a coordinated palette of eight colors.

T   F   5. Most presentation programs come with built-in collections of clip art images or CDs containing clip art files.

T   F   6. You can modify pictures inserted on a slide.

T   F   7. If a sound file is smaller than 100 KB, it will be embedded in the presentation, or stored as part of the presentation file itself.

T   F   8. Notes pages and handouts have the same headers and footers.

T   F   9. Typically, when you create overheads you should use a dark background with light text.

T   F 10. Package a presentation with a viewer if you want to be able to deliver it on a computer that does not have the presentation program installed.

MATCHING

Match the correct term in Column 1 to its description in Column 2.

Column 1

___ 1. Slide

___ 2. Color scheme

___ 3. Marker

___ 4. Fill effect

___ 5. Table

___ 6. WAV

___ 7. Timings

___ 8. Service bureau

___ 9. Hyperlink

___ 10. Publish

Column 2

A. A symbol inserted to the left of items in a list.

B. A company that takes slide information and reproduces it on 35-mm slides for a fee.

C. The intervals that control the length of time a slide is displayed before the transition to the next slide.

D. A single screen of information within a presentation.

E. To save a file in a Web-compatible format on a Web server so that viewers can access it using a Web browser.

F. A set of data arranged in columns and rows.

G. A sound file format frequently used to accompany slide transitions.

H. Text or an object that you click to display a destination location.

I. A set of coordinated colors used for the background, titles and other text, shadows, fills, bullets and other accents, and hyperlinks.

J. A pattern, gradient, picture, or texture that you apply to the background of a slide.

FILL IN THE BLANK

Complete the following sentences by writing the correct word or words in the blanks provided.

1. Usually, the default view in a presentation program is _____ View.

2. The slide _____ determines the location of different types of content on the slide, such as text blocks and graphics objects.

3. A(n) _____ template is a presentation template that includes prompts, formatting, and slides organized for a specific presentation type.

4. The color marked as _____ on a color palette is the default scheme color for the selected element.

5. In most presentation programs, a chart is linked to the data you key in a(n) _____.

6. You might use a(n) _____ chart to show the relationship between managers and subordinates in a company division, or to depict a family tree.

7. In a presentation, a(n) _____ is either an animated GIF file or a video clip file.

8. When applying animations, select a(n) _____ effect to control how an element comes into view on the slide.

9. When you want changes to affect all notes pages in a presentation, edit and format the Notes _____.

10. A(n) _____ show is a presentation created from selected slides within a presentation.

PROJECTS

In these projects, you will create a presentation about Niagara Falls.

PROJECT U3-1

1. Launch your presentation graphics program to create a new, blank presentation file.

2. Save the file as **Falls1**.

3. Click the Title placeholder and key **Niagara Falls**.

4. Click the Subtitle placeholder and key **A Remarkable Natural Wonder**.

5. Insert a new slide that has a layout with placeholders for a title and a bullet list. For example, in PowerPoint, select the Title and Text layout.

6. Click the Title placeholder and key **About the Falls**.

7. Click in the Text placeholder and key the following list:
   The Niagara Falls are created by water from the Great Lakes flowing into the Niagara River. There are actually three Falls:
       American Falls
       Bridal Veil Falls
       Horseshoe Falls

8. Click in the Notes pane and key: **American Falls and Bridal Veil Falls are sometimes just called American Falls. They are on the American side of the Niagara River. Horseshoe Falls are on the Canadian side of the river.**

9. Insert a new slide that has a layout with placeholders for a title and two bullet lists. For example, in PowerPoint, select the **Title and 2-Column Text** layout. Click the Title placeholder and key **Compare the Falls**.

10. Click the Text placeholder on the left and key the following list:
Horseshoe Falls
    Height: 167 feet
    Width: 2,600 feet
    Volume of water: 600,000 gallons/second

11. Click the Text placeholder on the right and key the following list:
American Falls & Bridal Veil Falls
    Height: 176 feet
    Width: 1,060 feet
    Volume of water: 150,000 gallons/second

12. Insert a new slide that has a title and text layout. Key the title **Fun Facts, Part 1.**

13. Click the text placeholder and key the following list:
Falls started flowing more than 12,000 years ago.
Niagara Falls erodes about 4 feet per year.
The depth of the river under Horseshoe Falls is as deep as the height of the Falls.
More than 10 million people visit the Falls every year.

14. Insert a new slide that has a title and text layout. Key the title **Fun Facts, Part 2.**

15. Click the text placeholder and key the following list:
The first person over the Falls in a barrel was Annie Taylor on October 24, 1901.
At least 13 others have taken the plunge, but not all survived.
Using man-made attractions, you can go under the Falls, over the Falls, and through the Falls.

16. Click in the Notes pane and key the following: **Not everyone survives the trip. Some are seriously injured and some are killed. Some attractions include the Maid of the Mist boat ride, the Cave of Winds tour down the gorge, and Journey Behind the Falls.**

17. Insert a new slide that has a title and text layout. Key the title **Sources.** Click the text placeholder and key the following list (note that your program automatically formats the URLs as hyperlinks):
http://www.niagarafallslive.com
http://www.niagarafalls.ca
http://www.niagarafrontier.com

18. Apply the **Ocean** design template (or one that is appropriate to the content of this presentation) to all slides in the presentation.

19. Change the color scheme to one with a teal background and an olive green arrow.

20. Apply the **Fade Smoothly** transition (or something comparable) to the first slide, at slow speed, set to advance on a mouse click.

21. Apply the **Shape Circle** transition (or something comparable) to the remaining slides, at slow speed, set to advance on a mouse click.

22. Check the spelling in the presentation and correct any errors.

23. Preview the presentation in Slide Show View, clicking the screen to advance through the slides. At the end of the presentation, return to Normal View.

24. Save the changes and close **Falls1**. Leave your presentation program open to use in the next project.

PROJECT U3-2

1. Open **Project2a** and save it as **Falls2**.

2. Make **Slide 2** current and display the slide master. Insert the JPEG formatted graphics file **Project2b** on to the slide master.

3. Resize the image to **10.0** inches wide by **7.5** inches high, so it fills the slide, and then send it to the back so it displays behind other content.

4. Create a title master slide. For example, click the **Insert New Title Master** button on the Slide Master View toolbar.

5. Delete the background image from the title master, and then close Master View.

6. Make **Slide 1** current. Insert the animated GIF file **Project2c** on to the slide. Resize it to **2.0** inches high (the width should adjust automatically) and position it under the subtitle, centered horizontally on the slide.

7. Change the color of the background on Slide 1 to a custom color. Set the RGB values as follows: Red: **150**, Green: **195**, and Blue **250**, and apply the custom color to Slide 1 only.

8. Insert the **Project2d** sound file on Slide 1, set to play automatically.

9. Edit the sound object to hide the icon during the slide show.

10. Insert the **Project2d** sound file on Slide 6, set to play automatically. Edit the sound object to hide the icon during the slide show and to loop the sound until stopped.

11. Change the font of the title text to **54** point **Tahoma**.

12. Apply the **Fade in All** animation scheme (or something comparable) to all slides.

13. Create custom timings using the Rehearse timings feature. Allow time to read all text on each slide. Save the timings.

14. Preview the presentation in Slide Show View, using the customized timings. At the end of the show, return to Normal View.

15. Package the presentation on a CD, naming the CD **Niagara Falls** and including the viewer program so it will automatically play when the CD is inserted in a CD drive.

16. Set up the presentation for a live delivery, without the timings or animations. (If the sound icon displays during the presentation after you set the slide show options, drag it into the lower-left corner of the slide so it is out of the way.)

17. Practice delivering the presentation as if you are in front of a live audience. Use the Pen tool to highlight the height of the falls. At the end of the presentation, save the annotations.

18. Save and close **Falls2**. Keep your presentation program open to use in the next project.

PROJECT U3-3

1. Open **Project3** from the data files and save it as **Falls3**.

2. Make **Slide 5** current and then insert a new slide using a layout with a placeholder for a title and a table. Key the title **Waterfall Comparison**.

3. Insert a table with three columns and four rows.

4. Key the following data in the table:

Name	Location	Height (in feet)
Angel Falls	Venezuela	3,212
Victoria Falls	Zambia	350
Horseshoe Falls	Canada	167

5. Center the text in the first row, and make it bold.

6. Right-align the numbers in the third column.

7. Apply a solid-line, 3-point, black border around the outside of the table.

8. Apply a dotted-line, 3-point, black border between the rows and columns.

9. Apply a light gray fill color to all cells in the table.

10. Insert a new slide using a title and chart layout. Key the title **Niagara is Small!**

11. Insert a chart and replace the data in the datasheet with the following, deleting all sample data that is not replaced:

	Height
Angel Falls	3212
Victoria Falls	350
Horseshoe Falls	167

12. Change the chart type to **Clustered Column with 3D Effect** (or something comparable).

13. Edit the Chart Options to add the title **Feet** to the Y axis.

14. Format the chart area with a light gray fill.

15. Make **Slide 8** current and add the following bulleted item to the end of the list:
    http://www.world-waterfalls.com.

16. Select **Slides 6** and **7** and apply a transition so the slides advance on a mouse click, or automatically after 15 seconds.

17. Preview the presentation in Slide Show View.

18. Create handouts for the presentation with 3 slides per page, in portrait orientation. Add a header with today's date fixed, and a footer with your name and page numbers on all handout pages.

19. Print the handouts in color.

20. Publish the entire presentation on the Web, using the default options, and preview the presentation in your browser. Use the navigation controls to browse through the presentation, and test some of the links on the last slide. Close your browser when you are finished.

21. Save **Falls3** and close it. Close your presentation program.

SIMULATION

The owner of the Lighthouse View Inn, a bed and breakfast located on the coast of Maine, is planning a marketing campaign to attract a wider range of clients. You believe that a central part of the campaign should be developing slide presentations that can be delivered live to travel agents, set up as a self-running presentation for either travel agents or travelers at conventions, trade shows, and other locations, and published on the inn's Web site. In the following exercises you will play different roles to develop the presentations. You will research travel and the state of Maine, outline and plan the presentations, and then create presentations.

Before beginning your presentation program, read through each task completely. Take time to plan what you will need to accomplish the job, and how you will do it. Working alone or with a partner, review the steps and then create a schedule for completing the job. Set up a timeline with appropriate milestones. Establish criteria that you believe should be met for each stage of the project, and create a rubric that you can use to gauge your accomplishments.

JOB U3-1

Lighthouse View Inn has hired you to conduct market research to determine what will bring clients to the inn.

The first step in creating a successful presentation for your client is to focus on the message you want to convey. Your goal is to convince travel agents to direct clients to Lighthouse View Inn, or to convince travelers themselves to come to the inn. Therefore, you must emphasize the positive aspects of the area and of the inn in a way that makes a Maine vacation look fun and appealing.

Once you define your goals, you should start gathering the information you will need. Use the Internet or travel books and magazines to look up interesting travel facts about Maine. (You may want to gather pictures that you can use as well, but remember that you must have permission to use someone else's work.) Record the data on paper, in a word processing document, or in a spreadsheet. Remember to record all source information, including Web site addresses. If you create a computer file, save it as **Job1_Info**, and include your name and today's date at the top of the file.

As you work, try to organize the information into the following categories: Information About Travel and Bed and Breakfasts, General Information About Maine, and Activities in Maine. You may use other categories and subcategories as well, and even format the categories using heading styles.

A good place to start your research is http://www.visitmaine.com. Other useful Web sites include http://bandb.about.com, http://www.meliving.com, and http://www.visitingnewengland.com. You may find other useful sites as well. Following are some questions you should try to answer:

Why do people like to stay in a bed and breakfast?

What's the difference between a bed and breakfast and a hotel?

What is the average number of vacation days around the world each year?

How large is Maine?

What is the weather like in each of the four seasons?

How many miles of coastline are there in Maine?

How many lakes, ponds, and other freshwater beaches are there in Maine?

Are there any national parks in Maine?

How many state parks are there in Maine?

What types of activities can people participate in during each of the four seasons?

Ask a classmate to review the research and offer suggestions about additional topics you might want to include. When you have completed your research, save and print all files.

JOB U3-2

Now that the research has been completed, a content developer needs to mold this information into an appealing presentation.

You begin by planning an outline for the presentation. Draw up the outline on paper, or in a word processing file. Save the word processing file as **Job2_Outline**. Include your name and today's date at the top of the file.

To organize the outline, refer to the **Job1_Info** document you created in Job 1. Interpret and rewrite the material for your presentation. Include content for each slide you want in the presentation, including the title slide. For example, key the presentation title text **Lighthouse View Inn**, and the subtitle text, **Your Home Away from Home**. Assign a main heading style to content you want on all title slides, such as the categories that can be sections in the presentation, and possibly even custom shows. Assign the next subheading style to the text you want to use for titles on the slides in each section, and the use regular text for the bulleted items on each slide. If necessary, do more research to fill in gaps. A sample outline is shown in Figure UR3-1.

FIGURE UR3-1
A sample outline

Title: Lighthouse View Inn
Your Home Away from Home
Title: Maine: The Pine Tree State

Slide: Fast Facts
Area: 33,215 square miles
Coastline: 5,500 miles
542,629 acres of state and national parks
6,000 lakes and ponds
32,000 miles of rivers and streams
Nearly 90% of all American lobsters are caught in Maine

Slide: Maine's Appeal
Magnificent coastline
Acadia National Park
Baxter State Park
Fresh, outdoor lifestyle
Quaint towns
Outlet shopping
Fine dining
A four season destination

Slide: Spring
Cool weather and blue skies
No crowds.

Slide: Summer
Warm days and cool nights
There are not enough hours in the day

Slide: Autumn
Autumn shines with foliage
Catch a glimpse of a moose while picnicking in a park

Slide: Winter
Winter glistens with bright sunshine reflecting off snow.
Play outside, or sit around a warm fire with friends.

Title: Activities in Maine

Slide: Outdoor Recreation
Hiking
Biking
Downhill skiing
X-Country skiing
Snowshoeing
Snowmobiling
Ice climbing
Kayaking
Canoeing
River rafting
Fishing
Hunting
Sailing

Slide: Shopping
Outlet towns for bargains
Quaint local shops
Specialty stores and boutiques

Slide: Dining
Fresh fish
Local produce
Elegant restaurants
Country Inns
Seafood Shanties
Lobster, lobster, and more lobster!

Title: Lighthouse View Inn

Slide: Why a B & B?
Personal service
Friendly guests
High-quality food
Quaint accommodations

Slide: About Lighthouse View Inn
A fully-restored antique home
Ten guestrooms
Baths and showers in each room
Restaurant on the premises

Slide: Lighthouse View Inn Amenities
Four season operation
Magnificent ocean views
Easy access to all Maine has to offer
Reasonable rates

Slide: Join Us
For information, contact us at:
56778 Ocean Drive
Wells, ME 04090
(207) 555-5555

As you work, think about graphics such as pictures, tables, or charts that you could use to reinforce your content. Also consider if you want to include sound or movies. Add notations in the outline for the type of content you want to include. If you locate and save pictures, you should save the graphics files. Name the first one **Job2_Pic1**, and then name each additional picture using the next consecutive number. Insert them in the outline in the appropriate location, if you want. Remember to record the source information. When you complete the outline, ask a classmate to review it and offer suggestions and then make improvements as necessary. When you are finished, save and print the outline file.

JOB U3-3

As the marketing assistant, use the outline to create a presentation that you can deliver live to travel agents. (If you did not complete the outline in JobU3-2, you can use the outline document **Job3a**.)

You may start your presentation program, create a new file, and then key the text. (Some programs let you export an outline from a word processing document to your presentation program to create a presentation. For example, open **Job3a** in Word, click File on the menu bar, click Send To, and then click Microsoft Office PowerPoint. This may save you time keying text, but you may have to edit and reformat some of the content.) Save the presentation file as **Job3_Pres1**.

Apply a design template such as **Leaves**, with a color scheme that has a light background, such as white, or gray. Apply slide transitions and animations if you want. Use the information in your **Job1_Info** file to create speaker notes to use during a live presentation For example, you may want to key information about beaches or about Acadia National Park. Check the spelling, and proofread all slides. Correct all errors.

Enhance the presentation using graphics, movies, and sound. Insert the graphics file **Job3b** on all title slides in the lower-left corner. This is a version of the graphics logo you created in the Unit Review of Unit 1. Search for and insert appropriate clip art or animated GIF files on the title slides used for each section, and on other slides, if you want. If necessary, use the graphics file **Job3c**, and the animated GIF files **Job3d** and **Job3e**. Insert pictures on other slides. If you do not have any pictures, use the files **Job3f** and **Job3g**. Insert an appropriate sound clip that you locate, or use **Job3h**.

Create at least two custom shows. For example, create a custom show named **Maine** using slides about Maine, and one named **Inn** about Lighthouse View Inn. Insert hyperlinks in the presentation to link to each custom show.

Preview the presentation in Slide Show View, and practice delivering it live. Rehearse your narration, and practice advancing the slides. Add notes if you think of things you might want to say, and prepare for questions the audience might have. After practicing, ask a classmate to listen to you and make suggestions for how you could improve. Practice some more. Create handouts to give to the audience. Include a header with today's date fixed, and a footer with your name and the page number. Print the handouts in color. Deliver the presentation to your class.

Package the presentation and copy it to a CD. Name the CD **LVI**, and include the viewer program. (If it is not possible for you to write to a CD, then copy the files to a folder.) Test the CD. To prepare a self-running version of the presentation for use at conventions or shows, save the **Job3_Pres1** file as **Job3_Pres2**. Insert action buttons so the viewer can navigate through the presentation, but also set slide timings. Set slide show options to run the presentation at a kiosk, but choose to display only the **Maine** custom show. Test the presentation in Slide Show View.

Save another version of the file as **Job3_Pres3**. This one will be for the Inn's Web site. Set slide show options to play all slides in the show for a live audience. Remove the hyperlinks to the custom shows. Publish the file as a Web page. Change the page title to **Visit Lighthouse View Inn**. Do not include the slide navigation controls. Preview the published file in your Web browser. Use the action buttons to navigate through the presentation, and then close your browser.

Save the **Job3_Pres3** file and close it. Close your presentation program.

DESKTOP PUBLISHING

Unit 4

Estimated Time for Unit: 8.5 hours

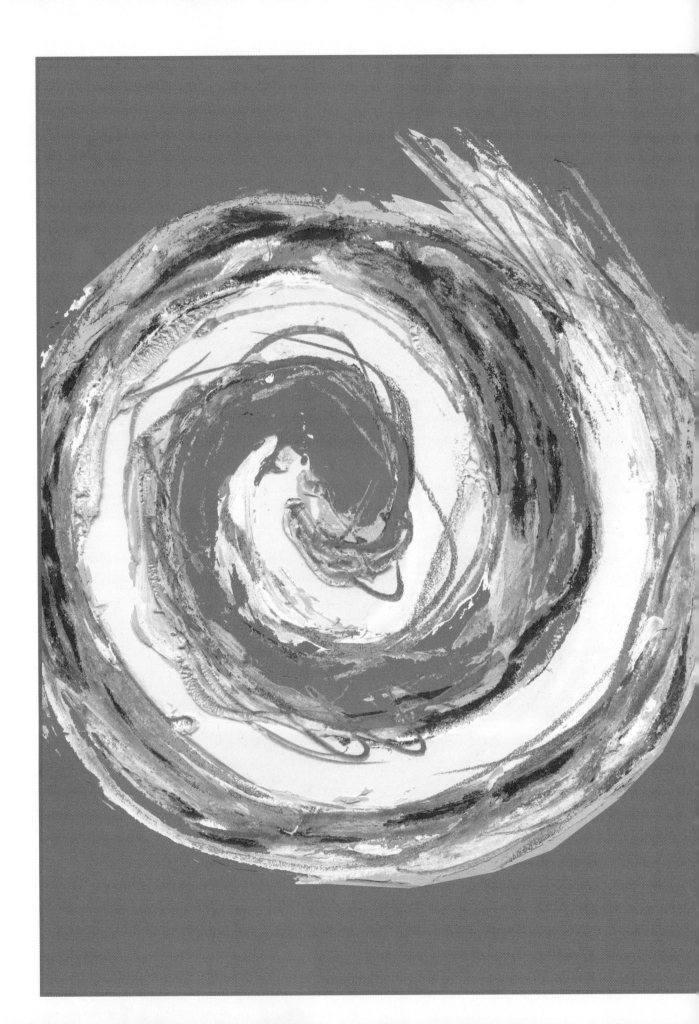

WORKING WITH DOCUMENTS

OBJECTIVES

Upon completion of this lesson, you should be able to:

- Plan a publication.
- Create a new file.
- Save, close, and reopen a document.
- Change the document view.
- Add and edit text.
- Use Undo and Redo.
- Insert a picture.
- Check spelling.
- Preview and print a document.

Estimated Time: 1.5 hours

VOCABULARY

Binding

Boundaries

Double-sided printing

Frame

Galleys

Mock-up

Page navigation buttons

Page size

Paper stock

Proofreader's marks

Publication type

Scratch area

Sheet size

Single-sided printing

Text box

Toggles

Desktop publishing is used to design and produce printed documents such as business cards, brochures, booklets, nametags, product packaging, posters, banners, calendars, invitations, and newsletters. Although all desktop publishing programs have features you can use to arrange and format text and graphics, the programs differ in their level of sophistication. For example, programs designed for professional use, such as Microsoft Publisher or Adobe InDesign, include features used to prepare a document for commercial printing, while home-use programs, such as Microsoft Greetings or Microsoft Works, assume you will print your documents on a desktop printer. Some word processing programs also offer low-level desktop publishing features for simple documents such as letters, memos, and reports. In this book, you will learn how to use a full-featured desktop publishing program to design, create, and publish professional-level documents.

No matter which program you use, there are six basic steps to producing a desktop publishing document:

1. Plan the document.

2. Select a design.

3. Insert text.

4. Insert graphics.

5. Prepare the document for publication.

6. Print the document.

In this lesson, you will learn to use these steps to create a document quickly and easily. Later lessons cover these steps in greater detail.

Plan a Publication

The first phase of desktop publishing is to plan the basic format for your document. You must make decisions about the physical aspects of the document, such as the page size, the paper stock, color scheme, single-sided or double-sided printing, binding options, and the number of copies. The *page size* is the dimensions of the finished document page. *Paper stock* refers to the specifications for the sheets of paper, such as the size, type, weight, and opacity. *Single-sided printing* means to print on one side of a sheet of paper, and *double-sided printing* means to print on both sides of the paper. *Binding* is the method used to attach or secure pages or sections of a book or booklet, usually using stitching, staples, wire, plastic, tape, or glue.

As you think about these issues, you should keep your budget in mind. The amount of money you have available significantly affects the type of document you can produce. For example, color printing costs more than black and white, and paper stocks range widely in price.

You should also consider the program you are using. Make sure it supports all the features you want to include and that it is compatible with other programs and hardware devices you may need to use. For example, can you use your desktop publishing program to create graphics, or will you need to import graphics from another source, such as a graphics program, a scanner, or a digital camera? Can you easily enter as much text as you need, or will you need to copy the text from a word processing program?

> **Hot Tip**
>
> Looking at existing documents for ideas can be helpful in the planning process. You can find many types of documents in your home, classroom, and library, including newsletters, flyers, banners, and brochures.

You also need to make decisions about the content of the document: Who will be reading it? What is its goal? There are many different reasons for creating a publication. Marketing publications, such as direct mail postcards, are designed to sell a product, whereas informational publications, such as corporate newsletters, are designed to educate and inform. Invitations, playbills, and product packaging have very different purposes, and therefore require different approaches. The content of a brochure to be distributed at a conference for neurosurgeons will certainly differ from the content of a flyer that is part of a mass mailing to the customers of a retail store.

To ensure the success of your publication, you should create a *mock-up*, which is a rough draft or sample of the publication. Like a storyboard for an animation or video, a mock-up for a publication represents the finished product, without including fine details. It lets you map out and plan the overall concept of the publication. Creating a mock-up also lets you experiment with page size, *sheet size*—which is the dimensions of the paper—and orientation as well as positioning text and graphics. Recall that orientation is the position of the paper in relation to the printed content. Portrait orientation—sometimes called tall—prints the content across the short side of the page, while landscape orientation—sometimes called wide—prints the content along the long side of the page.

>
> **Note**
>
> It is important to note that in desktop publishing, page size and sheet size are not the same thing. Page size is the dimensions of the finished document page, whereas sheet size—which is sometimes called paper size—is the size of the paper on which the document is printed.

Although you may be able to use your desktop publishing program to preview sample documents, the most effective method for creating a mock-up is to actually take a piece of paper the same size and shape that you envision for the finished product, and then mark it with the location of text and graphics. For example, you can create a mock-up of a tri-fold brochure by folding a standard 8.5-inch by 11-inch sheet of paper into thirds. Or you can create a mock-up of a postcard mailer by using a ruler to draw a rectangle the size of the postcard on a sheet of paper, and then using a pencil to indicate the placement of an address label, text, and graphics.

S TEP-BY-STEP 18.1

1. Hold a blank sheet of 8.5-inch by 11-inch paper with the 8.5-inch sides at the top and bottom. This is portrait orientation. You are going to make a mock-up of a postcard mailer. The page size of the mailer is approximately 8.5 inches wide by 5.5 inches high, which is about half the sheet size. The postcard has two pages—the front and the back.

2. Fold the top edge of the sheet down to meet the bottom edge, and then unfold the page. If you plan to print on 8.5-inch by 11-inch paper, you can fit two postcards on a sheet—one above the fold and one below the fold.

STEP-BY-STEP 18.1 Continued

3. Using a ruler, draw 0.5-inch margins on all sides of the rectangle above the fold, and then mark the locations where you would position the information on the front, or page 1. For example, include a headline, informational text, company contact information, a company logo, and a picture. Refer to Figure 18-1.

FIGURE 18-1
Mock-up of a postcard mailer

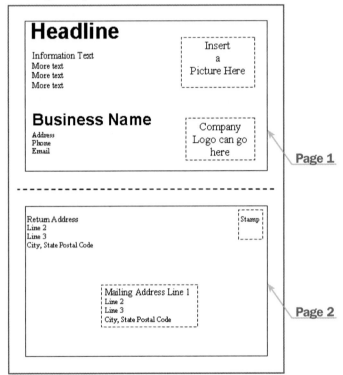

4. Draw the same margins below the fold, and then mark the locations of the information for the back, or page 2, such as the mailing address, return address, and stamp.

5. Keep this sheet of paper as a reference for creating a postcard mailer in the rest of this lesson.

Create a New File

To create a new desktop publishing file, use the New command on the File menu, or click the New button on the main or standard toolbar. There are many variations or options for creating a new publication, depending on the program you are using. Some programs automatically create a blank file using the default settings for options, such as page size and orientation, but most programs display a dialog box where you can select the *publication type*—which is the kind of document you want to create, such as a newsletter or a calendar—and then select the publication design, or template, or where you can customize the settings. Recall that a template is a file used as a model for creating other files. In a desktop publishing program, templates usually contain page layout and text formatting settings as well as objects such as sample text and graphics.

Using a template is the fastest and easiest way to create a professional-looking document, because it already has a coordinated font scheme, color scheme, and layout. All you have to do is replace the sample text and graphics. You can select options to customize the individual settings at any time.

Depending on your program, the available publications are listed in a New dialog box, a Templates dialog box, or New Publication task pane, similar to the one in Figure 18-2. When you select a publication type, most programs list the designs or templates available for that type, often sorted into categories. In some programs, actual thumbnail-sized previews display in the dialog box or in a window called a Design Gallery. Click the design or template you want to use to create the new document, and then, if necessary, click a button such as Open or Create Publication.

FIGURE 18-2
Publication types listed in a task pane

Publication types

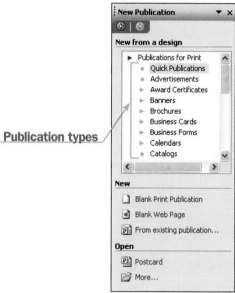

Some desktop publishing programs prompt you to enter personal information such as your name, a business name, address, and phone number when you create a document based on a template. The program automatically enters the data in a new publication so that you do not have to retype the information each time you create a document. You may have supplied some of this information when you installed the program, or you can key it in the appropriate dialog box. You can edit the information at any time.

New files usually have a generic name such as Publication or Untitled and are numbered consecutively. So, the first file you create is Publication1; the second is Publication2; and so on. You customize the name when you save the file. Most programs let you have more than one file open at a time, although only one can be active.

STEP-BY-STEP 18.2

1. Launch your desktop publishing program. A dialog box or task pane for creating new documents displays. It may be called the New dialog box, Templates dialog box, or New Publication task pane. If the program is already open, or the dialog box is not open, click **File** on the Menu bar, and then click **New**. If you are using Adobe InDesign, click **New from Template** on the Welcome screen. If necessary, click **Help** on the Menu bar and then click **Welcome Screen** to display the Welcome screen.

> **Note**
>
> If you are using Adobe InDesign, you use the Adobe Bridge program to locate and display available templates. Adobe Bridge is a program that comes with Adobe Creative Suite and Adobe Production Studio that you use to organize, browse, and locate assets, including template files.

2. Select **Publications for Print** if necessary, and then select a **Postcards** publication type. A postcard is usually a simple, two-page document similar to the mock-up you created in the previous exercise. One page is set up for entering text and graphics and the other page is set up for entering address information and postage. Once you select a publication type, the available designs display on the screen, as shown in Figure 18-3.

FIGURE 18-3
Sample designs for postcard mailers

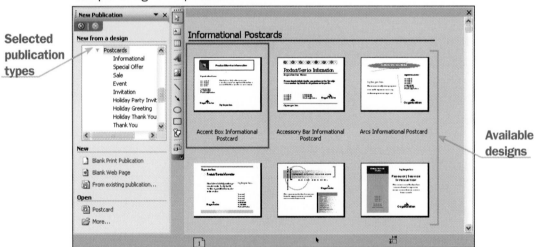

3. Scroll through the list of designs to see what is available, and then click a simple design such as the **Level Informational Postcard** design in Microsoft Publisher. If necessary, click the **Open** or **Create Publication** button to create the document. If you are using InDesign and there is no simple postcard design available, locate and open **Step18-2** in the Data files for this lesson.

> **Note**
>
> If you cannot find postcards in the list of publications, your program probably uses a different name, such as Mailers, or lists them as a category under Cards. Also, don't worry if your screen looks different from the one in the illustration. You may be using a program that lists the publications and designs in a different format, such as in a dialog box or without previews.

STEP-BY-STEP 18.2 Continued

4. If prompted, cancel the dialog box that asks you to enter personal information. Your program creates and displays the publication on screen with default sample information. Depending on your program and the publication type, options for changing the layout and content may display as well.

> **Note** ☑
>
> If your program displays a dialog box listing font substitutions necessary for the template you selected, you may choose another font or accept the default substitution. You will learn more about fonts in Lesson 19.

5. If available, select the option to change the size of the document from Quarter-page (4.25 inches x 5.5 inches) to Half-page (5.5 inches x 8.5 inches). The document should look similar to Figure 18-4. Leave the publication open to use in the next exercise.

FIGURE 18-4
Sample page of postcard document

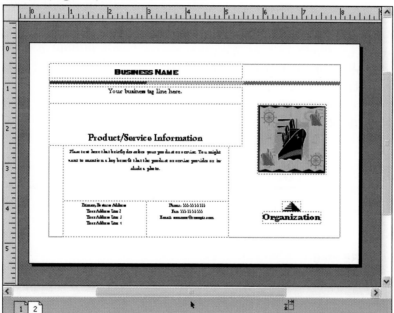

Save, Close, and Reopen a Document

As with other programs, the first time you save a publication, use the Save As command on the File menu to give it a name and select a storage location. You should use filenames that help identify the file contents, and, of course, you must follow standard filename rules. That means you cannot use the following characters: /, \, >, <, *, ?, ", !, :, ;. By default, most programs save a new publication file in the My Documents folder on your local hard disk, or in the same folder where you most recently saved a file. However, you can select a different location. Once you have saved a file for the first time, you can use the Save command or the Save button on the Standard toolbar to save changes. You can use the Save As command to save the file with a new name or in a new location. The original file will remain unchanged.

When you have finished using a publication file, you should close it. You can close a file by using the Close command on the File menu. Some programs remain open after you close a file so you can continue working, while others close unless there are other publication files still open.

If you have not saved the file before selecting the Close command, the program displays a dialog box asking if you want to save. Click the Yes button to save the changes and close the file. Click the No button to close the file without saving the changes. Click the Cancel button to close the dialog box and continue working in the file. If you close the file without saving, all changes that you made since the last time you saved will be lost.

To work again with a file you have already closed, you must open it in your desktop publishing program. You can use the Open button on the main or Standard toolbar or the Open command from the File menu to display the Open dialog box. In some programs you can select the command from a task pane or Welcome screen. You can use the Open dialog box to locate and select the file you want to open.

Important

Save your files frequently! In the event of a mechanical problem or a power failure, all data you have entered or edited since the last time you saved will be lost. Saving is the only way to ensure that your work is safe.

Hot Tip

You can close the program and all open files at the same time if you are finished using the program. Use the Exit command on the File menu. If you haven't saved an open file, the program will prompt you to save before closing.

S TEP-BY-STEP 18.3

1. Click **File** on the Menu bar, and then click **Save As**. The Save As dialog box displays, as shown in Figure 18-5.

FIGURE 18-5
Save As dialog box

STEP-BY-STEP 18.3 Continued

2. In the *File name* text box, with the default name already selected, key **Postcard**. This will be the name of the new file.

3. From the *Save in* drop-down list, select the location where you want to store the file.

4. Click **Save** in the dialog box. The file is saved with the new name in the selected storage location.

5. Click **File** on the Menu bar, and then click **Close**. The **Postcard** file closes.

6. Click **File** on the Menu bar, and then click **Open**. The Open a File or Open Publication dialog box displays, as shown in Figure 18-6. (Don't worry if your Open dialog box does not look exactly the same as the one in the figure.)

FIGURE 18-6
Open Publication dialog box

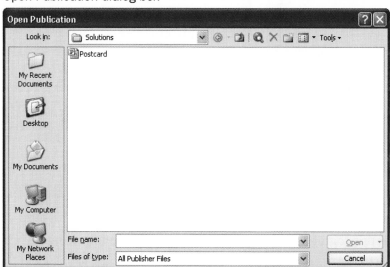

7. If the **Postcard** file is not listed in the dialog box, click the *Look in* list drop-down arrow and then select the location where the file is stored.

8. In the list of files, click **Postcard**.

9. Click the **Open** button in the dialog box. The file opens in the program window. Leave the **Postcard** file open to use in the next exercise.

> ### Hot Tip
>
> Some programs also have a command for opening recently used files. The most recently used files may be listed at the bottom of the File menu, so you can simply click the File menu and then click the name of the file you want to open. Or, recently used files may be listed on a submenu. Click the File menu, click a command such as Open Recent or Recent Publications to display the submenu, and then click the name of the file you want to open.

Change the Document View

When a publication file is open, it may display in a program window similar to Figure 18-7. The appearance of the screen depends on the program you are using as well as on default options set for your computer. However, most desktop publishing programs have a number of standard screen elements in common, such as a document window, Menu bar, toolbars, scroll bars, rulers, and panels or task panes where you can select options.

FIGURE 18-7
Typical desktop publishing window

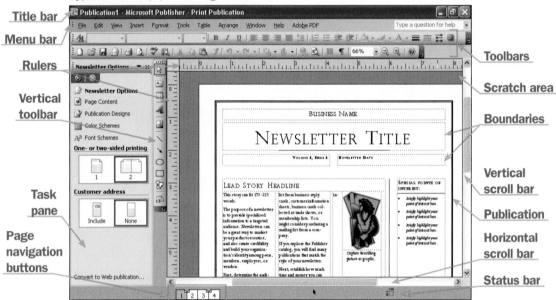

In addition, your program probably has some or all of the following:

- Nonprinting gridlines, guides, and *boundaries*—lines that mark the borders of text boxes and other objects—that help you align objects on a page;

- *Page navigation buttons*, which are icons you can click to shift the display to show a different page;

- A *scratch area*, or pasteboard, which is a portion of the screen outside the document page where you can temporarily store text and graphics.

Even if the element names are not the same in all programs, you should find that you have functions that are similar.

View Options

While you are working in your desktop publishing program, you may want to change the view to get a different look at your publication. The view is the way your file is displayed onscreen. Most programs let you display your file in different view modes such as normal or standard, whole page or two-page spread, or preview. You can also choose to show or hide specific elements such as the rulers, the task pane, the guides, and the toolbars.

Most of the commands you use to change the view are located on the View menu. Other commands may be on a different menu, such as the Arrange menu or the Window menu, or available as buttons on a toolbar. Notice that many commands controlling the way a program is displayed are *toggles*, which means they are either on or off. Each time you select the command, it switches from on to off, or off to on. When a command is on, it usually has a check mark beside it on the menu.

S TEP-BY-STEP 18.4

1. Click the command to toggle the rulers. For example, in Publisher, click **View** on the Menu bar and then click **Rulers**. If the rulers were not displayed before, this command toggles them on. If they were displayed, the command toggles them off.

2. Choose the command that shows or hides the Formatting toolbar, or a different toolbar. For example, in Microsoft Publisher click **View** on the Menu bar, point to **Toolbars**, and then click **Formatting** on the submenu. This toggles the Formatting toolbar on or off. In Adobe InDesign click **Window** on the Menu bar, and then click **Tools** to toggle the toolbox on or off.

3. Repeat steps 1 and 2 until the rulers and the Formatting toolbar (or toolbox) display. In other words, toggle the rulers and toolbar on.

4. Use the page navigation feature in your program to display page 2 of the postcard. For example, in Publisher, click the **Page 2** icon on the Status bar; in InDesign, click the **Next Page** arrow in the Status bar. (If page 2 is already displayed, display page 1.) Page 2 in the Postcard document is the reverse side of the mailer, as shown in Figure 18-8. Use the same feature to switch back to page 1. In some programs, you can press the **Page Up** or **Page Down** key to change pages.

FIGURE 18-8
Page 2 of the postcard mailer

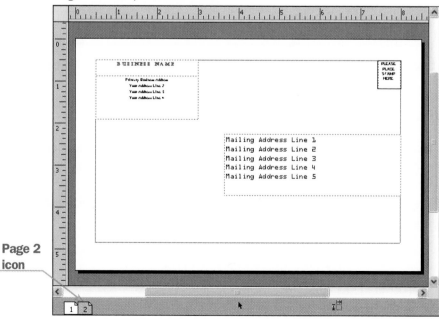

Page 2 icon

STEP-BY-STEP 18.4 Continued

5. If your program has a task pane or panel displayed, select the command to close it. For example, click **View** on the Menu bar, and then click **Task Pane**. In InDesign, click **Window** and then click **Pages** to close the Pages panel.

6. Practice toggling other elements on and off to change the view, including options that may be on different menus. For example, show and hide special characters or boundaries and guides. Leave the default features such as the toolbars and rulers displayed onscreen when you are finished. Leave **Postcard** open to use in the next exercise.

> **Did You Know?**
>
> Most panels and task panes have close buttons in the upper-right corner. Click the button to close the task pane or panel. They may also have drop-down arrows you can click to display option menus.

Change the Zoom

When you need to get a closer look at a publication, zoom in. Recall that zooming increases or decreases the magnification of the file on your screen by a percentage of its original size. For example, zoom in to 200% to display the file at twice its actual size, or zoom out to 50% to display it at half its actual size. Zooming in gives you a closer look and makes it easier to see and work with a particular area, whereas zooming out makes the publication look smaller and lets you get an overall look at the composition.

You can use commands on the View menu such as Zoom or Zoom To to select a magnification percentage from a list. Some programs have a Zoom box on a toolbar or the Status bar in which you may key a specific percentage, or select a magnification from a drop-down list. You can also simply click the Zoom In tool to zoom in or the Zoom Out tool to zoom out.

STEP-BY-STEP 18.5

1. In the **Postcard** file, change the magnification to **200%**. The magnification increases so you get a closer look at the publication.

2. Zoom out to **150%**. The magnification decreases.

3. Adjust the zoom to **75%**. For example, click the **Zoom** box, key **75**, and press **Enter**. The magnification is adjusted to 75% of the document's actual size. It should look similar to Figure 18-9. (The actual appearance depends upon your screen size and resolution. You may have to select different zoom percentages to make your screen look the same as in the Figure.) Leave **Postcard** open to use in the next exercise.

STEP-BY-STEP 18.5 Continued

FIGURE 18-9
File displayed at 75% of its actual size

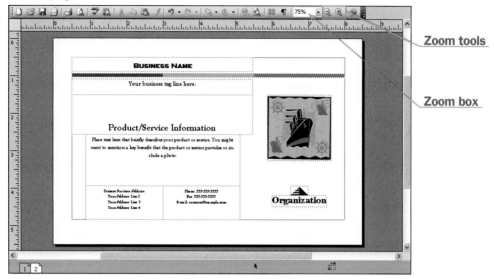

Zoom tools

Zoom box

Add and Edit Text

Text in a desktop publishing file is inserted in a *text box* or *frame*. A text box or frame is an object you can easily move and resize, which makes it easy to position and format the text in the publication. (Some programs have an additional feature called a text block, which is also used for holding text.) When you create a publication file based on a design or template, your program automatically inserts text boxes to hold the contact information and sample text. You replace the sample text to customize the publication. You can also enter new text and edit existing text at any time, as well as insert new text boxes. You learn more about working with text in Lesson 19.

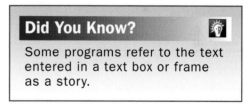

Did You Know?

Some programs refer to the text entered in a text box or frame as a story.

Enter Text

In some programs, such as Microsoft Publisher, you simply click the mouse pointer in the text box to position the insertion point so you can enter and edit text. In other programs, such as Adobe InDesign, you first select the Text Tool in the toolbox, and then click in the text box. When the insertion point is inside the text box, sizing handles and/or a border may display, as

Note

In some programs, if a text box contains boilerplate or sample text, when you click the text, it is automatically selected.

shown in Figure 18-10. In some programs, a rotation handle displays as well. To select the text box, click its boundaries with the mouse pointer, or click the Selection Tool in the toolbox and then click the boundaries.

FIGURE 18-10
Selected text box

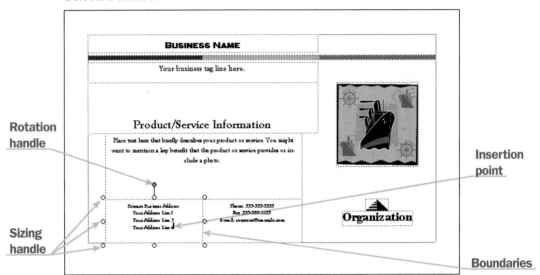

In most desktop publishing programs, you use the same standard text entry, editing, and selection commands that you use in other programs to move the insertion point within a text box or frame and to make changes to the text. For example, to select text, simply drag the mouse across it, or, with the keyboard, position the insertion point at the beginning of the selected text, press and hold Shift, and then press arrow keys to define the selection. To insert new text, simply position the insertion point and begin keying. Table 18-1 describes some of the common keystrokes used to work with text.

> **Hot Tip**
>
> To select more than one text box at a time, select the first one, then press and hold Shift and select another one.

TABLE 18-1
Common text-editing keystrokes

PRESS THIS KEY	TO DO THIS
Up arrow	To move insertion point up one line.
Down arrow	To move insertion point down one line.
Left arrow	To move insertion point one character to the left.
Right arrow	To move insertion point one character to the right.
Backspace	To delete the character to the left of the insertion point.
Delete	To delete the character to the right of the insertion point.
Enter	To start a new paragraph.

As you type in a text box, the text is automatically formatted according to the settings determined by the publication type and design. For example, the text may automatically be centered within the text box, or aligned to the right or left. Usually, the text is automatically sized to fit within the text box. Also, you do not have to press Enter to start a new line, because the text wraps within the text box. When text wraps, it automatically starts a new line when the current line is full. If automatic hyphenation is on, words that are split from one line to the next are automatically hyphenated. Although you can change the formatting, in most cases, the default design formatting is appropriate for the publication type and design you have selected.

S TEP-BY-STEP 18.6

1. Replace sample information with the specific company information given below. (You may have to switch pages to enter all the information, and some information may be entered more than once.)

a. Locate and select sample text for the company name (such as *Business Name* or *Organization*) and zoom in, if necessary, to get a better view. Then, key **Backstage Dance Studio**.

b. Locate and select sample text for the company address and key the following street address:
622A Chestnut Street
Cleveland Heights, OH 44118

> **Note**
>
> Some programs use sample text designed to help you decide where to enter replacement text, while other programs may use gibberish or foreign language text as placeholders.

c. If there are extra address lines, delete them.

d. Locate and select sample text for other contact information and key the following replacement text:
Phone: 216-555-5555
Fax: 216-555-5558
Email: jcrane@mail.com

e. If you see sample text for a company tag line or slogan, select it and key **Exceptional Training in All Types of Dance**.

2. Locate the sample headline (such as *Product/Service Information*) in the publication and select the sample text.

> **Hot Tip**
>
> To resize a text box, select it and then drag a sizing handle. To delete a text box, select it and then press Delete.

3. Key **New Class Offerings**. The new text replaces the selected text.

4. Select the sample text in the text box below the headline, or wherever there is a text box for entering information, and key the following text. (Remember, you do not have to press Enter to begin a new line.)
Backstage Dance Studio is pleased to announce a full range of ballroom dance classes beginning January 8th. Each class will meet twice a week for six weeks. Separate sessions will be available for beginners, intermediate dancers, and advanced students. Contact us for a complete schedule, including class times and fees.

STEP-BY-STEP 18.6 Continued

5. Switch to page 2. In some programs, the organization name and address were automatically replaced on this page of the postcard when you changed this information on the previous page. Locate and select the sample mailing address for the postcard and replace it with your name and address.

6. Replace any other sample text in the document (check both pages of the postcard). For example, select the sample Logo text *Organization* (on page 1), and replace it with the text **Backstage Dance**. In most programs, the text is automatically resized to fit within the text box. If it is not resized, you can resize the text box by selecting it and dragging a sizing handle.

   Now, go back and edit some existing text.

7. Click the text *New Class Offerings* with the Pointer or Text Tool. The insertion point appears where you clicked.

8. Select the text *Class Offerings* and replace it with the text **for Winter**. The document should look similar to the one in Figure 18-11.

FIGURE 18-11
Postcard with replacement text

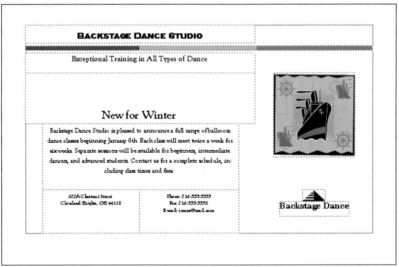

9. Save the changes to the **Postcard** file and leave it open to use in the next exercise. If your program prompts you to save the organization information, click **No**.

Use Undo and Redo

As in other types of programs, if you are unhappy with the results of a command or selection in your desktop publishing program, you can use the Undo command to reverse it. Undo lets you reverse the most recent action, or, in some programs, a series of actions. You can use the Redo command to reverse the results of an Undo action. Undo and Redo are available as commands on the Edit menu and may also be available as buttons on a toolbar. The first time you use the command, the most recent action is reversed. Repeat the command to reverse the action prior to that, and so on.

S TEP-BY-STEP 18.7

1. Double-click the word *Exceptional* to select it, and then replace it with the word *Outstanding*.

2. Select the **Undo** command from the **Edit** menu, or click the **Undo** button on the toolbar. Your program undoes the most recent action, which is the replacement of the text *Exceptional*.

3. Select the **Redo** command from the **Edit** menu, or click the **Redo** button on the toolbar. The previous action is reversed.

4. Click **Undo** again.

5. Save the changes if necessary, and leave **Postcard** open to use in the next exercise.

Insert a Picture

When you create a publication file based on a design or template, your program may automatically insert sample graphics such as shapes or clip-art images, sized and positioned to enhance the document. Though you probably want to keep the shapes that are part of the publication design, you may just as likely want to replace the sample clip art with something that represents the content of the publication. To replace the clip art, open a dialog box in which you locate and select the graphics file you want to insert instead.

In some programs, such as Microsoft Publisher, you can right-click the object you want to replace, click Change Picture on the shortcut menu, and then click one of the options to open a dialog box for inserting a picture from a variety of sources. In other programs, such as Adobe InDesign, you select the object to replace, click File on the Menu bar, and then click Place to open the Place dialog box. In either case, you then locate and select the file you want, and select the command to insert it in the publication.

S TEP-BY-STEP 18.8

1. Select the command to open the dialog box where you can locate and select the picture file you want to insert. For example, in Publisher, right-click the picture you want to replace, point to **Change Picture**, and then click **From File**. In InDesign, select the object to replace, click **File** on the Menu bar, and then click **Place**. In the Place dialog box, verify that the **Replace selected item** check box is selected.

2. Locate and select **Step18-8** in the Data files.

3. Click the command to insert the graphics file. For example, in Publisher, click Insert. In InDesign, click Open. The replacement graphic in the postcard should look similar to Figure 18-12.

FIGURE 18-12
Replacement picture in the Postcard file

4. Save the changes and leave **Postcard** open to use in the next exercise.

Check Spelling

At a minimum, most desktop publishing documents include some text, such as a caption on a poster. Other documents include a lot of text, such as an eight-page newsletter. Spelling errors can take all the credibility out of a publication, so it is very important to check the spelling before you print a document or send it to be published. You might also consider the cost of reprinting a publication if you discover an error after it has already been printed.

All desktop publishing programs include a spelling checker feature that you can use to locate and correct spelling errors. The spelling checker compares the words in the document to a built-in dictionary. If the spelling checker cannot find the word, it highlights the word. You can correct the spelling, ignore the word, or add the word to the dictionary so that it will not be marked as incorrect in the future.

Some programs also offer a feature that checks spelling as you type and automatically flags words that may be incorrect with a visual mark on the screen, such as a wavy colored underline. You can ignore the flag and continue typing, correct the spelling, or add the word to the dictionary.

> **Extra for Experts**
>
> If your program automatically inserts text stored in your personal information into a publication file, it will not mark the text as misspelled, even if it includes a proper name or an unusually spelled word. The program recognizes that these words may not be in its dictionary.

Of course, even the best spelling checker won't catch all spelling errors. *Form* and *from* are both words that are spelled correctly but they have very different meanings. Additionally, spelling checkers cannot distinguish between homophones—words that sound the same but are spelled differently and have different meanings. So, if you key the word *threw* when you mean to key *through*, the spelling checker does not identify the mistake. The only way to be certain your text is correct is to proofread it carefully.

To start a spelling checker in your desktop publishing program, click in the text box you want to check, then click the Spelling button on the toolbar, or select the check spelling command. (Your program may open the text box's text in a story editor window, which is a separate window used for editing text.) When the spelling checker identifies a word that is not in the dictionary, it displays a dialog box similar to the one in Figure 18-13. Select the correct spelling in the list and then click the Change or Replace button, or click one of the other command buttons, such as Ignore or Add to Dictionary. There may also be an option to extend the spell check to all text boxes (or stories) in the document.

FIGURE 18-13
Check Spelling dialog box

If your program has an automatic spelling checker, you may already have noticed flagged words. The program checks the spelling as you key new text and marks words that are not in the dictionary. To correct the spelling, you can delete the error and rekey the text, or you can right-click the word and select an option from the shortcut menu that displays. Usually, you can choose the same options that are available in the spelling dialog box, including selecting the correct spelling, ignoring the error, or adding the word to the dictionary.

S TEP-BY-STEP 18.9

1. Click in the headline text *New for Winter* and change the *e* in *New* to an **a**, then change the *t* in *Winter* to a **b**. Click the text box border to select the text box. If your program has an automatic spelling checker, it probably flagged the incorrectly spelled words *Naw* and *Winber*. (If it does not flag the word, the automatic spelling checker may not be active. The option for turning the automatic spelling checker off or on is usually found in a Spelling Options dialog box or it may be a toggle on a Spelling submenu.)

STEP-BY-STEP 18.9 Continued

2. If your program displays a wavy underline beneath the word *Naw*, right-click the word. A shortcut menu displays, similar to the one in Figure 18-14.

FIGURE 18-14
Spelling shortcut menu

3. Click the correctly spelled word **New** on the shortcut menu. Your program corrects the spelling.

Now use the spelling checker to locate other errors in the publication.

4. Click the **Spelling** button on the toolbar, or select the command to start the spelling checker. You may need to click the Start button in the Spelling dialog box to begin the check.

5. If you have not already corrected the word *Naw*, your program will highlight it. Select the correct word (**New**), if necessary, and click the **Change** button to replace the incorrect word.

6. The spelling checker highlights the word *Winber*. Select **Winter** in the list of suggestions and click **Change**, or key the correct spelling and click **Change**.

7. Select the option to check all text boxes or stories in the document. You may need to ignore some text that is not misspelled but is not in the spell check's dictionary, such as the e-mail address. When the check is complete, close all open dialog boxes and/or the story editor window(s).

8. Save the changes to **Postcard** and leave it open to use in the next exercise.

FIGURE 18-15
Common proofreaders' marks

INSTRUCTION	MARK IN MARGIN	MARK IN TEXT
Delete	℘	the ~~happy~~ dog
Insert	*happy*	the˰dog
Let it stand	*stet*	the happy dog
Make capital	*cap*	the dog
Make lowercase	*lc*	the Dog
Set in italics	*ital*	the dog
Set in boldface	*bf*	the dog
Transpose	*tr*	dog the
Close up space	⌒	d og
Insert a space	#	thedog
Start a paragraph	¶	"where is the dog?"˰"Over there"
Move left	[	⊏the dog
Move right	]	the⊐ dog
Align	‖	the dog the dog the dog

Historically Speaking

PROOFREADERS' MARKS

Before computers took over so many publishing tasks, authors and editors checked text on long sheets of proofs called ***galleys***. They marked the text using standard ***proofreaders' marks*** that printers and typesetters understood to specify changes in the text. Although computers have automated a good part of document production, some jobs are still best done the old-fashioned way, and that includes proofreading. For best-quality results, final proofs should still be printed, read, and marked by hand. Reading a document for errors is a vital part of creating a first-class publication.

Figure 18-15 illustrates just a few of the standard proofreaders' marks used to indicate errors and changes. One mark is made in the margin beside the text, and one mark is made in the text itself. An editor or production specialist reading the marked copy knows immediately how to correct the document. You can find a complete list of proofreaders' marks in most standard dictionaries or on the Internet.

Preview and Print a Document

The goal of creating a desktop publishing document is to see it in print. Even if you intend to have the actual publication prepared by a commercial printer, you can use your program to preview the publication onscreen the way it will look when it is printed and to quickly print a sample copy.

To preview a document before printing, you can simply change the zoom setting or use a Print Preview button or menu command if available. Programs with Print Preview usually display the entire first page, as shown in Figure 18-16. The Print Preview may also have a toolbar with buttons you can use to change pages, display multiple pages at the same time, change the zoom, change some printer settings, and print the document.

FIGURE 18-16
Postcard in Print Preview

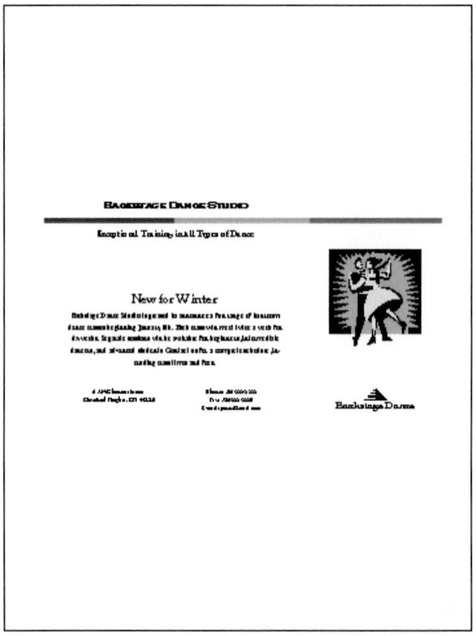

To quickly print a single copy using the default print settings, you can usually click the Print button on the toolbar. If you want to change any print settings, you must select the Print command from the File menu to open the Print dialog box. The Print dialog box, shown in Figure 18-17, lists options such as the number of copies to print, whether to use two-sided printing, and even which printer to use. The options depend on the specific printer and program you are using. In Lesson 22, you learn how to prepare a publication for printing on your desktop or network computer and for commercial printing.

FIGURE 18-17
Print dialog box

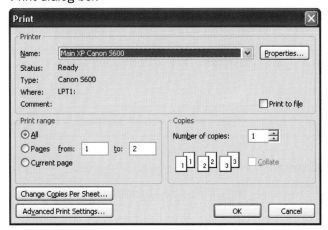

By default, most programs are set up to print a single page of a document on a single sheet of paper. If you want to see how a two-sided publication will look, you must use two-sided printing. Most desktop printers cannot print on two sides at the same time, so you print one side and then reinsert the paper into the printer and print the other side. Some printers will instruct you on how to position the paper in the paper feed to be sure the document prints correctly, or you can consult the printer manual. In some cases, you may have to experiment by feeding a sheet through and marking the top, bottom, back, and front.

If your printer supports two-sided printing, you may select that option before completing the following steps. Otherwise, follow the steps to manually print the publication on two sides. In addition, make sure your printer is correctly connected to the computer or network that it is on, and that there is paper in the paper feeder.

S TEP-BY-STEP 18.10

1. Click to preview the **Postcard** document. For example, click the **Print Preview** button on the toolbar if available, or select the command to change to print preview.

2. Display page 2—the reverse side of the postcard—by clicking the **Page Down** button on the Print Preview toolbar, pressing **Page Down** on your keyboard, or clicking the **Next Page** button on the Status bar.

3. Change back to page 1 and then close the Print Preview window if you have one open, or change the view back to **Normal**.

4. Click **File** on the Menu bar, and then click **Print**. The Print dialog box displays.

5. Choose to print only page 1 by keying **1** in a page range box, or keying **1** in both the *from* and the *to* boxes. You may also be able to choose a **Current Page** option.

6. Click the **OK** or **Print** button. The page prints. Return the page to the printer feeder, being sure to insert it correctly so that the second page prints on the blank side, top to bottom.

7. Click **File** on the Menu bar, and then click **Print**. Choose to print only page 2 of the publication.

STEP-BY-STEP 18.10 Continued

8. Click the **OK** or **Print** button. The page prints. You can cut the blank areas off the paper and compare the printed document to the mock-up you created at the beginning of this exercise.

9. Save the changes and close **Postcard**. Close your desktop publishing program.

SUMMARY

In this lesson, you learned:

■ Desktop publishing programs are used to produce printed documents.

■ Some desktop publishing programs differ in their level of sophistication. Some programs are designed for professional use and others are designed for home use.

■ It is a good idea to plan a publication before you create it using your desktop publishing program.

■ Most programs have built-in templates and designs that you can use to quickly create a professional-looking document that includes formatting, text, and graphics.

■ You can change the way a file is displayed onscreen and toggle screen elements off and on.

■ In a desktop publishing file, text is inserted in a text box or frame.

■ You can enter and edit text using standard word-processing commands.

■ You can insert pictures into a desktop publishing file.

■ Desktop publishing programs come with spelling checkers that can help you locate and correct spelling errors.

■ You can preview and print a publication at any time.

VOCABULARY *Review*

Define the following terms:

Binding	Page navigation buttons	Scratch area
Boundaries	Page size	Sheet size
Double-sided printing	Paper stock	Single-sided printing
Frame	Proofreaders' mark	Text box
Galleys	Publication type	Toggles
Mock-up		

REVIEW *Questions*

TRUE / FALSE

Circle T if the statement is true or F if the statement is false.

T   F   1. You should never enter personal information in a desktop publishing program.

T   F   2. Most desktop publishing programs have non-printing gridlines to help you align objects on the page.

T   F   3. Zooming changes the magnification of the file on the screen, not the actual size of the data in the file.

T   F   4. Sizing handles display around a selected text box.

T   F   5. The Undo and Redo commands do not work in most desktop publishing programs.

T   F   6. You can replace sample clip-art images in a publication.

T   F   7. An automatic spelling checker marks spelling errors as you type.

T   F   8. To quickly print a single copy using the default print settings, you can usually click the Print button.

T   F   9. Most desktop printers can easily print on two sides of a sheet of paper at the same time.

T   F   10. All paper stocks cost the same.

WRITTEN QUESTIONS

Write a brief answer to each of the following questions.

1. What is the difference between page size and sheet size?

2. What are some benefits of using a template to create a publication?

3. Give three examples of spelling errors that a spelling checker might not catch.

4. What are the six steps to producing a desktop publishing document?

5. Name at least three issues to consider when you are planning a publication.

FILL IN THE BLANK

Complete the following sentences by writing the correct word or words in the blanks provided.

1. You can experiment with page size, sheet size, and orientation by creating a(n) _____ of a publication.

2. Most desktop publishing programs have a(n) _____ area where you can temporarily store text and graphics.

3. _____ is the method used to attach or secure pages or sections of a book or booklet.

4. The kind of document you want to create is called the _____ type.

5. In a desktop publishing program, a(n) _____ usually contains page layout and text formatting settings as well as objects such as sample text and graphics.

6. Most desktop publishing programs let you display your file in different _____ modes such as normal or standard, whole page or two-page spread, or preview.

7. When a command is toggled on, it may have a(n) _____ beside it on a menu.

8. When you need to get a closer look at a publication, _____ in.

9. Another word for a text box is _____.

10. If you want to change any print settings, you must use the _____ dialog box.

PROJECTS

PROJECT 18-1

Plan a flyer to announce the annual open house of the human resources department at a medium-sized corporation.

1. Try to locate actual flyers that announce events, so you can look at them for ideas, or look at the designs or templates that come with your desktop publishing program.

2. Make decisions about the physical aspects of the flyer.
   A. A standard flyer usually has a sheet size of 8.5 × 11 inches.
   B. Flyers are usually printed on one side only.
   C. Flyers may be printed in black and white or color.
   D. Flyers are usually printed on standard copy paper stock.
   E. Flyers are usually printed in large quantities.

3. Make decisions about the content you want to include.
   A. You must include facts, such as the name of the event, the location, the date, and the time.
   B. You should include paragraph text describing the event.
   C. You may want to include facts about the corporation.
   D. You may want to include graphics.

4. Create a mock-up of the flyer using an 8.5 × 11 inch sheet of paper. (You may want to refer to sample flyers, or to the designs or templates that come with your program.)
   A. Draw margins.
   B. Draw text boxes where you want to place text.
   C. Draw frames where you want to place graphics.

5. Write your name and today's date on the back of the mock-up and save it to reference in the following project.

PROJECT 18-2

1. Launch your desktop publishing program and choose to create a flyer.

2. Select a simple design or template appropriate for advertising an event. For example, in Publisher, select the **Ascent Event** design. If you are using InDesign, select the **Flyer3** template.

3. If the Personal Information dialog box displays, you may cancel it, or you may choose to key some of the data provided in step 6 in the appropriate boxes and then click Save.

4. Save the file as **OpenHouse**.

5. Close the task pane if there is one, and then zoom in to **75%**, or greater.

6. Replace the sample text with the following information, deleting extra sample lines as necessary (If you are using InDesign, you may have to make decisions about where to insert the replacement text, and you may have to change font size or resize text boxes in order to fit the text.):
   Business Name: **Human Resources Department**
   Business tag line: **We're Here for You.**
   Date: **April 21**
   Time: **10:00 a.m. until 5:00 p.m.**
   Event title: **Open House**
   Description: **The Human Resources staff invites you to join us for our annual department open house! We will be available to discuss policies, procedures, and other issues, as well as to answer questions about forms, job opportunities, benefits, and all topics relating to our department. Of course, there will also be refreshments! Please stop by anytime between 10 and 5. We look forward to seeing you then.**

Highlights: **Tours**
            Refreshments
            Ask the Manager
Location: **Suite 311**
Contact person: **Liz Jackson, ext. 201**
Business Address: **677 Maple Street**
                Gardner, MA 01440
Business Numbers: **Phone: 978-555-5555**
                Fax: 978-555-5566
                E-mail: contact@mail.com
Logo text: **Sugar Hill Communications**

7. Replace the sample picture with **Project18-2** from the Data files. Adjust the size of the graphic frame if necessary.

8. Check the spelling in the file. Remove any unnecessary text boxes, frames, or graphics.

9. Preview the file, and then print a single copy.

10. Save changes and close the **OpenHouse** file. (If necessary, select not to save the logo as part of the information file or to make the information entered the primary business information.) Leave your desktop publishing program open to use in the next project.

PROJECT 18-3

1. Plan a fax cover form for Liz Jackson in the Human Resources Department of Sugar Hill Communications. A fax cover is a form you send with a facsimile transmission. The form usually includes information about the business sending the fax, such as the name and address, information about the recipient, such as a name, phone number, and fax number, the name and phone number of the sender, and the number of pages in the fax. There may also be space for notes or comments.

2. In your desktop publishing program, choose to create a fax cover form using a basic design or template, such as the **Straight Edge Fax Cover** design (from the Business Forms category) in Publisher or the **Fax** template in InDesign (located in the Forms category of the InDesign templates).

3. Save the file as **Fax**.

4. Close the task pane if there is one, and then zoom in to **75%** or greater.

5. Replace the sample text with the following information, deleting extra sample lines, as necessary. (You may need to adjust fonts, font sizes, and text box sizes in some programs.)
Logo text: **Sugar Hill Communications**
Organization: **Sugar Hill Communications**
Organization Address: **677 Maple Street**
                    Gardner, MA 01440
Organization Numbers: **Phone: 978-555-5555**
                    Fax: 978-555-5566
                    E-mail: contact@mail.com

To: **Nancy M. Landry**
  902 Millwood Avenue
  Gardner, MA 01440
  Phone: 978-555-9999
  Fax: 978-555-8888
From: **Liz Jackson**
Status: **Urgent**
Date sent: **Today's Date**
Number of pages: **2**
Message: **On behalf of Sugar Hill Communications, I am pleased to send you this offer of employment. After you review the offer, please contact me.**

6. Check the spelling in the publication. Delete any text boxes or graphics you don't need.

7. Preview the publication, and then print one copy.

8. Save the changes, close **Fax**, and close your desktop publishing program.

WEB PROJECT

Assume you have been hired to work for the campaign of a local political candidate. One of your jobs will be to produce advertising documents such as flyers and mailers. Use the Internet to look up information about desktop publishing programs so that you can make a purchasing recommendation. Try to find at least two programs designed for professional use and at least two programs designed for home use. Research cost, features, and compatibility and then record the information in a spreadsheet or table so you can compare the information. You should also consider whether you will be able to produce the publications on a desktop printer, or if you will have to have them printed by a commercial print shop.

To start, try searching for desktop publishing, or looking up the Web sites of software companies you know sell desktop publishing programs, such as Microsoft and Adobe. Most sites have feature lists that you can save or print, as well as pricing information. When you have gathered the information, analyze it and then write a report of at least 250 words recommending a product. Use your research to support your decision.

TEAMWORK PROJECT

Many businesses and organizations use newsletters to distribute information to members, employees, and customers. Though not as lengthy or as formal as a newspaper or magazine, a newsletter can present information in a variety of formats including articles, pictures, tables, and charts. It can be a single page, multiple pages, black and white, or color.

In this project, work together to plan a two-sided newsletter for your class. Start by meeting to plan the development and production of the publication. You may want to try to locate some professional newsletters to look at for ideas. There may be some in the school library or office, or your instructor may have some. You can also assign roles to your team members. For example, someone may be the managing editor, responsible for the budget, someone may be the production editor, responsible for setting production specifications, someone may be a designer, responsible for designing the layout, and so on.

Determine the target audience and the message you want the publication to convey. You can even select content ideas for the first issue. Agree on how you want the finished product to look, how it will be printed, and how it will be distributed. If possible, research the costs of producing the publication, including paper costs, printing costs, and delivery costs. You can call or write to a commercial printer to ask for a price list, or consult your school administrator to find out about paper and copying costs. Enter the pricing information into a spreadsheet, or record it in a table so you can compare and analyze it. See if you can save money by changing some of the project specifications. For example, could you print fewer copies, use black and white instead of color, or distribute the publication by hand instead of mail? Once you have settled on a budget and a publication plan, try making a mock-up that you can share with the class.

CRITICAL *Thinking*

Use your desktop publishing program to create a thank-you card that you can send to someone who has helped you recently, such as a classmate, friend, or relative, or a school administrator, instructor, or volunteer. Start by planning how you want the card to look. For example, do you want it to be a single, unfolded sheet of paper, or do you want it to be folded? Do you want to include graphics? Color? Will you leave space to handwrite a personal note? Do you have card stock to print it on or will you use plain paper?

Once you have made decisions about the publication, look at the designs or templates available in your program for ideas; then create a mock-up that shows how the paper will fold and how the content will be arranged. Create the document by selecting the publication type and design. Replace the sample text and graphics with customized text and graphics. Before you print the card, be sure to check the spelling and proofread your work for other errors.

WORKING WITH TEXT

OBJECTIVES

Upon completion of this lesson, you should be able to:

- Create a blank document.
- Insert, delete, resize, and position text boxes.
- Select a font and font size, and apply font styles, effects, and color.
- Align text.
- Set indents and tabs and create lists.
- Set character, line, and paragraph spacing, and set margins in a text box.
- Copy, move, and import text.
- Create columns, connect text boxes, and control line and paragraph breaks.

Estimated Time: 2 hours

VOCABULARY

Ascenders

Baseline

Descenders

Frame inset

Gutter

Horizontal alignment

In port

Indents

Kerning

Leading

Margin guides

Margins

Newsletter-style columns

Orphan

Out port

Overflow text

Overset text

Paragraph spacing

Tab leaders

Tabs

Threading text

Tracking

Typography

Vertical alignment

White space

Widow

Text is an important component of most desktop publishing documents. Sometimes, the text makes up the bulk of the publication, such as in a newsletter that includes lengthy articles. Other times, the text is used to highlight or complement other content. For example, a sales flyer may use short bullet lists or a travel brochure may have photo captions. All desktop publishing programs include tools that help you enhance the appearance of your publications and ensure that the text is easy to read. Most of the tools are similar to those found in word processing programs that allow you to apply boldface or indent a paragraph. Other tools are designed specifically for fine-tuning documents for publication, such as adjusting spacing between lines, characters, and paragraphs. In this lesson, you learn how to create a blank document, insert and delete text boxes, format text, and control text flow.

Create a Blank Document

In Lesson 18 you learned to create a publication using your program's built-in designs or templates. If none of the templates or designs is suitable for your publication, you can create a new blank document and start from scratch. This gives you the freedom to insert objects, key text, and apply formatting to arrange and design the publication any way you want. You are not constricted by the design elements of the template, and your publication will not look just like a publication that someone else designed using the same template.

Although some desktop publishing programs start with a new blank document open on the screen, most start displaying a dialog box or task pane listing designs or templates. You need to click the option for creating a blank document or publication to display a default blank document. Alternatively, click the New button on the toolbar. Some programs first display a dialog box in which you can select settings to control the appearance of the new document or just click OK to create a document with the default settings. In most programs, the default blank document is a full 8.5-inch by 11-inch page with 1-inch *margins* marked by *margin guides* on all sides. Margins are the area between the edge of the page and the objects in the publication. Margin guides are nonprinting lines that indicate the position of the margins. Some programs may have different default margins.

Note

Some programs display an option for creating a blank Web page, or publications for Web use. These pages are optimized for display on the World Wide Web. See Lesson 22 for more information on preparing publications for the Web.

Note

Some programs use picas as the default measurement unit for publications, whereas other programs use inches. A pica is equal to ⅙ of an inch, or 12 points. To change the measurement unit, open a dialog box such as Options or Preferences, locate the unit setting on a tab such as General or Units & Increments, and select the unit you want to use. You can usually choose inches, picas, points, or centimeters. Click OK to apply the change.

STEP-BY-STEP 19.1

1. Launch your desktop publishing program and select the command to create a new, blank full-page document with **1.0 inch** (**6 picas**) margins on all sides. If necessary, close the template dialog box or window, first. Your program creates and displays a document similar to the one shown in Figure 19-1.

FIGURE 19-1
Blank full-page document

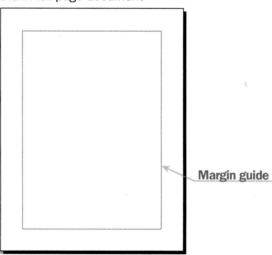

Margin guide

2. Save the file as **Mentors** and leave it open to use in the next exercise.

> **Note** ☑
>
> You should always use proper typography and keyboarding when keying text in a publication.

> **Note** ☑
>
> Working with text boxes is similar to working with text blocks in graphics and animation files. Refer to Lesson 4 for information on working with text in a graphics file, and Lesson 7 for working with text in an animation file.

Work with Text Boxes

As explained in Lesson 18, text in a desktop publishing document is inserted in a text box, which is sometimes called a frame or text frame. When you create a document based on a template or design, your program automatically inserts and formats text boxes. You can manually insert text boxes at any time, and you can delete text boxes you no longer need. Once a text box is inserted in a document, you can easily change its size and/or position on the page.

Insert and Delete Text Boxes

To insert a text box, select a tool such as Text Box or Type and then click and drag to draw the text box in the publication. As you drag, guidelines appear on both the horizontal and vertical ruler. Use these lines to help you gauge the text box dimensions. Most programs also display the object size and position somewhere onscreen, such as the Status bar or Control palette. When you release the mouse button, the new text box displays in the document, and it is selected.

The appearance of a selected text box varies depending on the program you are using. Most display sizing handles and a nonprinting border, like other selected objects. Some also display *in ports* and *out ports*, which are larger handles that you use when connecting one text box to another. You learn how to connect text boxes later in this lesson.

Usually, the new text box has an insertion point flashing in it, but in some programs, you have to click a Type Tool and then click in the new frame to place the insertion point. (Recall that an insertion point is a flashing vertical bar that indicates where keyed text will display.) New text is generally inserted to the left of the insertion point. You use standard text entry and editing techniques to key text in a desktop publishing program. To delete a text box, click its border to select it, and then press Delete, or choose Delete or Clear from the Edit menu.

S TEP-BY-STEP 19.2

1. Adjust the zoom to at least **75%** so you have a good look at the top part of the document.

2. Click the tool that allows you to insert a text box or text frame, and then position the mouse pointer along the top margin halfway across the page, at about **4.25 inches** on the horizontal ruler.

3. Press and hold the mouse button and drag diagonally down and to the right to draw a box about **1 inch** high and **3 inches** wide. Use the rulers for help sizing the object. Release the mouse button to insert the object in the file. It should look similar to Figure 19-2.

FIGURE 19-2
Blank text box

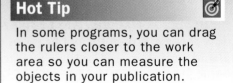

Text Box tool

Insertion point

Blank text box

Text box position on Status bar

Text box dimensions on Status bar

4. If necessary, click in the text box with the Text Tool to position the insertion point, and then key the text **Mentoring Volunteers**. The text displays in the default formatting.

Hot Tip

In some programs, you can drag the rulers closer to the work area so you can measure the objects in your publication.

STEP-BY-STEP 19.2 Continued

5. Select the **Text Box** or **Type Tool** again, and then position the mouse pointer in the lower-left corner of the document, where the left and bottom margins intersect.

6. Press and hold the mouse button and drag diagonally up and to the right to draw an object about **2 inches** high and **6 inches** wide. Again, use the rulers to help size the object. Release the mouse button to insert the object in the file.

7. Key the text **Join us on Friday**.

Now, try deleting a text box.

8. Use the pointer or selection tool to click the border of the text box you drew in step 6 to select it, and then press **Delete**. The text box is removed from the file.

9. Save the changes and leave **Mentors** open to use in the next exercise.

> **Note**
>
> Some programs display pop-up tips as you work. For example, in Publisher the Office Assistant may display a tip advising you to zoom in on text for a closer look. Click the tip to remove it. To hide the Office Assistant, click Help, and then click Hide the Office Assistant. To turn it off, right-click the Office Assistant, click Options, click to deselect the Use the Office Assistant check box, and then click OK.

Resize and Position Text Boxes

To resize a text box, select it and then drag a sizing handle. When the mouse pointer is positioned over a sizing handle, it may change to a resize pointer, which is usually a double-headed arrow. Drag a top or bottom handle to change the text box height. Drag a side handle to change the width, or drag a corner handle to change both the height and width at the same time.

To position a text box, select it, position the mouse pointer over the object's border, and then drag the object to a new location. When the mouse pointer is over the border, it may change to a move pointer, which is usually a four-headed arrow.

As mentioned previously, most programs display a selected object's size and position onscreen to help you with sizing and positioning. The position references the X and Y coordinates. Recall that the X coordinate is the horizontal position and the Y coordinate is the vertical position, relative to the page. Programs usually set the X and Y coordinate based on the upper-left corner of the object (Publisher) or the center of the object (InDesign). For more information refer to Lesson 21.

STEP-BY-STEP 19.3

1. Select the text box.

2. Position the mouse pointer over the object's border, and then press and hold the mouse button and drag the object to the upper-left corner of the document, where the top and left margins meet. Release the mouse button to move the object.

3. Position the mouse pointer over the sizing handle in the lower-right corner of the text box.

STEP-BY-STEP 19.3 Continued

4. Press and hold the mouse button and drag across to the right margin and down to the **3-inch** mark on the ruler to draw an object **6.5 inches** wide by **2 inches** high, as shown in Figure 19-3. As you drag, the mouse pointer may change to a cross-hair, and a dashed line may define the text box size. Release the mouse button to resize the object.

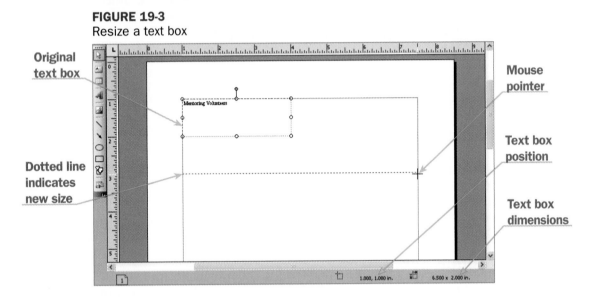

FIGURE 19-3
Resize a text box

5. Save the changes and leave **Mentors** open to use in the next exercise.

Work with Fonts

You can change the look of text in a publication using font formatting. Recall that a font is the typeface or design of a set of characters, including letters, numbers, and symbols. In publishing, the technique of selecting typefaces and arranging type in a publication is called *typography*.

Although the main goal in selecting a font is to make text easy to read, appropriate use of fonts can also make an impact in your publications and help define the tone and message you want to convey. Fonts can be elaborate or simple, decorative or plain. It is worth spending some time to select just the right font or combination of fonts to complement your publication.

In addition to selecting a font, you can set font size, font style, font effects, and font color. You can apply font formatting to selected text, or you can select the options before you key new text. Many font formatting options can be set using toolbar buttons, palette options, or menus. In addition, most programs have a Font or Character dialog box similar to the one shown in Figure 19-4, in which you can select font formatting options. To open the Font dialog box, click the Menu bar command for formatting text, such as Format in Publisher, or Type in InDesign, and then click the command to display the dialog box. For example, click Font in Publisher or Character in InDesign.

FIGURE 19-4
Font dialog box

Select a Font and Font Size

As discussed in Lesson 4, there are two basic types of fonts: *serif* fonts and *sans serif* fonts. Serif fonts have serifs — which are short lines and curlicues at the ends of the lines that make up each character. Serif fonts are generally easy to read and so are often used for lengthy paragraphs, reports, or letters. Some common serif fonts include Times New Roman, Garamond, and Century. Sans serif fonts have straight lines without serifs and are often used for headlines and titles. Some common sans serif fonts are Arial, Impact, and Tahoma. Other types of fonts include script fonts, which imitate handwriting, decorative, or fantasy fonts, and symbol fonts, which include sets of symbols you can insert as characters into text.

> **Note** ☑
>
> The concepts and techniques for working with fonts and font formatting in a publication are the same as in other types of documents. Refer to Lesson 4 for information on using fonts in a graphics file, Lesson 7 for information on working with fonts in an animation file, and Lesson 13 for working with fonts in a presentation file.

Your program probably has a default font and font size for text inserted in a blank document. For example, in Microsoft Publisher, the default font is 10-point Times New Roman. To choose a font, locate your program's font list on a menu, toolbar, palette, dialog box, or task pane. In most cases, the fonts are listed in alphabetical order, and you can sometimes see a preview of a font when you select it in the list. Most desktop publishing programs come with a long list of built-in fonts, and you may have other fonts available on your computer as well. You can also buy and install font sets you need, or locate free fonts on the Internet.

Too many fonts can make a publication difficult to read. In general, you should try to use no more than three fonts on a page, and you should avoid mixing similar fonts on the same page. You typically use a serif font for body text and a sans serif font for headlines. You can add a third font for captions or subheadings, or better yet, change the size and/or style of one of the other fonts you are already using.

Font size is the height of an uppercase letter in the font set, measured in points. Recall that there are 72 points in an inch. Select a new font size by locating your program's font size list on a toolbar, menu, palette, or dialog box. You can choose one of the sizes on the list or key a size in the font size box. Many programs have Increase Font Size and Decrease Font Size toolbar buttons that you can use to quickly change the font in 1-point increments.

Some programs have a copy fitting or AutoFit option, which automatically adjusts the size of text to fit within a text box. Copy fitting is usually a toggle that is turned on or off using a menu command or a dialog box. When copy fitting is on, text you key in a text box automatically resizes to fit within the text box borders. When copy fitting is off, text is sized according to the current font size selection.

If a text box is too small to display all of the text it contains, the hidden text is called either *overflow* or *overset text*. Most programs display an icon indicating that there is hidden text. In Publisher, the icon is an *A* followed by an ellipses. In InDesign, a red plus sign displays in the frame's out port.

> **Note** ☑
>
> If you open a file that uses a font that is not installed on your computer, your program may automatically substitute a similar font, or it may display a dialog box asking if it is OK to substitute a font.

> **Hot Tip**
>
> Some programs let you scale the height or width of selected text by a percentage of its original size. For example, set the horizontal scale to 200% to stretch the text to twice its original width. Set the vertical scale to 50% to shrink it to half its original height.

S TEP-BY-STEP 19.4

1. Select all of the text in the text box.

2. Click the **Font** box drop-down arrow on the toolbar or Character Formatting Controls palette, and then click **Arial** on the list of fonts. You may have to scroll to the top of the list to locate the correct font. (If you are using InDesign you may have to click the Character Formatting Controls button to display the font options.)

3. Click the **Font Size** box on the toolbar or palette and key **36**, or click **36** on the Font Size list. Deselect the text. It should now be formatted in 36-point Arial, as shown in Figure 19-5.

STEP-BY-STEP 19.4 Continued

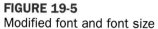

FIGURE 19-5
Modified font and font size

Font

Font size

Modified text

4. Save the changes and leave **Mentors** open to use in the next exercise.

Apply Font Styles, Font Effects, and Font Color

Recall that *font style* is used to call attention to specific text without changing the font itself. *Font style* is the slant and weight—or thickness—of characters in a font set, such as bold and italic. Some programs also offer underlining as a font style. Bold is usually used to highlight text and make it stand out, while italic is usually used for subtle emphasis. Click a toolbar button to apply a style, or select it in the Font dialog box.

Font effects are attributes applied to characters such as superscript, subscript, shadows, or small caps. Font effects are sometimes used for decorative purposes, but are sometimes necessary for correct typography. For example, to key the chemical formula for water correctly you need to use a subscript 2: H_2O. Font effects are usually available in the Font dialog box or Character Formatting Controls palette. You can often combine effects to achieve different results.

Font color is simply the color used for text. By default, font color is usually black. In most programs, you change the font color by selecting the text and then clicking the Font Color button on the toolbar to display a palette of available colors from which you click the color you want. In some programs, font color is determined by the current fill color, which is usually set by double-clicking the Fill button and then selecting a color in a dialog box or palette. You learn more about using color in a publication in Lesson 21.

> **Note** ☑
>
> The concepts and techniques of working with color in a publication file are very much the same as working with color in other types of documents. Refer to Lesson 5 for more information about working with color in a graphics program and Lesson 13 for information about working with color in a presentation program.

STEP-BY-STEP 19.5

1. Select all of the text in the text box and apply the bold font style. This is usually done by clicking the **Bold** button on a toolbar.

2. Apply the Small caps effect to the selected text. For example, in Publisher, open the Font dialog box, select the **Small caps** check box, and then click **OK**. In InDesign, click **Type** on the Menu bar and then click **Character** to display the Character palette. Click the **Options** button in the top right corner of the Character palette, and then click **Small Caps** on the drop-down menu.

> **Hot Tip**
>
> Use the Font dialog box to make multiple changes to font formatting, and to preview the results before applying them. You can select a font, font size, font style, font effects, and font color.

3. Change the font color to blue. If you are using Publisher, click the **Font Color** drop-down arrow on the Formatting toolbar and then click the **blue** color swatch on the color palette. If you are using InDesign, double-click the **Fill Tool** to display the Color Picker, select blue by keying the following RGB values: R:**0**, G:**0**, B:**255**, and then click **OK**. Once you deselect the text, it should look similar to Figure 19-6.

FIGURE 19-6
Modified font style, effect, and color

Font Color button

Bold button

Modified text

MENTORING VOLUNTEERS

4. Save the changes and leave **Mentors** open to use in the next exercise.

> **Hot Tip**
>
> In InDesign you can add a color to the Swatches panel by selecting it in the Color Picker dialog box and then clicking the Add RGB Swatch button.

Align Text

In desktop publishing programs you can set text alignment to position paragraphs in relation to the borders of a text box, just like you can align text in a text block in a graphics file (Lesson 4) or animation file (Lesson 7), or in a placeholder in a presentation file (Lesson 13). You can set the *horizontal alignment* of text to adjust the position of paragraphs in relation to the left and right margins of the text box. You can set the *vertical alignment* to adjust the position of all text in a text box in relation to the top and bottom margins of the text box. (To see an example of different text alignments refer to Figure 4-8.)

Horizontal Alignment

Most programs offer four horizontal alignment options:

- *Left align*, which positions a paragraph so that text is even with the left margin;
- *Right align*, which positions a paragraph so that text is even with the right margin;
- *Center align*, which positions a paragraph so text is centered between the margins; and
- *Justify*, which spaces the text so that both the left and right margins are even. (Some programs may also have a variety of justify options to control the alignment of the last line in a justified paragraph.)

To set horizontal alignment, position the insertion point within a paragraph or select multiple paragraphs and then click an alignment button on the toolbar or Paragraph Formatting Controls palette. You can also select an alignment before you key new text. You may also select alignment options from a menu or in the Paragraph dialog box or panel. Horizontal alignment is carried forward to the next paragraph when you press Enter. However, each paragraph of text can have a different horizontal alignment.

Vertical Alignment

Most programs offer three vertical alignments:

- *Top*, which positions the text to start immediately below the top border;
- *Bottom*, which positions the text to end immediately above the bottom border; and
- *Center*, which positions the text between the top and bottom borders.

In most programs, you set vertical alignment in a dialog box such as Format Text Box or Text Frame Options. You can set only one vertical alignment for a text box, no matter how much text it contains.

> **Note**
>
> Do not confuse vertical alignment, which spaces text within a text box, with vertical text direction, an effect in which text characters are positioned vertically instead of horizontally. To achieve a vertical text effect, you usually have to create a graphics object using a different program or a utility such as WordArt. Using WordArt is covered in Lesson 22.

S TEP-BY-STEP 19.6

1. Make sure the insertion point is positioned in the text, and then click the **Align Right** button. If you are using InDesign, you may have to click the **Paragraph Formatting Controls** button on the Control palette to display the alignment buttons.

2. Click the **Center** button. The text is centered between the left and right margins.

3. Select the command to open the dialog box in which you can set vertical alignment. If you are using Publisher, click **Format** on the Menu bar and then click **Text Box**. If necessary, click the **Text Box** tab. If you are using InDesign, click **Object** on the Menu bar, and then click **Text Frame Options**.

<u>**STEP-BY-STEP 19.6 Continued**</u>

4. Select the option to center the text vertically. For example, click the *Vertical alignment* drop-down arrow and click **Middle** or **Center**.

5. Click the **OK** button in the dialog box. The text should look similar to Figure 19-7.

FIGURE 19-7
Text is centered vertically and horizontally

6. Print one copy of the **Mentors** file.

7. Save the changes and close **Mentors**. Leave your desktop publishing program open to use in the next exercise.

Set Indents and Tabs and Create Lists

You can set indents and tabs within a text box in much the same way you do in a standard word processing document. *Indents* set temporary margins for a paragraph or series of paragraphs. *Tabs* adjust the horizontal position of text across a single line. To set indents and tabs for a single paragraph, simply position the insertion point in the paragraph and then select the options you want to apply. To format multiple paragraphs, select the paragraphs before selecting the options. You can also select the options before you key new text. Indents and tabs are carried forward to new paragraphs when you press Enter.

Lists are an effective way to present information so that readers can quickly identify and digest the important points you are trying to make. In addition, lists are useful for breaking up the layout of a page to make it more interesting and appealing. Use numbered lists when the order of items matters and use bulleted lists when the order does not matter. For instance, you would number directions to a building but you would bullet facts about a product or service.

Most programs offer many different methods to apply indents, tabs, and lists. Usually, you can set precise values or select options in a dialog box or control palette, but it is often faster and easier to simply drag the indent or tab markers on the horizontal ruler or on the Tabs ruler.

When formatting paragraphs, it may help to display nonprinting characters such as paragraph marks, tabs, and spaces. Paragraph marks look something like a backwards *P*, tab marks look like right arrows, and spaces are dots. To display nonprinting characters, you can click the Special Characters button on the toolbar, or select the appropriate menu command.

> **Note** ☑
>
> Most desktop publishing programs automatically hyphenate words that break at the end of a line. You can usually use options in the Hyphenation or Character dialog box to insert discretionary and manual hyphens, change the width of the hyphenation zone, and turn automatic hyphenation off or on.

Set Indents

Most programs offer five types of indents:

- A *first-line indent* indents the first line of a paragraph from the left margin.

- A *left indent* indents all lines in a paragraph from the left margin.

- A *right indent* indents all lines from the right margin.

- A *double* or *quotation indent* indents all lines from both the left and right margins.

> **Note** ☑
>
> Some desktop publishing programs automatically replace double-hyphens with an em dash character.

- A *hanging indent* indents all lines except the first line from the left margin.

Indents may be set by dragging indent markers on a ruler, by specifying values in a Control palette, or by using a dialog box. Some programs have Increase Indent and Decrease Indent toolbar buttons that you can use to quickly adjust a left indent in 0.5-inch increments. In Publisher, the indentations options are on the Indents and Spacing tab of the Paragraph dialog box. Click Format on the Menu bar and then click Paragraph. Click the Indents and Spacing tab, if necessary. If you are using InDesign and the Control palette is not displayed, click Window > Control. Click the Paragraph Formatting Controls button to make the indents options available. To display the Tabs ruler, click Type on the Menu bar and then click Tabs. Your instructor may want you to use a particular method to complete the following exercise. If not, select the method you want to use.

S TEP-BY-STEP 19.7

1. Open **Step19-7** from the data files and save it as **Meeting**. This publication is similar to the **Mentors** file you worked with earlier in this lesson, but it includes additional text.

2. Increase the zoom to at least **75%**, and then select the command to display nonprinting characters, if they are not already displayed. In Publisher click the **Special Characters** button on the **Formatting** toolbar. In InDesign, click **Type** on the Menu bar and then click **Show Hidden Characters**.

3. Select the text of the quotation, including the quotation marks, but not the speaker's name or title. Apply a double or quotation indent by indenting the text **0.5 inches** from both the left and right margins. You can do this by dragging the indent markers on the horizontal or Tabs ruler, or by setting values on the Indents and Spacing tab of the Paragraph dialog box in Publisher, or the Paragraph Formatting Controls palette in InDesign.

STEP-BY-STEP 19.7 Continued

4. Select the speaker's name and title and indent the lines **3 inches** from the left margin. When you deselect the text, the text box should look similar to the one in Figure 19-8.

FIGURE 19-8
Indents applied to text

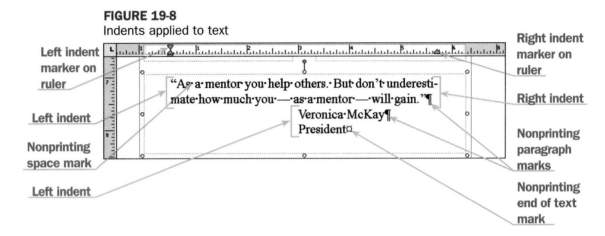

Left indent marker on ruler

Left indent

Nonprinting space mark

Left indent

Right indent marker on ruler

Right indent

Nonprinting paragraph marks

Nonprinting end of text mark

"As a mentor you help others. But don't underestimate how much you — as a mentor — will gain."

Veronica McKay
President

5. Save the changes and leave **Meeting** open to use in the next exercise.

Set Tabs

A tab is a stop indicator at a specific point along the horizontal ruler. Each time you press the Tab key, the insertion point advances to the next tab stop. There are four types of tab stops in most programs:

■ *Left* sets text to start flush with the tab stop.

■ *Right* sets text to end flush with the tab stop.

■ *Center* centers text on either side of the tab stop.

■ *Decimal* aligns decimal points or periods flush with the tab stop.

Most programs have default left tab stops set every 0.5 inch. In most programs, you can also apply *tab leaders*, which are characters repeated on the line preceding the tab stop. Common tab leader characters include dots, lines, dashes, and bullets.

To set tabs, use the Tabs dialog box, or click on the horizontal ruler or the Tabs ruler to position the tab. First, select the tab stop type, then click the ruler, or key the position and then click Set. You can usually change one type of tab to another by double-clicking the tab to display a dialog box where you can select the new tab type. Move a tab if necessary by simply dragging it on the ruler. To delete a tab, drag it off the ruler or use a dialog box to delete it.

STEP-BY-STEP 19.8

1. Position the insertion point to the left of the word *Date:* in the last text box on the page.

2. Set a right tab stop at **1.5 inches** on the horizontal ruler or on your program's Tabs ruler and then set a left tab stop at **2.0 inches** on the horizontal ruler or on your program's Tabs ruler.

STEP-BY-STEP 19.8 Continued

3. Press **Tab** to move the word *Date:* to the first tab stop.

4. Move the insertion point to the right of the word *Date:* and press **Tab** to move the insertion point to the second tab stop. Key **Saturday, March 22**, and then press **Enter**. (Close or move the Indents/Tabs ruler if necessary.)

5. Press **Tab**, key **Time:**, press **Tab**, and key **10:00 a.m.**

6. Press **Enter**, press **Tab**, key **Location:**, press **Tab**, and key **Cafeteria**. The text box should look similar to the one in Figure 19-9.

FIGURE 19-9
Align text using tabs

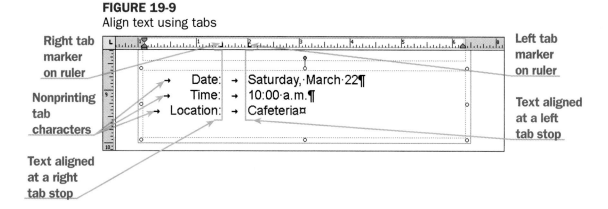

7. Save the changes and leave **Meeting** open to use in the next exercise.

Create Lists

To create a list, you simply apply a list format or style to the current paragraph or to selected paragraphs. Most lists are formatted automatically using a hanging indent, which means the bullet is flush with the left margin (or first line indent setting), and the text lines are indented. Usually, the formatting is carried forward when you press Enter. You can also select the list format before you key new text.

Most programs include a set of built-in bullet styles that you can quickly apply to lists. Click the Bullets button on the toolbar to apply the default bullet style or the most recently used bullet style to the current paragraph, or select the bullet size and other options in a dialog box.

Likewise, most programs include built-in number formats. Click the Numbering button on the toolbar to quickly apply the default number style or the most recently used number style to the current paragraph. Options for customizing the separator character and indent are usually found in a dialog box.

> **Note** ☑
>
> The techniques for creating and customizing lists in a publication are similar to those used in a presentation file. Refer to Lesson 13 for more information on working with lists.

S TEP-BY-STEP 19.9

1. Select the five lines (4 paragraphs) of text under the heading *Morning Agenda*. Do not select the heading.

2. Apply the default bulleted list formatting. For example, click a button such as **Bullets** or **Bulleted List**.

3. In the text box to the right of the one where you created the bulleted list, select the last three lines of text in the text box: *Pick up an application*, *Fill out an application*, and *Submit an application*.

4. Apply the default numbered list formatting. For example, click a button such as **Numbering** or **Numbered List**. When you deselect the text, it should look similar to Figure 19-10. Don't worry if the formats of the numbers and bullets are not the same as in the illustration. Your program may have different defaults.

FIGURE 19-10
Text formatted as lists

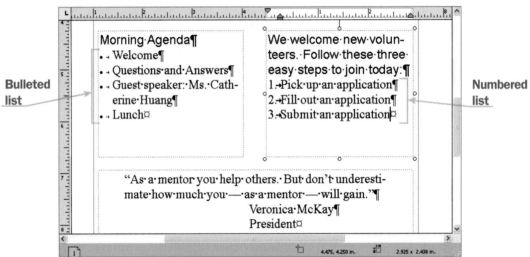

5. Save the changes and leave **Meeting** open to use in the next exercise.

Adjust Spacing

When you create a desktop publishing document, you should consider the amount of white space in and around text boxes as part of the overall composition of the page. *White space* is the area on a page that has no text or graphics. Spacing between characters, spacing between lines in a paragraph, and spacing between paragraphs can greatly affect the appearance of the page as well as its readability.

In most programs, there are many ways to control the amount of space in and around your text. Four of the most common methods include:

■ *Tracking* controls the space between all characters in a text box.

■ *Kerning* controls the space between two specific characters.

- *Leading*, or line spacing, controls the amount of space between lines of text.

- *Paragraph spacing* controls the amount of space before and/or after a paragraph.

You can also set top, bottom, left, and right margins within a text box to control the amount of white space between the text and the text box borders.

Set Character Spacing

Tracking, or the amount of space allotted for the width of each character, is determined by the font set. You can increase or decrease the spacing between all characters in a selection by setting the tracking. Kerning is used when you can see uneven spacing between a pair of characters within a word. Uneven spacing causes the reader's eye to hesitate, making it harder to read the text. Good kerning spaces characters so that the reader views each word as a single unit.

> **Note**
>
> Pay particular attention to kerning in larger-sized text, such as headlines or titles; in text typed in all uppercase letters; and when using light-colored characters on a darker background. These situations tend to make spacing problems stand out more.

You can usually set tracking and kerning values in a dialog box, or you may be able to select options or key values on a control palette. To open the dialog box, click Format on the Menu bar and then click Character Spacing. To open the Control palette, click Window on the Menu bar and then click Control. (You may have to click the Character Formatting Controls button to make the character formatting options available.)

Tracking is usually set as a percentage of the original spacing. However, some programs let you select relative spacing, such as *tight*, which decreases spacing, or *loose*, which increases spacing. Relative spacing adjusts the spacing relative to the default spacing instead of by a specific amount. (InDesign measures tracking in thousandths of an em, which is the width of the character *m* in the current font set.)

In most programs, you increase or decrease the kerning between a selected pair of characters by a specific number of points. In some programs, you select to expand or condense the spacing between the selected pair and then enter the distance in points. In some programs, you position the insertion point between the two characters, and then set the kerning. Some programs have automatic kerning options you can set to automatically increase the space between wide characters when the text is larger than a specified size.

> **Extra for Experts**
>
> In some programs you can insert three types of relative spaces in place of regular spaces—em spaces (double the width of a regular space), *en spaces* (half the width of an em space), and *thin spaces* (one quarter the width of an em space). Unlike regular spaces, relative spaces change width in relation to point size and font only, even when text is justified.

S TEP-BY-STEP 19.10

1. Select the heading text *We welcome new volunteers. Follow these three easy steps to join today:.*

2. Open the Character Spacing dialog box or the Control palette and change the tracking to **80%** of the original tracking or **-75 thousandths of an em**. Click **OK**. This decreases the amount of spacing between all characters. As a result, some character pairs may appear to run together.

STEP-BY-STEP 19.10 Continued

3. Adjust the kerning in the word *join* so that the *o*, *i*, and *n* do not run together. In Publisher, select the word, open the character spacing dialog box, and expand the kerning to **1 pt**. Then click **OK**. In InDesign, position the insertion point between the *i* and the *o* and set the kerning to **25**.

4. Repeat step 3 to expand the kerning in the words *welcome*, *Follow*, *these*, and *today*.

5. Save the changes and leave **Meeting** open to use in the next exercise.

Set Line and Paragraph Spacing

Line spacing, or leading (pronounced to rhyme with wedding), controls the vertical space between lines of text. It is measured from the *baseline*—which is the bottom of the line—of one line to the baseline of the next. If there is too much or too little space between lines, the reader's eye has trouble following from one line to the next. Sometimes, if the leading is too close, *ascenders*, which are the parts of characters that extend above the rest of the text, may run into the text in the line above, and *descenders*, which are the parts of characters that extend below the baseline, may run into the text in the line below. In general, you want the space between lines to be greater than the space between words, but some situations, such as short lines of text, call for tighter leading.

In most programs, you can set the leading on the Indents and Spacing tab of the Paragraph dialog box or on the Character Formatting Controls palette. To open the dialog box, click Format on the Menu bar and then click Paragraph. If necessary, click the Indents and Spacing tab. You can usually use either lines or points as the unit of measure. If you use lines and then change the font size, the line spacing adjusts automatically. If you use points, the line spacing remains constant, no matter what font size you apply.

Paragraph spacing helps break content into chunks that are easier to locate and read than one long continuous stream of text. You usually set the amount of space to leave before and after the current paragraph in points.

Both paragraph spacing and line spacing can be applied to the current paragraph, to selected paragraphs, or to new paragraphs before you key the text. The formatting is carried forward to the next paragraph when you press Enter. Line and paragraph spacing options are usually available in a dialog box or on the Paragraph Formatting Controls palette.

Note

You should set paragraph and line spacing instead of pressing Enter to insert extra lines. Setting spacing options gives you greater control over the appearance of your publication and makes editing and rearranging text much easier.

Hot Tip

Instead of trying to fit many paragraphs into one text box, break the text up into multiple text boxes. Using multiple text boxes gives you more flexibility in terms of position, size, alignment, and other formatting and layout options.

STEP-BY-STEP 19.11

1. Select all of the text in the text box containing the quotation.

2. Using the appropriate dialog box or menu, set the leading or line spacing to **18 points**. You may have to key the unit of measure (such as *pt*, which is the abbreviation for point) in order to switch from lines to points. Setting the spacing to 18 points decreases the amount of space between lines.

3. Deselect the text and then position the insertion point anywhere within the quotation.

4. Set the spacing before the paragraph to **3pt** and the spacing after the paragraph to **6pt**. In InDesign, you may have to key a unit of measure before keying the value in a Control palette box such as **p3** or **p6** to set the spacing in points. When you are finished, the text box should look similar to the one in Figure 19-11.

FIGURE 19-11
Adjusted line and paragraph spacing

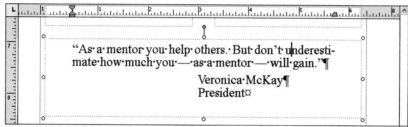

5. Save the changes and leave **Meeting** open to use in the next exercise.

Set Margins in a Text Box

To control the amount of space between text and the text box border, set the text box margins, which are sometimes called the *frame inset*. Your program probably has a narrow default text box margin size, such as 0.04 inch. You can increase a margin by increasing the width, or decrease a margin by decreasing the width. Each margin can be set independently of the other margins. In most programs, the text box margins are set in a dialog box. You can set the margins for one text box or for selected text boxes at the same time.

STEP-BY-STEP 19.12

1. Select the two text boxes containing the lists. To select both boxes at the same time, select one, press and hold **Shift**, and then select the other.

2. Open the dialog box in which you can set text box margins. For example, in Publisher, click **Format** on the Menu bar, click **Text Box**, and then click the **Text Box** tab. In InDesign, click **Object** on the Menu bar and then click **Text Frame Options**.

STEP-BY-STEP 19.12 Continued

3. Set the left, right, top, and bottom margins (Inset Spacing in InDesign) to **0.2 inch**, and then click the **OK** button in the dialog box. The margins in the text boxes increase, as shown in Figure 19-12.

FIGURE 19-12
Increase text box margins

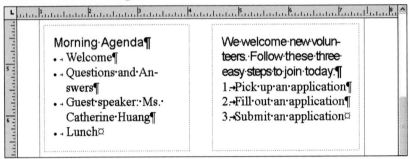

4. Save the changes and leave **Meeting** open to use in the next exercise.

Copy, Move, and Import Text

To save yourself the trouble of rekeying, you can easily copy, move, or import text into a desktop publishing document. The Copy, Cut, and Paste commands are used in all Windows programs to copy and move text as well as objects from one location to another. The copied or cut items are stored temporarily on the Clipboard, which is a temporary storage area in your computer's memory. When you select the Paste command, the item is inserted at the current location. A cut item is removed from the original location, whereas a copied item remains in both the original and new locations. Cut, Copy, and Paste commands are available as toolbar buttons or on the Edit menu.

Using the Clipboard, you can copy or move selected text within a text box or from one text box to another. You can also copy or move an entire text box and its contents. You can even copy and move text from one document to another, even if the documents are different types. For example, you can copy a chart from a spreadsheet into a publication document, or a paragraph from a word processing document into a text box in a publication. Note that if you include the nonprinting paragraph mark at the end of a paragraph when you select text to cut or copy, you include the paragraph formatting, too.

When you want to import an entire text file into your desktop publishing document, you use the Insert > Text File command or the File > Place command. Locate and select the file you want to insert, and then click OK. Depending on your program, you may be able to insert text-only files, or you may be able to import and preserve text that has been formatted in a word processing document. When you insert a file, the entire file is inserted into a text box.

When copying or importing text, you may find that the text box or frame is not large enough to hold all

> **Note** ☑
>
> Some programs let you use the Import command to import a word processing or other type of file into your desktop publishing program. When you use the Import command, the file is converted to a new desktop publishing document.

text. If a text box cannot show all text, it usually displays a symbol near the bottom, such as *A...* or a red triangle in the bottom handle (or out port) of the frame. If you see such a symbol, increase the size of the text box or frame or decrease the font size, until all text shows.

S TEP-BY-STEP 19.13

1. Select the text *Guest speaker: Ms. Catherine Huang* in the bullet list. Do not select the paragraph mark at the end of the line. (You may have to use the Shift and the arrow keys to not select the paragraph mark.) You want to copy this text into the headline text box at the top of the page, but you do not want to copy the bullet list formatting with it. If you copied the paragraph mark, the line would retain its bullet list formatting. (In some programs, the bullet list format may be copied, even if the paragraph mark is not selected.)

2. Copy the text to the Clipboard using either the **Copy** button or command.

3. Position the insertion point at the end of the headline text in the text box at the top of the page, and press **Enter** to start a new paragraph.

4. Select the command to paste the text. For example, click the **Paste** button or click **Edit** on the Menu bar and then click **Paste**. (If you accidentally copied the paragraph mark, too, the line will retain its bullet list formatting. Simply click the **Bullets** button on the toolbar to remove the bullet. You may also need to center the text horizontally.)

5. Click the **Text Box** or **Type Tool** on the toolbar and insert a new text box between the headline text box and the text boxes containing the lists. Size the box to fill the open area—about **6.3 inches** by **1.1 inches**.

6. Select all the text in the quotation text box, including the speaker's name and title and all paragraph marks. Cut the selection to the Clipboard and then click in the new text box and select the command to paste the selection. If a dialog box displays asking if you want to use AutoFlow, click **No** to continue. Don't worry if some of the text is hidden. You can adjust the size of the box later. The top part of your document should look similar to Figure 19-13.

FIGURE 19-13
Copy and move text in a document

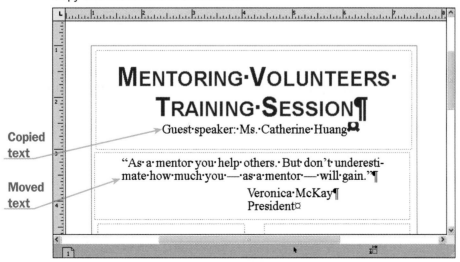

STEP-BY-STEP 19.13 Continued

7. Position the insertion point in the empty text box that originally held the quotation, and select the command to insert a text file. If you are using Publisher, click **Insert** on the Menu bar, and then click **Text File**. If you are using InDesign, select the empty frame, then click **File** > **Place**. Locate and select **Step19-13** from the data files, and then click **OK** to insert the text into the text box.

8. Select the inserted text and change the font to **Arial** and the font size to **14 points**.

9. Set the left and right indents to **0.25 inches** and justify the horizontal alignment.

10. Check the spelling in the document and correct all errors, then display the page in Print Preview. It should look similar to Figure 19-14. If some of the text is hidden, adjust the size and position of the text boxes until all text shows.

FIGURE 19-14
Completed publication

MENTORING VOLUNTEERS
TRAINING SESSION
Guest speaker: Ms. Catherine Huang

"As a mentor you help others. But don't underestimate how much you — as a mentor — will gain."
Veronica McKay
President

Morning Agenda
- Welcome
- Questions and Answers
- Guest speaker: Ms. Catherine Huang
- Lunch

We welcome new volunteers. Follow these three easy steps to join today.
1. Pick up an application
2. Fill out an application
3. Submit an application

Mentoring Volunteers is a non-profit organization that pairs experienced professionals with high school students in order to provide role models, encourage the students to set and achieve goals, and help develop intergenerational bonds.

Date: Saturday, March 22
Time: 10:00 a.m.
Location: Cafeteria

11. Print one copy of the file.

12. Save the changes and close **Meeting**. Leave your desktop publishing program open to use in the next exercise.

Control Text Flow

In some desktop publishing programs, you can control the way text flows within a text box by dividing the text box into *newsletter-style columns*. In newsletter-style columns, text flows from the bottom of a column to the top of the next column to the right. With newsletter-style columns, the columns are fixed within the size and position of the text box, so you do not have a great deal of flexibility when it comes to arranging the text in the publication.

To provide more flexibility, some programs let you connect text boxes so text that does not fit in the first text box automatically flows into the next connected text box. Sometimes, this is called *threading text*. When you use connected text boxes, you can size and position each text box independently. You can even connect text boxes on different pages.

Some desktop publishing programs have commands for controlling line and paragraph breaks. For example, you can select to keep lines together or with the next line on the same page or in the same column, and you can control widows and orphans. A *widow* is the last line of a paragraph that displays alone at the top of a page, and an *orphan* is the first line of a paragraph that displays alone at the bottom of a page.

Divide a Text Box into Columns

The command for dividing a text box into columns is usually in a dialog box, such as Columns in Publisher, that you open by clicking a button in the Format Text Box dialog box, or Text Frame Options in InDesign. You key the number of columns you want to apply, and then specify the width of the *gutter*, which is the space between columns. You may also be able to set a precise column width. If there is already text in the text box, your program divides it into the columns. When you key new text in the text box, text is entered in the left-most column first. When you reach the bottom of the left-most column, the text automatically wraps to the top of the next column to the right.

S TEP-BY-STEP 19.14

1. Open **Step19-14** from the data files and save it as **Reminder**.

2. Increase the zoom to at least **75%**, and then select the second text box from the top.

3. Open the dialog box where you set options for columns. If you are using Publisher, click **Format** on the Menu bar, click **Text Box**, click the **Text Box** tab, and then click the **Columns** button. In Indesign, click **Object** on the Menu bar and then click **Text Frame Options**.

STEP-BY-STEP 19.14 Continued

4. Set the number of columns to **2** and the gutter width spacing to **0.25** and then click **OK** to apply the change. Click **OK** again, if necessary to close all dialog boxes and return to your document. The text box should look similar to Figure 19-15.

FIGURE 19-15
Two columns in a text box

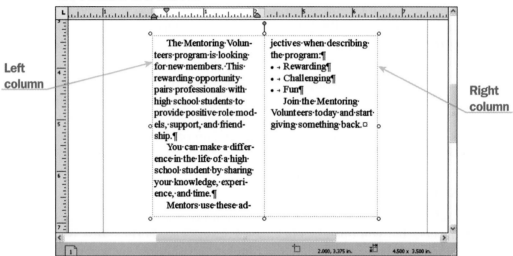

Left column

Right column

5. Save the changes and leave **Reminder** open to use in the next exercise.

Connect Text Boxes

In most programs, you connect text boxes by selecting the first text box, clicking a linking tool such as Create Text Box Link, and then clicking the next text box to connect. Or you may be able to simply click the out port of one frame and then click in the next frame. The box to connect must be blank, but the first box may contain text. Repeat the procedure to connect additional boxes. The text will flow from one box to the next in the order in which you connect the boxes. To break the link connecting boxes, click in the box and then use a tool such as Break Forward Link. When you select a linked text box, a link box displays below it to indicate whether the linked text flows forward to the next text box or back to the previous text box. You can click the link box to jump from one linked box to another, which may be particularly useful if the linked boxes are not on the same page.

STEP-BY-STEP 19.15

1. Click in the text box containing the text *For more information*.

2. Create a text box link with the blank text box to the right. If you are using Publisher, display the Connect Text Boxes toolbar if necessary, click the **Create Text Box Link** button, and then click the blank text box to the right. If you are using InDesign, select the text box, click in the out port handle and then click the blank text box to the right.

STEP-BY-STEP 19.15 Continued

3. Click back in the previous text box and position the insertion point at the end of the text and press **Enter** to start a new line. Notice that the insertion point jumps to the connected text box.

4. Key **The next training session is March 22!** and then press **Enter**. Key **Call 555-5555 to register today!** Notice that the last line does not display in the text box.

5. Link the current text box to the next blank text box, below the other two. The overflow text displays in the newly connected box, as shown in Figure 19-16.

FIGURE 19-16
Linked text boxes

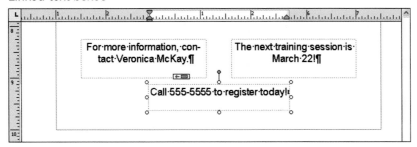

6. Save the changes and leave **Reminder** open to use in the next exercise.

Control Line and Paragraph Breaks

In most desktop publishing programs you can use options in the Paragraph dialog box or palette to control line and paragraph breaks. Typically, you can select to keep selected lines together or keep the current lines with the next line. In some programs, you can automatically control widows and orphans, and you can select to start a paragraph or line in the next available text box.

STEP-BY-STEP 19.16

1. Click in the text box that is divided into two columns.

2. Click in the paragraph that starts *Mentors use,* at the bottom of the left column. Notice that this paragraph breaks across the two columns.

3. Select the command to display the dialog box that has options for controlling line and paragraph breaks. If you are using Publisher, click **Format** on the Menu bar, click **Paragraph**, and then click the **Line and Paragraph Breaks** tab. In InDesign, click **Type** on the Menu bar, click **Paragraph**, click the menu arrow, and then click **Keep Options**.

4. Select the option to keep all lines in the paragraph together. In Publisher, click to select the **Keep lines together** check box, and then click **OK**. In InDesign, click the **Keep Lines Together** check box, click the **All lines in Paragraph** option button, and then click **OK**. All lines in the paragraph move to the right column.

STEP-BY-STEP 19.16 Continued

5. Check the spelling in the document and then display it in Print Preview. It should look similar to Figure 19-17.

FIGURE 19-17
Completed publication

6. Save the changes and close **Reminder**. Close your desktop publishing program.

SUMMARY

In this lesson, you learned:

■ When you want to create a publication from scratch, create a blank publication.

■ You can create new text boxes at any time, and delete text boxes you no longer need.

■ You can resize and reposition text boxes.

■ Apply font formatting to enhance the appearance of a publication and make the text easier to read. Font formatting includes the font set, font size, font style, font effects, and font color.

■ Horizontal alignment controls the position of text relative to the left and right text box margins, and vertical alignment controls the position of text relative to the top and bottom text box margins.

■ Set indents to create temporary margins for a paragraph in a text box. Most programs have five types of indents: first-line, left, right, double or quotation (justify), and hanging.

- Set tabs to position text along a single line. Most programs have four types of tab stops: left, right, center, and decimal.

- Lists are an effective way to communicate important points of information. Use bullet lists when order doesn't matter, and use numbered lists when order does matter.

- You can change the spacing between characters, lines, and paragraphs to make your text easier to read and to control the amount of white space in a document.

- The Clipboard is the easiest way to copy and move text and objects, but you can also insert an entire text file into a text box.

- You can control text flow by creating columns within a text box and by connecting text boxes. You can also control paragraph and line breaks.

VOCABULARY *Review*

Define the following terms:

Ascenders	Leading	Tab leaders
Baseline	Margin guides	Tabs
Descenders	Margins	Threading text
Frame inset	Newsletter-style columns	Tracking
Gutter	Orphan	Typography
Horizontal alignment	Out port	Vertical alignment
In port	Overflow text	White space
Indents	Overset text	Widow
Kerning	Paragraph spacing	

REVIEW *Questions*

TRUE / FALSE

Circle T if the statement is true or F if the statement is false.

T   F   1. Once you insert a text box in a document you cannot change its size or position.

T   F   2. Font size is the height of an uppercase letter in the font set, measured in points.

T   F   3. Use tabs to adjust the horizontal position of text across a single line.

T   F   4. Leading is measured from the baseline of one line to the baseline of the next line.

T   F   5. It is a good idea to press Enter to leave a blank line instead of adjusting paragraph and line spacing options.

T   F   6. You can use tabs to set up newsletter-style columns.

T F 7. A serif font imitates handwriting.

T F 8. Use the justify alignment option when you want to space text so that both the left and right margins are even.

T F 9. Most lists are formatted automatically using a double indent.

T F 10. If there is too much or too little space between lines, the reader's eye may have trouble following from one line to the next.

WRITTEN QUESTIONS

Write a brief answer to each of the following questions.

1. What is typography?

2. What is the difference between horizontal alignment and vertical alignment in a text box?

3. Explain at least four common methods of controlling the amount of space in and around text in a publication.

4. Explain at least three ways of controlling text flow in a publication.

5. What are at least two reasons for creating a publication from scratch?

FILL IN THE BLANK

Complete the following sentences by writing the correct word or words in the blanks provided.

1. The left _____ is the space between the left edge of the page and the objects in the publication.

2. Arial is a common _____ font.

3. Text that is hidden because it cannot fit in the text box is called _____ or overset.

4. _____ set temporary margins for a paragraph or series of paragraphs.

5. Tab _____ are characters repeated on the line preceding a tab stop.

6. White _____ is the area on a page that has no text or graphics.

7. A(n) _____ is a part of a character that extends below the baseline.

8. Margins in a text box are sometimes called the frame _____.

9. Copied or cut items are stored temporarily on the _____.

10. The last line of a paragraph that displays alone at the top of a page is called a(n) _____.

PROJECTS

PROJECT 19-1

1. Launch your desktop publishing program and create a new blank document with **1-inch** margins and save the file as **Opening**.

2. Increase the zoom to at least **75%** and display nonprinting characters.

3. Insert four text boxes or frames as follows:
   A. Draw one text box starting in the upper-left corner of the document, where the left and top margins meet. Size the box approximately **2 inches** high and **6.5 inches** wide (the width of the page from margin to margin).
   B. Start the second text box immediately below the first (with no space between the boxes), and size it to approximately **2.5 inches** high and **6.5 inches** wide.
   C. Repeat step B above to draw a third text box immediately below the second.
   D. Draw the fourth text box immediately below the third, sizing it to fill the remaining area at the bottom of the document—approximately **2 inches** high by **6.5 inches** wide.

4. Click in the first text box at the top of the page, and key and format text as follows:
   A. Select a sans serif font such as **Gill Sans MT** in **48-point** and key **Gamer's Delight**.
   B. Press **Enter**, change the font size to **36**, and key **Grand Opening Celebration**.
   C. Center the text horizontally and vertically in the text box.
   D. Select the text in the text box and apply the **Small caps** font effect.

5. Click in the next text box down, and key and format text as follows:
   A. Using the same sans serif font you used in step 4, in **26-point** font size, key the text **Join in the Excitement,** and then press **Enter** to start a new line.
   B. Change to an 18-point, serif font such as **Georgia** and set a left indent of **2 inches.**
   C. Key the following five lines of text, pressing **Enter** after each line:
      Contests
      Food
      Live Music
      Free Stuff
      Special Guests
   D. Select all five lines and apply the default bullet list formatting.
   E. Center the first line of text in the text box, then select it and apply bold, italics, and an underline.
   F. Set the paragraph spacing to leave **12 points** of space after the selected paragraph.
   G. Expand the kerning between the *E* and the *x* in the word *Excitement* to add space, then condense the kerning between the *x* and the *c* to remove space.

6. Click in the third text box, and key and format text as follows:
   A. Using the same 26-point sans serif font you used in step 4, key the text **Enter to Win,** and then press **Enter** to start a new line.
   B. Change to the 18-point **Georgia** font you used earlier. Set a left indent of **2 inches** and a right indent of **1 inch.**
   C. Key the following three lines of text, pressing **Enter** after each line:
      Fill out an entry form.
      Drop it off at any Gamer's Delight store.
      Wait for the call announcing that you are the winner!
   D. Select all lines but the first and apply the default numbered list formatting.
   E. Center the first line of text in the text box, then select it and apply bold, italics, and an underline.
   F. Set the paragraph spacing to leave **12 points** of space after the selected paragraph.

7. Click in the last text box, and key and format text as follows:
   A. Set the horizontal alignment to center.
   B. Using the same 18-point serif font you used earlier, key the text **Gamer's Delight** and then press **Enter.**
   C. Change the font size to **16 points,** key **The Source for Your Video and Online Gaming Needs** and then press **Enter.**
   D. Change the font size to **14 points,** and then key **5151 South City Turnpike.** Press **Enter,** key **West Hill, NH 03300,** and then press **Enter** to start a new line.
   E. Set the horizontal alignment to left, and then set a left tab stop at 2.5 inches on the horizontal ruler.
   F. Key the text **Monday – Saturday.** Press **Tab** and key the text **10:00 a.m. until 9:00 p.m.** Press **Enter** to start a new line.
   G. Key the text **Sundays,** press **Tab,** and key the text **12:00 p.m. until 9:00 p.m.** Press **Enter** to start a new line.
   H. Delete the left tab stop and set a right tab stop at **6.0 inches** on the horizontal ruler. Key the text **For information contact:,** press **Tab,** and key **Jay Hewitt, Store Manager.** Press **Enter** to start a new line.
   I. Press **Tab** and key **555-555-5433.**

J. Select all text in the text box and set the leading (line spacing) to **14 points**.

K. Click anywhere on the line with the city, state, and zip code, and set spacing to leave **6 points** of space after the current paragraph.

L. Set the vertical alignment in the text box to **Bottom**.

8. Check the spelling in the document and make corrections as necessary. If necessary, adjust text box size and position to display all text.

9. Print one copy of the document.

10. Save the changes and close **Opening**, but leave your desktop publishing program open to use in the next project.

PROJECT 19-2

1. In your desktop publishing program, create a new blank full-page document with **1-inch** margins and save the file as **Invite**.

2. Insert a text box the full size of page 1.

3. Select a decorative font, such as **Comic Sans MS**. Set the font size to **36 points**, change the font color to **blue**, set the horizontal alignment to **Center**, and key the text **Gamer's Delight is having a Grand Opening Sale!**

4. Press **Enter** to start a new line, change the font color to **black**, the font size to **26 points**, and key the following lines of text. (Press **Enter** at the end of each line.)
You're Invited!
Friday April 10
4:30 p.m.

5. Start a new line, change the font size to **20 points** and key the following lines:
5151 South City Turnpike
West Hill, NH 03300

6. Select all text in the document and set the line spacing to leave **6 points** of space before and after each paragraph.

7. Start a new line, and then insert the **Project19-2** text file from the data files.

8. Select the newly inserted text and change the font to a 28-point casual script, such as **Freestyle Script**, and justify the alignment.

9. Indent the paragraph **.5 inches** from the left and the right, and set line spacing to leave **36 points** of space before the paragraph.

10. Check the spelling in the document and then print it.

11. Save the changes and close **Invite**. Leave your desktop publishing program open to use in the next project.

PROJECT 19-3

1. In your desktop publishing program, create a new blank full-page document with **1-inch** margins and save the file as **Entry**.

2. Insert a text box starting in the upper-left corner of the document, where the left and top margins meet. Size the box approximately **2 inches** high and **6.5 inches** wide.

3. Select a decorative font such as **Comic Sans MS**. Set the font size to **36 points**, change the font color to **blue**, set the horizontal alignment to **Center**, and key the text **Gamer's Delight**, press **Enter** to start a new line, and then key **Official Entry Form**.

4. Insert a new text box immediately below the first, and size it to approximately **2.0 inches** wide by **2.5 inches** high. Set the font to **16-point, bold, black, Arial** and set the horizontal alignment to **Align Right**. Adjust the paragraph spacing to leave **1.5 points** after each paragraph.

5. On the first line, key **Name:** and then press **Enter**. Key **Address:** and press **Enter** four times. Key **Telephone:**, press **Enter**, key **E-Mail:**, press **Enter**, and then key **Age:**.

6. Insert a new text box starting at about **4 inches** on the horizontal ruler and **3 inches** on the vertical ruler (to the right of the second text box) and size it to about **3.5 inches** wide by **2.5 inches** high. Set the font to **16-point, bold, black, Arial** and set the horizontal alignment to **Left**. Adjust the paragraph spacing to leave **1.5 points** after each paragraph.

7. On the first line, key 25 underscore characters across the width of the text box and then press **Enter**. Repeat this step 7 times to create 8 lines in the text box.

8. Insert a new text box starting at about **2.5 inches** on the horizontal ruler and **6 inches** on the vertical ruler. Size the box to about **4 inches** wide by **1 inch** high. Set the font to **12-point**. **Times New Roman**, flush left, and set paragraph spacing to leave **2 points** after each paragraph.

9. Key the following lines of text:
   Detach the top portion of this form and submit it to any Gamer's Delight location by 5:00 p.m. on April 10.
   Winner will be selected at random from all entries.
   Grand Prize is a video gaming system.

10. Insert a new text box starting on the left margin at about **7.5** on the vertical ruler and size it approximately **6.5 inches** wide by **.5 inches** high. Set the font to **14-point**. **Times New Roman, bold**. Center the text horizontally and vertically.

11. Key the text **Official Rules and Regulations**.

12. Insert one more text box, starting on the left margin at about **8.0 inches** on the vertical ruler (immediately below the previous box) and size it approximately **6.5 inches** wide by **2.0 inches** high.

13. Divide the text box into two columns, leaving .25 spaces between the columns.

14. Set the font to **14-point Times New Roman**, flush left, and then key the following lines of text:
    Open to anyone 18 years of age or older.
    No purchase necessary.
    Official entry form must be received by 5:00 p.m. on April 10.

Grand Prize winner will be announced on April 11.
Winner does not have to be present at drawing.
If winner does not claim prize within 60 days, a new winner will be selected.
For a list of winners, write to Gamer's Delight, P.O. Box 555, West Hill, NH 03300.

15. Select all lines and apply the default numbered list formatting.

16. If necessary, click in the last line of text in the left column and set line and paragraph breaks to keep all lines in the paragraph together.

17. Check the spelling in the document and make corrections as necessary.

18. Print one copy of the document.

19. Save the changes and close **Entry**. Close your desktop publishing program.

 ## WEB PROJECT

For a project on Japan, use the Internet to research the Japanese alphabet. See if you can find information about different characters and what they mean. Then see if you can find a Japanese character font that you can download for free to use in a publication. If you have trouble locating a Japanese character font, see if you can find an English-language font that is designed to simulate Japanese characters. Create a publication (for example, you may design a poster or banner using the Japanese characters) and ask your classmates to review it and to offer comments and suggestions. Revise the publication using the suggestions, and then print it. Share it with your class.

 ## TEAMWORK PROJECT

As a group, plan and design a publication announcing an upcoming event at your school or in your community. For example, you may want to create a flyer, banner, or poster to announce a concert or play, a sporting event, a parade, or a meeting. You can work together on each stage of creating the flyer, or you can assign different roles so each person is responsible for different tasks.

Write the text you want to use in the publication. Remember, lists are an effective way to communicate important concepts and ideas. Create a mock-up of the publication so you can determine the page size and how you want the text positioned on the page. For example, determine whether all the text should be in one text box, or if you should split it into multiple text boxes, and then indicate spacing and alignment on the mock-up as well. Decide which text should be large and which should be smaller, and discuss the types of fonts you want to use. You can use your desktop publishing program to test different fonts, font sizes, and font effects. Try to find a combination of two or three fonts that you think work well together, and print sample text to see how they look when printed. Select colors that you think complement each other. Finally, create the publication.

You can start with a blank document, or use a template or design that matches your mock-up. Apply font formatting, spacing, and alignment to make the publication appealing and easy to read. When you are finished, check the spelling. Ask your classmates to review it and offer comments and suggestions. Revise the publication using the suggestions, and then print it. Present it to your class. With permission, post it in the school office or lobby, or anywhere it will get the attention of people who might be interested in the event.

CRITICAL*Thinking*

Use your desktop publishing program to create a business card for yourself. Create a mock-up so you can size and position all the information you want to include. Include at least your name, address, phone number, and e-mail address. If you have a job, you should include your title, or you may want to make up a job you would like to have. When you are ready, start with a blank document, or use one of your program's templates or designs. Use text boxes to position the text the way you planned on the mock-up. Use two fonts, and any colors, styles, and effects that you think enhance the card. Try different alignments and spacing. When you are finished, check the spelling and print one copy. If you are happy with the result, you can purchase blank cards and print additional copies.

FORMATTING PAGES

OBJECTIVES

Upon completion of this lesson, you should be able to:

- Set up pages.
- Apply built-in layout options.
- Set guides.
- Use master pages.
- Insert page numbers.
- Insert and delete pages.
- Save a publication as a template and create a publication based on a custom template.
- Apply a color scheme and font scheme.
- Use styles.

Estimated Time: 2 hours

VOCABULARY

Baseline guides

Column guides

Document master

Facing pages

Field

Gutter

Layout guides

Master pages

Master page spread

Mirrored pages

Page layout

Page setup

Recto

Row guides

Ruler guides

Two-page spread

Verso

Watermark

Good page formatting uses the basic principles of design, including contrast, balance, and consistency, to capture a reader's attention. Your desktop publishing program has many tools to help you use these principles when you format your publication. When you create a document using a template or design, your desktop publishing program automatically applies page formatting options suitable for the publication type. The formatting includes a *page setup* that defines settings such as page size, margin width, number of pages in the publication, and page orientation. You can also format pages on your own by selecting options manually. For example, you may set a custom page size for a brochure, change the orientation for a booklet, or add pages to a catalog. That way, you can customize built-in designs, and you can create your own designs from scratch. You can even save your own designs as a template for creating future documents. In this lesson, you learn how to format pages by applying layouts and other options.

Set Up Pages

Page setup options usually are set automatically when you select a template or design, or when you select the publication type. They affect the entire publication, and they generally include settings such as the page size, paper size, and page orientation. As discussed in earlier lessons, the page size is the height and width of the printed page, and the page orientation is the position of the paper in relation to the content. The paper size, which is sometimes called the sheet size, is the size of the actual sheet of paper on which the publication is printed.

You can change the individual default page setup options in a dialog box such as Page Setup in Publisher (shown in Figure 20-1), or Document Setup in InDesign. In addition to settings such as page size, paper size, and orientation, you may be able to set the number of pages in the publication, specify how many copies to print per sheet, specify double-sided printing, or create a *two-page spread*. A two-page spread consists of two *facing pages* that are sometimes called *mirrored pages* because their layout and margins are not identical, but reversed.

FIGURE 20-1
Page Setup dialog box

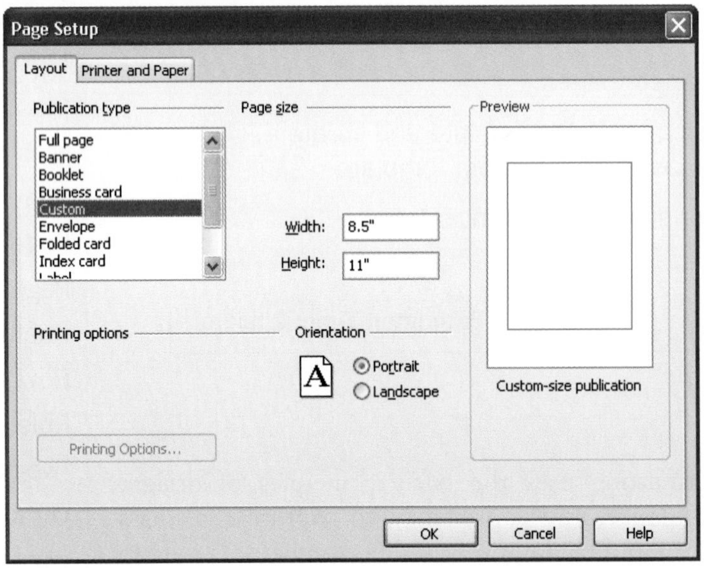

S TEP-BY-STEP 20.1

1. Launch your desktop publishing program, and select the command to create a new, blank document. If the Document Setup dialog box displays, skip step 2. (If the Template dialog box opens, close it.)

2. Select the command to display the dialog box that has the options for controlling page setup. For example, in Publisher, click **File** on the Menu bar, and then click **Page Setup**. In InDesign, click **File** > **Document Setup**.

3. Set the orientation to **Landscape**.

4. Click **Custom** in the *Publication type* or *Page size* list and then set the page size dimensions to **7** inches wide by **5** inches high.

STEP-BY-STEP 20.1 Continued

5. Click the **OK** button in the dialog box. The publication should look similar to the one in Figure 20-2. (Close the task pane, if necessary.)

FIGURE 20-2
Custom page size

6. Save the file as **Notice**.

7. Open the dialog box that has the options for controlling page setup again.

8. Click **Postcard** in the *Publication type* list, and then click **1/4 page Letter** in the *Page size* list. Alternatively, set the custom page size to **5.5** inches wide by **4.25** inches high, still in **Landscape** orientation.

9. Click the **OK** button to change the publication layout.

10. Save the changes and leave **Notice** open to use in the next exercise.

Apply Built-In Layout Options

Page layout, or the way you organize and arrange objects and white space on a page, significantly affects the overall impact of a publication. Page layout involves the use of alignment, size, and position to lead the reader's eye across the page. A well-designed page layout makes it easy for the reader to locate and absorb information. For example, a two-column layout may make a newsletter easier to read, while the position of a picture may lead the reader's eye to a particular article.

In some programs, you can apply built-in page layout options to change the appearance of pages. In Publisher, for instance, you can select layout options in the task pane. To apply a built-in option, display the task pane and select the type of option you want to change, or select the type of option directly from the Format menu. Then, click the option to apply it. The available options change depending on the current publication type, and sometimes even depending on the current page.

If you want, for example, to include a customer address on the back of a catalog publication, create the catalog publication using a catalog template (or open an existing catalog publication), and then click Catalog Options in the task pane or on the Format menu. Then, click Include in the customer address section. Your program automatically changes the layout and design of the back page of the catalog to include the address. To remove the address, click None. To change a catalog page from two columns of all text to one column with graphics, click Page Content in the task pane or on the Format menu, make the page you're planning to modify active, and then click the option to apply it.

Not all programs offer built-in options. Adobe InDesign is one that does not. If your program does not, skip this exercise, close the Notice file, but leave your desktop publishing program open to use in the following exercise.

STEP-BY-STEP 20.2

1. Click **Format** on the Menu bar, and then click **Quick Publication Options**.

2. In the task pane rest your mouse pointer on each layout option to display its description in a ScreenTip.

3. Click the **No picture** layout. It may be the second choice from the bottom in the middle column.

4. Click the **Message only** layout in the task pane. The publication changes to reflect the selection.

5. Click the **Sidebar heading, picture at the bottom** layout and then close the task pane. The file should look similar to the one in Figure 20-3.

FIGURE 20-3
Apply a built-in layout option

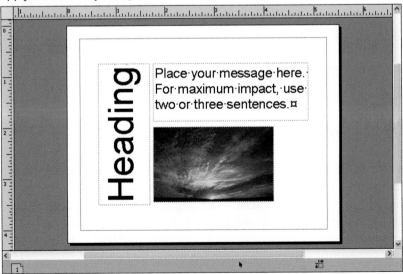

6. Save the changes and close **Notice**. Leave your desktop publishing program open to use in the next exercise.

Set Guides

All desktop publishing programs have *layout guides* or nonprinting lines that you can display on the screen while you work to help you position and align objects on a page. Different programs use different terms to identify guides. Your program may use *column guides* or *row guides* to define columns and rows; margin guides to define the top, bottom, left, and right margins; and *ruler guides* to define any point along the vertical or horizontal ruler. Most programs also have *baseline guides*, which are horizontal guides that define the baseline of each line of text.

Sometimes, each type of guide displays onscreen in a different color so you can differentiate between them. In most programs, you set column, grid, and margin guides for the entire publication, but you can set ruler guides on any page. Figure 20-4 shows different guides in a desktop publishing document.

Hot Tip

In some programs, you can insert ruler guides simply by clicking on the ruler and then dragging the guide into the document window.

Note

If guides are not displayed on your screen, you may have selected the command to toggle them off. Click View on the Menu bar, and then click the command to show guides.

FIGURE 20-4
Guides in a blank publication

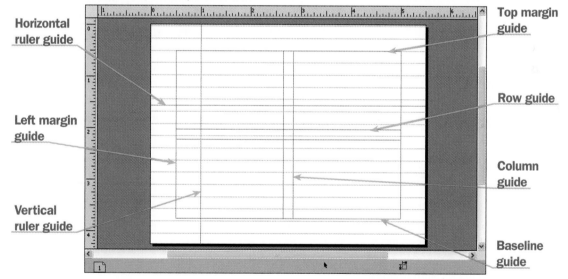

Horizontal ruler guide

Left margin guide

Vertical ruler guide

Top margin guide

Row guide

Column guide

Baseline guide

Usually, you toggle the guides on or off on-screen using commands on the View menu. You can set the position of guides using a dialog box such as Layout Guides in Publisher, which is shown in Figure 20-5. In InDesign you set margins and columns in the Margins and Columns dialog box. You customize grid and guide options in the Preferences dialog box.

FIGURE 20-5
Layout Guides dialog box

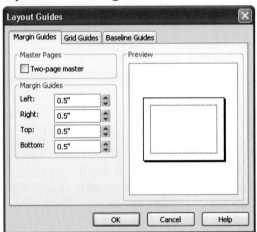

Note that margins are usually set for the top, bottom, left, and right of a page. If you are going to bind or fold a publication, you need to leave extra space along the inside page edges, or **gutter**. The gutter is usually the left edge of right-hand or odd-numbered pages—sometimes called **recto** pages, and the right edge of left-hand, or even-numbered pages—sometimes called **verso**. In Publisher, the gutter between columns is called spacing. (Recall that a gutter—or alley—is also the term used to describe the space between columns.) Sometimes, depending on the program and publication type, the left and right margin settings are actually called inside and outside margins. *Inside* refers to the edge that may be bound or folded, and *outside* refers to the edge opposite the binding or fold.

S TEP-BY-STEP 20.3

1. Create a new blank **8.5**-inch by **11**-inch single-page document. If you are using a program that prompts you for document setup options, such as InDesign, clear the *Facing Pages* check box, and accept the default margins.

2. Save the file as **April Meeting**.

3. Select the command to display margin and column guides, if necessary. If you are using Publisher, click **View** on the Menu bar and then click **Boundaries and Guides**. (A check mark next to the command indicates that it is already toggled on.) If you are using InDesign, click **View** on the Menu bar, click **Grids & Guides**, and then click **Show Guides**. (If the available command is *Hide Guides*, it is already toggled on.)

4. Select the command to open the dialog box for setting margin guides. In Publisher, click **Arrange** on the Menu bar, and then click **Layout Guides**. In InDesign, click **Layout** on the Menu bar and then click **Margins and Columns**.

STEP-BY-STEP 20.3 Continued

5. Key **1.25** in the *Left*, *Right*, *Top*, and *Bottom* boxes to set all margins to 1.25 inches.

6. Create two columns in the document with a **.2**-inch gutter. In Publisher click the **Grid Guides** tab in the Layout Guides dialog box and key **2** in the *Columns* box. (The spacing defaults to .2.) In InDesign, key **2** in the *Number* box and key **.2** in the *Gutter* box.

7. Click the **OK** button to apply the changes.

8. Display a horizontal ruler guide **3** inches below the top of the page. You may click on the horizontal ruler and drag down to create the guide, or use a command such as Publisher's **Arrange > Ruler Guides > Add Horizontal Ruler Guide**, and then drag the guide to position it.

> **Note** ☑️
>
> You can change the unit of measure in most desktop publishing programs to inches, centimeters, picas, or points.

9. Zoom in on the top part of the document (about **66%**). Insert a text box or text frame between the top margin and the horizontal ruler guide, sized to the width of the page between the left and right margins (**6.0** inches wide by **1.75** inches high).

10. Select a sans serif font such as **Arial**; set the font size to **48**; apply **boldface**; and set the horizontal alignment to **Center**. Key **Sales Department April Meeting**. The document should look similar to the one in Figure 20-6.

FIGURE 20-6
Text added to April meeting

Horizontal ruler guide

Two column guides with .2-inch gutter

1.25-inch margins on all sides

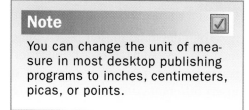

11. Save the changes and leave **April Meeting** open to use in the next exercise.

Use Master Pages

Most desktop publishing programs include some form of a *master page* to help you maintain consistency through a multipage publication. A master page is a model or template used to contain text and/or objects that display on every page in a publication. Usually a master page is used to store objects that are repeated on every page of a publication, such as page numbers, a *watermark*, or a logo that you want in the corner of every page. A watermark is a semi-transparent object that displays behind other objects on pages in a publication. (You will learn more about watermarks in Lesson 21.) In some programs, master pages also store basic page setup options.

To understand master pages, imagine a background that displays standard and consistent elements on every page in a publication. On each page of the publication, you overlay a sheet of tracing paper. You can see through the tracing paper to the background elements, and you can insert different content on the tracing paper to customize the foreground of each page.

No matter which program you use, changes that you make to a master page affect every page formatted with that master, while changes that you make to the publication page affect only that page. To modify a master page, you must switch to that master page. Otherwise, the changes are applied to the foreground page only.

Most programs automatically create a *document master*, which is a single master page for an entire publication, when you create the document. Usually, this master is called *Master A*. If the publication uses facing pages or two-page spreads, the program may automatically create a *master page spread*, which includes a left page master page and a right page master page. In Publisher, however, you must manually create a master page spread by selecting the option in the Layout Guides dialog box.

To work on a master page, switch to Master Page view. This is done in Publisher, by choosing a command such as Master Page on the View menu, or using the Apply or Edit Master Page task pane. In InDesign, this is done by selecting the master page from a list on the Status bar, or in the Pages palette.

> **Note** ☑
>
> In some programs, such as InDesign, you can create as many master pages as you want, and each master may include multiple layers.

S TEP-BY-STEP 20.4

1. Switch to Master Page view. If you are using Publisher, click **View** on the Menu bar and then click **Master Page**. In InDesign, click the page number drop-down arrow on the Status bar and click **A-Master**, or double-click **A-Master** in the Pages palette. The elements, such as margin guides, that are automatically stored as part of the master document display, while objects such as the text box that you created on the publication page no longer display. If a task pane displays, close it.

> **Note**
>
> In Publisher, column guides display on the master page, but in InDesign they do not.

STEP-BY-STEP 20.4 Continued

2. Insert a text box or frame the width of the page between the left and right margins, about **1/4** inch high, along the bottom margin. Select a sans serif font such as **Arial**, set the font size to **14**, and the horizontal alignment to **Center**. Key **Contact the department coordinator to add an item to the agenda**. The page should look similar to Figure 20-7.

> **Note** ☑
>
> If you are using InDesign, and a two-page spread displays in Master page view, you did not clear the Facing Pages check box in the Document Setup dialog box when you first created the document. Click the menu arrow in the Pages palette and then click Master Options for "A-Master". Change the Number of Pages value to 1 and then click OK.

FIGURE 20-7
A master page

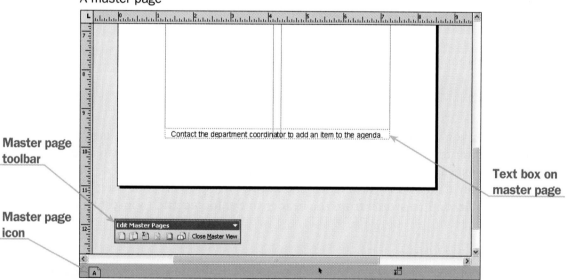

Master page toolbar

Master page icon

Contact the department coordinator to add an item to the agenda.

Edit Master Pages
Close Master View

Text box on master page

3. Change back to normal page view. The content on the master page and the foreground page both display.

4. Save the changes and leave **April Meeting** open to use in the next exercise.

Insert Page Numbers

Page numbers are an important feature of multipage documents. They help readers locate specific items based on a table of contents or an index. In most desktop publishing programs, page numbers are inserted on a master page as a *field* or marker. A field is a code instead of an actual number so the page number updates if you add, delete, or move pages within the publication. Usually, page numbers are inserted in either the page header or footer. Recall that a header displays information repeated at the top of every page in the area between the top margin and the top edge of the page, and a footer repeats information at the bottom of every page in the area between the bottom margin and the bottom edge of the page.

To insert page numbers, switch to the master page and then select the command to insert the page number. In Publisher, click Insert on the Menu bar and then click Page Numbers. A page numbers dialog box similar to the one in Figure 20-8 displays so you can select options such as the location of the number on the page,

> **Important**
>
> You should always insert a page number as a field, not as a specific number. If you insert a specific number, that number will display on every page in the publication.

the number format, and whether a number should appear on the first page. In InDesign, first position the insertion point where you want to place the page number. Click Type on the Menu bar, click Insert Special Character, and then click Auto Page Number.

FIGURE 20-8
Page Numbers dialog box

In Publisher, you can insert page numbers and other fields, such as the date or time, using the Header and Footer toolbar. Select the View > Header and Footer command to display the Header and Footer toolbar and the header area on the screen. The header area is defined by boundary lines. You can key data directly into either the header or footer area, or use the toolbar buttons described in Table 20-1 to switch from the header to the footer, and to insert fields.

TABLE 20-1
Header/footer toolbar buttons

ICON	BUTTON NAME	CLICK TO
[#]	Insert Page Number	Insert automatically updating page numbers.
[📅]	Insert Date	Insert automatically updating current date.
[🕐]	Insert Time	Insert automatically updating current time.
[⊞]	Show Header/Footer	Switch between the header and footer areas.
Close	Close	Click to close the toolbar and return to the previous document view.

S TEP-BY-STEP 20.5

1. Change to Master Page view.

2. Insert page numbers in the center of the footer. If you are using Publisher, click **Insert** on the Menu bar, and then click **Page Numbers**. In the Page Numbers dialog box, select **Bottom of page (Footer)** from the *Position* list, and select **Center** from the *Alignment* list. Make sure the option to display numbers on the first page is selected, and then click the **OK** button. If you are using InDesign, create a text frame in the horizontal center of the page in the footer area, and set the font to **10 points**. Click **Type** on the Menu bar, click **Insert Special Character**, and then click **Auto Page Number**. If necessary, adjust the alignment of the character and the text frame to make sure it is centered horizontally.

3. Zoom in on the bottom of the page to at least **100%** magnification. It should look similar to Figure 20-9. Because you are in Master Page view, a field code displays in place of the actual page number. In Publisher the code is a number sign; in InDesign it is the letter *A*.

FIGURE 20-9
Page number field code in Master Page view

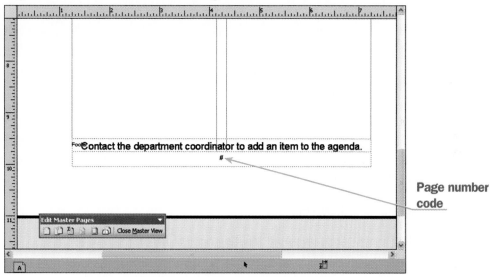

Page number
code

STEP-BY-STEP 20.5 Continued

4. Change to normal page view. The footer area should look similar to Figure 20-10.

FIGURE 20-10
Page number in normal page view

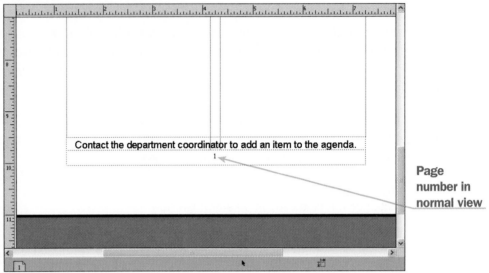

Contact the department coordinator to add an item to the agenda.

Page number in normal view

5. Change back to Master Page view.

6. Create a header with the current date left aligned. If you are using Publisher, click **View** on the Menu bar, and then click **Header and Footer**. Click the **Insert Date** button on the Header and Footer toolbar, and then click **Close** on the Header and Footer toolbar. If you are using InDesign, create a text frame in the header area and key today's date.

7. Change to normal page view.

8. Save the changes and leave **April Meeting** open to use in the next exercise.

Insert and Delete Pages

A fundamental way to change the layout of a publication is to change the number of total pages. In most programs, you can easily insert new pages or delete pages you don't need. To insert a new page, use a command such as Insert > Page in Publisher or Layout > Pages > Insert Pages in InDesign to display a dialog box similar to the one in Figure 20-11, in which you select options such as how many pages to insert, where to insert them, and whether to create content on the new page(s). In some programs, you also select the master page to apply to the new pages.

FIGURE 20-11
Insert Page dialog box

To delete a page, make it active by selecting it and then selecting the Delete Page command. In Publisher, the command is on the Edit menu; in InDesign, it is on the Pages palette. In some programs a dialog box prompts you to confirm the deletion. Be careful when deleting pages because all the content on the page is deleted at the same time. You can use the Undo command to reverse the action if you delete a page by mistake.

STEP-BY-STEP 20.6

1. Make sure you are in normal page view, and then select the command to insert one blank page after the current page. The new page displays on the screen. It should look similar to Figure 20-12. Notice that all the content you inserted on the master page is on the new page, but the content you inserted on the foreground page is not.

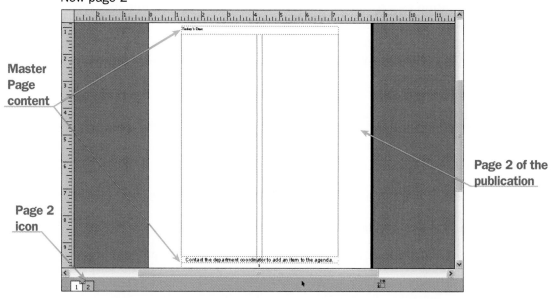

FIGURE 20-12
New page 2

Master Page content

Page 2 icon

Page 2 of the publication

2. Insert another new blank page after page 2. Now, the publication has three pages.

Now, try deleting a page.

STEP-BY-STEP 20.6 Continued

3. Switch to page 2, and then select the command to delete it. If you are using Publisher, click the **page 2** icon in the Status bar, click **Edit** on the Menu bar, and then click **Delete Page**. If you are using InDesign, click the **page 2** icon in the Pages palette, and then click the **Delete** icon. If necessary, click the **OK** button in any confirm dialog boxes to complete the deletion.

4. Save the changes and leave **April Meeting** open to use in the next exercise.

> **Hot Tip**
>
> In Publisher, you can reposition pages within a document by dragging the page icons on the Status bar.

> **Note**
>
> In InDesign, you may have to apply a master page to the foreground pages. To do so, make the master page active. Click the menu arrow in the Pages palette and then click Apply Master to Pages. In the To Pages box, key the page number of the page to which you want to apply the master. You may key multiple page numbers separated by commas. Click OK to apply the master.

Create a Template

Once you have a publication set up just right, you can save it as a template so you can base future documents on it. Saving a publication as a template ensures that new documents are created with uniform page setup and formatting characteristics. In addition, your template can include elements that you want to be the same in every new document, such as page numbers, disclaimer text, and even a corporate logo.

Save a Publication as a Template

Save a publication as a template using the familiar Save As command. In the Save As dialog box, key a template name and select the template file type from the *Save as type* list. In some programs, the template file is automatically stored in the Templates folder with other publication templates. In other programs, you can store the template file in any folder.

STEP-BY-STEP 20.7

1. Switch to page 1 and edit the text in the text box to change the word *April* to the word **Monthly**. Format the word *Monthly* in Bold Italic.

2. Click **File** on the Menu bar, and then click **Save As**. The Save As dialog box opens.

3. Key **Monthly Sales Meeting** in the *File name* text box.

4. Click the **Save as type** drop-down arrow and select the option to save the file as a template. In Publisher click **Publisher Template**. In InDesign, click **InDesign Template**.

> **Hot Tip**
>
> It is a good idea to use a name that describes the template.

STEP-BY-STEP 20.7 Continued

5. If necessary, select the location where you want to store the template. (In some programs, the location for the template will default to a Templates folder on the local hard drive. You will have to select a different location if you want to store your template with your solution files.)

6. Click the **Save** button in the Save As dialog box. The file is saved as a template.

7. Close the **Monthly Sales Meeting** template file, and leave your desktop publication program open to use in the next lesson.

Create a Publication Based on a Custom Template

Once you have saved a custom template, you can use it to create a new publication based on the template. Depending on your program, you either use the File > New command or the File > Open command to locate and open the template file. If you are using Publisher you click File on the Menu bar and then click New to display the New Publication task pane. Click *From existing publication* to open a dialog box, then locate and open the template. If you are using InDesign, click File on the Menu bar and then click Open to display the Open a File dialog box in which you locate and open the template.

S TEP-BY-STEP 20.8

1. Create a new publication based on the Monthly Sales Meeting template. In Publisher, click **File** on the Menu bar and click **New**. In the task pane, click **From existing publication**. Locate and select the **Monthly Sales Meeting** template file, and then click **Create New**. In InDesign, click **File** on the Menu bar, click **Open**, locate and select the **Monthly Sales Meeting** template file, and then click **Open**.

2. Save the file as **May Meeting**. This file is a publication file, not a template file.

3. Edit the word *Monthly* in the text box to **May**. Remove the italic font style, leaving the text formatted in bold.

4. Save the changes and close **May Meeting**. Leave your desktop publishing program open to use in the next exercise.

Apply a Color Scheme and Font Scheme

As you have already learned, publications based on a template or design are created with a particular color scheme and font scheme. The color scheme is a set of coordinated colors used in the publication. A font scheme is a set of coordinated fonts applied to text. In Publisher you can change the font scheme or color scheme simply by picking a new scheme. Some programs, such as InDesign, do not have options for applying font schemes and color schemes. In such a program you must change the color or font for each element individually.

Change the Color Scheme

Most color schemes have three or more colors that are automatically applied to different elements of a document. Usually, the main color is used for text, and additional colors are used for accents such as bullets, lines, and shading. To select a color scheme, use the Format > Color Schemes command to open the Color Schemes task pane and click the scheme you want to apply. The Color Schemes task pane looks similar to the one in Figure 20-13.

FIGURE 20-13
Color Schemes task pane

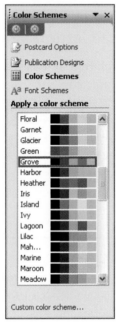

Don't worry if your program doesn't support color schemes. You learn more about working with color in Lesson 21, including how to define colors, modify colors, create custom color schemes, and import colors. In the meantime, you can complete the following steps by changing the color of individual elements in the publication.

STEP-BY-STEP 20.9

1. Open **Step20-9** from the data files and save it as **Dance**. (This is a version of the **Postcard** file you created in an earlier lesson.) If your program warns you that it must use substitute fonts, click **OK** to continue.

   If your program does not offer color schemes, leave this file open and go on to the next exercise, or manually change the color of different elements in the publication using the colors described in step 4.

2. Click **Format** on the Menu bar, and then click **Color Schemes** to open the Color Schemes task pane or palette.

STEP-BY-STEP 20.9 Continued

3. Scroll through the list of color schemes. Click a color scheme that has bright colors, such as **Wildflower**. Note the change in the document.

4. Scroll through the list of color schemes and click one that includes only shades of brown, such as **Brown**. If you are manually changing the colors, use the following RGB color codes:

Background graphics fill on pages 1 and 2: R: **194**, G: **173**, B: **153**

Background graphics stroke on pages 1 and 2: R: **133**, G: **92**, B: **51**

All text on pages 1 and 2: R: **102**, G: **51**, B: **0**

5. Close the task pane or palette. The file should look similar to the one in Figure 20-14.

FIGURE 20-14
Dance with the Brown color scheme

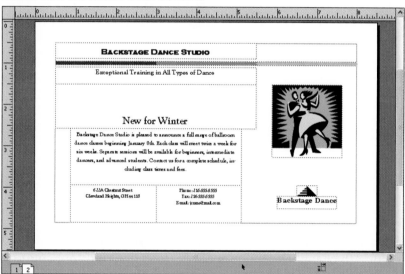

6. Save the changes and leave **Dance** open to use in the next exercise.

Change the Font Scheme

If your program has built-in font schemes, they usually include two fonts: a main font for headings and a minor font for body text. To select a font scheme, display a task pane or dialog box such as the Font Schemes task pane or palette. The Font Schemes task pane looks similar to the one in Figure 20-15. Simply click the scheme you want to apply.

FIGURE 20-15
Font Schemes task pane

If your program does not have font schemes, you can still experiment with the fonts available on your system. You can change the font, font style, font size, and font color to give your publication a different look.

STEP-BY-STEP 20.10

1. Click **Format** on the Menu bar, and then click **Font Schemes** to open the Font Schemes task pane.

   If your program does not have font schemes, apply the fonts manually as described in step 3.

2. Scroll through the list of font schemes. Click a font scheme that combines two versions of a similar font, such as the **Foundry** font scheme, which uses *Rockwell Extra Bold* as the main font and *Rockwell* as the minor font. Note the changes in the document.

3. Scroll through the list of font schemes and click one that uses a script font for headings, such as **Monogram**, which uses *Edwardian Script ITC* as the major font and *TW Cen MT* as the minor font. If you are manually changing the fonts, apply the **Edwardian Script ITC** to at least one heading, and **TW Cen MT** to subheadings and regular text. Note that you may apply variations of the font, such as condensed or bold. You may also change the font size as necessary.

STEP-BY-STEP 20.10 Continued

4. Close the task pane or palette. The file should look similar to the one in Figure 20-16.

FIGURE 20-16
Dance with the Monogram font scheme

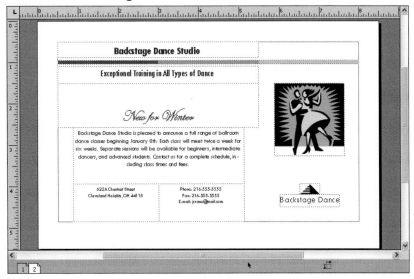

5. Save the changes and leave **Dance** open to use in the next exercise.

Use Styles

A *style* is a collection of formatting settings that you can apply to text, paragraphs, and, in some programs, to objects. A style might include the font, the font size, the alignment, and the font effect. Most programs include a list of paragraph styles for formatting text, headings, lists, and other parts of a publication. Styles can be very useful in helping you maintain consistent formatting throughout a document, and they can save you time. To apply a style, click in the paragraph to format, or select the text to format, and then open the Styles task pane or palette and select the style to apply. You can also select a style and then key new text.

> **Hot Tip**
>
> In Publisher, you can use the Style box on the Formatting toolbar to quickly apply a style. Click the drop-down arrow to display the style list, or key the style name directly in the Style box, and then press Enter.

STEP-BY-STEP 20.11

1. Open the task pane or palette that lists styles. If you are using Publisher, click **Format** on the Menu bar, and then click **Styles and Formatting**. If you are using InDesign, click **Type** on the Menu bar, and then click **Paragraph Styles**.

STEP-BY-STEP 20.11 Continued

2. Click anywhere in the company name text *Backstage Dance Studio* at the top of the page, and then scroll through the list of styles. Click the first body text style in the list. It may be called **Body Text** or simply **Body**. The style is applied to the text.

3. Scroll through the list of styles and click the second **Organization Name** style or the **Head** style.

4. Click in the tagline *Exceptional Training in All Types of Dance*, and then click the second **Organization Name** style again, or the **Subhead** style. The document should look similar to the one in Figure 20-17.

FIGURE 20-17
Text formatted with styles

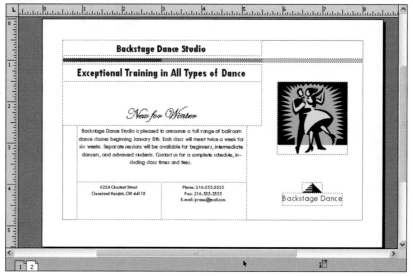

5. Print one copy of the publication.

6. Save the changes. If prompted, click **No** to save without modifying the personal information.

7. Close **Dance** and your desktop publication program.

SUMMARY

In this lesson, you learned:

■ Page formatting controls the layout and organization of objects on a page.

■ The basic page setup options include page size, paper size, and page orientation.

■ Some programs have built-in layout options you can apply to quickly change the page layout for a publication.

■ Guides help you arrange and position objects on a page.

- There are four types of guides in most desktop publishing programs: column or grid guides, margin guides, baseline guides, and ruler guides.

- Master pages help you maintain consistency in multipage documents.

- You can use a master page to store objects that you want to display on all pages, such as a tagline or date.

- In some programs, master pages can also store page layout and formatting information.

- You should insert page numbers on a master page.

- Page numbers are usually inserted as field codes, so that they update on each page.

- You can save a document as a template so that you can create new documents based on it.

- Some programs have color schemes and font schemes you can quickly apply to any publication to insure consistent formatting.

- Use a style to quickly apply a set of formatting characteristics to paragraphs in a publication.

VOCABULARY *Review*

Define the following terms:

Baseline guides	Layout guides	Recto
Column guides	Master page	Row guides
Document master	Master page spread	Ruler guides
Facing pages	Mirrored pages	Two-page spread
Field	Page layout	Verso
Gutter	Page setup	Watermark

REVIEW *Questions*

TRUE / FALSE

Circle T if the statement is true or F if the statement is false.

T   F   1. Page setup options are usually set automatically when you select a template or design.

T   F   2. Page orientation is sometimes called sheet size.

T   F   3. Facing pages are sometimes called mirrored pages.

T   F   4. Not all desktop publishing programs have a feature for applying built-in layout options.

T   F   5. You cannot change the position of a ruler guide.

T   F   6. Right-hand pages are usually odd numbered.

T F 7. All desktop publishing programs have a feature for applying a color scheme.

T F 8. Most font schemes include a main font for headings and a minor font for body text.

T F 9. Different types of guides usually display on-screen in different colors.

T F 10. Changes that you make to a master page affect every page formatted with that master.

WRITTEN QUESTIONS

Write a brief answer to each of the following questions.

1. What is the difference between ruler guides and margin guides?

2. What is the benefit of inserting a page number code in a field instead of keying the actual page number?

3. Describe at least two reasons for saving a publication as a template.

4. Describe at least three settings that help define page setup.

5. What are three basic principles of design that affect page formatting?

FILL IN THE BLANK

Complete the following sentences by writing the correct word or words in the blanks provided.

1. If you are going to bind a publication, you need to leave extra space along the _____ page edges, or gutter.

2. Right-hand pages are sometimes called _____ pages.

3. Left-hand pages are sometimes called _____ pages.

4. A(n) _____ page is a model or template that you use to contain text and/or objects that display on every page in a publication.

5. A(n) _____ is a collection of formatting settings that you can apply to text, paragraphs, and, in some programs, to objects.

6. Page _____ is the way you organize and arrange objects and white space on a page.

7. To work on a master page you must switch to Master Page _____.

8. Place a page number in the _____ if you want it to display at the bottom of the page.

9. A two-page _____ consists of facing pages.

10. All desktop publishing programs have layout _____ that you can display on the screen to help you position and align objects on a page.

PROJECTS

PROJECT 20-1

Before beginning this project, create a mock-up of a two-sided 8.5-inch by 11-inch newsletter with two columns on both pages and a banner headline that extends across the top of the first page. You need space for four articles on each page, but the articles may not be of equal length.

Use a ruler and a pencil to draw columns on both sides of a letter-sized sheet of paper. Leave a gutter of approximately .2 inches.

Use a ruler and a pencil to draw horizontal rules indicating the location of the banner headline on page 1 and possible divisions for positioning the four articles on each page.

1. Launch your desktop publishing program and open **Project20-1** from the data files. This file contains all the content you need to create a two-sided newsletter, already formatted and divided into text boxes. However, you must size and position the text boxes to create a layout that is appealing and easy to read.

2. Save the file as **ArtsNews**.

3. Increase the zoom to at least **75%** and take some time to examine the content. Look at both pages. Notice that some of the text boxes are overflowing with text. At least one is overlapping the margins.

4. Change to Master Page view and divide the page into two columns of equal width, with a gutter of .2 inches. If you are using InDesign, apply the master to both pages 1 and 2. (Click the menu arrow in the Pages palette, click **Apply Master to Pages**, in the To Pages box, key **1,2**, and then click **OK**.) Close Master Page view.

5. Make page **1** active and move all text boxes except the headline box, which is the one containing the text *Our Arts News* at the top of the page out into the scratch area (the gray or white area around the outside of the page).

6. Format the page as follows:
   A. Set horizontal ruler guides at **2.25**, **2.5**, and **6.75** inches on the vertical ruler. You can check the position of your ruler guides using the coordinates in the status bar or Control palette.
   B. Size and position the headline text box to fit vertically between the top margin and the first ruler guide, and horizontally across the width of the page, between the page margins.
   C. Size and position the text box containing the date and volume number vertically between the first and second ruler guides, and horizontally across the width of the page, between the page margins.
   D. Now move the second ruler guide down **0.25** inch, to the **2.75**-inch mark on the vertical ruler.
   E. Size and position the text box with the headline *A Night of the Arts* vertically between the second and third ruler guides and horizontally within the left column.
   F. Move the third ruler guide down **0.25** inch to the 7-inch mark on the vertical ruler. Size and position the text box with the headline *Volunteer News* vertically between the third ruler guide and the bottom margin, and horizontally within the left column. Notice that there is still overflow text.
   G. Insert a new blank text box or frame sized and positioned vertically between the second and third ruler guides and horizontally within the right column. Connect the text box at the bottom of the left column with the blank text box at the top of the right column. The overflow text should flow into the new text box.
   H. Size and position the remaining text box—*Donations Needed*—vertically between the third ruler guide and the bottom margin, and horizontally within the right column. Page 1 is now complete.

7. Make page **2** active and drag all of the text boxes into the scratch area.

8. Format the page as follows:
   A. Insert a horizontal ruler guide at **5** inches on the vertical ruler.
   B. Size and position the text box with the headline *Officer Nominations* to fit vertically between the top margin and the horizontal ruler guide, and horizontally within the left column.
   C. Size and position the text box with the list of editors and officers to fit vertically between the ruler guide and the bottom margin, and horizontally within the left column.
   D. Move the ruler guide up to **2.5** inches on the vertical ruler, and then size and position the text box containing the text *Don't Forget!* to fit vertically between the top margin and the ruler guide and horizontally within the right column.
   E. Move the ruler guide down to the **2.75**-inch mark on the vertical ruler, and then size and position the remaining text box within the remaining space.

9. Print both pages, either on separate sheets of paper or on a double-sided sheet.

10. Save the changes and close **ArtsNews**, but leave your desktop publishing program open to use in the next project.

PROJECT 20-2

Before beginning this project, create a mock-up of a 4-page booklet using a blank letter-sized sheet of paper:

Hold the sheet in Landscape orientation (with the long side on top) and then fold it in half left to right.

Mark the front as **page 1** and the back as **page 4**. Mark the left inside page as **page 2** and the right inside page as **page 3**.

Unfold the sheet and note that each side of the sheet is a two-page spread—the front is pages 2 and 3 and the back is pages 1 and 4.

1. Create a new blank document in your desktop publishing program and save it as **ArtsNight**.

2. Set page setup options to create a 4-page booklet, with pages sized to **5.5** inches wide by **8.5** inches high, in Landscape orientation. (If your program asks permission to add pages, click the **Yes** button.)

3. Set margins to **.75** inches on the inside and outside and **.5** on the top and bottom. If you are using InDesign, make sure the *Facing Pages* option is selected, and set the number of pages in the document to **4**.

4. Change to **Master Page** view and set up the pages on the master page spread as follows:
   A. Insert a horizontal ruler guide across the top of the sheet at the **1.0**-inch mark on the vertical ruler, and another horizontal ruler guide across the bottom of the sheet at the **7.5**-inch mark on the vertical ruler. (If you are using InDesign, you must insert the guides on each page.)
   B. Draw four text boxes—one at the top of each page between the ruler guide and the top margin, the width of the column, and one at the bottom of each page, between the ruler guide and the bottom margin, the width of the column.
   C. Using the default font in **10** points in both top text boxes, key **Our Arts Alliance**. Left-align the text on the left page and right-align the text on the right page.
   D. Using the same font and font size in both bottom text boxes, key **Page**, leave a space, and then insert the page number field. Again, left-align the text on the left page and right-align the text on the right page.

5. Change to regular page view and make page 1 active if necessary. Set up the page as follows:
   A. Insert three horizontal ruler guides positioned at **2.0**, **4.0**, and **6.0** inches on the vertical ruler.
   B. Draw two text boxes sized to fit between the inside and outside margins—one between the first and second ruler guides you just added and one between the second and third ruler guides.

6. Enter and format text in the text boxes as follows:
   A. Display the Font Schemes list and select a decorative but sophisticated font scheme such as **Etched**, which uses *Copperplate Gothic Bold* and *Garamond*. If your program does not offer font schemes, you can apply font formatting as suggested in the following steps.

B. In the top text box that you just created, key **Our Arts Alliance**. (The text may display in all uppercase characters because of the font selection.) Display the Styles and Formatting list and apply the **Title** style to the text. If the title style is not available, apply a style such as **Headline** style. If there are no styles available, apply the **Copperplate Gothic Bold** font. Select the text and change the font size to **48**.

C. In the bottom text box that you just created, key **A Night of the Arts**. (Again, the text may display in all uppercase characters.) Apply the **Body Text 5** style to the text. If the Body Text 5 style is not available, apply a style such as **Subhead 1**, or apply the **Copperplate Gothic Light** font. Select the text and change the font size to **22**.

D. Center the text in both text boxes horizontally and vertically, if necessary.

7. Display pages 2 and 3 and insert two vertical ruler guides. Position one **1** inch from the left edge of page 2 and the other **1** inch in from the right edge of page 3.

8. On page 2, insert a text box sized to fit between the vertical ruler guide on the left and the inside margin on the right (**3.75** inches wide) and the top and bottom horizontal guides (**6.5** inches high). Enter and format text as follows:

A. Apply the **Body Text 2** style (or use **12**-point **Garamond**, aligned left) and key the following paragraphs:

A Night of the Arts is presented by Our Arts Alliance, a community organization devoted to promoting the arts in our community. This night is intended to celebrate many types of performing and visual arts through music, dance, theater, and exhibition. The program is free, but we will happily accept donations. We welcome you and hope you enjoy the evening. [Enter]

Our Arts Alliance was founded in 1995 by a small group of arts lovers in order to support the arts in the public schools. Over the years the organization has grown both in terms of membership and programs. Where we once offered only two programs a year, we now offer more than 100! [Enter]

We gratefully acknowledge the support of the following, without whom we would not exist:

B. Press **Enter** to start a new line and then apply the first **List Bullet** style (or the default bullet formatting). Increase the font size to **12** (if necessary) and key the following list (pressing **Enter** after each item):

The Board of Selectmen
The Chamber of Commerce
Our community volunteers

C. Center all text vertically in the text box.

9. On page 3, insert a text box sized to fit between the vertical ruler guide on the right and the inside margin on the left (**3.75** inches wide) and the top and bottom horizontal ruler guides (**6.5** inches high).

A. Apply the **Heading 1** style and increase the font to **18** points, or apply the **Copperplate Gothic Bold** font in 18 points. Key **Performers**. (The text may display in all uppercase characters because of the font selection.)

B. Set the line spacing to leave **6 pt** before and **36 pt** after the paragraph, and then press **Enter**.

C. Apply the first **List Bullet** style (or the default bullet formatting using the **Garamond** font) and change the font size to **14** points. Set the line spacing to leave **6 pt** before and after each paragraph. Key the following paragraphs:

Windfire Dance Troupe
Our Arts Community Band

Uncle Jim's Barbershop Quartet
Comedy by Collective
Hip Hop Revelry
Bella A Cappella
Jazz Sensations
Our Arts Community Players
The Drama Queens
Artwork by local artists

    D. Center the text vertically in the text box.

10. Make page 4 active and draw a text box sized to fit between the top and bottom horizontal guide and left and right margins.

    A. Apply the Body Text style. (Or select **Garamond**, apply italics, and set the font size to **38.3**. Center the paragraph horizontally.) Set line spacing to leave **6 pt** of space before the paragraph, and **36 pt** after. Key **Special Thanks To**, and then press **Enter** to start a new line.

    B. Apply the Body Text 5 style. (Or, select **Copperplate Gothic Light**.) Change the font size to **18** points and key the following paragraph:
Everyone at town Hall, Jennifer Harwich, Copy Shop Printers, Main Street Electrical Supply, The Chadwick Family, Purple Cow Arts and Crafts, Jeffrey and Helene Gould, and Our Arts Volunteers!

    C. Center the text vertically in the text box.

11. Apply a color scheme that uses different shades of blue, such as **Dark Blue** in Publisher (or apply color to the fonts manually).

12. Check the spelling in the entire document and then print it. Fold the printed page into a booklet.

13. Save the changes and close **ArtsNight**. Keep your desktop publishing program open to use in the next project.

PROJECT 20-3

1. Create a new blank document and save it as **Reminder**.

2. Change the page setup to create a 1/4 page postcard-sized document—**5.5** inches wide by **4.25** inches high, in **Landscape** orientation. Set the margins to .25 on each side. If necessary, set it to print only one copy per sheet. (It is not necessary in InDesign.) In Publisher, use the following steps:

    A. In the Page Setup dialog box, click the Change Copies Per Sheet button.

    B. In the Small Publication Print Options, select the Print one copy per sheet option button.

    C. Click **OK**, and then click **OK** again to close the Page Setup dialog box.

3. If available, apply the **No picture** layout to the publication. Alternatively, create two text boxes as follows:

    A. Insert a text box **4.3** inches wide by **1.2** inches high, with its upper-left corner positioned at **.75** on the vertical ruler (Y) and **.6** on the horizontal ruler (X).

    B. Insert a second text box **4.3** inches wide by **1.6** inches high directly below the first text box (**1.95** on the vertical ruler (Y) and **.6** on the horizontal ruler (X)).

4. If available, apply a font scheme such as **Casual**, which uses *Comic Sans MS* for both the major and minor font, or just apply the font as you key text.

5. In the top text box, key the text **Reminder** (replacing sample text if you applied a layout in step 3). If necessary, apply **54.2**-point **Comic Sans MS** in **Bold, Centered**.

6. In the bottom text box, change the style to **Body Text 2**, or select **Comic Sans MS**, 12-point regular, with **6** points of space after each paragraph. Center the text horizontally, and then key the following lines:
Our Arts Alliance presents A Night of the Arts!
Saturday, March 21.
Doors open at 6:30 p.m.
Admission is free but donations are gladly accepted.

7. Apply **Bold** to the text **A Night of the Arts!**

8. If available, apply a color scheme that uses shades of red, such as **Red** (in Publisher), or change the font color of the word *Reminder* to red.

9. Insert a new, blank page after the current page.

10. Insert a text box sized to **1.75** inches wide by **.75** inches high in the upper-left corner of the publication page (where the left margin meets the top margin).

11. Apply the **Address** style, or set the font to **Comic Sans MS**, **10.9** point, red, centered horizontally, and key the following lines:
Our Arts Alliance
1515 Main Street
Sudbury, MA 01776

12. Insert another text box sized to **2.0** inches wide by **1.0** inch high. Position it with its upper left corner at **2.0** inches on the horizontal ruler (X) and **2.0** inches on the vertical ruler (Y).

13. Apply the **Body Text 3** style, or set the font **Comic Sans MS**, **9**-point regular, aligned left, with **5** points of space after each paragraph. Key the following lines:
First and Last Name
Address1
Address2
City, State Postal Code

14. Check the spelling in the entire document and then print it. You may print each page on a separate sheet, or use double-sided printing.

15. Save the changes and close **Reminder**. Close your desktop publishing program.

WEB PROJECT

Because the goal of using a desktop publishing program is to produce printed publications, it is important to have a desktop printer that you can rely on to print high-quality pages at a reasonable price. In this exercise, compare and analyze desktop printers for a classroom environment so that you can make a purchasing recommendation. First, use the Internet to research desktop printers. Look up types of printers, such as ink jet, bubble jet, and laser, and the features they offer. Are some designed for a specific purpose, such as photo printing? Do some offer features that make them more suitable for desktop publishing than others? Take note of specifications such as resolution and speed. Pick three to five printers and make a comparison chart. You can use a spreadsheet program if you have one, a word-processing program, or write the chart by hand. Include the cost of the printer as well as the cost of the consumables such as ink or toner for each printer. When you have compiled all of the information you need, decide which printer you think is the best value. Write a report of at least 500 words explaining your decision, and present it to the class.

 TEAMWORK PROJECT

Booklets are common publications used for purposes ranging from a performance program to information about how to fill out tax forms. A booklet may be as simple as a single letter-sized piece of paper folded in half to create four pages, or as complex as a multipage bound document. As a group, plan and design a 4-page booklet about your class or for a school or community organization. The booklet may provide general information such as the name of the instructor and the subjects you are studying, or it may be for a specific event, such as a school play or an art show.

Start by creating a mock-up so you have a general idea of the size, layout, and appearance. Remember that page 1 is the front cover, pages 2 and 3 are facing pages in a two-page spread, and page 4 is the back cover, and design the publication accordingly. Decide if there are any objects you want displayed on all pages, such as the organization's name, or page numbers. If so, plan to use master pages. Assign roles to each member of the team so that everyone contributes. For example, someone might be responsible for gathering information, someone might be responsible for organizing the layout, someone might be responsible for keying the text, and someone might be responsible for proofreading and editing.

When you are ready, use your desktop publishing program to create the publication. Select the page setup options appropriate for the booklet, such as the orientation and page size. Use layout options to help you arrange and position the text on the page. Use master pages as necessary. Select a font scheme if one is available, and use styles to format the headings and the body text. You can modify the formatting if you want to change the alignment, indents, or font formatting. Select a color scheme if there is one available, or develop your own set of coordinated colors. When you are finished, check the spelling and then print one copy. Remember, if you are using double-sided printing, you may have to reinsert the paper in the printer to print the second side. Ask a classmate to review the booklet and offer suggestions and comments. Make changes as necessary to improve the booklet. With your instructor's permission, print enough copies to distribute to the class. Save the booklet as a template so that you can use it again to create new booklets for different purposes.

CRITICAL *Thinking*

For a social studies project, use your desktop publishing program to create a 3-panel brochure about a place you would like to visit or have visited. Start by looking at brochures you might find in a local business, library, or school office for ideas. You can also look at designs or templates that come with your program. Next, create a mock-up so you can size and position all of the information you want to include. In a 3-panel brochure, you usually use a single letter-sized piece of paper, folded in thirds. On your mock-up, you can indicate which panel is the front, which is the back, and so on.

When you are ready, start with a blank document, or use one of your program's templates or designs. If available, you can select built-in layout options to customize the page layout. Use layout guides and ruler guides to set up the pages, and then insert text boxes to enter the content. Use a master page to insert content you want to print on every page. Apply a font scheme, or select any fonts you want to use. Likewise, select a color scheme, or customize the colors manually. Don't forget to use text formatting such as alignment, lists, and color to enhance the publication. When you are finished, check the spelling and print one copy. Ask a classmate to review it and make comments and suggestions. Make changes as necessary to improve the brochure. With your instructor's permission, print enough copies to distribute to the class. Save the brochure as a template so that you can use it again to create new brochures in the future.

ENHANCING PUBLICATIONS

Upon completion of this lesson, you should be able to:

- Insert objects such as pictures and drawing objects.
- Position and align objects as well as set text to wrap within an object.
- Work with color in a publication and apply color appropriately.
- Enhance objects with patterns, textures, gradients, shadows, and 3-D effects.
- Enhance text by using dropped capitals, text art, and adding text to shapes.
- Insert horizontal rules.
- Apply border art.
- Use design objects such as mastheads, tables of content, and logos.
- Create a watermark.

Estimated Time: 1.5 hours

VOCABULARY

Brand recognition

Color system

Dropped capital

Horizontal rules

Letterhead

Logo

Masthead

Picture frame

Process color

Reference point

Spot color

Standoff

Table of contents

Text wrap

When you add visual details and enhancements to a document, you make the publication more appealing. A bold graphic or eye-catching color can be the difference between someone reading your document or tossing it in the trash. You can also use enhancements to create *brand recognition*, which is when people associate a certain color or shape with a specific organization. Think of the font and colors of Coca Cola, or Apple Computer's white apple logo. In this lesson, you learn how to use desktop publishing tools to enhance publications with graphics, special effects, and color. You can add shadows and 3-D effects to objects to make them stand out on a page. You can apply borders and rules to visually separate elements on a page, and you can add graphics and watermarks to pages as decoration or part of an overall publication design. You can even use text as a decoration by turning it into a graphics object or starting a paragraph with a dropped capital letter.

Insert Objects

Objects are the text boxes, charts, shapes, pictures, and other elements you insert in a publication to provide information, organize a page, and improve visual appeal. With most desktop publishing programs, you can use drawing tools to draw objects such as shapes and text boxes directly in a publication file or you can import objects from a variety of sources, including digital cameras, graphics programs, and scanners. You can manipulate, format, and control the object once it is in the publication.

The processes for acquiring, inserting, and working with objects in a desktop publishing program are similar to those used in other programs. Refer to Lesson 1, Creating Graphics, for information about using drawing tools. Refer to Lesson 2, Importing and Exporting Graphics, for information about scanning images, using a digital camera, and acquiring clip art. Refer to Lesson 14, Working with Graphics Objects, for information on importing and drawing objects, creating tables, charts, and diagrams, and formatting objects.

Insert a Picture

In most desktop publishing programs you can define a blank *picture frame*—which is a frame in which you insert a graphics object—anywhere on a publication page. The frame acts as a placeholder so you can organize and arrange the content on the page. You then use the Change Picture or Edit > Place command to insert a picture in the frame. You can also use the Insert > Picture or Edit > Place command to insert a picture directly from a file, from your program's clip art collection, or from a device such as a scanner or camera. In that case, the picture is inserted as a floating object that you can size and position anywhere on the page.

To define a blank frame, click the appropriate frame tool, such as the Picture Frame tool in Publisher, or the Rectangular Frame Tool in InDesign. If necessary, click the option to draw an empty picture frame, and then click and drag to define the frame. To insert the picture, select the frame, and then select the command to insert the picture from a file, from your program's clip art collection, or from a device such as a scanner or camera.

In some programs the picture is automatically sized to fit in the frame. In other programs you may have to select a command to fit the contents to the frame. In InDesign, for instance, you must select the Object > Fitting > Fit Contents to Frame command.

STEP-BY-STEP 21.1

1. Launch your desktop publishing program, and open **Step21-1a** from the data files. Save the file as **Class**.

2. Select the tool for drawing a blank rectangular picture frame. If you are using Publisher click the **Picture Frame** tool and then click **Empty Picture Frame**. If you are using InDesign, click the **Rectangular Frame Tool**.

3. Click and drag to draw a frame in the upper-left corner of the page, sized to approximately **2.0** inches square.

4. With the blank frame selected, select the command to insert a picture from a file into the frame. In Publisher, right-click the frame, click **Change Picture**, and then click **From File**. In InDesign, click **Edit** on the Menu bar, and then click **Place**.

STEP-BY-STEP 21.1 Continued

5. Locate and select the graphics file **Step21-1b** from the data files for this lesson, and insert it into the frame. If necessary, select the command to fit the contents to the frame. In InDesign, click **Object** on the menu bar, click **Fitting**, and then click **Fit Contents to Frame**. The top of the page should look similar to Figure 21-1.

FIGURE 21-1
A picture inserted in a publication

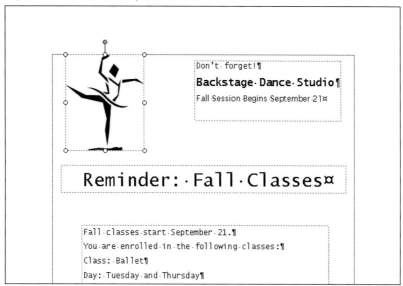

6. Save the changes to **Class** and leave it open to use in the next exercise.

Insert a Drawing Object

Use the drawing tools in your desktop publishing program to insert basic shapes such as lines, ovals, and rectangles. You can usually use a polygon tool to draw multisided shapes or stars. To insert a shape, click the tool, and then click and drag to draw the shape. The color of the *fill* (the area within the shape) and *stroke* (the line that defines the outline of the shape) depend on your program. In Publisher, new shapes have no fill and a .75 point black stroke. In InDesign, the default fill is no fill, and the default stroke is 1.0 point black, but new shapes are drawn using the current fill and stroke colors.

Some programs, such as Publisher, have an AutoShapes tool that you can use to select and draw more complex shapes such as stars, lightning bolts, and hearts. Simply click the AutoShapes tool to display a menu of palettes. Click a palette to see the available AutoShapes, and then click the AutoShape you want to insert.

S TEP-BY-STEP 21.2

1. Select the tool for drawing an oval, or ellipse. If necessary, set the fill to no fill, and the stroke to **3/4 pt.** (.75 pt.) **black**. (You may have to adjust the stroke after drawing the shape.)

2. Click and drag in the white space to the left of the address text box near the bottom of the page to draw an oval approximately **2.0** inches wide by **1.5** inch high.

3. Select the tool for drawing a five-pointed star. If you are using Publisher, click the **AutoShapes** tool, point to **Stars and Banners**, and then click the **5-Point Star**. If you are using InDesign, double-click the **Polygon Tool**, set the number of sides to **5**, set the star inset to **60%**, and then click **OK**. If necessary, set the fill to **no fill**, and the stroke to **3/4 pt.** (.75 pt.) **black**. (You may have to adjust the stroke after drawing the shape.)

4. Click and drag in the oval shape to draw a star approximately **1.5** inches wide and **1.4** inches high. If necessary, drag the star to center it in the oval. The bottom of the page should look similar to Figure 21-2.

FIGURE 21-2
Insert drawing shapes

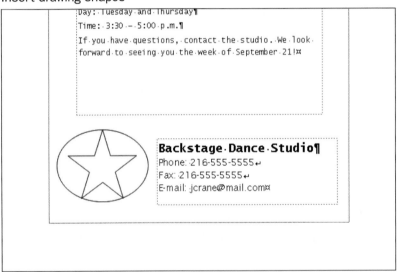

5. Save the changes to **Class** and leave it open to use in the next exercise.

Arrange Objects

Although you can size, format, and position objects in a publication using the same techniques that you use in most other types of programs, most publication programs also provide commands for fine-tuning alignment and position. For example, you can drag an object to a new location, or you can set a precise position relative to the page.

> **Note**
>
> You can group, ungroup, and set the stacking order of objects in a publication using commands similar to those in other programs. For more information, refer to Lesson 3.

In most programs, the position of objects is modified based on a *reference point*, which is a fixed spot used as a control for moving and modifying objects. The default reference point depends on the program you are using, but it is often the center of the object (InDesign) or the upper-left corner (Publisher). Although many programs do not let you move the reference point, some programs do, and it can greatly affect modifications made to the object. For example, if you set the precise position of two identical objects to 2 inches horizontal and 2 inches vertical, and then set one reference point at the center of an object and the other in the upper-left corner of the object, the objects will be positioned in different places on the page. The following exercises assume that the default reference point is the upper-left corner of the object.

> **Note**
>
> If you are using InDesign, you can easily move the reference point to the upper-left corner of an object: Select the object and then click the square in the upper-left corner of the Reference Point diagram at the left end of the Control palette.

Position an Object Precisely

To position an object precisely in some programs you use the Format Object dialog box to specify the horizontal and vertical location relative to either the upper-right corner, the upper-left corner, or the center of the page. In other programs, you set the horizontal (X) and vertical (Y) coordinates. Recall that the coordinates are specific points laid out in an invisible grid that starts in the upper-left corner of the page, with the coordinates of 0, 0. As you move an object to the right, the X coordinate increases. As you move down, the Y coordinate increases. In Publisher you can view an object's coordinates in the Status bar; in InDesign the coordinates display in the Control palette. As in most programs, you can usually group multiple objects together so that you can manipulate them as one, and you can change the stacking order to place them in front of or behind other objects.

STEP-BY-STEP 21.3

1. Using the Selection Tool, if necessary, click the oval shape, press and hold **Shift**, and then click the star shape to select both the oval and the star shapes.

2. Select the command to group the two objects. If you are using Publisher, click **Arrange** on the Menu bar, and then click **Group**. If you are using InDesign, click **Object** on the Menu bar, and then click **Group**.

3. Choose the command to open the dialog box or palette where you enter values to position an object. In Publisher, click **Format** on the Menu bar, click **Object**, and then click the **Layout** tab. In InDesign, display the Control palette, if necessary.

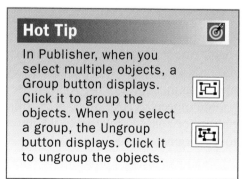

> **Hot Tip**
>
> In Publisher, when you select multiple objects, a Group button displays. Click it to group the objects. When you select a group, the Ungroup button displays. Click it to ungroup the objects.

4. Click in the *Horizontal* or *X* text box, select the current value if necessary, and key **4**. If necessary, click the *From* drop-down list and select **Top Left Corner**.

5. Click in the *Vertical* or *Y* text box, select the current value if necessary, and key **5**. Again, if necessary click the *From* drop-down list and select **Top Left Corner**.

STEP-BY-STEP 21.3 Continued

6. Click **OK**. The object moves to the specified position, interfering with the text in the text box. (You learn how to control text wrap later in this lesson.)

7. With the group still selected, select the command to send it behind the text box. If you are using Publisher, click **Arrange** on the Menu bar, click **Order**, and then click **Send to Back**. If you are using InDesign, click **Object** on the Menu bar, click **Arrange**, and then click **Send to Back**. The page should look similar to Figure 21-3.

FIGURE 21-3
Position objects as a group

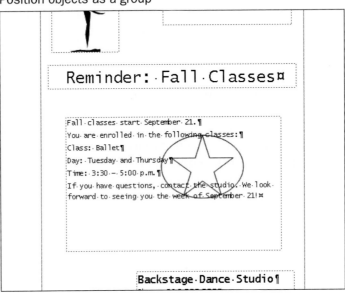

8. Save the changes and leave **Class** open to use in the next exercise.

Align Objects

You have already learned how to use guidelines to visually align objects on a page. Most desktop publishing programs also have tools for making sure objects are precisely aligned. You can toggle on the *Snap to* feature if you want objects to automatically align to the guides. You can use the Nudge command or the arrow keys to move an object up, down, left, or right in small increments. In most programs, you can use options on an Align menu or Align palette to align and distribute objects in relation to other objects. In some programs, such as Publisher, you can align an object horizontally relative to the left and right margins, and vertically relative to the top and bottom margins.

If you are using a program that does not have options for fine-tuning alignment, or aligning objects relative to the margins, you can complete the following exercise by dragging the objects or setting the X and Y coordinates.

Hot Tip

Use the Distribute command to space multiple objects evenly between either the top and bottom margins or the left and right margins.

STEP-BY-STEP 21.4

1. Select the grouped shapes, if necessary. (You may have to send the text box behind the group to do this.)

2. Select the command to align objects relative to the margins. If you are using Publisher, click **Arrange** on the Menu bar, point to **Align or Distribute**, and then click **Relative to Margin Guides**. InDesign does not have a command for aligning objects relative to the margins.

3. Select the command to align the group centered between the left and right margins. If you are using Publisher, click **Arrange** on the Menu bar, point to **Align or Distribute**, and then click **Align Center**. (If you are using InDesign, drag the object to the center of the page.)

4. Select the command to center the group between the top and bottom margins. If you are using Publisher, click **Arrange** on the Menu bar, point to **Align or Distribute**, and then click **Align Middle**.

5. If available, use the Nudge command to nudge the object up until its top aligns with the top of the text box. In Publisher, click **Arrange** on the Menu bar, click **Nudge**, and then click **Up**. Repeat the command or press the **Up arrow** key on the keyboard as many times as necessary, until the top of the grouped objects aligns with the top of the text box. If your program does not have a Nudge command, drag the object into position. The page should look similar to the one in Figure 21-4.

FIGURE 21-4
Objects aligned in publication

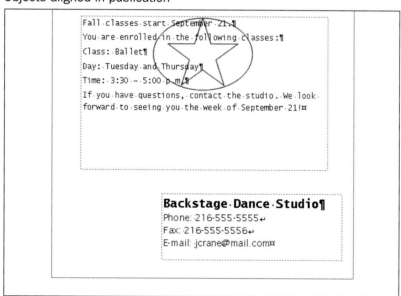

6. Save the changes and leave **Class** open to use in the next exercise.

Set Text Wrap

To adjust the width, shape, and position of white space between text and objects on a page you can select a *text wrap* style. Most desktop publishing programs have a selection of text wrap styles and options you use to control the way text wraps to make room for objects. Most programs offer five wrapping styles, as described in Table 21-1.

TABLE 21-1
Text wrap styles and options

BUTTON	STYLE NAME	DESCRIPTION
▣	Square	Wraps text evenly around four sides of an object.
▣	Tight	Wraps text along the contours of an object.
▣	Through	Continues lines of text through transparent backgrounds of objects.
▣	Top and Bottom	Wraps text evenly on the top and bottom of an object.
▣	None	Does not wrap text. Instead, text is stacked behind or in front of the object.

In most programs, the text wrapping options are listed in a dialog box, such as Format Object or a palette called Text Wrap. Simply select the object, and then open the dialog box or palette and select the style you want to apply. Alternatively, click the Text Wrap button on a toolbar, such as the Picture toolbar, and then click the style on the pop-up palette that is displayed. Depending on the style you select and your program, you may also be able to set text flow options to control the way text flows around the object. For example, if you select Square, Tight, or Through, you can select whether to wrap the text on both sides of the object, only the left side, only the right side, or just on the largest side of the object. If you select the Square wrapping style, you can enter the specific distance you want to maintain between the object and any of its four sides. This is sometimes called the *standoff*.

STEP-BY-STEP 21.5

1. Select the grouped shape, if necessary, and change the stacking order to bring it to the front, if necessary. In some programs, the text wraps around all sides of the object by default.

2. With the group selected, set the wrapping style to Top and Bottom. If you are using Publisher, click the **Text Wrapping** button on the Picture toolbar, and then click **Top and Bottom**. You may need to display the Picture toolbar to locate the Text Wrapping button. If you are using InDesign, click **Window** on the Menu bar, click **Text Wrap** to display the Text Wrap palette, and then click the **Jump objects** text wrap style.

3. Change the text wrapping style to **Tight**. (In InDesign it is called **Wrap around object shape**.)

STEP-BY-STEP 21.5 Continued

4. If available, select the option to wrap the text on the left side of the object only. In Publisher, click **Format** on the Menu bar, click **Object**, and then click the **Layout** tab. Make sure the **Tight** wrapping style is selected, and then click the **Left only** option button. Click **OK** to apply the change. In InDesign, select the **Wrap around bounding box** option and then set the Right Offset to a value great enough to force the text to the left of the group—about **1.5** inches. The page should look similar to Figure 21-5.

FIGURE 21-5
Text wrapped on the left side of the group

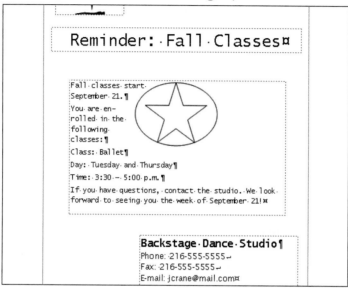

5. Save the changes and leave **Class** open to use in the next exercise.

Work with Color

Color, which is also called hue, is frequently the first thing a reader sees and responds to. Whereas some publications, such as some newspapers, use only two colors—black and white—many incorporate at least one additional color for emphasis and effect, and some use a wide spectrum of colors for reproducing photographs and other full-color images.

About Color in a Publication

When you work with color in a desktop publishing program, the most important thing to keep in mind is that the way colors display on your computer screen is not necessarily the way they will look when printed. Many factors affect the way colors appear on your screen and in print, including the specific printer model, the specific monitor model, and your software program. But the most important factor is that printers and monitors use different *color systems*. Recall that a color system—which may be called a color model—is a method for defining standard colors. (Refer to Lesson 5, Creating Special Effects, for more information about color systems.)

The color system used for displaying colors on a monitor is called RGB. The RGB system creates colors by combining different values of red, green, and blue. The main color system used for defining colors in print is called *CMYK* (or CMY). The CMYK system creates colors by combining percentages of cyan (blue), magenta (red), yellow, and black. These colors—often called *process colors*—are the colors of the ink used in four-color printing. Process color is usually used for publications that contain many colors, such as brochures that include photographs or high-definition graphics.

When a publication designer wants to use a specific color of ink instead of mixing the color during printing, he or she can select a *spot color* from a color system or library such as the *Pantone Matching System*. A spot color is ink that is premixed before the printing process. You use spot colors when it is necessary to have an exact color such as matching a client's logo color, or when printing with only one or two colors, or when using special inks for emphasis. You can use both spot colors and process colors in the same publication. Spot color printing on its own is usually less expensive than process color printing.

> **Important**
>
> If a publication will be printed by a commercial printer, you should discuss the color system with the printer prior to designing the publication, and if you make any color changes.

Apply Color

Applying color to elements of a publication is similar to applying color in other types of files. You usually select the element you want to color, and then open a palette where you can select a color swatch. You can also open a dialog box or palette where you can select a standard color, or define a custom color. The new color may be added to the palette automatically, or you may have to click a button such as *Add RGB Color Swatch* to add the color to the palette.

There are two basic methods for defining a custom color. The first method is to simply select a color from a *color bar* in a dialog box such as Colors in Publisher—

> **Did You Know?**
>
> RGB, CMYK, and the Pantone Matching System are not the only color systems. Other common process color systems include HSL (Hue, Saturation, Lightness) and Grayscale, which uses percentages of black to create shades of gray. Other spot color systems include Toyo Color Finder and DIC Color Guide.

shown in Figure 21-6—or Color Picker in InDesign (or the Color palette in InDesign). The second method is to select a color system and then key the color system values for a particular color. In either case, start by selecting the element to color and opening the appropriate dialog box or palette. Select the Custom tab, if necessary. Then, either click the color you want to apply, or select the color system and then key the values for each color. Units used for values differ by system. For example, RGB values usually range from 0 to 255, but CMYK values use percentages.

FIGURE 21-6
Custom tab of the Colors dialog box

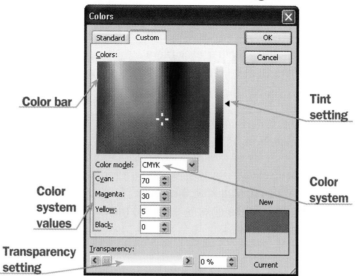

Color bar

Tint
setting

Color
system
values

Color
system

Transparency
setting

You can also usually modify a color by changing its *tint* and/or *transparency*. Recall that tint, which is sometimes called *brightness*, is the range of a color from black to white. When you add white to a color, you increase its brightness. Add black to shade or decrease the brightness. Transparency, which is sometimes, called *opacity*, measures the degree to which you can see through a color. To make a color completely opaque, set the transparency to 0%. To see through a color, increase the transparency. The options for changing tint and/or transparency may be found in the color dialog box or palette.

Extra for Experts

Some programs come with color charts for particular color systems that you can use to select a specific color. When you select the color system from the list in the custom color dialog box, a color chart displays. Click the color you want to use, and then click OK.

S TEP-BY-STEP 21.6

1. Ungroup the star from the oval shape. (If the text wrapping reverts to the default, reset it to the left side only with both objects selected.) Select the oval shape and display the Fill color palette. If your program does not have a Fill color palette, display the Fill Color Picker dialog box.

2. Click the beige color swatch labeled **Accent 2**, which is the third swatch from the left. If your program does not have a Fill color palette, or only displays standard colors in the Swatches palette, key the following RGB color values in the Fill Color Picker dialog box: R: **194**, G: **194**, B: **173**, click the **Add RGB Color Swatch** button to add the color to the palette, and then click **OK**.

3. Select the star shape. (If necessary, select the command to send the oval shape back behind the star, and then select the star.)

Hot Tip

Look on the Web to find color system tables listing values for the entire range of colors. Such a table can save you time in experimenting with color values to find the one you want.

STEP-BY-STEP 21.6 Continued

4. Open the dialog box or palette for selecting custom fill colors. If you are using Publisher, click the **Fill Color** drop-down arrow on the Formatting toolbar, click **More Fill Colors**, and then click the **Custom** tab. If you are using InDesign, display the Fill Color Picker dialog box.

5. If necessary, change to the CMYK color system. In Publisher, click the **Color model** drop-down arrow and then click **CMYK**.

Extra for Experts

Some desktop publishing programs have a Set Transparent Color tool or command that you can use to make colors in some bitmap graphics and clip art files transparent. The transparent colors will not print.

6. Key the following values: Cyan: **70**; Magenta: **30**; Yellow: **5**; Black: **0**. In InDesign, click the **Add RGB Color Swatch** button to make sure the color is added to the Swatches palette.

7. Click **OK** as many times as necessary to close all dialog boxes and apply the color to the shape. The publication should look similar to Figure 21-7.

FIGURE 21-7
Custom color fill

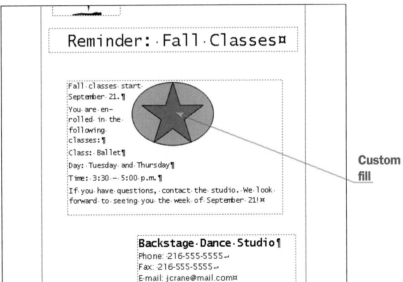

Custom fill

8. Save the changes and leave **Class** open to use in the next exercise.

Enhance Objects

Many programs provide options for formatting objects with special effects such as shadows, 3-D, textures, gradients, and patterns. Patterns, textures, and gradients are usually applied as fill or stroke effects, whereas shadows and 3-D effects are applied to entire objects. The methods for applying special effects to objects vary depending on your program, and not all programs offer all types of effects.

To apply fill effects such as gradients, textures, or patterns, you usually select the object to format, open the basic fill color palette, then click Fill Effects to open the Fill Effects dialog box. There may be multiple tabs in the dialog box, each one offering options for applying specific fill effects. Locate the effect you want to use, click it, and then click OK. (For more information on fill effects, refer to Lesson 13, Enhancing a Presentation.) To apply a stroke pattern, you usually select the object to format, open the basic stroke color palette, and then click Patterned Lines to open the Patterned Lines dialog box. Locate the pattern you want to use, click it, and then click OK. Sometimes there are alternative methods for applying such effects. For example, in Publisher you can select the object, and then select the Format > Object command to open a dialog box. You would then click the Colors and Lines tab to access options for setting stroke and fill colors and styles.

Apply Patterns, Textures, and Gradients

Patterns are simply repetitive designs such as grids or hatch marks. By default, they are black on white, but you can usually select a foreground color and a background color. Patterns may be applied to both fills and strokes. *Textures* are bitmap graphics files used as fills. You can select from a list of built-in textures, or select a picture file to use as a texture. Not all programs support patterns and/or textures. InDesign, for example, does not.

Gradients are a blend of colors that gradually change in brightness or tint. You usually select one or more colors to include in the gradient, and then select a pattern or style. A *radial gradient* blends colors out from a central point, while a *linear gradient* blends the colors horizontally. There may be other gradient options available in your program as well, such as variations of the selected style or a list of preset colors and styles. Shadows and 3-D effects are applied to an entire object.

S TEP-BY-STEP 21.7

1. Zoom in on the oval and star shapes to about **200%**. Select the star shape if it is not already selected. If you are using a program such as InDesign that does not have texture effects, skip ahead to step 4.

2. Click the **Fill Color** drop-down arrow on the Formatting toolbar, click **Fill Effects**, and then click the **Texture** tab to open the dialog box that contains options for applying texture fill effects.

3. Click a blue, heavy texture, such as **Denim** in Publisher. Click **OK** to apply the effect to the shape.

4. Open the dialog box or menu for applying stroke pattern effects. If you are using Publisher, click the **Line Color** drop-down arrow on the Formatting toolbar, click **Patterned Lines**, and then click the **Pattern** tab. If you are using InDesign, display the Stroke palette.

5. Click a wavy or zig-zag line pattern. If necessary, click the **OK** button to apply the effect.

6. Select the oval shape and then select the command for applying gradient fill effects. In Publisher, click the **Fill Color** drop-down arrow on the Formatting toolbar, click **Fill Effects**, and then click the **Gradient** tab. In InDesign, click the **Gradient Tool** and then click the fill to format. (If necessary, reset the starting fill color to R: **194**, G: **194**, and B: **173**.)

STEP-BY-STEP 21.7 Continued

7. Select a vertical linear gradiant that shades from the original fill color on the left to black on the right. If necessary, click **OK** to apply the effect. It should look similar to Figure 21-8.

> **Note** ☑
>
> If you have trouble selecting the gradient start color in InDesign, you may want to use the commands in the Swatches palette to create a Gradient Color Swatch that has the correct custom fill color as the start and black as the stop.

FIGURE 21-8
Texture fill, gradient fill, and patterned line

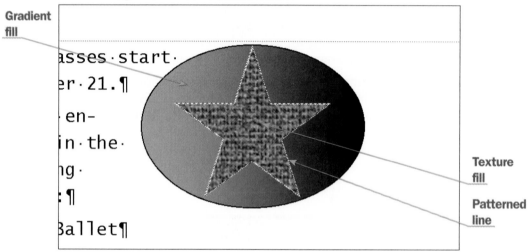

Gradient fill

Texture fill

Patterned line

8. Save the changes and leave **Class** open to use in the next exercise.

Apply Shadows and 3-D Effects

A *shadow*—or *drop shadow*—adds shading on one side of the outer edge of an object to create the illusion of depth and highlights. A *3-D effect* also creates the illusion of depth by adding or extending shapes along one or two sides of an object. To apply a shadow, select the object to format, and then select the command to open a palette of available styles. For example, in Publisher, click the Shadow Style button on the Formatting toolbar. Click the style you want to apply. You may also be able to use toolbar buttons to adjust options such as the position, color, and size of shadows.

The procedure for applying 3-D effects is basically the same. Select the object to format,

> **Note** ☑
>
> Usually, you cannot combine shadows and 3-D effects on the same object.

> **Note** ☑
>
> To apply an effect such as a shadow directly to text, use the Font Effects options as described in Lesson 19.

click the button to open a palette of 3-D styles, then click the style you want to apply. You also may be able to use toolbar buttons to adjust options such as the depth, direction, tilt, and lighting of the 3-D effect. Not all programs support 3-D effects. InDesign, for example, does not.

STEP-BY-STEP 21.8

1. Select the oval shape, if necessary, and then open the dialog box or menu for applying a shadow. If you are using Publisher, click the **Shadow Style** button on the Formatting toolbar. If you are using InDesign, click **Object** on the Menu bar and then click **Drop Shadow**.

2. Click the style that applies a shadow extending from the bottom of the shape down and to the right. In Publisher select **Shadow Style 6**. In InDesign, click the **Drop Shadow** check box and then set the opacity to about **40%**.

3. Select the star shape, and then open the dialog box or menu for applying 3-D effects. In Publisher click the **3-D Style** button on the Formatting toolbar. If you are using a program that does not support 3-D effects (such as InDesign), skip to step 5.

4. Click a style that tilts the face of the object down and to the right and extends the top and left sides of the object up and to the left. In Publisher this is called **3-D Style 2**. The shapes should look similar to Figure 21-9.

FIGURE 21-9
Drop shadow and 3-D effect

5. Save the changes and leave **Class** open to use in the next exercise.

Note

You can rotate and flip objects in a publication using similar techniques as in other programs. Refer to Lessons 3 and 14 for more information.

Enhance Text

In addition to formatting text with fonts and font formatting, many desktop publishing programs provide tools for creating sophisticated effects using text. Most programs have a feature for creating a *dropped capital*—sometimes called a *drop cap*—a decorative effect in which the first character in a paragraph is larger than the other characters. The drop cap may be offset to the left of the lines of text in the paragraph or inset to the right.

Additionally, some programs offer a utility that lets you create text objects that include special effects formatting such as shadows and 3-D just as you did with other objects. And some programs let you simply add text to shapes.

Create Dropped Capitals

Dropped capital letters are often used to dress up the first paragraph of a chapter in a book or for emphasizing the first paragraph in a newsletter or magazine article. When you apply a dropped capital, the first letter in the paragraph is scaled to the specified size, which is usually measured in lines. In some programs, you can select additional options for formatting the dropped capital, including whether you want the character to drop down into the paragraph or extend up above the paragraph. You may also be able to select more than one character to drop and to change the font formatting. Some programs come with a selection of built-in dropped capital styles.

In some programs, to apply a dropped capital, position the insertion point in the paragraph to format, and then open the dialog box where you can select options such as a style, the number of lines to drop, and so on. In Publisher, click Format on the Menu bar, and then click Drop Cap. In InDesign, select the character to format, and then key the number of lines to drop in the Drop Cap Number of Lines box in the Paragraph Formatting Controls palette.

STEP-BY-STEP 21.9

1. Position the insertion point in the paragraph of text beginning with *Fall classes*. If you are using InDesign, select the letter *F* at the beginning of the paragraph. (You may need to zoom out.)

2. Select the command to drop the letter by **3** lines. If you are using Publisher, click **Format** on the Menu bar, click **Drop Cap**, click the **Custom Drop Cap** tab, and then click the **Dropped** option. Key **3** in the *Size of letters* box, and then click **OK**. If you are using InDesign, click the **Paragraph Formatting Controls** button in the Control palette, and then key **3** in the *Drop Cap Number of Lines* box. The paragraph should look similar to Figure 21-10. If necessary, increase the height of the text box a bit so that all of the text displays.

STEP-BY-STEP 21.9 Continued

FIGURE 21-10
Dropped capital

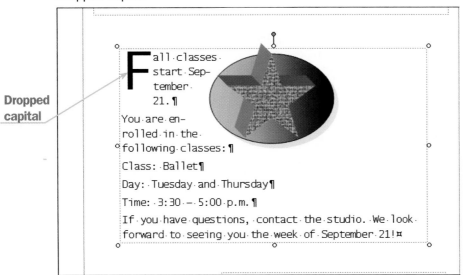

Dropped capital

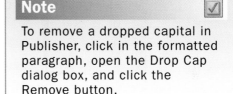

3. Save the changes and leave **Class** open to use in the next exercise.

> **Note** ☑
>
> To remove a dropped capital in Publisher, click in the formatted paragraph, open the Drop Cap dialog box, and click the Remove button.

Create Text Art

Some desktop publishing programs, such as Publisher, have a feature that lets you turn your text into graphics objects. Creating an object from text characters lets you remove the constraints of the text box and adds flexibility in terms of formatting, sizing, and positioning the text. You can format the object with special effects such as fills and shadows, scale it, and position it anywhere on the page. However, not all desktop publishing programs include a feature for creating text art. If you are using a program such as InDesign that does not, you may be able to create a text art object in a graphics program and insert it as an object into your publication.

To create a text art object, start the utility provided with your program. If you are using Publisher, click Insert on the Menu bar, click Picture, and then click WordArt. Alternatively, click the appropriate toolbar button to start the utility. In most cases, you then select a style and click OK. Key the text you want included in the object and select font formatting. Click OK to create the object.

You can use standard techniques to format the entire object, such as scaling, moving, and rotating. In addition, buttons on a toolbar enable you to modify the text art itself. You may be able to change the shape, edit the text, or select a different style for the text. Other options may include changing to vertical text, adjusting character height and spacing, and selecting an alignment.

> **Hot Tip** ◎
>
> Select existing text before starting the utility program to automatically enter that text in the text art object.

STEP-BY-STEP 21.10

1. Delete the text box that contains the text *Reminder: Fall Classes*.

2. Start the utility for creating text art. If you are using Publisher, click the **Insert WordArt** button on the Objects toolbar. If your program does not support text art, draw a blank frame approximately **6.0** inches wide by **.5** inches high, position it centered horizontally with its top at **3.5** inches from the top margin, and insert **Step21-10** from the data files. Fit the contents to the frame, if necessary, and then continue with step 7 below.

3. Click a style that displays blue and green text in a wave shape (fifth column, third row in the Publisher WordArt Gallery), and then click **OK**.

4. Key the text **Reminder: Fall Classes** to replace the sample text, and then click **OK**. Your program creates the text object and inserts it in the publication.

5. Resize the object to approximately **1.0** inches high by **5.5** inches wide.

6. Center the object horizontally between the left and right margins, and position it vertically **3.25** inches from the top-left corner of the page. It should look similar to Figure 21-11.

FIGURE 21-11
Text as a graphics object

7. Save the changes and leave **Class** open to use in the next exercise.

Add Text to Shapes

In some programs, such as Publisher, you can add text to shapes inserted in a publication. Simply select the shape and key the text. The program automatically inserts a text box that is sized and positioned to constrain the text within the shape. You can key and format the text as you would in any text box. Not all programs have a feature for adding text to shapes. InDesign, for example, does not. But you may be able to create the same effect by layering a text box on top of the shape.

STEP-BY-STEP 21.11

1. Select the star shape.

2. Key the text **Ballet**. If your program does not support adding text to shapes, insert a text box or frame sized to fit within the star. (You may have to select an option to ignore the text wrap settings in the Text Frame Options dialog box.)

3. Select the text and change the font to **14** point **Times New Roman** in **white**. Deselect the text. It should look similar to Figure 21-12.

FIGURE 21-12
Text added to a shape

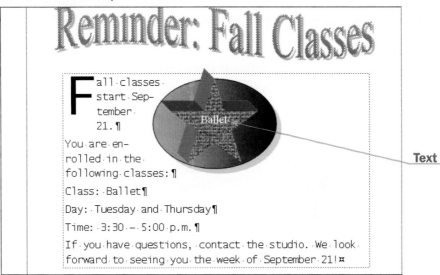

4. Save the changes and leave **Class** open to use in the next exercise.

Insert Horizontal Rules

Horizontal rules are printing lines that can be inserted before or after a paragraph of text. In most programs, you apply a rule using a dialog box such as Horizontal Rules or Paragraph Rules. First, position the insertion point in the paragraph to be formatted. Second, open the dialog box for applying rules and select the option to apply a rule before the paragraph and/or after the paragraph. (For example, in Publisher, click Format on the Menu bar, and then click Horizontal Rules. Or, in InDesign, click Type on the Menu bar, click Paragraph, display the panel's menu, and then click Paragraph Rules.) Third, select formatting options for each rule such as the line weight, the line style, and the line color. You can also specify to indent the rule from the left and/or right text box margin, and you may be able to specify how much space to leave between the text and the rule. Last, click OK to apply the rule. To remove a rule, open the dialog box and deselect the option for applying the rule before and/or after the paragraph.

STEP-BY-STEP 21.12

1. Click in the first line of text in the text box in the upper-right corner of the page, and then open the dialog box for applying horizontal rules.

2. Select options to apply a 2-point, single-line rule before the paragraph. Change the line color to the custom blue you created earlier in this lesson, then click **OK** to apply the rule. In InDesign, you may have to set the Offset to **0.15** to position the rule above the text. (Click the **Preview** check box in the Paragraph Rules dialog box to see the rule before you click **OK**.)

3. Position the insertion point in the last line of text in the same text box and display the dialog box for applying horizontal rules. Select options to apply a 2-point, single-line rule after the paragraph. Change the line color to the custom blue you created earlier in this lesson, then click **OK** to apply the rule. In InDesign, you may have to adjust the Offset to **.04**. The text box should look similar to Figure 21-13.

FIGURE 21-13
Horizontal rules applied before and after paragraphs

Horizontal rule before first paragraph

Horizontal rule after last paragraph

4. Save the changes and leave **Class** open to use in the next exercise.

Apply Border Art

Some desktop publishing programs, such as Publisher, come with a collection of built-in border art pictures you can apply around rectangular objects such as text boxes and squares. To apply border art, select the object, and then open the Format Object dialog box. Click the Border Art button to open the Border Art dialog box. Click the border you want to apply, and then click OK. Click OK again to close the Format Object dialog box and apply the border. Not all programs have a feature for applying Border Art. InDesign is one program that does not have a Border Art feature. You can, however, apply a stroke around rectangular objects.

> **Hot Tip**
>
> To create a page border in InDesign, draw a frame the size of the margins on the master page, and then apply a border to it. The border then appears in the background on all pages in the publication.

In some programs, you can create a custom picture border, which you can save and reuse. Simply click the Create Custom button in the Border Art dialog box and then click the Select Picture button. Locate and select the picture file you want to use, and then click OK. Key a name for the new border and then click OK again. The new border is added to the list of available borders. You may also be able to insert a Design Gallery Border Object and resize it to fit around any object. Inserting Design Objects is covered in the next exercise.

STEP-BY-STEP 21.13

1. Select the picture frame containing the picture of the ballerina.

2. Click **Format** on the Menu bar, click **Picture**, click the **Colors and Lines** tab, and then click the **BorderArt** button to open the BorderArt dialog box. If you are using a program such as InDesign that does not have a feature for applying border art, apply a custom **blue 3**-point triple-line stroke (thin, thick, thin) on the outside of the object, and then skip to step 5.

3. Select the **Weaving...Strips** border, and then click **OK** . If the Weaving...Strips border is not available, select any border.

4. On the Colors and Lines tab of the Format Picture dialog box key **6** in the Weight text box, and then click **OK**.

5. Display the publication in Print Preview. It should look similar to Figure 21-14. (If you do not have a color printer, your print preview may be in black, white, and shades of gray.)

FIGURE 21-14
The completed publication

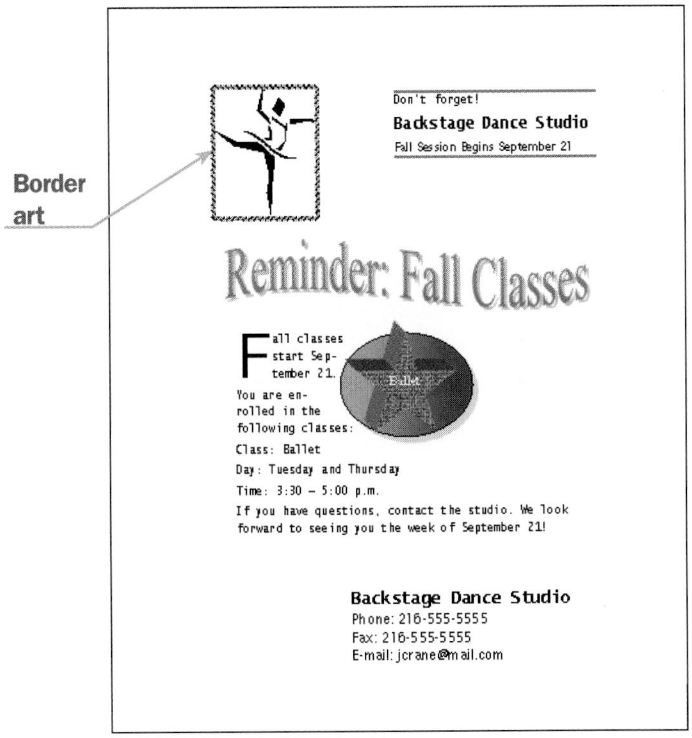

STEP-BY-STEP 21.13 Continued

6. Check the spelling in the publication and correct all errors. Print one copy.

7. Save the changes and close **Class**. Leave your desktop publishing program open to use in the next exercise.

Use Design Objects

Many desktop publishing programs, including Publisher, come with tools for automatically setting up and formatting elements of a publication that otherwise have to be created manually. You may be able to quickly insert features such as tables of contents, logos, forms, borders, and *mastheads*. A masthead is the information displayed across the top of a newsletter or newspaper, including, but not limited to, the title, the date, and the volume number. (It may also be a section inserted in a newspaper or magazine that lists the names and positions of the publication's staff.) Unfortunately, not all desktop publishing programs include tools for automating the creation of these features. If you are using a program such as InDesign that does not, you can manually insert and format text and graphics and design these features on the page.

If your program includes pre-designed publication elements, they are probably listed in a design gallery or dialog box. To open the gallery, click the Design Gallery Object button on the Objects toolbar, or click Insert on the Menu bar, and then click a command such as Design Gallery Object. In the gallery, click the category of the element you want to create, click the design you want to use, and then click Insert Object. The element is inserted as an object, or a group of objects, in the publication. You can customize the object by replacing sample text and graphics, by sizing it and positioning it on the page, and even by changing formatting, such as the font or color scheme or applying special effects.

Mastheads

As mentioned, a masthead is the information displayed across the top of a newsletter or newspaper. It usually includes text, such as the title, the date, and the volume number, as well as graphics elements such as borders or rules. Some include quotes, slogans, color, and pictures. You can set up a masthead manually by positioning text boxes and graphics across the top of the page and applying formatting. However, if your program cannot automatically set up a masthead, you can easily select one from the program's built-in list and insert it in your publication. To customize the masthead, replace the sample text with the correct information and make any formatting changes you want, such as modifying the color or font scheme.

S TEP-BY-STEP 21.14

1. Open **Step21-14** from the data files and save the file as **Studio**. This is the front page of a newsletter.

2. Click **Insert** on the Menu bar and then click **Design Gallery Object**, or click the **Design Gallery Object** button on the Objects toolbar to open the gallery or dialog box that lists available design objects. If your program does not offer design objects, you can set up the masthead yourself using text boxes and formatting. Ask your instructor for more information.

3. Select the **Mastheads** category, and then click the **Checkers Masthead** design. Click **Insert Object** to insert the object into the publication.

4. Align the object vertically with the top of the page, relative to the page margins, and center it horizontally.

5. Replace the sample text *Newsletter Title* with the text **Studio News**.

6. Replace the sample text *Business Name* (or *Your organization*) with the text **Backstage Dance Studio**.

7. Replace the sample text *Newsletter Date* with the text **Fall**.

8. Change the color scheme to **Iris**. The top portion of the newsletter should look similar to Figure 21-15.

FIGURE 21-15
Masthead object in publication

9. Save the changes and leave **Studio** open to use in the next exercise.

Tables of Contents

Use a *table of contents* to direct the reader to specific articles, stories, or chapters in a publication. Although traditionally associated with long publications, a table of contents can be useful in short publications such as newsletters as well. A table of contents usually includes a list of the headlines or titles on the left and the page numbers where the items begin on the right. It may or may not have dot leaders along the line between the two columns.

If your program can automatically set up a table of contents, you simply select the design you want to use, replace the sample text with the correct headlines, titles, and page numbers, and then size and position the object in the publication. If you are using a program such as InDesign that does not include design objects, either manually create a table of contents as shown in Figure 21-16, or skip the following exercise.

S TEP-BY-STEP 21.15

1. Open the gallery or dialog box that lists available design objects.

2. Select the **Tables of Contents** category, and then select the **Checkers Table of Contents** design. Click **Insert Object** to insert the object into the publication.

3. Size and position the object to fit in the left column between the masthead and the existing article.

4. Replace the list of titles (*Inside Story*) with the following list so it looks similar to Figure 21-16:
   Welcome Back
   Dance Around Town
   Meet the Owner: An Interview with Virginia Caplan
   Letters to the Editor
   Fall Schedule
   Check This Out! Links to Interesting Web Sites
   Staying Fit

FIGURE 21-16
Table of contents in publication

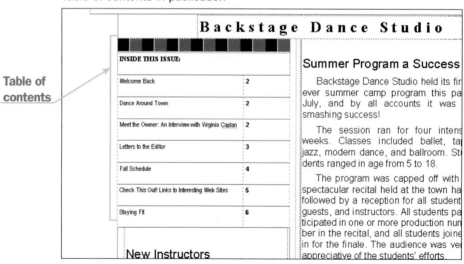

5. Save the changes and leave **Studio** open to use in the next exercise.

Logos

A *logo* is a symbol representing a company or organization, which may include text, graphics, or both. Usually, logos are designed using a different program, such as a graphics program, or by hand, but they are often printed in publications as part of stationery *letterheads*, in the masthead of a newsletter, or even as a watermark. A letterhead is the area on a sheet of stationery where the name, address, and other information about a company or individual are printed. If a logo has been saved as a graphics file, you can simply insert it in a publication as you would any graphics file. If it has been drawn or printed, you can scan it in. If you don't have an existing logo, you may be able to use your desktop publishing program to create one by inserting, sizing, and positioning text and graphics.

If you are using a program, such a Publisher, that can automatically create a logo, you simply select the logo design you want to use, replace the sample text with the name of your organization, and then replace the sample picture with the picture of your choice. You can size and position the logo anywhere in the publication. The result is a professional-looking logo in minutes.

S TEP-BY-STEP 21.16

1. Open the dialog box or gallery that lists available design objects. If your program does not have a design gallery, you can insert the graphics file **Step21-16a** into the white space in the lower-right corner of the page, and then skip to step 6.

2. Select the **Logos** category, and then select the **Open Oval Logo** design. Click **Insert Object** to insert the object into the publication.

3. Drag the object over into the white space in the lower-right corner of the page.

4. Replace the picture (the pyramid shape above the text) with the picture file **Step21-16b** from the data files.

5. Replace the sample text with the text **Backstage Dance Studio**. (The font size should adjust automatically.)

6. Resize the object to fill the white space—about **3** inches wide by **1.75** inches high.

STEP-BY-STEP 21.16 Continued

7. Display the publication in Print Preview. It should look similar to Figure 21-17. (If you do not have a color printer, your print preview may be in black, white, and shades of gray.)

FIGURE 21-17
Completed page

8. Print one copy of the **Studio** file.

9. Save the changes and close the file. Leave your desktop publishing program open to use in the next exercise.

Create a Watermark

A *watermark* is a semitransparent image usually inserted in the background of printed publications. Watermarks can be found on many types of publications, but they are often used on stationery and business cards to provide a subtle identification or brand mark, and they are even used on currency and checks, as they are difficult to forge and can be proof of authenticity. In most programs, watermarks must be created from a picture file. You insert the picture file on the page and adjust its size and position. Then, adjust the image control settings to make the picture semitransparent. The image control settings may be in a dialog box or on a toolbar, such as the Picture toolbar. Send the image to the back of the stacking order so it is layered behind all other objects on the page. If you want a watermark to appear on every page of a publication, you can insert it on a master page.

Some programs have options that automatically adjust the color and transparency to settings appropriate for a watermark. For example, in some programs such as Publisher, you click the

Color button on the Picture toolbar and then click Washout, or select the option on the Picture tab of the Format Picture dialog box. In other programs, such as InDesign, you must manually adjust the opacity setting in the Transparency palette.

STEP-BY-STEP 21.17

1. Open the file **Step21-17a** from the data files and save it as **Letter**.

2. Change to Master Page view.

3. Insert the picture file **Step21-17b** from the data files on the master page.

4. Resize the picture to approximately **7.6** inches wide—the height should adjust automatically, but if it does not, set it to about **4.45**. If you are using InDesign, select the command to fit the content in the frame. Select the options to create a watermark. In Publisher, set the image control to **Washout**. In InDesign, display the Transparency palette and set the opacity to about **15%**.

5. Center the picture horizontally and vertically relative to the page margins. (If you are using InDesign, drag it into position.) If necessary, close any open dialog boxes by clicking **OK**.

6. Close Master Page view and display the publication in Print Preview. It should look similar to the one in Figure 21-18.

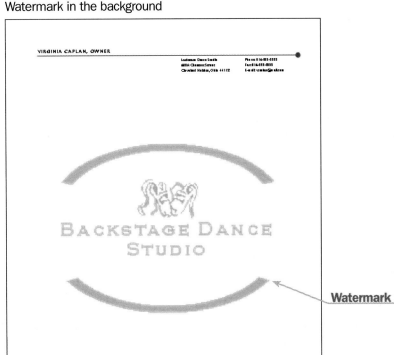

FIGURE 21-18
Watermark in the background

7. Print one copy of **Letter**.

8. Save the changes and close **Letter**. Close your desktop publishing program.

SUMMARY

In this lesson, you learned:

- You can insert objects such as text boxes, pictures, shapes, and charts into a publication.

- You can acquire objects from a variety of sources, including files, digital cameras, scanners, and clip art.

- Once you insert an object, you can scale, move, and format it.

- Most desktop publishing programs have tools for fine-tuning the position of an object on the page.

- You can set text wrap options to adjust the width, shape, and position of white space between text and objects on a page.

- The RGB color system is used to define color on monitors, and the CMYK color system is used to define color in print.

- You can define custom colors by using a color bar or by keying a color system value.

- You can add a gradient, pattern, or texture to a fill, and a pattern to a stroke.

- Shadows and 3-D effects create the illusion of depth on the page.

- A dropped capital is a decorative effect that makes the first letter in a paragraph stand out from the rest of the text.

- Some programs have utilities that let you turn text into graphics objects, and some programs let you add text to shapes.

- You can insert horizontal rules before and/or after a paragraph.

- Some programs let you apply pictures as borders around rectangular objects.

- Some programs come with objects already designed for use as logos, mastheads, and tables of contents.

- You can insert a watermark in the background of any page in a publication.

VOCABULARY *Review*

Define the following terms:

Brand recognition	Logo	Spot color
Color system	Masthead	Standoff
Dropped capital	Picture Frame	Table of contents
Horizontal rules	Process color	Text wrap
Letterhead	Reference point	

REVIEW *Questions*

TRUE / FALSE

Circle T if the statement is true or F if the statement is false.

T   F   1. There is no such thing as a blank frame in desktop publishing.

T   F   2. You can use drawing tools to insert basic shapes in a publication.

T   F   3. The horizontal coordinate is usually called Y.

T   F   4. Use the Nudge command to move an object up, down, left, or right in small increments.

T   F   5. RGB is the main color system used for defining colors in print.

T   F   6. You cannot use both spot colors and process colors in the same publication.

T   F   7. Transparency is sometimes called brightness.

T   F   8. All desktop publishing programs have command that you can use to apply 3-D effects to objects.

T   F   9. Horizontal rules regulate the way you align objects in relation to the left and right margins.

T   F   10. A masthead it the figure on the front of old sailing ships.

WRITTEN QUESTIONS

Write a brief answer to each of the following questions.

1. What are two methods of positioning an object precisely on a page?

2. Explain the difference between process color and spot color.

3. Describe at least three design elements that some programs—such as Publisher—include as part of a design gallery to help you quickly design and format publications.

4. Name at least two reasons for using a watermark.

5. What are three ways you can acquire objects for use in a publication?

FILL IN THE BLANK

Complete the following sentences by writing the correct word or words in the blanks provided.

1. You can use Publisher's _____ tool to draw complex shapes such as stars and lightning bolts.

2. In most desktop publishing programs, the position of objects is modified based on a(n) _____ point.

3. Select a text _____ style to adjust the width, shape, and position of white space between text and objects on page.

4. The _____ color system creates colors by combining percentages of blue, red, yellow, and black ink.

5. _____ is the range of a color from black to white.

6. A(n) _____ is a blend of colors that gradually change in brightness or tint.

7. Apply a(n) _____ capital effect when you want the first character in a paragraph to display larger than the other characters.

8. In some programs, such as Publisher, you can use the _____ to move an object up, down, left, or right in small increments.

9. A(n) _____ is a symbol representing a company or organization.

10. If you want a watermark to display on every page of a publication you should insert it on the _____ page.

PROJECTS

PROJECT 21-1

In this project, design letterhead stationery for an assisted living center.

1. Launch your desktop publishing program and create a new blank full-page document with 1-inch margins. If necessary, deselect the **Facing Pages** check box.

2. Save the file as **SAC.**

3. Change to Master Page view. (Because you want the letterhead information displayed on all pages, even in multipage documents, you will insert the data on the master page.)

4. Insert a horizontal ruler guide at **2** inches on the vertical ruler, and another one at **9** inches on the vertical ruler.

5. Insert a text box **6.5** inches wide by **1.5** inches high. Align the bottom of the text box on the top ruler guide, and center it horizontally on the page. (The text box will extend into the top margin.)

6. Insert and format text as follows:
   A. On the first line in the text box, use a **36**-point serif font such as **Sylfaen** and key **Sunshine Assisted Care, Inc.**
   B. Center the text horizontally and vertically in the text box.
   C. Insert a 1-point horizontal, black rule below the paragraph, sized to extend from the left margin to the right margin. If you are using InDesign, set the offset to **.05.**

7. Insert another text box **6.5** inches wide by **1.5** inches high. Align the top of the text box on the bottom ruler guide, and center it horizontally.

8. Insert and format text as follows:
   A. On the first line in the text box, use the same serif font you used in step 6 in **14** points to key **320 Matheson Street ~ Healdsburg, California ~ 95448**, and then press **Enter.**
   B. Key **Telephone (707) 555-5555 ~ Fax (707) 555-6666 ~ Email mail@gha.com.**
   C. If the tilde characters (~) appear too high in relation to the other text on the line, format them using the Subscript font effect, or adjust the baseline shift to about **-5 pt.**
   D. Center both lines horizontally, and align them vertically with the bottom of the text box.
   E. Position the insertion point in the first line of text, and insert a 1-point horizontal rule above the paragraph, sized to extend from the left margin to the right margin. If you are using InDesign, set the Offset to about **.15.**

9. Insert a sun shape near the top of the page, sized at **0.5** inches by **0.5** inches. If necessary, set the stroke to **3/4 (.75)** pt. solid line, **black.** (If you cannot draw a sun using your program's drawing tools, draw a different shape such as a star.)

10. Position the shape horizontally **1** inch from the upper-left corner and vertically **0.5** inches from the upper-left corner. Set the text wrap to **None.**

11. Create a custom fill color for the sun shape as follows:
    A. Open the custom color dialog box and select the **CMYK** system.
    B. Enter the following values: Cyan: **4**; Magenta: **5**; Yellow: **90**; Black: **0.** Add the swatch to the palette, if necessary, and then apply the color to the shape.

12. If possible, apply a **3-D** effect to the shape, such as **3-D Style 10**, which tilts the face down and to the right and extends the top and left sides. If your program does not support 3-D effects, try applying a different transformation, such as rotating the object **25** degrees. Keep in mind, however, that this may effect the positioning of the object because it moves the reference point.

13. Use the Copy and Paste commands to duplicate the shape. Flip or reflect the shape horizontally, or apply a reverse 3-D effect such as **3-D Style 9**. Position the duplicate horizontally **7** inches from the upper-left corner and vertically **0.5** inches from the upper-left corner. If necessary, change the object's reference point, or simply drag it into position opposite the original object.

14. Create a watermark as follows:
    A. Insert the picture file **Project21-1** from the data files.
    B. Set the image control color to washout, or adjust the opacity to about **15%**.
    C. Size the picture to about **5** inches high (the width should adjust automatically but if it does not, set it to about **3.37"**), and center it horizontally and vertically relative to the margins.

15. Check the spelling in the document and correct errors as necessary.

16. Change back to regular view.

17. Print one copy of the publication.

18. Save the changes and close **SAC**. Leave your desktop publishing program open to use in the next project.

PROJECT 21-2

Enhance a newsletter using pictures and shapes.

1. Launch your desktop publishing program and open **Project21-2a** from the data files.

2. Save the file as **ArtNews2**.

3. Insert the graphics file **Project21-2b** from the data files into the blank frame in the upper-left corner of page 1.
   A. Size the picture to about **1.25** inches high by about **1.344** inches wide, if necessary, and fit the content to the frame.
   B. Position the picture about **1.0** inch from the top left corner horizontally and **0.625** inches from the upper-left corner vertically. If you are using InDesign, you may have to change the reference point to the upper-left corner of the object.

4. Insert the graphics file **Project21-2c** to illustrate the story with the headline *Donations Needed* in the lower-right corner of page 1. Format the picture as follows:
   A. Size the picture to about **0.75** inches high by **0.75** inches wide, and fit the content to the frame.
   B. Set the text wrap for the picture to Tight.
   C. Position the picture **4** inches from the upper-left corner horizontally, and **6.75** inches from the upper-left corner vertically. (If you are using InDesign, you may have to change the reference point.) It will overlap the column guides to the left of the headline. Fine-tune the position as necessary so that all of the text fits in the text box.

5. Change to page 2 and draw a smiley face on the page near the letter to the editor. You may draw the face using an AutoShape, or by using basic shapes.
   A. Size the smiley face to **0.5** inches by **0.5** inches.
   B. Fill the shape with the custom color blue C: 83, M: 3, Y: 0, K: 0.
   C. Set the text wrap to **Square**.

   D. Position the shape to the left of the text *Dear Editor*, at approximately **4.25** from the upper-left corner horizontally and **2.5** from the upper-left corner vertically, then fine-tune the position as necessary, so all of the text fits in the text box.

6. Print both pages, either on separate sheets of paper or on a double-sided sheet.

7. Save the changes and close **ArtNews2**. Leave your desktop publishing program open to use in the next project.

PROJECT 21-3

Enhance a newsletter using borders, lines, dropped capitals, and other effects.

1. In your desktop publishing program, open **Project21-3** from the data files.

2. Save the file as **ArtNews3**.

3. On page 1, insert a masthead design object in a simple style, such as **Frames Masthead**. Format the object as follows. (If your program does not have masthead design objects, use text boxes to insert the masthead information.)
   A. Center the object horizontally, and position it vertically **0.5** inches from the upper-left corner of the page.
   B. Replace the sample text *Newsletter Title* with the text **Our Arts News**.
   C. Replace the sample text *Business Name* (or *Your organization*) with the text **Our Arts Alliance**.
   D. Replace the sample text *Newsletter Date* with the text **Winter/Spring**.
   E. Change the color scheme to **Green**, or any scheme that uses shades of green. If no color schemes are available, create a custom green for the headline font. For example, C: **82**; M: **10**; Y: **100**; K: **14**, and a different green for accents such as strokes or line: C: **75**, M: **3**, Y: **96**, K: **3**.

4. On page 1, insert a table of contents design object in the same style you used for the masthead. Format the object as follows. (If your program does not have table of contents design objects, use text boxes to insert the information.)
   A. Replace the first three story names (*Inside Story*) with the following: **Officer Nominations, Donations Needed, Letters to the Editor**. Each story is on page 2.
   B. Delete the remaining items in the table. (Select the items to delete, click **Table** on the Menu bar, click **Delete**, and then click **Rows**.)
   C. Size and position the object to fit in the white space in the lower-right corner of the page, and then increase the font size of the text *Inside this issue:* to **14** points, apply bold, if necessary, and change the font size of the article headlines to **12** points.

5. Apply a dropped capital letter sized to drop 3 lines to the first character in the first paragraph under the headline *A Night of the Arts*. Increase the height of the text box depth, if necessary, to display all text again.

6. Position the insertion point in the headline text *Volunteer News*, and apply a 2-point green horizontal rule before the paragraph.

7. Switch to page 2 and select the text box containing the text *Don't Forget....* Apply a simple art border, such as **Circles and Rectangles**, sized to **8** points, around the object. If your program does not have art borders, apply a heavy, dashed line border. If necessary, increase the height of the text box so that all text fits.

8. Insert a green 2-point horizontal rule before the first paragraph (the headline) and after the last paragraph in the text box in the top, left of the page.

9. Position the insertion point in the first paragraph under the headline *Donations Needed* and create a dropped capital letter that drops 2 lines. Adjust text boxes as necessary to show all text.

10. Print one copy of each page—either using double-sided printing or on two sheets.

11. Save the changes and close **ArtNews3**. Close your desktop publishing program.

 ## WEB PROJECT

For a science project, use the Internet to research a famous scientist or inventor. Look up facts such as when and where the person was born and went to school, and what contributions he or she made to science. Try to locate a picture of the person and of any inventions. You might also try to learn some personal information such as whether he or she had a family, where they lived, and so on.

When you have completed your research, use your desktop publishing program to create a brochure or flyer about the person. Start by creating a mock-up that indicates where text and objects will be positioned. Then, create the document from scratch, or using one of your program's templates or designs. Write the text and insert and position objects. Apply formatting and enhancements to make the document interesting to look at. When the publication is complete, check the spelling and correct errors. Ask a classmate to review the document and offer comments and suggestions. Incorporate the suggestions to improve the document. Print the document, and then present it to your class.

 ## TEAMWORK PROJECT

As a group, plan and design a flyer or brochure advertising a historic or well-known site in your community as a tourist destination. Start by selecting the site, and then work together to research it so you have all of information to include in the publication. You may want to assign jobs to each team member. Someone might be a photographer responsible for using a digital camera to take pictures of the site to include in the document, or to locate existing pictures that you might be able to use. (Don't forget to get permission, if necessary!) Other jobs might include a copywriter to write the text for the publication, a designer to design the layout, a proofreader to check the text and design for errors, and a manager to organize all aspects of the process.

As with other publications, you should decide the page setup, including how many pages to include, and whether you will use double-sided or single-sided printing. Then, mock up the publication so you have a general idea of its size, layout, and appearance. Remember to include the general size and position of objects such as the pictures you plan to include.

When you are ready, use your desktop publishing program to create the publication document. You can start with a blank document, or use one of your program's templates or designs. Insert all text and objects, and position them on the pages so the document is appealing and easy to read. When you are finished, check the spelling and then print the publication. Ask a classmate to review the document and offer comments and suggestions. Incorporate the suggestions to improve the publication. Present the completed product to your class.

CRITICAL *Thinking*

For a language arts or reading project, use your desktop publishing program to design and create a book jacket for a book you have read. Plan the publication carefully, considering the page size and sheet size and all the components that must be included. The document will be printed only on one side, but it will probably have five pages: a back page, a front page, and a spine (the strip along the binding between the back and front), as well as folds for the front and back covers. Use a ruler to measure the actual book so you know how large a sheet to use and how large the pages must be. Write the text and either create or locate the graphics, and then insert the data into the publication. Adjust the size and position of all objects, and enhance the publication using color, horizontal rules, and other effects. When you are satisfied with the publication, check the spelling, print it, and share it with your class.

PUBLISHING A DOCUMENT

OBJECTIVES

Upon completion of this lesson, you should be able to:

- Plan for publication.
- Check page design and print page proofs.
- Set properties for desktop printing.
- Prepare color separations.
- Enable trapping.
- Prepare a file for commercial printing.
- Compress files for delivery to a commercial printer on a storage device or electronically.
- Publish to the Web.

Estimated Time: 1.5 hours

VOCABULARY

Bleed

Camera-ready film

Color separations

Composite

Crop marks

Filtered HTML

PostScript®

PostScript® Printer Description file (PPD)

Preflight

Print properties

Printer's spread

Proof

Publish

Reader's spread

Trapping

Web publication

Zip

A document created with a desktop publishing program is not really complete until it is *published*. Publishing is the method used to output the document so you can distribute it to readers. The two main methods of publishing are printing the document on your desktop printer or having it printed by a commercial printer. A third option is to print a copy on your desktop printer, and then have it reproduced at a copy shop. In some programs you can also publish a document to the World Wide Web by storing the file on a Web server so it can be opened by anyone connected to the Internet. In this lesson, you learn how to decide the type of publication best suited for a particular project and how to prepare a document for publishing.

Plan for Publication

You make some decisions regarding publication before you even start a project. As you learned in Lesson 18, you should always start by determining the physical aspects of the publication, such as page size, paper stock, method of binding, number of colors, and the number of copies you will need. And, of course, you must consider your budget. You can also decide whether you want to print the publication at all, or publish it on the Web. All these factors affect the decision of how to publish the completed document. For example, if your desktop printer cannot accommodate the physical aspects of the job—such as the paper size—you must consider a commercial printer. If you plan to fold a booklet or staple a newsletter in the upper-left corner, you might not need a commercial printer. But if you want a more sophisticated binding you may have no other choice. Other things to consider include how fast you need the document published; the quality you expect in the finished product; and extra options, such as embossing or foil stamping.

Select a Publication Method

As mentioned, the basic choices for publishing a document are to use your desktop printer, a commercial printer, a copy shop, or publish to the World Wide Web. Use the following guidelines to decide which method is best for a particular job.

- In general, if you need only a few copies of a publication and are working within a tight budget, your desktop printer may be the best choice. Keep in mind, however, that the quality of the publication depends a great deal on the specific printer you are using. A laser printer provides the best quality output, followed by an inkjet printer. Other considerations include the time you must spend operating the printer, the cost of ink or toner, the necessity of folding or binding by hand, and whether your printer can handle the project specifications such as page size, color, or double-sided printing.

- Use a copy shop if you need to produce many copies, if you have a tight budget, or if you need the publication in a hurry. A copy shop may also be able to handle folding or basic binding techniques such as stapling. When you use a copy shop, the quality of the finished product depends on the quality of the original being reproduced, as well as on the available equipment. Before you commit to a copy shop, consider generating a test copy so you can determine if it meets your standards.

- Use a commercial printer if you want the highest quality product and if you can afford it. Other benefits of using a commercial printer include access to more binding options, the ability to handle special orders, and the knowledge and advice an experienced printer can provide.

- Finally, publish to the Web if you want to make the publication available over the Internet.

Select a Commercial Printer

If you decide to use a commercial printer, then the next step is choosing one. The cost of the job should not be the only factor to influence your decision. You will have to work closely with the printer from the very outset of the project, so you should find someone you are comfortable with and who you trust. Following are some of the questions you should ask a commercial printer before you even begin designing the publication:

- What type of color will be used—spot, process, or a combination—and must you use a specific color matching system?

■ How does the commercial printer want the file delivered? Can it be on a disk or CD, or sent electronically on the Internet?

■ If you can submit a file, does the commercial printer want the document file in a particular format, such as PostScript®, or is your program's file format suitable?

■ Can you submit a *composite*, or does the printer want *color separations*? A composite is a file or a printed proof that contains all color information, while color separations are files or printed proofs showing the layout of each color—black, cyan, magenta, and yellow for process color printing, and each spot for spot color printing—on separate sheets of paper.

■ Can you prepare the proof on your desktop printer, or does the printer require *camera-ready film*? Camera-ready film is film made of the finished pages that can be used to publish the document.

■ Does the printer have in stock the type and quantity of paper you've selected?

■ Does the printer have the necessary facilities for folding or binding the publication as required?

■ For bound or folded publications, should you submit pages formatted as *printer's spreads* or *reader's spreads*? Reader's spreads are basically facing pages—such as page 2 on the left and page 3 on the right. In printer's spreads, the pages are arranged in the order that they must be printed for the page order to be correct when the publication is bound. For example, in a 4-page folded booklet, page 4 is on the left of the sheet and page 1 is on the right of the sheet.

> **Note**
>
> Most desktop publishing programs automatically format multi-page documents as printer's spreads. If you want to print reader's spreads for proofing, you probably have to select an option in the Print dialog box.

Perform Prepress Checks

No matter which method of publication you select, before you publish the document, you should perform a quality check. The check should include using a spelling checker and proofreading the file for errors. (Checking spelling is covered in Lesson 18.) You should also look over the design and layout to determine if there are any improvements to make. You may need to nudge the location of a headline in a newsletter, or expand the size of a text box so all the text is displayed. You can use tools in your program to perform these checks, and then you should print a proof of the publication so that you can check it manually.

> **Hot Tip**
>
> Often we read what we expect to read instead of what is really there. To catch spelling errors and other problems you might otherwise miss, try looking at the words in reverse order from the end of a story to the beginning. It's also a good idea to have someone else proofread as well.

Check Page Design

Some desktop-publishing programs, such as Publisher, include tools for checking the design of a publication. A design checker works similar to a spelling checker. It locates and highlights design problems, such as too much text to fit in a text box. To start the checker, select a command such as Tools > Design Checker. The design checker displays in a task pane or dialog box.

Publisher, for example, lists items in the task pane. You can click the item's drop-down arrow to select from a list of options, such as *Go to the Item*, automatically *Fix* the item, or *Never Run this Check Again*. You can also click *Explain* to start the Help program and display information about how to fix the problem.

If your program has a design checker, use it to complete the following exercise. If you are using a program such as InDesign that does not have a design checker, you can complete the exercise simply by examining the publication on your computer screen to find problems and correct them.

STEP-BY-STEP 22.1

1. Launch your desktop publishing program, and open **Step22-1** from the data files. (If a message asks you if it is OK to accept macros from this source, click **Enable Macros** to continue.) Save the file as **Mailer**.

2. Run a spelling checker to identify spelling errors. If the checker finds any errors, correct them.

3. Start the design checker if one is available in your program. If you are using Publisher, click **Tools** on the Menu bar, and then click **Design Checker**. The Design Checker displays, as shown in Figure 22-1.

FIGURE 22-1
Design Checker task pane

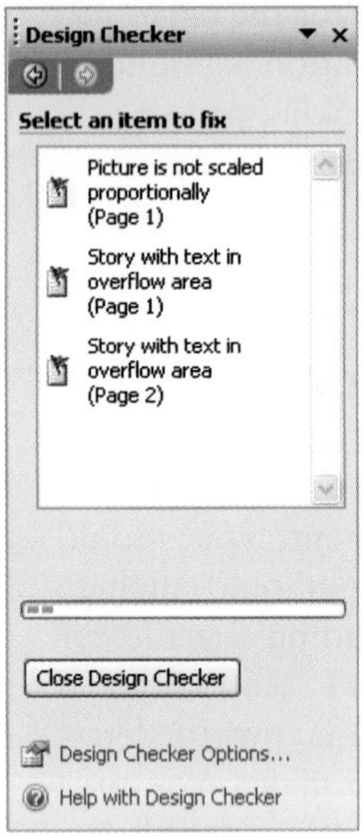

4. Select the first item in the list—*Picture is not scaled proportionately (Page 1)*, click the drop-down arrow, and then click **Go to this Item** to select the problem object. If your program does not have a design checker feature, try to locate the object on page 1 that does not display correctly.

5. Click the drop-down arrow on the first item in the Design Checker again, and click **Fix: Rescale Picture**. Your program automatically fixes the problem. Manually realign the object in the center of the page, if necessary. Notice that the item in the Design Checker displays as corrected, and is then removed from the list. If your program does not have a design check feature, resize the object manually so that it displays correctly.

STEP-BY-STEP 22.1 Continued

6. Click the drop-down arrow of the next item in the check box—*Story with text in overflow area (Page 1)*—and click **Go to this Item**, or manually locate the text box that has overflow text. Resize the text box so it is about **1.0** inch high. Once the box has been resized, all of the text displays.

7. Go to the next item in the Design Checker, which is a text box on page 2 that is too small to display all the text it contains.

8. Resize the text to **12** points.

9. Correct or ignore any other problems that the Design Checker identifies, and then close it.

10. Save the changes and leave **Mailer** open to use in the next exercise.

Print Page Proofs

You should always print a sample copy or *proof* of the publication to review before you print all copies or send the publication to a commercial printer. You should proofread the printout for spelling errors that your spelling checker does not catch, and for design problems such as inconsistent line weight, misaligned objects, or mismatched colors that show up more clearly in print. Also, you can see the entire publication in its actual size when you print it, and you can give it to someone else to check as well. For desktop printing, you can also use a proof to determine if the colors you have selected reproduce the way you expect.

Before printing, make sure the desktop printer is correctly set up for use with your computer. This means it is physically attached to your computer or network and the printer driver software has been correctly installed. You should also make sure that the proper size paper is correctly loaded in the printer and the printer is turned on. If you are concerned with color quality, you may want to install fresh ink cartridges or toner before printing.

As you have already learned, to print a copy of a publication on your desktop or network printer, click File on the Menu bar and then click Print to display the Print dialog box. Click the OK or Print button in the Print dialog box to generate the file. Alternatively, to print a single copy of the document using the default settings, click the Print button on the toolbar.

STEP-BY-STEP 22.2

1. Click **File** on the Menu bar and then click **Print**.

2. Click **OK** or **Print** to print one copy of each page on a separate sheet of paper.

3. Proofread the printout for spelling and design errors. There are two spelling errors that the spelling checker probably did not find, and one layout error where text is not properly aligned. When you locate the errors, circle them on the printout in red, and then correct them in the file.

4. Save the changes and leave **Mailer** open to use in the next exercise.

Set Properties for Desktop Printing

Print properties are the settings that control the way a publication prints on your desktop printer. They fall into two basic categories: printer options, which are specific to the printer model you are using; and print options, which are specific to the program and the publication document. Printer options may include the draft quality, whereas print options might include whether to print graphics or how many copies of a page to print on one sheet of paper.

You access the print properties through your program's Print dialog box. The available options and the way they are organized depend on your desktop publishing program, your printer, and the publication with which you are working. Usually, however, you click a button such as Properties or Setup to open your printer's Properties dialog box, which should be similar to Figure 22-2.

FIGURE 22-2
Canon S600 printer Properties dialog box

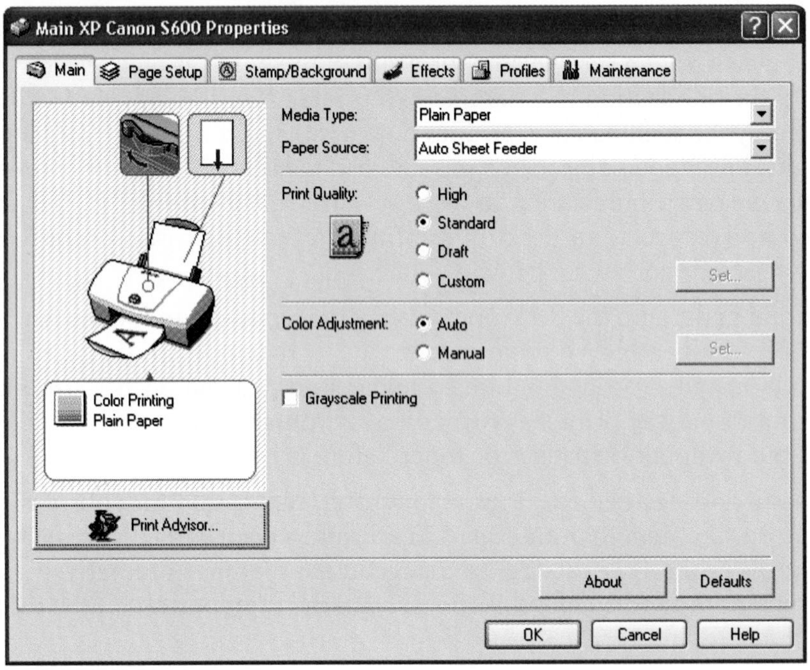

Some programs, such as InDesign, make print options available in the Print dialog box. In other programs, such as Publisher, you click a button such as Advanced Print Settings to open an Advanced Print Settings dialog box. The Page Setting tab should look similar to Figure 22-3.

FIGURE 22-3
Page Settings tab of the Print Settings dialog box

In addition to properties, keep in mind that certain types of publications require special setup or handling to print correctly. For example, duplex (double-sided) printing may require you to print one page, then reinsert the paper correctly in the printer to print the next page. Banners and posters may print on multiple sheets of paper, which must then be arranged to create the complete publication. Conversely, you may be able to print more than one postcard on the same sheet, and then trim them to size.

Some effects also require special handling. For instance, you print a *bleed*, which is an effect created by an object running off the edge of the page, by using options in the Page Setup dialog box to set the publication to print on a sheet size larger than the page size. Position the object in the document so it extends beyond the edge of the page. After printing, you crop, or trim, the paper to the appropriate page size.

Did You Know?

Some desktop printers have a nonprintable region, which is the area on the top, bottom, left, and right of a page on which data cannot be printed. If your printer has a nonprintable region, it is listed in the printer-specific Properties dialog box.

Table 22-1 lists some common print properties. Keep in mind, however, that because the specific properties available on your computer depend on the printer and the program you are using, you may not have all the properties listed, or you may have more.

TABLE 22-1
Common print properties

PROPERTY	DESCRIPTION
Printer	Select the printer to print the document. Other options may change depending on the printer selected.
Number of copies	Key the number of copies of each page that you want to print.
Collate	Select this option to print pages consecutively. Deselect this option to print all copies of each page before proceeding to the next page.
Print range	Use these options to specify the exact pages to print. Select All to print all pages, key a range separated by a hyphen to print all pages within the range, and/or key specific page numbers separated by commas to print only those pages. Other options may be available, such as printing the current page only, printing only odd- or even-numbered pages, or printing blank pages.
Orientation	Select either landscape or portrait orientation.
Reverse	Select this option to print pages from the end of the document to the beginning, rather than from the beginning to the end.
Printer's marks	Use these options to specify whether to print elements such as **crop marks**, which indicate where the paper should be cut or trimmed down to the correct page size; or color bars, which are used to gauge the printed colors. Marks are displayed only if the paper size is at least 1 inch taller and wider than the page size.
Fonts	Use these options to specify whether to allow font substitution.
Page setup	Depending on your printer, you may be able to scale the output by a percentage of the original size or select an option to control the way the document fits on the printed page. For example, you may be able to select Poster printing or Banner printing to print thumbnails of each page, and to choose how many copies of each page to print per sheet. Other options may include printing reader's spreads or printer's spreads and tiling the pages.
Graphics or Proof	Use these options to specify whether to include graphics in the printout.
Print quality	Select the quality level you want to use. The higher the quality, the better the output. This option usually determines the resolution, the amount of ink, or the number of colors used to print a document.
Color	Use these options to specify grayscale, black-and-white, or four-color printing. In some programs, or for some publications, you may be able to set options for printing color separations, screens, and/or bleeds.

*S*TEP-BY-STEP 22.3

1. Click **File** on the Menu bar and then click **Print**.

2. If available, select the option for high-quality printing. Print quality options are usually found in the printer's Properties dialog box. (You may need to select a Properties or Setup/Preferences button to see this dialog box.)

3. Select the option to print crop marks. This option may be available on the **Page Settings** tab of the Advanced Print Setting dialog box (in Publisher) or on the **Marks and Bleed** tab of the Print dialog box (in InDesign).

4. Select to print page 1 only. If you are using Publisher, click the **Current Page** option in the Print dialog box. If you are using InDesign, click the **Range** option and then key **1** in the Range text box.

5. Click in the *Copies* or *Number of copies* box and key **2** to select to print two copies of the page.

6. Click **OK** or **Print** to print two copies of page 1.

7. Reinsert the printed sheets into your printer, positioned correctly to print page 2 on the reverse side.

8. In the document, make page 2 active, click **File** on the Menu bar, and then click **Print**.

9. Select to print two copies of page 2, and then print the pages. You should now have two copies of the **Mailer** publication.

10. Using the crop marks as guides, trim the paper to the publication page size. You can use scissors, but to get a straighter edge, use a paper cutter.

11. Save the changes and leave **Mailer** open to use in the next exercise.

Prepare Color Separations

A commercial printer will probably want you to submit a final composite proof, which is an accurate copy of the publication, as well as separations, which are printouts showing the layout of each color—black, cyan, magenta, and yellow for process color printing, and each spot for spot color printing—on separate sheets of paper. A composite is the default method of printing. All components and all colors are printed on each page. (You printed a composite of the Mailer file earlier in this lesson.)

Important
In most desktop publishing programs you can only print separations on a printer that supports PostScript® language Level 2 or higher. Level 2 was introduced in 1991, so if you purchased your printer after 1991, it should be able to print separations. For more information, consult your instructor or the Web site of your printer manufacturer.

In some programs, the option to print separations instead of a composite is available in the Print dialog box. In InDesign, it is on the Output tab of the Print dialog box. In other programs the option is in a print settings dialog box. In Publisher, the option is in the Output list in the Advanced Print Settings dialog box. Note that separations generally print in black and white because they are used to note the position of each color, not to match colors.

STEP-BY-STEP 22.4

1. Click **File** on the Menu bar, and then click **Print** to display the Print dialog box.

2. Select the option to print all separations. In Publisher, click the **Advanced Print Settings** button, click the **Output** drop-down arrow, click **Separations**, and then click **OK**. In InDesign, click the **Output** tab, click the **Color** drop-down arrow, and then click **Separations**. If Separations is not available, click the **Printer** drop-down arrow and click **PostScript® File**, then click the **PPD** drop-down arrow and click **AdobePDF 7.0**. Then, click **Separations** in the Color list.

3. Click **OK** or **Print** to print the separations. One page prints for each color. If your printer does not support PostScript® language level 2, a warning box displays. Click **OK** to continue without printing the separations.

4. Save the changes and leave **Mailer** open to use in the next exercise.

Enable Trapping

Sometimes adjoining colors are printed slightly out of register, which means they are not aligned properly. When that happens, there may be gaps or overlaps between the colors. *Trapping* is a technique used to adjust the position of adjoining colors to avoid such gaps or overlaps. Most desktop publishing programs have automatic trapping that you can turn off or on. By default, your program uses typical trapping settings appropriate for most publications. You can adjust the trapping settings in most desktop publishing programs to fine-tune the way trapping is applied. For instance, you may be able to specify the trap width or set custom trapping for objects.

To enable trapping for a publication, open the dialog box that displays trapping preferences, and then select the Automatic trapping option. If you are using Publisher, click Tools on the Menu bar, click Commercial Printing Tools, click Registration Settings, and then click Publication. If you are using InDesign, trapping is enabled on the Output tab of the Print dialog box. It may only be available when you select to print separations.

STEP-BY-STEP 22.5

1. Open the trapping preferences dialog box. In Publisher click **Tools** on the Menu bar, click **Commercial Printing Tools**, click **Registration Settings**, and then click **Publication**. In InDesign, click **File** on the Menu bar, and then click **Print**. Click the **Output** tab, if necessary.

2. Select the option to enable trapping. In Publisher, the dialog box should look similar to Figure 22-4.

FIGURE 22-4
Enable automatic trapping

Select to enable trapping

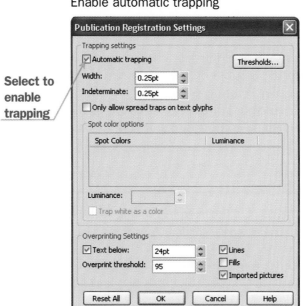

3. Click **OK** to apply the change.

4. Save the changes and leave **Mailer** open to use in the next exercise.

Save a File for Commercial Printing

Before you deliver a publication to a commercial printer, you must correctly prepare your publication files. Usually, that means saving the file in a format that the commercial printer can use and conducting a *preflight*. A preflight is a quality check that can be performed before delivering a publication to the printer or it can be performed by the printer before publication. The preflight includes, among other things, making sure that all graphics and fonts used in the publication are available. You may also have to specify colors for commercial printing. If your commercial printer uses the same program you use, or has the capability to convert your file, you may be able to submit the file in its native, or default, file format. You must, however, be sure that all graphics and fonts are embedded in the file, or you must submit the graphics and font files as well.

Luckily, most desktop publishing programs have a tool for preparing a file for commercial printing. This utility, which is usually called something like *Pack and Go* or *Package*, automatically sets up all the files needed to generate the publication, including the publication file, fonts, and graphics. In some cases, it actually packs all the files together in one new file. In other cases, it simply copies and organizes the necessary files.

If the commercial printer cannot use your file in its default file format, you may have to convert to a different format. Many commercial printers request files in *PostScript®* format. PostScript® is a page description language used to define page layout and design for printing specifically on PostScript® printers, which are printers that use the PostScript® language.

> **Note** ☑
>
> Always consult your commercial printer before submitting files and proofs. Most printers have a list of requirements detailing exactly what you need to provide.

Set up a File for Commercial Color Printing

If you are using a program such as Publisher, you can use the Color Printing dialog box to specify commercial color printing settings. Click Tools on the Menu bar, click Commercial Printing Tools, and then click Color Printing. Select the type of printing process you want to use, and then click OK. You can select spot color, process color, or a combination of the two. Your program may also offer RGB or single-color options. If you are using InDesign, skip this exercise.

STEP-BY-STEP 22.6

1. Click **Tools** on the Menu bar, point to **Commercial Printing Tools**, and then click **Color Printing** to display the dialog box where you can specify options for commercial printing.

2. Select the option to print **Process colors (CMYK)**. A dialog box displays informing you that all colors will be converted to process colors. Click **OK**. The Color Printing dialog box should look similar to Figure 22-5.

FIGURE 22-5
Set commercial printing colors

STEP-BY-STEP 22.6 Continued

3. Click **OK**.

4. Save the changes and leave **Mailer** open to use in the next exercise.

Check for Missing Elements

When you submit a file to a printer, it must include all graphics and fonts. If the elements are embedded in the file, they should be available to the printer. If they are linked, or stored on your system, you must supply them as separate files along with the publication file.

You can use your program's tools to identify missing elements. Some programs, such as InDesign, have an automated preflight check that identifies missing fonts and graphics, as well as other possible problems. In other programs, you can use tools to list font and graphics information so you can locate any items that may be missing. This is the case in Publisher, where you can display a list of all fonts used in a publication. If a font is marked as *Printer*, it means it is not embedded in the file and must be supplied separately. You can also select options such as whether to embed the fonts when saving. In Publisher, you can use the Graphics Manager task pane to display information about graphics used in the publication.

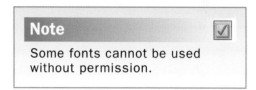

> **Note** ☑
>
> Some fonts cannot be used without permission.

S TEP-BY-STEP 22.7

1. Start the feature to check for missing fonts. If you are using Publisher, click **Tools** on the Menu bar, point to **Commercial Printing Tools**, and then click **Fonts**. A Fonts dialog box similar to the one in Figure 22-6 displays. If you are using InDesign, click **File** on the Menu bar and then click **Preflight**. In the Preflight dialog box, click the **Fonts** tab.

FIGURE 22-6
Fonts dialog box

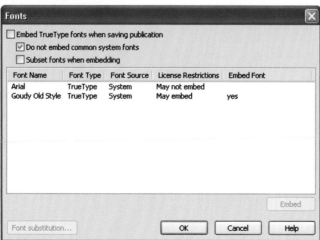

STEP-BY-STEP 22.7 Continued

2. Read the information to determine if any fonts are unavailable or protected.

3. If available, select the option to **Embed TrueType fonts when saving the publication**. Deselect the option not to embed common system fonts if it is available.

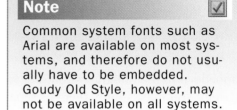

> **Note** ☑
>
> Common system fonts such as Arial are available on most systems, and therefore do not usually have to be embedded. Goudy Old Style, however, may not be available on all systems.

4. If the dialog box displays only font information, click **OK** to close it. If you are using InDesign, leave the Preflight dialog box open.

5. Start the feature to check for missing graphics. In Publisher, click **Tools** on the Menu bar and then click **Graphics Manager**. The Graphics Manager task pane displays, similar to the one in Figure 22-7. In InDesign, click the **Links and Images** tab in the Preflight dialog box.

FIGURE 22-7
Graphics Manager task pane

6. Read the information to determine if any graphics are missing or unavailable. If a file is embedded, it is stored with the publication information; if it is linked, you must supply the source file when you submit the publication to the printer.

7. Close the task pane or dialog box.

8. Save the changes and leave **Mailer** open to use in the next exercise.

Pack the Publication Files

To reproduce the document correctly, the commercial printer must be able to open and use all components of the publication file including the fonts and graphics. Most desktop publishing programs have a file preparation utility that you can use to be sure all components are available. In addition to compiling the necessary files and packing them into a single folder, most programs also generate a list of the packed files, including information such as whether a font is embedded or if a graphics file is linked. Usually, the utility also creates a Readme, Report, or Instructions file that contains information about the packed publication and, possibly, how to unpack the data for use. The printer can open the Readme file for instructions.

The steps for using an automatic file preparation utility vary depending on the program you are using. Usually, you start the utility and then select options to control where the packed file is saved and exactly what is included in it. In any case, you start the utility by clicking File on the Menu bar, clicking a command such as Pack and Go or Package, and then clicking a command such as Take to a Commercial Printing Service. Select options, if necessary, and click the Next button to proceed through the steps necessary to complete the process, or click Save to save the file.

If your program does not have an automatic file preparation feature, you must make sure to deliver all font and graphics files to the commercial printer along with the publication file. Most printers will request a file list as well.

> **Hot Tip**
>
> Save the packed file to a floppy disk or CD so it is ready for delivery to the commercial printer.

STEP-BY-STEP 22.8

1. Create a new folder named **Step22-8** that you can use to store the packed files. Ask your instructor where to place the folder.

2. In the **Mailer** file, start the file preparation utility that comes with your program. In Publisher, click **File** on the Menu bar, point to **Pack and Go**, and then click **Take to a Commercial Printing Service**. In InDesign, click **File** on the menu and then click **Package**.

3. In Publisher click **Next**, or in InDesign click **Continue**. If prompted to enter instructions, click **Continue** again.

4. Select or key the location where you want to store the packed file—the **Step22-8** folder you created in step 1. If you are using InDesign, key the folder name **Mailer** (the **Mailer** folder will be stored in the **Step22-8** folder). In Publisher, click **OK** in the Choose Location dialog box, and then click **Next**.

5. Select options to include embedded fonts and linked graphics, and to create or update links for graphics.

6. Click the button to package the file. In Publisher, click **Next** and then click **Finish**. In InDesign, click **Package**, and then click **OK** in the Font Alert box.

7. If a dialog box prompts you to print separations or composites, clear the selections, then click **OK**. The packed file is stored in the specified location. Leave **Mailer** open to use in the next exercise.

Save a PostScript® File

Most desktop publishing programs have tools for converting a file to PostScript® format. In some programs, such as Publisher, you start off using the Save As command just as you do to save the file in any other format. However, if you select PostScript® from the *Save as type* list and then click the Save button, the Save as PostScript® File dialog box opens. You must select a PostScript® printer from the Printer list. If you do not have a PostScript® printer, you can select Adobe PDF. You can click the Advanced Printer Settings option to select additional options, and then click the Save button to save the file.

Note

Your commercial printer can supply you with print properties necessary for preparing the PostScript® file.

In other programs, such as InDesign, you create the PostScript® file using the Print Options dialog box. Click File on the Menu bar, and then click Print. From the Printer list, select a PostScript® printer, and then select the appropriate *PostScript® Printer Description file (PPD)*, which is a file that provides information about the printing device, from the PPD list. (You should ask your commercial printer which printer and PPD to use.) Select additional printer options as necessary, and then click the Save button. Key a name and specify a location for the PostScript® file, and then click Save.

S TEP-BY-STEP 22.9

1. Select the command for saving the file in PostScript® format. If you are using Publisher, click **File** > **Save As**. If you are using InDesign click **File** > **Print**.

2. If you are using Publisher, select **PostScript®** from the *Save as type* list, or select a PostScript® printer from the Printer list and an **AdobePDF** format from the PPD list. If you are using InDesign, click the **Output** tab, select **Composite CMYK** from the Color list, and then click **Save**.

3. Select the location where you want to store the file and key the filename **PSMailer**. Click **Save**. If you are using InDesign, the program saves the PostScript® file and you can skip to step 6.

4. If you are using Publisher, select a PostScript® printer from the *Name* list, or select **Adobe PDF**. If you choose Adobe PDF, click the **Properties** button, deselect the **Do not send fonts to "Adobe PDF"** check box, and then click **OK**. Click the **Advanced Print Settings** button to display the Advanced Print Settings dialog box. Select **Composite CMYK** from the Output list, and then click **OK**.

5. Click **Save** to save the file. (If a message box displays, click **OK** to continue.)

6. Save and close **Mailer** and your desktop publishing program.

Note

If you make changes to a publication file after preparing it for printing, be sure to update all font and graphics information and generate new proofs.

Deliver Files to a Commercial Printer

When the files are 100 percent ready to go, you must deliver them to the commercial printer. You usually have two choices for delivery: on removable media, such as a Flash drive, CD-R, CD-RW, or electronically via the Internet. Ask your printer which method you should use.

Remember, you may have to deliver the font and graphics files in addition to the publication file. Font files are stored in the Fonts folder, which is in the Windows folder on your hard drive (or network). A Fonts folder window is shown in Figure 22-8. Be sure to deliver font files for all styles of the font used in the publication. For example, include the bold and italic versions of the font.

FIGURE 22-8
Fonts folder window

If you are submitting more than one file, your commercial printer may want you to compress or *zip* them into one file. A compressed file is smaller than a lot of individual files and is usually easier to manage. The printer can unzip or extract the files as necessary.

Compress Files

Although you do not have to compress the files before delivery, it is easier to send one compressed file over the Internet instead of many other files. Also, the printer may request a compressed file. Some versions of Windows come with a compression utility you can use to zip or compress the files, or you can use any compression utility. Select all the files you want to compress, then right-click the selection and click the appropriate command for zipping or compressing the files. For example, with the Windows compression tool, click Send to. On the submenu, click Compressed (zipped) Folder. Windows compresses the files into one folder. You can identify the zipped folder because its icon has a zipper on it, as shown in Figure 22-9. By default, the zipped folder has the same name as the first compressed file. To rename the folder, right-click it and click Rename. Key the new name and then press Enter. To extract the files, right-click the zipped file or folder and click Extract All.

FIGURE 22-9
Compressed folder icon

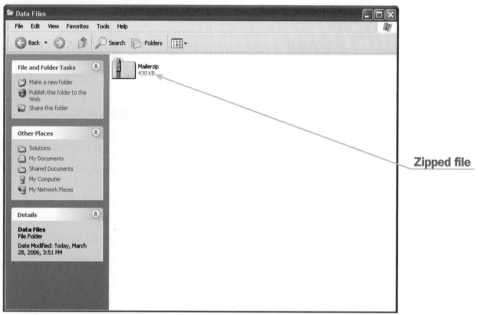

In the following exercise, you use data files and font files supplied with this book. Your instructor may want you to use the actual PostScript® file or the packed files you created in previous exercises, as well as the font files stored in the Fonts folder in the Windows folder on your computer.

STEP-BY-STEP 22.10

1. From the Windows desktop, use My Computer or Windows Explorer to navigate to the folder where the data files for this lesson are stored, and then copy the following files to the folder where your solutions are stored: **Step22-10a**, **Step22-10b**, **GOUDOS**, **GOUDOSB**, and **Arial**.

2. Use Windows to navigate to your **Solutions** folder, then press and hold **Ctrl** and click the following files to select them: **Step22-10a** (the PostScript® file), **Step22-10b** (a GIF graphics file), **GOUDOS** (Goudy Old Style font), **GOUDOSB** (Goudy Old Style Bold font), and **Arial** (Arial font).

3. Use your compression utility to compress the files. For example, if you are using the Windows compression utility, right-click the selection and click **Send To** on the submenu, then click **Compressed (zipped) Folder**. (Depending on your compression utility, you may have to key a name—**Mailerzip**—and then click the **Add** button in order to compress the files. If so, skip step 4.)

4. Right-click the compressed folder and click **Rename**. Key the filename **Mailerzip**, and then press **Enter**.

Deliver Files on Removable Media

If your commercial printer requests the file(s) on a removable storage device, simply use the Send To command to transfer the necessary files to the device. If you are copying a lot of files, you may want to compress or zip them first.

You transfer files to a removable device using your operating system. First, insert the destination disk in the appropriate storage device, or connect the device to the appropriate port. For example, insert the CD-R in the CD-R drive or attach the Flash drive to a USB port. Then, navigate to the window where your publication files are stored. Right-click the file or files to copy, click the Send To command, and then click the device where you want to store the files. If you are burning the files to a CD, use your CD-burning utility to complete the process. You should attach a label to the device and write the filename, your name, and the date on it, as well as any other information to help the commercial printer identify the contents. You can then hand deliver or ship the disk along with the composite and separations and a file list.

STEP-BY-STEP 22.11

1. Insert the destination disk into the appropriate storage device. For example, insert a CD-R or CD-RW into a CD-R drive or insert a Flash drive into a USB port.

2. From the Windows desktop, navigate to the folder where the data files are stored.

3. Right-click the **Step22-11** compressed folder, click **Send To**, and then click the device where you want to store the files. If the device is a disk or Flash drive, Windows copies the files and you can skip to step 5. If the device is a CD, you must use your CD-burning software to complete the process.

4. Navigate to the My Computer window and open the window for the CD drive. Click the **Write these files to CD** command. Follow the prompts to name the CD and copy the files. Click **Finish** when the process is complete.

5. Remove the disk and label it with the filename, your name, and the date. It is now ready to deliver to the commercial printer.

6. Use a word processing program, a text editor, a database program, a spreadsheet program, or a piece of paper and a pen to create a list of all the files you have copied to the disk so that you can supply it to the printer as well.

Deliver Files Electronically

If your commercial printer requests the file(s) electronically, send them via e-mail using your e-mail account. Log on to the Internet using your ISP account, and then start your e-mail program. Create a new message and key the recipient's e-mail address in the *Send to* text box. Key descriptive information in the Subject text box, such as the job number or the publication name. Attach the file or compressed file to the message, and then send the message. Ask the printer to confirm

> **Note**
>
> Your printer may have an FTP site to which you can upload files. To use an FTP site, you need FTP client software (which is built in to many popular Internet browsers), an account number, and a password. Ask your printer for more information.

receipt or set your e-mail for receipt confirmation. You may need to ship the file on a disk as well, along with all proofs and file lists.

STEP-BY-STEP 22.12

1. Log on to your Internet Service Provider, and start your e-mail program.

2. In the To text box, key the address of the commercial printer.

3. In the Subject text box, key **Files for postcard mailer**.

4. In the message text area, key **Please reply to confirm receipt**, and then key your name and e-mail address.

5. Click the button for attaching a file, then locate and select the **Step22-12** compressed folder.

6. Click the **Send** button in your e-mail program to send the message and its attachment.

7. Close your e-mail program and log off. If necessary, disconnect from the Internet.

Publish to the Web

Many desktop publishing programs have tools you can use to publish a document to the Web. If the document was designed as a Web publication, you can usually use a command such as File > Publish to the Web to select a file server storage location, and save the file in a Web-compatible format. If the document was designed for print, you may have to convert it to a Web publication before you can save it to the Web. A *Web publication* is one that is optimized for display on a Web browser. Features that may not display properly on a Web page, such as text wrapping around graphics, are disabled. When you publish to the Web, most desktop publishing programs save the file in *filtered HTML* format, which is a version of HTML that is smaller than standard HTML. Associated graphics files are stored in a separate folder, usually named with the HTML filename, followed by an underscore and the word *files*. The folder must be stored on the file server with the HTML document or the Web page will not display correctly.

If your program does not have tools for publishing to the Web skip this exercise. Close your desktop publishing program.

> **Note**
>
> InDesign does not have tools for publishing directly to the Web. However, you can use the File > Package for GoLive command to prepare files for use in Adobe's GoLive Web page design program.

S TEP-BY-STEP 22.13

1. In your desktop publishing program open **Step22-13**.

2. Select the command to convert it to a Web publication. If you are using Publisher, click **File** on the Menu bar and then click **Convert to Web Publication**. Click **Next** to continue.

3. Select not to include a navigation bar, and then click **Finish** to convert the publication. Notice that the text wrapping is disabled so that the graphics overlap the text.

4. Save the file as **DancePage**.

5. Select the text box containing the text *Backstage Dance Studio* near the top of the page and move it to the right so that it abuts the logo object instead of overlapping it.

6. Select the picture of the dancers and drag it to the right so it does not overlap any text. The top of the page should look similar to Figure 22-10.

FIGURE 22-10
Web publication

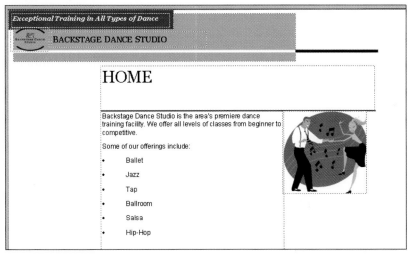

7. Select the command to publish the file to the Web. In Publisher, click **File** on the Menu bar and then click **Publish to the Web**. If a dialog box about file server storage displays, click **OK**. The Publish to the Web dialog box displays.

8. In the *File name* text box, key **HomePage**, and then select the location where you want to store the file.

9. Click **Save**. If a dialog box explaining filtered HTML displays, click **OK**.

10. Save the changes to the **DancePage** publication and close it. Close your desktop publishing program.

SUMMARY

In this lesson, you learned:

■ You can use a desktop printer to publish a document if you need only a few copies or are concerned about the cost.

■ You can have a copy shop reproduce a publication if you need many copies, are in a hurry, and are concerned about the cost.

■ You should have a commercial printer publish a document if you want the best quality, need many copies, have special printing requests, and have enough money in the budget.

■ You can publish to the Web to make a publication available for viewing on the Internet.

■ Before printing, you should check the spelling and design in a publication.

■ Some programs have a design checker utility that can locate problems such as too much text in a text box, or pictures that are out of proportion.

■ You set print properties to control the way a document prints, but the properties vary depending on your printer, your desktop publishing program, and the publication.

■ Commercial printers usually require a composite proof and separations.

■ Trapping helps eliminate gaps and overlaps between adjoining colors.

■ Many programs have a utility that automatically prepares a file for commercial printing.

■ You may have to save a file in PostScript® format for your commercial printer.

■ You can deliver a publication file to a commercial printer on disk or electronically.

■ In some cases, you must deliver font and graphics files as well.

■ You may have to convert a print publication into Web format before you can publish it to the Web.

■ Some features that are used in a print publication may not be supported in a Web publication. For example, text wrapping is not supported, so you may have to rearrange graphics so they do not overlap text.

■ When you publish a file to the Web, it is saved in filtered HTML format.

VOCABULARY *Review*

Define the following terms:

Bleed	PostScript®	Proof
Camera-ready film	PostScript® Printer	Publish
Color separations	Description file (PPD)	Reader's spread
Composite	Preflight	Trapping
Crop marks	Print properties	Web publication
Filtered HTML	Printer's spread	

REVIEW *Questions*

TRUE / FALSE

Circle T if the statement is true or F if the statement is false.

T F 1. You should use a copy shop to produce your publication if you want the highest quality product.

T F 2. A commercial printer will proofread your publication before printing it and will correct errors.

T F 3. Some programs include a tool that checks the publication design for errors, such as text in the overflow area.

T F 4. All desktop printers have the same printer options.

T F 5. Separations usually print in black and white.

T F 6. Some fonts are copyright protected and can only be used with permission.

T F 7. If a graphics object is linked to a publication, you do not have to supply it to the printer in a separate file.

T F 8. Usually, a packing utility generates a Readme, Report, or Instructions file that contains information about the packed publication.

T F 9. In order to generate a PostScript® file, you must select a PostScript® printer or Adobe PDF from the Printer list.

T F 10. Most publication files are too large to transmit via e-mail.

WRITTEN QUESTIONS

Write a brief answer to each of the following questions.

1. What are four methods of publishing a document that you create with a desktop publishing program?

2. List at least three things to consider when deciding which method to use to publish a document.

3. Why should you print a proof before publishing a document?

4. What are the two most common ways to deliver publication files to a commercial printer?

5. Name at least one feature that may not display the same when you convert a print publication to a Web publication.

FILL IN THE BLANK

Complete the following sentences by writing the correct word or words in the blanks provided.

1. Print _____ are the settings that control the way a publication prints on your desktop printer.

2. A(n) _____ is an effect created by an object running off the edge of the page.

3. The print _____ setting usually determines the resolution, the amount of ink, or the number of colors used to print a document.

4. Printouts showing the layout of each color in a publication are called _____.

5. A printout showing all components and all colors on each page is called a(n) _____.

6. _____ is a technique used to adjust the position of adjoining colors to avoid gaps or overlaps.

7. Perform a(n) _____ to make sure that all graphics and fonts used in the publication are available.

8. Many commercial printers request files in the _____ format.

9. A(n) _____ file is smaller than a lot of individual files and is usually easier to manage.

10. _____ HTML is a version of HTML that is smaller than standard HTML format.

PROJECTS

PROJECT 22-1

In this project you prepare a newsletter for publishing on your desktop printer.

1. Launch your desktop publishing program, and open **Project22-1** from the data files. Save the file as **ArtNews5**.

2. Run the spelling checker. Ignore people's names, and correct any other spelling errors as necessary.

3. Run the design checker to locate and address the following issues, and any other issues you or the checker find. If your program does not have a design checker, manually look for and fix design problems.
   A. The picture at the top of page 1 is not scaled properly. Select the option to automatically fix the problem or resize the object to **1.34** inches wide by **1.25** inches high.
   B. The text box containing the headline *Donations Needed* is not large enough to fit all the text. Fix the problem by increasing the height of the text box as necessary.
   C. There is white space between the top of text boxes at the top of page 2 and the top margin. You do not have to take action to change this, or you can adjust the size of the text boxes as necessary. If available, select the option to **Explain** this issue, read the information, and then close the Help panel.

4. Set printer properties to print one draft-quality composite proof of each page on separate sheets of paper, without crop marks.

5. Print the proofs.

6. Proofread the proofs for spelling and grammatical errors that the spelling checker did not catch, and for design problems that the design checker did not catch. Mark the problems on the printed proofs, and fix them in the publication file.
   A. The text box containing the *Volume number*, *issue number*, and *date* is not aligned correctly with the margins. Center the text box horizontally relative to the margin guides.
   B. There are two spelling errors in the third paragraph of the story headlined *A Night of the Arts*.
   C. The text wrapping for the smiley face object on page 2 should be set to **Square**.
   D. There are design problems with horizontal rules above and below the paragraph that begins with the text *Don't forget!* The rule above is thicker than the rule below. Change the thickness of the top rule to **1 pt**.

7. Set printer properties to print two high-quality, double-sided color copies of the **ArtNews5** file, and then print the publication. If necessary, print page 1, then reinsert the sheet in the printer and print page 2 on the reverse side.

8. Save the changes and close **ArtNews5**. Leave your desktop publishing program open to use in the next project.

PROJECT 22-2

In this project, you prepare a newsletter for publishing by a commercial printer.

1. In your desktop publishing program, open the file **Project22-2**. Save the file as **ArtNews6**.

2. Check for missing elements such as fonts or graphics. Select to **Embed TrueType fonts**, but not common system fonts.

3. Set up the publication for commercial color printing using both spot and process colors.

4. Set print options to print separations.

5. Enable trapping.

6. If you have a PostScript® Level 2-compatible printer, print the separations.

7. Change the print options to print a CMYK composite of the publication, including all available printer's marks.

8. If your program has an automatic file preparation utility, use it to prepare the publication files for the commercial printer. Ask your instructor whether to save the files on a removable device such as a CD-R or Flash drive, or a new folder set up for this purpose, named **Project22-2**.

9. Save a copy of the publication in PostScript® format, with the name **PSArtNews**.

10. Save the changes and close **ArtNews6**. Leave your desktop publishing program open to use in the next project.

PROJECT 22-3

In this project, you publish a document to the Web. If your program does not support publishing to the Web, skip this exercise.

1. In your desktop publishing program, open the file **Project22-3**. If a dialog box displays prompting you to install a wizard, click **Yes** to continue.

2. Convert the file to a Web publication without adding a navigation bar.

3. Save the file as **Calendar**.

4. Move the picture to the right of the calendar.

5. Adjust the size and position of the text boxes at the top of the page so that all text displays.

6. Publish the file to the Web, with the name **CalendarPage**.

7. Save the changes and then close **Calendar**. Close your desktop publishing program.

WEB PROJECT

Publishing a document to the Web may be less expensive than printing, and it may make a publication available to a wider audience. Use the Internet to research some of the differences between designing a page for printing and designing a page for publishing on the World Wide Web. Start by looking for information about the basic principles of design as used for printed documents and for Web pages. Look for the different ways to use color; for example, most printed documents use dark text on a light background, while many Web pages use light text on a dark background. Are there different concepts concerning alignment or white space? See if you can find information about fonts that look better on-screen than in print, or why you should select certain types of graphics for use on the Web and others for use in print. Use the information you find to write a report of at least 500 words explaining what you have learned. Alternatively, use a spreadsheet program to create a chart comparing print publishing design with Web publishing design.

 TEAMWORK PROJECT

As a group, use a telephone book or other business directory to compile a list of commercial printers and copy shops in your community. If you have a database program or a spreadsheet program, use it to enter information about each business, including the name, address, telephone number, fax number, and e-mail address. You may want to include additional information such as specialties, a contact's name, or even the hours of operation. If you do not have a database or spreadsheet program, you can record the information in a notebook.

Think of a publication you would like to create for your class, school, or community. You can pick any type of publication, such as a newsletter, a poster, a banner, a flyer, a brochure, an advertisement, or a booklet. If you like, you can even use one of the publications you planned and created in an earlier lesson. Plan the publication from scratch, including paper stock, sheet size, color, page setup, and number of copies. Contact at least two commercial printers on your list and ask them for assistance planning the publication. Tell them up front that this is a class project, and that it is unlikely you will actually be contracting with them to print the publication. If they are uncooperative, thank them and then try a different business in your list. Things you might consider asking them include the type of color process they use, what type of files they prefer working with, and how they like the files delivered. You should also ask them if they have any advice about paper stock, what the time frame for completing the job would be, and, of course, how much it would cost. Record the answers along with the other information about the printer.

Contact at least two copy shops and ask them for information about reproducing copies of the publication. Ask them if they have color copying, if they have self-service options, and if they have any advice based on the type of publication and the number of copies you need. Also, remember to ask them the cost, and how long it would take.

Based on the information you have gathered, decide whether you would want to use a commercial printer, a copy shop, or simply print the publication yourselves on your desktop printer. Use a word-processing program to write a proposal for producing the publication. Include specifications about the publication and a recommendation for how and where to publish the document. Include the reasons for your recommendation. If you do not have a word-processing program, handwrite the proposal. Present the proposal to your class.

CRITICAL *Thinking*

Design and create a booklet providing tips and hints about desktop publishing that could be used as a handout in a desktop publishing class. Start by planning the booklet from scratch. Think about the audience and how you want to present the information. Consider how the booklet will be published, its size and its length, and whether you will use color in it or just black-and-white text and graphics. Also consider how long it will take to create the booklet and develop a realistic schedule to guide you through the process. Include time to have your classmates review your work at each stage so you can improve it as you go along. Record specifications in a word-processing or spreadsheet document so you can refer to them as you create the booklet.

Next, organize the information to include in the booklet. Do you want to include technical information about printers and software programs, or just information about design and organization? If necessary, research the information to include using books or the Internet, or by talking to an instructor or commercial printer. Use a word-processing program or text editor to store the information electronically.

Plan how to format the text in the booklet. Will you simply key paragraphs of information, or do you want to use different elements to break up the text and make the booklet more appealing visually? Look at other publications to see how they do it. (Look at this book for ideas, such as the list of objectives at the beginning of each lesson, the way the headings are formatted, and how tips and notes are presented in boxes.) Select or create a font scheme, and select the appropriate font sizes to use for each element. Record the specifications in a word-processing or spreadsheet document so you can refer to them when you create the booklet. Having specifications ensures consistency throughout the booklet.

Decide what type of graphics to include. Do you want to use lines or borders? Are there pictures to include? If so, are they already in a graphic file format, or do you need to convert them or create them? Do you have permission to use them? Prepare the graphics files so you have them ready to insert. Think of a title for the booklet and how you want the cover page to look.

Use your desktop publishing program to create the booklet. Set up the pages to match the specifications that you planned. Copy and paste the text from the word-processing or text editor document, or key the text directly into the publication. Apply the text formatting specifications you selected. Insert, size, and position graphics objects to complement the text. Print a draft copy of the booklet and ask your classmates to review it and make comments. If necessary, make changes or adjustments to improve the booklet.

Prepare the booklet for publication. Check the spelling and the design. Print another proof and review it carefully for errors. Make improvements, if necessary, and then review it again. When you are satisfied that the booklet is complete, print it and share it with your class.

DESKTOP PUBLISHING

REVIEW *Questions*

TRUE / FALSE

Circle T if the statement is true or F if the statement is false.

T F   1. Text in a desktop publishing file is usually inserted in a text box or frame.

T F   2. You can depend on a spelling checker to catch all typographical errors.

T F   3. In general, you should try to use at least five fonts on every page in a publication.

T F   4. The space between objects and the edge of the page is called the gutter.

T F   5. Effective page formatting uses the basic principles of design, including contrast, balance, and consistency, to capture a reader's attention.

T F   6. In most desktop publishing programs, page numbers are inserted as a field so the number updates if you add, delete, or rearrange pages.

T F   7. The only color system available in most desktop publishing programs is RGB.

T F   8. A horizontal rule is a printing line that can be inserted before or after a paragraph of text.

T F   9. Separations are the default method of printing in most desktop publishing programs.

T F 10. Many commercial printers request files in PostScript® format.

MATCHING

Match the correct term in Column 1 to its description in Column 2.

<table>
<tr><td colspan="2" align="center">**Column 1**</td><td colspan="2" align="center">**Column 2**</td></tr>
</table>

	Column 1		Column 2
___	1. Page layout	A.	The dimensions of the paper on which a publication is printed.
___	2. Reference point	B.	Colors of ink used in four-color printing.
___	3. Page size	C.	Colors of ink that are premixed before the printing process.
___	4. Spot colors	D.	The technique of selecting typefaces and arranging type in a publication.
___	5. Verso		
___	6. Crop marks	E.	The way you organize and arrange objects and white space on a page.
___	7. Sheet size	F.	A stop indicator at a specific point along the horizontal ruler.
___	8. Process colors	G.	Lines printed on a proof to indicate where the paper should be cut or trimmed down to the correct page size.
___	9. Tab		
___	10. Typography	H.	The dimensions of the finished document page.
		I.	A fixed spot used as a control for moving and modifying objects.
		J.	A left-hand or even-numbered page.

FILL IN THE BLANK

Complete the following sentences by writing the correct word or words in the blanks provided.

1. A(n) _____ is a rough draft or sample that lets you map out and plan the overall concept of the publication.

2. The _____ area is the portion of the screen outside the document page where you can temporarily store text and graphics.

3. Font _____ are attributes applied to characters such as superscript, subscript, shadows, or small caps.

4. _____ alignment adjusts the position of all text in a text box in relation to the top and bottom margins of the text box.

5. Facing pages are sometimes called _____ pages because their layout and margins are not identical, but reversed.

6. A(n) _____ is a semi-transparent object that displays behind other objects on pages in a publication.

7. The distance between an object and text wrapped around any of its four sides is sometimes called the _____.

8. _____-ready film is film made of the finished pages that can be used to publish a document.

9. If an object is _____ in a publication file, you do not have to supply the source file to the commercial printer.

10. Use a(n) _____ shop to publish a document if you need to produce many copies, if you have a tight budget, or if you need the publication in a hurry.

PROJECTS

PROJECT U4-1

1. Launch your desktop publishing program and create a new blank document using the default settings.

2. Save the document as **Poster**.

3. Set up the page layout for the **Poster** publication as follows:
   A. Publication type: **Poster**
   B. Page size: **18** inches wide by **24** inches high
   C. Paper size: **Letter**
   D. Orientation: **Portrait**
   E. Page overlap: **0.5** inches. (In some programs you specify overlap—or tiling—when you print, not when you set up the page layout.)
   F. Margins: **1.5** inches on all sides
   G. No double-sided printing
   H. No facing pages

4. Insert a horizontal ruler guide at **13** inches on the vertical ruler.

5. Insert the picture file **Project1a** into the **Poster** publication. Resize and position the picture to fill the space above the horizontal ruler guide—approximately **15** inches wide by **11.5** inches high.

6. Insert another horizontal ruler guide at **16.75** inches on the vertical ruler, and then insert a text box or text frame sized to fit in the space between the two horizontal ruler guides—approximately **15** inches wide by **3.75** inches high.

7. In a **42**-point sans serif font, such as **Arial Rounded MT Bold**, key the following five lines of text.
   Calling All Singers!
   Perfect Pitch Community Chorus
   Needs You!
   All Ages
   All Levels of Ability

8. Format the text as follows:
   A. Apply the **Small Cap** text effect to the second line of text.
   B. Adjust the paragraph spacing before and after the second line of text to **12** points.
   C. Change the leading (or line spacing) between the last three lines of text to **0.9** lines (about 40 points). All the text should fit within the text box, but if not, increase the text box height slightly.
   D. Center all text horizontally.

9. Insert two new horizontal ruler guides, one at **17.5** inches and one at **19.5** inches on the vertical ruler, and then insert a text box sized to fit between them. The text box should be approximately **15** inches wide by **2** inches high.

10. Using a **26**-point serif font, such as **Georgia**, justified alignment, and leaving **3** points of space before and after each paragraph, key the following two paragraphs of text:
    Rehearsals are Wednesdays from 7 p.m. to 9 p.m. in the HHS Chorus Room. Concerts are scheduled for October, December, February, and April. Registration fee is $25.00.
    For more information or to sign up call Nelson Beauchamp, Director, at 555-1234, or email him at nbeauchamp@ppcb.org.

11. Insert the graphics files **Project1b**, **Project1c**, and **Project1d** into the space between the bottom margin and the lower text box.
    A. Size each object to approximately **2** inches high. Let the width adjust automatically. (If necessary set the approximate widths for **Project1b** to **1.9** inches, for **Project 1c** to **2.0** inches, and **Project1d** to **1.9** inches.)
    B. Select all three objects and then select the command to distribute them horizontally to space them evenly across the page.
    C. Align **Project1b** and **Project1d** vertically with the bottom margin, and align **Project1c** vertically with the bottom of the text box above it.

12. Check the spelling in the publication and then print a draft-quality proof (it will take about 9 sheets of paper to print the entire poster). Proofread the printed document for errors, and make corrections in the file.

13. Print at least one copy of the completed publication. Crop and assemble the individual sheets to complete the poster.

14. Save the changes and close **Poster**. Leave your desktop publishing program open to use in the next project.

PROJECT U4-2

1. Create a mock-up of a four-page booklet to use as a program for the Perfect Pitch Community Chorus' Spring concert.
   A. The booklet is to print on two sides of a single sheet of 8.5-inch by 11-inch paper, which will be folded in the middle.
   B. You need to include a title and the date on the front (page 1), a list of chorus members on page 2, the list of music on page 3, and information about the chorus on the back (page 4).

2. In your desktop publishing program, open **Project2a** from the data files. This file contains all the text you need to complete the publication.

3. Save the file as **Program**.

4. On page 1, size the text box to 3 inches wide by 0.5 inches high. Center it horizontally between the left and right margins, and position it vertically 3.5 inches from the top of the page.

5. Draw a new text box, sized to 3 inches wide by 1 inch high. Align it with the right margin horizontally and with the bottom margin vertically. Connect the first text box to the new text box, and then format the text as follows:
   A. Apply **28-point Arial** to the first line in the first text box. Center the text horizontally.
   B. Apply **14-point Arial** to the remaining two lines. Leave 4 points of space before and after each paragraph. Right-align both paragraphs horizontally, and align them vertically with the bottom of the text box.

6. Use WordArt or another text art program to create two graphics text objects as follows. (If you do not have a text art program, create text boxes, use a decorative font to key the text, and then modify and format the text as desired.)
   A. Create an object using a wave style and a two-color horizontal gradient fill.
   B. Key the text **Perfect Pitch** in a 36-point serif font such as **Times New Roman**.
   C. Center the object horizontally relative to the margins, and align it with the top margin vertically.
   D. Create a second object using the same style and colors.
   E. Key the text **Community Chorus** in a 28-point serif font such as **Times New Roman**.
   F. Center the object horizontally, and position it **2.5** inches from the top of the page vertically.

7. On page 2, resize the top text box to **3.25** inches wide by **0.75** inches high and position it horizontally **1.0** inch from the top-left corner (between the column boundaries) and vertically **1.25** inches from the top-left corner. Format the text as follows:
   A. Apply **14**-point **Arial** or a similar sans serif font in bold to the first line.
   B. Apply **12**-point **Times New Roman** or a similar serif font in bold and italic to the second line.
   C. Insert a **green, 2**-point thick horizontal rule after the second line. (Try the custom color C = 78; M = 0; Y = 99; K = 0.)

8. Resize the second text box on page 2 to **3.25** inches wide by **4.0** inches high, and divide it into two columns, with .08 inches of space between the columns. Position the text box vertically **2.0** inches from the top-left corner and horizontally **1.0** inch from the top-left corner.

9. Format the text in the text box in **12**-point **Times New Roman** and then modify the formatting as follows:
   A. Set the leading (line spacing) to **1** space (about 14 points) and leave **3** points of space after every paragraph. Leave **3** points of space before every paragraph except the first—*Soprano*. (If necessary, adjust the height of the text boxes so all text is displayed.)
   B. Apply **14**-point **Arial, bold** to the headings *Soprano, Alto, Tenor,* and *Bass*.

10. On page 3, resize the top text box to **3.25** inches wide by **.5** inches high and position it horizontally **6.75** inches from the top-left corner and vertically **1.5** inches from the top-left corner. (Recall that the "top-left corner" refers to the sheet of paper on which the publication will print, not the publication page.) Format the text as follows:
    A. Apply **14**-point **Arial** or a similar sans serif font.
    B. Insert a **green, 2**-point thick horizontal rule after the line of text. (Try the custom color C = 78; M = 0; Y = 99; K = 0.)

11. Resize the second text box on page 3 to **3.25** inches wide by **5.5** inches high. Position it horizontally **6.75** inches from the top-left corner and vertically **2.0** inches from the top-left corner. Format the text as follows:
    A. To the name of each piece of music, apply **14**-point **Arial**, bold, with **3** points of space before and after each paragraph.
    B. To the paragraphs listing the composers' and/or arrangers' names, apply **14**-point **Times New Roman**, with **12** points of space after each paragraph.
    C. Apply a **0.25**-inch left indent to the paragraphs listing the composers' and arrangers' names.

12. On page 4, resize the text box to **3** inches wide by **3** inches high and align it in the center horizontally, relative to the margins, and vertically with the bottom margin. Format the text as follows:
    A. Apply **12**-point **Arial**, with **10** points of space after each paragraph to all of the text.
    B. Justify the first paragraph of text.
    C. Convert the remaining lines into a bulleted list, using a simple round black bullet.

13. On page 4, insert the graphics file **Project2b** from the data files. Size it to approximately **3** inches high by **2.75** inches wide. Align it in the horizontal center, relative to the margins, and vertically with the top margin.

14. On page 1, insert the graphics file **Project 2c** from the data files. If necessary, size it to approximately **2.0** inches wide by **1.8** inches high. Align in it the horizontal center, relative to the margins, and position it vertically **4.5** inches from the top-left corner of the page.

15. Check the spelling in the document and then print a draft-quality proof. Proofread the print-out for errors and make corrections in the file.

16. Print at least one copy of the booklet using duplex or two-sided printing, if possible.

17. Save the changes to **Program**, close the file, but leave your desktop publishing program open to use in the next exercise.

PROJECT U4-3

If your program does not support publishing to the Web, skip this project.

1. Open **Project3** from the data files.

2. Convert the document to a Web publication. Do not add a navigation bar.

3. Publish the document to the Web, with the file name **PitchPage**.

4. Save the **PitchPage** document and close it. Close your desktop publishing program.

SIMULATION

The owner of the Lighthouse View Inn, a Bed and Breakfast located on the coast of Maine, wants to establish communication with current and potential guests. As a marketing assistant, you believe this goal can be accomplished using effective publications such as brochures and newsletters.

Before starting to work in your desktop-publishing program, take the time to plan each project completely. Working alone or with a partner, review the steps and then create a schedule for completing the job. Set up a timeline with appropriate milestones. Establish criteria that you believe should be met for each stage of the project, and create a rubric that you can use to gauge your accomplishments. Periodically, have your classmates review your work and offer comments. Incorporate their suggestions as you continue your work.

JOB U4-1

You want to create a brochure for guests and other people visiting the area. To begin, you create a mockup of the brochure, and then you create a new, blank publication. You insert pictures and text into the document to create the brochure.

1. Create a mock-up of a trifold brochure, using a standard 8.5-inch by 11-inch sheet of paper in landscape orientation.
   A. Fold the page into thirds, and mark the front panel with an F and the back panel with a B.
   B. Unfold the sheet of paper and number the panels on the inside 1, 2, and 3, and the panels on the outside 4, 5, and 6. The inside panels are all on page 1 of your document, and the outside panels, which include the front (panel 6) and back (panel 5), all appear on page 2 of your document.
   C. Label panels 1 through 4 follows:
   Panel 1: **Greetings from Lighthouse View**
   Panel 2: **About Maine**
   Panel 3: **Things to Do**
   Panel 4: **About Our Inn**

2. Using a pencil, draw horizontal ruler guides to divide each side of the page into thirds. Place one horizontal ruler line 2.5 inches from the top across the width of the page, and then define a second horizontal ruler line three inches from the bottom.

3. Define the areas on each panel where you will insert picture frames and text boxes.
   A. On panels 1, 2, and 3, define a text box at the top, a picture frame at the bottom, and another text box in the middle.
   B. On panel 4, define a text box at the top, a text box in the middle, and a picture frame at the bottom.
   C. On panel 5, define a large picture frame on the top two thirds of the panel, and a text box at the bottom.
   D. On panel 6, define a text box at the top, a picture frame in the middle, and a text box at the bottom.

4. Launch your desktop publishing program and create a new, blank publication. Save it as **Brochure**.

5. Change the page layout for the **Brochure** publication as follows:
   A. Publication type: **Custom**
   B. Orientation: **Landscape**
   C. Page size: **11** inches wide by **8.5** inches high
   D. Paper size: **Letter**
   E. Margins: .2 inch on all sides
   F. No double-sided printing
   G. No facing pages

6. Switch to Master Page view and divide the page into 3 columns, leaving .2 inches between columns. Insert two horizontal ruler guides—one at **2.5** inches on the vertical ruler and one at **5.5** inches on the vertical ruler. Switch back to regular page view.

7. Insert a second page. Remember, page 1 contains the content for the inside panels of the brochure, and page 2 contains the content for the outside panels of the brochure. The middle panel on page 2 is the back panel, and the right panel on page 2 is the front panel.

8. If available, select the **Foundation** font scheme, in which the major font is Times New Roman and the minor font is Arial Bold. (If that font scheme is not available, use Times New Roman for all headings and Arial Bold for all body text.)

9. Insert text boxes and empty picture frames on each panel as you planned them on the mock-up. Size the frames and text boxes using all the space available between the margins and the column guides.

10. On panel 1 (the left panel on page 1), insert content as follows:
    A. In the text box at the top, key **Greetings from Maine!**, change the font size to 26-points, and center the text horizontally and vertically.
    B. In the text box in the middle, key **We invite you to experience the year-round beauty of the Pine Tree State.** Apply the **Heading 4** style (or change the font size to **12** points and apply **bold**). Press **Enter**, apply the **List Bullet** style (or apply the default bullet list formatting), change the font to **12**-point **Arial**, leave 6 points of space after each paragraph, and key the following lines:
       Summer means warm days and cool nights.
       Fall brings bright foliage and blue skies.
       Winter is a wonderland of snow.
       Spring is a time of fresh air and renewed promise.
    C. In the picture frame at the bottom, insert the photo file **Job1a** from the data files. (Fit the contents to the frame, if necessary.) Size it to **2.75** inches high. If the width does not adjust automatically, set it to **1.83** inches. Position the picture horizontally **1.0** inch from the top-left corner and vertically **5.55** inches from the top-left corner (or aligned with the bottom margin).

11. On panel 2 (the middle panel on page 1), insert content as follows:
    A. In the text box at the top, key **Things to Know About Maine**, change the font size to 26-points, and center the text horizontally and vertically.

B. In the text box in the middle, key **Fast Facts About Maine:**. Apply the **Heading 4** style (or change the font size to **12** points and apply **bold**). Press **Enter**, apply the **List Bullet** style (or apply the default bullet list formatting), change the font to **12**-point **Arial**, leave 6 points of space after each paragraph, and key the following lines:
Maine covers a total area of 33,215 square miles.
There are more than 3,500 miles of coastline.
Maine has more than 542,600 acres of state and national parks.
The winter temperature averages 20 degrees Fahrenheit.
The summer temperature averages 70 degrees Fahrenheit.

C. In the picture frame at the bottom, insert the photo file **Job1b** from the data files. (Fit the contents to the frame, if necessary.) Size it to approximately **3.4** inches wide—or the width of the column. If the height does not adjust automatically, set it to **2.26** inches. Position the picture horizontally **3.8** inches from the top-left corner and vertically **6** inches from the top-left corner (or aligned with the bottom margin).

12. On panel 3 (the right panel on page 1), insert content as follows:
    A. In the text box at the top, key **Things to do in Maine**, change the font size to **26**-points, and center the text horizontally and vertically.
    B. In the text box in the middle, create two columns. Then, insert the text file **Job1c** from the data files. Delete the first line of the imported text, and then apply the **List Bullet** style (or apply the default bullet list formatting) to the remaining items. Change the font to **12**-point **Arial** and leave 6 points of space after each bulleted item. Select all items after *Kayaking* at the bottom of the left column and apply paragraph formatting to keep them with the next line. This should force all items from *Canoeing* to the end of the list to display in the right column.
    C. In the picture frame at the bottom, insert the photo file **Job1d** from the data files. Size it to approximately **3.4** inches wide—or the width of the column. If the height does not adjust automatically, set it to **2.26** inches. (Set the content to fit the frame, if necessary.) Position the picture horizontally **7.4** inches from the top-left corner and vertically **6.0** inches from the top-left corner (or aligned with the bottom margin).

13. Change to page 2. On panel 4 (the left panel), insert content as follows:
    A. In the text box at the top, key **About Our Inn**, change the font size to **26**-points, and center the text horizontally and vertically.
    B. In the text box in the middle, insert the text file **Job1e** from the data files. (Do not use autoflow.) Edit the first line of text to **Lighthouse View Inn offers:**, and then format it in the **Heading 4** style (or change the font size to **12** points and apply **bold**). If necessary, format the seven items in the list in the **List Bullet** style (or apply the default bullet list formatting). Change the font to **12**-point **Arial** and leave 6 points of space after each item. Cut and paste the last four lines of text to the text box at the bottom of panel 5.
    C. In the picture frame at the bottom of panel 4, insert the photo file **Job1f** from the data files. Size it to approximately **3.4** inches wide—or the width of the column. If the height does not adjust automatically, set it to **2.31** inches. (Fit the content to the frame, if necessary.) Position the picture horizontally **.2** inches from the top-left corner and vertically **6.0** inches from the top-left corner (or aligned with the bottom margin).

14. On panel 5 (the back), insert content as follows:
    A. In the picture frame, insert the graphics file **Job1g** from the data files. Size it to approximately **3.25** inches wide. If the height does not adjust automatically, set it to **4.53** inches. (Fit the content to the frame, if necessary.) Position the picture horizontally **3.87** inches from the top-left corner and vertically **1** inch from the top-left corner.

B. In the text box at the bottom, apply the **Address** style to all four lines (or change the font to **Arial**), and then change the font size to **18**-points. Center the text horizontally and vertically in the text box.

15. On panel 6 (the front), insert content as follows:
   A. In the text box at the top, key **Lighthouse View Inn**, change the font size to **26**-points. Center all text horizontally and vertically.
   B. In the picture frame in the middle, insert the photo file **Job1h** from the data files. Size it to approximately **3.0** inches high. If the width does not adjust automatically, set it to **2.4** inches. (Fit the content to the frame, if necessary.) Position the picture horizontally **7.87** inches from the top-left corner and vertically **2.5** inches from the top-left corner.
   C. In the text box at the bottom, key **"Your Home Away From Home"**. Apply the **Heading 7** style to the text (**14**-point **Times New Roman, italic**), and center it horizontally and vertically.

16. Check the spelling in the document, and then print a draft-quality proof. Proofread the document and examine the design for errors. Make corrections in the file.

17. Print the **Brochure** file, using double-sided or duplex printing, if possible. Save it and close the file, but leave your desktop publishing program open to use in Job U4-2.

JOB U4-2

The owner of the Inn thinks it would be a good idea to distribute a newsletter to guests to keep them up-to-date on events and activities planned for the Inn. Because the publication will be generated four times each year, you decide you should create a template for it. The template will insure consistency in design for each issue.

1. In your desktop publishing program, create a new blank publication using the default settings.

2. Save the file as a template with the name **NewsTemp**.

3. Adjust the page setup as follows:
   A. Publication type: **Full page**
   B. Orientation: **Portrait**
   C. Page size: **8.5** inches wide by **11** inches high
   D. Paper size: **Letter**
   E. Margins: **1** inch on all sides
   F. No double-sided printing
   G. No facing pages

4. Change to Master Page view and create two columns, with **.25** inches between the columns.

5. Insert page numbers in the lower-right corner of the page. Precede the number with the word **Page**. (You can do this by creating a footer or by inserting a text box or text block.)

6. Change to normal view.

7. Insert a new page so there are a total of two pages in the publication.

8. On page 1, insert a horizontal ruler guide at **3** inches on the vertical ruler.

9. If available, insert the **Crossed Lines Masthead** design object, and align it relative to the margin guides with the top vertically, and centered horizontally. Replace the sample text *Business Name* (or *Your Business*) with the text **Lighthouse View Inn**. Replace the sample text *Newsletter Name* with the text **A Maine View**. Replace the sample text *Newsletter Date* with the text **Season**. If the design object is not available, create the masthead as follows:

   A. Insert a text box sized about **0.5** inches high and **5** inches wide, aligned with the top and left of the page. In the text box, key the text **Lighthouse View Inn**, using a **13**-point serif font (such as Times New Roman) in **bold** all-capital letters. Center the text vertically. Fill the text box with a **bright blue** color, and change the font color to **white**. Apply a **1**-point **white** (or paper) horizontal rule after the paragraph.

   B. Insert another text box sized about **1.25** inches high and **5** inches wide. Position it vertically so its top is aligned with the bottom of the other text box, and horizontally with the left of the page. Using the same serif font in about **56** points, key the text **A Maine View**. Fill the box with the same **bright blue**, and change the font color to **white**.

   C. Insert two more text boxes, each sized about **0.5** inches high by **1.5** inches wide. Position them to the right of the other text boxes, one above the other, so the top of one is aligned with the bottom of the other. The top box should be aligned with the top margin of the page. Using a **12**-point, sans serif font, such as **Arial Narrow**, key **Volume 1, Issue 1** in the top text box, and **Season** in the bottom text box. Adjust font size and style as desired.

   D. If necessary, adjust the size and position of the text boxes to improve the appearance of the masthead. Select all four text boxes and group them.

10. On page 2, insert a text box sized to approximately **3.12** inches wide (or the width of the column) by **3.0** inches high.

11. Key the following lines of text:
    A Maine View is published quarterly by Lighthouse View Inn, Inc.
    Information contained in this newsletter is meant for Lighthouse View employees and guests. For more information, call (941) 555-5555.

12. Format the text with an **18**-point serif font, such as **Times New Roman**. Justify the text. Apply a **light gray** fill or shade to the text box (R: **204**, G: **204**, B: **204**) and a **4**-point **blue** border line on all sides. (If necessary, adjust the inset to leave space between the text and the border.) Set paragraph spacing to leave **3** points before and after each paragraph. Align the text box in the lower-left corner of the page, where the left margin and the top of the footer area meet.

13. Save the changes and close the template file. Leave your desktop publishing program open to use in the next exercise.

JOB U4-3

Now, you can use your **NewsTemp** template to create the first issue of the newsletter.

1. In your desktop publishing program, create a new document based on the **NewsTemp** template.

2. Save the file as **InnNews**.

3. Replace the text *Season* in the masthead with the text **Winter**.

4. Insert three text boxes on page 1. Create two that are sized to **3.12** inches wide (or the width of the column) by **6.0** inches high. Position one in the left column, with its top aligned with the horizontal ruler guide; and position the other in the right column, also with its top aligned with the horizontal ruler guide. Create the third sized to **6.5** inches wide by **1.0** high, and position it across the page above the footer.

5. Switch to page 2, and insert three text boxes as follows:
   A. Size one text box to approximately the width of the column (**3.12** inches wide) by **3.25** inches high and position it in the upper-left part of the page.
   B. Size one text box to approximately the width of the column (**3.12** inches wide) by **1.5** inches high, and position it in the upper-right part of the page.
   C. Size the third text box to approximately the width of the column (**3.12** inches wide) by **4.0** inches high and position it in the lower-right part of the page.

6. Open the file **Job3a** from the data files. You may open this text file in your desktop publishing program, or in a text editor such as Notepad. The text in this file is organized into six articles with the following headlines: *Winter Carnival, Renovations Complete, Book Your Summer Vacations, Themed Events, Send in Your Ideas,* and *Winter Specials.* Copy and paste the headlines and text for each article into the text boxes in the **InnNews** file as follows:
   A. Copy and paste the *Winter Carnival* article into the text box in the left column of page 1.
   B. Copy and paste the *Renovations Complete* article into the text box in the right column of page 1.
   C. Copy and paste the *Book Your Summer Vacations* article into the text box across the bottom of page 1.
   D. Copy and paste the *Themed Events* article into the text box at the top of the left column on page 2.
   E. Copy and paste the *Send in Your Ideas* article into the text box at the top of the right column on page 2.
   F. Copy and paste the *Winter Specials* article into the text box at the bottom of the right column on page 2.

7. Close the **Job3a** text file without saving any changes.

8. Format the text as follows:
   A. Format all headlines (the first line in each text box) with a sans serif font, such as **Arial,** in **16**-points.
   B. Format the remaining text with a serif font, such as **Times New Roman,** in **12**-points.
   C. Set the line spacing of all text to **1** space between lines and **6**-points before and after each paragraph. (It may be necessary to increase the height of some text boxes to accommodate the increased spacing.)
   D. Apply a **2**-line dropped capital to the first letter of the first paragraph of each article.

9. Apply a **2**-point, **blue** horizontal rule above the headline *Book Your Summer Vacation* on page 1.

10. Insert pictures as follows:
    A. On page 1, insert the graphic file **Job3b**. Size it to **2.5** inches wide. If the height does not adjust automatically, set it to **2.75**. (If necessary, fit the contents to the frame.) Align the picture in the center of the page, relative to the margin guides, (or position it horizontally **3.0** inches from the top-left corner and vertically **4.0** inches from the top-left corner) and set the text wrapping to square.
    B. On page 2, insert the graphic file **Job3c**. Size it to **3.12** inches wide (the width of the column) and **2.78** inches high. (If necessary, fit the contents to the frame.) Position it horizontally **4.4** inches from the top-left corner and vertically **2.8** inches from the top-left corner.
    C. Also on page 2, insert the graphic file **Job3d**. Size it to **2.0** inches wide and **2.78** inches high. (If necessary, fit the contents to the frame.) Position it horizontally **1.62** inches from the top-left corner and vertically **4.25** inches from the top-left corner.

11. Check the spelling in the document and then print a draft-quality proof. Proofread the document and check the design for errors. Make corrections as necessary in the file.

12. Print the publication, using double-sided printing if possible.

13. Save **InnNews** and close it. Close your desktop publishing program.

WEB SITE DEVELOPMENT

Unit 5

Estimated Time for Unit: 10 hours

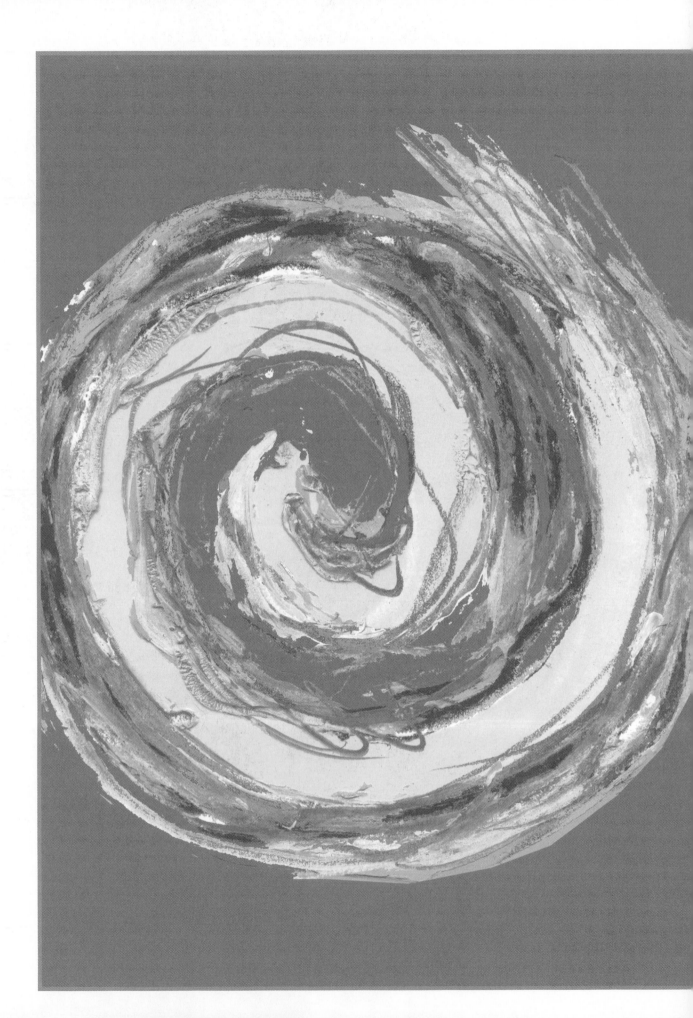

CREATING A WEB PAGE

OBJECTIVES

Upon completion of this lesson, you should be able to:

- Describe how the World Wide Web is organized.
- Use a Web browser to locate a Web page, navigate a Web site, and display HTML source code.
- Create folders to store Web page files.
- Use a text editor to define and save an HTML file.
- View an HTML file as a Web page in your browser.
- Use HTML tags to modify Web page content.
- Use HTML Heading Tags to format text.

Estimated Time: 2 hours

VOCABULARY

ASCII

Domain

Element

Home page

HTML tags

HTTP (Hypertext Transfer Protocol)

Hyperlinks

Hypertext Markup Language (HTML)

Internet Service Provider (ISP)

Navigation bar

Password

Protocol

Uniform Resource Locator (URL)

User name

Web browser

Web client

Web pages

Web server

Web site

World Wide Web (WWW)

You are probably familiar with the Internet (also called the Net) and the World Wide Web. This fascinating system of interconnected computers links people and places together in ways that could only be dreamed about as recently as 1990. People who "surf the Net" are actually locating, opening, and reading documents—called Web pages—that are stored on computers anywhere around the globe. In this unit, you learn how to create Web pages using a variety of programs, features, and tools.

In this lesson, you begin your study of Web site development by using a text editor such as Windows Notepad to create a simple Web page. You learn how to use the Hypertext Markup Language (HTML) to define, modify, and format Web page content. In later lessons, you use a more sophisticated Web design program, such as Macromedia Dreamweaver or Microsoft FrontPage, to create and format Web pages. You also learn how to use other applications, such as a word processing program, presentation program, or spreadsheet program, to create Web pages and add information to a Web site.

How the Web Is Organized

The *World Wide Web*, often simply called the Web, is a global network of Web server computers on which Web pages are stored. *Web pages* are documents or files stored in *Hypertext Markup Language* (*HTML*) format and stored on a Web server computer so that anyone with access to the World Wide Web can access the Web page. Web pages can contain text, graphics, multimedia effects, or some combination of all three (see Figure 23-1). HTML is an authoring language that uses codes, called *HTML tags*, to define data on the page so that it can be interpreted and displayed by a Web browser. A Web page can be of any length. However, individual Web pages generally contain approximately one screen's worth of content. If there is more content about a specific topic, there are *hyperlinks*—often called links—you can click to jump to a different page for more information.

FIGURE 23-1
A Web page contains text, graphics, and multimedia effects

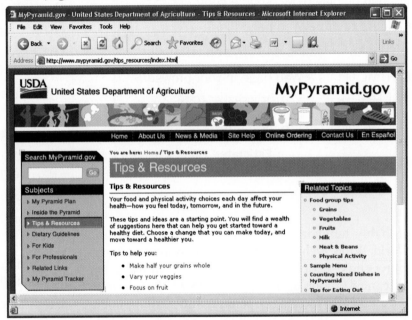

Web sites are multiple Web pages connected using hyperlinks. Once two Web pages on a similar topic are linked, a Web site is born! Generally, Web pages on a Web site deal with different aspects of the same topic. For example, the Microsoft Web site at www.microsoft.com includes information about Microsoft products, service, and support. The Library of Congress Web site at www.loc.gov includes information about different aspects of American history and government.

Web servers are computers on which you can store Web site and Web page data so that other people can access it. *Web clients* are computers that are linked via a network to a Web server. When you use your *Web browser*—a software program that you use to locate Web pages and interpret the HTML coding to display the pages on your computer—your computer is acting as a Web client. There are a number of Web browsers on the market, including Internet Explorer, Netscape, Mozilla Firefox, and Opera.

Use a Web Browser

As mentioned, you use your Web browser to locate a Web page you want to view. When you start your Web browser, you may have to key your user name and password in order to log in to your *Internet Service Provider (ISP)*, which is a company that provides Internet access for a fee. Your *user name* is the name that identifies you to the system and your *password* is a secret word or code that confirms your identity.

When your browser opens, it usually displays a default *home page*. A home page is a main point of entry into a Web site. From there, you can access any Web page by keying the page's *Uniform Resource Locator (URL)* in your browser's address bar, and clicking a button such as Go, or by pressing Enter. A URL is the string of characters that specifies the path to the location where the page is stored. From one page, you can access other pages in the same site by clicking the available links.

Understand a URL

Every URL on the Web includes a path statement that describes how to get to the page, just as a home address written on an envelope enables letters to be delivered to the correct individual's house. Understanding the path is the key to finding Web pages. The first part of a URL identifies the correct protocol to use. A *protocol* is a standard format used for transmission. On the Web, the protocol is *http (Hypertext Transfer Protocol)*, so all Web addresses properly begin with the characters *http://*.

The second part of a URL identifies the *domain*, which is the name that identifies the computer, or Web server, where the page is stored. Usually, the domain starts with the characters *www* for World Wide Web. Next comes a period—called a *dot*—followed by the registered site name, followed by another dot, followed by an abbreviation that identifies the type of domain. Some common domain types are listed in Table 23-1.

TABLE 23-1
Common domain types

DOMAIN	DESCRIPTION
.com	Used by commercial businesses.
.edu	Used by educational institutions such as schools and universities.
.gov	Used by government agencies.
.org	Used by associations and non-profit agencies.
.mil	Used by the U.S. military.
.net	Used by networks and communications companies.

After identifying the domain, a URL path names the folder or subfolders on the Web server where the page is stored. Just as you store documents in folders on your computer to keep them organized, pages on a Web server may be organized into folders as well. The folder names are separated from the domain and each other by slashes.

Finally, the last part of the URL is the actual Web page file name.

So, in the URL: *http://www.mypyramid.gov/tips_resources/index.html*, *http://* tells the Web browser to use the HTTP protocol. *www* tells the browser to look on a Web server. *mypyramid.gov* is the name of the domain. *tips_resources* is the name of a folder on the domain. And *index.html* is the name of the Web page.

In the following exercise, you launch your browser and locate a Web page using a URL. In order to complete the exercise, you must have a Web browser installed on your computer, and an account with an ISP.

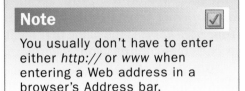

Note ☑

You usually don't have to enter either *http://* or *www* when entering a Web address in a browser's Address bar.

STEP-BY-STEP 23.1

1. Launch your Web browser. If necessary, enter your user name and password to log on to the Internet.

2. Click in your browser's Address bar, and replace the default text by keying **http://www.si.edu.** Click the **Go** button, or press **Enter.** The home page of the Smithsonian Institution displays, as shown in Figure 23-2.

FIGURE 23-2
The Smithsonian Institution home page

STEP-BY-STEP 23.1 Continued

3. Click in your browser's Address bar, and key **http://mypyramid.gov**. Click **Go**, or press **Enter**. The home page of the MyPyramid Web site, which is part of the United States Department of Agriculture's Web site, displays, as shown in Figure 23-3. Leave your Web browser open to use in the next exercise.

FIGURE 23-3
The MyPyramid home page

URL in Address bar

Go button

Navigate a Web Site

Most Web sites have a home page that displays when you first access the site. This page probably includes content welcoming new visitors and directing them to click the links to access specific information on other pages within the site. You can usually identify a link because it is in a different color or font, and has an underline. A picture may be a link as well. When you rest a mouse pointer on a link, the pointer changes to the link pointer, which is a hand with a pointing finger. A ScreenTip may display the destination page name, and the destination URL may display in the Status bar. After you click a link it may display in a different color, indicating that it has been used.

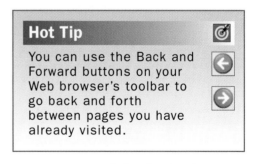

Hot Tip

You can use the Back and Forward buttons on your Web browser's toolbar to go back and forth between pages you have already visited.

Many Web pages have a *navigation bar*, which is a row of links, similar to a menu. They may also have a table of contents or an index, which is a list of links. These navigation tools help you move to the main sections of the Web site.

STEP-BY-STEP 23.2

1. On the MyPyramid home page, rest the mouse pointer on the link **Tips & Resources** in the index on the left side of the page. The Link pointer displays, along with a ScreenTip, as shown in Figure 23-4.

FIGURE 23-4
Use links to navigate among pages in a Web site

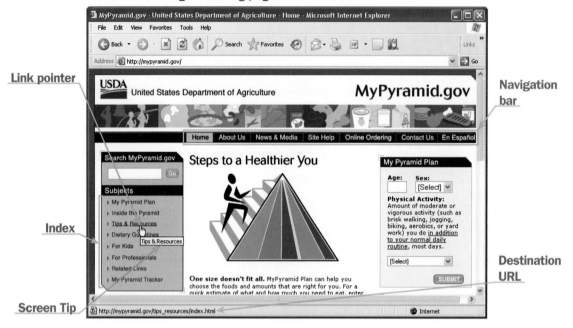

2. Click the **Tips & Resources** link to display the Tips & Resources page.

3. In the bulleted list of *Tips to help you*, click the **Focus on fruit** link to display a page of tips on eating fruit, as shown in Figure 23-5.

STEP-BY-STEP 23.2 Continued

FIGURE 23-5
View another page on the same site

Current
page URL

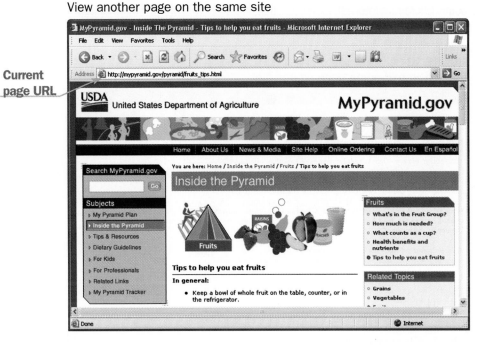

4. Scroll down the page to view all of the content.

5. In the navigation bar across the top of the page, click **Home** to return to the site's home page. Leave your browser open to use in the next exercise.

Display HTML Source Code

Although the Web pages display as regular text and graphics in your Web browser window, behind the scenes they are coded in HTML format, which means that HTML tags keyed in the file describe how the page should display. Your Web browser interprets the HTML tags in order to display the colors, pictures, text, formatting, and links on your screen. Most browsers have a command that you can use to display the HTML source code formatting.

STEP-BY-STEP 23.3

1. With the MyPyramid home page displayed, click the command to display the HTML source code. If you are using Microsoft Internet Explorer, click **View** on the Menu bar and then click **Source**. The source file displays in a text editing program such as Notepad, as shown in Figure 23-6.

FIGURE 23-6
The MyPyramid home page source file

HTML tags

Netiquette

PROTECT YOUR PRIVACY

The Web is a vast, public environment where anyone can write anything and make it available to everyone. Social networking Web sites like MySpace.com and Friendster.com make it easy and fun to create your own Web page profiles, write blogs, post photos and videos, share music, and communicate with other people. Sometimes, it's easy to forget that some of the people viewing your pages are strangers. To maintain your privacy and protect your security, never give out personal information, such as your full name, address, phone number, password, and even your daily schedule. Of course, strangers aren't the only ones viewing your posts! Your parents, teachers, classmates, and employers all have access to the Web. So, when you're writing your blog keep this old saying in mind: If you don't have anything nice to say, don't say anything at all. On the Web, you never know who's listening.

STEP-BY-STEP 23.3 Continued

2. Scroll down in the HTML code to see the kinds of tags used to create the page. The HTML tags are enclosed in angle brackets < >.

3. Click **File** on the Menu bar and then click **Exit**, or click the **Close** button in the upper-left corner of the window to exit the text editor program.

4. Close your Web browser. If necessary, log off from your ISP.

Create HTML Web Site Folders

A Web site can consist of many HTML files, as well as associated files such as graphics or video. It is important to keep all of the files stored together in the same folder so that the pages can display properly when accessed on the Web. Generally, you should create one main folder for the site and then add subfolders as necessary to store related files. For example, within the site folder you might have a folder named *Graphics* for storing all pictures and images. (You learn more about using graphics files and other types of files on a Web page in Lesson 25. You learn more about site folders, which may be called root level folders, in Lesson 26.) It takes a little more work in the beginning to organize your Web site using folders, but it means less confusion later when you can neatly store your related files in the proper location.

You can create all your Web pages and organize all of your files on your personal computer, using your computer's file management system (for example, Windows Explorer). When the site is complete you can upload the site folder to a Web server so that is available to anyone browsing the Web.

In the following exercise, you create a main folder for your Web site. Because you do not use associated files in this lesson, you do not have to create any subfolders.

STEP-BY-STEP 23.4

1. Launch a file management program such as Windows Explorer. In Windows, click the **Start** button and then click **My Documents**.

2. Navigate to the folder where you want to store the Web site folder.

3. Click **File** on the Menu bar, click **New**, and then click **Folder** to create a new folder.

4. Key **Australia** and then press **Enter** to name the folder.

STEP-BY-STEP 23.4 Continued

5. Open the **Australia** folder. The window should look similar to Figure 23-7.

FIGURE 23-7
Web site folder

Web site folder is current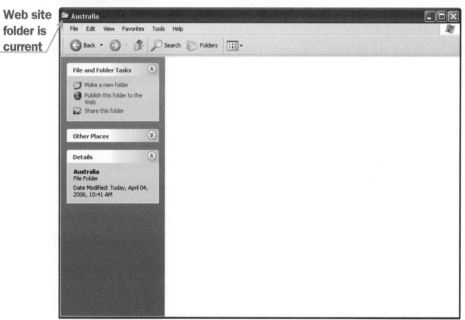

6. Close your file management program window.

Use a Text Editor to Define an HTML File

Now that you have seen a variety of Web pages and even looked at a few HTML tags, it's time to create a simple Web page of your own. Every HTML document is a simple text file created with an ASCII-standard text editor. *ASCII*—which stands for American Standard Code for Information Interchange—is a system that assigns a code to every key on a keyboard and some special characters as well, so that all computers can interpret the characters the same way. Most text editors including Windows' Notepad use ASCII characters. You key the text in the text file, including HTML tags, and then save the file in HTML format.

> **Extra for Experts**
>
> You can use other types of editors, including word processing programs, as long as you save the file correctly in HTML format. You learn more about using other programs to create Web pages later in this unit.

Create an HTML File

Text editors such as Notepad contain a number of familiar features to those who have used a word processor. You can save and print documents. You can use commands such as Cut, Copy, and Paste, to move or copy text. You can select text and use Backspace and Delete to remove text. But your options for formatting text are limited.

You use the text editor to key the HTML tags that define the structure and formatting for your Web page. (Formatting is covered in Lesson 24.) The tags must be keyed according to strict rules, so that all Web browsers can interpret the codes correctly. Some of the basic rules include the following:

■ An HTML tag begins with a left angle bracket character < and ends with a right angle bracket character >. Between the angle brackets is an *element*, which is the actual tag name, such as BODY or FONT. So, a correct tag looks like this: <BODY>. (Some elements have attributes, which describe properties of the elements. You learn about attributes in Lesson 24.)

■ Most tags are used in pairs. The first in the pair is an opening tag, which displays at the beginning of a section, and the second is a closing tag, which displays at the end of the section. The closing tag includes a slash character to the left of the tag name. So, <BODY> would be an opening tag at the beginning of the BODY section, and </BODY> would be the closing tag at the end.

■ Text that you enter between a pair of HTML tags is formatted with the code specified by those tags. For example, if you key <H1>Graphics</H1> in a file, a browser will turn on H1 formatting at the opening tag, apply it to the text *Graphics*, and then turn off H1 formatting at the closing tag.

■ You can use either uppercase or lowercase letters in HTML tags. For example, a Web browser will interpret <HTML> and <html> the same way. You may want to use all uppercase letters so that you can easily identify the tags when you look at your file.

Table 23-2 lists some commonly used HTML tags.

TABLE 23-2
Common HTML tags

OPENING TAG	CLOSING TAG	DESCRIPTION
<HTML>	</HTML>	Identifies the content as HTML format.
<HEAD>	</HEAD>	Defines the header of an HTML document.
<TITLE>	</TITLE>	Defines the Web page title, which displays in the browser's title bar.
<BODY>	</BODY>	Defines the body of an HTML document.
<P>	</P>	Starts a new paragraph by inserting a blank line after the closing tag.
 		Inserts a line break after the tag.
<H1>	</H1>	Applies HTML heading 1 formatting to the content between the tags. Headings 2 through 6 are also available.
<CENTER>	</CENTER>	Center aligns the content between the tags.
<B>	</B>	Applies bold formatting to the content between the tags.
<I>	</I>	Applies italic formatting to the content between the tags.

In the following exercise, you use a text editor to create a Web page file, then key the text and HTML codes to define the page content.

STEP-BY-STEP 23.5

1. Launch your text editor. For example, to start Notepad, click the **Start** button on the Windows taskbar, click **All Programs**, click **Accessories**, and then click **Notepad**. A new, untitled document opens.

2. Key the following lines exactly as shown. Your text editor window should resemble Figure 23-8 when you finish.

```
<HTML>
<HEAD> <TITLE> </TITLE> </HEAD>
<BODY> Hello, World Wide Web! </BODY>
</HTML>
```

FIGURE 23-8
Text file with HTML tags

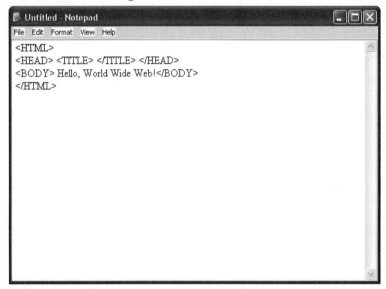

3. Leave the file open to use in the next exercise.

Save the HTML File

You save an HTML text document the same way you save files in other programs. Use Save or Save As on the File menu to open a Save As dialog box, navigate to the location where you want to store the file (such as in your Web site folder), and then key a name for the file.

It is important that you key the correct *file extension* along with the file name when you save an HTML file in a text editor. Recall that a file extension is a dot followed by three or four characters that indicate the format of the file. By default, most text editors save files in text format with a .txt file extension. For a Web browser to identify a file that contains HTML tags, it must have either an .html or .htm file extension.

> **Note**
>
> It is not necessary to leave spaces before or after HTML tags. The tags work with spaces or without. However, there cannot be spaces between the angle brackets and the tag name.

You can give your Web page any name but, traditionally, the first page a Web browser looks for when it finds a new Web site is the *index.html* file. Increasingly, browsers use other file names to find the main or home page of a Web site, such as default.html or default.asp.

After you save a file, you can continue working in it or close it. Usually, closing a text file closes the text editing program as well. If you have made any changes, the program will prompt you to save before closing. You can also use the File > Save command to save changes while you work.

Extra for Experts

If you are using a word processing program as a text editor, key a file name that includes an .htm or .html file extension and then select the plain text file type. Click Save to save the file correctly.

STEP-BY-STEP 23.6

1. Click **File** on the Menu bar, and then click **Save As**. The Save As dialog box displays.

2. From the *Save in* drop-down list, navigate to and open the **Australia** folder you created previously.

3. In the *File name* box, with the default name already selected, key **index.html** as shown in Figure 23-9.

FIGURE 23-9
Key the file name and extension

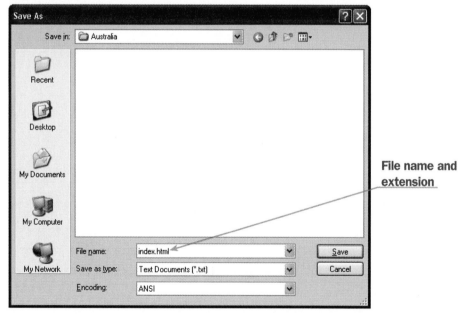

File name and extension

4. Click **Save**.

5. Click **File** on the Menu bar and then click **Exit** to close your text editor.

View Your Web Page in a Browser

To see how your Web page will look to someone browsing the Web, you can open it in your Web browser. While you are building Web pages on your computer, you do not have to log on to the Internet to access your files. Instead, you can use your browser's File > Open command to locate the page by either keying a path to the file, or by browsing to locate the file.

The exercise below gives instructions for viewing a page using Internet Explorer on a Windows computer. If you are using a different browser, the commands may be different.

STEP-BY-STEP 23.7

1. Launch Internet Explorer. You do not have to connect to your ISP.

2. Click **File** on the Menu bar, and then click **Open** to display the Open dialog box.

3. Click **Browse**. A dialog box similar to the Open dialog box in other program displays.

4. Navigate to your **Australia** folder. It should look similar to Figure 23-10.

FIGURE 23-10
Locate the index.html file

5. Select the **index.html** file, click **Open**, and then click **OK** in the Open dialog box. Your page displays in the browser and should look similar to Figure 23-11. Notice that the tags do not display.

STEP-BY-STEP 23.7 Continued

FIGURE 23-11
Your Web page in a browser

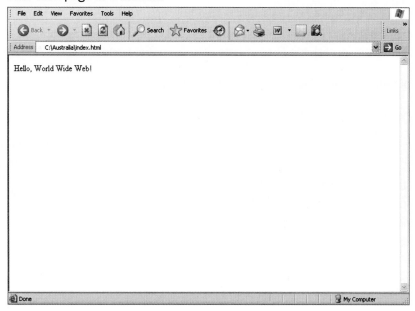

6. Click **View** on the Menu bar and then click **Source** to display the HTML source code for the page. The **index.html** file opens in your text editor.

7. Close the text editor and then minimize your browser. (You will need it open to use in the next exercise.)

Use HTML Tags to Modify Web Page Content

You can modify your Web page by keying additional content in the HTML file, or by editing existing content. You can easily delete or replace existing text, key new tags, or replace tags.

To edit the Web page file, start your text editing program and use the File > Open command to locate and open the HTML file. The file may not display in the Open dialog box at first, because it is in HTML format and only text formatted files display by default. Select *All files* from the *Files of type* drop-down list to add HTML files to the list, select the file, and then click the Open button.

To see how the changes affect the page, you must view it in your browser. Instead of opening and closing the page each time you want to see a change, you can use your browser's Refresh button to update the page.

STEP-BY-STEP 23.8

1. Launch your text editor and select the command to open an existing file. For example, click **File**, on the Menu bar and then click **Open**.

2. In the Open dialog box, navigate to your Australia folder and open it. Select the command to display all files. For example, click the **Files of type** drop-down arrow and then click **All Files**.

3. Select your **index.html** file and then click the **Open** button.

4. Select the text *Hello, World Wide Web!* between the `<BODY>` `</BODY>` tags and press **Delete** to remove the text.

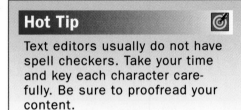

Hot Tip

Text editors usually do not have spell checkers. Take your time and key each character carefully. Be sure to proofread your content.

5. Position the insertion point after the opening `<BODY>` tag and press **Enter** to start a new line. Key the following lines of text, pressing **Enter** at the end of each line. When you are finished, it should look similar to Figure 23-12.

```
Cities in Australia
Sydney
Melbourne
Perth
Hobart
Cairns
Brisbane
```

FIGURE 23-12
Edited Web page content

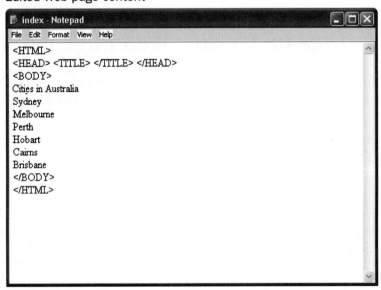

6. Click **File** on the Menu bar, and then click **Save** to save the changes. Minimize your text editing program.

STEP-BY-STEP 23.8 Continued

7. Maximize your browser. (If necessary, launch your browser and open the **index.html** page.) Click **Refresh** or select **View** > **Refresh**. The page should look similar to Figure 23-13. Note that the content displays on a single line, not on separate lines the way you keyed it in the text file. You must format the content using HTML tags in order to insert blank lines and line breaks.

FIGURE 23-13
View your modified content

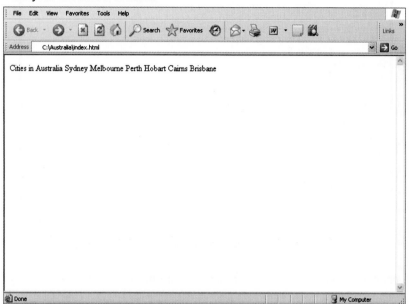

8. Minimize your browser and restore the text editor window.

Try using HTML tags to insert a blank line. The tag is `<P> </P>`, and the line is inserted after the closing tag.

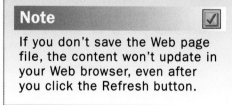

> **Note** ☑️
>
> If you don't save the Web page file, the content won't update in your Web browser, even after you click the Refresh button.

9. Position the insertion point to the left of the *C* in the word *Cities* and key the opening tag `<P>`. Move the insertion point to the end of the line, to the right of the word *Australia* and key the closing tag `</P>`.

Now, try using HTML tags to insert line breaks. The tag is `<BR>`. You only need one tag, which will be followed by the break.

10. Position the insertion point at the end of the word *Sydney* and key `<BR>`. Move the insertion to the end of the next line and key `<BR>`. Repeat this step to insert a line break tag at the end of each of the next four lines.

Now, use tags to create a Web page title. The tag is `<TITLE> </TITLE>`, and the text between the tags displays in the Web page's title bar when the page opens in a browser.

STEP-BY-STEP 23.8 Continued

11. Position the insertion point between the opening `<TITLE>` and closing `</TITLE>` tags, and then key **Cities in Australia**. When you are finished, the file should look similar to Figure 23-14.

FIGURE 23-14
Use tags to insert breaks, blank lines, and a page title

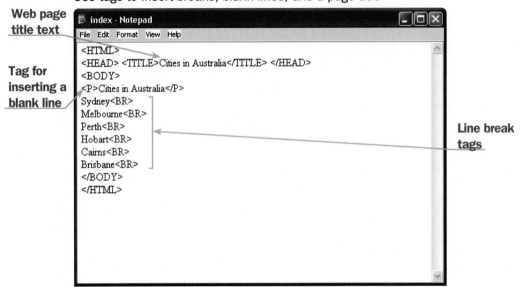

12. Save the changes, restore your browser, and refresh the page to view the changes. It should look similar to Figure 23-15.

FIGURE 23-15
View the modified file in your browser

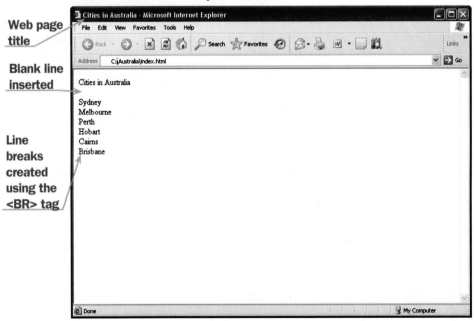

STEP-BY-STEP 23.8 Continued

13. Minimize your browser and restore the text editor window. Leave **index.html** open to use in the next exercise.

Note

If your Web page does not look the way you expect, you may not have saved the text file, or you may have made an error when keying the tags. Be sure to include both the opening and closing tags where necessary, and the slash character (/) in the closing tag.

Use HTML Heading Tags to Format Text

There are six HTML heading tags you can apply to quickly change the size of text. They are used in pairs and are numbered from 1 to 6:

<H1> Very Large Heading </H1>

<H2> Large Heading </H2>

<H3> Medium Size Heading </H3>

<H4> Slightly Smaller Heading </H4>

<H5> Small Heading </H5>

<H6> Very Small Heading </H6>

STEP-BY-STEP 23.9

1. Position the insertion point to the left of the `<P>` opening tag and key `<H1>`. Move the insertion point to the end of the line, after the `</P>` closing tag, and key `</H1>`.

2. Save the changes, restore your browser, and refresh the page. The text *Cities in Australia* is now formatted using the HTML heading 1 style.

3. Minimize your browser and, in the text editing window, position the insertion point to the left of the *S* in the word *Sydney*, and key `<H3>`. Move the insertion point to the right of the *y* in the word *Sydney*—to the left of the `<BR>` tag—and key `</H3>`.

STEP-BY-STEP 23.9 Continued

4. Position the insertion point to the left of the *M* in *Melbourne*, and key **<H4>**. Move the insertion point to the end of the word Brisbane—to the right of the e and to the left of the **
** tag—and key **</H4>**. The file should look similar to Figure 23-16.

FIGURE 23-16
Use heading tags to format text

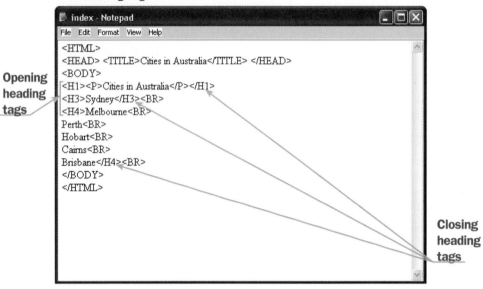

5. Save the changes and close **index.html**.

6. Restore your browser, and refresh the page. It should look similar to Figure 23-17.

STEP-BY-STEP 23.9 Continued

FIGURE 23-17
The formatted text in your browser

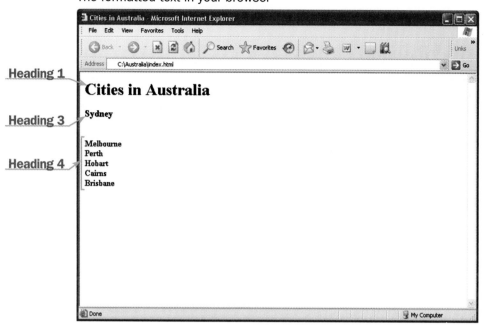

7. Close your browser.

SUMMARY

In this lesson, you learned:

■ The World Wide Web is a collection of Web pages and Web sites stored on Web servers that can be accessed by Web clients.

■ A uniform resource locator (URL) identifies the storage location of a Web page.

■ You can use a Web browser to locate and display pages stored on the World Wide Web.

■ To keep all of the files you need for a Web site organized, you should create a folder and subfolders to store them.

■ You can use a simple text editor such as Notepad to create a Web page file using HTML tags to define the structure and formatting of the Web page content.

■ HTML tag names are enclosed in angle brackets.

■ Many HTML tags are used in pairs, with an opening tag and a closing tag. The closing tag includes a slash in front of the tag name.

■ When you save a Web page file in a text editing program, you must key the .html or .htm file extension after the file name.

■ You can open the file in your text editing program to make changes.

■ You can use your browser to preview the Web page without logging on to the Internet, and you can refresh the page to see the changes you make.

VOCABULARY *Review*

Define the following terms:

ASCII	Hypertext Markup Language	User name
Domain	(HTML)	Web browser
Element	Internet Service Provider	Web client
Home page	(ISP)	Web pages
HTML tags	Navigation bar	Web server
HTTP (Hypertext Transfer	Password	Web site
Protocol)	Protocol	World Wide Web (WWW)
Hyperlinks	Uniform Resource Locator	
	(URL)	

REVIEW *Questions*

TRUE / FALSE

Circle T if the statement is true or F if the statement is false.

T   F   1. ASCII is an authoring language that uses codes to define data on a Web page.

T   F   2. Web addresses properly begin with the characters http://.

T   F   3. A Web browser interprets HTML tags in order to display a Web page properly.

T   F   4. All HTML tags are used in pairs.

T   F   5. All HTML tags begin with a left angle bracket character and end with a right angle bracket character.

T   F   6. A closing HTML tag has a hyphen character in front of the tag name.

T   F   7. You can key an HTML tag name in either uppercase or lowercase letters.

T   F   8. To see how changes you make in a Web page file using a text editor affect the page, you must view the page in your Web browser.

T   F   9. Most text editors do not have spelling checkers.

T   F   10. Mozilla Firefox is a type of Web server.

WRITTEN QUESTIONS

Write a brief answer to each of the following questions.

1. Identify and describe at least four common domain types.

2. What are some of the ways you can identify a link on a Web page?

3. Name the two file extensions that indicate to a Web browser that a text file contains HTML tags.

4. What are the four main parts of a URL?

5. Name and describe at least three HTML tags you can use to format a Web page.

FILL IN THE BLANK

Complete the following sentences by writing the correct word or words in the blanks provided.

1. A Web _____ is a collection of multiple Web pages connected using hyperlinks.

2. A Web _____ is a computer that is linked via a network to a Web server.

3. When you start your Web browser, it usually displays a default _____ page.

4. A(n) _____ is the string of characters that identifies the address where a Web page is stored.

5. Use the _____ HTML tag to insert a line break.

6. Click your browser's _____ to update a page.

7. Many Web pages have a(n) _____ bar, which is a row of links, similar to a menu.

8. HTTP is the _____ used to transmit data on the World Wide Web.

9. The period character, which is called a(n) _____, separates parts of the domain name.

10. A Web _____ is a software program that you use to locate and display Web pages.

PROJECTS

PROJECT 23-1

In this project, you explore the White House Web site.

1. Launch your Web browser and log on to the Internet.

2. In the Address bar, key **http://www.whitehouse.gov**, and then click **Go**, or press **Enter** to display the home page for the White House Web site.

3. Click the link to **History & Tours** near the top-right corner of the page.

4. If available, click the link to the **Oval Office Video Tour**. This will play a video in a Real Player window. When the video is finished, close the Real Player window.

5. Locate the link for information about **White House Tours**, and then click it to go to the White House Tours page. Read the page.

6. Display the source code for the page in a text editor. If you are using Internet Explorer, click **View** on the Menu bar and then click **Source**.

7. Examine the way HTML tags are used to structure and format the page.

8. With your instructor's permission, print the text document so you can compare the HTML source code with the Web page in your browser.

9. Close your text editor program.

10. Try any other links in the Web site to view information that interests you. When you are finished exploring the site, click the **Home** link to return to the White House Web site home page.

11. Close your browser.

PROJECT 23-2

In this project, you create a home page for a Web site about pets.

1. Use a file management program to create a folder named **Pets** where you can store the files for this project.

2. Start your text editor program. Save the text file as **pets_index.html**, and store it in the Pets folder you created in step 1.
   A. Click **File** on the Menu bar and then click **Save As**.
   B. Navigate to the **Pets** folder.
   C. In the *File name* box, key **pets_index.html** to replace the default file name.
   D. Click the **Save** button.

3. Key the following lines, including the HTML tags.

```
<HTML>
<HEAD> <TITLE>All About Pets</TITLE> </HEAD>
<BODY>
Welcome to a Web site that is All About Pets!
In this Web site you will find information about common types of pets,
how to choose a pet,
and how to care for a pet.
Click any link to start learning All About Pets.
</BODY>
</HTML>
```

4. Click **File** on the Menu bar and then click **Save** to save the changes to the file.

5. Launch your Web browser and open the **pets_index.html** Web page.
   A. Click **File** on the Menu bar and then click **Open**.
   B. Click the **Browse** button.
   C. Navigate to the **Pets** folder.
   D. Select the **pets_index.html** file and then click the **Open** button.
   E. Click the **OK** button in the Open dialog box.

6. Switch back to the text editor.

7. Enclose the text *Welcome to a Web site that is All About Pets!* in Heading 1 HTML tags as follows:

```
<H1>Welcome to a Web site that is All About Pets!</H1>
```

8. Enclose the entire line, including the Heading 1 tags, in Paragraph tags as follows:

```
<P><H1>Welcome to a Web site that is All About Pets!</H1></P>
```

9. Enclose the next sentence in Heading 3 tags, and the last sentence in Heading 4 tags as follows:

```
<H3>In this Web site you will find information about common types of pets,
how to choose a pet,
and how to care for a pet.</H3>
<H4>Click any link to start learning All About Pets.</H4>
```

10. Key a line break tag after each line in the second sentence as follows:

```
<H3>In this Web site you will find information about common types of
pets,<BR>
how to choose a pet,<BR>
and how to care for a pet.</H3><BR>
<H4>Click any link to start learning All About Pets.</H4>
```

11. Save the file, switch to your browser, and refresh the page to see the Web page.

12. Close your browser. Close your text editor.

PROJECT 23-3

In this project, you create a Cats page for the Web site about pets.

1. Start your text editor program. Save the text file as **cats.html**, and store it in the **Pets** folder you created in Project 23-2.
   A. Click **File** on the Menu bar and then click **Save As**.
   B. Navigate to the **Pets** folder.
   C. In the *File name* box, key **cats.html** to replace the default file name.
   D. Click the **Save** button.

2. Key the following lines, including the HTML tags.

```
<HTML>
<HEAD> <TITLE>All About Pets - Cats</TITLE> </HEAD>
<BODY>
Cats Make Great Pets
Cats are:
Independent
Loving
Beautiful
Before you get a pet cat, ask yourself the following questions:
Do you have the time?
Do you have the space?
Will you take care of it?
Use the links on this page to learn more about types of cats.
</BODY>
</HTML>
```

3. Click **File** on the Menu bar and then click **Save** to save the changes to the file.

4. Launch your Web browser and open the **cats.html** Web page.
   A. Click **File** on the Menu bar and then click **Open**.
   B. Click the **Browse** button.
   C. Navigate to the **Pets** folder.
   D. Select the **cats.html** file and then click the **Open** button.
   E. Click the **OK** button in the Open dialog box.

5. Switch back to the text editor.

6. Enclose the text *Cats Make Great Pets* in Heading 1 HTML tags follows:

```
<H1>Cats Make Great Pets</H1>
```

7. Enclose the next line in Heading 3 tags, as follows:

```
<H3>Cats are:</H3>
```

8. Enclose the next three lines in Heading 4 tags. Key a line break tag after the text *Independent* and *Loving*, as follows:

```
<H4>Independent<BR>
Loving<BR>
Beautiful</H4>
```

9. Enclose the next line in Heading 3 tags, as follows:

```
<H3>Before you get a pet cat, ask yourself the following questions:</H3>
```

10. Enclose the next four lines in Heading 4 tags, as follows:

```
<H4>Do you have the time?
Do you have the space?
Will you take care of it?
Use the links on this page to learn more about types of cats.</H4>
```

11. Key a line break tag at the end of each of the three questions, and enclose the last line in paragraph tags, as follows:

```
<H4>Do you have the time?<BR>
Do you have the space?<BR>
Will you take care of it?<BR>
<P>Use the links on this page to learn more about types of cats.</H4></P>
```

12. Save the file, switch to your browser, and refresh the page to see the Web page.

13. Close your browser. Close your text editor.

PROJECT 23-4

In this project, you create a Dogs page for the Web site about pets.

1. Start your text editor program. Save the text file as **dogs.html**, and store it in the **Pets** folder you created in Project 23-1.
   A. Click **File** on the Menu bar and then click **Save As**.
   B. Navigate to the **Pets** folder.
   C. In the *File name* box, key **dogs.html** to replace the default file name.
   D. Click the **Save** button.

2. Key the following lines, including the HTML tags.

```
<HTML>
<HEAD> <TITLE>All About Pets - Dogs</TITLE> </HEAD>
<BODY>
Dogs Make Great Pets
Dogs are:
Fun
Loving
Playful
Before you get a pet dog, ask yourself the following questions:
Do you have the time?
Do you have the space?
Will you take care of it?
Use the links on this page to learn more about types of dogs.
</BODY>
</HTML>
```

3. Click **File** on the Menu bar and then click **Save** to save the changes to the file.

4. Launch your Web browser and open the **dogs.html** Web page.
   A. Click **File** on the Menu bar and then click **Open**.
   B. Click the **Browse** button.
   C. Navigate to the **Pets** folder.
   D. Select the **dogs.html** file and then click the **Open** button.
   E. Click the **OK** button in the Open dialog box.

5. Switch back to the text editor.

6. Enclose the text *Dogs Make Great Pets* in Heading 1 HTML tags as follows:

   ```
   <H1>Dogs Make Great Pets</H1>
   ```

7. Enclose the next line in Heading 3 tags, as follows:

   ```
   <H3>Dogs are:</H3>
   ```

8. Enclose the next three lines in Heading 4 tags. Key a line break tag after the text *Fun* and *Loving*, as follows:

   ```
   <H4>Fun<BR>
   Loving<BR>
   Playful</H4>
   ```

9. Enclose the next line in Heading 3 tags, as follows:

   ```
   <H3>Before you get a pet dog, ask yourself the following questions:</H3>
   ```

10. Enclose the next four lines in Heading 4 tags, as follows:

    ```
    <H4>Do you have the time?
    Do you have the space?
    Will you take care of it?
    Use the links on this page to learn more about types of dogs.</H4>
    ```

11. Key a line break tag at the end of each of the three questions, and enclose the last line in paragraph tags, as follows:

    ```
    <H4>Do you have the time?<BR>
    Do you have the space?<BR>
    Will you take care of it?<BR>
    <P>Use the links on this page to learn more about types of dogs.</H4></P>
    ```

12. Save the file, switch to your browser, and refresh the page to see the Web page.

13. Close your browser. Close your text editor.

 ## WEB PROJECT

As discussed in this lesson, you can use your Web browser and a text editing program to display the HTML source code for any Web page. In this exercise, use your Web browser to display the home page for your school, a different school, or an organization in your community. Display the source code for the page and examine it to see how the HTML tags are used. With your instructor's permission, print the source code file and compare it to the Web page displayed in your browser. See if you can interpret how the tags provide the structure and formatting for the page.

 ## TEAMWORK PROJECT

For your science class, plan and create a Web page about a topic you are studying now, or studied earlier in the year. As a team, select the topic. For example, if you are studying botany, you might select a plant and list five to ten facts about it. If you are studying zoology, you might select an animal. If you are studying chemistry, you might select a specific chemical. Next, agree on the information you want to include. You may want to include a descriptive paragraph, list facts, or do both. If necessary, research the topic so that you have the best information available.

When you have gathered the information, work together to create the Web page. Start by creating the folder (or folders) that you will need to store your files. Then, use your text editor to create and save the Web page file. Take turns keying the text and the HTML tags. Refer to the exercises in this lesson to see how to use the structural tags. Use tags to insert paragraph and line breaks and to format the content in headings. As you work save the changes and display the page in your browser so you can see how your Web page looks. Make changes as necessary. When you are finished, save the text file. Display the page in your browser for your class to see.

CRITICAL *Thinking*

For your social studies class, plan and create a Web page about a place you would like to visit. You might select a country, a city, a landmark, or even a vacation destination. Research the place to gather information that you want to include on your Web page. You might want to include information about the weather, the people, the language, the currency, activities or attractions, and possibly some historical or newsworthy facts.

When you have gathered the information, create the folder (or folders) that you will need to store your files. Then, use your text editor to create and save the Web page file. Key the text and the HTML tags to develop the content on the page. Use structural tags and formatting tags. As you work, save your changes and display the page in your browser so you can see how your Web page looks. Make changes as necessary. When you are finished, save the text file. Display the page in your browser for your class to see.

FORMATTING AND LINKING WEB SITE PAGES

OBJECTIVES

Upon completion of this lesson, you should be able to:

- Explain how Web sites are structured.
- Apply font formatting, including font face, font size, and font color.
- Align text.
- Add horizontal rules to a Web page.
- Create bulleted and numbered lists.
- Create consistent Web pages.
- Create hyperlinks on Web pages.

Estimated Time: 2 hours

VOCABULARY

Attribute

Hierarchical structure

Linear structure

Navigation system

Random access structure

Value

Web sites have been created on nearly every topic imaginable. Part of the reason for this is that all you need to develop a Web site is access to a Web server, a text editor, and a topic. Of course, if you want to attract a lot of visitors to your site, you should also add a little creativity.

Even if your Web page is made up of only text, you can make it interesting. There are HTML tags for formatting the font face, style, size, and even color. You can apply different alignments and format text as lists to make it easier to read. And, you can insert hyperlinks to connect your page to other pages, thereby creating a Web site.

In this lesson, you create a Web site on the topic of Australian animals. You learn how to format text using fonts, alignments, and lists. You also learn how to insert horizontal rules and how to link multiple Web pages using hyperlinks.

How Web Sites Are Structured

When two or more pages that relate to a common topic or purpose are linked together, they create a Web site. To get the most out of a Web site, visitors must be able to easily access the pages that contain the information they need, and this depends in great deal on how the site is organized. Most Web sites are organized using one of three basic structures, or a combination of any of the three:

■ Linear

■ Random access

■ Hierarchical

Linear structure is designed so that visitors view one page at a time, often in a specific order. The Web site designer sets the order, and therefore controls the way the visitor uses the site. This structure is suitable when your want your visitors to move through a Web site from beginning to end. For example, if a site provides instructions for building a birdhouse, a linear Web site can direct the visitor from the first step through the last step, in the correct order. Figure 24-1 is a diagram of a linear structure.

FIGURE 24-1
Diagram of a linear structure

Random access structure allows Web site visitors to jump to any page on the Web site from any other page. The Web site designer has no control over the way the visitor uses the site. This is a good organizational structure for sites that provide information that can be viewed in any order. For example, if a site provides information about tourist destinations in Paris, France, visitors can randomly access pages for any destination that interests them. Figure 24-2 is a diagram of a random access structure.

FIGURE 24-2
Diagram of a random access structure

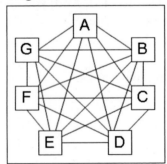

Hierarchical structure organizes pages into categories and subcategories. The Web site designer controls the content in each category, but the user can browse through the categories in any order. It is useful for organizing a large Web site that contains many pages and a lot of information. For example, a Web site for a school might have one category for students, with subcategories for the student handbook, athletics, clubs, and homework. It might have another category for parents, with subcategories for teacher contact information, the guidance department, and the school calendar. A third category might be for teachers, with subcategories of teacher resources, professional development, and job openings. Figure 24-3 is a diagram of a hierarchical structure.

FIGURE 24-3
Diagram of a hierarchical structure

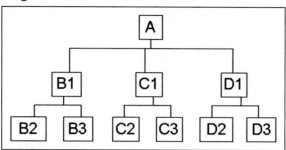

As a Web site designer, it is a good idea to select a site structure before you develop a site. You should examine the topic and the number of pages you will need to present all the information effectively. Ask yourself whether you want visitors to see the pages in any particular order. If so, you should use a linear structure. Consider if the content breaks down into categories. If so, you should use a hierarchical structure. If it is a relatively small site, and all pages relate directly to the main topic, you may want to use a random access structure.

For your Web site about Australian animals, a hierarchical structure makes a lot of sense. The index page can be at the top, and each animal can be a category. Start by creating the index page.

S TEP-BY-STEP 24.1

1. Use a file management program to create a folder for storing the files for this lesson. Name the folder **Aussie Animals**.

2. Launch your text editor. To use Windows' Notepad, for example, click the **Start** button on the Windows taskbar, click **All Programs**, click **Accessories**, and then click **Notepad**.

3. Save the text file as **an_index.html** in the **Aussie Animals** folder.

4. Key the following lines exactly as shown here.

```
<HTML>
<HEAD><TITLE>Animals of Australia</TITLE></HEAD>
<BODY>
<P>Aussie Animals</P>
<P>There are many animals that are native to Australia,<BR>
which means you cannot find them anywhere else in the world -- except in
zoos!</P>
<P>In this Web site you will find information about some of the most
interesting -- and unique -- Aussie Animals.</P>
<P>Kangaroos</P>
<P>Tasmanian Devils</P>
<P>Echidnas</P>
</BODY>
</HTML>
```

STEP-BY-STEP 24.1 Continued

5. Save the changes to the file.

6. Launch your Web browser and open the **an_index.html** page. In Internet Explorer, for example, click **File** on the Menu bar, click **Open**, and then click **Browse** in the Open dialog box. Navigate to the Aussie Animals folder, select **an_index.html**, and click the **Open** button. Click **OK** in the Open dialog box to display the page. It should look similar to Figure 24-4.

FIGURE 24-4
Index page in a browser

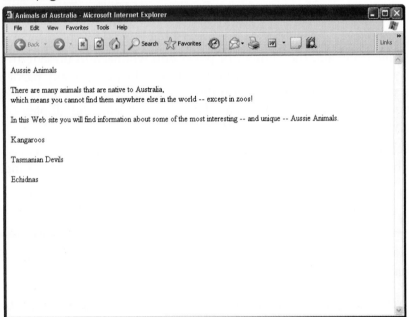

7. If necessary, make corrections to your Web page in the text editor, save the changes, and preview the page again.

8. Minimize your browser. Leave **an_index.html** open in the text editor to use in the next exercise.

Apply Font Formatting

Y ou have already learned a great deal about using font formatting to enhance text in documents created using multimedia programs. On a Web page, you can use the `<FONT> </FONT>` tag to apply font formatting including specifying a particular font, setting a font size, and changing the font color.

Because the same <FONT> tag controls all font formatting, you key an attribute in the opening tag to specify which property you want to set. An *attribute* is a term that describes the properties of an element. In fact, sometimes attributes are called *properties*. With the <FONT> tag, you can use the FACE attribute to specify the font, the SIZE attribute to specify the font size, and the COLOR attribute to specify the font color. You follow the attribute with an equals sign, and then key a *value*, which defines the specific property, such as the specific font name, font size, or color. The value is enclosed in quotation marks. You can specify one or more than one attribute in the same <FONT> tag. It is important to note that when you use the SIZE attribute, you do not specify an exact font size, such as 12 points, or 24 points. Rather, you key a value ranging from 1 (very small) to 7 (large).

For example, to format the text *Animals* in the font Arial, you would key:

```
<FONT FACE="Arial">Animals</FONT>
```

To format the text *Animals* in a large font size in Arial, you would key:

```
<FONT SIZE="7" FACE="Arial">Animals</FONT>
```

To format the text *Animals* in a large font size, in Arial, in blue you would key:

```
<FONT SIZE="7" FACE="Arial" COLOR="Blue">Animals</FONT>
```

Note

Refer to Lesson 4 for information on using fonts in a graphics file, Lesson 7 for information on working with fonts in an animation file, Lesson 13 for working with fonts in a presentation file, or Lesson 19 for working with fonts in a publication file.

Extra for Experts

If you specify a font that is not available, the visitor's browser uses a default font. You can include alternative font values in the tag, or even "serif" or "sans serif" so the browser will use a similar font. For example, key <FONT FACE="Georgia, Garamond, serif"> to specify the font Georgia, with Garamond as an alternative, or any serif font if neither Georgia nor Garamond are available.

S TEP-BY-STEP 24.2

1. Position the insertion point to the left of the <P> tag on the line with the text *Aussie Animals*.

2. Key <FONT SIZE="7" FACE="Arial Bold" COLOR="Blue">.

3. Position the insertion point at the end of the line, to the right of the </P> tag, and key </FONT>.

4. Save the changes, make your browser active, and refresh the page. It should look similar to Figure 24-5.

FIGURE 24-5
Use Font tags to format text

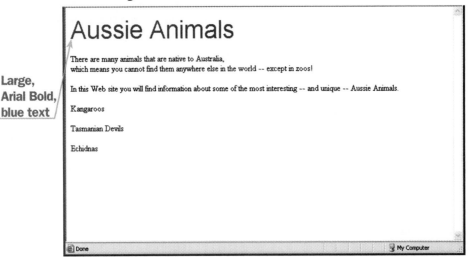

Large, Arial Bold, blue text

5. If necessary, make corrections to your Web page in the text editor, save the changes, and preview the page again.

6. Minimize your browser. Leave **an_index.html** open in the text editor to use in the next exercise.

Align Text

B_y default, HTML text is left-aligned, so all text lines up at the left margin of the Web page and forms a jagged edge on the right side of the page. You can use the <CENTER> </CENTER> tag to center-align content on a Web page, regardless of the size of the Web browser's window.

You can also align a paragraph using the <P> </P> tag with the ALIGN attribute. Use the value "right" to right-align the paragraph; "left" to left-align the paragraph; "center" to center the paragraph; or "justify" to justify the paragraph.

> **Note** ☑
>
> If the formatting does not display as you expect, check the syntax in the .html file. Common mistakes include omitting either an opening tag or a closing tag, or one of the angle brackets. Or, you might have omitted the slash from the closing tag. Also check that you keyed the equals sign between the attribute and the value, and that the value is enclosed in quotation marks.

> **Note** ☑
>
> Refer to Lesson 4 for information on aligning text in a graphics file, Lesson 13 for aligning text in a presentation file, or Lesson 19 for aligning text in a publication file.

S TEP-BY-STEP 24.3

1. Position the insertion point to the left of the `<FONT>` opening tag and key `<CENTER>`.

2. Move the insertion point to the right of the `</FONT>` closing tag and key `</CENTER>`.

3. Save the changes, make your browser active, and refresh the page. The text *Aussie Animals* should be centered on the page.

> **Note**
>
> When you enclose HTML tags within other HTML tags, it is called nesting. You learn more about nesting tags in Lesson 25.

4. Make your text editor active. Position the insertion point to the right of the closing `</P>` tag after the text *except in zoos!*. Press **Enter** to start a new line and then key the following lines:

```
<P ALIGN="right">Have you ever visited a zoo?<BR>
Some zoos have great Web sites.<BR>
Try this link to the San Diego Zoo<BR>
and take a virtual zoo tour!</P>
```

5. Save the changes, make your browser active, and refresh the page. The new text should be right-aligned on the page, as shown in Figure 24-6.

FIGURE 24-6
Align text on the page

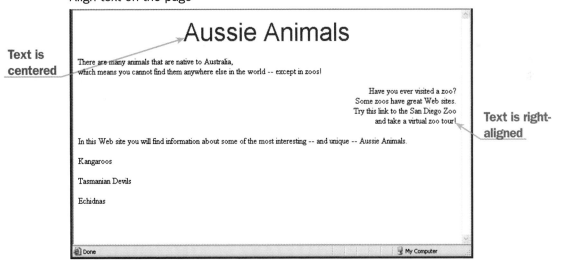

6. If necessary, make corrections to your Web page in the text editor, save the changes, and preview the page again.

7. Minimize your browser, but leave it and your text editor open to use in the next exercise.

Add Horizontal Rules

Horizontal rules are lines that stretch across the page from left to right. They are a nice way to enhance a Web page that uses a lot of text, because they can add balance, decoration, and define parts of the page. By separating the page into sections, they can make it easier for visitors to find the information for which they are looking. Rules can also draw attention to a heading or paragraph, and they can make the page more visually interesting. You use the <HR> tag to insert a horizontal line. You do not need a closing tag.

In this exercise, you create a new Web page for the Aussie Animals Web site. This page will be divided by a horizontal rule.

> **Note**
>
> For information on inserting horizontal rules in a publication file, refer to Lesson 21.

STEP-BY-STEP 24.4

1. In your text editor, create a new file and save it as **kangaroos.html** in the **Aussie Animals** folder.

2. In the new file, key the following lines:

```
<HTML>
<HEAD><TITLE>Animals of Australia: Kangaroos</TITLE></HEAD>
<BODY>
<CENTER><FONT SIZE="7" FACE="Arial" COLOR="Blue">
<P>Kangaroos</P></FONT></CENTER>
<FONT SIZE="5" FACE="Arial"><P>Red Kangaroo</P></FONT>
<HR>
<P ALIGN="justify"><FONT SIZE="4">The Red Kangaroo is the largest species
of kangaroo. It lives in the central, interior, part of the Australian
continent. It occupies mixed habitats of open shrub lands, grasslands,
mallee scrubs, mulga country, and desert. Red Kangaroos travel in groups
called mobs that can have up to several hundred members. They graze at
night, and can go for a long time without water.</FONT></P>
<HR>
</BODY>
</HTML>
```

3. Save the changes to the file.

4. Make your browser active and open **kangaroos.html**. It should look similar to Figure 24-7.

STEP-BY-STEP 24.4 Continued

FIGURE 24-7
Horizontal rules enhance a Web page

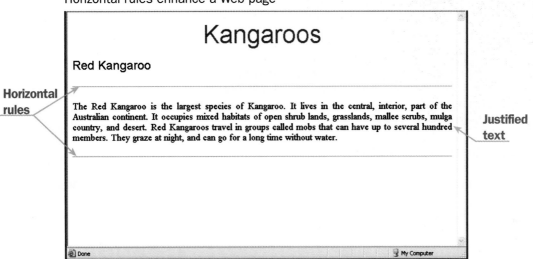

5. If necessary, make corrections to your Web page in the text editor, save the changes, and preview the page again.

6. Minimize your browser and leave **kangaroos.html** open in the text editor to use in the next exercise.

Create Lists on Web Pages

You can often improve the appearance and make a Web page easier to read by organizing lines of text into lists. You can use the <OL> </OL> tag to create an ordered—numbered—list when the order of items matters, such as in step-by-step instructions. You can use the <UL> </UL> tag to create an unordered—bulleted—list when the order does not matter, such as in a list of features or topics. For both types of list, you precede each line with the <LI> tag, which identifies it as a list item. The <LI> tag does not require a closing tag.

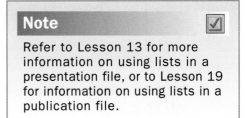

Note

Refer to Lesson 13 for more information on using lists in a presentation file, or to Lesson 19 for information on using lists in a publication file.

Create a Bulleted (Unordered) List

When you create a bulleted list on a Web page, the visitor's browser indents each item in the list, and inserts a marker at the beginning of each item. By default, the marker is a simple black dot.

Try adding a bulleted list to the kangaroos.html page.

STEP-BY-STEP 24.5

1. Position the insertion point to the right of the second <HR> tag at the end of the file and press **Enter** to start a new line.

2. Key the following lines:

```
<FONT SIZE="4"><P>Fast Facts<P>
<UL><LI>Red Kangaroos are marsupials.
<LI>Red Kangaroos can jump up to 29 feet.
<LI>They have been known to reach speeds of 25 miles per
hour.</UL></FONT>
```

3. Save the changes to the file.

4. Make your browser active and refresh the **kangaroos.html** file. It should look similar to Figure 24-8.

FIGURE 24-8
Organize text in a bulleted list

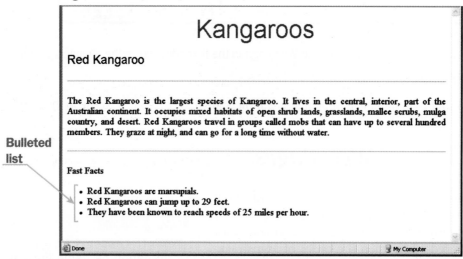

5. If necessary, make corrections to your Web page in the text editor, save the changes, and preview the page again.

6. Minimize your browser, but leave it and your text editor open to use in the next exercise.

Create a Numbered (Ordered) List

When you create a numbered list, the visitor's browser indents all lines in the list and inserts numbers at the start of each item. In this exercise, convert existing lines on your an_index.html page into a numbered list. At the same time, you can apply font formatting and horizontal rules to make the page more consistent with the formatting on the kangaroos.html page.

S TEP-BY-STEP 24.6

1. Open **an_index.html** in your text editor.

2. Position the insertion point to the left of the `<P>` tag on the line that begins *There are many animals...* and key `<FONT SIZE="5">` to change the size of the following text.

3. Move the insertion point to the right of the word *else* in the middle of the following sentence, and key `<BR>` to insert a line break. Press **Enter** to move the following text to the next line.

4. Move the insertion point to the right of the `</P>` tag after the text *zoos!* and key the closing font tag `</FONT>`.

5. Move the insertion point to the left of the `<P>` tag at the beginning of the next line and key `<FONT SIZE="3" FACE="Arial">`. Key the closing `</FONT>` tag to the right of the `</P>` tag after the text *tour!*

6. Press **Enter** to start a new line and key `<HR>` to insert a horizontal rule.

7. Move the insertion point to the left of the `<P>` tag at the beginning of the next line and key `<FONT SIZE="4">`.

8. Move the insertion point to the right of the `</P>` tag at the end of the line (after the text *Aussie Animals.*) and press **Enter** to start a new line. Key `<HR>` to insert a horizontal rule.

9. Move the insertion point to the beginning of the next line and then key `<OL><LI>` to start the numbered list.

10. Move the insertion point to the beginning of the next line and key `<LI>`, then move it to the beginning of the next line and key `<LI>`.

STEP-BY-STEP 24.6 Continued

11. Move the insertion point to the right of the `</P>` tag at the end of the line with the text *Echidnas* and key `</OL></FONT>` to end the list and the font formatting. The file should look similar to the one in Figure 24-9.

FIGURE 24-9
Key tags to add formatting to a page

12. Save the changes to the file. Make your browser active and open the **an_index.html** file. It should look similar to Figure 24-10.

FIGURE 24-10
View the formatted page

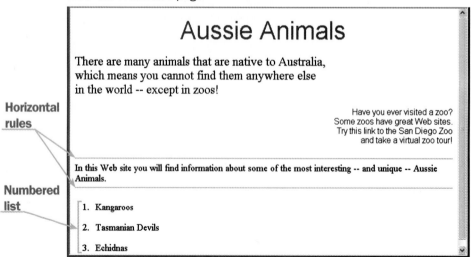

STEP-BY-STEP 24.6 Continued

13. If necessary, make corrections to your Web page in the text editor, save the changes, and preview the page again.

14. Minimize your browser, but leave it and your text editor open to use in the next exercise.

Create Consistent Web Pages

One of the key aspects of Web site design is to create an environment that helps visitors know that they are still on the same Web site no matter how many pages they visit in the site. To accomplish this, you should try to use a consistent design on all pages. The design can include the page structure, font formatting, language, and even design elements such as rules, graphics, and backgrounds. The consistency results in a "look and feel" that is carried through the entire site, making visitors feel comfortable and making it easy for them to navigate within the site. If you change the look and feel from page to page, the Web site becomes inconsistent, confusing, and it may end up being difficult to use.

One way to create new pages that have the same look and feel as existing pages is to use the File > Save As command in your text editor to save the existing .html page file with a new name, and then edit the text in the new file for the new page. This ensures that the tags you use on one page are also used on the new page. In this exercise, you will use the existing kangaroos.html page to create one page for Tasmanian Devils and another for Echidnas.

STEP-BY-STEP 24.7

1. Open the **kangaroos.html** file in the text editor.

2. Click **File** on the Menu bar and then click **Save As** to open the Save As dialog box.

3. Verify that the **Aussie Animals** folder is current and then key **devils.html** to replace the filename *kangaroos.* (Remember to key the filename extension.) Click **Save** to save the file with the new name.

4. In the Title text and the blue text, replace the word *Kangaroos* with **Tasmanian Devils**.

5. Replace the text *Red Kangaroo* with the text **Tasmanian Devil**.

6. Replace the paragraph that begins *The Red Kangaroo* and ends with *water.* with the following paragraph:

```
The Tasmanian Devil is the largest, meat-eating marsupial in Australia.
They are found only on the island of Tasmania and live in coastal scrub
and eucalyptus forests. They have very powerful jaws and sharp teeth.
They are fearful of people, but can be vicious with each other and other
animals. They get their name from the piercing scream they make when
fighting.
```

STEP-BY-STEP 24.7 Continued

7. Replace the text in the three items in the bulleted list with the following text:

```
Tasmanian Devils are nocturnal which means they sleep during the day.
Tasmanian Devils are scavengers that eat dead meat.
They are usually black with a white collar.
```

8. Save the changes to the file. Make your browser active and open **devils.html**. It should look similar to Figure 24-11.

FIGURE 24-11
Tasmanian Devils page

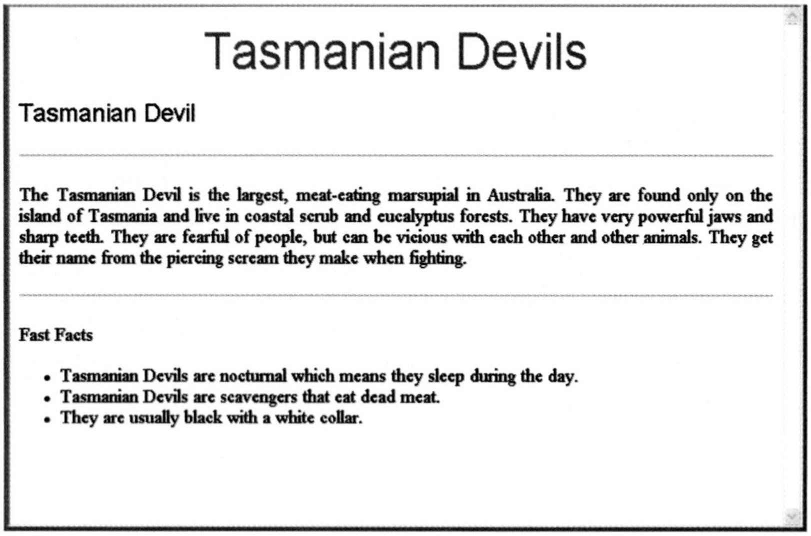

9. If necessary, make corrections to the page in the text editor, save the changes, and preview the page again.

10. Select **File** > **Save As** in your text editor and save the file as **echidnas.html**.

11. In the Title text and the blue text, replace *Tasmanian Devils* with **Echidnas**. On the next line of text, replace *Tasmanian Devil* with **Echidna**.

12. Replace the paragraph that begins *The Tasmanian Devil* and ends with *fighting.* with the following paragraph:

```
The Echidna is one of only two mammals in the world that lays eggs.
Echidnas have spiny quills like a porcupine, a pointy snout, and a long
sticky tongue like an anteater. They live all over Australia and can
survive in a wide range of temperatures and habitats.
```

13. Replace the text in the three items in the bulleted list with the following text:

```
Echidnas are nocturnal which means they sleep during the day.
Echidnas eat ants and termites.
A baby Echidna is called a puggle.
```

14. Save the changes to the file. Make your browser active and open the **echidnas.html** file. It should look similar to Figure 24-12.

STEP-BY-STEP 24.7 Continued

FIGURE 24-12
Echidnas page

Echidnas

Echidna

The Echidna is one of only two mammals in the world that lays eggs. Echidnas have spiny quills like a porcupine, a pointy snout, and a long sticky tongue like an anteater. They live all over Australia and can survive in a wide range of temperatures and habitats.

Fast Facts

- Echidnas are nocturnal which means they sleep during the day.
- Echidnas eat ants and termites.
- A baby Echidna is called a puggle.

15. If necessary, make corrections to the page in the text editor, save the changes, and preview the page again. Minimize your browser, but leave it and your text editor open to use in the next exercise.

Create Hyperlinks on Web Pages

Now that you have a set of four Web pages—an index, a page about kangaroos, a page about Tasmanian Devils, and a page about Echidnas—you can link them to form a Web site. To link the pages, you insert *hyperlinks*. Recall that a hyperlink is text or graphics that you click to go to a destination location. The way you set up hyperlinks determines the navigation system for your Web site. The *navigation system* is how hyperlinks are implemented to facilitate the way visitors browse from page to page in a Web site.

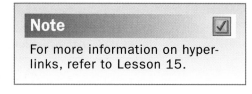

> **Note** ☑
>
> For more information on hyperlinks, refer to Lesson 15.

To define a hyperlink on a Web page, you use an anchor tag—<A> </A>—with an HREF attribute. The HREF attribute is the hyperlink reference. The value you key after the attribute is the name of the hyperlink destination file. If the pages are stored in the same folder, you can key only the filename and extension. If the pages are stored in different locations, you must key the full path.

Remember to use correct syntax when you key an anchor tag. You must follow the attribute (HREF) with an equals sign, and enclose the value (destination filename) in quotation marks. The text between the opening and closing anchor tags is formatted on the Web page as a hyperlink, which by default is usually a different color from the surrounding text and is underlined.

Once you define the link you should test it in your browser. If it works, the destination page displays. If it doesn't work, then either nothing happens or the wrong page displays. You must go back and edit the tag in the text editor to fix the link.

Link an Index Page to Topic Pages

In a hierarchical structure you should have links from the index page to the main categories, and then links from each category back to the index. In some Web site structures, you may have links from each page to the other pages, or a table of contents or navigation bar on each page to link to main topics or categories in the site.

In this exercise, you create links from the items in the numbered list on the an_index.html page to the three topic pages.

STEP-BY-STEP 24.8

1. Open the **an_index.html** file in your text editor.

   You want to format the text *Kangaroos* as a hyperlink, but not the number in the numbered list.

2. Position the insertion point to the left of the *K* in the word *Kangaroos* in the first item in the numbered list and key `<A HREF="kangaroos.html">`.

3. Move the insertion point to the right of the *s* in the word *Kangaroos* and key `</A>`, the closing tag.

4. Move the insertion point to the left of the *T* in the word *Tasmanian* in the second item in the numbered list and key `<A HREF="devils.html">`. Key the closing tag `</A>` to the right of the *s* in the word *Devils*.

5. Move the insertion point to the left of the *E* in the word *Echidnas* in the third item in the numbered list and key `<A HREF="echidnas.html">`. Key the closing tag `</A>` to the right of the *s* in the word *Echidnas*.

6. Save the changes to the file. Make your browser active and open **an_index.html**. It should look similar to Figure 24-13.

FIGURE 24-13
Index page with hyperlinks

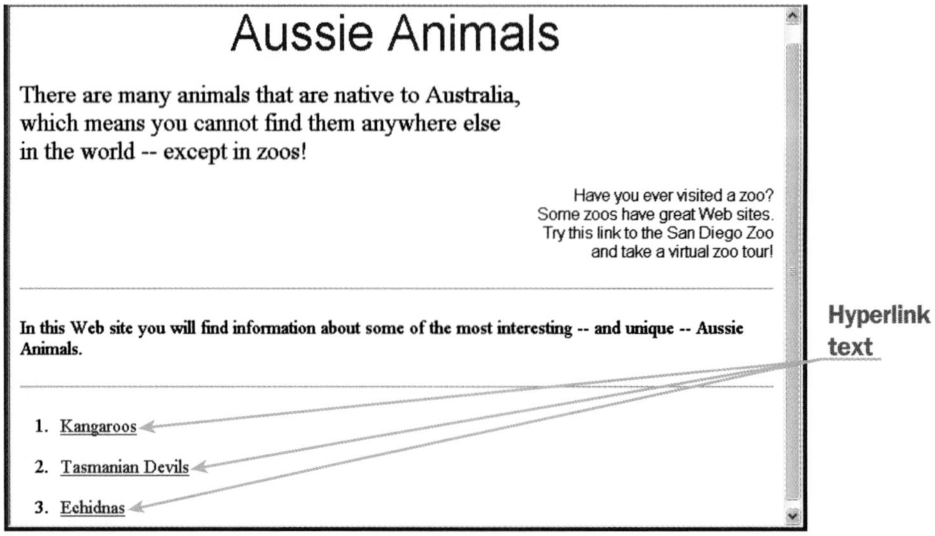

Hyperlink text

STEP-BY-STEP 24.8 Continued

7. If your index page does not appear similar to that shown in Figure 24-13, you may have keyed something incorrectly in your text editor, or you may have forgotten to save your changes. If this is the case, return to your text editor, correct any problems, and save the changes. Then return to your browser and refresh the **an_index.html** page.

8. Click the hyperlink text **Kangaroos**. The kangaroos.html page should display in your browser.

9. If necessary, edit an_index.html in your text editor to correct any problems and save the changes. Return to your browser, refresh the index page, and then test the link again.

10. Click **Back** on your browser's toolbar to return to the an_index.html page. Test the link to the devils.html page, return to the an_index.html page, and then test the link to the echidnas.html page.

11. If necessary, edit the an_index.html file in your text editor to correct any problems, save the changes, and test the links in your browser again. Return to your index page and minimize your browser. Leave the text editor open to use in the next exercise.

Link Topic Pages to an Index Page

Although you can usually use your browser's toolbar buttons to get back to previously viewed pages, it is important to make links available on all pages in your Web site to aid visitors in navigation. Determining the text to use as hyperlinks on the index page was fairly obvious—the topics were listed neatly on the page. Deciding what you want to use for hyperlink text on your topic pages, and where to position the hyperlinks, may require a bit more thought. You want to be sure the hyperlink text clearly indicates what will display when the visitor clicks the link so they do not have to guess where a link might lead. The text *Return* does not identify a specific location, whereas the text *Return to Home Page* does. In addition, the links should be visible and accessible, so visitors do not have to hunt around for them. Sometimes, you might even include more than one link to the same destination just to be sure the visitor can find it. A link to the home page, for example, may be at the top and at the bottom of a topic page.

In the following exercise, you insert a link to the an_index.html page at the bottom of each of the three topic pages. You will apply font formatting to the hyperlink text and will center it horizontally.

STEP-BY-STEP 24.9

1. Open the **kangaroos.html** file in your text editor.

2. Insert a blank line above the closing </BODY> tag near the end of the file, and then position the insertion point on the blank line.

3. Key the following:
```
<CENTER><FONT SIZE="4" FACE="Arial"><A HREF="an_index.html">Aussie
Animals Home</A></FONT></CENTER>
```

STEP-BY-STEP 24.9 Continued

4. Save the changes to the file. Make your browser active and click the hyperlink to the **kangaroos.html** page. It should look similar to Figure 24-14.

FIGURE 24-14
Hyperlink text added to the page

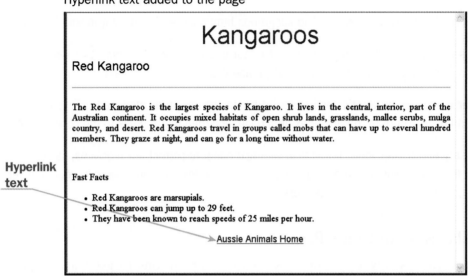

Hyperlink text

5. Click the link you created to the index page. The an_index.html page should display.

6. Return to your text editor and open the **devils.html** page. Repeat steps 2 through 4 to add the hyperlink to the page and test it in your browser.

7. Return to your text editor and open the **echidnas.html** page. Repeat steps 2 through 4 to add the hyperlink to the page and test it in your browser. You should now be able to go from the index page to each topic page, and from each topic page to the index page.

> **Hot Tip**
>
> Instead of rekeying all the text in step 3, you could select this text in the kangaroos.html file, copy it, and paste it into the other two files.

8. If necessary, edit the files in your text editor to correct any problems, save the changes, and test the links in your browser again. Leave your text editor open to use in the next exercise.

Link Your Web Site to Another Web Site

You can create hyperlinks from your Web pages to other Web pages on the Internet by keying the full URL path to the page in the anchor tag's HREF value. In this exercise, add a link to the San Diego Zoo's Web site to your an_index.html page.

STEP-BY-STEP 24.10

1. Open the **an_index.html** file in your text editor. Locate the text *Try this link to the San Diego Zoo and take a virtual tour!*

2. Position the insertion point to the left of the *S* in the word *San* and key:

```
<A HREF="http://www.sandiegozoo.org">
```

3. Move the insertion point to the right of the *o* in the word *Zoo* and key `</A>` the closing anchor tag.

4. Save the changes to the file. Make your browser active and refresh the **an_index.html** page.

5. Click the hyperlink text *San Diego Zoo.* If necessary, log on to the Internet. The home page of the San Diego Zoo Web site should display in your browser. Explore the site if you want.

6. Close your browser, log off the Internet, if necessary, and then close your text editor.

SUMMARY

In this lesson, you learned:

■ Most Web sites are organized using one of three basic structures, or a combination of any of the three: linear, hierarchical, or random.

■ You can use the <FONT> </FONT> tag to apply font formatting such as the font face, size, and color.

■ Some HTML tags require an attribute and a value in order to specify a property.

■ If a tag takes an attribute, you key the element, then the attribute, followed by an equals sign, and finally the value in quotation marks.

■ To set a font size, instead of keying a size in points you key a value ranging from 1, which is very small, to 7, which is large.

■ You can use the <CENTER> </CENTER> tag to center content on a Web page, or the <ALIGN> </ALIGN> tag to apply left-aligned, right-aligned, justified, or centered text to a paragraph.

■ You can use the <HR> tag to insert a horizontal rule on a Web page.

■ Horizontal lines help to organize information on Web pages.

■ You can use the <OL> </OL> tag to create a numbered—or ordered—list or the <UL> </UL> tag to create a bulleted—or unordered—list. Each item in the list must be preceded by the <LI> tag.

■ To maintain a look and feel throughout a Web site, you should create Web pages that have consistent layout and formatting.

■ One way to create consistent pages is to use your text editor's File > Save As command to save an .html Web page file with a new name, and then edit it to customize the content for a new page.

■ You can use the <A> </A> anchor tag to define a hyperlink on a Web page, and then use the HREF attribute to specify the destination Web page.

VOCABULARY *Review*

Define the following terms:

Attribute	Linear structure	Random access structure
Hierarchical structure	Navigation system	Value

REVIEW *Questions*

TRUE / FALSE

Circle T if the statement is true or F if the statement is false.

T   F   1. It is a good idea to select a site structure before you develop a site.

T   F   2. You can use the `<FACE> </FACE>` tag to apply font formatting.

T   F   3. On a Web page, all text must be between 1 point and 7 points in size.

T   F   4. An HTML tag element can have more than one attribute.

T   F   5. The `<CENTER>` tag does not require a closing tag.

T   F   6. The `<LI>` tag must precede items in both numbered lists and bulleted lists.

T   F   7. You can use your text editor's File > Save As command to create a copy of an .html text file.

T   F   8. If a hyperlink works when you test it in your browser, the Web site's home page displays.

T   F   9. You cannot apply font formatting to hyperlink text.

T   F   10. You can only link a Web page in your site to another Web page in your site.

WRITTEN QUESTIONS

Write a brief answer to each of the following questions.

1. What are the three basic structures used for most Web sites?

2. Name at least two reasons why you should try to use a consistent design on all pages in a Web site.

3. Name at least two things to consider when inserting hyperlinks on a Web page, and explain why each is important.

4. What are some common syntax errors that might cause a Web page to display incorrectly?

5. Name at least three ways you can make a text-only Web site more interesting and attractive to visitors.

FILL IN THE BLANK

Complete the following sentences by writing the correct word or words in the blanks provided.

1. A(n) _____ structured Web site is designed so that visitors view one page at a time, often in a specific order.

2. A(n) _____ is a term that describes the properties of a Web page element.

3. When you key a(n) _____ as part of an HTML tag, you must enclose it in quotation marks.

4. You can use the <P> </P> tag with the _____ attribute to justify text.

5. You can use the _____ tag to insert a horizontal line on a Web page.

6. You can use the _____ tag to create a bulleted list.

7. You can use the _____ tag to create a numbered list.

8. Using a consistent Web page design establishes a look and _____ for a Web site.

9. The _____ system is how hyperlinks are implemented to facilitate the way visitors browse from page to page in a Web site.

10. The value you key after the HREF attribute is the name of the hyperlink _____.

PROJECTS

PROJECT 24-1

In this project, you will create an index page for a hierarchical Web site for a realty office.

1. Use a file management program to create a folder named **Realty** where you can store the files for this project.

2. Start your text editor program. Save the text file as **realty_index.html**, and store it in the **Realty** folder you created in step 1.
   A. Click **File** on the Menu bar and then click **Save As**.
   B. Navigate to the **Realty** folder.
   C. In the *File name* text box, key **realty_index.html** to replace the default filename.
   D. Click the **Save** button.

3. Key the following lines:
```
<HTML>
<HEAD><TITLE>Clearview Realty</TITLE></HEAD>
<BODY>
<CENTER><FONT SIZE="7" FACE="Impact" COLOR="Green">Clearview
  Realty</FONT><BR>
<FONT SIZE="4" FACE="Arial" COLOR="Green">4141 Main Street<BR>
Framingham, MA 01701<BR>
(508) 555-5555</FONT><BR>
<FONT SIZE="5" FACE="Impact" COLOR="Green"><P>"Bringing Your Dreams into
  Focus"</P></FONT></CENTER>
<HR>
<HR>
<FONT SIZE="4" FACE="Arial"><P ALIGN="Justify">At Clearview Realty we work
  for the buyer, not the seller. Our staff is knowledgeable, professional,
  and hard-working. Our mission is to find you a home at the best possible
  price in the shortest amount of time. Call Clearview today and move in
  tomorrow!</P>
<OL><LI><P>Rentals</P>
<LI><P>Homes for Sale</P>
<LI><P>General Information</P></OL></FONT>
</BODY>
</HTML>
```

4. Save the changes to the file.

5. Make your browser active and open the **realty_index.html** file.
   A. Click **File** on the Menu bar and then click **Open**.
   B. Click the **Browse** button.
   C. Navigate to the **Realty** folder.
   D. Select the **realty_index.html** file and then click the **Open** button.
   E. Click the **OK** button in the Open dialog box.

6. Examine the page for errors, including spelling mistakes.

7. If the page does not display correctly—for example, if there are missing line breaks, alignments run together, or font sizes are too large or too small—make the text editor active and

look for missing tags, missing characters such as the slash in closing tags, the equals sign after attributes, and the quotation marks around values.

8. Make corrections as necessary, save the changes, and preview the page again.

9. Minimize your browser, but leave it and your text editor open to use in the next project.

PROJECT 24-2

In this project, you will create three Web pages for your realty Web site. To create a consistent look and feel, you will create the first page using some of the same formatting characteristics you used in the realty_index.html file. You will then use the File > Save As command to create the other two pages.

1. Click **File** on the Menu bar and then click **New** to create a new file in your text editor program. Save the text file as **rentals.html**, and store it in the **Realty** folder you created in Project 24-1.

2. Key the following lines:

```
<HTML>
<HEAD><TITLE>Clearview Realty: Rentals</TITLE></HEAD>
<BODY>
<CENTER><FONT SIZE="7" FACE="Impact" COLOR="Green">Rental
Information</FONT><BR></CENTER>
<HR>
<HR>
<FONT SIZE="4" FACE="Arial"><P ALIGN="Justify">Contact Clearview Realty for
help finding a home to rent. We have realtors who specialize in rentals, so
they are not distracted by selling homes. They all have intimate knowledge
of the area and the surrounding communities and they know what is available.
We have listings in all price ranges and all categories.</P>
Click a link for more information:
<UL><LI><P>Apartments</P>
<LI><P>Houses</P></UL></FONT>
<HR>
<HR>
<CENTER><FONT SIZE="6" FACE="Impact" COLOR="Green">Call Clearview today and
move in tomorrow!</FONT><BR>
<FONT SIZE="4" FACE="Arial" COLOR="Green">(508) 555-5555</FONT></CENTER>
</BODY>
</HTML>
```

3. Save the changes to the file, make your browser active, and open the **rentals.html** file.

4. Examine the page for errors, including spelling mistakes.

5. If the page does not display correctly—for example, if there are missing line breaks, alignments run together, or font sizes are too large or too small—make the text editor active and look for missing tags, missing characters such as the slash in closing tags, the equals sign after attributes, and the quotation marks around values.

6. Make corrections as necessary, save the changes, and preview the page again.

7. Display the **rentals.html** page in your text editor and then use the File > Save As command to save it as **sales.html**.
   A. Click **File** on the Menu bar and then click **Save As**.
   B. Navigate to the **Realty** folder.
   C. In the *File name* text box, key **sales.html** to replace *rentals*.
   D. Click the **Save** button.

8. Replace the text *Rentals* in the title and *Rental* in the first text line with the text **Sales**.

9. Replace the paragraph of text beginning *Contact Clearview Realty for help...* with the following paragraph:

   Contact Clearview Realty for help finding a home to buy. Our agents work for you, not for the seller. They are familiar with this town as well as the surrounding communities. They can find you a house or condo in any style and price range. They can access all listings in the state, and they do the legwork so you don't have to!

10. In the bulleted list replace the text *Apartments* with the text **Condos**.

11. Add a new item to the bulleted list as follows:
    A. Position the insertion point between the closing `</P>` tag and the closing `</UL>` tag on the last line of the list.
    B. Press **Enter** to start a new line.
    C. Key `<LI><P>New Construction</P>`.

12. Save the changes to the file, make your browser active, and open the **sales.html** file.

13. Examine the page for errors, including spelling mistakes. If the page does not display correctly, make the text editor active and look for missing tags, missing characters such as the slash in closing tags, the equals sign after attributes, and the quotation marks around values.

14. Make corrections as necessary, save the changes, and preview the page again.

15. Display the **sales.html** page in your text editor and then use the File > Save As command to save it as **info.html**.

16. Replace the text *Sales* in the title with the text **General Information**. Replace the text *Sales Information* in the first text line with the text **General Information**.

17. Replace the paragraph of text beginning *Contact Clearview Realty for help...* with the following paragraph:

    Clearview Realty offers professional sales and rental services. All agents are board-certified and can provide you with confidential, high-quality assistance locating your next home. We understand the market, we are familiar with the area, and we know how to make a deal.

18. Replace the items in the bulleted list as follows:
    A. Replace the text *Condos* with the text **About Our Agents**.
    B. Replace the text *Houses* with the text **About the Local Area**.
    C. Replace the text *New Construction* with the text **Listings**.

19. Save the changes to the file, make your browser active and open the **info.html** file.

20. Examine the page for errors, including spelling mistakes. If the page does not display correctly make the text editor active and look for missing tags, missing characters such as the slash in closing tags, the equals sign after attributes, and the quotation marks around values.

21. Make corrections as necessary, save the changes, and preview the page again.

22. Minimize your browser, but leave it and your text editor open to use in the next project.

PROJECT 24-3

In this project you will create links between the realty Web site index page and the three topic pages. You will create a new folder for storing the linked files. You may use the files you created in Projects 24-1 and 24-2, or you may use the data files provided.

1. Use a file management program to create a new folder named **CVSite**.

2. In your text editing program, open **realty_index.html** or open **Project24-3a**. Save the file as **cvsite_index.html** in the **CVSite** folder you created in step 1.

3. Open **rentals.html** or open **Project24-3b**. Save the file as **cvrentals.html** in the **CVSite** folder.

4. Open **sales.html** or open **Project24-3c**. Save the file as **cvsales.html** in the **CVSite** folder.

5. Open **info.html** or open **Project24-3d**. Save the file as **cvinfo.html** in the **CVSite** folder.

6. Open the **cvsite_index.html** file in your text editor.

7. Position the insertion point to the left of the *R* in *Rentals* in the numbered list and key `<A HREF="cvrentals.html">`.

8. Move the insertion point to the right of the *s* in *Rentals* and key `</A>`, the closing tag.

9. Move the insertion to the left of the *H* in the word *Homes* in the second item in the numbered list and key `<A HREF="cvsales.html">`. Key the closing tag `</A>` to the right of the *e* in the word *Sale*.

10. Move the insertion point to the left of the *G* in the word *General* in the third item in the numbered list and key `<A HREF="cvinfo.html">`. Key the closing tag `</A>` to the right of the last *n* in the word *Information*.

11. Save the changes and open the **cvsite_index.html** file in your browser. Test the links, using the **Back** button on your browser's toolbar to return to the **cvsite_index** page. If necessary, edit the file in the text editor to correct any problems and test the links again.

12. Open the **cvrentals.html** file in your text editor.

13. Position the insertion point after the opening `<BODY>` tag and press **Enter** to start a new line. On the new line, key `<FONT SIZE="4" FACE="Arial" COLOR="Green"><A HREF="cvsite_index.html">HOME</A></FONT>`.

14. Save the changes and open the **cvrentals.html** file in your browser. Click the **HOME** link in the upper-left corner of the page. The cvsite_index page should display. If necessary, edit the file in the text editor to correct any problems and test the link again.

15. Open the **cvsales.html** file in your text editor and repeat steps 13 and 14 to create a hyperlink to the **cvsite_index.html** page.

16. Open the **cvinfo.html** file in your text editor and repeat steps 13 and 14 to create a hyperlink to the **cvsite_index.html** page.

17. Test all of the links in your Web site and make corrections to the text files as necessary. When you are satisfied that the links work correctly. Close your browser and your text editor.

 WEB PROJECT

An effective Web site captures a viewer's attention, provides useful information, and makes it easy and intuitive to navigate from one page to another. In this exercise, use your Web browser to examine and compare at least three Web sites. Create a table or spreadsheet where you can record your observations comparing the sites. Select the features you want to compare, such as type of structure, ease of navigation, access to useful information, how quickly the pages download, the use of color, and the use of multimedia.

Select the sites you are going to compare. You may want to select different types, such as one commercial site, one educational site, and one government site, or you may want to compare three of the same type. Next, examine each home page and record the comparison information in your table. Test links to other pages and continue recording your information. When you are finished, review the information you have gathered. Write a report of at least 500 words explaining what you think makes a Web site effective or ineffective. Use examples from your research to support your opinion.

 TEAMWORK PROJECT

As a team, plan and create a Web site for your school's Math department. Decide the content you want to include, such as general information, a class list, and a list of instructors. You might even want to include a "problem of the day." Select enough topics so that there is at least one page for each team member to create. Once you have decided on the content, select the structure you are going to use. Finally, decide the type of formatting you want to use so that you can have a consistent look and feel throughout the site. For example, agree on a font for headings and one for body text. Decide whether you want to use color, horizontal rules, and different alignments.

Working together, create a folder for storing all of the files for the Web site. Then, design and create an index or home page. You may want to sketch it on paper before you begin working in your text editor. Use the formatting you agreed on and include the text that you will link to the other pages. Check the page in your browser frequently, and correct errors as you work. When the page is complete, split up and create your individual topic pages, using the same look and feel that you agreed on. Check your page in your browser as you work. When you are satisfied, ask a classmate to check your page for errors.

Get back together as a team and create the hyperlinks from the main page to the topic pages, and from the topic pages back to the main page. Check the Web site in your browser to make sure all of the links work. Ask your classmates to review the site.

CRITICAL*Thinking*

For your English or Language Arts class, plan and create a Web site about an author. You should include at least three pages in the site—a main or index page and at least two topic pages. The main or index page should include general information and provide links to the other pages. The other pages should provide information about books the author has written.

When you are ready, create the folder that you will need to store your files and then use your text editor to create the main page. Use the formatting tags covered in this lesson to create a look and feel for your site. Include the text that you plan to hyperlink to the other pages. Save and check the page in your browser as you work. When the main page is complete, create a page about one of the author's books. Use similar formatting as on the main page in order to maintain the look and feel of the site. Include the text you plan to link back to the main page. Save and check the page in your browser as you work. When the page is complete, use the File > Save As command in your text editor to create another page for the site. Edit the content for a different book. In this manner, create as many pages as you want in your site.

Edit the files in the text editor to create the hyperlinks. Make sure you link the main page to each of the other pages, and each page back to the main page. Test all of the links in your browser and make corrections as necessary until they function properly. When you are finished, ask your classmates to access and use your Web site. If they have suggestions for improving it, edit the text files and test the site again.

ENHANCING WEB PAGES

OBJECTIVES

Upon completion of this lesson, you should be able to:

- Apply custom colors to Web page text, backgrounds, rules, and links.
- Embed, size, and align graphics on a Web page.
- Format a graphic as a hyperlink.
- Embed animations, audio, and video on a Web page.

Estimated Time: 2 hours

VOCABULARY

Active content

Inline graphics

Nested tags

A text-only Web page might provide information, but it might also be boring, and a boring Web page will not attract visitors. You have already seen that you can use standard colors with the `<FONT> </FONT>` tag to make a Web page more appealing. You can also customize colors for fonts, backgrounds, horizontal rules, and hyperlinks. Other ways to spice up a Web page include inserting multimedia content, such as graphics, animations, video, and audio. Multimedia—when used appropriately—can bring a page to life. It can deliver your message in an exciting and vibrant format and make visitors want to return to your Web site time and time again.

In this lesson, you add custom colors to a Web page. You also learn how to add graphics, audio, video, and animations to the page.

Apply Custom Colors to Web Page Components

One way to create an appealing look and feel for a Web site is to develop a *color scheme*. Recall that a color scheme is a set of coordinated colors that you apply to different components in a document. As explained in Lesson 24, you can use the COLOR attribute with the `<FONT> </FONT>` tag to change the color of text. You can also apply color to other Web page components, including all text on a page, the page background, horizontal rules, and hyperlinks.

> **Note** ☑
>
> For more information, about hexadecimal values, refer to Lesson 1. For more information about working with color, refer to Lessons 5 (graphics), 13 (presentations), or 21 (publications).

To apply a standard color, such as red, blue, or green, key the color name as the value in quotation marks. When you want to use a custom color, you can specify a *hexadecimal code* as the value. Recall that hexadecimal codes use 16 characters—0, 1, 2, 3, 4, 5, 6, 7, 8, 9, A, B, C, D, E, and F—to define colors based on their components of red, green, and blue.

When you experiment with color, keep in mind that people will be viewing the page on-screen in a browser. For that reason you should select the colors carefully and make sure they work well together. For example, dark-colored text on a dark background may be difficult to read. Also, using too many different colors may make a site confusing, or just plain ugly. Also, in some cases, overlapping colors may not display the way you expect.

Apply Color to All Text on a Page

You can apply the same color to all text on a page using the TEXT attribute in the <BODY> </BODY> tag.

Note

Hyperlink color is not controlled by the same tags as other text. You learn to change hyperlink color later in this lesson.

STEP-BY-STEP 25.1

In this exercise, you will create a new home page for the Australian Animals Web site, and apply color to the text.

1. Use a file management program such as Windows Explorer to create a new folder named **Animals Site** where you can store the files for this lesson.

2. Launch your text editor and open the file **Step25-1** from the data files for this lesson. Save it as **aus_home.html** in your **Animals Site** folder.

Note

There are blank lines in the html file to make it easier to see the code. Blank lines do not affect the way the page displays in a browser.

3. Launch your Web browser and open the **aus_home.html** page. If you are using Internet Explorer, click **File** on the menu bar, click **Open**, click **Browse**, navigate to the **Animals Site** folder, select the **aus_home.html** page, click **Open**, and then click **OK**. It should look similar to Figure 25-1.

FIGURE 25-1
A plain-text Web page

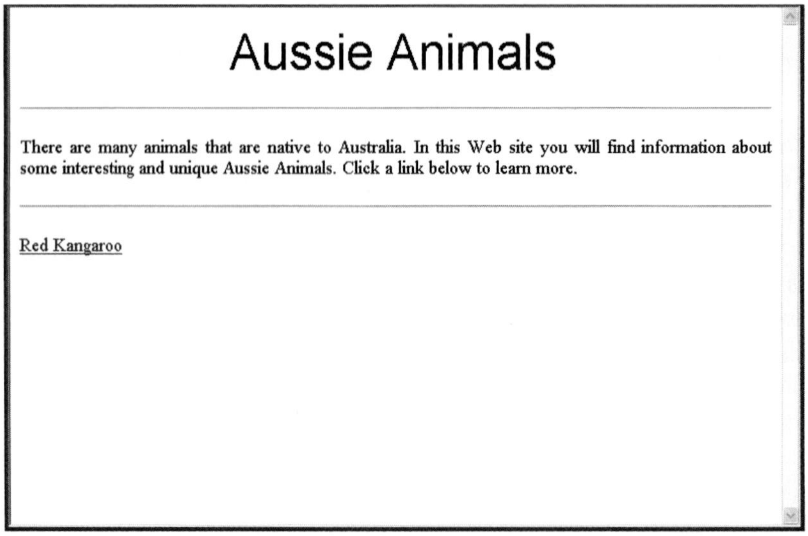

Aussie Animals

There are many animals that are native to Australia. In this Web site you will find information about some interesting and unique Aussie Animals. Click a link below to learn more.

Red Kangaroo

STEP-BY-STEP 25.1 Continued

4. Minimize your browser and switch to your text editor.

5. Position the insertion point between the Y and the right angle bracket in the opening <BODY> tag. Press the spacebar and then key **TEXT="green"**.

6. Save the changes and restore your browser window. Refresh the page. It should look similar to Figure 25-2.

FIGURE 25-2
Apply the same color to all text

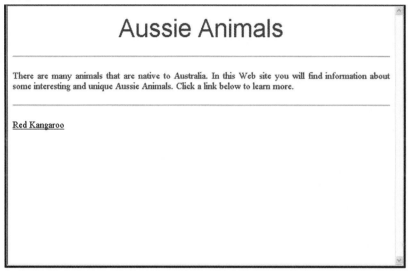

7. Minimize your browser. In the text file, replace the value *green* with the hexadecimal code **#669900**.

8. Save the changes and restore your browser window. Refresh the page. The color changes slightly to a custom green.

9. Minimize your browser but leave it and your text editor open to use in the next exercise.

Apply Color to Selected Text

To customize the color of selected text, key the hexadecimal value with the COLOR attribute in the <FONT> </FONT> tag.

Extra for Experts

All 216 *Web-safe colors*—which are colors that display the same in different browsers—can be defined using combinations of the same six pairs of hexadecimal codes: 00, 33, 66, 99, CC, and FF. For example, #0000FF is the code for a standard blue; #FF00FF is the code for a standard pink, and #FFFF00 is the code for a standard yellow. For more information on Web-safe colors, refer to Lesson 5.

STEP-BY-STEP 25.2

1. Position the insertion point between the quotation marks after the text *Arial* and the right angle bracket at the end of the first opening <FONT> tag.

2. Press the spacebar and key **COLOR="#663300"**.

3. Save the changes and restore your browser window. Refresh the page. The color of the text *Aussie Animals* should be brown, as shown in Figure 25-3.

FIGURE 25-3
Customize the color of selected text

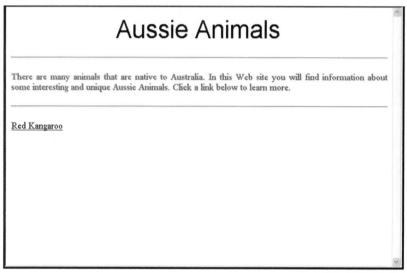

4. Minimize your browser but leave it and your text editor open to use in the next exercise.

Change the Background Color

By default, a Web page background is white. You can quickly enhance a Web page by applying a colored background. Use the BGCOLOR attribute with the <BODY> </BODY> tag to change the background color.

> **Note**
>
> Many Web pages use graphics as a background. You learn how to apply a graphic background in Lesson 27.

STEP-BY-STEP 25.3

1. Position the insertion point between the quotation marks after the hexadecimal code *#669900* and the right angle bracket at the end of the opening <BODY> tag.

STEP-BY-STEP 25.3 Continued

2. Press the spacebar and key **BGCOLOR="#CCCC99"**.

3. Save the changes and restore your browser window. Refresh the page. The background color should look similar to Figure 25-4.

FIGURE 25-4
Customize the background color

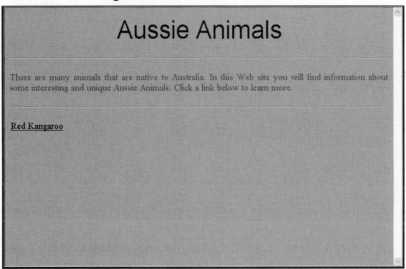

4. Minimize your browser but leave it and your text editor open to use in the next exercise.

Change the Color of Horizontal Rules

You can use the COLOR attribute with the <HR> tag to customize the color of a horizontal rule.

STEP-BY-STEP 25.4

1. Position the insertion point between the *R* and the right angle bracket in the first <HR> tag.

2. Press the spacebar and key **COLOR="#663300"**. (This is the same brown you applied to the text *Aussie Animals*.)

3. Position the insertion point between the *R* and the right angle bracket in the second <HR> tag, press the spacebar and key **COLOR="#663300"**.

STEP-BY-STEP 25.4 Continued

4. Save the changes and restore your browser window. Refresh the page. The rules should look similar to Figure 25-5.

FIGURE 25-5
Customize the color of horizontal rules

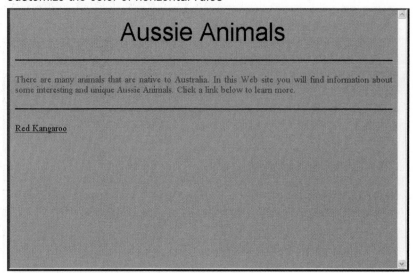

> # Aussie Animals
>
> _____
>
> There are many animals that are native to Australia. In this Web site you will find information about some interesting and unique Aussie Animals. Click a link below to learn more.
>
> _____
>
> Red Kangaroo

5. Minimize your browser but leave it and your text editor open to use in the next exercise.

Change the Color of Hyperlink Text

You can customize the color of hyperlink text using the LINK, VLINK, and ALINK attributes with the <BODY> </BODY> tag. The LINK attribute controls the color of the text before the link is clicked, and the VLINK attribute controls the color of the text after the link is clicked, or *visited*. The ALINK attribute controls the color of the link during the click.

STEP-BY-STEP 25.5

1. Position the insertion point between the quotation marks after the hexadecimal code *CCCC99* and the right angle bracket at the end of the opening <BODY> tag.

2. Press the spacebar and key **LINK="#336600" VLINK="#3399CC" ALINK="#33FF00"**.

3. Save the changes and restore your browser window. Refresh the page. It should look similar to Figure 25-6.

Note	

The link does not point to a valid page, yet. If you click it, a message displays in your browser telling you that the page cannot be found. You will create the destination page in an exercise later in this lesson.

STEP-BY-STEP 25.5 Continued

FIGURE 25-6
Customize the color of the hyperlink text

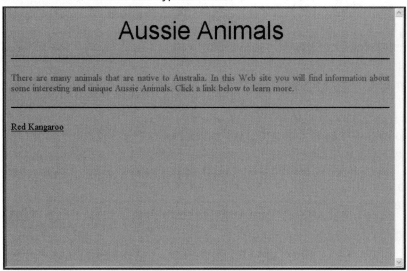

4. Minimize your browser but leave it and your text editor open to use in the next exercise.

Insert Graphics on a Web Page

You have seen in other units in this book that graphics can make almost any document more interesting, more informative, and more appealing. The same is true for Web pages. You can insert any graphics file on a Web page, including GIF and JPEG files. You can specify a size for the image, and position it relative to the surrounding text.

Insert and Size a Picture on a Web Page

To insert a graphics file on a Web page you use the <IMG> tag with the SRC attribute. IMG is short for image, and SRC is short for source. The value for the SRC attribute is the path to the source graphics file. Pictures are inserted in their actual size by default, but you can use the HEIGHT and WIDTH attributes with the <IMG> tag to change the size. You specify the value in pixels.

Extra for Experts

Most browsers keep track of visited pages in a History file. If a link displays in the VLINK color, you can purge the history file to see it in the LINK color. In Internet Explorer, click **Tools** on the menu bar, click **Internet Options**, click the **Clear History** button, and then click **OK**.

Note

For information on graphics file types, refer to Lesson 1.

To stay organized and to be sure that the visitor's browser will be able to locate graphics files, it is a good idea to store them in a folder named something like *Images* or *Graphics* that is a subfolder of the main folder you created for storing the Web site files. By keeping all files used in the

Web site in the same folder, you can easily move the entire folder when necessary without having to update all of the paths on all of the Web pages.

S TEP-BY-STEP 25.6

1. Use a file management program to create a folder named **Images** in the **Animals Site** folder.

2. Copy the graphics file **Step25-6** from the data files for this lesson to the **Images** folder, and rename it **Roo**. If necessary key the **.gif** file extension as well.

3. Switch to your text editor. Position the insertion point on the blank line below the second <HR> tag, above the linked text *Red Kangaroo*.

4. Key **<IMG SRC="Images/Roo.gif">**.

5. Save the changes and restore your browser window. Refresh the page. It should look similar to Figure 25-7.

FIGURE 25-7
Insert a picture on a Web page

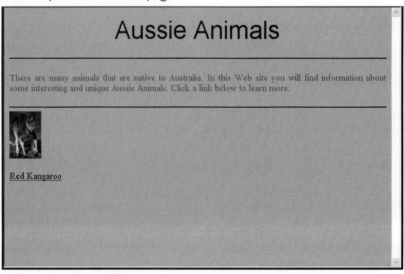

6. In the **aus_home.html** file, position the insertion point between the closing quotation marks and the right angle bracket in the <IMG> tag, press the spacebar and key **HEIGHT="102" WIDTH="75"**.

7. Save the changes and restore your browser window. Refresh the page. The picture should increase slightly in size.

8. Minimize your browser but leave it and your text editor open to use in the next exercise.

Align Graphics

If you want to integrate a picture on the same line as text, you must *nest* the <IMG> tag within the <P></P> tag that encloses the text. A nested tag is placed within another set of opening and closing tags. The nested tag is affected by the elements and attributes in the outer, nesting tag. (You used nested tags when you centered a paragraph in Lesson 24.)

By default, images are *inline* with the text, which means positioned along the same line as the text, with its baseline aligned with the text baseline. You can use the ALIGN attribute with the value "middle" to shift the picture so that the text aligns with the middle of the picture. Use the value "top" to align the text with the top of the picture.

Hot Tip

Use the ALIGN attribute in the <IMG> tag with the value "right" to right-align a picture on a Web page, or use the <CENTER> </CENTER> tag to center it on the page.

STEP-BY-STEP 25.7

1. In the **aus_home.html** file, click and drag to select the complete <IMG> tag. Click **Edit** on the menu bar and then click **Cut** to cut the selection to the Clipboard.

2. Move the insertion point down one line, and position it between the right angle bracket of the opening <P> tag and the left angle bracket of the opening <A> tag. Click **Edit** on the menu bar and then click **Paste** to paste the selection into the file, nested within the <P> </P> tag. The line should look like:

```
<P><IMG SRC="Images/Roo.gif" HEIGHT="102" WIDTH="75"><A HREF="roos.html">
Red Kangaroo</A></P></FONT>.
```

3. Save the changes and restore your browser window. Refresh the page. The picture should be inline with the text, as shown in Figure 25-8.

FIGURE 25-8
Position a picture inline with text

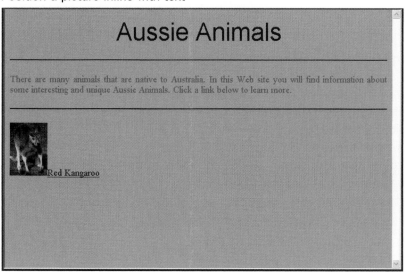

STEP-BY-STEP 25.7 Continued

4. In the **aus_home.html** file, position the insertion point between the closing quotation marks after the WIDTH value *"75"* and the right angle bracket of the IMG tag. Press the space bar and key **ALIGN="middle"**.

5. Save the changes and restore your browser window. Refresh the page. The middle of the picture should align with the text, as shown in Figure 25-9.

FIGURE 25-9
Align the middle of the picture with the text

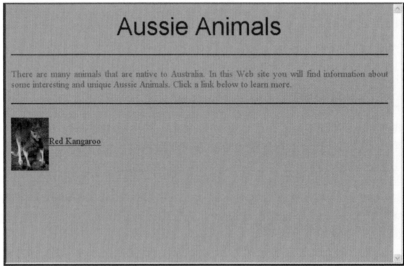

6. Minimize your browser but leave it and your text editor open to use in the next exercise.

Format a Graphic as a Hyperlink

You can easily format a picture as a hyperlink on a Web site using the same anchor tag that you use to format text as a hyperlink. Instead of enclosing the hyperlink text in the <A> </A> tag, just nest the <IMG> tag. You can even format both text and a graphic using the same <A> </A> tag.

Usually, a picture formatted as a hyperlink displays a thin border in the LINK—or VLINK, if the link has been clicked—color. You can use the BORDER attribute with the <IMG> tag to specify a width for the border. The value is measured in pixels.

> **Hot Tip**
>
> Use the BORDER attribute in the <IMG> tag to insert a border around any picture on a Web page, even one that is not a hyperlink.

S TEP-BY-STEP 25.8

1. In the **aus_home.html** file, click and drag to select the complete **<IMG>** tag. Click **Edit** on the menu bar and then click **Cut** to cut the selection to the Clipboard.

2. Move the insertion point to the right and position it between the right angle bracket of the opening <A> tag and the letter *R* in the text *Red*.

3. Click **Edit** on the menu bar and then click **Paste** to paste the selection, nested within the <A> </A> tag. The line should look like:

```
<P><A HREF="roos.html"><IMG SRC="Images/Roo.gif" HEIGHT="102" WIDTH="75"
ALIGN="middle">Red Kangaroo</A></P></FONT>
```

4. Position the insertion point between the closing quotation marks after the value *"middle"* and the right angle bracket, press the spacebar and key **BORDER="5"**.

5. Save the changes and restore your browser window. Refresh the page. The picture should now be formatted as a hyperlink, with a 5-pixel border, as shown in Figure 25-10.

FIGURE 25-10
Format a picture as a hyperlink

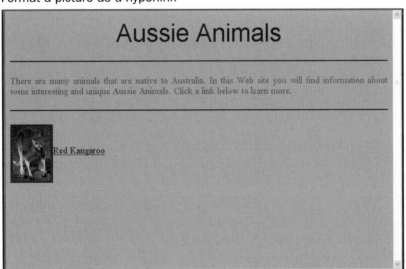

6. Rest the mouse pointer on the picture. It should change to the link pointer—a hand with a pointing finger. (Do not click the link, yet. It still does not point to a valid destination.)

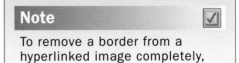

Note ☑

To remove a border from a hyperlinked image completely, set the BORDER value to "0".

7. Minimize your browser but leave it and your text editor open to use in the next exercise.

Embed Animations, Audio, and Video

People expect the Web to be lively and entertaining. If you want them to visit your Web page, you can use *active content* to bring the page to life. Active content includes elements that change, or that allows the visitor to interact with the Web page. For example, you can embed a flying logo animation to identify a sponsor or to add humor to a page. Place a video on a page to provide live-action information such as a product demonstration. Use music or sound to entertain or inform.

One of the simplest ways to embed active content on a Web page is to use the <EMBED> tag. It can be used with animations, video, and sound. Like the <IMG> tag, it uses the SRC attribute to identify the source file, the HEIGHT and WIDTH attributes to specify the size of the object on the page, and the ALIGN attribute to position the animation relative to the surrounding text.

You should also set up folders in your main Web site folder for storing the different types of multimedia files. As with graphics files, it will help you keep the files organized, make sure the visitor's browser will be able to locate the source files when it needs them, and make it easy to move the files if necessary.

As you add active content to your page, keep in mind that there are a few reasons you should not rely on the multimedia content to deliver your message, but rather use it to enhance the text on the Web page.

> **Note**
>
> If a visitor's browser cannot display active content, a red X in a frame displays in its place. You can use the ALT attribute with the <EMBED> tag to insert alternative text in place of the active content.

- Not all browsers will display the content the same way. The security settings may block the display of active content, or the browser may not support the HTML tags that you used to define the Web page.

- Not all systems will have the necessary hardware and software to play animations, video, or music.

- Too much of a good thing may become distracting or even annoying. Some people listen to music or talk on the phone while using the Internet. They may not appreciate a page that automatically plays music.

- Active content may significantly increase the size of your Web page, which may affect the download speed. Most people do not like to wait, and will move on to another page if it takes too long for the content to display in a browser.

> **Note**
>
> If a browser's security level is set so that it will not play active content by default, usually when a page that contains embedded active content loads, the browser displays a dialog box or security bar asking the viewer if it is OK to display the content. If you trust the source, you can follow the prompts to display the content.

Embed an Animation on a Web Page

You can insert an animated GIF file using the <IMG> tag that you use to insert regular GIF files. An animated GIF usually plays continuously on the Web page, without stopping. You can embed an .swf Flash animation file using the <EMBED> tag. Recall that the .swf file is the file generated from the completed animation, that you test and preview in the Flash Player

> **Did You Know?**
>
> *ActiveX* is a technology developed by Microsoft to enable active content on Web pages. It is widely used on the World Wide Web.

window. Most personal computers have the Flash Player installed, so Flash animations play correctly in most browsers. Flash animations play once by default when the page displays or when the page is refreshed.

> **Note** ☑
>
> For more information on Macromedia Flash, refer to Lessons 6, 7, and 8.

When you use the <EMBED> tag, at a minimum you must use the SRC attribute to identify the animation file. You can also use the HEIGHT and WIDTH attributes to specify the size of the animation on the page, and the ALIGN attribute to position the animation relative to the surrounding text.

STEP-BY-STEP 25.9

In this exercise, you will insert an animated GIF file on the aus_home.html page, and then replace it with a Flash animation.

1. Use a file management program to create a folder named **Animations** in the **Animals Site** folder.

2. Copy the animated GIF file **Step25-9a** and the Flash .swf file **Step25-9b** from the data files for this lesson to the **Animations** folder. Rename *Step25-9a* to **Hop** (if necessary, key the **.gif** file extension) and rename *Step25-9b* to **Flag** (if necessary, key the **.swf** file extension).

3. Switch to your text editor, position the insertion point between the right angle bracket after the <P> opening tag and the letter *A* in the word *Aussie Animals.* Key **<IMG SRC="Animations/Hop.gif">**.

4. Save the changes and restore your browser window. Refresh the page. The animated GIF of a hopping kangaroo should display to the left of the text *Aussie Animals.*

5. Minimize your browser. In the text editor, click and drag to select the <IMG> tag you inserted in step 3, and key **<EMBED SRC="Animations/Flag.swf" HEIGHT="175" WIDTH="200" ALIGN="middle">**.

STEP-BY-STEP 25.9 Continued

6. Save the changes and restore your browser window. Refresh the page. If necessary, click the warning bar that displays across the top of the page, click the option to allow blocked content, and then click **Yes**. An animation of an Australian flag with the text Aussie Animals should display to the left of the text Aussie Animals. When the animation completes, the page should look similar to Figure 25-11.

FIGURE 25-11
Embed an animation

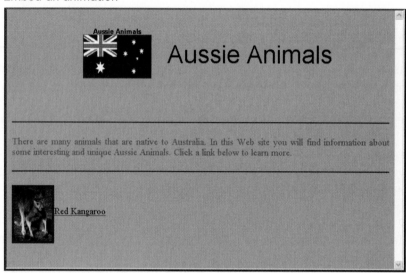

7. Minimize your browser but leave it and your text editor open to use in the next exercise.

Embed Sound on a Web Page

You can use the <EMBED> tag to insert a sound file on a Web page. Sound is a touchy subject when it comes to Web pages, because some people may not want to hear it. They may be in an office or classroom environment, where the sound might disturb others, or they may be listening to something else instead. They also might not have the necessary hardware to play sound, such as a sound card and speakers, or their browser may be set not to play active content. If you want, you can use the AUTOSTART and the CONTROLLER attributes to give visitors the option of playing the sound or not.

The AUTOSTART attribute determines whether the sound will play automatically when the page displays. You set the value to "true" if you want the sound to play, or "false" if you do not want it to play. The CONTROLLER attribute lets you insert a console with control buttons on the page. Visitors can use the buttons to start, stop, or pause the sound, and even to adjust the volume. You should also set the HEIGHT and WIDTH attributes in order to specify the size of the console on the page.

> **Note**
>
> You may also be able to use the HIDDEN attribute to show or hide the control buttons on the page. Set the value to "true" to hide the controls, or to "false to show the controls.

STEP-BY-STEP 25.10

In this exercise, you will insert a sound file that plays didgeridoo music. (A didgeridoo is a native Australian instrument.) You will start the music automatically, but display the controls so the visitor has the option of stopping the music at any time. You will position the controls in the bottom-right corner of the page so they are not obtrusive.

1. Use a file management program to create a folder named **Audio** in the **Animals Site** folder.

2. Copy the music file **Step25-10** from the data files for this lesson to the Audio folder. Rename it to **Music** (if necessary, key the **.aif** file extension).

3. Switch to your text editor, position the insertion point on the line with the hyperlinked image and text, between the letter o in the text *Kangaroo* and the left angle bracket before the </A> closing tag.

4. Key **<EMBED SRC="Audio/Music.aif" AUTOSTART="true" CONTROLLER="console" HEIGHT= "50" WIDTH="144" ALIGN="right">**. The text file should look similar to Figure 25-12.

FIGURE 25-12
The aus_home.html file

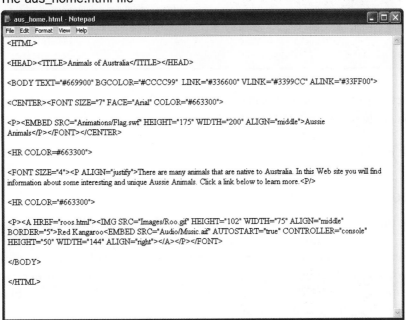

STEP-BY-STEP 25.10 Continued

5. Save the changes and restore your browser window. Refresh the page. If a dialog box prompting you to run an ActiveX control displays, click **OK** to continue. The music should start automatically, and the controls should display in the lower-right corner of the page, as shown in Figure 25-13.

FIGURE 25-13
Display sound controls

6. Use the controls to pause, start, and stop the sound. (You may have to click twice, or press **Enter** or the spacebar to make the controls active.)

7. Minimize your browser but leave it and your text editor open to use in the next exercise.

Embed Video on a Web Page

You can use the <EMBED> tag to insert a video on a Web page. Like audio files, you can select whether to play the video automatically, and whether to display controls. Keep in mind that some computers may not have the software and hardware required to display video in a browser, or may not be compatible with the video you embed on the page. If a browser cannot display the video, it may display a placeholder icon, or it may display the controls with a black background. In some cases, the video may display without the controls.

In this exercise, you will create a page about kangaroos for the Web site, and insert a video on it. You will also link the page to the home page.

S TEP-BY-STEP 25.11

1. Use a file management program to create a folder named **Video** in the **Animals Site** folder.

2. Copy the video file **Step25-11a** from the data files for this lesson to the **Video** folder. Rename it to **Scratch** (if necessary, key the **.mpg** file extension).

3. In your text editor, open the text file **Step25-11b** from the data files for this lesson and save it as **roos.html** in the **Animals Site** folder.

4. In the **roos.html** file, position the insertion point between the left angle bracket after the `<FONT SIZE="4">` opening tag and the letter *T* at the beginning of the word *The*.

5. Key **<EMBED SRC="Video/Scratch.mpg" AUTOSTART="false" CONTROLLER="console" HEIGHT= "200" WIDTH="200" ALIGN="right">**.

6. Save the changes and restore your browser window. Open the **roos.html** page. If necessary, click the warning bar that displays across the top of the page, click the option to allow blocked content, and then click **Yes**, or, if a dialog box prompting you to run an ActiveX control displays, click **OK** to continue. The first frame of the video and the video controls should display to the right of the paragraph, as shown in Figure 25-14. Some browsers may not display the controls.

FIGURE 25-14
Video with controls

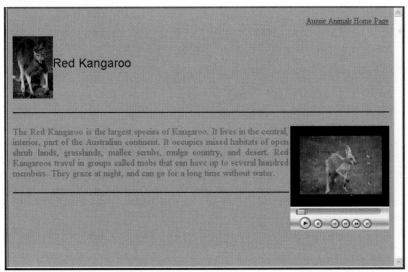

7. Click the **Play** button in the video controls to play the video. (You may have to click twice, or press **Enter** or the spacebar to make the controls active.) If the controls do not display in your browser, press the spacebar to start the video.

Note ☑
In some browsers, the video object may become smaller when it finishes playing.

STEP-BY-STEP 25.11 Continued

8. When the video finishes, click the **Aussie Animals Home Page** link in the upper-right corner of the page. The **aus_home.html** page should display in your browser. Again, if you are prompted to run an ActiveX control, click **OK** to continue. You may click the **Stop** button to stop the audio if you want.

9. Click the picture of the kangaroo. The **roos.html** page should display in your browser. Notice that the hyperlink color is different, now that the link has been clicked.

10. If necessary, make corrections to the code in the **roos.html** page and the **aus_home.html** page in your text editor, save the changes, and test the pages in your browser again.

11. When the pages are complete, close your browser and your text editor.

> **Extra for Experts**
>
> The steps in this lesson illustrate a very basic method of using the `<EMBED>` tag to insert animation, audio, and video on a Web page. There are many other attributes that you can use to control and position the multimedia content, and there are other tags for inserting active content, such as the `<OBJECT>` tag. If you are interested in learning more, there are many Web sites that can provide more information.

SUMMARY

In this lesson, you learned:

■ You can apply color to many Web page components, including text, backgrounds, horizontal rules, and links.

■ You can create custom colors by using hexadecimal codes.

■ You can use the `<IMG>` tag to insert graphics on a Web page.

■ You should store the files you insert or embed on a Web page in folders created for the specific type of file. For example, you should store graphics in an *Images* folder, music in an *Audio* folder, animations in an *Animations* folder, and movies in a *Video* folder.

■ You can use the HEIGHT and WIDTH attributes to specify the size of a graphic, animation, or video on a page.

■ If you want to integrate a picture, animation, or video on the same line as text, you must place the `<IMG>` tag within the `<P>` `</P>` tag with the text.

■ You can use the ALIGN attribute to adjust the position of a picture, animation, video, or sound controls in relation to the surrounding text.

■ You can turn a graphic into a hyperlink. To modify the look of the link, you can change the border width.

■ You can use the `<EMBED>` tag to insert multimedia files on a Web page.

- When you embed an audio or video file, you may want to set the AUTOSTART attribute to "false" so that the sound does not play automatically.

- You can display audio or video controls using the CONTROLLER attribute so the visitor can choose whether or not to play the file.

VOCABULARY *Review*

Define the following terms:

Active content	Inline graphic	Nested tags

REVIEW *Questions*

TRUE / FALSE

Circle T if the statement is true or F if the statement is false.

T F 1. You can use the BGCOLOR attribute with the <FONT> </FONT> tag to change the background color of a page.

T F 2. All horizontal rules on a Web page must be black.

T F 3. The LINK attribute controls the color of hyperlink text before the link is clicked.

T F 4. You can only insert GIF formatted graphics on a Web page.

T F 5. The value for the SRC attribute identifies the path to the source file.

T F 6. You can format a picture as a hyperlink.

T F 7. Animated GIF files usually play continuously on a Web page in a browser.

T F 8. Set the AUTOSTART attribute to "false" if you do not want a sound or video to play automatically when the Web page displays.

T F 9. All computers have the software and hardware required to display video in a browser.

T F 10. You can change the alignment of graphics, animations, and videos on a Web page.

WRITTEN QUESTIONS

Write a brief answer to each of the following questions.

1. What are four types of multimedia content you can place on a Web page?

2. Name at least two problems that might arise from adding color to a Web page.

3. Explain how to keep multimedia files used in a Web site organized, and why it is important.

4. What are some reasons people might not appreciate sound on a Web page?

5. Explain how to use the ALIGN attribute to position graphics in relation to the surrounding text.

FILL IN THE BLANK

Complete the following sentences by writing the correct word or words in the blanks provided.

1. Key the _____ code as the value for the COLOR attribute to create a custom color on a Web page.

2. The _____ attribute controls the color of hyperlink text after the link has been clicked.

3. Values entered for the HEIGHT and WIDTH attributes are measured in _____.

4. By default, images are inserted _____ with the text, which means positioned along the same line as the text.

5. In most browsers, the _____ attribute determines whether controls for playing sound or video display on the page.

6. If you want to integrate a picture on the same line as text, you must _____ the `<IMG>` tag within the `<P>` `</P>` tag that encloses the text.

7. You can use the BORDER attribute with the `<IMG>` tag to specify a(n) _____ for the border that displays around a graphic.

8. The _____ tag can be used to place animations, video, and sound on a Web page.

9. _____ animations play once by default when the page displays or when the page is refreshed.

10. If a browser cannot display a video, it may display a(n) _____ icon.

PROJECTS

PROJECT 25-1

In this project, you will add color to a home page for a realty office.

1. Use a file management program to create a folder named **Project 25-1** where you can store the file for this project.

2. Start your text editor program and open the file **Project25-1**. Save the file as **cv_home.html**, and store it in the **Project 25-1** folder you created in step 1.

3. Launch your Web browser and open the **cv_home.html** page to see what it looks like. It has no color, except for the hyperlinked text, which is the default blue.

4. Minimize your browser and make the **cv_home.html** page active in your text editor.

5. Position the insertion point between the *Y* and the right angle bracket in the `<BODY>` opening tag.

6. Press the spacebar and key **BGCOLOR="#0099FF"**.

7. Save the changes and restore your browser window. Refresh the page. The background color should be a custom blue.

8. Switch to your text editor. With the insertion point still to the left of the right angle bracket in the opening `<BODY>` tag, press the spacebar and key **LINK="#FFFF00" VLINK="#00FF00" ALINK="#FF9900"**. The complete opening `<BODY>` tag should look like:

```
<BODY BGCOLOR="#0099FF" LINK="#FFFF00" VLINK="#00FF00" ALINK="#FF9900">
```

9. Save the changes and restore your browser window. Refresh the page. The unclicked hyperlink color should be yellow. (The link does not yet point to a valid destination. If you click it, the message displays that the page cannot be found. Click the **Back** button on your browser's toolbar to return to the home page.)

10. Switch to your text editor. Position the insertion point between the right angle bracket and the quotation marks after the value *"Impact"* in the first opening `<FONT>` tag (that formats the text *Clearview Realty*). Press the spacebar and key **COLOR="#FF9966"**.

11. Move the insertion point between the right angle bracket and the quotation marks after the value "Impact" in the third opening <FONT> tag (that formats the text *Bringing Your Dreams into Focus*). Press the spacebar and key **COLOR="#FFFF00"**.

12. Position the insertion point to the left of the right angle bracket in the first <HR> tag, press the spacebar and key **COLOR="#FFFF00"**.

13. Repeat step 12 to apply the color to the second <HR> tag.

14. Save the changes and restore your browser window. Refresh the page. The company name should be in a custom orange, and the tag line and the two horizontal rules should be in the same yellow as the unclicked hyperlink text.

15. If the page does not display correctly, make the .html file active and make corrections as necessary. The file should look like the following:

```
<HTML>
<HEAD><TITLE>Clearview Realty</TITLE></HEAD>
<BODY BGCOLOR="#0099FF" LINK="#FFFF00" VLINK="#00FF00" ALINK="#FF9900">
<CENTER><FONT SIZE="7" FACE="Impact" COLOR="#FF9966">Clearview
Realty</FONT><BR>
<FONT SIZE="4" FACE="Arial">4141 Main Street<BR>
Framingham, MA 01701<BR>
(508) 555-5555</FONT><BR>
<FONT SIZE="5" FACE="Impact" COLOR="#FFFF00"><P>"Bringing Your Dreams into
Focus"</P></FONT></CENTER>
<HR COLOR="#FFFF00">
<HR COLOR="#FFFF00">
<FONT SIZE="4" FACE="Arial"><P ALIGN="Justify">At Clearview Realty we work
for the buyer, not the seller. Our staff is knowledgeable, professional,
and hard-working. Our mission is to find you a home at the best possible
price in the shortest amount of time. Call Clearview today and move in
tomorrow!</P>
<P><A HREF="cvsales.html">Homes for Sale</A></P></FONT>
</BODY>
</HTML>
```

16. Save the changes, and preview the page again.

17. Minimize your browser, but leave it and your text editor open to use in the next project.

PROJECT 25-2

In this project, you will add an animation and a sound to a version of the **cv_home.html** file. You will use the HIDDEN attribute to hide the audio control buttons.

1. Use a file management program to create a folder named **Project 25-2** where you can store the files for this project. In the folder, create one folder named **Animation** and another folder named **Audio.**

2. Copy the .swf animation file **Project25-2a** from the data files for this lesson to the **Animation** folder. Rename it **cv_logo** (key the **.swf** file extension if necessary).

3. Copy the .wav sound file **Project25-2b** from the data files for this lesson to the **Audio** folder. Rename it **cv_sound** (key the **.wav** file extension if necessary).

4. In your text editor, open the text file **Project25-2c** from the data files for this lesson and save it as **cv_home2.html** in the **Project 25-2** folder.

5. Position the insertion point to the left of the first <CENTER> opening tag and key **<EMBED SRC="Animation/cv_logo.swf">**.

6. Click and drag to select the opening <CENTER> tag. Click **Edit** on the menu bar and then click **Cut** to cut it to the Clipboard.

7. Move the insertion down to the left of the second opening <FONT> tag (formatting the address). Click **Edit** on the menu bar and then click **Paste** to paste the <CENTER> tag into the file.

8. Save the changes and open the **cv_home2.html** page in your browser. If necessary, click the warning bar that displays across the top of the window, click the option to display blocked content, and then click **Yes**, or click **OK** in the dialog box prompting you to play ActiveX controls. The animation should display to the upper left of the company name. The address text should still be centered.

9. Switch to your text editor. Position the insertion point on the blank line above the <EMBED> tag you inserted in step 5 and key **<EMBED SRC="Audio/cv_sound.wav" AUTOSTART="true" HIDDEN="true">**.

10. Save the changes and restore your browser window. Refresh the page. The sound file should play applause. No controls should display.

11. If the page does not display correctly, make the .html file active and make corrections as necessary. The text file should look like the following:

```
<HTML>
<HEAD><TITLE>Clearview Realty</TITLE></HEAD>
<BODY BGCOLOR="#0099FF" LINK="#FFFF00" VLINK="#00FF00" ALINK="FF9900">
<EMBED SRC="Audio/cv_sound.wav" AUTOSTART="true" HIDDEN="true">
<EMBED SRC="Animation/cv_logo.swf"><FONT SIZE="7" FACE="Impact"
COLOR="#FF9966">Clearview Realty</FONT><BR>
<CENTER><FONT SIZE="4" FACE="Arial">4141 Main Street<BR>
Framingham, MA 01701<BR>
(508) 555-5555</FONT><BR>
<FONT SIZE="5" FACE="Impact" COLOR="#FFFF00"><P>"Bringing Your Dreams into
Focus"</P></FONT></CENTER>
<HR COLOR="#FFFF00">
<HR COLOR="#FFFF00">
<FONT SIZE="4" FACE="Arial"><P ALIGN="Justify">At Clearview Realty we work
for the buyer, not the seller. Our staff is knowledgeable, professional, and
hard-working. Our mission is to find you a home at the best possible price in
the shortest amount of time. Call Clearview today and move in tomorrow!</P>
<P><A HREF="cv_sales.html">Homes for Sale</A></P></FONT>
</BODY>
</HTML>
```

12. Save the changes, and preview the page again.

13. Minimize your browser, but leave it and your text editor open to use in the next project.

PROJECT 25-3

In this project you will add graphics and video to a Web page, and you will link it to a home page. You must start by organizing all of the files you need for the Web site.

1. Use a file management program to create a new folder named **Project 25-3** where you can store the files for this project. In the folder, create one folder named **Images**, one named **Video**, one named **Animation**, and one named **Audio**.

2. Copy the .gif graphics file **Project25-3a** from the data files for this lesson to the **Images** folder. Rename it **house** (key the **.gif** file extension if necessary).

3. Copy the .mpg video file **Project25-3b** from the data files for this lesson to the **Video** folder. Rename it **video** (key the **.mpg** file extension if necessary).

4. Copy the .swf animation file **Project25-3c** from the data files for this lesson to the **Animation** folder. Rename it **cv_logo** (key the **.swf** file extension if necessary).

5. Copy the .wav sound file **Project25-3d** from the data files for this lesson to the **Audio** folder. Rename it **cv_sound** (key the **.wav** file extension if necessary).

6. Open the text file **Project25-3e** from the data files for this lesson, and save it as **cv_home3.html** in the **Project 25-3** folder.

7. Open the text file **Project25-3f** from the data files for this lesson, and save it as **cv_sales.html** in the **Project 25-3** folder. (This file contains embedded links to the animation and audio files.)

8. Position the insertion point between the right angle bracket at the end of the opening <A> tag and the letter *H* in the text *HOME*, and then key:
   <IMG SRC="Images/house.gif" HEIGHT="100" WIDTH="100" ALIGN="middle" BORDER="3">.

9. Move the insertion point down to the next blank line, and key:
   <EMBED SRC="Video/video.mpg" HEIGHT="200" WIDTH="200" AUTOSTART="false" CONTROLLER="console" ALIGN="right">.

10. Save the changes and open the **cv_sales.html** page in your browser. If necessary, click the warning bar that displays across the top of the window, click the option to display blocked content, and then click **Yes**, or click **OK** in the dialog box prompting you to play ActiveX controls. The picture should display as a hyperlink in the upper-left corner of the page, and the video with controls should display—but not play—on the right side of the page. Your browser may not display the controls.

11. Click the **Play** button on the video controls to play the video. You may have to click twice, or press **Enter** or the spacebar first to activate the controls. If the controls are not available, press the spacebar to start the video. When the video is finished, test the link to the *Home* page, and from the *Home* page, test the link back to the *Sales* page.

12. If the page does not display correctly, make the .html file active in your text editor and make corrections as necessary. The **cv_sales** text file should look like the following:

```
<HTML>
<HEAD><TITLE>Clearview Realty: Sales</TITLE></HEAD>
<BODY BGCOLOR="#0099FF" LINK="#FFFF00" VLINK="#00FF00" ALINK="#FF9900">
<FONT SIZE="4" FACE="Arial" COLOR="#FF9966"><A HREF="cv_home3.html"><IMG
SRC="Images/house.gif" HEIGHT="100" WIDTH="100" ALIGN="middle"
BORDER="3">HOME</A></FONT>
<EMBED SRC="Video/video.mpg" HEIGHT="200" WIDTH="200" AUTOSTART="false"
CONTROLLER="console" ALIGN="right">
<CENTER><FONT SIZE="7" FACE="Impact" COLOR="#FF9966">Sales
Information</FONT><BR></CENTER>
<HR COLOR="#FFFF00">
<HR COLOR="#FFFF00">
<FONT SIZE="4" FACE="Arial"><P ALIGN="Justify">Contact Clearview Realty for
help finding a home to buy. Our agents work for you, not for the seller.
They are familiar with this town as well as the surrounding communities.
They can find you a house or condo in any style and price range.  They can
access all listings in the state, and they do the legwork so you don't have
to!</P>
<HR COLOR="#FFFF00">
<HR COLOR="#FFFF00">
<CENTER><FONT SIZE="6" FACE="Impact" COLOR="#FFFF00">Call Clearview today
and move in tomorrow!</FONT><BR>
<FONT SIZE="4" FACE="Arial" COLOR="#FFFF00">(508) 555-5555</FONT></CENTER>
</BODY>
</HTML>
```

13. Save the changes, and preview the page again.

14. Close your browser and your text editor.

 ## WEB PROJECT

Respecting intellectual property as well as ownership of copyrighted material is an important part of using the Web. There are many sites that make material available for free, some that ask you to reference the source, and others that ask you to pay a fee to use content that you find online. In this project, use the Internet to research the issue of copyrights on the Web. You should be able to find legal information, as well as opinions from different sources about what should be copyrighted and how people can respect copyrights. Using the information you gather, form your own opinion. Write a report of at least 500 words explaining the issues and your position. Do not forget to cite your sources!

 ## TEAMWORK PROJECT

As a team, plan and create a Web site for your school's Science department. (If you created a Web site for the Math department in Lesson 24, you may want to use it as a basis for the new site, or you may want to improve the Math site by adding color and multimedia content.) Choose the content you want to include, such as general information, a class list, and a list of instructors. Select enough topics so that there is at least one page for each team member to create. Once you have decided on the content, select the structure you are going to use. Finally, decide on the type of formatting you want to use so that you can have a consistent look and feel throughout the site. For example, agree on a font for headings and one for body text. Agree on a color scheme, and look up the hexadecimal codes for the colors you want to use. Decide whether you want to use color, horizontal rules, or different alignments.

Locate or create multimedia files that you can use, such as pictures of the instructors, students, or facilities, or an animation that has something to do with science. If possible, you might record a video of a class, a lab, or a student explaining a science project to include.

Working together, create a folder for storing all of the files for the Web site. Remember to create separate folders for the different types of multimedia files. Then, design and create an index or home page. Use the formatting you agreed on and include the text that you will link to the other pages. Insert any multimedia files that you want on the home page. Check the page in your browser frequently, and correct errors as you work.

When the page is complete, split up and create your individual topic pages, using the same look and feel that you agreed on. Again, insert multimedia files as necessary. Check your page in your browser as you work. When you are satisfied, ask a classmate to check your page for errors.

Get back together as a team and create the hyperlinks from the main page to the topic pages, and from the topic pages back to the main page. Check the Web site in your browser to make sure all of the links work. Ask your classmates to review the site.

CRITICAL*Thinking*

Embellish the Web site you created in Lesson 24 for your English or Language Arts class about an author. (If you did not complete the project, start from scratch.) Develop a color scheme and apply it to the pages in your site. Locate or create multimedia content that you can add to the site, such as a picture of the author or of the book covers. You might record yourself or a classmate reading a selection from one of the books, and then insert the sound file on a page, or you might want to record a video. Remember to store the multimedia files in appropriately named folders in the main Web site folder. You may want to experiment with different alignments for graphics and animations, and try hiding and showing controls for sound and video. Preview the pages in your browser frequently, and make corrections and improvements as you work. Remember to test all of the links in your browser. When you are finished, ask your classmates to access and use your Web site. If they have suggestions for improving it, edit the text files and test the site again.

WORKING IN A WEB SITE DESIGN PROGRAM

Keying HTML tags into a text file provides you with a great deal of control over the development of a Web page. It is also a time-consuming job that requires strong attention to detail. Luckily, there are Web site development programs such as Macromedia Dreamweaver and Microsoft Office FrontPage that let you develop Web sites without keying any HTML code unless you want to. Using a Web site development program frees you from the necessity of focusing on the syntax of HTML code so that you can spend your time developing exciting and attractive Web pages.

> **Note**
>
> If you do not have an HTML editing program, you can still complete the exercises in this lesson by keying the code in your text editor.

In this lesson you learn the basics of how to use a Web site development program to create a Web site. The figures show the Macromedia Dreamweaver 8 program interface, but steps are provided for both Dreamweaver 8 and Microsoft Office FrontPage 2003. If you are using a different program, the steps may be different, but the basic concepts should be similar.

Explore Your Web Site Design Software

When you first start your Web site development program, you will notice that it is much more like other application programs than it is like a text editor. For example, if you use Dreamweaver you will recognize the similarity of the workspace to other Macromedia programs, including Fireworks and Flash. If you use FrontPage, you will see that the program window is similar to Microsoft's other Office programs, such as PowerPoint and Publisher. Both programs have menus and toolbars as well as panels or task panes that you can use to access the features you need to develop your Web site. You can customize the workspace to display the tools you need, and you can change the view to see the HTML source code.

Use the Web Site Design Window

Most Web site development programs start in Design view, with a new blank HTML file open in the document window, or they display a Start screen from which you can select to open an existing file or create a new one. *Design view* is the view you use to enter and format content in a Web page without keying code. The blank file is usually named something like Untitled-1 or new_page_1. The workspace usually has features that are similar to other programs, such as a document window, title bar, and Menu bar. In addition they have panels, toolbars, and task panes that are specific to developing Web sites. You can usually customize the workspace to display the tools you need using the commands on the View or Window menu. You can usually show or hide different panels or task panes, rulers, grids, and guides and in some programs you can collapse and expand panels.

STEP-BY-STEP 26.1

In this exercise, you launch your HTML editing program and practice customizing the workspace by expanding the document window, toggling the ruler and grids, and displaying the options for working with behaviors. *Behaviors* are codes that allow visitors to interact with the Web page.

1. Click the **Start** button on the Windows taskbar, click **All Programs**, open the folder that contains your program, and then click the program name to launch your Web design software. Your program may display a Start page, a blank document window, the most recently used Web page or Web site, or a new blank document in the document window. If a new blank document displays in the document window, skip to step 3. If a recently used page or site displays, close it (click **File** on the Menu bar and then **Close** to close a page, or **Close Site** to close a Web site).

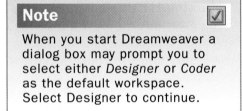

Note ☑

When you start Dreamweaver a dialog box may prompt you to select either *Designer* or *Coder* as the default workspace. Select Designer to continue.

2. If necessary, select the command to create a new blank HTML document. In Dreamweaver, Click **File** on the Menu bar, click **New**, choose the **General** tab if necessary, click **Basic page** in the *Category* column, click **HTML** in the *Basic page* column, and then click **Create**. In FrontPage, click **File** on the Menu bar and then click **New** to display the New task pane. Click **Blank page**. A new, blank document displays in the document window, as shown in Figure 26-1. Your program may display a different workspace.

Hot Tip ⊚

If the Start page displays in Dreamweaver, simply click HTML under Create New to create a new HTML document.

STEP-BY-STEP 26.1 Continued

FIGURE 26-1
The default Dreamweaver workspace

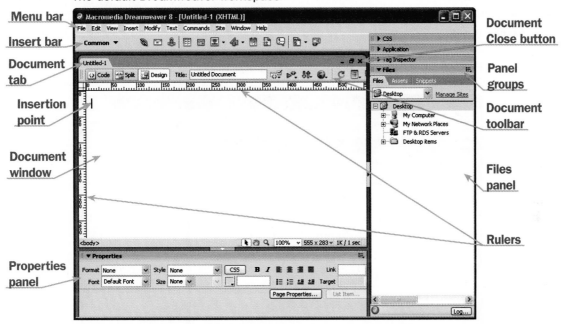

3. Expand the document window area. In Dreamweaver, click the right-pointing expand arrow on the right side of the document window to hide the panel groups, or in FrontPage, click the **Close** button in the task pane.

4. Select the command to toggle the ruler display off, if necessary. (In Dreamweaver, the rulers usually display by default, whereas in FrontPage they do not.) Click **View** on the Menu bar, click a command such as **Rulers** or **Ruler and Grid**, and then click **Show** or **Show Ruler**.

5. Select the command to toggle the grid on. For example, click **View** on the Menu bar, click **Grid** or **Ruler and Grid**, and then click **Show** or **Show Grid**.

STEP-BY-STEP 26.1 Continued

6. Select the command to display options for working with behaviors. In Dreamweaver, click **Window** on the Menu bar, then click **Behaviors** to display the Behaviors panel. In FrontPage, click **Format** on the Menu bar and then click **Behaviors** to display the Behaviors task pane. Your display should look similar to Figure 26-2.

FIGURE 26-2
Customize the workspace

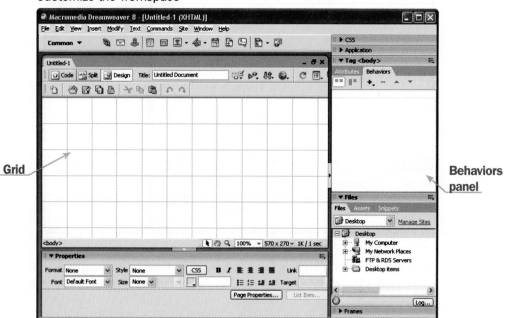

7. Close the Behaviors panel or task pane, expand the document window to the right, toggle the grid off, and display the rulers.

8. Leave your Web site development program open to use in the next exercise.

Open an Existing Web Page and View the Code

You can easily open an existing HTML Web page document in your HTML editing program using the File > Open command. Simply click File on the Menu bar and then click Open to display the Open File dialog box. Navigate to the location of the Web page document, select the page, and then click Open. In some programs, you can click the Open button on a toolbar to display the Open File dialog box.

The page opens looking similar to the way it looks in a browser. To view the HTML source code, you can switch to Code view. *Code view* displays the HTML tags the way you see them in a text editor. You can edit the tags in Code view. Most programs also have a *Split view* that lets you display Design view and Code view in the same document window with one view on the top half of the screen and the other on the bottom half. Usually, you click a button such as *Code* to change to Code view, Design to change back to *Design* view, and *Split* to display both at the same time. In Dreamweaver, the view buttons are on the Document toolbar across the top of the document window; in FrontPage, they are in the lower-left corner of the window.

When you are finished working with the document, you can use the File > Close command or the document's Close button to close it.

S TEP-BY-STEP 26.2

1. In your Web site development program, click **File** on the Menu bar, and then click **Open**.

2. Navigate to the folder where the Data files for this lesson are stored, and select the **Step26-2** HTML file. Click the **Open** button. The page opens in the document window in Design view. It should look similar to Figure 26-3.

FIGURE 26-3
Web page in Design view

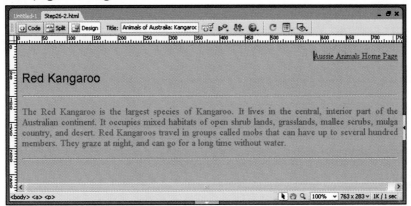

3. Click the **Code** button to change to Code view. If necessary, collapse the Properties panel so you can see the entire file. It should look similar to Figure 26-4. Notice that each line is numbered along the left side of the window to help you identify the location of the content. Also notice that certain items display in different colors. For example, tags and attributes may display in dark blue or red, values may be bright blue, and hyperlinks may be green.

FIGURE 26-4
Web page in Code view

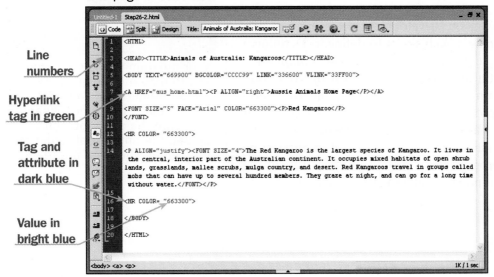

STEP-BY-STEP 26.2 Continued

4. Click the **Split** button to change to Split view. Most programs display Code view on the top half of the screen, and Design view on the bottom half, as shown in Figure 26-5.

FIGURE 26-5
Web page in Split view

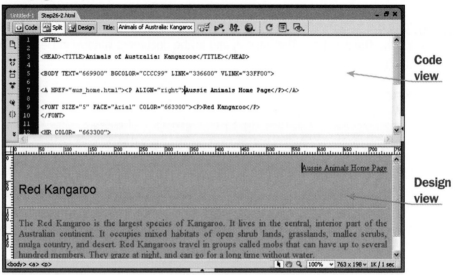

5. Click the **Design** button to change to Design view.

6. Click the **Close** button in the upper-right corner of the document window, or click **File** on the Menu bar and then click **Close** to close the Web page.

7. Close the blank, unnamed document, as well. Leave your Web site development program open to use in the next exercise.

Define a Web Site

In most Web site development programs the first step in developing a Web site is to define it. Defining a site gives the site a name and identifies—or *maps*—the path to the main site folder stored locally on your computer. The main folder may be called the *root level folder*. Some programs will create the root level folder automatically, but you may want to create it manually using a file management program, or select an existing folder. Some programs also create subfolders for storing content such as images and a blank index page.

> **Note**
>
> Your program may also prompt you to map a corresponding remote folder on a Web file server, but it is not necessary to create the site. You can upload the entire root folder to the server when you are ready.

Define a New Web Site

You usually define a Web site by selecting a command such as Site > New Site or by selecting a Web site template in the New task pane and then following the prompts to name and/or locate the root level folder. Once you define the site, the folder and its contents display onscreen in a panel such as Files or Folder List.

S TEP-BY-STEP 26.3

In this exercise, you create a folder named *My Aussie Web Site* and then use your Web site development program to define it as a Web site. If you are using Dreamweaver, you will create and save a new index page for the site.

1. Use a file management program such as Windows Explorer to create a new folder named **My Aussie Web Site** in the location where you plan to store the solutions for this lesson.

2. In your Web site development program, select the command to create a new Web site. In Dreamweaver, click **Site** on the Menu bar, and then click **New Site** to display the Site Definition dialog box. Click the **Basic** tab, if necessary, to display the Basic options. In FrontPage, click **File** on the Menu bar, click **New** to display the New task pane, and then click **One page Web site** to display the Web Site Templates dialog box. Skip to step 4.

3. In the Site Definition dialog box replace the text *Unnamed Site 1* with the name **My Aussie Web Site**. Leave the http:// address blank, and then click **Next**. Click to select the option **No, I do not want to use server technology**, and then click **Next**. If necessary, select the option **Edit local copies on my machine...**.

4. Click the command to locate the root level folder. If you are using Dreamweaver, click the folder icon next to the path to the default storage location to open the *Choose local root folder* dialog box. If you are using FrontPage, click the **Browse** button in the Web Site Templates dialog box to open the New Web Site location dialog box.

5. Navigate to the location of the *My Aussie Web Site* folder, select the folder, and click **Open**. In Dreamweaver, click **Select** to return to the Site Definition dialog box and continue with step 6. In FrontPage, click **OK** to define the site, creating a private subfolder and an images subfolder and an index Web page. Leave your Web design program open, but skip the rest of this exercise.

STEP-BY-STEP 26.3 Continued

6. In Dreamweaver, click **Next**. Click the **How do you connect to your remote server?** drop-down arrow and then click **None**. Click **Next**. The Summary page should look similar to Figure 26-6.

FIGURE 26-6
Site Definition Summary page

7. Click **Done**. Dreamweaver creates the site and displays it in the Files panel. Leave your Web site development program open to use in the next exercise.

Add a Page to a Site

You can use the File > New command to add pages to your site at any time. To add a new page to a Web site, use a command such as New on the File menu, or click a New toolbar button to display the New Document dialog box or the New task pane. You may need to choose the type of document you want to create from a list of page types. For example, choose blank page or HTML to create a basic HTML file.

A new page does not become part of the Web site until you save it. Use a familiar command such as Save or Save As on the File menu to open a Save As dialog box where you can specify a name for the page and make sure it is saved in the current Web site. Most programs give a new page a default title, such as Untitled Document, or the name of the file. You can change the title at any time. In Dreamweaver, you change the title in the Title box on the Document toolbar. In FrontPage, you change the title in the Properties dialog box.

> **Note** ☑
>
> If you are using FrontPage, your instructor may ask you to practice creating a new page. To create a page in FrontPage, click File on the Menu bar, click New, and then click Blank page in the New task pane. To delete it, right-click the file name in the Folder List and then click Delete.

STEP-BY-STEP 26.4

In this exercise, you will create and save a new page, named *index*. You will view the code and then change the title. If you are using FrontPage, your program automatically created an index page when you defined the site. You may skip steps 1 and 2 and begin with step 3.

1. Create a new, blank HTML file. In Dreamweaver you may do this by clicking **HTML** on the Start page, or by using the File > New command as follows: Click **File** on the Menu bar, click **New**, choose the **General** tab if necessary, click **Basic page** in the *Category* column, click **HTML** in the *Basic page* column, and then click **Create**.

2. Save the file as **index** in the My Aussie Web Site. Click **File** on the Menu bar and then click **Save As**. Navigate to the **My Aussie Web Site** folder, if necessary. Key **index** in the File name text box, and then click **Save**. The page is stored in the site, and displays in the Files panel, as shown in Figure 26-7.

FIGURE 26-7
The index page in Design view

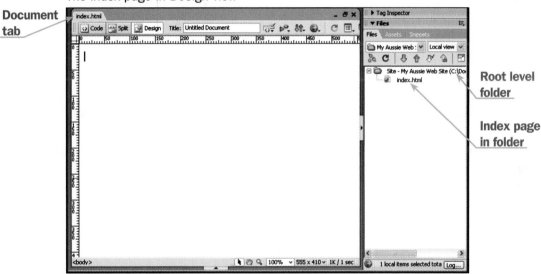

Document tab

Root level folder

Index page in folder

STEP-BY-STEP 26.4 Continued

3. Display the **index** page in Code view. The page should look similar to Figure 26-8. Notice that your program automatically entered HTML tags to specify HTML as the language, and to set up the head, title, and body. Some programs add other code to define the type of page and its storage location.

FIGURE 26-8
The index page in Code view

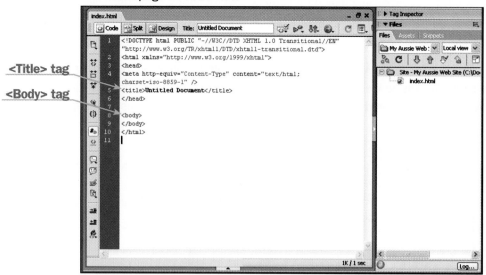

4. Locate or display the location where you can change the page title. In Dreamweaver, the Title text box displays on the Document toolbar. In FrontPage, click **File** on the Menu bar and then click **Properties** to open the Properties dialog box.

5. Select the default page title, key **Australia Destinations**, and then press **Enter**. The page title changes. Notice that the new title displays in the `<title> </title>` tag on the page in Code view.

6. Change to Design view and save the changes to the page. Leave your Web site development program open to use in the next exercise.

 **Computer Ethics**

ACCEPTABLE USE POLICIES

Almost every corporate, education, and government Web site has rules called *Terms of Use* or *Acceptable Use Policies* (AUPs) designed to protect the site and its visitors. These policies outline the rights and responsibilities of users on networks and Web sites. Although they may differ depending on the sponsoring organization, most include rules about using the Web site to publish or distribute libelous, slanderous, obscene, or inappropriate literature, graphics, or other offensive materials. They may also include rules forbidding the use of copyrighted material without permission.

Add Text to a Web Page

The real value of using a Web site development program becomes obvious when you start to add content such as text. You do not have to enter the HTML tags to format text. Instead, you can simply key your text in a document window and then use toolbar buttons, menu commands, or a properties panel to apply formatting.

Enter Text and Check Spelling

You can use the same methods for entering and editing text on a Web page that you use in other types of documents. Characters that you key display to the left of the insertion point. Use the directional arrow keys or the mouse to move the insertion point to a new location. Press Backspace to delete the character to the left of the insertion point or press Delete to delete the character to the right of the insertion point. You can click and drag to select text, and use the Cut, Copy, and Paste commands on the Edit menu to copy or move a selection.

Most Web site development programs have a spelling checker utility similar to those found in other programs so you can check for incorrectly spelled words. To start the checker, select a command such as Check Spelling on the Text menu or Spelling on the Tools menu. Some spelling checkers will also catch grammatical errors such as repeated words or incorrect capitalization. For more information about using a spelling checker, refer to Lessons 4, 12, and 18.

> **Note**
>
> Remember that even the best spelling checker utility will not catch all errors, such as correctly spelled words that are used incorrectly. Proofread your text carefully before making your Web page available for the whole world to see.

S TEP-BY-STEP 26.5

In this exercise you key text in your Web page that includes spelling errors. You then check and correct the spelling.

1. If necessary, expand the **index** page document window, and then key **Things to See and Do in Australia**. Press **Enter** to start a new line.

2. Key **Australia is a large and beautiful country with many interesting things to sea and do. Click a link below to learn more about a specific topic.** Press **Enter**.

STEP-BY-STEP 26.5 Continued

3. Key **Ayers Rock**, press **Enter**, and then key **The Great Barrier Reaf**. The document should look similar to Figure 26-9.

FIGURE 26-9
Text, including spelling errors

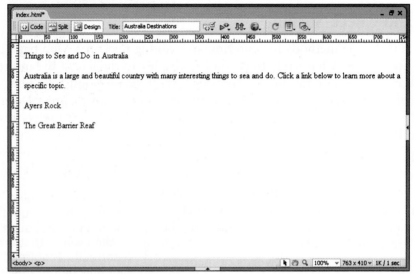

4. Move the insertion point to the beginning of the document and start the spelling checker. In Dreamweaver click **Text** on the Menu bar and then click **Check Spelling**. In FrontPage, click **Tools** on the Menu bar and then click **Spelling**. The spelling checker starts and locates an incorrectly spelled word: *Reaf*.

5. In the Suggestions list, click the correctly spelled word **Reef**, and then click the **Change** button. Your program corrects the errors and continues checking the document. If there are other errors, correct them as necessary.

6. In the spelling check complete dialog box, click **OK**.

7. Proofread the text. Note that the spelling checker did not identify the word *sea* as an error because it is spelled correctly. However, the word should be spelled *see*.

8. Select the word *sea* and key **see**.

9. Save the changes to **index** and leave it open to use in the next exercise.

Format Text

You can use typical font formatting commands to format the text in a Web page document. You can select a font from a list of available fonts and apply a color using a color palette or Color Picker dialog box. In some programs, such as Dreamweaver, font formatting commands are available on the Text menu or in the Properties panel. In other programs, such as FrontPage, they are on the Format menu or Formatting toolbar. Although you can usually apply any font installed on you computer, some Web site development programs organize fonts into series, such as a series of sans serif or serif fonts. When you select a series, the first font is applied to the text, but other fonts are included in the HTML tag as alternatives in case the visitor's browser does not have the first font installed.

STEP-BY-STEP 26.6

1. If necessary, display the onscreen element that provides the text formatting commands. In Dreamweaver, display the Properties panel. In FrontPage, display the Formatting toolbar.

2. Select the first line of text in the document.

3. Apply **Arial**, or a sans serif series of fonts that starts with Arial, to the selected text. In Dreamweaver, click the **Font** drop-down arrow in the Properties panel, and then click **Arial, Helvetica, sans serif**. In FrontPage, click the **Font** drop-down arrow on the Formatting toolbar and then click **Arial**.

4. Click the **Size** drop-down arrow and then click **24** to increase the font size to **24** points. (If necessary, change the unit of measure to points.)

5. Click the **Align Center** button in the Properties panel or the **Center** button on the Formatting toolbar to center the text on the page.

6. Change the font color to **Blue** (hexadecimal **#0000FF**). In Dreamweaver, click the **Text Color** button in the Properties panel and then click the **Blue** color swatch. In FrontPage, click the **Font Color** drop-down arrow on the Formatting toolbar and then click the **Blue** color swatch.

7. Select the second paragraph of text and change the font to **Georgia**, or a serif series of fonts that starts with Georgia.

8. Change the font size to **16** points.

STEP-BY-STEP 26.6 Continued

9. Select the last two paragraphs and change the font size to 14 points. Deselect the text. The document should look similar to Figure 26-10.

FIGURE 26-10
Formatted text

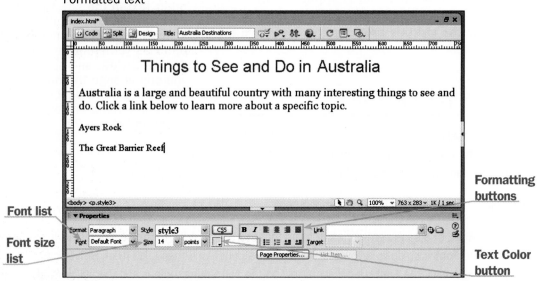

10. Change to Code view to see the HTML code for the formatted text, and then change back to Design view.

11. Save the changes to **index** and leave it open to use in the next exercise.

Format a Web Page

You already know that you can improve the appearance and readability of a Web page by using color and elements such as horizontal rules. Most Web site development programs make it easy to apply such formatting to a page using menu commands and toolbar buttons.

Insert Horizontal Rules

Most programs have commands on the Insert menu for inserting horizontal rules. You can set properties for the rule to change its height, width, and alignment, and you can select whether to display it as a solid color or as a shaded line.

Hot Tip

In Dreamweaver, use the Insert > HTML > Special Characters command to insert other HTML tag elements such as line breaks.

Note

By default, a horizontal rule is as wide as the window. You can set it to a specific length in pixels, or as a percentage of the window. Rule height is always measured in pixels.

S TEP-BY-STEP 26.7

In this exercise, you insert and format a horizontal rule.

1. Position the insertion point to the left of the *A* in the word *Australia* at the beginning of the second line of text.

2. Select the command to insert a horizontal rule. In Dreamweaver, click **Insert** on the Menu bar, click **HTML**, and then click **Horizontal Rule**. The Properties panel displays options for the Horizontal rule. In FrontPage, click **Insert** on the Menu bar and then click **Horizontal Line**. Right-click the line and then click **Horizontal Line Properties** to display the Properties dialog box.

3. In the H or Height box, key **6**.

4. Select the option to display a solid line. In Dreamweaver, click to clear the **Shading** box. In FrontPage, click to select the **Solid line (no shading)** box, and then click **OK** to close the Properties dialog box. The page should look similar to Figure 26-11.

FIGURE 26-11
Insert a horizontal rule

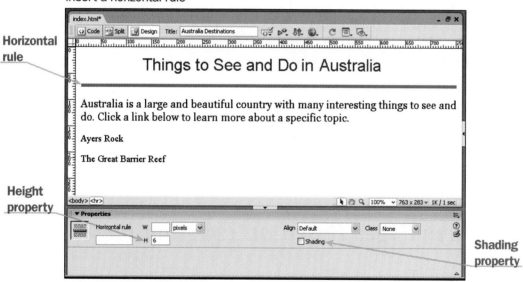

5. Save the changes to **index** and leave it open to use in the next exercise.

Change the Background Color

In most programs you set the background color for the page in the Page Properties dialog box. To display the Page Properties dialog box, select a command such as Modify > Page Properties in Dreamweaver or Format > Background in FrontPage. You can then select a color from the Background palette, or specify a custom color.

STEP-BY-STEP 26.8

In this exercise, you apply a background color to the Web page.

1. Select the command to display the Page Properties dialog box. In Dreamweaver, click **Modify** on the Menu bar and then click **Page Properties**. In FrontPage, click **Format** on the Menu bar and then click **Background**.

2. Click the **Background color** drop-down arrow. If necessary, click **More Colors** to display a full color palette.

3. Click a dusty peach color swatch (hexadecimal **#FFCC99**) and then click **OK**. If necessary, click **OK** again. The background color changes, as shown in Figure 26-12.

FIGURE 26-12
Change the page background

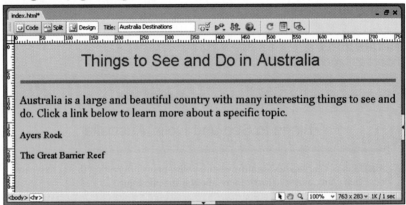

4. Save the changes to **index** and leave it open to use in the next exercise.

Create New Pages Based on Existing Pages

As you learned in Lesson 24, a Web site looks better and is easier to use when it includes consistent formatting on all pages. You can easily use the File > Save As command in your Web site development program to save an existing file with a new name, and then edit the page content to create a new page that has the same formatting as the original page.

> **Note** ☑
>
> Make sure you save changes to a page before you save it with a new name. If you do not save the changes, the original page will not retain the most recent changes. A page that has not yet been saved has an asterisk after the page name on the Document tab in the document window.

STEP-BY-STEP 26.9

In this exercise, you use the File > Save As command to create two new pages for your Web site. You will edit the page title and text on each new page.

1. Click **File** on the Menu bar and then click **Save As** to display the Save As dialog box. Verify that My Aussie Web Site is the current storage location.

STEP-BY-STEP 26.9 Continued

2. In the *File name* text box, key **ayers_rock** and then click **Save** to save the page with a new name. Your program automatically adds either an *.htm* or an *.html* file extension.

3. Change the page title to Ayers Rock. In Dreamweaver, select the text in the Title text box on the Document toolbar, key **Ayers Rock**, and then press **Enter**. In FrontPage, click **File** on the Menu bar, click **Properties**, key **Ayers Rock**, and then click **OK**.

4. Select the first line of text on the ayers_rock page and then key **Ayers Rock (Uluru)** to replace the existing text.

5. Select the paragraph of text after the horizontal rule and then key: **Ayers Rock is a large sandstone rock formation in central Australia. It is more than 986 feet high and 5 miles around. The Aboriginal people call it Uluru and consider it sacred. Visit at sunrise or sunset to observe the way it changes color in different light.**

6. Click the **Justify** button in the Properties panel or on the Formatting toolbar to justify the paragraph alignment.

7. Select the next line of text—*Ayers Rock*—and key **Home**. The page should look similar to Figure 26-13.

FIGURE 26-13
Ayers Rock page

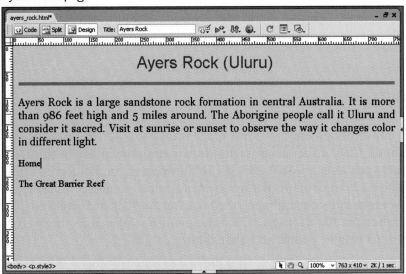

8. Check the spelling on the page and correct any errors, and then save the changes to the page.

9. Save the page as **reef** in the My Aussie Web Site. Change the page title to **Great Barrier Reef**.

10. Select the first line of text on the reef page and then key **The Great Barrier Reef**.

11. Select the paragraph of text after the horizontal rule and then key: **The Great Barrier Reef is the largest coral reef in the world. Located off the east coast of Australia, it is actually a system of more than 3000 reefs scattered with many lovely islands. It is home to more than 1500 species of fish.**

STEP-BY-STEP 26.9 Continued

12. Select the last line of text—The Great Barrier Reef—and key **Ayers Rock**. The page should look similar to Figure 26-14.

FIGURE 26-14
The Great Barrier Reef page

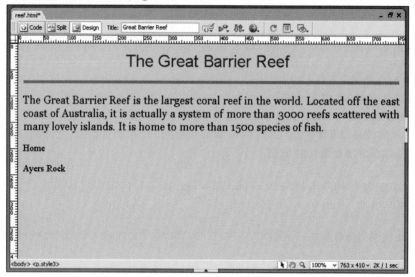

13. Check the spelling on the page and correct any errors, and then save the changes to the page. Leave it open to use in the next exercise.

Insert Pictures

Most Web site development programs make it easy to insert pictures using any one of a variety of methods. One of the easiest methods is to drag the image to the document window from a panel such as Files or Assets (in Dreamweaver) or Folder List (in FrontPage). You can also usually use a command on the Insert menu, such as Insert > Image in Dreamweaver or Insert > Picture > From File in FrontPage, or click a button such as Images to display a dialog box where you can select the file to insert. Once the picture is placed in the Web page, you can set properties such as its height, width, and alignment.

Keep in mind that you must be sure that the image files are stored in an appropriately named folder in the root level Web site folder. This is necessary for uploading to the Web server with the other Web site files so that a browser will be able to locate them correctly.

STEP-BY-STEP 26.10

In this exercise, you create an *images* folder in your *My Aussie Web Site* folder and then copy two graphics files to it. You then insert the pictures on your Web pages. If you are using FrontPage, your program automatically created an images folder when you defined the Web site, so you can skip step 1.

1. Use a file management program such as Windows Explorer to create a new folder named **Images** in your *My Aussie Web Site* folder.

STEP-BY-STEP 26.10 Continued

2. Use the file management program to copy the graphics files **Step26-10a** and **Step26-10b** from the Data files for this lesson to the **Images** folder. Rename *Step26-10a* to **reef**, and rename *Step26-10b* to **rock**. (If necessary, key the **.gif** file extension.)

3. Display the Files panel in Dreamweaver, or the Folder List panel in FrontPage, if it is not already displayed. In Dreamweaver, click **Window** on the Menu bar and then click **Files**. In FrontPage, click **View** on the Menu bar and then click **Folder List**.

4. Expand the **Images** folder. It should look similar to Figure 26-15.

FIGURE 26-15
Picture files in the Images folder

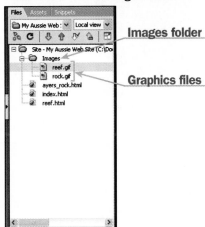

5. Click and drag the **reef.gif** file from the panel to the document window, and drop it when the mouse pointer is positioned to the left of the first line of text. If a dialog box displays prompting you to key alternative text, click **OK** to continue.

STEP-BY-STEP 26.10 Continued

6. Expand the width of the document window, if necessary, and display the Properties panel or dialog box. In Dreaweaver, if the Properties panel is not open, click **Window** on the Menu bar and then click **Properties**. In FrontPage, right-click the picture and then click **Picture Properties**. Click the **Align** or Alignment drop-down arrow and then click **Middle**. Click **OK** if necessary to close the Picture Properties dialog box. The document should look similar to Figure 26-16.

FIGURE 26-16
Picture in the Web page file

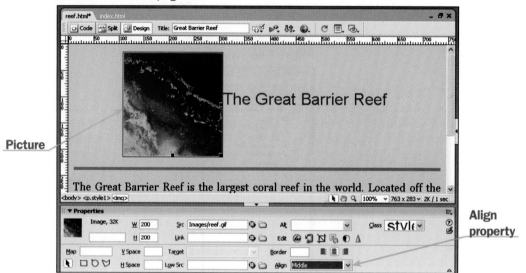

7. Save the changes to the **reef** file and then open the **ayers_rock** file. You can do this using the command for opening recently used files on the File menu, or by double-clicking the file name in the Files or Folder List panel. (Both files will be open.)

8. Click and drag the **rock.gif** file from the Files or Folder List panel to the document window, and drop it when the mouse pointer is positioned to the left of the first line of text. If a dialog box displays prompting you to key alternative text, click **OK** to continue.

9. Expand the width of the document window, if necessary, and display the Properties panel or dialog box. Click the **Align** or Alignment drop-down arrow and then click **Middle**. Click **OK** if necessary to close the Picture Properties dialog box.

10. Save the changes to **ayers_rock**. Leave it and the **reef** file open to use in the next exercise.

Link Pages in a Web Site

You can create hyperlinks in a Web site development program by selecting the text or object you want to link, and then selecting the destination file in a dialog box. You may access the dialog box by clicking a button such as Browse for File or Insert Hyperlink. In most programs, links are not active by default, which means you cannot just click the link to jump to the destination. To make the link active, you can press and hold the Ctrl key while you click or double-click.

Usually, you can display a navigation or map view of a site to see how pages in the site are linked. This visual display shows the navigational structure and relationship between pages in a site, and can be very useful as a site grows to include many pages. To display the navigational structure you change the view by selecting it from a View drop-down list, the View menu, or by clicking a View button. In FrontPage, you must add existing pages to the navigational structure in order to display them in Navigation view.

S TEP-BY-STEP 26.11

In this exercise, you link the three Web pages in the My Aussie Web Site and test the links. You also display the links in the map view.

1. Select the text *The Great Barrier Reef* at the bottom of the **ayers_rock** page.

2. Select the command to insert a hyperlink. For example, click a button such as **Browse for File** (next to the Link text box) in the Properties panel in Dreamweaver, or **Insert Hyperlink** on the Standard toolbar in FrontPage. A dialog box similar to the Select File dialog box shown in Figure 26-17 displays.

FIGURE 26-17
Select File dialog box

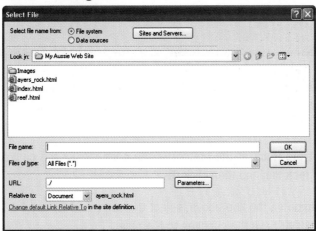

3. Select the **reef** file (the extension may be .htm or .html) and then click **OK**. The text is formatted as a hyperlink.

STEP-BY-STEP 26.11 Continued

4. Select the text **Home** on the line above, select the command to insert a hyperlink, select the **index** file, and then click **OK**. The text is formatted as a hyperlink. Deselect the text. The page should look similar to Figure 26-18.

FIGURE 26-18
Hyperlinks on the page

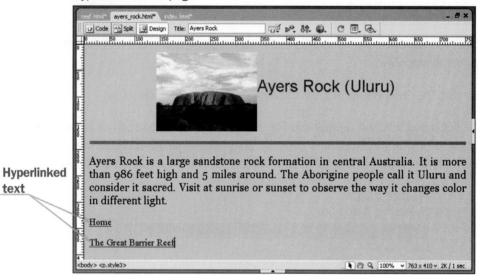

Hyperlinked text

5. Save the changes to the page and then press and hold **Ctrl** and double-click the link **The Great Barrier Reef**. (If you are using FrontPage, you only have to click once.) The Great Barrier Reef page should display.

6. Select the text **Ayers Rock** at the bottom of the page, select the command to insert a hyperlink, select the **ayers_rock** file, and then click **OK**.

7. Select the text **Home** on the line above, select the command to insert a hyperlink, select the **index** file, and then click **OK**. Save the changes to the page.

8. Press and hold **Ctrl** and double-click the link **Home**. (If you are using FrontPage, you only have to click once.) The **index** page should display.

9. Select the text **The Great Barrier Reef** at the bottom of the page and insert a hyperlink to the **reef** page. Select the text **Ayers Rock** and insert a hyperlink to the **ayers_rock** page. Save the changes to the page. Now, all pages are linked.

10. Press and hold **Ctrl** and double-click (or click) the link **The Great Barrier Reef**. Use the **Home** link to return to the index page, and test the **Ayers Rock** link. Test the links on each page.

11. Change the view to display the navigational structure. In Dreamweaver, click the **View** drop-down arrow in the Files panel and then click **Map view**. In FrontPage, click **View** on the Menu bar and then click **Navigation**. Right-click the **index** page icon, click **Add Existing Page**, click **reef** and then click **OK**. Right-click the **index** page icon again, click **Add Existing Page**, click **ayers_rock**, and then click **OK**.

STEP-BY-STEP 26.11 Continued

12. If available, click the plus sign to the left of the ayers_rock file in the Map view to expand it. In Dreamweaver, the Map view should look similar to Figure 26-19.

Note

If all pages do not display in Map view, make sure you saved the most recent changes to each page, and then refresh the view by pressing F5 or by clicking the Refresh button.

FIGURE 26-19
Map view

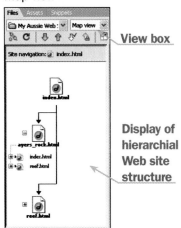

View box

Display of hierarchial Web site structure

13. Change back to local view. In Dreamweaver, click the **View** drop-down arrow in the Files panel and then click **Local view**. In FrontPage, click **View** on the Menu bar and then click **Page**.

14. Close the **Ayers Rock** and **The Great Barrier Reef** pages, saving changes, if necessary. Leave the **index** page open to use in the next exercise.

Preview a Web Site

One of the key reasons to use a Web site development program is the ease with which you can view and manage an entire Web site. To preview a Web page in a browser, simply click a button such as Preview in Browser and, if necessary, select the browser you want to use. Your browser opens to display the current page. You can test the links in your browser, or just check the colors and alignment of objects and text. You must save the changes to a page before you can preview it in a browser.

Extra for Experts

Some programs have a utility for testing links to find problems. Select a command such as Site > Check Links Sitewide in Dreamweaver or Tools > Recalculate Links in FrontPage and your program will check the links for breaks or links to nonexistent pages and display the results. Some programs even repair problems.

Note

Some programs, such as FrontPage, have a Preview button you can click to see how a page looks in the browser without actually displaying it in the browser.

STEP-BY-STEP 26.12

In this exercise, you preview your Web site in your browser.

1. Select the command to preview the **index** page in your browser. For example, click the **Preview/Debug in Browser** button. If necessary, click the browser you want to use. Your browser starts, and displays the page.

2. Click the link to the **Ayers Rock** page. The page displays in the browser window.

3. Click the link to the **Great Barrier Reef** page, and then click the link to the **Home** page.

4. Continue testing the links in your browser. When you are finished, close the browser.

5. Close the **index** page and then close your Web site development program.

SUMMARY

In this lesson, you learned:

- A Web site development program lets you develop and create Web sites without having to key HTML code.

- Most Web site development programs have familiar menus, toolbars, panels, or task panes that you can use to access features and select commands.

- You can customize the program workspace to make the tools you need available.

- By default, most Web site development programs display a document in Design view, but you can switch to Code view or split the window to see both views at the same time.

- You define a Web site by mapping the root level folder on your computer.

- Some programs automatically create folders and an index page when you define the Web site, or you can manually create the folders and new pages as you need them.

- You use standard text entering and edit commands to add text to a Web page.

- Most Web site development programs have spelling checkers that you can use to identify and correct spelling errors.

- You can easily apply formatting such as fonts, font styles, and font effects to text on a Web page.

- You can improve the appearance of a Web page by inserting horizontal rules and changing the background color.

- You can use the File > Save As command to save a Web page file with a new name. This can help insure consistent formatting on all pages in a Web site.

- One of the easiest ways to insert a picture on a Web page is to drag the image file from a panel to the document. Alternatively, you can open a dialog box and select a file to insert.

- You can create hyperlinks by selecting the hyperlink text and then selecting the destination file in a dialog box.

- Usually, you can display a map view to see how pages relate to each other in a navigational structure.

- Most Web site development programs make it easy to preview Web pages in a browser.

VOCABULARY *Review*

Define the following terms:

Behaviors	Map	Root level folder
Code view	Map view	Split view
Design view		

REVIEW *Questions*

TRUE / FALSE

Circle T if the statement is true or F if the statement is false.

T   F   1. Most Web site development program windows look a lot like a text editing program window.

T   F   2. You can customize the Web site development program workspace to display the tools you need.

T   F   3. You cannot use a Web site development program to open or edit Web pages created in a text editor.

T   F   4. You can use the File > New command to add pages to a site at any time.

T   F   5. A new page does not become part of a Web site until you save it.

T   F   6. You cannot size text in points in a Web site development program.

T   F   7. You can drag an image from a panel to the document window to insert it on a Web page.

T   F   8. You cannot control the size or alignment of pictures when you are using a Web site development program.

T   F   9. In most Web site development programs, hyperlinks are not active by default.

T   F   10. You must save the changes to a Web page before you can preview it in a browser.

WRITTEN QUESTIONS

Write a brief answer to each of the following questions.

1. What is a primary benefit of using a Web site development program instead of a text editor to create a Web page?

2. What are two common Web site development programs?

3. What is an acceptable use policy?

4. Why do graphics files used on a Web page have to be stored within the main site folder?

5. How can you test a hyperlink using the Web site development program?

FILL IN THE BLANK

Complete the following sentences by writing the correct word or words in the blanks provided.

1. _____ view is the view you use to enter and format content in a Web page without keying code.

2. _____ view is the view you use to display and edit HTML tags.

3. When you _____ a Web site, you give it a name and identify the main site folder.

4. The main site folder may be called the _____ level folder.

5. _____ view, which is sometimes called navigation view, shows the navigational structure and relationship between pages in a site.

6. _____ are codes that allow visitors to interact with the Web page.

7. _____ view lets you display Design view and Code view in the same document window.

8. In Dreamweaver, you change the Web page title in the Title text box on the _____ toolbar.

9. When you select a(n) _____ of fonts, the first font is applied to the text, but other fonts are included in the HTML tag as alternatives in case the visitor's browser does not have the first font installed.

10. Set _____ for a horizontal rule to change its height, width, and alignment.

PROJECTS

PROJECT 26-1

In this project, you will define a new Web site and add a new Web page to it.

1. Use a file management program to create a new folder named **Policies** that you can map as the root level folder for a new Web site.

2. Launch your Web site development program and select the command to create a new Web site. In Dreamweaver, do the following:
   A. Click **Site** on the Menu bar.
   B. Click **New Site** to display the Site Definition dialog box.
   C. Replace the text *Unnamed Site 1* with the name **Acceptable Use**. Leave the http:// address blank.
   D. Click **Next**.
   E. Click to select the option **No, I do not want to use server technology**, and then click **Next**.
   F. If necessary, select the option **Edit local copies on my machine....**

   In FrontPage, do the following:
   A. Click **File** on the Menu bar.
   B. Click **New** to display the New task pane.
   C. Click **One page Web site** to display the Web Site Templates dialog box.

3. Click the command to locate the root level folder. If you are using Dreamweaver, click the folder icon next to the path to the default storage location to open the *Choose local root folder* dialog box. If you are using FrontPage, click the **Browse** button in the Web Site Templates dialog box to open the New Web Site location dialog box.

4. Navigate to the location of the **Policies** folder, select the folder, and click **Open**. If you are using FrontPage, click **OK** to define the site and skip to step 9.

5. In Dreamweaver, click **Select** to return to the Site Definition dialog box, and then click **Next**.

6. Click the **How do you connect to your remote server?** drop-down arrow and then click **None**. Click **Next** to display the Summary page.

7. Click **Done**.

8. Click **HTML** on the Start page to create a new, blank HTML file. If the Start page is not open, do the following:
   A. Click **File** on the Menu bar and then click **New**.
   B. Click **Basic page** in the *Category* column.
   C. Click **HTML** in the *Basic page* column.
   D. Click **Create**.

9. Save the file as **intro** in the **Policies** folder. If you are using FrontPage, rename the default **index.html** file to **intro**. (Right-click the file name in the Folder List, click **Rename**, key **intro** and then press **Enter**.)

10. Change the page title to **AUP: Intro**. In Dreamweaver, select the text in the Title text box on the Document toolbar and then key **AUP: Intro**. In FrontPage, click **File** on the Menu bar, click **Properties**, select the default page title and then key **AUP: Intro**.

11. Key the following paragraphs in the **intro** file:

    Acceptable Use Policy

    Introduction

    This Acceptable Use Policy (AUP) is intended to help enhance the use of the Internet by pre-venting unacceptable use. All users, including those who access some of our services but do not have accounts, as well as those who pay a monthly service fee to subscribe to the services must comply with this policy.

    We support the free flow of information and ideas over the Internet and do not actively monitor use under normal circumstances. We do not exercise editorial control over the content of any Web site or electronic mail transmission. However, we reserve the right to remove any materials that, in our sole discretion, may be illegal, may subject us to liability, or which may violate this policy.

12. Save the changes to the file and then preview it in your browser.

13. Close your browser. Close the **intro** file, but leave your Web development program open to use in the next project.

PROJECT 26-2

In this project, you will add and format a version of the **intro** page and insert a graphics object.

1. Use a file management program to create a new folder named **Images** in your **Policies** root level folder.

2. Copy the graphics file **Project26-2a** from the Data files for this lesson to the **Images** folder in the **Policies** root level folder. Rename the file **Next**. If necessary, key the **.gif** file extension.

3. In your Web development program, open the HTML file **Project26-2b** and save it as **page1** in the **Policies** folder. If necessary, click **Yes** to update links. Change the Web page title to **Acceptable Use Policy: Introduction**.

4. Format the first line in a **bold, 16**-point sans serif font such as **Arial,** or a series of sans serif fonts beginning with Arial, and center align it on the page. Change the text color to blue hexadecimal **#003399.**

5. Format the second line in a **14**-point sans serif font such as **Arial,** or a series of sans serif fonts beginning with Arial, and leave it left-aligned.

6. Format the remaining two paragraphs in a **12**-point serif font such as **Georgia,** or a series of serif fonts beginning with Georgia, and justify the alignment.

7. Change the page background color to light gray hexadecimal **#CCCCCC.**

8. Insert the **Next** graphics file on the last line in the file. If prompted, key **Next** as the alternative text.

9. Right-align the object on the page.

10. Save the changes to the file and leave it open to use in the next project.

PROJECT 26-3

In this project, you will use the page1 file to create two additional files for your Web site. You will then link all of the files together in a linear structure.

1. Copy the graphics file **Project26-3a** from the Data files for this lesson to the **Images** folder in the **Policies** root level folder. Rename the file **Back.** If necessary, key the **.gif** file extension.

2. In your Web development program, use the **File > Save As** command to save a copy of the *page1* file as **page2** in your **Acceptable Use Web** site.

3. Change the Web page title to **Acceptable Use Policy: Guidelines.**

4. Replace the text *Introduction* with the text **Guidelines.**

5. Delete the two paragraphs of text and then key the following list:

Users must respect the privacy of others.

Users shall not intentionally seek information on, or represent themselves as, another user unless explicitly authorized to do so by that user.

Users shall not obtain copies of, or modify files, other data, or passwords belonging to others.

Users must respect the legal protection applied to programs, data, photographs, music, written documents and other material as provided by copyright, trademark, patent, licensure and other proprietary rights mechanisms.

Users shall not intentionally develop or use programs that harass other users or infiltrate any other computer, computing system or network and/or damage or alter the software components or file systems of a computer, computing system or network.

Use of the service for malicious, fraudulent, or misrepresentative purposes is not acceptable.

The service may not be used in ways that violate applicable laws or regulations.

Unsolicited advertising is not acceptable.

Repeated, unsolicited and/or unwanted communication of an intrusive nature is strictly prohibited.

6. Format the list items as a numbered list.
   A. Select all list items.
   B. Click the **Ordered list** button in the Properties panel (Dreamweaver) or **Numbering** button on the Formatting toolbar (FrontPage).

7. Format the list items in a **12**-point serif font such as **Georgia,** or a series of serif fonts beginning with Georgia.

8. Insert a new blank line at the end of the file and then insert the **Back** graphics file on the last line. If prompted, key the alternate text **Back.**

9. Select the **Back** graphic and insert a hyperlink to the page1 file.

10. Save the changes, then right-click the graphic and click **Open linked page** to display the page1 file.

11. Select the **Next** graphic and insert a hyperlink to the **page2** file.

12. Save the changes, then right-click the graphic and click **Open linked page** to display the page2 file.

13. Save the *page2* file as **page3** in your **Acceptable Use Web site.**

14. Change the Web page title to **Acceptable Use Policy: Conclusion.**

15. Replace the text *Guidelines* with the text **Conclusion.**

16. Delete the numbered list items, and remove the numbered list formatting.

17. Key the following two paragraphs of text in place of the numbered list:

    The intent of this policy is to identify certain types of uses that are not appropriate, but this policy does not necessarily enumerate all possible inappropriate uses.

    If we learn of possible inappropriate use, we will notify the responsible party, who must take immediate remedial action and inform us of its action. We will assist in identifying the nature and source of the inappropriate use and in implementing remedial action if requested. If remedial action is taken promptly, we will take no further action. If we are unable to contact the responsible party, or if there is no remedial action taken, we reserves the right to pursue remedial action independently. Wherever possible, we will pursue remedial action with the least impact to the overall service.

18. Format the two paragraphs in a **12**-point serif font such as **Georgia,** or a series of serif fonts beginning with Georgia, and justify the alignment.

19. Delete the **Next** graphic and the line it was on.

20. Edit the hyperlink destination for the **Back** graphic to **page2.**

21. Save the changes, then right-click the graphic and click **Open linked page** to display the **page2** file.

22. Select the **Next** graphic and insert a hyperlink to the **page3** file.

23. Save the changes, then right-click the graphic and click **Open linked page** to display the **page3** file.

24. Preview the page in your browser and test the **Back** link. From the Guidelines page, test the **Back** link to display the Introduction page. From the Introduction page, test the **Next** link to display the Guidelines page. From the Guidelines page test the **Next** link to display the Conclusion page.

25. Close your browser and close all open files, saving changes as necessary. Close your Web site development program.

 WEB PROJECT

In this project, use the Internet to research different acceptable use policies for different types of Web sites. Try to locate a policy for a government site, a corporate site, and an educational site, and then compare them to see the similarities and the differences. In addition, see if you can locate general information about how to develop an acceptable use policy of your own. If you do not understand some of the terms and conditions, do your best to find definitions and explanations online. Alternatively, ask your instructor, a librarian, or a Web site developer in your area for an explanation. Use the information you locate to write an acceptable use policy of your own for the sites you have created in this unit. You can write the policy by hand, in a word processing program, or in an HTML file that you can add to your Web sites.

 TEAMWORK PROJECT

As a team, create a budget for developing and maintaining a department Web site. Start by selecting a project manager who can keep everyone organized and focused on completing assignments. Next, decide what information you need to create the budget. Some things you might ask include:

- How many people do you need to work on the Web site?

- How long will it take, and much will they be paid?

- What type of hardware and software will you need and how much will it cost?

- How much will it cost to store the site on a Web file server?

- How long will the planning and creation of the site take? How much time will be spent on maintenance?

Give each team member the responsibility of finding specific information. If necessary, use the Internet to try to find answers to these questions, or contact a Web developer in your area who will be willing to talk to you. When you have gathered the information you need, create a spreadsheet or table listing each item and its cost, and then calculate the total cost. Write a report of at least 250 words explaining the budget, and then present it to your class.

CRITICAL *Thinking*

Throughout this unit you have primarily created hierarchical Web sites and at least one linear Web site. (For a refresher on different navigational structures, refer to Lesson 23.) The random-access structure is generally used the least because it is only effective in a site with a small number of pages. If there are too many pages it becomes unwieldy for the developer and confusing for the visitor. However, in a small site, it may be a useful structure for making information available. In this exercise, consider when a random-access Web site might be useful. Think about the type of information you might want to make available for a site visitor to access in any order. What is the maximum number of pages you would want to include, keeping in mind that every page should link to every other page? Select a topic that you think would work as a random-access Web site, and draw a diagram showing how the pages would link. Then, use your Web site development program to define and create the site. Preview the pages frequently, and make corrections and improvements as you work. Remember to test all of the links. When you are finished, ask your classmates to access and use your Web site. If they have suggestions for improving it, edit the text files and test the site again.

POLISHING AND PUBLISHING YOUR WEB SITE

In order to make a Web site available to others, you must *publish* it. Basically, publishing means transferring the HTML files to a remote site, such as a Web file server. Before you publish the site you want to be sure it is as professional as possible. One method of insuring consistent formatting is to use style sheets. You can also insert background graphics to create an eye-catching page design. Finally, you can add pages created with other programs to your Web site to make sure the best and most current information is available. If you add content to a Web page, or add new pages to a site, you must update the site by republishing.

Use Cascading Style Sheets

Creating a look and feel using a Web site development program may be easier than keying HTML tags in a text editor, but it still leaves room for error. Most Web site development programs offer a feature called *Cascading Style Sheets (CSS)* that help insure consistent formatting throughout a Web site, even when the site is displayed on different browsers, or different systems. CSS are a collection of formatting settings that you can attach to a Web page and then use as the default styles for formatting text and objects on the page. There are three types of style sheets:

■ *External style sheets*, which are sometimes called linked style sheets, are stored in a separate file in a Web site. They may be used to format elements on any page in the site.

- *Embedded style sheets* are stored in the <HEAD> section of a page and are used to format elements on that page only.

- *Inline style sheets* are used to format individual elements on a page.

You can use all three types of style sheets in a single Web page, as shown in Figure 27-1.

FIGURE 27-1
Three types of style sheets in a Web page

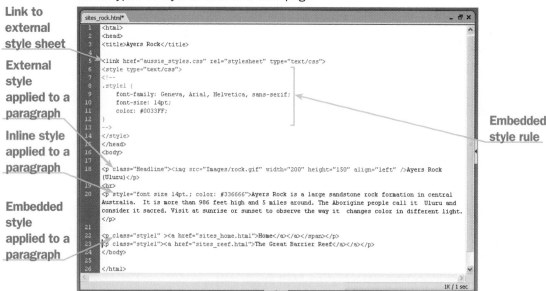

Link to external style sheet

External style applied to a paragraph

Inline style applied to a paragraph

Embedded style applied to a paragraph

Embedded style rule

The rules are applied in cascading order, which is where the name *cascading style sheet* comes from.

- First, the rules in the external sheet are applied.

- Next, the rules in the embedded style sheet are applied, taking precedence over the external sheet rules.

- Finally, the inline rules take precedence over the other two.

By using CSS, you can separate the Web page structure, which is defined by HTML tags on the page itself, from the presentation formatting, which is defined by the style sheet. For example, you can insert HTML tags to identify the structure of the headings and paragraph elements on the Web page. You can define the formatting for the headings and paragraphs by creating CSS rules in your style sheet.

A *CSS rule* is the code that defines the style. It consists of two parts—the selector and the declaration. The *selector* is the name you assign to identify the rule. The *declaration*—which may be called the *definition*-contains the attribute(s) and the value(s) that determine the formatting. The declaration is always enclosed in brackets. The following CSS rule is named *violet*, and it sets the color to violet:

```
violet {COLOR: #9966CC}
```

There are two basic types of rules: class styles and HTML tag rules.

- *Class styles*, which may be called *Custom CSS rules* or *User-defined styles*, can be applied to any range or block of text. Usually, class styles start with a period, which your program will insert automatically. To apply a class rule to an element on a page, you key the CLASS attribute with the rule selector as the value in the element's tag. For example, the following tag applies the violet rule to the text *Welcome*:

```
<P CLASS=".violet">Welcome</P>
```

■ *HTML tag rules* change the formatting for a particular tag, such as <P> or <H1>. When you create or modify an HTML tag rule, all text formatted with that tag is changed; you do not have to key any additional attributes or values. For example, the following tag changes the color of all horizontal rules on a page to violet:

```
hr {color: #9966CC}
```

 Communication Skills

CITING WEB SOURCES

It is usually illegal, not to mention unprofessional, to use work that is not your own without providing citations, even when the source is a Web page. There are eight key elements for citing an Internet source. If not all of the information is available, use as much as you can locate. The elements are usually presented in this order:

1. Author's name.
2. Title of work.
3. Book title, publication, magazine, or title of Web page (as it appears in the title bar of your browser), underlined or italicized.
4. The page number (section number or identifying feature), if accessible.
5. The date the material was originally published.
6. The electronic address or URL in angle brackets: e.g., <http://www.mla.org>.
7. Begin the first line at the left margin and indent all the following lines in the citation.
8. Use periods, not commas, to separate parts of the citation.

For example:

To cite a professional Web page:

The Nebraska Writer's Project. Ed. Ben Rand. Nebraska State University.
    27 May 1998 <http://www.nstate.edu/writer/>.

To cite a corporate Web page:

Barksdale, Karl. "Corporate View: Corporate Communications Style Guide."
    Corporate View. 27 May 1998 <http://www.corpview.com/
    intranet/Mission-CriticalFunctions/CorpCommunications/sgcite.htm>.

To cite a personal Web page:

Welsh, Shari. Web page. 1 July 1999 <http://www.handwritingsolutions.com>.

To cite an online article:

Rutter, Michael. *"Catching Lake Trout."* Outdoor Life. 1 May 1999
    <http:// www.outdoorlife.com>.

To cite an e-mail:

Barksdale, Karl. *Amazon River Pollution Tests.* 22 May 1999
    kbarksdale@handwritingsolutions.com.

Although you can define and apply CSS rules manually by keying the code, it is much simpler to let your Web site development program do the work. Some programs automatically generate embedded CSS code when you apply formatting. However, to maintain control over your page formatting, it is a good idea to create the styles first, and then apply them to the elements you want to format. You can create embedded styles to apply to a single page, or you can create the styles in an external style sheet so you can apply them to any page.

Create an Embedded CSS

To create an embedded style, open a dialog box or panel and select the command to create a new style. You key a new style name, and then select formatting options. In Dreamweaver, use the CSS Styles panel. In FrontPage use the Style dialog box.

Did You Know?

If you use Dreamweaver, in Lesson 26 when you selected font formatting the program automatically generated the CSS rules, added them to the page HEAD, and entered the code in the document.

Extra for Experts

This section only touches on the power of CSS. For more information, ask your instructor, use your program's Help system, or consult the Internet.

S TEP-BY-STEP 27.1

1. Use a file management program such as Windows Explorer to create a new folder named **Aussie Sites** in the location where you plan to store the solution files for this lesson.

2. Copy the HTML files **Step27-1a**, **Step27-1b**, and **Step27-1c** from the data files for this lesson to the Aussie Sites folder. Rename *Step27-1a* to **sites_home**, *Step27-1b* to **sites_rock**, and *Step27-1c* to **sites_reef**. If necessary, key the **html** file extensions.

3. Launch your Web site development program and select the command to create a new Web site named **Aussie Sites**, defining the **Aussie Sites** folder as the root level folder. If necessary, leave the *http://* address blank, do not use server technology, and select to **Edit local copies on your machine....** Specify **None** as the method of connecting to the server. (Refer to Lesson 26 for complete instructions of defining a new Web site.)

4. If necessary, in the **Aussie Sites** folder, create a folder named **Images**. (If you are using FrontPage, the program may have created the Images folder automatically.) This can be done in either Windows Explorer or in the Files panel of Dreamweaver.

5. Switch to Windows Explorer if necessary and copy the graphics files **Step 27-1d** and **Step27-1e** from the data files to the **Images** folder in the **Aussie Sites** Web site folder. Rename *Step27-1d* to **reef** and *Step27-1e* to **rock**. If necessary, key the **gif** file extensions.

6. Switch back to your Web site development program and open the **sites_home** Web page file. Select the command to create a new style or CSS rule. In Dreamweaver, click **Window** on the Menu bar and then click **CSS Styles** to display the CSS Styles panel, and then click the **New CSS Rule** button. The New CSS Rule dialog box should look similar to Figure 27-2. In FrontPage, click **Format** on the Menu bar and then click **Style** to display the Style dialog box.

STEP-BY-STEP 27.1 Continued

FIGURE 27-2
New CSS Rule dialog box

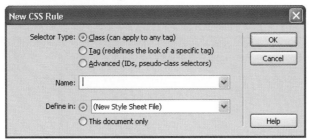

7. Select the option to create a class or user-defined style. In Dreamweaver, click the **Class** option button. In FrontPage, click the **List** drop-down arrow, click **User-defined styles**, and then click the **New** button.

8. In the **Name** text box, key **Headline**.

9. In Dreamweaver, click to select the **This document only** option button, if necessary, and then click **OK**. In FrontPage, click the **Format** button and then click **Font**.

10. Select font formatting as follows:
    a. From the **Font** drop-down list, select a sans serif font such as **Arial**, or select a sans serif series that begins with Arial.
    b. Set the Font Size to **24** points.
    c. Set the Font Style to **normal**.
    d. Set the Variant to **small-caps**.
    e. Set the color to hexadecimal **#003399**.

11. In Dreamweaver, click **Apply**. In FrontPage, click **OK**. Select the command to display paragraph formatting options. In Dreamweaver, click **Block** in the *Category* list. In FrontPage, click the **Format** drop-down arrow and then click **Paragraph**.

12. Set the text alignment to **center**, and then click **OK**. (If you are using FrontPage, click **OK** repeatedly to close all dialog boxes.) The style is embedded in the <HEAD> section of the page and added to the list of available styles.

STEP-BY-STEP 27.1 Continued

13. Display the page in Code view. It should look similar to Figure 27-3.

FIGURE 27-3
An embedded style

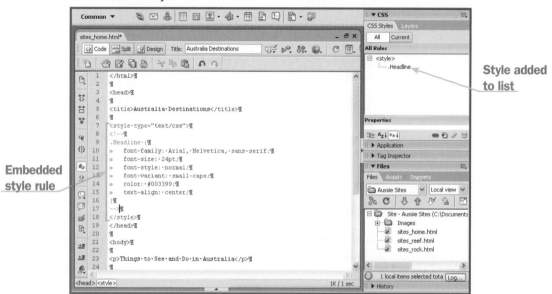

14. Change back to Design view. Save the changes to the page and leave it open to use in the next exercise.

Apply an Embedded CSS

To apply an embedded style to an element, select the element and then select the style from the Style list. In Dreamweaver, the Style list is in the Properties panel. In FrontPage, it is on the Formatting toolbar.

STEP-BY-STEP 27.2

1. Make sure the insertion point is positioned in the first line of text on the **sites_home** page, and then click the **Style** drop-down arrow to display the list of available styles. In Dreamweaver, the Style drop-down arrow is in the Properties panel; in FrontPage, it is on the Formatting toolbar.

2. Click **Headline** on the drop-down list of styles. The formatting is applied to the paragraph as shown in Figure 27-4.

STEP-BY-STEP 27.2 Continued

FIGURE 27-4
Formatted text

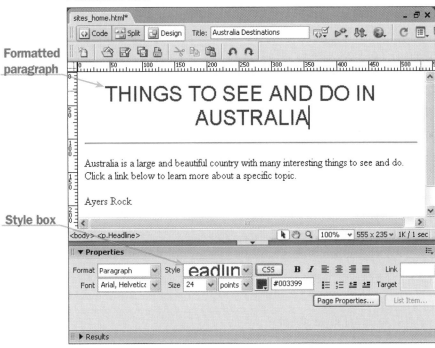

Formatted paragraph

Style box

3. Change to Code view. Notice that the `class` attribute with the `Headline` value has been added to the opening `<P>` tag for the text.

4. Change back to Design view. Save the changes and leave **sites_home** open to use in the next exercise.

Create an External CSS

The process of creating a style rule for an external CSS is basically the same as for an embedded CSS. The difference is that you save the style in the external style sheet file instead of in the `<HEAD>` tag of a particular page. Usually, you use the File > New command to create a new style sheet. You then save it, create the style rules you want to include, and then link it to a Web site.

Note

Some programs, including Dreamweaver, let you select an existing style sheet or create a new style sheet at the same time that you create the new rule. Click the New CSS Rule button in the CSS Styles panel, select the type of rule and key a rule name, then click the (New Style Sheet) option button to create a new sheet, or select an existing sheet from the drop-down list.

STEP-BY-STEP 27.3

1. Click **File** on the Menu bar and then click **New** to create a new file.

2. Select to create a new, blank, CSS file. In Dreamweaver, select the **General** tab if necessary, click **Basic page** in the *Category* list, click **CSS** in the *Basic page* list, and then click **Create**. In FrontPage, click **More page templates** in the New task pane, click the **Style Sheets** tab, click **Normal Style Sheet**, and then click **OK**.

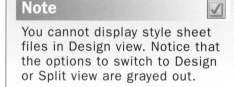

> **Hot Tip**
>
> In Dreamweaver, on the Start page, click CSS under Create New to create a new style sheet file.

3. Save the CSS file as **aussie_styles** in the **Aussie Sites** Web folder, click **File** on the Menu bar and then click **Save As**. In the *File name* text box, key **aussie_styles**. Select **Style Sheets** (Dreamweaver) or **CSS Files** (FrontPage) from the *Save as type* drop-down list, and then click **Save**. The style sheet is added to the Web site, as shown in Figure 27-5.

> **Note**
>
> You cannot display style sheet files in Design view. Notice that the options to switch to Design or Split view are grayed out.

FIGURE 27-5
New, blank external style sheet

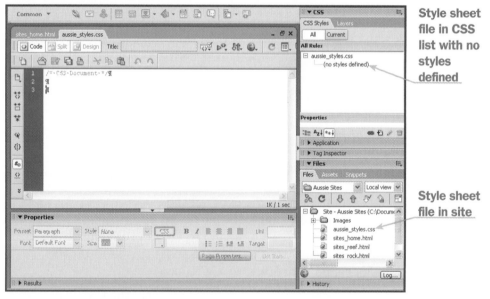

4. Create a new class style named **Body_Text** in the current document, as follows:

   a. Select the command to create a new style or CSS rule.

   b. Select the option to create a class or user-defined style.

   c. In the Name text box, key **Body_Text**.

   d. In Dreamweaver, click to select the **This document only** option button, if necessary, and then click **OK**. In FrontPage, click the **Format** button and then click **Font**.

STEP-BY-STEP 27.3 Continued

5. Select formatting for the style as follows:

   a. Set the font to a sans serif such as **Verdana**, or a sans serif series that begins with Verdana.

   b. Set the font size to **14** points.

   c. Set the font style to **normal**.

   d. Set the font weight to **bold**.

   e. Set the font color to **black** (hexadecimal **#000000**).

   f. Set the text alignment to **justify**.

6. Click **OK** (repeatedly, if you are using FrontPage) to create the style. The style sheet should look similar to Figure 27-6.

FIGURE 27-6
Define a style in an external style sheet

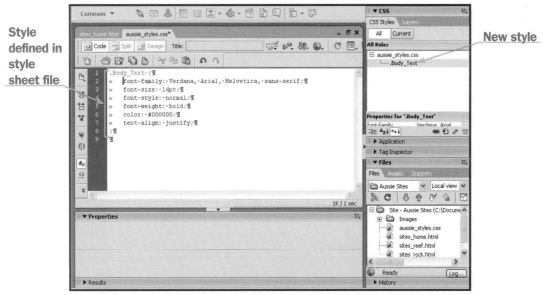

7. Save the changes and close the **aussie_styles** style sheet file. Leave **sites_home** open to use in the next exercise.

Attach a Style Sheet to a Web Page

You can easily link a style sheet to any Web page. Simply open the page, select the command to attach a style sheet, and then locate and select the style sheet file. Your program inserts the code that links the page to the style sheet into the page <HEAD> section. In Dreamweaver, click the Attach Style Sheet button in the CSS Styles panel. In FrontPage, click Format on the Menu bar and then click Style Sheet Links.

Extra for Experts

Most programs include external style sheet templates that already include style rules for different formatting. Select a style sheet template to create a new style sheet for your Web site. You can use the existing styles as is, or modify them to customize your page formatting.

STEP-BY-STEP 27.4

1. Select the command to attach a style sheet to the **site_home** page. In Dreamweaver, click the **Attach Style Sheet** button in the CSS Styles panel, or click the **Style** drop-down arrow in the Properties panel and then click **Attach Style Sheet**. In FrontPage, click **Format** on the Menu bar and then click **Style Sheet Links**. The Attach External style sheet dialog box, shown in Figure 27-7, displays.

FIGURE 27-7
Attach External Sheet dialog box

2. In the dialog box, click **Browse** (Dreamweaver) or **Add** (FrontPage).

3. Locate and select **aussie_styles.css**, and then click **OK** twice to attach the style sheet.

4. Click anywhere in the paragraph of text beginning *Australia is a large....*

5. Click the **Style** drop-down arrow and then click **Body_Text**. The style is applied to the paragraph.

6. Change to Code view. It should look similar to Figure 27-8. Notice the link to the style sheet in the <HEAD> tag, and the class attribute that applies the style to the paragraph text.

FIGURE 27-8
Link to an external style sheet

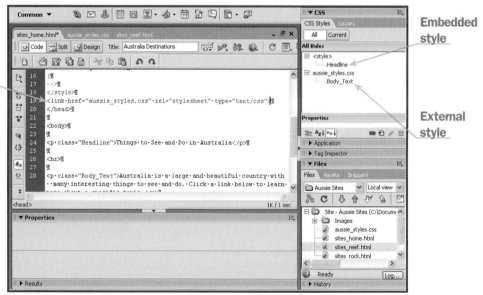

Page is linked to an external style sheet

Embedded style

External style

STEP-BY-STEP 27.4 Continued

7. Save the changes to **site_home** and leave it open to use in the next exercise.

Copy Embedded Styles to a Style Sheet

If you want to use embedded styles from one page to format other pages, you could recreate the styles in a style sheet, or you can copy the code to a style sheet file.

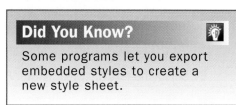

Did You Know?

Some programs let you export embedded styles to create a new style sheet.

S TEP-BY-STEP 27.5

1. Select the eight lines of code beginning with .*Headline {* (in Dreamweaver, it is lines 9 through 16). These are the lines that define the Headline style rule.

2. Click **Edit** on the Menu bar and then click **Cut**.

3. Open the **aussie_styles** style sheet file in your Web page development program and position the insertion point on a blank line at the end of the file.

4. Click **Edit** on the Menu bar and then click **Paste**. The file should look similar to Figure 27-9.

FIGURE 27-9
Copy embedded style code to a style sheet

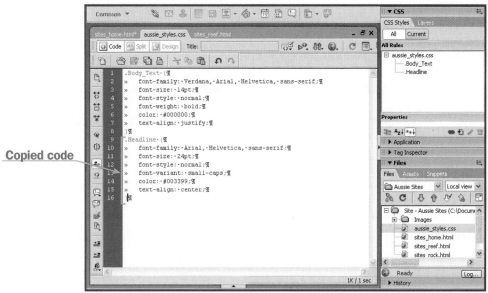

Copied code

5. Save the changes and close the **aussie_styles** file.

6. In the **sites_home** page, delete the five lines of the `<style>` tag (lines 7 through 11 in Dreamweaver). This code is no longer needed because the style rule has been removed. Do not delete the code linking to the external style sheet (`<link href="aussie_styles.css" rel="stylesheet" type="text/css">`).

STEP-BY-STEP 27.5 Continued

7. Change to Design view.

8. Select the text *Ayers Rock* and create a hyperlink to the **sites_rock** file. (For information on creating hyperlinks, refer to Lesson 26.)

9. Select the text *The Great Barrier Reef* and create a hyperlink to the **sites_reef** file.

10. Save the changes.

11. Test the *Ayers Rock* link. (In Dreamweaver, press and hold **Ctrl** and double-click the link. In FrontPage, press and hold **Ctrl** and click the link.) The **sites_rock** page should display.

12. Save all the changes and leave **sites_rock** open to use in the next exercise.

Use One Style Sheet to Format a Web Site

Once you create an external style sheet, you can easily attach it to any page in a Web site and use it to apply consistent formatting on all pages.

STEP-BY-STEP 27.6

1. Attach the **aussie_styles** style sheet to the **sites_rock** Web page.

2. Apply the **Headline** style to the first line of text.

3. Apply the **Body_Text** style to the main paragraph of text.

4. Select the text *Home* and create a hyperlink to the **sites_home** Web page.

5. Select the text *The Great Barrier Reef* and create a hyperlink to the **sites_reef** Web page. Save the changes to the page.

6. Test the link to *The Great Barrier Reef*. The **sites_reef** page should display.

7. Attach the **aussie_styles** style sheet to the **sites_reef** Web page.

8. Apply the **Headline** style to the first line of text and the **Body_Text** style to the main paragraph of text.

9. Select the text *Home* and create a hyperlink to the **sites_home** Web page.

10. Select the text *Ayer's Rock* and create a hyperlink to the **sites_rock** Web page. Save the changes to the page.

11. Test the link to **Home**. The **sites_home** page should display. Leave it open to use in the next exercise.

Apply a Background Graphic

Applying color to the background of a Web page is one way to get away from a plain white screen. But, if you want to create a page background that identifies the content and adds texture to the page, you can use background graphics. Background graphics are usually small, washed out images that will not distract too much from the page content. Often, a company might use its logo as a background image, but any graphic will do.

Some programs, including Dreamweaver, *tile* the images by default, which means they are repeated in columns and rows over the entire page. Some programs, including FrontPage, simply insert a single image on the page. In Dreamweaver you can select whether or not you want to repeat the image but in FrontPage you cannot. Keep in mind, however, that other page content must display over—or in front of—the image. Therefore, you want to keep the image small and somewhat transparent.

To apply a background graphic you add the BACKGROUND attribute to the <BODY> tag and then specify the graphic file name as the value. Most Web site development programs generate the code automatically when you select the graphic as a background. Usually, you specify the background graphic in the Page Properties dialog box.

Hot Tip

Use a graphic of a geometric pattern to achieve the appearance of texture on the page.

Extra for Experts

In FrontPage, you can tile a background image by using a table on the Web page. Ask your instructor for more information or consult the FrontPage Help program.

Hot Tip

If necessary, you can edit the image in a graphics program to increase its transparency.

S TEP-BY-STEP 27.7

1. Use a file management program to copy the graphics file **Step27-7** from the data files to the **Images** folder in the **Aussie Sites** folder. Rename it **roo**. Key the **gif** file extension if necessary.

2. Open the Page Properties dialog box. In Dreamweaver, click **Modify** on the Menu bar and then click **Page Properties**. In FrontPage, click **Format** on the Menu bar and then click **Background**. If necessary, select the option to use a Background picture.

Note

You may want to set a background color as well as a background image. If the visitor's browser is set not to display graphics, the color will display instead.

STEP-BY-STEP 27.7 Continued

3. Click the *Background image* **Browse** button and then locate and select the **roo** graphics file in the **Images** folder. Click **OK**. The Page properties dialog box should look similar to Figure 27-10.

FIGURE 27-10
Page Properties dialog box

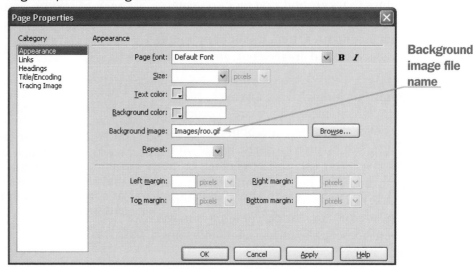

4. Click **OK**. The image is inserted on the page background using the default settings. It should look similar to Figure 27-11. (In FrontPage, a single image the size of the page displays.)

FIGURE 27-11
Background graphics on a page

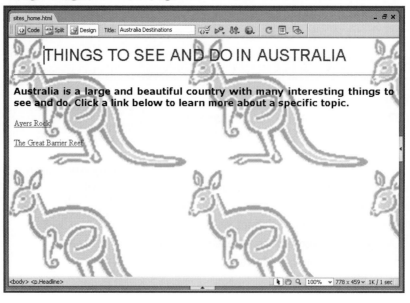

5. Save the changes to **sites_home**. Leave it open to use in the next exercise.

Define a Remote Site

The procedures for publishing a Web site are different depending on the Web site development program, but in general you must prepare for publication by defining the *remote site*. The remote site is the storage location of the published Web site. It might be on a Web server maintained by an Internet Service Provider (ISP), on an Intranet server maintained by your company, or even on your computer's hard disk, if your computer is acting as a Web server.

Defining the remote site usually includes specifying the URL of the site and selecting the method you will use to transfer the files. Frequently you will use *File Transfer Protocol (FTP)*, which is a file transfer system that allows you to *upload*, or *put*, files on an Internet server located somewhere on the World Wide Web. It also allows you to *download*, or *get*, files from a server on the Web and transfer them to your computer. In some programs, you may also have to specify the URL of the host Web server, and the protocol that you will use to transfer your site files.

In most programs, you provide all of the remote site data in a single dialog box. In Dreamweaver, you use the Advanced tab of the Site Definition dialog box. In FrontPage you use the Remote Web Site Properties dialog box.

If you do not have access to a Web server, you can publish your Web site to a folder on your own computer or on a local network.

S TEP-BY-STEP 27.8

The following exercise assumes you will be using a local folder. Your instructor may want you to use a location on a Web server if one is available.

1. Use a file management program to create a new folder name **Remote Site** in the location where you are storing the solutions for this lesson.

2. Switch back to your Web site development program and select the command to open the dialog box for setting up a remote site. In Dreamweaver, click **Site** on the Menu bar, and then click **Manage Sites**. Select the **Aussie Sites** folder and then click **Edit**. The Site Definition dialog box displays. Click the **Advanced** tab and then click **Remote Info** in the *Category* list. In FrontPage, click **View** on the Menu bar and then click **Remote Web Site**. Click the **Remote Web Site Properties** button at the top of the page to display the Remote Web Site Properties dialog box.

3. Select the option for storing in a local folder. In Dreamweaver, click the **Access** drop-down arrow and then click **Local/Network**. In FrontPage, click the **File System** option button. (If your instructor wants you to use a Web server, select **FTP** and then fill in the required information.)

4. Enter the path to the remote folder. For example, click the **Browse** button and navigate to the **Remote Site** folder you created in step 1. Click **Select** in Dreamweaver or **Open** in FrontPage.

STEP-BY-STEP 27.8 Continued

5. Click **OK**. If your program prompts you to create or recreate the Web site or cache at the specified loca-tion, click **OK**. If you are using Dreamweaver, click **Done** to close the Manage Sites dialog box. If you are using FrontPage, both the local Web site and the Remote Web site folders display on your screen in Remove Web site view. Leave your Web site development program open to use in the next exercise.

Publish a Site

Once you have defined the remote Web site, you can transfer your Web site files and folder to the remote site to make them available to the world. Most Web site development programs let you view both the local Web site and the remote Web site onscreen at the same time, so you can easily transfer the files from one to the other. In FrontPage, you use Remote Web site view. In Dreamweaver, you click the *Expand to show local and remote sites* button to expand the Files panel to show both the Local view and the Remote view at the same time.

To transfer the files, upload them from the local site to the remote site. In some pro-grams, including Dreamweaver, you select the folder(s) or file(s) you want to upload, but in other programs, including FrontPage, all items that have changed since the last upload are uploaded by default. To make the transfer, select the command to upload. In Dreamweaver, you click the Put button. In FrontPage, you select the *Local to Remote* option, and then click the Publish Web site button. After the transfer, you will see the Web site folders and files in both locations.

STEP-BY-STEP 27.9

1. If you are using Dreamweaver, click the **Expand to show local and remote sites** button in the Files panel. The panel expands to show both, as shown in Figure 27-12. If necessary, click the Refresh button or press F5 to refresh the display. (In FrontPage, Remote Web site view should be displayed from the previous exercise. If not, click **View** on the Menu bar and then click **Remote Web Site**.)

STEP-BY-STEP 27.9 Continued

FIGURE 27-12
View remote and local sites side by side

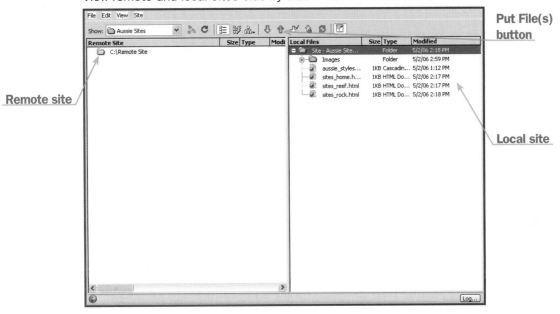

2. If necessary, select the **Aussie Sites** root level folder. If you are using FrontPage, click the **Local to remote** option button.

3. Click the button to upload the files. In Dreamweaver, click the **Put File(s)** button, and then click **OK**. In FrontPage, click the **Publish Web site** button. Your program uploads the files to the remote site. When the transfer is finished, it should look similar to Figure 27-13.

FIGURE 27-13
Uploaded files on remote site

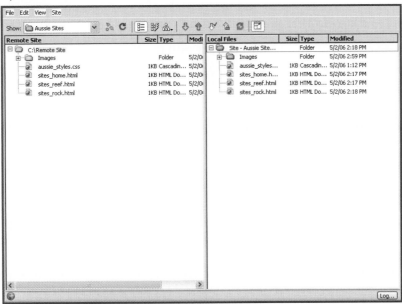

STEP-BY-STEP 27.9 Continued

4. Change back to the default Design workspace view. In Dreamweaver, click **Collapse to show only local or remote site**. In FrontPage, click **View** on the Menu bar and then click **Folders**.

5. Launch your Web browser and open the **sites_home** file stored in the **Remote Site** folder. (If you used a Web server as a remote site, browse to the home page URL.) Test the links to the other two pages in the site, and then close your browser. Leave your Web site development program open to use in the next exercise.

> **Note**
>
> Your program may automatically generate a folder named _notes that includes an .xml-formatted file that specifies certain design information.

Add a Web Page Created with a Different Program to Your Site

You can add Web pages created with different programs to your Web site simply by storing them in your Web site folder. This is useful if you want to make information created in a different format available on your Web site. You might want to include spreadsheet data, a presentation file, or a publication form for visitors to print. Or you might have information already stored in a word processing document that can supplement the information on your Web pages. It also makes it possible for coworkers or team members to supply information for the site even if they are not familiar with HTML or Web site development programs.

Many types of programs let you save files in Web page format. For example, in Unit 3 you learned how to save a presentation file as a Web page, and in Unit 4 you learned how to create a Web publication. You can then incorporate the page into your Web site design by creating links to and from the page or by attaching the site's style sheet so you can apply consistent formatting.

There are two ways to store a file in your Web site folder:

■ Open the file in its native program and use the File > Save As command or the Publish to the Web command to select the storage location.

■ Use your file management program to copy it into the Web site folder.

After you add content to your Web site, or modify existing content, you must be sure to republish to update the remote site.

Add a Word Document Web Page to a Site

Most major word processing programs such as Microsoft Office Word let you save a document in HTML format. The same document can then be opened in the original program as well as in a browser. When the original program saves the document in HTML format, it adds code that is only necessary if you plan to open the document again in the original program. Once you add the file to your Web site, you can use tools in your Web site development program to remove the unnecessary code.

> **Note**
>
> Not all Web site development programs have a tool for cleaning up Word HTML code.

STEP-BY-STEP 27.10

1. Use a file management program to copy the HTML Word document **Step27-10** from the data files to the **Aussie Sites** folder. Rename it to **wildlife**. Key the **html** file extension if necessary.

2. Open the **wildlife** Web page in your Web site development program. It should look similar to Figure 27-14.

FIGURE 27-14
Word HTML document

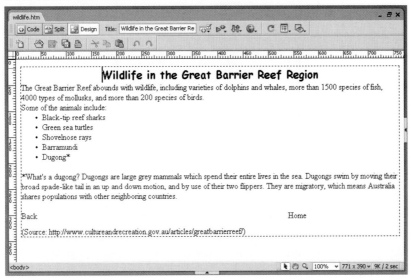

3. Select the command to clean up the Word HTML. If you are using Dreamweaver, click **Commands** on the Menu bar and then click **Clean Up Word HTML**. A dialog box listing elements that can be cleaned displays, as shown in Figure 27-15. If the command is not available in your program, skip to step 6.

FIGURE 27-15
Clean up Word HTML dialog box

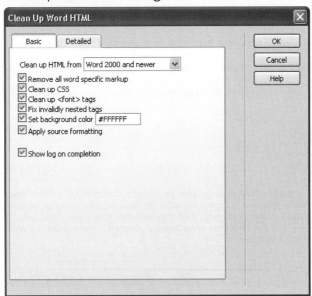

STEP-BY-STEP 27.10 Continued

4. Verify that all check boxes are selected, and then click **OK**. Your program cleans the document and displays a results dialog box, similar to the one in Figure 27-16.

FIGURE 27-16
Results of the HTML code clean-up

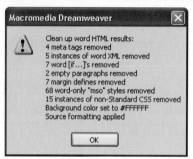

5. Click **OK**.

6. Attach the **aussie_styles** style sheet to the **wildlife** page.

7. Apply the **Headline** style to the first paragraph and the **Body_Text** style to all paragraphs except the items in the bulleted list, the words *Back* and *Home*, and the source information on the last line. (Remember, embedded and inline formatting will override the external style sheet formatting.)

8. Select the word **Back** and create a hyperlink to the **sites_reef** page.

9. Select the word **Home** and create a hyperlink to the **sites_home** page. The page should look similar to Figure 27-17.

FIGURE 27-17
Formatted Word document

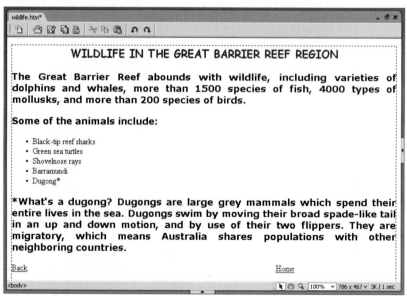

STEP-BY-STEP 27.10 Continued

10. Save the changes to the page and then test the **Back** link. The **sites_reef** page should display.

11. Position the insertion point at the end of the main paragraph and key **Click here for more information about reef wildlife**.

12. Select the sentence you keyed in step 11 and create a hyperlink to the **wildlife** file.

13. Save the changes to the file and then test the hyperlink. Test the **Home** link on the **wildlife** page.

14. Close all open pages and leave your Web site development program open to use in the next exercise.

Update the Remote Site

Now that you have added content to your Web site, you must republish it to make sure the remote site is current, as well. You can use the same steps that you used to upload the files originally to upload the revised content.

STEP-BY-STEP 27.11

1. Display both the remote site and the local site onscreen at the same time. If you are using Dreamweaver, click the **Expand to show local and remote sites** button in the Files panel. If you are using FrontPage, click **View** on the Menu bar and then click **Remote Web Site**.

2. If necessary, refresh the page to display all files.

3. Upload all files in the **Aussie Sites** Web site folder, or upload all changed pages. In Dreamweaver, select the **Aussie Sites** folder on the local site, click the **Put File(s)** button, and then click **OK**. In FrontPage, select the **Local to remote** option button and then click **Publish Web site**.

4. When the transfer is complete, the remote site should include the **wildlife** Web page document.

5. Close your Web site development program.

6. If you want, test the Web site in your browser. When you are finished, close the browser.

SUMMARY

In this lesson, you learned:

■ Most Web site development programs let you use cascading style sheets to ensure consistent formatting throughout a Web site.

■ External style sheets are stored in a separate file in a Web site.

■ Embedded style sheets are stored in the <HEAD> section of a page.

■ Inline style sheets are used to format individual elements on a page.

- Each CSS rule includes a selector and a declaration, which is always enclosed in brackets.
- You can use class styles to format any range or block of text.
- You can use an HTML tag rule to change the formatting for any existing tag.
- You can use background graphics on a Web page.
- When a Web site is finished, you can upload it to a remote Web site so anyone can access it.
- If you do not have access to a Web server, you can publish your Web site to a folder on your own computer or on a local network.
- You can add Web pages created with different programs to your Web site simply by storing them in your Web site folder.
- If you make changes to a Web site that has already been published, you can update the remote site by republishing.

VOCABULARY *Review*

Define the following terms:

Cascading Style Sheet (CSS)	External style sheet	Put
Class styles	File Transfer Protocol (FTP)	Remote site
CSS rule	Get	Selector
Declaration	HTML tag rules	Upload
Download	Inline style sheet	
Embedded style sheet	Publish	

REVIEW *Questions*

TRUE / FALSE

Circle T if the statement is true or F if the statement is false.

T F 1. Macromedia Dreamweaver is the only Web site development program that uses Cascading Style Sheets.

T F 2. By using CSS, you can separate the Web page structure from the presentation formatting.

T F 3. A CSS rule is the code that defines the style.

T F 4. When you create or modify an HTML tag rule, all text formatted with that tag is changed.

T F 5. You can copy embedded style sheet code to an external style sheet file.

T F 6. You can only attach an external style sheet to one Web page at a time.

T   F   7. The procedures for publishing a Web site are the same in all Web site development programs.

T   F   8. If you do not have access to a Web server, you cannot publish your Web site.

T   F   9. To publish a Web site, you transfer the Web site files from a local site to a remote site.

T   F   10. Most major word processing programs, such as Microsoft Office Word, let you save a document in HTML format.

WRITTEN QUESTIONS

Write a brief answer to each of the following questions.

1. Explain the order in which style sheet rules are applied.

2. Why should you use a small, somewhat transparent image as a background graphic?

3. List at least two pieces of information you need to know in order to set up a remote Web site.

4. What are some reasons you might want to include Web pages created with different programs in a Web site, and what types of data could you include?

5. Why do you have to republish a Web site?

FILL IN THE BLANK

Complete the following sentences by writing the correct word or words in the blanks provided.

1. _____ style sheets, which are sometimes called linked style sheets, are stored in a separate file in a Web site.

2. _____ style sheets are stored in the <HEAD> section of a page and are used to format elements on that page only.

3. _____ style sheets are used to format individual elements on a page.

4. In a CSS rule, the _____ identifies the element that will be affected by the rule, such as a paragraph or heading.

5. In a CSS rule, the _____, which may be called the definition, contains the attribute and the value that determines the formatting.

6. You can apply _____ styles, which may be called Custom CSS rules or User-defined styles, to any range or block of text.

7. You can _____ an image on the background if you want it repeated in columns and rows over the entire page.

8. To apply a background graphic you add the _____ attribute to the <BODY> tag and then specify the graphic file name as the value.

9. The _____ site is the storage location of the published Web site.

10. File Transfer Protocol (FTP) is a file transfer system that allows you to upload, or _____, files on an Internet server located somewhere on the World Wide Web.

PROJECTS

PROJECT 27-1

In this project, you will create an external style sheet that includes style rules for a major heading, a subheading, and body text.

1. Launch your Web site development program and select the command to create a new external style sheet file.

   In Dreamweaver, do the following:
   A. Click **File** on the Menu bar.
   B. Click **New**.
   C. Click **Basic** page in the *Category* list.
   D. Click **CSS** in the *Basic page* list.
   E. Click **Create**.

In FrontPage, do the following:
   A. Click **File** on the Menu bar.
   B. Click **New** to display the New task pane.
   C. Click the **Style Sheets** tab.
   D. Click **Normal Style Sheet**.
   E. Click **OK**.

2. Save the CSS file as **ex_styles** in the folder where you are storing the solution files for this lesson.

3. Create a new class style named **Head1** in the current document.

4. Select formatting options as follows:
   A. Set the font to a sans serif such as **Verdana**, or a sans serif series that begins with Verdana.
   B. Set the font size to **36** points.
   C. Set the font style to **normal**.
   D. Set the font weight to **bold**.
   E. Set the font color to **#996600**.
   F. Set the text alignment to **center**.

5. Create a new class style named **Subhead** in the current document.

6. Select formatting options as follows:
   A. Set the font to a sans serif such as **Arial**, or a sans serif series that begins with Arial.
   B. Set the font size to **14** points.
   C. Set the font style to **italic**.
   D. Set the font color to **#CC6600**.
   E. Set the text alignment to **left**.

7. Create a new class style named **Body_Text** in the current document.

8. Select formatting options as follows:
   A. Set the font to a serif such as **Times New Roman**, or a serif series that begins with Times New Roman.
   B. Set the font size to **12** points.
   C. Set the font style to **normal**.
   D. Set the font color to **black** (#000000).
   E. Set the text alignment to **justify**.

9. Save the changes to **ex_styles**, and then close it. Leave your Web site development program open to use in the next exercise.

PROJECT 27-2

In this project, you will define a new Web site and add three Web pages and a version of the **ex_styles** style sheet to it. You will use the style sheet to format the pages and you will create hyperlinks among the pages.

1. Use a file management program to create a new folder named **Bears Site** that you can define as the root folder for a new Web site.

2. Copy the CSS file **Project27-2a** and the HTML files **Project27-2b, Project27-2c,** and **Project27-2d** from the data files for this lesson to the **Bears Site** folder. Rename the files as follows (if necessary, key the file extension):

Project27-2a	**bears_styles**
Project27-2b	**bears_home**
Project27-2c	**bears_brown**
Project27-2d	**bears_polar**

3. Use your Web site development program to create a new Web site named **Bears Site,** defining the **Bears Site** folder as the root level folder. If necessary, leave the *http://* address blank, do not use server technology, and select to **Edit local copies on your machine.** Specify **None** as the method of connecting to the server.

4. If necessary, create a folder named **Images** in the **Bears Site** folder. Copy the graphics files **Project27-2e** and **Project27-2f** to the **Images** folder. Rename the files as follows (key the **gif** file extension, if necessary):

Project27-2e	**brown_bear**
Project27-2f	**polar_bear**

5. Open the **bears_home** Web page and change the page title to **All About Bears.**

6. Attach the **bear_styles** style sheet to the bears_home Web page.

7. Apply the **Head1** style to the first line of text.

8. Apply the **Subhead** style to the second line of text.

9. Apply the **Body_Text** style to the paragraph of text.

10. Select the text *Brown Bears* and create a hyperlink to the **bears_brown** Web page.

11. Select the text *Polar Bears* and create a hyperlink to the **bears_polar** Web page.

12. Save the changes to the file and test the link to the **Brown Bears** page.

13. In the **bears_brown** Web page, change the page title to **Brown Bears,** and then insert the **brown_bear** graphics file to the right of the paragraph beginning *Brown bears are sometimes called....*

14. Repeat steps 6 through 9 to attach the style sheet and format text.

15. Apply the **Subhead** style to the text: *Facts about brown bears:.*

16. Select the next three lines and apply bullet list formatting.

17. Select the text *Home* and create a hyperlink to the **bears_home** page.

18. Select the text *Polar Bears* and create a hyperlink to the **bears_polar** page.

19. Save the changes and test the link to the **Polar Bears** page.

20. In the **bears_polar** Web page, change the page title to **Polar Bears,** and then insert the **polar_bear** graphics file to the right of the paragraph beginning *Polar bears are the largest bears in the world.*

21. Repeat steps 6 through 9 to attach the style sheet and format text.

22. Apply the **Subhead** style to the text: *Facts about polar bears:*.

23. Select the next four paragraphs and apply bullet list formatting.

24. Select the text *Home* and create a hyperlink to the **bears_home** page.

25. Select the text *Brown Bears* and create a hyperlink to the **bears_brown** page.

26. Save the changes and test the link to the **Brown Bears** page.

27. Preview the Web site in your browser and test all of the links. Close your browser.

28. If necessary correct errors. Save the changes and close all open pages. Keep your Web site development program open to use in the next exercise.

PROJECT 27-3

In this project, you will define a new Web site using a copy of the **Bears Site**. You will add a Word document to the site, which you will format using the external style sheet. You will also add background graphics to the page and set up hyperlinks to it. Finally, you will publish the site.

1. Use a file management program to copy the **Bears Site** folder and its contents. Rename the copied folder **Bears Site2**.

2. Copy the Word HTML file **Project27-3a** from the data files to the **Bears Site2** folder. Rename the file **bear_species**, keying the **html** file extension if necessary.

3. Copy the graphics file **Project27-3b** from the data files to the Images folder in the **Bears Site2** folder. Rename the file **bg_bear**, keying the **gif** file extension if necessary.

4. Use your Web site development program to create a new Web site named **Bears Site2**, defining the **Bears Site2** folder as the root level folder. If necessary, leave the *http://* address blank, do not use server technology, and select to **Edit local copies on your machine**. Specify **None** as the method of connecting to the server.

5. Open the **bear_species** Web page in your Web site development program.

6. Clean up the Word HTML on the page.

7. Attach the **bear_styles** style sheet to the **bear_species** page.

8. Apply the **Head1** style to the first line of text.

9. Apply the **Subhead** style to the second line of text.

10. Select the eight species of bears and apply bullet list formatting.

11. Apply the **Body_Text** style to the last line of text.

12. Select the URL *http://www.bearden.org*, click in the **Link** box in the Properties panel and key **http://www.bearden.org**. Press **Enter** to create a hyperlink to the Web page.

13. Select the word *Home* and create a hyperlink to the **bears_home** Web page.

14. Insert the **bg_bear** graphics file as a background image on the **bear_species** Web page. If possible, select to repeat it along the X axis—or across the top—of the page. For example, in Dreamweaver:

    A. Click **Modify** on the Menu bar and then click **Page Properties**.
    B. Click the *Background image* **Browse** button and locate and select the **bg_bear** file.
    C. Click the **Repeat** drop-down arrow and then click **Repeat - x**.
    D. Click **OK**.

15. Save the page and test the **Home** link to the **bears_home** page.

16. On a blank line at the bottom of the page, key **Other species of bears**, select the text and insert a link to the **bear_species** page.

17. Save the page and test the link.

18. Preview the site in your browser and test all of the links, including the link to the *bearden.org* Web site. When you are satisfied that all of the links work correctly, close your browser.

19. Define a remote Web site. If you have access to a Web server, use it for the remote site. Alternatively, set up the remote site in a folder named **Bears Remote Site** on your computer or network.

20. Publish the **Bears Site2** Web site to the remote site.

21. Test the remote site in your browser.

22. If necessary, make corrections to the local pages and then republish the site.

23. Close your browser, all open files, and your Web site development program.

 ## WEB PROJECT

Cascading style sheets can greatly simplify the chore of formatting multiple pages in a Web site by making the same styles available for all pages. Most Web site development programs come with a few built-in CSS templates that include basic styles for formatting text. You can also find CSS templates on the Internet that are available to download for free. Use the Internet to research cascading style sheets to learn more about how you can use them to format Web sites. With your instructor's permission, locate and select one or two CSS templates that you can download for free. Attach them to a Web site and use them to format the pages.

 ## TEAMWORK PROJECT

In this teamwork project, work together to develop a Web site about an aspect of your local community. For example, you might want to focus on the history of the community, about interesting places in the community, or even about the geography of your community.

Assign each team member one topic to research and about which to create a Web page. Work together to develop your ideas and to create a presentation design for your site. For example, select a color scheme, font scheme, and page organization. Decide the type of navigation system you want to use. You might want to develop styles and store them in an external style sheet so each team member can use them to format different pages.

Define a Web site and store all of the pages in the Web site folder. If anyone is using graphics or other multimedia files, make sure they are all stored in a graphics folder in the root folder. Work together to design a home page for your site, and then create hyperlinks to the other pages, and from the other pages back to the home page. Test the Web site in a browser. Ask classmates to review the site and offer suggestions for improving it. Make the improvements and test the site again. When the site is complete, publish it to a Web file server or to a remote site folder on your local computer.

CRITICAL *Thinking*

Use the information you have learned about cascading style sheets to simplify the code in the Web site you developed for your English/Language Arts class in Lessons 24 and 25. You may want to copy the files from the site to a new site, and remove all formatting code in order to start from scratch. You can develop an external style sheet and use it to apply consistent formatting to all pages in the site, and then customize formatting as necessary using embedded or inline styles. When you complete the project, preview the site in a browser. Ask a classmate to review it as well, and offer suggestions for improvement. Make the changes and preview the Web site again. When you are satisfied with the results, publish the Web site.

WEB SITE DEVELOPMENT

REVIEW *Questions*

TRUE / FALSE

Circle T if the statement is true or F if the statement is false.

T F 1. You must have a Web site development program in order to create an HTML file.

T F 2. All HTML tags are used in pairs.

T F 3. You can apply font formatting to text on a Web page.

T F 4. In an HTML tag, an attribute value must be enclosed in question marks.

T F 5. You can use the BGCOLOR attribute to change the background color of a Web page.

T F 6. Graphics must always be aligned in the top-left corner of a Web page.

T F 7. Most Web site development programs let you display Code view and Design view on-screen at the same time.

T F 8. Most Web site development programs have a spelling checker utility.

T F 9. You cannot update the content on a Web site that has already been published.

T F 10. Many different types of programs let you save a document in HTML format so you can incorporate it into a Web site.

MATCHING

Match the correct term in Column 1 to its description in Column 2.

Column 1

___ 1. Web site

___ 2. Active content

___ 3. Root level folder

___ 4. Navigation system

___ 5. Cascading Style Sheet

___ 6. HTML tags

___ 7. Attribute

___ 8. External style sheet

___ 9. Acceptable Use Policy

___ 10. ALINK

Column 2

A. Codes that define data on a Web page so that it can be interpreted and displayed by a Web browser.

B. Rules that outline the rights and responsibilities of users on networks and Web sites.

C. A term that describes the properties of an element.

D. A collection of formatting settings that you can attach to a Web page and then use to format text and objects on the page.

E. A file that stores formatting rules, which can be linked to a Web page.

F. Multiple, related Web pages connected using hyperlinks.

G. Elements on a Web page that change, such as video or animations, or elements that allow the visitor to interact with the Web page.

H. The attribute that controls the color of a hyperlink when the link is being clicked.

I. The main folder where you store the files and subfolders for a Web site.

J. How hyperlinks are implemented to facilitate the way visitors browse from page to page in a Web site.

FILL IN THE BLANK

Complete the following sentences by writing the correct word or words in the blanks provided.

1. A Web _____ is a computer on which you can store Web site and Web page data so that other people can access it.

2. In a URL, the _____ is the name that identifies the computer, or Web server, where the page is stored.

3. A(n)_____ Web site structure allows Web site visitors to jump to any page on the Web site from any other page.

4. A(n) _____ Web site structure organizes pages into categories and subcategories.

5. When you want to use a custom color on a Web page, use a(n) _____ code.

6. If you want to integrate a picture on the same line as text, you must _____ the <IMG> tag within the <P> </P> tag that encloses the text.

7. In most Web site development programs the first step in developing a Web site is to _____ it.

8. Use the _____ tag to start a new line on a Web page.

9. Usually, the code that defines an embedded style is stored in the _____ section of a Web page.

10. The _____ site is the storage location of a published Web site.

PROJECTS

PROJECT U5-1

In this project you will use a text editor to create a home page for a Web site about music.

1. Use a file management program to create a folder named **Music** where you can store the files for this project.

2. Use a file management program to create one folder named **Images** and another named **Audio** in the **Music** folder.

3. Copy the graphics files **ProjectU5-1a** and **ProjectU5-1b** from the data files for this lesson to the **Images** folder. Rename *ProjectU5-1a* to **notes1** and rename *ProjectU5-1b* to **notes2**. Key the **gif** file extension, if necessary.

4. Copy the audio file **ProjectU5-1c** from the data files for this lesson to the **Audio** folder. Rename it **jazz**. Key the **aif** file extension if necessary.

5. Start your text editor program and save the new blank file as **index.html** in the **Music** folder.

6. Key the following HTML code:

```
<HTML>
<HEAD><TITLE>Music F.Y.I</TITLE></HEAD>
<BODY BGCOLOR="#FFCCCC">
<CENTER><IMG SRC="Images/notes1.gif" HEIGHT="100" WIDTH="150">
<IMG SRC="Images/notes1.gif" HEIGHT="100" WIDTH="150">
<IMG SRC="Images/notes1.gif" HEIGHT="100" WIDTH="150">
<IMG SRC="Images/notes1.gif" HEIGHT="100" WIDTH="150"></CENTER><BR>
<EMBED SRC="Audio/jazz.aif" AUTOSTART="true" CONTROLLER="console"
  HEIGHT="50" WIDTH="144" ALIGN="right">
```

```
<P><FONT SIZE="7" FACE="Arial" COLOR="#003399">My Music Web Site</FONT></P>
<HR COLOR="#6600CC">
<FONT SIZE="4"><P ALIGN="justify"><IMG SRC="Images/notes2.gif" HEIGHT="102"
  WIDTH="75" ALIGN="left">What's your favorite type of music? Is it Hip
  Hop? Techno? Classic Rock? It doesn't matter whether you load your MP3
  player with jazz, classical, or opera as long as you are listening! From
  this Web page you can find out a little bit about some different types
  of music. Learn some history, find out the names of some notable
  musicians, and maybe even feel the rhythm!</P></FONT>
<HR COLOR="#6600CC">
<FONT SIZE="5" FACE="Arial"><P>Types of Music</P>
<UL><LI>Jazz
<LI>Rock and Roll
<LI>Hip Hop
</UL></FONT>
</BODY>
</HTML>
```

7. Save the changes to the HTML file.

8. Launch your browser and open the **index.html** file. Enable active content as necessary. The page should look similar to Figure U5-1.

FIGURE U5-1
index.html page in browser

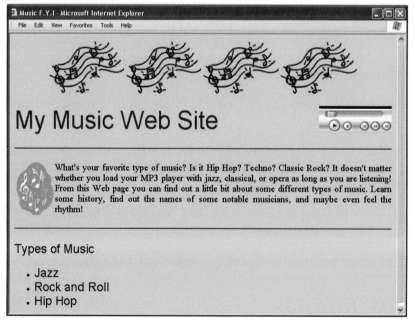

9. Check the file for errors, including typographical errors, and test the audio controls.

10. Minimize your browser and edit the HTML file in your text editor to correct any problems, and then save the changes.

11. Restore your browser window and refresh the page.

12. Close your browser and your text editor.

PROJECT U5-2

In this project you will use a Web site development program to develop and publish a version of the music Web site.

1. Use a file management program to copy the entire folder **ProjectU5-2** from the data files for this lesson to the location where you are storing the solutions. Rename the folder **Music2**.

2. Launch your Web site development program and select the command to create a new Web site named **Music F.Y.I.**, defining the **Music2** folder as the root level folder. If necessary, leave the *http://* address blank, do not use server technology, and select to edit local copies on your machine. Specify **None** as the method of connecting to the server.

3. Open the **index.html** file in your Web site development program. This is a version of the **index** file you created in Project U5-1, but all formatting has been removed.

4. Create a new external style sheet named **music_styles** in the **Music2** folder.

5. Create a class style in the CSS document named **Head1**, using the following formatting:
   A. Set the font to a sans serif such as **Verdana**, or a sans serif series that begins with Verdana.
   B. Set the font size to **24** points.
   C. Set the font style to **normal**.
   D. Set the font weight to **bold**.
   E. Set the font color to **#003399**.

6. Create a class style in the CSS document named **Body_Text**, using the following formatting:
   A. Set the font to a serif such as **Georgia**, or a serif series that begins with Georgia.
   B. Set the font size to **12** points.
   C. Set the font style to **normal**.
   D. Set the font weight to **bold**.
   E. Set the font color to **black** (**#000000**).
   F. Set the text alignment to **justify**.

7. Create a class style in CSS document named **Subhead**, using the following formatting:
   A. Set the font to a sans serif such as **Arial**, or a sans serif series that begins with Arial.
   B. Set the font size to **14** points.
   C. Set the font style to **normal**.
   D. Set the font color to **#003399**.

8. Save the changes to the **music_styles** style sheet and then attach it to the **index** Web page.

9. Apply styles to the index page as follows:
   A. Apply the **Head1** style to the first line of text.
   B. Apply the **Body_Text** style to the main paragraph.
   C. Apply the **Subhead** style to the text *Types of Music*.

10. Apply the background color **#FFCCCC** to the index page.

11. Select the bullet item *Jazz* and create a hyperlink to the **jazz.html** Web page in the **Music F.Y.I.** site.

12. Select the bullet item *Hip Hop* and create a hyperlink to the **hip_hop.html** Web page in the **Music F.Y.I.** site.

13. Save the changes to the page.

14. Test the link to the **jazz** page.

15. Change the Web page title to **Jazz F.Y.I.**

16. Attach the **music_styles** style sheet to the **jazz** Web page.

17. Apply styles to the jazz page as follows:
    A. Apply the **Head1** style to the first line of text.
    B. Apply the **Body_Text** style to the main paragraph.
    C. Apply the **Subhead** style to the text *Notable Jazz Musicians.*

18. Apply the background image **sax** that is stored in the **Images** folder in the **Music2** folder to the **hip_hop** page. If available set the repeat to **Repeat-Y**, or to display in a single column along the left edge of the window. (This option will not be available in FrontPage.)

19. Select the text **HOME** and create a hyperlink to the **index.html** page.

20. Save the changes to the page and test the **HOME** link.

21. Test the **Hip Hop** link.

22. Change the Web page title to **Hip Hop F.Y.I.**

23. Attach the **music_styles** style sheet to the **hip_hop** Web page.

24. Apply styles to the **hip_hop** page as follows:
    A. Apply the **Head1** style to the first line of text.
    B. Apply the **Body_Text** style to the main paragraph.
    C. Apply the **Subhead** style to the text *Notable Hip Hop Performers.*

25. Apply the background image **rapper** that is stored in the **Images** folder in the **Music2** folder to the **hip_hop** page. If available set the repeat to **Repeat-Y**, or to display in a single column along the left edge of the window. (This option will not be available in FrontPage.)

26. Select the text **HOME** and create a hyperlink to the **index.html** page.

27. Save the changes to the page and test the **HOME** link.

28. Test the Web site in your browser. If necessary, make corrections to the three pages using your Web site development program and then test the site again.

29. Define a remote Web site. If you have access to a Web server, use it for the remote site. Alternatively, set up the remote site in a folder named **Music Remote Site** on your computer or network.

30. Publish the **Music F.Y.I.** Web site to the remote site.

31. Test the remote site in your browser.

32. If necessary, make corrections to the local pages and then republish the site.

33. Close your browser, all open files, and your Web site development program.

SIMULATION

The owner of the Lighthouse View Inn, a bed and breakfast located on the coast of Maine, has asked you to help increase the inn's presence on the World Wide Web. As a Web site developer, you have proposed the following two projects:

Create an HTML page that can be displayed in any browser on any platform. Other organizations such as a travel bureau or Chamber of Commerce can link to the page to incorporate the information into their Web sites.

Create a Web site for the inn, using lots of graphics and simple text to provide general information for potential customers and travel agents.

Before starting each job, take the time to read through the explanation and instructions so you have a solid understanding of what you must do. Working alone or with a partner, review the steps and then create a schedule for completing the job. Set up a timeline with appropriate milestones. Establish criteria that you believe should be met for each stage of the project, and create a rubric that you can use to gauge your accomplishments. Periodically, have your classmates review your work and offer comments. Incorporate their suggestions as you continue your work.

JOB U5-1

In this project you will use a text editor to create an HTML file that provides general information about the inn and the area. You will include text, graphics, and animation. You will use color, font formatting, horizontal rules, and lists to make the page interesting and appealing.

1. Use a file management program to create a folder named **Inn Page** where you can store the files for this project.

2. Use a file management program to create one folder named **Images** and another named **Animations** in the **Inn Page** folder.

3. Copy the animation file **JobU5-1a** from the data files for this lesson to the **Animations** folder. Rename it **light**. Key the **gif** file extension if necessary.

4. Copy the graphics file **JobU5-1b** and **JobU5-1c** from the data files for this lesson to the **Images** folder. Rename *JobU5-1b* to **view** and rename *JobU5-1c* to **sunset**. Key the **jpg** file extension, if necessary.

5. Start your text editor program and save the new blank file as **inn_page.html** in the **Inn Page** folder.

6. Key the following HTML code:

```
<HTML>
<HEAD><TITLE>Lighthouse View Inn</TITLE></HEAD>
<BODY FONT="Garamond" BGCOLOR="#66CCFF">
<IMG SRC="Animations/light.gif" HEIGHT="150" WIDTH="150" ALIGN="left">
<P><CENTER><FONT SIZE="7"><B>Lighthouse View Inn</B></FONT><BR>
<FONT SIZE="5" FACE="Garamond"><B><I>"Your Home Away From
   Home"</I></B></FONT></CENTER></P>
<HR COLOR="#333399"><BR><BR><BR>
<P><IMG SRC="Images/view.jpg" HEIGHT="150" WIDTH="200" ALIGN="right">
```

```
<FONT SIZE="5">Come for the Beauty<BR></FONT>
<FONT SIZE="4"><UL><LI>Wake up to the smell of salt air.
<LI>Gaze across the bay over your morning coffee.
<LI>Stroll the beaches in the afternoon light.
<LI>Watch the sunset shoot fingers of gold across the sky.
<LI>Bask in the cool evening breeze.
<LI>Count the stars overhead.
</UL><P/></FONT>
<HR COLOR="#333399">
<P><IMG SRC="Images/sunset.jpg" HEIGHT="150" WIDTH="125" ALIGN="right">
<FONT SIZE="5">Stay for the Fun<BR></FONT>
<FONT SIZE="4"><UL><LI>Ride the waves.
<LI>Raft the rivers.
<LI>Climb the mountains.
<LI>Hike the trails.
<LI>Fish the ocean.
<LI>Sail the waters.
</UL><P/>
<HR COLOR="#333399">
<CENTER>To learn more about Lighthouse View Inn:<BR>
56778 Ocean Drive<BR>
Wells, ME 04090<BR>
(207) 555-5555<BR>
inquiries@lvi.mail.net</CENTER></FONT>
</BODY>
</HTML>
```

7. Save the changes to the HTML file.

8. Launch your browser and open the **inn_page.html** file. Enable active content as necessary.

9. Check the file for errors, including typographical errors.

10. Minimize your browser and edit the HTML file in your text editor to correct any problems, and then save the changes.

11. Restore your browser window and refresh the page.

12. Close your browser and your text editor.

JOB U5-2

In this project you will use your Web site development program to create a Web site for the Lighthouse View Inn. You will plan the design and navigational structure, gather the content that you want to include, and then define and create the site. You may want to use files that you created in the Unit Review lessons of the other units in this book, such as a graphics logo, as well as research on Maine or inns that you completed previously. Alternatively, you may use the data files provided with this lesson.

To begin, decide how many pages you want in your site. You should include at least three—a home page or index, and two content pages. You might have a page that lists information about the inn, such as the types of rooms and other amenities available. (Refer to the Word document file **JobU5-2a** provided.) A second page might list things to do in Maine. (Refer to the Word document file **JobU5-2b** provided.) You might want to have a page with information about seasonal activities planned at the inn. (Refer to the Word document file **JobU5-2c** provided.) You might even want to include a Word document saved in HTML format in your Web site.

Next, decide on the type of navigational structure. Do you want visitors to move from page to page in a linear fashion, or do you want to create a hierarchical structure? Would a random-access structure make sense for this site? You might want to draw a diagram of your site, indicating how the pages will link to each other. Create a root level folder named **Lighthouse View Site** and create any subfolders that you will need.

When you are satisfied with the navigational structure, think about design issues. You may want to pick a color scheme and look up the hexadecimal codes for the colors before you begin. You should gather all of associated files you want to use, including graphics and animations. If you cannot locate files on your own, you might want to use **JobU5-2d** (the LVI logo), **JobU5-2e** (an animated .gif), or the animated .gif you used in Job U5-1. You might also want to use a graphic background, such as the file **JobU5-2f**. Give the files identifiable names, and store them in the appropriate subfolders in your site folder.

When you are ready, launch your Web site development program and define the Web site. You may want to start by creating an external style sheet that you can use to apply styles to all pages in the site. Name the style sheet something like **lvi_styles**. Create your index page and give it a name such as **lvi_index**. Use styles and other formatting tools to make it appealing and interesting. Include text or graphics for linking to the other pages. Don't forget to add appropriate page titles. Check your work as you go, and test it in a browser. Create and format the additional pages, testing the links to make sure they work. Check your spelling and watch for grammatical errors as well.

When you are satisfied with the Web site, publish it to a remote site on a Web server or on your local computer or network. Test the site, and ask your classmates to test it as well. Ask them what they liked or did not like about the site, and make improvements if possible. Republish the site, if necessary.

INTEGRATED SIMULATION

Introduction

BioTarium, a small, not-for-profit museum of natural science in Kansas City, Missouri, is dedicated to making science and nature accessible to people of all ages. It provides a hands-on learning center for the entire family, with four levels of indoor exhibitions and over three acres of outdoor space. Permanent exhibits include small mammals, reptiles, birds of prey, ecosystems of the world, and a working beaver dam. It has nature trails for self-guided tours, and it runs educational programs in the classroom and out. BioTarium has received a large donation from the estate of a wealthy patron. The museum trustees want to use a portion of the funds to increase community awareness of the facilities and programs, and to attract new visitors. They have hired you to assist in the planning and development of multimedia marketing and business materials.

The following jobs step you through the process of creating these materials and are set up to challenge your creativity and critical thinking skills. They provide suggestions instead of specific steps so you can develop your own ideas to explore the possibilities of multimedia applications. Each job requires the use of two or more multimedia programs such as graphics, animation, video, presentation systems, desktop publishing, or Web page development. Jobs may also require use of supplementary programs such as word processors, text editors, spreadsheets, or databases. You may complete each job on your own or work in teams. For example, each team member could be responsible for completing the tasks associated with one program, and then the entire team could work together to integrate the results.

As you complete the jobs, keep in mind everything you have learned about multimedia design and creation. Consider such factors as the audience and the message, as well as the basic principles of design and color. Think about whether a file will be printed or viewed on a computer screen and how that affects your work. At different stages, ask your classmates to review your work, and then use their suggestions to make improvements.

The following information is the company name, tagline, street address, telephone, fax, and Web site address that you should use when necessary in your documents and files:

BioTarium

"It's Your World; Discover It"

1522 E. 16th Street

Kansas City, Missouri 64108

Tel. (816) 555-5555

Fax (816) 555-5556

www.biotarium.org

mail@biotarium.org

JOB 1

The museum director wants a new logo for the BioTarium to use on printed documents such as stationery, postcard mailers, and brochures. In this job, design and create the logo using a graphics program, and then use the logo to design and create a template for letterhead stationery using your desktop publishing program.

1. Use your graphics program to design and create the logo in a file saved with a descriptive name such as **BioLogo1**. You may start with an existing image, such as a .gif-formatted drawing of an animal or plant, or you may start from scratch. Either way, you should include the museum name and appropriate graphics elements. **Hint:** Adjust the size of the drawing area to just fit the graphic. That way, you will not export unnecessary blank space around the graphic. You may also want to change the background color from white to transparent if you have that option.

2. When the logo is complete, optimize and export the file in a format suitable for use in printed documents, and save it with a descriptive name such as **BioLogo2**.

3. Use your desktop publishing program to plan and create a template for letterhead stationery. The publication should be a standard, letter-sized page with 1-inch margins. It should include the logo graphics file as well as the museum name, address, phone, fax, and Web site information either in the header or footer area. You may want to use color, horizontal rules, and shapes to enhance the appearance of the publication, but the main body of the page should be blank.

4. When the template file is complete, save it with a descriptive name such as **BioLetterhead** and close it.

5. Create a new document based on the template and save it with a descriptive name such as **BioLetter**.

6. Write a letter to your school principal providing information about the Biotarium and inviting classes to visit.

7. When the letter is complete, print it. Save and close all open files and programs.

JOB 2

The museum trustees have seen the logo and love it. They would like to see it animated so that it can be used in presentations, videos, and on the museum's Web site. In this job, use your graphics program to modify the logo image for use in an animation program. Export the file so you can import it into your animations program, and then create an animated logo.

1. Start by planning how you want to animate the logo. You may want to animate it as a whole, or you may want to animate individual parts. You could have the entire logo spin in place, or you could animate just the text. You might want parts of the logo to fly into place, or change size. Use storyboarding to visualize and plan the animation.

2. Use your graphics program to save a copy of the original image that you can modify as necessary to prepare it for animation, or create a new image file to animate.

3. Save the file with a descriptive name, such as **BioLogo3**.

4. When the image is ready, optimize and export it in a format suitable for use in an animation, with a descriptive name such as **BioLogo4**. Alternatively, export it directly to your animation program or launch your animation program and import the file.

5. Use your animation program to animate the logo as you planned in step 1. **Hint:** Make sure the Stage is just large enough to hold the animation.

6. Test the animation to make sure it plays smoothly and optimize it as necessary. Play it for your classmates, ask for their feedback, and incorporate their suggestions into the animation.

7. When the animation is complete, publish it. Save the changes and close all open files and programs.

JOB 3

The museum director wants to create an automated, computer-based presentation about one of the live animal exhibits. The presentation can run in the museum lobby, or it can be sent to schools and other groups in the community so people can see what the museum has to offer. In this job, select a topic such as reptiles and amphibians, small mammals, or birds of prey. Research the topic on the Internet or in your library and use the information to create the presentation. Look for information such as fun facts on the different animals. Locate pictures that you can use for free—but remember to cite the source! You may even be able to locate free video clips that you can use with permission. (Alternatively, use a camcorder to capture your own video, import the clip into your video-editing program, and then export it to a format suitable for use in a presentation.)

1. Use the Internet to gather information about the animals you have selected. Look for interesting facts that can be presented in bullet lists on slides, as well as photos, clip art, and videos that you can use for free, with permission. Record your research in a word processing document, including the citations for each source. Save the document with a descriptive name, such as **PresInfo**. Consider organizing the information as an outline to help you create the presentation.

2. Use your graphics program to optimize and export the original logo file in a format suitable for use in a presentation. Save the file with a descriptive name such as **PresLogo**.

3. Use your presentation program and the information you have gathered to create a presentation of at least seven slides. Save it with a descriptive name such as **BioPres**. Alternatively, if you set up your research as an outline in the word processing file, import it into your presentation program to create the presentation file.

4. Format the presentation using an appealing design template, colors, and fonts. Insert graphics, such as the pictures you downloaded from the Internet. If you were able to locate video, insert that as well. Consider recording narration or adding music to accompany the slides.

5. Insert the logo on the presentation's slide master, so it is displayed on every slide in the presentation. Size and position the image for the best effect.

6. Apply slide transitions and animations as necessary, keeping in mind that the presentation will play on an unattended computer monitor in the museum lobby. You may want to create customized timings.

7. Test the presentation and show it to your classmates. Incorporate their suggestions in the presentation file.

8. When you are satisfied with the results, optimize the presentation for delivery as a stand-alone presentation.

9. Deliver the presentation to your classmates.

10. Save the file and close all open files and programs.

JOB 4

It is now time to begin development of a Web site for the BioTarium. Start by deciding what information you want to include on the site, and the type of navigational structure you want to use. Consider the data you already have that you can incorporate into the Web site, such as the logo, the animated logo, and the information you gathered for the presentation. Plan a color scheme, using the Web-safe palette, and decide if you want to have additional graphics, animation, sound, or video. If so, locate or create the files, remembering to obtain permission as necessary. Decide whether you want to use a text editor and key HTML code, a Web site development program, or a combination of the two. Also, decide whether you want to include a cascading stylesheet to use to format the different pages. You can start with an index page and one or two informational pages; the site can grow from there.

1. Use a file management program to create the root level folder for your Web site and sub-folders for the associated files you plan to include. Copy all necessary files into the subfolders so they will be available when you need them. If you are using a Web site development program to create the site, define the root level folder as your Web site.

2. Use your Web site development program or text editor to create a home page for Biotarium. Save the home page in the root level folder with a descriptive name, such as **bio_index**. Don't forget to include a description Web page title.

3. On the home page, include short paragraphs or pictures that you can link to the other pages you plan to include, such as general information, information about the animals, or information about educational programs. Insert the animated logo or the static logo on the index page.

4. Format the page using color, horizontal rules, and font formatting.

5. Preview the page in your Web browser as you work, so you can correct problems as they arise. Don't forget to check the spelling and grammar on the page, as well.

6. Create the other pages for your site, saving them in the root level folder with descriptive file names. You may want to save the index page with a new name to insure consistent formatting and to save time, or you may want to start with a new blank page. Don't forget to include description Web page titles. Modify the text and formatting as necessary, and insert graphics, animations, sound, or videos if you want. Preview the page in your browser as you work.

7. Create hyperlinks among the pages, and test the links to make sure they all work as expected.

8. When you are satisfied with the results, define a remote site and upload the root level folder and its contents to the remote site.

9. Test the remote site in your browser. If necessary, make changes locally and republish the site.

10. Save and close all files and programs.

JOB 5

In this job, you save the presentation you created in Job 3 as a Web site and then link it to the BioTarium Web site.

1. Use a file management program to create a subfolder in your Web site root level folder where you can store the presentation Web site.

2. Use your presentation graphics program to save the presentation as a Web site, in the appropriate folder in your root level folder. Give the Web site file a descriptive name, such as **WebPres**, and include a descriptive Web page title.

3. Test the presentation Web site, set properties, and make changes as necessary. If necessary, republish the site.

4. Use your Web site development program to incorporate the presentation Web site as part of the Biotarium site. Add a link from the index page to the presentation. Add a link from the presentation back to the index page. (You may have to use your presentation graphics program for this, and then republish the presentation site.)

5. Test the site in your browser and check the links. Make changes and improvements as necessary.

6. When you have finished, republish the Web site to the remote site. Ask your classmates to visit the site.

7. Save and close all files and programs.

JOB 6

The museum director wants a short video highlighting some of the museum's educational programs. The video can be used on the Web site, in standalone presentations, or maybe as an advertisement on the local access cable channel. In this job, you prepare the video and then insert it on a new Web page that you link to the Web site.

1. Start by planning a storyboard for the video. Decide what you want to show in the video that will make the museum appealing to viewers. The entire sequence should be about 30 seconds long. You can make creative use of the area where you live or go to school to simulate the museum environment. For example, you can shoot video that could be used to illustrate a nature trail while you are walking through trees; you might be able to capture video of small animals such as squirrels or chipmunks, or of birds such as pigeons or robins. You can even stage a scene using friends in a classroom or outside, conducting an experiment. Alternatively, you may find some video clips on the Internet that are available for free with permission. You can also take "still" pictures with a digital camera to use as source clips and then add transitions, effects, and titles to animate the sequence.

2. Use a video camera to record the scenes you need for your storyboard, or locate clips on the Internet that you can use for free, with permission.

3. Create a new project in your video-editing program, and save it with a descriptive name, such as **BioVideo**.

4. Capture the source video into the project, or import source video clips and still images into the project. If you want to include sound or music, import those files as well. You may want to rename the clips in order to better identify them in the project.

5. Assemble the clips into a sequence based on your storyboard. Use your video-editing program to edit and enhance the video. Include transitions and effects, and titles if you want.

6. Preview the video while you work and make improvements as necessary.

7. When you are satisfied with the video, export it in a format suitable for streaming on the Web, saving it with a descriptive file name such as **WebVideo**. Also export it in a format suitable for display on a computer screen or television monitor, saving it with a descriptive file name such as **TVVideo**. You may want to export it directly to a CD or DVD, and then show the video to your classmates.

8. Copy the **WebVideo** file into the appropriate subfolder in your Web site root level folder.

9. Use your text editor or Web development program to create a new Web page file about the Biotarium's Education programs. Save the page in your Biotarium Web site root level folder with a descriptive name, such as **ed_page**.

10. Using consistent formatting, add a heading and a brief paragraph of text describing some of the educational programs. Don't forget to include a descriptive Web page title.

11. Insert the WebVideo on the Web page, sizing it for the best display. If possible include controls so the visitor can start, stop, and pause it.

12. Test the page in your browser and make corrections and adjustments as necessary.

13. Add a hyperlink from the Index page to the Educational Programs page, and from the Educational Programs page back to the Index page. Test the links in your browser.

14. When you are satisfied with the new page, republish the site to the remote site. Ask your classmates to visit the site and play the video.

15. Save and close all open files and programs.

APPENDIX A

THE WINDOWS OPERATING SYSTEM

Microsoft Windows is the operating system that controls the way your computer works. An operating system is a software program that provides the instructions that allow you to communicate with your computer and all of its attached devices. Among other things, you use Windows to launch and exit programs, to find and open files, and to install new programs and hardware devices. This appendix covers some useful Windows features.

About Windows

There are different versions of Windows, but they all function in basically the same way. Information is displayed in windows, or rectangular areas, on your desktop. Some windows, called folders, are used to store files just like paper folders hold paper files in your desk drawer. When you open a folder window, it displays a list of all the files stored in that folder. Other windows, called program windows, are used to display a running program. There are also windows called dialog boxes that convey information between you and your computer.

Windows has a *graphical user interface* (GUI), which means you use easy-to-understand visual elements to communicate with your computer. Pictures called *icons* represent programs. Plain English commands are listed on easy-to-find *menus*. You can use a mouse or a keyboard or a combination of the two to make selections. One of the most convenient features of Windows is that it provides a common platform for all Windows programs. This means there are similarities in the way different programs look and function, so they are easier to learn and use.

The Windows Desktop

Depending on your version of Windows and the way your computer or network is set up, when you turn on your computer, you see either the Windows *desktop* or a *sign-in* screen. The Windows desktop is the main screen or workspace from which you can access all the tools you need to use your computer. The sign-in screen lists the names of all the people authorized to use the computer. From the sign-in screen, you click your name and then enter your password, if necessary, to display the desktop.

The default Windows XP desktop is shown in Figure A-1. Your desktop may look quite different because different versions of Windows have different default desktops, and your computer may be customized with different programs, different colors, and a different background. In any case, you should be able to locate the components described in Table A-1. You can also use

ScreenTips to identify elements on your screen. ScreenTips are descriptions that appear when the mouse pointer rests on an item such as an icon or a *button*.

FIGURE A-1
Windows XP desktop

Mouse pointer

Recycle Bin icon

Quick Launch toolbar

Start button

Taskbar

Notification area

Recycle Bin

start   9:52 AM

TABLE A-1
Desktop Components

COMPONENT NAME	DESCRIPTION
Start button	A button on the taskbar used to open the Start menu, from which you can access everything stored on your computer, including programs and files.
Taskbar	A row that usually appears at the bottom of the screen (though it can be on the top or either side), used to display buttons and icons that provide quick access to common tasks. The taskbar displays the Start button, the Notification area, and buttons representing open programs and files. You can also opt to display toolbars such as Quick Launch on the taskbar.
Quick Launch toolbar	A list of icons representing commonly used programs. Click an icon to launch the program.
Recycle Bin icon	An icon representing the Recycle Bin folder, where deleted files and folders are stored until you remove them permanently.
Notification area	An area at the end of the taskbar used to display information about system components. Usually, the clock/calendar is displayed in the notification area, as well as information about hardware devices such as printers and networks that are currently in use.
Mouse pointer	The mouse pointer indicates the current location of the mouse on your screen. It usually looks like an arrow, but the mouse pointer can change in shape depending on the current action. For example, it looks like an hourglass when the computer is busy processing a command.

Use the Mouse

You use your mouse and keyboard to make selections and issue commands in Windows. The mouse pointer represents the current location of the mouse on your screen. You move the mouse pointer by sliding the mouse on your desk or on a mouse pad. The four basic mouse actions are click, double-click, right-click, and click-and-drag.

- Click means to press and release the left mouse button. This action is usually done to select an item, but sometimes is used to launch a program or open a window.

- Double-click means to press and release the mouse button twice in rapid succession. Use this action to launch a program or open a window.

- Right-click means to press and release the right mouse button. Right-click is used to open a short-cut menu of common commands.

- Click-and-drag means to press and hold the left mouse button, and then slide the mouse to a different location. Click-and-drag is used for moving selected items. When you release the mouse button, the item drops into the new location.

Your mouse may also have a scroll wheel. Spin the wheel to shift the screen display up and down through the contents of a window.

> **Note**
>
> If the taskbar is not displayed, your computer probably has been customized to hide it when it is not in use. This leaves more room to display data on the screen. Move the mouse pointer to the side of the screen where the taskbar is usually displayed (try the bottom first), and it should appear.

Use the Keyboard

In addition to the standard text characters and numbers, most computer keyboards have special keys for quickly accessing computer features and commands. Table A-2 describes some common Windows keys.

> **Note**
>
> By default, mice are set up for right-handed users. If you are left handed, ask your instructor for information about setting up the mouse for your use.

TABLE A-2
Common Windows keys

KEY	DESCRIPTION
Modifier keys (Ctrl, Alt, Shift)	These keys are used in combination with other keys or mouse actions to select commands or perform actions. For example, pressing the Ctrl key and the S key at the same time usually saves the current file.
Directional keys	The directional keys include the up, down, left, and right arrows, as well as the Home, End, Page Up, and Page Down keys. These keys move the insertion point or selection box around the screen, or shift the display to show a different part of a window.
Enter key	The Enter key is used to execute a command or to start a new paragraph when you are keying text.

TABLE A-2 Continued
Common Windows keys

KEY	DESCRIPTION
Escape key (Esc)	The Escape key is used to cancel a command.
Editing keys	The editing keys include Insert, Delete, and Backspace. They are used when you are keying data to control the way information is entered.
Function keys (F1–F12)	Usually found in a row above the standard keyboard keys, these keys are often assigned as shortcut keys for commands in programs. For example, F9 is often used to update information, and F2 is often used to repeat the most recent action.
Windows logo key	Usually located on either side of the spacebar, this key is used to open or close the Start menu, and in combination with other keys for other purposes.
Application key	Usually found to the right of the spacebar, this key is used in place of a right-click to open a shortcut menu of commands.

Launch a Program

Depending on how your computer is set up, there may be program icons displayed on the desktop or the taskbar. If so, click or double-click an icon to launch the program. If the program is not represented by a desktop icon, use the Start menu. The Start menu displays links to commonly used programs. Click the program name to launch the program. Figure A-2 shows both the Windows XP Start menu (on the left) and the Classic Windows Start menu (on the right).

FIGURE A-2
Windows XP Start menu (left) and Classic Windows Start menu (right)

To access any program installed on your computer, use the All Programs menu. Click the Start button to open the Start menu, and then click Programs or All Programs. A list of all programs installed on your computer is displayed, as shown in Figure A-3. Some of the programs may be grouped into folders. If so, move the mouse to point to the folder, which will display a menu of programs in the folder. Click the name of the program you want to launch. The program opens in a program window on the desktop.

FIGURE A-3
All Programs menu

Most program windows have common elements, such as a title bar, a Menu bar, and a toolbar. To exit a program, you can click the Program Close button, which is an X in the upper-right corner of the window, or you can click File on the Menu bar, and then click Exit. A typical program window is shown in Figure A-4.

Note

If there is a right-pointing arrow-head next to a menu item, that means the item has a *submenu*. Click the item to open the sub-menu, and then click the pro-gram you want to launch. If there is an ellipse (...), it means the command opens a dialog box. If there is a shortcut key combination, press that combi-nation to quickly select the com-mand without using a menu.

FIGURE A-4
Microsoft WordPad program window

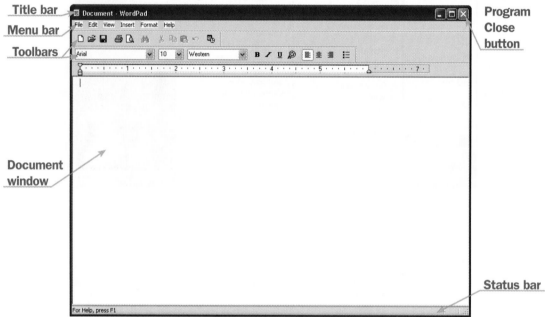

Title bar

Menu bar

Toolbars

Document window

Program Close button

Status bar

The Windows Filing System

One of the main functions of Windows is to help you keep the contents of your computer organized. Windows uses a file management program called Windows Explorer to help you keep track of *files* and *folders*. Files are the documents that store data, and folders are storage areas where you place files and other folders so you can find them easily. The files and folders are stored using a multilevel—or hierarchical—filing system, which means files are stored in folders, and folders may be stored in other folders.

Storage Devices

At the base of the filing system are the *disk drives* or other storage devices, which are the hardware devices on which the file and folder data is written electronically. Local storage devices are attached directly to your computer. Network storage devices may be attached anywhere on the network. You may have one or more of the following attached directly to your computer or to your network:

■ Hard disk drive, which is fixed inside the computer case.

■ Floppy disk drive, which has a slot so you can insert and remove a disk.

■ CD or DVD drive, which has a drawer in which you can insert and remove a CD or DVD disk.

■ Removable jump drive, flash drive, or memory key, which attaches directly to a universal serial bus (USB) port on your computer.

Disk drives are named using letters. A floppy disk drive is always named drive A. If there is a second floppy disk drive, it is called drive B. The hard disk drive stored in your computer is usually called drive C. Additional drives are named using consecutive letters, so a CD drive may be drive D, a DVD drive may be drive E, and so on. You can usually add descriptive names or labels to the drive letter to help identify the storage device. To see a list of your local storage devices, click the Start button and then click My Computer on the Start menu. The My Computer window opens as shown in Figure A-5. Alternatively, double-click the My Computer icon on the Windows desktop. Remember, the contents of the My Computer window vary depending on the contents of your computer system.

Did You Know?

There are two basic types of CD drives: CD-ROM drives, which can read but not write information on a CD; and CD-RW drives, which can read and write information on a CD. To write information on a CD, you must have a CD-RW drive and CD-R or CD-RW discs. DVD drives can usually read data from CDs. If you have a DVD burner, your computer can write information on DVDs, as well.

FIGURE A-5
My Computer window in Windows XP

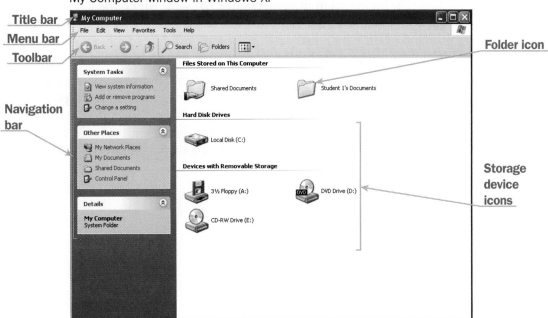

Folders

Files can be stored directly on a disk, but to keep things organized, you usually store them in folders. Windows comes with some default folders used for storing system information and data files. You can create new folders at any time. The default folders are usually listed on the Start menu or are represented by icons on the desktop. The following list describes some of the Windows default folders:

- *My Documents* is the default storage location for data files.

- *Shared Documents* is used to store documents that can be opened by anyone on the network.

- *My Computer* displays the components of your computer system, such as disk drives and other attached devices.

- *Control Panel* provides access to your computer components so you can customize and control settings and options.

- *Recycle Bin* is used to store deleted files and folders until you choose to remove them permanently.

Navigate Through the Contents of Your Computer

To view the contents of a disk or folder, you open the window that displays the item, and then open the item itself. For example, to see the contents of a floppy disk in drive A, you click the Start button to open the Start menu and then click My Computer to open the My Computer window. In the My Computer window, you double-click the drive A icon to open the drive A window.

Most folder windows have similar characteristics, including a title bar, a Menu bar, and possibly toolbars. The contents list is displayed in the main folder window. Some versions of Windows display additional information in the Explorer Bar pane along the left side of the window. You can change the contents of the Explorer Bar depending on what you are doing. By default, it displays the links bar, which lists links to common folders such as My Computer or My Documents. Click a link to open the folder.

You can change the Explorer Bar to display Folders if you want to navigate using a hierarchical tree diagram as shown in Figure A-6 (in versions of Windows prior to Windows XP, this feature is called Windows Explorer). Click the Folders button to display the hierarchical tree. Click an item in the tree to display its contents in the main folder window. Click a plus sign next to an item to expand the tree, or click a minus sign to collapse the tree.

FIGURE A-6
Folders Explorer Bar in Windows XP

Folders button

Selected folder

Folder tree

Contents of selected folder

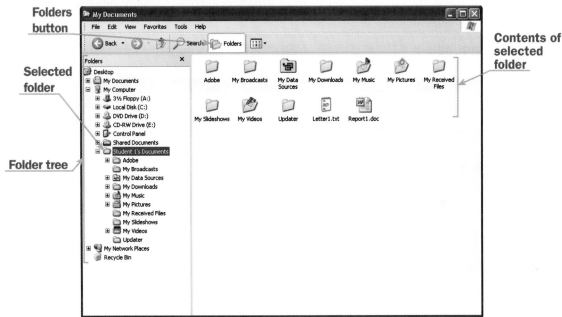

There may also be Back, Forward, and Up buttons on the toolbar at the top of the window. Click Back or Forward to scroll through all of the windows you have opened recently, and click Up to open the folder in which the current folder is stored.

Change the Window Display

You can change the way items are displayed in a folder window. Click the Views button on the toolbar or the View command on the Menu bar, and then click one of the following:

■ *Thumbnails* to display an icon or picture with the item name.

■ *Tiles* to display a smaller icon or picture with the item name, type, and size.

■ *Icons* to display a smaller icon or picture with the item name.

- *List* to list the items by name.

- *Details* to list the items including specific information such as name, type, size, and modification date, as shown in Figure A-7.

FIGURE A-7
Folder in Details view

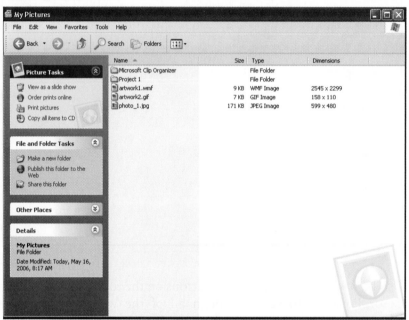

You can also change the sort order and grouping of the items in a folder window. Click View on the Menu bar and then click Arrange Icons by. Click the sort order or grouping option you want to use. You can also click the heading at the top of the column by which you want to sort.

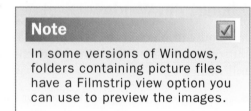

Note

In some versions of Windows, folders containing picture files have a Filmstrip view option you can use to preview the images.

Work with Windows

As mentioned, information is displayed in windows on the Windows desktop. The two basic types of windows are program windows, used to display an open program, and folder windows, used to display the contents of folders and storage devices. You can have more than one window open at a time, but only one can be active. The active window is the one in which you are currently working. All open windows have a button on the taskbar. To make a different window active, click its taskbar button. If there is not enough room on the taskbar to display buttons for each open window, Windows may group the buttons according to program and display one button for each group. When you click a group button, a menu of windows appears so you can click the specific window you want to make active.

Size and Position Windows

Windows open in the size and position they were when you last used them. All windows have control buttons in the upper-right corner that you can use to change the window's size and position.

- Click the Maximize button to increase the size of a window to fill the entire desktop.

- Click the Minimize button to reduce a window so it is just a button on the taskbar.

- Click the Restore Down button to restore a maximized window to its previous size and position. The Restore Down button is available only in a maximized window.

- Click the Close button to close the window.

You can also drag a window by its title bar to move it to a different location on the desktop, and you can drag the borders of a window that is not maximized to change its size.

To arrange all open windows on the desktop, right-click a blank area of the taskbar and select one of the following commands:

> **Note** ☑
>
> The current document or file may also have control buttons in the upper-right corner of the window. The program control icons are on the title bar, whereas the document control buttons are on the Menu bar.

- *Cascade Windows* to overlap the windows, showing only the title bars. The active window is on top, as shown in Figure A-8.

- *Tile Windows Horizontally* to arrange the windows across the width of the screen. You can see a portion of all windows. The title bar of the active window is brighter than the others.

- *Tile Windows Vertically* to stack the windows from the top to the bottom of the screen. You can see a portion of all windows, and the title bar of the active window is brighter than the others.

FIGURE A-8
Cascading windows

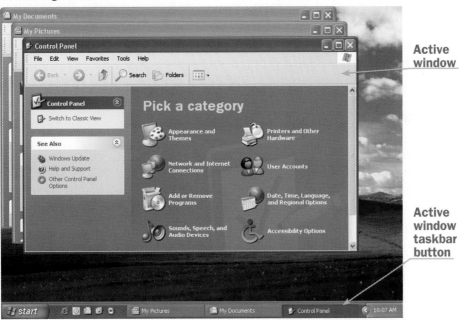

Install a Program

If you purchase a new program, you must install it on your computer so you can use it. Usually, you install a program from a CD-ROM. When you insert the CD-ROM in the CD-ROM drive, the installation usually begins automatically. You simply follow the instructions on the screen to install and set up the program. During the installation, you may have to enter information about your computer or about the program you are installing. For example, you may have to enter a key or code number and select the folder in which you want to store the program files. If the program does not start automatically, you can use the Add New Programs command in the Control Panel. If you use the Add New Programs command, you need to know the name of the installation or set-up file. Usually, it is setup.exe or install.exe.

> **Note**
>
> You may need to obtain permission from a system administrator or network administrator before installing a new program.

Before you purchase a new program, read the package to make sure it is compatible with your computer system. The system requirements are usually listed on the back or side of the package. Most stores do not let you return opened software. To determine if a program is compatible, ask yourself the following questions:

- Does the program run on the version of Windows you have installed?

- Does your computer have enough memory to run the program?

- Does your computer have enough disk space to install the program?

- Does the program require a particular hardware device or component, such as a video adapter card or specific monitor resolution?

You can locate information about your computer system in the System Properties dialog. To open the System Properties dialog box, right-click the My Computer icon and then click Properties, or open the Control Panel and either double-click the System icon, or click *See basic information about your computer*. In the System Properties dialog box, you can locate such information as the version of Windows running on your computer, the amount of memory you have installed, and the processor speed.

To find out how much disk space you have available, open My Computer, right-click on the icon for your hard drive, and click Properties.

Install a Hardware Device

Hardware devices are components that are connected to your computer system and controlled by your computer's microprocessor. Hardware devices can include your printer, modem, scanner, digital camera, video camera, microphone, speakers, keyboard, monitor, mouse, and disk drives.

Before you can use a hardware device, you must install it on your computer. The first step in hardware installation is to connect the device to the computer. Some devices, such as internal modems, are attached to slots inside the computer, and other devices, such as printers, are attached by cables to ports on the outside of the computer. Still others, such as a wireless mouse, communicate via wireless connections such as infrared or satellite. Local devices are attached directly to your computer, and network devices are attached to the network. If a device installs inside the computer, you may want to consult a professional. If the device connects to a port outside the computer, you can install it yourself.

Next, you must install the correct device driver, which is a software program that provides the instructions that let the device communicate with Windows. Usually, the device driver comes on a floppy disk or CD-ROM with the device. Alternatively, you may be able to download it from the manufacturer's Web site. Windows comes with drivers for common hardware devices.

In most cases, when you plug the device into your computer, Windows detects it automatically and begins the installation procedure. Simply follow the instructions displayed on your screen to complete the installation and setup. If the installation does not start automatically, you can use the Add New Hardware command in the Control Panel.

> **Note** ☑
>
> You may need permission from a system administrator or network administrator to install a hardware device.

Use a Help Program

Windows and most Windows programs come with built-in help programs you can use to get information while you work. The Help program depends on the version of Windows you are using.

To start the Windows XP Help program, click the Start button to open the Start menu and then click Help and Support. The Help and Support Center screen is displayed, as shown in Figure A-9. You can click a link to go to a general topic page, from which you can click links to locate the specific information you need, or you can key a topic in the Search box and click the Go button. Windows displays a list of links to information about the topic.

FIGURE A-9
Windows XP Help and Support Center

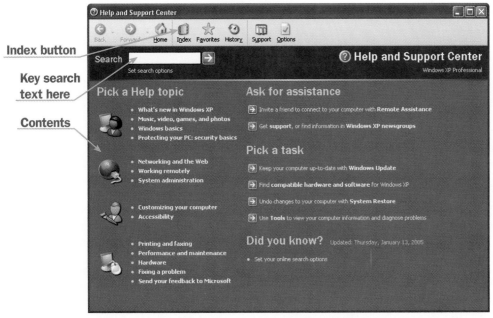

To start the Help program in a version of Windows prior to XP, click the Start button to open the Start menu and then click Help.

The program Help window has two panes. On the left you can select to use the Contents, Index, or Search tools. The specific help information is displayed on the right.

- *Contents* lists the major topics for which help is available. Click a book icon to display a list of subtopics, and then click a subtopic to display the information.

- *Index* provides an alphabetical list of help topics. You can scroll through the list to find the topic you need, or you can key a topic in the keyword search box to jump to that topic. Click a topic in the list to display the information.

- *Search* lets you search through all of the available help pages for a keyword. Key the word in the keyword search box, and then click the List Topics button to display a list of topics that contain that word. Click a topic in the list to display the information.

APPENDIX B

CROSS-CURRICULUM PROJECTS

Many projects in the *Multimedia Basics* text book can be used in cross-curriculum activities in order to show the students how the multimedia skills can be used in real-life scenarios. The following table lists the project and indicates which cross-curriculum subject(s) is integrated into the project content.

PROJECT	SOCIAL STUDIES/ HISTORY	ENGLISH/ LANGUAGE ARTS	SCIENCE	MATH
Lesson 1 Web Project	X			
Lesson 2 Teamwork Project		X		
Lesson 2 Critical Thinking		X		
Lesson 3 Web Project		X		
Lesson 4 Web Project	X			
Lesson 5 Critical Thinking	X			
Lesson 5 Teamwork Project		X	X	
Unit 1 Review Job 3	X	X		
Lesson 6 Teamwork Project	X	X	X	
Lesson 7 Teamwork Project				X
Lesson 8 Teamwork Project			X	
Lesson 8 Critical Thinking	X	X		
Lesson 9 Web Project		X		X
Lesson 9 Critical Thinking		X		
Lesson 10 Web Project		X		
Lesson 10 Teamwork Project	X			
Lesson 10 Critical Thinking		X		
Lesson 11 Web Project		X		
Lesson 11 Teamwork Project	X			

PROJECT	SOCIAL STUDIES/ HISTORY	ENGLISH/ LANGUAGE ARTS	SCIENCE	MATH
Lesson 11 Critical Thinking			X	
Lesson 12 Web Project		X		
Lesson 12 Teamwork Project	X	X	X	X
Lesson 12 Critical Thinking		X		
Lesson 13 Web Project		X		
Lesson 14 Web Project		X		
Lesson 14 Teamwork Project	X			
Lesson 14 Critical Thinking				X
Lesson 15 Web Project			X	
Lesson 15 Teamwork Project	X			
Lesson 15 Critical Thinking		X		
Lesson 16 Web Project	X	X		
Lesson 16 Teamwork Project	X			
Lesson 16 Critical Thinking		X		X
Lesson 17 Web Project		X		X
Lesson 17 Critical Thinking	X			
U3 Review Project 1	X			
U3 Review Project 2	X			
U3 Review Project 3	X			
U3 Review Job 1	X			
U3 Review Job 2	X			
U3 Review Job 3	X			
Lesson 18 Web Project		X		X
Lesson 18 Teamwork Project		X		X
Lesson 18 Critical Thinking		X		
Lesson 19 Web Project	X			
Lesson 19 Teamwork Project		X		
Lesson 19 Critical Thinking		X		
Lesson 20 Web Project		X		X
Lesson 20 Teamwork Project		X		
Lesson 20 Critical Thinking	X			
Lesson 21 Web Project			X	

PROJECT	SOCIAL STUDIES/ HISTORY	ENGLISH/ LANGUAGE ARTS	SCIENCE	MATH
Lesson 21 Teamwork Project	X			
Lesson 21 Critical Thinking		X		
Lesson 22 Web Project		X		
Lesson 22 Teamwork Project		X		
Lesson 22 Critical Thinking	X			
Lesson 23 Web Project		X		
Lesson 23 Teamwork Project			X	
Lesson 23 Critical Thinking	X			
Lesson 24 Web Project		X		
Lesson 24 Critical Thinking		X		
Lesson 25 Web Project	X	X		
Lesson 25 Teamwork Project			X	
Lesson 25 Critical Thinking		X		
Lesson 26 Web Project	X	X		
Lesson 26 Teamwork Project		X		X
Lesson 27 Teamwork Project	X			
Lesson 27 Critical Thinking		X		
Integrated Simulation Job 1		X		
Integrated Simulation Job 3		X	X	
Integrated Simulation Job 4		X	X	
Integrated Simulation Job 6		X	X	

GLOSSARY

24p An HD format that runs 24 progressive frames per second.

A

Acceptable Use Policy (AUP) The rules that protect a Web site and network from unauthorized use, hackers, and abuse. Also called *Terms of Use* policy.

Actions A set of instructions that cause an event.

Action button A graphics element that a viewer can click or rollover to cause an action to occur.

ActionScript A programming language used in Macromedia's Flash to write script statements.

Active Current, or in use.

Active content Elements on a Web page that change, or allow the visitor to interact with the page.

Additive colors Colors that, when combined in full value, add up to white. Red, green, and blue are additive colors.

Align Position an object horizontally or vertically relative to the top, bottom, left, or right of the drawing area or the page, or relative to other objects.

All-over balance A type of balance in which objects are positioned using a grid-like design with focal points scattered throughout in order to direct the eye through the design.

Alpha The setting that controls the transparency of an object.

Amplitude A measure of volume, or loudness.

Analogous colors Colors that are next to each other on the color wheel.

Animated GIF A GIF-formatted file that includes two or more graphics cycles that create an animation effect.

Animation Graphics combined with motion. Also called *movies* or *animated graphics*.

Animation scheme Collections of animation settings and transitions that you can apply to a single slide or all slides.

ANSI An acronym for American National Standards Institute. A set of standard text-based characters that all computers can read and understand.

Ascenders The parts of characters that extend above the rest of the text.

ASCII An acronym for American Standard Code for Information Interchange. It is a system that assigns a code to every key on a keyboard and some special characters as well, so that all computers can interpret the characters the same way.

Aspect ratio The ratio that compares the width of an image to the height of the image.

Assets Digital content such as video clips, text, drawing, sounds, and still images used to create a movie, Web page, or animation.

Attribute A part of an HTTP tag that describes the properties of an element. Sometimes called a property.

Audio track The audio portion of recorded video or audio, or of a sequence.

AutoPlay DVD A DVD that starts playing the movie automatically when it is inserted in a DVD player.

AutoShape In some programs, a built-in, predrawn object such as a star or lightning bolt.

AVI An acronym for Audio Video Interleave file format. The most common video file format used on the Windows platform.

B

Balance A basic principle of design that describes the visual weight of objects and the way they are arranged.

Bandwidth The speed at which a network or modem transfers data. Also called *connection speed*.

Bandwidth target The maximum size for optimum download performance, such as the maximum size of a frame in an animation file.

Baseline The bottom of a line of text.

Baseline guides Horizontal guides that define the baseline of each line of text.

Behaviors Code that allows visitors to interact with a Web page.

Bevel An effect used to create the illusion of three-dimensionality by making the object appear to rise out of the drawing area.

Binding The method used to attach or secure pages or sections of a book or booklet, usually using stitching, staples, wire, plastic, tape, or glue. Also, the material used in the binding.

Bins In some programs, such as Adobe Premiere Pro 2.0, folders used to organize clips in a project.

Bitmap A type of graphics in which the image is created using a series of dots.

Bleed An effect created by an object running off the edge of the page.

Blinds A transition that gives the illusion of window blinds opening over a slide or frame.

Boundaries Nonprinting lines that mark the borders of text boxes and other objects.

Bounding box A rectangular shape with selection handles displayed around a selected object.

Brand recognition The association of a certain color or shape with a specific organization.

Brightness A measurement of the amount of white or black added to a hue. Sometimes called *tint*.

Broadcast To display a presentation to an invited audience via the Internet or an intranet.

Bullet A marker such as a dot, check mark, or asterisk.

Button An object on a toolbar, in a dialog box, or on a Web page that a user can click to access a feature or command, or to link to a target destination.

Button symbol A symbol that a viewer can click to interact with an animation.

C

Camera-ready film Film made of the finished pages that can be used to publish a document.

Canvas In some programs, the term used to describe the drawing area.

Capture To import video footage from a camcorder into a video editing program.

Cascading Style Sheet A collection of formatting settings that you can attach to a Web page and then use as the default styles for formatting text and objects on the page.

CD burner A drive that writes data on to a CD using a laser to burn the data on the disc.

Cell The rectangular area at the intersection of a column and a row.

Chart A graphical representation of table data.

Class styles Styles that you can apply to any range or block of text. Sometimes called *custom CSS rules* or *user-defined styles*.

Clip A video segment.

Clip art Pictures and other types of files that can be inserted into a document.

Clipboard A temporary storage area in the computer's memory where data that has been cut or copied is stored until it is pasted into a new location.

CMY A color system or model used for printing, which creates colors by blending different levels of cyan, magenta, and yellow.

CMYK A color system or model used for printing, which creates colors by blending different levels of cyan, magenta, yellow, and black.

Code Instructions to a computer that are written in a programming language, such as HTML tags.

Code view A view in a Web site development program in which you can view and edit HTML tags.

Codec (Compressor/decompressor) A system for compressing a large amount of data into a smaller file.

Color bar A linear palette that displays gradations of color ranging from red to violet.

Color depth The number of colors used in an image or on a screen.

Color palette A set of up to 256 colors that may be used in a file.

Color scheme A set of coordinated colors.

Color separations Files or printed proofs that show the layout of each color—black, cyan, magenta, and yellow for process color printing, and each spot for spot color printing—on separate sheets of paper.

Color system A system used to define standard colors, such as RGB (Red, Green, Blue), which is used for computer monitors, or CMYK (Cyan, Magenta, Yellow, Black), which is used for printing. Sometimes called a *color model*.

Color tweening Animation in which the color of an object changes over time.

Color wheel A palette that displays gradations in color ranging from red to violet.

Column guides Nonprinting lines that define columns on the page.

Column A vertical component of a table, or a vertical section of a page.

Compatible file format Able to work together.

Complementary colors Colors that are opposite each other on the color wheel.

Composite A file or a printed proof that contains all color information.

Compress Reduce in size.

Compression The process of reducing the space required to store data by efficiently encoding the content.

Connection speed The speed at which a network or modem transfers data. Also called *bandwidth*.

Consistency The use of repetition to create a uniform and predictable design.

Content Text, graphics, video, animation, and other items and objects that comprise a file.

Content template A template that includes prompts, formatting, and data organized for a specific type of document. The prompts provide instructions and tips for creating the document.

Contrast The degree of separation between the color values of different parts of the same image. Also, a basic principle of design in which elements with opposite or complementary features are juxtaposed in order to create visual interest.

Cool colors The colors ranging from green to violet on the color wheel.

Coordinates Points on the drawing area or page used to position an object. The X coordinate positions the object horizontally and the Y coordinate positions the object vertically.

Crawl An effect that causes a single line of text to move horizontally across a frame.

Crop To cut or remove portions of an image.

Crop marks Printer's marks that can be printed in a publication in order to indicate where the paper should be cut or trimmed down to the correct page size.

Cross-dissolve A video transition that fades out the previous clip while fading in the next.

CSS rule The code that defines a style used to format content on a Web page.

Custom show A presentation created from selected slides within a presentation. The custom show has its own name, but the slides remain stored in the original presentation.

Cut line The break where one video clip ends and the next begins.

D

Data rate The amount of video information that must be processed each second during playback.

Data series One set of data displayed in a chart.

Datasheet A set of cells linked to a chart. You enter the data you want illustrated by the chart into the datasheet.

Declaration The part of a CSS rule that contains the attribute and the value that determines the formatting. Sometimes called the *definition*.

Default A standard setting or mode of operation.

Descenders The parts of characters that extend below the baseline.

Design template A set of built-in formats that you can apply in one step.

Design view The default view in most Web site design programs in which you can enter and format content without keying code.

Desktop The main screen or workspace in the Windows operating environment.

Destination The target location of a hyperlink. Also, the location to which you copy a file or paste a selection.

Device driver A software program that enables a computer to communicate with a hardware device.

Diagram A particular type of chart used to display conceptual information rather than data.

Digital camera A camera that captures pictures in digital format.

Digital video recorder A device that records digital video, such as a camcorder.

Digital video Video in which all of the information representing images has been digitized so that you can edit and display it on a computer.

Disk drive A hardware device that reads and writes information to and from storage disks.

Distort To change the height or width of an object without retaining the original proportions.

Distribute Adjust the space between objects in an image.

Dithering A process used to approximate colors that are not part of a file's color palette.

Document master A single master page used for an entire publication.

Document properties In an animation program, the settings that determine the dimensions and color of the Stage as well as the speed at which the animation plays. In other programs, document properties are settings that determine qualities and characteristics about a document or file.

Domain The registered name that identifies the computer, or Web server, where the page is stored.

Double-sided printing To print on both sides of a sheet of paper.

Double-sided transition A video transition that involves the end of one clip and the beginning of the next clip.

Download Copy files from one computer to another, usually from a network to a computer on the network.

Drawing area The area within the document window in which you draw and edit images. Sometimes called the *canvas* or *stage*.

Drawing objects Shapes that you draw in a document using a programs, drawing tools. Usually, drawing objects are vectors.

Dropped capital A decorative effect in which the first character in a paragraph is larger than the other characters. Sometimes called a *drop cap*.

Duplex printing Printing on both sides of a sheet of paper.

DVD burner A drive that writes data on to a DVD using a laser to burn the data on the disc.

E

Ease The rate at which change occurs in a tweened animation.

Element An HTML tag name, which is enclosed by angle brackets.

Em dash A special character that is roughly the width of a letter M. Usually used in place of two hyphens.

Embed Store an object or file as part of a file.

Embedded style sheet Style codes stored in the <HEAD> section of a page that are used to format elements on that page only.

Emboss An effect used to make an object appear to be inset into the drawing area. A raised emboss effect makes the object appear to rise out of the drawing area.

Emphasis The use of color, lines, or shapes in order to highlight or focus attention on a particular aspect of an image.

En dash A special character that is roughly half the width of an em dash. Usually used in place of the words *to* or *through*.

Event sound A sound that plays independently of the animation timeline. Event sounds must download completely before they can begin to play.

Expandable text block A text block that increases in width as characters are keyed so all characters fit on one line.

Export Save a file in a format that can be used by a different program.

External style sheet Style codes stored in a separate file in a Web site. Pages in the site are attached to the file to make the styles available for formatting. They are sometimes called *linked style sheets*.

F

Facing pages A two-page spread, which is a left-most page and a rightmost page facing each other in a publication. The pages are sometimes called *mirrored pages*.

Fade A transition in which the slide or frame content is gradually revealed through black.

Field A code that displays in place of actual data.

File A document that stores data.

File format The way data in a file is saved. Usually a file format is associated with a particular program, so that the program can read the data in the file.

File Transfer Protocol (FTP) A file transfer system that you use to upload, or put, files on an Internet server located somewhere on the World Wide Web.

Fill The area inside a shape.

Fill effect A pattern, gradient, picture, or texture that you apply to the fill of an object or the background of a slide.

Filtered HTML A version of HTML that requires less storage space than standard HTML.

Firewire An IEEE 1394 connection. Also called *iLink*.

Fixed-width text block A text block of a predetermined size in which text wraps from one line to the next.

.fla The file extension of files in the Flash file format.

Flip To reverse an image horizontally or vertically.

Floating object An object that can be sized and positioned anywhere on a page.

Folder A storage area in which you place files and other folders so you can find them easily. In some programs, folders are called bins or directories.

Font A set of characters in a particular typeface.

Font effects Attributes applied to a character in a font set, such as strikethrough or superscript.

Font scheme A collection of coordinated fonts.

Font size The size of characters in a font, measured in points.

Font style Attributes such as bold and italic that are applied to a font.

Footage Raw, unedited video material.

Footer The area across the bottom of each page or slide in a file.

Frame A placeholder object used to contain text or graphics. Also, a single image in a video or animation sequence.

Frame inset Margins within a text box.

Frame rate The speed at which frames progress in an animation or video. Frame rate is usually measured as frames per second (fps).

Frame-by-frame animation Animation in which you manually change the content on frames in a sequence.

G

Galleys The pages used for proofreading a publication before printing.

Get Download files from a remote Web site.

GIF An acronym for Graphics Interchange Format. GIF files are popular for use on the World Wide Web. They can contain up to 256 colors. They are used for cartoons, logos, graphics with transparent areas, and animations.

Glow An effect that applies a highlight to an object. Glows apply a band of color around all edges, while inner glows apply a band of color inside the edges.

Gradient Color that shades gradually from a dark hue to a light hue.

Graphic symbol A static image comprised of drawing objects, groups, or imported graphics.

Graphics tablet A hardware device on which you write or draw with a stylus in order to input data into your computer.

Graphics Images that you use to enhance the appearance of a variety of projects, including drawings, photographs, cartoons, charts, and maps.

Graphical user interface (GUI) A type of interface that uses icons, menus, and plain English commands so that users can interact with a computer program without using a programming or command language.

Grayscale A color scheme that uses a range of blacks, whites, and grays.

Grid guides Nonprinting lines used to define columns and rows in the document window of many types of programs.

Group To combine multiple objects together into one unit. Also, a unit comprised of multiple objects that have been grouped.

Guides Nonprinting gridlines used to help align and position objects in a document.

Gutter The space between columns, which may also be called the *alley*. Also, the space left along the inside edge of a page for binding or folding. The gutter is usually the left edge of rightmost or odd-numbered pages and the right edge of leftmost, or even-numbered pages.

H

Handle Extra frames before the in point or after the out point of a clip.

Handouts Printed pages that you can give to the audience before or after a presentation. They usually include a small thumbnail of each slide and space where viewers can handwrite their own notes.

Hanging indent A type of indent where the beginning of the first line is indented to one spot, and the beginning of the following lines are indented more.

Hardware device A component that is connected to a computer system and controlled by the computer's microprocessor.

Header Information repeated at the top of every page, slide, or frame in a document. Also, the area between the top margin and the top of a document.

Hexadecimal code A standard alphanumeric value used to identify colors based on their components of red, green, and blue.

Hierarchical structure A Web page organization structure designed like a flow chart, with a main or index page at the top that links to category or topic pages, which may link to subcategory or subtopic pages, and so on.

High Definition (HD) video Progressive video that delivers in a wide screen format with a 16:9 aspect ratio so the quality is significantly better than standard resolutions.

Home page A main point of entry into a Web site.

Horizontal alignment The position of text or objects in relation to the left and right margins of a text box, page, or drawing area.

Horizontal printing order An option for printing items such as slides, images, or even spreadsheets in which consecutive items are printed across the page horizontally left to right, and then to the next line.

Horizontal rules Printing lines that can be inserted before or after a paragraph of text.

HSL A color model that defines color based on its hue, saturation, and luminance. Sometimes called *HSB*.

HTML tag rules Styles that change the formatting for a particular tag, such as <P> or <H1>. When you create a CSS rule for an HTML tag, all text formatted with that tag is changed.

HTML tags Codes used to define the structure and formatting of content on a Web page.

HTTP An acronym for Hypertext Transfer Protocol, which is the protocol used to transmit data on the World Wide Web.

Hue Color.

Hyperlink Text or graphics formatted so that when you click it, a different page or location displays. Often called *links*.

Hyperlink base A folder in which you store all hyperlink destination files.

Hypertext Markup Language (HTML) An authoring language that uses codes, called HTML tags, to define data on a Web page so that it can be interpreted and displayed by a Web browser.

Hyphen A character used to indicate the break in a word from the end of one line to the beginning of the next line.

Hyphenation zone In some programs, the area along the right margin in which words are automatically hyphenated.

I

I-beam The shape of the mouse pointer when you are working in a text-entering or text-editing mode.

Icon A small picture displayed onscreen to represent a command or program.

IEEE 1394 A two-way digital connection that transfers data at up to 400 megabits per second. Also called *Firewire* or *iLink*.

iLink An IEEE 1394 connection. Also called *Firewire*.

Import Open a file created with one program in a different program.

Imposition The placement and position of multiple pages printing on a single sheet of paper.

In point The beginning of a clip.

In port A handle that displays in the upper-left of a selected text frame in some desktop publishing programs, such as Adobe's InDesign. A blue arrow displays in the In port when the frame is connected to another frame.

Indent A temporary left or right margin for a paragraph or series of paragraphs.

Inline graphics Graphics positioned along the same line as text.

Inline object An object positioned along the same line as text.

Inline style sheet Style codes used to format individual elements on a Web page.

Input source The device used to acquire sound.

Insertion point A flashing vertical line that indicates where characters will be inserted.

Instance One occurrence of a symbol.

Interactive Controls that allow a user to communicate with a program such as an animation by selecting an option that causes an action.

Interlaced video Video that alternates between drawing the even-numbered lines and the odd-numbered lines to create an image on the screen.

Intermediate frames Frames between the beginning keyframe and the ending keyframe in a sequence.

Internet Service Provider (ISP) A company that provides Internet access for a fee.

Intranet A private Web site usually reserved for specific groups of people, such as employees of a corporation.

J

JPEG An acronym for Joint Photographic Experts Group. This format is used for photographs and other high-color images. It supports millions of colors and can be compressed. It does not support transparency.

Justified An alignment option in which words are spaced so that the ends of lines are even with both the left and right margins.

K

Kerning Spacing between specific pairs of characters.

Key term A word or phrase that is used in a file or on a Web site, or that describes that file or Web site. Also called a *key word*.

Keyframe A frame in which a change occurs.

Knock out In some programs, the term used to describe hiding an object as part of a special effect.

L

Landscape orientation The orientation in which data is printed across the widest side of a sheet of paper. Sometimes called *wide*.

Layer An invisible sheet used to separate and organize content on the Stage in an animation or on the canvas in a graphics file. Layers may also be used in video-editing and Web site development programs.

Layout guides Nonprinting lines that you can display on the screen while you work to help you position and align objects on a page.

Layout The arrangement of text and objects on a slide, frame, Web page, or document page.

Leading Spacing between lines.

Legend The key that identifies a data series by color.

Letterhead The area on a sheet of stationery where the name, address, and other information about a company or individual are printed.

Library A folder in which you organize and store objects you use in an animation file and in some other programs.

Line spacing The amount of white space between the base of one line and the top of the next line. Sometimes called *leading*.

Linear gradient A gradient pattern in which the colors blend horizontally across an object.

Linear structure A Web page organization structure designed so that visitors view one page at a time, often in a specific order.

Link *See Hyperlink.*

List marker The symbol inserted to the left of items in a list.

Live presentation A presentation that you deliver in front of a live audience.

Lobby page A Web page that displays in the user's browser window while he or she is waiting for a broadcast to begin.

Logo A symbol representing a company or organization, which may include text, graphics, or both.

Loop Play repeatedly from beginning to end without stopping.

Loss setting A setting used to control compression by balancing file size with image quality.

Lossless A codec that does not cause a loss of quality.

Lossy A codec that causes a loss of quality by actually removing pieces of data during the compression.

M

Map To identify the path to a folder in a Web site.

Map view A view of the navigational structure or relationship between pages in a Web site. Sometimes called the *Navigation view*.

Margin The area between the edge of the page and the objects in the publication.

Margin guides Nonprinting lines that indicate the position of the margins.

Mask An effect used to hide or accentuate a specific portion of an image.

Master page A model or template used to contain text and/or objects that display on every page in a publication.

Master page spread A master page for a two-page spread. It includes a left page master and a right page master.

Masthead The information displayed across the top of a newsletter or newspaper, including, but not limited to, the title, the date, and the volume number. Also, a section inserted in a newspaper or magazine that lists the names and positions of the publication's staff.

Menu A list of commands or options.

Merge Combine multiple items to create a single item. For example, to combine cells in a table to create one cell.

MIDI An acronym for Musical Instrument Digital Interface. A common sound file format in which the file contains data that represents individual notes on a musical scale, rather than entire wave forms.

Mirrored pages Two facing pages, or a two-page spread, which is a leftmost page and a rightmost page facing each other in a publication.

Mock-up A rough draft or sample of the publication that represents the finished product, without including fine details.

Monochromatic A color scheme that uses black and one other color.

Motion guide A layer used in path animation on which you draw the motion path. Objects on layers linked to the motion guide will follow the path.

Movie   An animation or video file. In a presentation, a movie is either an animated GIF file or a video clip file.

Movie clip symbol   A symbol comprised of a frame sequence.

MP3   A sound file format.

MPEG   An acronym for Motion Pictures Expert Group. A common file format for video.

N

Native file format   The default file format for a particular program.

Navigation bar   A row of links to main sections of a Web site, usually positioned across the top or bottom of a Web page.

Navigation system   The organization and use of hyperlinks to facilitate the way visitors browse from page to page in a Web site.

Nested tags   HTML tags that are placed within another set of opening and closing tags.

Newsletter-style columns   Columns in which the text flows from the bottom of the column on the left to the top of the column on the right.

Non-linear editing   Editing that randomly accesses video scenes and clips in any order.

Notes master   A template that determines layout and formatting for all notes pages in a presentation.

Notes pane   An area onscreen in a presentation program where you can key text notes about each slide.

NTSC   An acronym for National Television Systems Committee. The standard television format used primarily in the United States.

Numbered list   A list in which each item is preceded by a number or letter, in consecutive order.

O

Objects   The elements, such as lines and shapes, that comprise a drawing. Also, digital content inserted in a file.

Onion skin   A feature that lets you view multiple frames in an animation sequence on the Stage at the same time.

Opacity   A measurement of the level of transparency of color.

Optimize   Prepare a file for export by selecting options to achieve the best combination of file size and quality. Also, to set options that best suit a particular purpose.

Orientation   The way text is positioned horizontally or vertically in a text block. Also the way a document is printed across either the long side (landscape orientation) or the short side (portrait orientation) of a page.

Orphan   The first line of a paragraph that displays alone at the bottom of a page.

Out point   The end of a video clip.

Out port   A handle that displays in the lower-right of a selected text frame in some desktop publishing programs, such as Adobe's InDesign. When there is overset text, a red plus sign displays in the Out port. When the text frame is connected to another frame, a blue arrowhead displays in the Out port.

Overflow text   Text that is hidden because it does not fit within its text box. Sometimes called *overset text*.

Overset text   Text that is hidden because it does not fit within its text box. Sometimes called *overflow text*.

P

Package   To copy all required files and a viewer program to a CD so you can deliver a presentation on a different computer system.

Page layout   The way you organize and arrange objects and white space on a page.

Page navigation buttons   Icons you click to move among the pages in a publication.

Page setup   Page formatting that defines settings such as page size, margin width, the number of pages in the publication, and the page orientation.

Page size   The dimensions of a finished document page.

PAL   An acronym for phase alternating line. The standard television format used primarily in Europe.

Pan   The action of scrolling the drawing area to display a part that might otherwise be hidden outside the document window.

Panels   On-screen elements used in some programs to provide quick access to common commands and features.

Pantone Matching System A color system or model used to define spot color.

Paper size The dimensions of a sheet of paper on which a document is printed. Also called *sheet size*.

Paper stock The specifications that define sheets of paper, such as the size, type, weight, and opacity.

Paragraph spacing The amount of white space before or after a paragraph.

Password A secret word or code that confirms your identity when you log on to a computer system or network.

Pasteboard The area around the stage in an animation program where you can store content that you do not want to display in an animation. Also called the work area.

Path The address of a folder or file, including the folder or filename and storage location.

Path animation Animation in which objects are forced to move along a specific path.

Pattern A bitmap graphic used as a fill in some graphics programs. Also, a repetitive graphic design used in an image.

Peel A video transition that gives the appearance of peeling away one clip to reveal another clip underneath.

Picture frame A frame in which you insert a graphics object.

Pixel A single tiny dot used as a unit of measure and to define images on a computer screen. Short for *picture element*.

Placeholder A rectangular object that defines a specific area on a slide, Web page, or other document.

Playback rate The speed at which a computer plays a file, such as the frames of an animation or video.

Player A program used to play a media file.

Playhead A marker that indicates the current location on the timeline in an animation program.

Plug-in A player that is loaded into a Web browser program so it can play a file such as an animation on a Web page when a user requests it.

PNG An acronym for Portable Network Graphic. This format is often used for graphics on the World Wide Web. It can support up to 32-bit color as

well as effects such as transparency. It is the native file format for Macromedia's Fireworks MX graphics program.

Points A unit of measure used in printing and publishing. There are 72 points in an inch.

Portrait orientation The page orientation in which data is printed across the shorter side of the page. Also called *tall*.

PostScript A page description language used to define page layout and design for printing specifically on PostScript printers, which are printers that use the PostScript language.

PostScript Printer Description file (PPD) A file that provides information about a PostScript printing device.

Preflight A quality check performed before delivering a publication to a printer that includes, among other things, making sure that all graphics and fonts used in the publication are available.

Presentation program A program you can use to create a professional slide presentation for a classroom, corporate training session, business seminar, or similar situation.

Presenter view A view available when you deliver a live presentation using two monitors. In this view controls are displayed that allow you to quickly navigate through the presentation, view your notes, and perform other tasks that help you deliver the presentation.

Primary colors The basic colors from which all other colors can be derived. Specifically, red, blue, and yellow.

Primary level The main level, usually in an outline or list.

Primary monitor In a two-monitor setup, the monitor you will use to display the files and programs you want to see.

Print properties Settings that control the way a publication prints on your desktop printer.

Printer's spread A spread in which the pages are arranged in the order that they must be printed for the page order to be correct when the publication is bound. For example, in a 4-page folded booklet, page 4 is on the left of the sheet and page 1 is on the right of the sheet.

Process color   Cyan, magenta, yellow, and black, which are the colors of ink used in four color printing.

Progressive download   A download in which the file begins to play before it is completely downloaded.

Progressive video   Video that draws each line of an image on the screen progressively from the top to the bottom.

Project   A file that stores the sequences assembled to create a movie, along with references to the assets that are associated with the sequences and the instructions for how to assemble and display the video.

Projector   An application file that includes the data as well as a built-in player so the file can be displayed anywhere, on any computer.

Proof   A sample copy that you can examine for errors.

Proofreader's marks   Symbols written on galleys to indicate the edits that should be made before printing.

Proportion   A basic principle of design that describes the size and location of an object in relation to other objects in an image.

Protocol   A standard format used for transmission on a network.

Publication type   The kind of document you want to create, such as a newsletter or a calendar.

Publish   To create a version of a file that you can deliver in a selected environment, such as on the World Wide Web, or as a printed publication.

Publish settings   Properties that control the way a file is published.

Put   Upload files to a remote Web site.

Q

QuickTime   A cross-platform multimedia format that is compatible with both Microsoft Windows and Apple Macintosh systems.

R

Radial balance   A type of balance in which objects are distributed evenly around a focal point.

Radial gradient   A gradient pattern in which the colors blend out from a center point.

Random access structure   A Web page organization structure designed so that visitors can jump to any page on the Web site from any other page.

Raster image   Bitmap image.

Reader's spread   Facing pages—such as page 2 on the left and page 3 on the right.

Recording level   A setting that controls the volume at which sound such as a narration for a presentation is recorded.

Recto   A rightmost, or odd-numbered page.

Reference point   A fixed spot used as a control for moving and modifying objects.

Remote site   The storage location of a published Web site.

Resolution   The quality or sharpness of an image, usually measured in pixels per inch or pixels per centimeter. Sometimes it is written as an equation, like this: vertical dots per inch × horizontal dots per inch.

RGB   A color system or model used on computer monitors, which creates colors by blending different levels of red, green, and blue.

Rich text format (.rtf)   A file format that saves all text and most formatting. It is compatible with many programs that read text, such as word processing and desktop publishing programs.

Roll   An effect that causes lines of text to move vertically through a frame.

Rollover   The action of moving the mouse pointer over an object.

Root level folder   The main folder of a Web site, in which all files and subfolders for that site are stored.

Rotate   To pivot an object around its center point.

Row   The horizontal component of a table.

Row guides   Nonprinting lines that define rows on the page.

Ruler guides   Nonprinting lines that define any point along the horizontal or vertical ruler.

S

Sample   The smallest unit of a digitized sound, typically an 8- or 16- bit value that represents the audio signal at a particular moment.

Sample rate The number of audio samples per second used to represent a sound.

Sans serif A font that has straight lines without serifs and that is often used for headlines and titles.

Saturation A measurement of the intensity of color.

Scale To change the size of an object. Scaled also can mean simply the size of an object.

Scanner A hardware device used to transfer printed images or text into a computer file.

Scratch area The portion of the screen outside the document page where you can temporarily store text and graphics.

ScreenTip A text description that displays when the mouse pointer rests on a screen element, such as an icon, command, or button.

Script Assist A feature of Macromedia's Flash 8, used for writing script statements even without knowledge of a programming or scripting language.

Script statements Coded instructions.

Search site A Web site that provides tools for locating other Web sites even if you don't know a specific address.

Secondary colors The colors created by mixing the primary colors. Specially, orange, green, and violet.

Secondary monitor In a two-monitor setup, the monitor on which others view content, such as the monitor on which an audience will view a presentation.

Selection handles Small rectangles that are displayed around the edges of the current or selected object. They can usually be used to resize the object.

Selector The part of a CSS rule that identifies the element that will be affected by the rule, such as a paragraph or heading.

Self-running presentation A presentation that plays automatically in an unattended situation.

Sepia A brown tint.

Sequence A series of frames, or video clips assembled to create a movie.

Serif A font that has serifs, which are short lines and curlicues at the ends of the lines that make up each character.

Service bureau A company that takes slide information and reproduces it on the 35 mm slides, for a fee.

Shadow An effect that creates the illusion of depth and dimension. Drop shadows add shading along two sides of the outer edge of an object. Inner shadows add shading along two inside edges.

Sheet size The dimensions of a sheet of paper.

Sign-in screen A screen that lists the names of all people authorized to use a computer. From the sign-in screen, you click your name and then enter your password, if necessary, to display the desktop.

Signature A group of pages printed on the same sheet of paper.

Single file Web page A file stored in metafile hypertext markup language (MHTML) format with an .mht file extension. All supporting files such as graphics, sounds, and video are integrated into the same file; no supporting folder is required.

Single-sided printing To print on one side of a sheet of paper.

Single-sided transition A video transition that involves only the beginning or end of one clip.

Size report A text file that includes the size of each frame in an animation as well as the total size of the entire animation file.

Skew To slant an object along its horizontal or vertical axis.

Slide A single screen of information within a presentation. Also, a video transition in which one clip slides off one side of the frame while the next clip slides in from the opposite side.

Slide layout The settings that control the location of different types of content on a slide, such as text blocks and graphics objects.

Slide master A template that stores certain layout and formatting characteristics for all slides formatted with a specific design template.

Slide pane The main area of a presentation program window where you view and edit slides.

Slide show The display of slides in consecutive order the way they would appear in a presentation.

Slide show file A file that opens in full-screen slide show view, not in a presentation program window.

Smoothing The degree of sharpness allowed along edges in an image.

Snap Align an object to a point, a path, or another object.

Sound card A hardware device that enables a computer to control and output sound, and sometimes to record sound.

Sound fade A change in the sound over time, such as increasing in volume in the left speaker while decreasing in volume in the right speaker.

Source clip An original clip imported into a video-editing program.

Split To divide one item to create multiple items. For example, to divide a single cell in a table into multiple cells, or to divide a single video clip into multiple clips.

Split view A view in a Web site design program in which Design view and Code view display side by side.

Spot color A process used primarily in printing, in which a color is premixed to a color standard such as the Pantone Matching System, not mixed during the printing process.

Stack Arrange objects in overlapping layers.

Stage In some programs, the term used to describe the drawing area, or canvas.

Standalone player A player than can be installed on any computer to play files without requiring a Web browser or access to the Internet, or access to the program originally used to create the file.

Standoff The specific distance between an object and other content such as text on any of its four sides.

Starting value The number used for the first item in a list.

Static motion video Images that are recorded and saved as a file for playback.

Still title A static image that does not move.

Stock *See Paper stock.*

Streaming rate The speed at which a computer can download a file, such as frames in an animation or video.

Streaming sound Sound that is synchronized with an animation. A streaming sound file plays without downloading.

Streaming video Video that plays without downloading.

Streaming video server A computer on the Internet that is configured to deliver video files by streaming or progressive downloading.

Stroke The line used to draw an object.

Style A collection of saved formatting settings.

Stylus A pen-like device used with a graphics tablet and other touch-sensitive devices including personal digital assistants.

Submenu A menu list that displays when you select an item from a main menu. Also called a nested menu.

Subordinate level A level that is indented under the primary level, usually in an outline or list.

Subtractive colors Colors that absorb light. Cyan, magenta, yellow, and black are subtractive colors.

SVCD An acronym for super video compact disc. A video format used for storing video on a CD in MPEG-2 format at a resolution of about 480 by 480.

Swatches Blocks of color displayed on a color palette.

.swf The file extension of files in the Flash Player file format.

Symbol In some programs such as Flash, a reusable object stored in a file's library.

Symbol font A font such as Monotype Sorts, Symbol, Webding, Wingding, and ZapfDingbats that includes symbol characters.

Symmetrical balance A type of balance in which a design is the same on both sides of a center axis, either horizontally or vertically.

T

Tab A nonprinting character used to position text along a single line.

Tab leader Characters repeated on the line leading up to a tab stop.

Table   A set of data arranged in columns and rows.

Table borders   The horizontal and vertical lines that define columns and rows in a table.

Table of contents   A list of sections in a publication. Usually, the section headings or titles display on the left, and the page numbers where the items begin are on the right.

Tag   An HTML command.

Task pane   An area that displays on the side of the window in some programs, providing quick access to frequently used commands and features.

Text block   An object used to contain lines of text in a graphics file.

Text box   A rectangular object or placeholder in which you key and format text. Also called a frame.

Text editor   A program used to create and edit text-based documents.

Text flow   The direction in which text is read—either left to right or right to left.

Text wrap   A feature used to adjust the width, shape, and position of white space between text and objects on a page.

Texture   A pattern applied to a fill or stroke to make it look as if color is applied over a textured surface.

Threading text   In some desktop publishing programs, the process of connecting text boxes so that text flows from one box to another.

Thumbnails   Small pictures that represent larger images or slides.

TIFF   An acronym for Tagged Image File Format. TIFF files are used for storing bitmap images. This format is commonly used in desktop publishing and other multimedia applications.

Tile   To repeat an image in columns and rows.

Timebase   A setting that specifies the time divisions a video program uses to calculate the time position of an edit.

Timeline   The area in an animation or video-editing program where you organize and control content over time.

Timings   Intervals that control the length of time a slide is displayed before the transition to the next slide.

Tint   The brightness of a color.

Title master   A slide master specifically designed for title slides.

Titles   Text labels used to identify items, such as elements of a chart, or a slide. Also, text or graphics that are added to a video sequence.

Toggle   A feature or command that can be turned on or off. Also, the action of turning a feature or command on or off.

Tonal range   The distribution of pixels in a bitmap image.

Toolbox   An onscreen element used to display a collection of tools or buttons. In graphics programs, it usually displays the drawing and editing tools.

Tracking   A setting that controls the space between all characters in a text box.

Transform   Modify an object by either scaling, distorting, skewing, rotating, or flipping.

Transition   In a video, the frames that are used to phase out one scene or clip and phase in the next. In a presentation, the effects used to advance from one slide to the next during a slide show.

Transparency   A medium used for slides and over-head projectors. Also, the level of opacity of a color.

Transparency film   A thin film medium used to create a positive image that can be viewed or projected by transmitted light.

Trapping   A technique used to adjust the position of adjoining colors to avoid such gaps or overlaps.

Trigger   A control that allows you to coordinate the start of one effect with the start of another on the same slide.

TrueType fonts   Fonts that reproduce the same when printed as when displayed onscreen.

TWAIN   The software language used by devices such as scanners and some digital cameras. It interprets data so that it can be read by a computer.

Tweened animation   Animation in which you specify the content in the beginning keyframe and the ending keyframe and the animation program automatically fills in the intermediate frames.

Two-page spread   A leftmost page and a rightmost page facing each other in a publication. The pages are sometimes called mirrored pages, because their layout and margins are not identical, but reversed.

Typography   The art and technique of selecting typefaces and arranging type in a publication.

U

Uniform Resource Locator (URL) The string of characters that identifies where a Web page is stored.

Upload To transfer data from a local computer to a remote computer, usually on a network.

User name The name that identifies you to a computer system or network.

V

Value The range from black to white in a hue. Also, the part of an HTTP tag that defines a specific property. Also, any number, term, or code that defines a property.

Variety A term used to describe the use of various elements of design in order to create visual interest in an image.

VCD An acronym for video compact disc. A CD on which video is stored in MPEG-1 format at a resolution of about 352 by 480 pixels.

Vector A type of graphics in which the image is created using lines and curves defined by mathematical formulas.

Verso A leftmost, or even-numbered page.

Vertical alignment The position of text or objects in relation to the top and bottom margins of a text box, page or drawing area, or in relation to other objects.

Vertical printing order An option for printing items such as slides, images, or even spreadsheets in which consecutive items are printed from the top of the page to the bottom, and then to the top of the next column.

Video conferencing A meeting set up and transmitted on the Internet using video and audio.

Video effects Changes that add a special visual or audio characteristic to a video.

Video track The video portion of recorded video or of a sequence.

View The way a file is displayed on-screen.

Viewer A program that lets you play a presentation even if the presentation program is not installed on the computer.

Voice over Spoken text that plays while other content such as a presentation slide, video, or animation displays.

W

Warm color The colors ranging from red to yellow on the color wheel.

Watermark A semi-transparent object that displays behind other objects on pages in a publication.

WAV A high-quality sound file format.

Waveform A graphics representation of the amplitude of sound over time.

Web browser A software program that locates Web pages and then interprets the HTML coding to display the pages on your computer.

Web client A computer linked via a network to a Web server.

Web page title The text that displays in the Web browser title bar when the presentation displays.

Web pages Documents or files stored in Hypertext Markup Language (HTML) format and stored on a Web server computer so that anyone with access to the World Wide Web can access the Web page.

Web publication A publication file that is optimized for display on a Web browser. Some features that may not display properly on a Web page, such as text wrapping around graphics, are disabled.

Web server A computer connected to the World Wide Web on which Web page files are stored.

Web site Multiple Web pages connected using hyperlinks, usually all related to the same or similar topic.

Web-based motion video Streaming video in which images are captured in real time and transmitted over an Internet connection, such as video conferencing or webcams.

Webcam A video camera attached to a computer that transmits the video to a Web page.

Webcast A broadcast delivered over the Internet.

Websafe colors Colors that display the same way on different systems, which makes them suitable for use on Web pages.

Weight The width or thickness of a line or stroke.

White space The area on a page that has no text or graphics. The space between visual elements in an image. It does not have to be white.

Widow The last line of a paragraph that displays alone at the top of a page.

Wizard An automated series of dialog boxes that prompts you through the steps necessary to complete a procedure.

Work area The area around the Stage in an animation program where you can store content that you do not want to display in an animation. Also called the *Pasteboard*.

Workspace The arrangement of panels and tools in a program window.

World Wide Web (WWW) A global network of Web server computers on which Web pages are stored. Usually called the *Web*.

Wrap To flow text automatically from the end of one line to the beginning of the next.

X

X-axis The category axis that displays the categories in a chart.

Y

Y-axis The value axis that displays the values in a chart.

Z

Zip To compress one or more files.

Zoom The action of adjusting the magnification of a file by a percentage of its actual size. Also the feature used for this purpose.

INDEX